THE PROVINCE OF QUEBEC AND THE EARLY
AMERICAN REVOLUTION

KENNIKAT AMERICAN BICENTENNIAL SERIES

Under the General Editorial Supervision of
Dr. Ralph Adams Brown
Professor of History, State University of New York

THE PROVINCE OF QUEBEC AND THE EARLY AMERICAN REVOLUTION

A STUDY IN ENGLISH-AMERICAN COLONIAL HISTORY

BY

VICTOR COFFIN, Ph. D.

KENNIKAT PRESS
Port Washington, N. Y./London

THE PROVINCE OF QUEBEC AND
THE EARLY AMERICAN REVOLUTION

Originally published in 1896 as Vol. 1, No. 3 of the
Economics, Political Science, and History Series of
The University of Wisconsin
Reissued in 1970 by Kennikat Press
Library of Congress Catalog Card No: 74-120873
ISBN 0-8046-1266-8

Manufactured by Taylor Publishing Company   Dallas, Texas

KENNIKAT AMERICAN BICENTENNIAL SERIES

PREFACE.

The present study was undertaken as one in English colonial history, and my first thought was closely to investigate governmental conditions in those parts of North America that did not join in the movement of revolt, not only just before and during the War of Independence, but also for such a period beyond that struggle as might show its more immediate effects on English colonial policy. The claims of other work have required the abandonment of the greater part of this undertaking, and the present publication deals only with the Province of Quebec, from its acquisition in 1760 down into the Revolution. As an institutional study the investigation ends with the Parliamentary settlement of the constitution of the province by the Quebec Act of 1774; but as a contribution to the history of the American revolution it has gone far enough into the first years of the war to show the main connections of Canada with that event. These connections seemed to offer an important and unexplored field of investigation, and have therefore been emphasized to a degree not originally intended. On both sides of my work — institutional and revolutionary, — the Quebec Act becomes the central point.

With regard to the institutional aspect I have kept in mind, not only the ordinary tasks of government, but also the rarer and more difficult problem of the grafting of English governmental ideas on an alien society. The effort to contribute to American revolutionary history has been guided in the first instance by the idea of tracing, through the critical years immediately preceding the outbreak, the bearing of the Imperial government in an obscure corner

iii

where a freer hand was given to it than elsewhere; later
there are encountered the obscure and important questions
connected with the general colonial bearing of the Quebec
Act, with its special influence on the early revolutionary
struggle, and with the attitude of the Canadians toward
that event. On these latter points I have been obliged,
though entering upon the investigation without bias or
controversial intent, to present my results in more or less
of a controversial style and to go somewhat largely into
the evidence. For in regard to them I am strongly at
variance with the hitherto prevailing opinions; being
forced to conclude both that the provisions of the Quebec
Act were neither occasioned nor appreciably affected by
conditions in the other colonies, and that, far from being
effectual in keeping the mass of the Canadians loyal to the
British connection, the measure had a strong influence in
precisely the opposite direction. The Canadians were *not*
kept loyal, and Canada was preserved at this crisis to the
British Empire through the vigor and ability of its British
defenders, and through the mismanagement of their cause
on the part of the revolutionists. As to the hitherto
accepted belief with regard to the origin and aims of the
Act, I need direct attention only to the Declaration of Independence and other utterances of the Continental Congress, and to the almost unvarying statements of American historians ever since. The belief in its beneficial
influence in Quebec has been nearly as uninterruptedly
held; even by those who admit its disastrous influence
on the course of events in the other colonies, it has
been constantly regarded as a *chef-d'oeuvre* of political
wisdom and humanity.[1] With this view I have no sym-

---

[1] Lecky, though laying stress upon its distastefulness to the other colonies, speaks of
it as especially important in the history of religious liberty, and as the result of the
government having resolved, "as the event showed very wisely, that they would not
subvert the ancient laws of the Province, or introduce into them the democratic system
which existed in New England." (*History of England in the Eighteenth Century*, III,
399). For modern Canadian expressions of similar views, as well as for asseverations con-

pathy, and I have steadily combated it in the conviction that the Quebec Act is really one of the most unwise and disastrous measures in English Colonial history. It will be shown below that it was founded on the misconceptions and false information of the Provincial officials; that though it secured the loyal support of those classes in Canada,—the clergy and the noblesse,—whose influence had been represented as all important, at the critical juncture this proved a matter of small moment. For the noblesse were found to have no influence, and that of the clergy was found in main measure paralyzed by the provision which had again laid on the people the burden of compulsory tithes. Without the Act the old ruling classes, there is every reason to believe, would have taken precisely the same attitude, and the people would not have been exposed to those influences which ranged them on the side of the invader. Apart from Canadian affairs, the disastrous effect of the measure on public feeling in the older provinces must be strongly considered in any estimate as to its expediency.

Judgment as to the general political wisdom, in distinction from the expediency, of this settlement of the constitution (and as it proved, largely of the history), of Quebec, will depend mainly on the view taken of certain general political facts and problems connected with the later history of British North America; aspects which I revert to more specially in my conclusion. A factor in the decision must, however, be the opinion held of the character and spirit of the administration to which that settlement was immediately due. An examination of the antecedents of the Act will indeed, I think, establish the conviction that the main desire of the authors of the measure was to further the security and

cerning the unshaken loyalty of the French Canadians, see Watson, *Constitutional History of Canada;* Lareau, *Hist. Droit Canadien;* Ashley, *Lectures on Canadian Constitutional History;* Bourinot, *Parliamentary Procedure and Practice in Canada.* Mr. Kingsford, the latest and best of Canadian historians, while admitting the disaffection of the Canadians at the beginning of the war, represents it as only momentary, and warmly defends the policy, expediency, and success of the Act.

prosperity of the Province and fulfill treaty obligations toward the French Canadians, and will show that there is practically no evidence of more insidious aims with regard to colonial affairs in general. But it will also appear that the step was accompanied by manifestations of an arbitrary policy, and that it was taken at a moment when its authors were exhibiting in other ways real evidences of hostility to the free spirit of American self-government. It would be surprising indeed to find a high degree of wisdom and enlightenment displayed in any colonial measure that emanated from the ministry of Lord North. The careful and candid student will on the whole, I think, come to the conclusion that though there are in the annals of that ministry many more discreditable achievements than the Quebec Act, no single step taken by it has been more politically disastrous than that which, beside increasing the colonial difficulties of the moment, is mainly responsible for the continued burdening of modern Canadian life with a steadily growing problem of national divergence.

My sources of information are stated in detail in Appendix II. The main study is based almost entirely on the manuscript copies of British State Papers in the Canadian Archives (the more important ones being also examined in the originals or original duplicates of the London Colonial and Record offices); though I have used with profit all the later material that was available, I am not conscious of any such obligations as would call for more special notice than has been given throughout in my notes. An exception however must be made in regard to Dr. William Kingsford's *History of Canada*, now in course of publication. The high value of Dr. Kingsford's book has been already fully recognized, and I very heartily concur in the recognition. My own main work on the period he has already covered has been done indeed in entire independence, and our conclusions frequently differ; but still my more intensive investigation owes a great deal to his more general and most

suggestive views. The material used for the general Western aspects of this study has been found mainly in the invaluable library of the State Historical Society of Wisconsin.
With regard to personal assistance, I am heavily indebted to
Dr. Douglas Brymner, the well-known Canadian Archivist,
and to the late Professor Herbert Tuttle of Cornell University. Dr. Brymner has not only facilitated in every way
my use of both the Canadian and the English Archives,
but has supplemented this assistance by the steady help
of that wide and accurate knowledge and keen judgment to
which American historical scholarship already owes so
much. In Professor Tuttle's seminary the study was begun
in the ordinary course of post-graduate work; that early
stage of it owes a great deal to his searching and suggestive criticism, as does its whole progress to the abiding inspiration of his own work and methods. I wish also to express my obligation to Professor Frederick J. Turner, the
Editor of this series, for very helpful discussion on various points, and for careful and suggestive proof-reading
throughout.

TABLE OF CONTENTS.

INTRODUCTION.

CHAPTER I.

THE FRENCH CANADIANS.

A. General.

B. The Noblesse and the Clergy.

CHAPTER II.

THE BRITISH SETTLERS.

A. Numbers, Origin, Occupations, Character.

B. Political Attitude.

C. Relations with the French Canadians.

CHAPTER III.

THE PROVINCIAL GOVERNMENT.

A. General Status.

CHAPTER IV.

THE SPIRIT AND DEVELOPMENT OF ADMINISTRATION.

A.   The Provincial Governors.

B.   The Imperial Office.

CHAPTER V.

THE QUEBEC ACT, — ITS ORIGINS AND AIMS.

A.   Preliminaries.

B. History of Main Provisions.

a. Boundaries.

b. Religion.

C. *Application of the Act.*

CHAPTER VI.

THE QUEBEC ACT AND THE AMERICAN REVOLUTION.

A. *The Revolution in the Province of Quebec.*

APPENDIX I.

APPENDIX II.

THE PROVINCE OF QUEBEC AND THE EARLY AMERICAN REVOLUTION.

INTRODUCTION.

What was known under the French as Canada or New France came into English possession through the capitulation of Montreal, September 8, 1760, and was finally ceded to England by the Treaty of Paris, February 10, 1763, closing the Seven Years' War. As thus ceded, no definite limits were assigned to "Canada, with all its dependencies," the only boundary line mentioned in regard to it being the Mississippi river. The British government was thus given a free hand in defining its extent, subject to the fixed boundaries and well-established claims of the adjacent colonies, to the indefinite possessions of the Hudson's Bay Company, and, more or less, to the conceptions of the Canadians themselves. Many causes intervened to delay a final settlement of the matter of boundaries, and meanwhile, by the Royal Proclamation of October 7, 1763, the new Province was defined so as to embrace, for the time being, a rectangular district of not more than 100,000 square miles, extending along both sides of the St. Lawrence river from the mouth of the River St. John to the point where the St. Lawrence is intersected by the 45th degree of north latitude.

From the date of the capitulation till August 10, 1764, the new acquisition was governed by the commanders of the

English forces in occupation, and the period is therefore known as that of the Military Rule. The investigation of political conditions in the Province does not necessarily have much to do with this preliminary suspension of civil government; but a brief statement of the general character of the Military Rule is necessary for several reasons, especially to show what had been the earliest experience of the French Canadians under British government, and with what anticipations they were likely to view its permanent establishment. It may be safely asserted that the military character of the government, so far as felt by the people in ordinary affairs, was to a large extent merely nominal. The final authority of course resided in the military arm, and the courts established for the administration of justice were of a military form; but these courts were not governed by the principles of martial law, at least in matters where the old French law or custom could be discovered or applied. French Canadians had a share in their administration,[1] while such instruments of local government as existed under the French seem to have been largely retained.[2] All contemporary testimony from the French Canadians is unmistakeable in its appreciation of the justice and humanity of the general proceedings of the military, and of the hopes the people had thus acquired for the future.[3] The official statements throughout the period as to the very satisfactory conduct of the French Canadians must be admitted to show a large degree of at least external harmony. We may conclude therefore that the conduct of the British authorities during this difficult time

---

[1] See Lareau, *Hist. de droit Canadian, II,* 87. For evidence of the satisfaction of the French with these courts see reference to petitions for their retention. (Canadian Archives, Q. 2. p. 273).

[2] See as to continuance of the office and functions of the captains of militia, Ordinance concerning sale of fire wood, Nov. 27, 1765, Vol. of Ordinances in Can. Archives.

[3] See *Report Canadian Arch.*, 1888, p. 19. See also *N. Y. Colonial Documents,* X., 1155, for a French memoir (1763) concerning the possibility of exciting a rebellion in Canada. It speaks of the people having been further drawn from their allegiance to France by the "mild régime of the English, the latter in their policy having neglected nothing to expedite the return of that comfort and liberty" formerly enjoyed.

had been such as to win in large degree the confidence of the conquered people, and that civil government was established in 1764 under favorable auspices.

It was on the model of the other Crown Colonies in America that British civil government was introduced on August 10, 1764, in pursuance of the Proclamation of October 7, 1763, and under a commission appointing Gen. James Murray, one of the resident military officers, " Captain-General and Governor-in-Chief in and over our Province of Quebec." Under this official and his successor, Col. Guy Carleton, government was conducted throughout the whole period covered by my investigation. Until 1775 the Proclamation of 1763, a purely executive act, continued to form the basis of administration; for the Quebec Act, passed May, 1774, and going into force one year later, was the first interference of the Imperial Parliament in Canadian affairs.   This remained the constitution of Canada from 1775 to 1791, at which latter date its provisions, so far as they affected the western part of the country, then being settled by the United Empire Loyalists and now known as the Province of Ontario, were repealed by the *Constitutional Act*.   As affecting however the settled regions acquired from the French and distinctively known after 1791 as Lower Canada, the Quebec Act, in its main provisions, still continues in force.   It has kept alive in British North America a French nation, never so united or self-conscious as at the present time.   One of the main objects of this inquiry is to investigate closely the conditions which led to this Act, and the state of government which it was intended to amend, with reference to the general wisdom and expediency of the measure and to its special connections with the American Revolution.

As I must constantly anticipate in my references to the Quebec Act it will be well perhaps to introduce here a short statement of its main provisions.[1]   With the accompanying Revenue Act it enacted:

---

[1] See App. I. for full reprint.

1. That the province of Quebec should be extended to include all the territory which the French had been supposed to lay claim to under the name of Canada, i. e., on the east to Labrador, on the west to the boundaries of Louisiana and the Hudson Bay Company's territory, and on the south to the boundaries of the other provinces and the Ohio; including therefore to the southwest and west the regions which now form the states of Ohio, Michigan, Indiana, Illinois, Wisconsin, and part of Minnesota.

2. That all previous governmental provisions in regard to Quebec as before constituted or to any part of the added territory should be annulled, and that the Provincial government should for the future consist of a governor and council, both appointed by the king, and together invested with a strictly limited legislative and money power. That a revenue should be provided for the province by customs duties imposed by the Imperial government, said revenue being entirely at the disposition of the Imperial authorities.

3. That full toleration of the Roman Catholic religion should exist in the province, including the removal of all disabilities by test oaths; and that the Church of Rome should " hold, receive and enjoy " its accustomed dues and rights with respect to its own adherents.

4. That though the English criminal law should continue to prevail, the inhabitants should "hold and enjoy their property and possessions, together with all customs and usages relating thereto, and all others their civil rights," according to the ancient laws and customs of Canada; these laws and customs to remain in exclusive possession until altered by provincial ordinances.

It may readily be imagined that Canada emerged from the final struggle of French and English in no very prosperous condition. Authorities agree in their doleful descriptions of the greatly weakened and almost destitute state of the colony in 1759, on the eve of the great contest; and the efforts of the two following years still further reduced it. During the first or military stage of the British occupation we meet with frequent official references to the danger of famine, and the dependence of the people on the government. But this state was not of long duration. When civil government is established, August, 1764, the crisis seems past, and the colony may be said to have again attained the position it had held on the eve of the

conquest. The new blood and capital that had been introduced, together with the unbroken peace of four years, had
stimulated all branches of industry and had opened the way
for the remarkable growth that is clearly traceable down
to 1775. The inhabitants cultivated their lands and pursued
the Indian trade and the fisheries in peace and with comparatively little molestation from the new state of things.
Content to be left alone, they concerned themselves little
about public affairs, and it is not till 1775 that we meet with
any general political manifestations on their part. Har-
vests steadily increased; the fear of famine died away; the
fanciful schemes for the commercial salvation of the
province which we meet with in the early years gradually
disappeared. Trade, at least in the wholesale and foreign
branches, fell into the hands chiefly of the small but enterprising body of new English-speaking settlers who, attracted by the fur trade and the fisheries, had followed in
the wake of the conqueror; and it soon received from them
a very notable impulse. The cultivation of the soil, remaining almost entirely in the hands of the French
Canadians, shared more slowly in the general improvement. The old French methods of culture had always been
bad, and it was not till the latter part of the French régime
that the country had produced enough for its own sub-
sistence; but before the year 1770 a considerable quantity
of grain was being exported.[1] In the opening up of new

---

[1] Striking evidence as to the comparatively prosperous condition of the people in the
latter part of the period is furnished in scattered references of the more observing revolutionists who visited the province, 1775-6. Charles Carroll (*Journal*, Maryland Hist.
Soc. Papers, 1876, p. 98), writes in May, 1776, that the country along the Sorel "is very
populous, the villages are large and neat, and joined together with a continued range
of single houses, chiefly farmers;" and after contrasting the prosperity of these farmers
with the poverty of the seigneurs, adds: "It is conjectured that the farmers in Canada
cannot be possessed of less than one million pounds sterling in specie; they hoard up
their money to portion their children; they neither let it out at interest nor expend it
in the purchase of lands." The writer of Henry's *Account of the Campaign* directed
special attention to the *habitant*, and testifies to his economy and prosperity. "It
seemed to me that the Canadians in the vicinage of Quebec lived as comfortably in gen -
eral as the generality of the Pennsylvanians did at that time in the County of Lancas-
ter." (Albany, 1877, p. 95.)

lands, however, very little progress was made in the early years; not indeed until the old French form of grant was reverted to.[1] Manufactures were primitive and unimportant. The policy of the government with regard to them does not seem to have differed in the main from that followed contemporaneously in the other colonies; though there are evidences of more enlightened conduct in the latter part of the period.[2]

The growth in population of the province during this period cannot be very accurately stated, but a comparison of the various conflicting estimates with general data leads to conclusions that are probably not much astray. A considerable decrease was occasioned by the removal to France, on the conquest, of most of the official and a large part of the noble and commercial classes;[3] and in 1762 the official returns give a total of 65,633 for the settled parts of the province. Beyond this there was by 1775 a scattered population in the upper western country of about 1,000 families, as well as fishing colonies around the mouth of the St. Lawrence. The growth throughout the period was almost entirely a natural one. Cramahé writes in 1773 that "fourteen years' experiences have proved that the increase of the province must depend upon its own population." But the French Canadians then as now needed no outside assistance in this matter, and it is probably safe to estimate them at 90,000 in 1775. Higher estimates, (and the contemporary ones of Carleton and Masères are much higher),[4] are manifestly inaccurate in view of the fact that the official census of 1784 asserts a total of only 113,012.

The population from the beginning was divided into two well defined sections of very unequal strength; (1) the French Canadians, who are constantly referred to in the official correspondence as the "new subjects," and (2) the

---

[1] See below.

[2] See Can. Arch., Q. 5–2, pp. 760, 839; Q. 6, p. 15.

[3] Murray states July 17, 1761, that the population was then 10,000 less than in 1759.

[4] Evidence before Commons in Quebec Act debate, Cavendish, *Report*.

small new English-speaking element, designated as regularly as the "old subjects." These sections, in their distinctive features and activities, will be later considered separately. Suffice it now to say that the British element was almost exclusively a trading one, and that but a very small part of it devoted itself to agricultural pursuits. It had been attracted to the province by the fur or Indian trade, and we shall find that the influence on the fortunes of the colony thus early exerted from this quarter was destined to be of the utmost importance throughout the period.

CHAPTER I.

THE FRENCH CANADIANS.

A. General.

It does not come within the possibilities of this investigation to present any close character study of the French Canadian, though it will be readily conceded that some such study is indispensable to the proper understanding of the conditions under which we must consider the new rule. For such a picture we can, however, go to Parkman, whose latest sketches bring the *habitant* and *gentilhomme* before us as the English conqueror found them; the former a loyal, ignorant, easily-led, but somewhat unstable peasantry of military extraction and training, with a decided taste for the wild, free life of the woods; the latter an entirely military semi-nobility, who from their first appearance had as the basis of existence the Court and the Camp, and who were almost as poor and ignorant and politically powerless as the *habitant*, whom up to this time they had found a docile follower, and of whose wild and hardy life they had been full sharers. In less romantic but not less pleasing colors is the *habitant* described by Governor Murray in 1762 —"a strong, healthy race, plain in their dress, virtuous in their morals, and temperate in their living;" in general entirely ignorant and credulous, they had been prejudiced against the English, but nevertheless had lived with the troops "in a harmony unexampled even at home;" and needed only to be reassured on the subject of the preservation of their religion to become good subjects.[1] Two years later the same authority writes of the French Canadians generally as "perhaps the bravest and best race upon the globe, a race, who, could they be indulged with a

---

[1] *General Report*, 1762, (Can. Arch., B. 7, p. 1).

few privileges which the laws of England deny to Roman
Catholics at home, would soon become the most faithful
and useful set of men in the American empire." [1]   And
November, 1767, Carleton describes them as comprising
10,000 men who had served in the late war, "with as much
valor, with more zeal, and more military knowledge for
America than the regular troops of France that were
joined with them." Indeed, this military origin and training of the people must be always kept in mind in
estimating their attitude and the causes likely to influence
them. Easily led, they were by no means timid or spirit-
less.

The clearly marked upper class sections of the French
Canadian population — the noblesse and the clergy — will be
considered more particularly later; for though small in
numbers their political weight was very great. Meanwhile,
I shall have regard to general features, so far as they can
be discerned. And here we are not always free of uncertainty; for when the new English observers speak of the
"French Canadians," or the "new subjects," or the "people," in a general way, it is by no means always easy to
determine how much worth the observation has as a general one, or to what extent the observer's vision is
narrowed by special conditions. There can be little doubt
that most of the representations of the officials as to the
attitude and character of the "new subjects" are really applicable only to the small section of them that came more
immediately and easily under view, — the noblesse. These
were continually hanging about the governmental steps and
obscuring the mass of the people; the latter, with no
knowledge of their former leaders' designs, and steadily
growing out of sympathy with their whole life, stolidly
pursued the work that was nearest to their hands, content
to be let alone, and troubling themselves very little about
changes of government or law.

---

[1] To Board of Trade, October 29th, 1764. Can. Arch., Q. 2, p. 233.

One of the first unmistakably general observations by the new rulers is an assertion by Murray in 1762 that the people are not ripe for the same form of government as in the other colonies. Their strong attachment to the church of their fathers and the great influence the clergy had exercised and could still exercise over them, are frequently spoken of and insisted upon; though as early as 1762 (after two years of peace and English government), we find Murray stating in his official report that "they do not submit as tamely to the yoke, and under sanction of the capitulation[1] they every day take an opportunity to dispute the tithes with their curés."[2] A year later (October 23, 1763),[3] he urges on the home government the necessity of caution in dealing with religious matters; adding however, that the people would not stickle for the continuance of the hierarchy, but would be content with the preservation of the priesthood as a devotional and educational body. Several petitions in regard to religious matters accompany this letter, and these are undoubtedly the first general manifestations within our period of French Canadian opinion on any subject.[4] They appear on the eve of civil government, being called forth probably by the news of the definite ceding of the country to England. Of their genuineness and representative character there can be little doubt, and making all allowance for the spirit of humility and modesty which the situation would be likely to engender, we cannot escape the conclusion that the body of the people had no desire for anything more in regard to religion than the measures necessary for the complete en-

---

[1] In the 27th article of the capitulation (September 8, 1760), the French commander had demanded that the people should be obliged by the English to pay the customary dues to the Church — a demand which was referred by Amherst to the will of the king. The clause was undoubtedly instigated by the clergy, and may be interpreted as showing that the latter were not at all disposed to trust to voluntary contributions. The point should be kept in mind in considering the attitude of the Canadians towards the Quebec Act, which re-established compulsory payment.

[2] Can. Arch., B. 7, p. 1.

[3] Ib., Q. 1, p. 251.

[4] Ib., Q. 1, pp. 226–47.

joyment of its voluntary features, and that they were already distinctly opposed to its legal establishment with compulsory powers.

As to the relations between the *habitants* and their old secular leaders, the noblesse, we have few indications previous to the Quebec Act. Murray, in a general report[1] immediately after his recall, (while still governor, but under the shadow of disapproval and investigation), represents the state of things as perfectly satisfactory, in the sense of the *habitants* being still of a submissive and reverent spirit; saying that they are shocked at the insults offered the noblesse by other classes in the community. This must be taken very cautiously, for Murray's object was to represent the noblesse, with whom he had been very closely associated against those other classes, as thoroughly in sympathy with the great mass of the people. Nor of much greater weight, probably, is Carleton's representation, March 15th, 1769, as to the advisability of admitting some of the noblesse to the Council on account of their influence over the lower classes (and over the Indians).[2] For he too seems to have remained in error on this point until roughly awakened by the utter failure of the seigneurs in 1775 in their attempt to assert, for the first time since the conquest, the old influence. This will appear more fully later; at present we need only notice the statement by Chief Justice Hey, that Carleton "has taken an ill measure of the influence of the Seigneurs or clergy over the lower orders of the people, whose principle of conduct, founded in fear and the sharpness of authority over them now no longer exercised, is unrestrained, and breaks out in every shape of contempt and detestation of those whom they used to behold with terror, and who gave

---

[1] Can. Arch., B. 8, p. 1. (Aug. 20, 1766.)

[2] Can. Arch., Q. 6, p. 34. See also to Shelbourne, Jan. 20, 1768 (Q. 5-1, 370), and Nov. 5, 1767 (Q. 5-1, 260). The latter is printed in full in *Rep. Can. Arch.*, 1888, p. 41.

them, I believe, too many occasions to express it."[1] Our
later investigation will show that there can be little doubt
that the influence of the noblesse had steadily declined
from the first hour of English domination, and that the
habitant had come with remarkable rapidity to look upon
the seigneur merely in the light of an obnoxious landlord.[2]
The causes of this change are not obscure and include a
clearer perception of the changed character of government
than the Canadians are generally credited with. For the
main reason, no doubt, was the greatly altered position of
the noblesse under the new regime, and their utter deprivation of that real military and nominal judicial authority which they had formerly enjoyed.[3] The contemporary
social relations in old France will at once suggest themselves to the reader; and I need here only remark that this
is not the only indication we have that social conditions in
the New France were not so different as has usually been
supposed.

Coming more particularly to the matter of general political attitude we are at once struck by the fact that the
trouble shortly before experienced with the Acadians seems
to have no parallel in Canada down to the American invasion. At the capitulation the Canadians acquiesced by the
most complete submission in the new rule, and during the
period that elapsed before the fate of the country was
finally decided we have in the reports of the commanding
officers only the strongest expressions of content with the
manner in which they are conducting themselves. Murray's
testimony (already quoted), is amply supported by that of
others representing all sections of the country.   Burton
(commanding at Three Rivers), says that they "seem very
happy in the change of their masters," and "begin to feel

---

[1] To the Lord Chancellor, Aug. 28, 1775. Can. Arch., Q. 12, p. 203.

[2] See Masères' *Account of the Proceedings, etc.;* also Cramahé to Hillsborough, July
25, 1772. (Can. Arch., Q. 8, p. 160.)

[3] The influence of military position upon the *habitant* was early perceived by Murray,
who in 1764 strongly urges on the home government the necessity on this account of the
military and civil authority in the Province being united. (Can. Arch., Q. 2, p. 206.)

that they are no_longer slaves."[1] Gage (at Montreal), writes that "the people in general seem well enough disposed towards their new masters."[2] The strongest assertions come from Haldimand, a French-speaking Swiss soldier, (Carleton's successor in 1778 as governor of the province), who may be supposed not only to have been best able to make himself acquainted with the real attitude of the people, but also to have been the least easily swayed in his conclusions. August 25th, 1762,[3] he writes in the most emphatic manner in regard to the groundlessness of the fears that had been expressed lest the Canadians should be dangerously affected by a recent success of the French in Newfoundland, and later asserts that, with the exception of the noblesse and clergy they are not uneasy as to their fate, and will easily console themselves for the change of rulers.[4] Allowance must probably be made in these representations for the natural desire of the military authorities to put their management of the country in the best light possible; but making all such we can still have no doubt that matters were in a per-fectly pacific (perhaps, rather, lethargic), state, and that from the conquerors' standpoint the conduct of the *habitant* left little to be desired.

The people were indeed thoroughly exhausted from the recent struggle and all thought of further resistance had departed with their leaders, the most irreconcilable of whom had gone to France at the capitulation. They had been stimulated in their efforts against the English by representations of the tyranny the latter if successful would immediately institute,— representations which had been the more easily credited from their knowledge of the fate which had overtaken the Acadians.[5] But that this fear was

---

[1] Official report, May, 1763. Can. Arch., B. 7, pp. 61–83.

[2] Official report, March 20, 1762. Ibid., B. 7, p. 84.

[3] Ibid., B. 1, p. 216.

[4] To Amherst, December 20, 1762, and February, 1763. Ibid., B. 1, pp. 262, 266.

[5] Murray to Halifax, March 9, 1764. Can. Arch., Q. 2, p. 78.

rapidly dispelled is strongly indicated by the statistical statement with regard to the emigration to France, which had been provided for in the treaty, and which was open without restriction to all for eighteen months from its conclusion. As we have already seen the leading French of the official, military and commercial classes had left before the cession; it is safe to conclude that these for the most part had never been very strongly rooted in the country, and were first of all, Frenchmen. The later records show that those who had any landed interests in Canada joined but little in this movement, and that still fewer of the mass of the people went.[1] The term of facilitated emigration extended through the summer of 1764, and in August Murray, after collecting statistical statements from the different commanders, writes that only 270 are going from the whole province, most of whom "are officers, their wives, children and servants." The tone with which the people finally accepted the irrevocable handing over of the country to England is very plainly to be seen in the religious addresses which have already been referred to as the first movement in any sense common that we meet with on the part of the Canadians. The tone is a manly one, and without any hypocritical professions of pleasure at the state of affairs, indicates a readiness (recognizing "que toute autorité vient de Dieu") to make the best of a bad business.

In general, therefore, with regard to the lower classes, we do not find throughout the period preceding the Quebec Act any indication that might have made the rulers uneasy. And certainly if anybody had profited by the change of government it was the *habitant*. He had been relieved from very grievous burdens, and at least during the earlier years, does not seem to have felt much new pressure in their stead. His peace and security had formerly cost him con-

---

[1] Emigration on their part was of course a much more serious matter. And the Canadians were early remarkable for love of their native country. (See Cramahé to Hillsborough, July 25, 1772. Can. Arch., Q. 8, p. 160.)

stant and often most critical military service; now it cost him nothing. And that he was not slow in appreciating some aspects of the change in government is shown by a difficulty those in charge of the *batteaux* service met with in the autumn of 1765. This service (of transporting by water troops and supplies to the garrisons in the upper country), was a constantly necessary one, and had been performed during the military period (i. e., 1760–4) without any difficulty by means of impress warrants,— the people apparently regarding as a matter of course what they had been accustomed under the old régime to do as a part of their regular militia duty. On the separation of the civil from the military authority such demands upon the people in time of peace became illegal,[1] and the service had not been otherwise provided for. During the first year of civil government it seems to have been continued, however, in a moderate way without opposition that we hear of; but October, 1765 the officer in charge reports great difficulties. Governor Murray had refused to grant impress warrants, sending instead to the local authorities recommendations of a peremptory nature; but we find it stated that half of the parishes applied to had refused to send a man, and that in one place the people had threatened to beat the bailiff. The military officer reports that " the bailiffs disregarded the orders given and the people were adverse and corrupted," and again that "the Canadians are now poisoned in their minds and instructed that they cannot be forced on such services." And it was not until an impress warrant of full power had been issued by the governor (on the plea of unavoidable necessity), that the service could be performed.[1] But it would seem that it was only on its military side of relief from oppressive duty and the immediate control of the seigneur or captain of militia, that the change of government seems thus to have

---

[1] See opinion of Prov. Att.-Gen., October 5th, 1765. Can. Arch., Q. 3, p. 81.

[2] Lords of Trade to Colonial Secretary, May 16th, 1766, with enclosures. Can. Arch., Q. 3, pp. 53–120.

been appreciated. In a letter to Shelbourne of December 24th, 1767, Carleton, after discussing the fact that the French Canadians still continued to transact their minor legal affairs in ways which would be invalid in the higher courts, writes that he has met only one Canadian "who sees the great revolution [1] in its full influence," and that he anticipates general consternation as the situation comes to be known.

In January, 1768, we find Carleton declaring that the exclusion of the Canadians from office, though directly concerning but a few (as but few were eligible), indirectly affected the minds of all, being regarded as a national slight and prejudice. There is strong reason for doubting the accuracy of this statement and for believing that on the whole the body of the people did not trouble themselves about the matter. It is difficult to come to a decision as to how far a similar opinion may be justified in regard to the movement that undoubtedly gained ground, or at least more confident expression, every year, with reference to the full restoration of the ancient civil laws.[2] But we are safe in taking whatever general expression we find on this head in a much more representative light, for every presumption would lead in that direction, and the influence of the clergy was a constant factor therefor.[3] As stated above, the earlier years do not show any very decided steps, and no doubt the more resolute stand of the later years is largely attributable to political education on the part of a few, and to the increasing pressure of the new system, which was daily augmenting the points of contact. It must from year to year have been found more difficult to follow the course with which the people have been

---

[1] He is referring more especially to the laws, supposedly *in toto* changed by the Proclamation of 1763.

[2] English criminal law was never objected to, and probably touched the people on few points. See evidence of Carleton before House of Commons, 1774, Cavendish's *Report.*

[3] See in connection here the later discussion of the extent to which French and English law was actually used.

credited, of avoiding the courts (for the Canadians were naturally a litigious people).[1] Not many petitions or memorials on this subject have come down to us from these years, but there were undoubtedly more than we know of. It was Carleton's policy to discourage this or any other form of popular demonstration,— a policy which his known sympathy with the objects of the French and the hopes he held out of their being soon attained, enabled him to follow out pretty successfully. August 7th, 1769, he writes that when last at Montreal he had succeeded in suppressing "the rough draft of a memorial to the king for the ancient laws," which had been "communicated for my approval."[2] October 25th, of the same year, he says that the lack of petitions on this subject was due solely to himself, and that if there had been given any hint that such were thought requisite, "there is not a Canadian from one extremity of the province to the other that would not sign or set his mark to such a petition."[3] He seems to have succeeded in inspiring the Canadians who were so minded with confidence in his advocacy of their wishes, and when he left the province in the autumn of 1770 (going expressly, as was well known, to give advice preparatory to a decisive settling of the government), he was presented by the French Canadians only with some addresses in regard to education, which they beg him to add to the points to be represented on their behalf.

In a word it may be safely asserted that there was nothing in the attitude of the people during this period to give the government serious disquietude. And we have evidence that the officials both at home and in the province were keeping a close watch for all symptoms of discontent, and were predisposed to see them if they existed. March 27th, 1767, Carleton writes to Sir William Johnson (in answer to

[1] Memorial of Pierre du Calvet, October, 1770. Can. Arch., Q. 7, p. 279.
[2] Can. Arch., Q. 6, p. 115.
[3] Can. Arch., Q. 6, p. 151. Reasons for doubting this assertion will be presented later.

an opinion expressed by the latter that the Canadian traders were tampering with the Indians): — "Ever since my arrival I have observed the Canadians with an attention bordering upon suspicion, but hitherto have not discovered either actions or sentiments which do not belong to good subjects."[1] November 20, 1768,[2] he writes to Hillsborough (apparently in answer to some uneasiness at home), that his observation of the people has not revealed anything to cause him to give any credit to alarming reports; adding, however, (now evidently referring only to the noblesse), that he has not the least doubt of their secret attachment to France, and that the non-discovery of traces of a treasonable correspondence was not to him sufficient proof that it did not exist. Early in 1772 Hillsborough transmits to Quebec a copy of a treasonable letter to France, alleged to have been signed by members of the Canadian noblesse.[3] In answer Cramahé declares his disbelief in its genuineness, but shows himself by no means satisfied of the trustworthiness of any class. However, the latest utterance we have previous to the Quebec Act is a statement by the same official, December 13th, 1773, that the people are tractable and submissive.[4]

It will be inferred from what has been said above that we are not to look for reflections of the public mind in the form of public meetings. Such demonstrations had been jealously prohibited by the French government for more than a century before the advent of the English, and while there is no indication throughout this period that the people generally expressed any wish for such a privilege,[5] the attitude of the provincial government was

[1] Can. Arch., Q. 4, p. 122.

[2] Letter printed in full in *Report Canadian Arch.*, 1888, p. 48.

[3] Can. Arch., Q. 8, p. 111.

[4] Can. Arch., Q. 10, p. 22.

[5] Carleton testified before the House of Commons in the debate on the Quebec Bill that he had never heard of petitions from the inhabitants to meet in bodies. The statement was supported by Chief-Justice Hey, who said that he knew of no conference among the Canadians regarding forms of government. That some popular movement,

evidently not much more liberal than during the old régime. All popular movements, not only by way of public meetings, but also through addresses, petitions, etc., were frowned upon by the authorities. Both Murray and Carleton were men of autocratic temper and of military training, and seem to have regarded all such attempts to influence governmental action as partaking of the nature of treason.

Very little need be said with regard to such administrative aspects of the new régime as might be considered factors, however slight, in the political education of the French Canadians. It will be remembered that under the old régime the highly centralized government had acted in local matters entirely by officials appointed from headquarters. The situation is but very slightly different in this first stage of English rule. The only trace of local self-government that is to be found is with regard to the parish bailiffs, (in large measure replacing the French captains of militia), who, beside their duties as administrative officers of the courts of justice, acted also in their several districts as overseers of highways and bridges, as fence viewers, and sometimes as coroners. These officials and their assistants were appointed by the government out of a list of six names annually furnished by the householders in each parish.[1] That the regulation was observed throughout the period and that the people seem on the whole to have complied with it, though not very eagerly,

---

however, early took place among the French of the town of Quebec is shown by a paper in the Haldimand collection. It is an answer by Murray to a charge that he occasioned discord among the old and new subjects by allowing some of the latter to meet in a deliberative way; his explanation being that this had been permitted only under careful restrictions, and with the desire of guarding the dependent French dealer against the influence of the English trader. That at least one such meeting took place is certain; but it is equally evident that there were very few, if any, more. It is most probable that the movement was due to a small group of professional men at Quebec, whom I shall have occasion to refer to later as very rapidly taking the place of the noblesse in the leadership of the people. The matter is of importance also with respect to the dreaded influence of the English trader.

[1] Ordinance of Sept. 17, 1764.

(probably, as in the case of juries, regarding it more as a burden than as a privilege), is shown by hints from the Council minutes.[1] Further than this we have no trace of participation by the people in their own government; such local affairs as were not managed by the bailiffs being in the hands of the justices of the peace or other direct appointees of the central government. Of direct representation of the people in regard to the central government there was of course none during the period, the Assembly which had been promised in the proclamation of 1763 never being established.[2] We need not delay over what might be regarded as forms of indirect representation,—as through the requirement that the council should consist only of residents, and through grand juries whose duty it was to report grievances, and whose report we find in one instance the direct occasion of new legislation; for these could contribute little or nothing to political education.

But yet that such political education was proceeding the following study will, I think, furnish considerable indirect and cumulative evidence. Just now I shall point only to some striking direct evidence as to the progress made up to the American invasion. It is the statement of a revolutionary officer stationed at Three Rivers, and entrusted

---

[1] Can. Arch., Q. 5–1, p. 295; Ib. 5–2, p. 876.

[2] In regard to the assembly we meet at the outset a curious uncertainty as to whether any measures were actually taken for the bringing of it together. The modern French Canadian historian, Garneau, asserts that it was actually convoked by Murray, and that its sitting was prevented by the refusal of the Canadians to take the oaths. Marriott, in his report to the Crown, 1774, says in regard to an assembly that "the fact is, though summoned and chose for all the parishes but Quebec by Gov. Murray, it has never sat." On the other hand Masères states in 1769 that "no assembly has hitherto been summoned." The probability of fact is with Masères, for it seems incredible that such an important step as the summoning in the much-debated matter of an assembly, not to say an actual election, could have taken place without any indication being given in an unbroken official correspondence which goes minutely into comparatively insignificant matters. Marriott, (who is probably Garneau's authority), was possibly misled by some notice of the election of bailiff-lists. It is certain that no assembly was ever constituted, and that whether the French Canadians were or were not given an opportunity to refuse to take the religious oaths required, these oaths were the main cause of the delay. That delay is dwelt upon elsewhere in connection with general imperial policy and the enesis of the Quebec Act.

through that district (containing seventeen parishes), with the task of replacing the militia officers appointed by Carleton by others in the interest of the revolutionary cause. Such was the public feeling in this district that this was done by popular election, the account of which shows the existence of a high degree of interest among the Canadians in the proceeding.   "In some parishes there are three or four candidates for the captaincy, and I receive information that bribery and corruption is already beginning to creep into their elections.   At some the disputes run so high that I am obliged to interfere."[1]   July 5, 1776, Gen. Wooster writes to Congress that he had caused similar elections to be held in every parish (apparently of the District of Montreal).[2]   The political advance of the French Canadians will best be appreciated through the examination later of their general attitude toward the Quebec Act and the American invasion. One of the conclusions of this study is that under the discouraging and unprogressive conditions which marked the few years of misgovernment between the conquest and the American revolution they had yet made such advance in the comprehension and appreciation of English government as to justify the strongest confidence in the possibility of a rapid and harmonious Anglicizing of the new province.

I had purposed treating of the *bourgeoisie* separately, but the material seems on the whole scarcely to warrant a sharp distinction between this class and the general body of the *habitants*. In the former term I include the great majority of the inhabitants of the towns,[3] as well as the retail dealers throughout the country and out of it among the Indians; and the social conditions of old France at the time would lead us to look for almost as wide a chasm between

---

[1] Amer. Arch., IV. 5, 481. "Extract of a letter from an officer in the Continental Army, dated Trois Rivières, March 24, 1776."

[2] 5 *Amer. Archives*, I. 12.

[3] The population of Quebec and Montreal is given in 1765 by Murray as 14,700.

the *bourgeois* and the *habitant* as between either and the
seigneur.   But this is a point in which we do not find the
social conditions of old and new France corresponding; for
in Canada the *bourgeois* attitude was in the main that of the
peasantry from which it had largely sprung, and with
which it had constant and close intercourse.[1]   It is probable
indeed that in the absence of manufactures and the great
possession of trade by the English element, a large part
of the urban population was directly connected with the
land, having been attracted to the town by reasons of security and convenience.[2]   Garneau asserts, indeed, that the
merchant class went to France at the conclusion of peace;
but the statement is probably true in regard only to the
more considerable dealers.   We are told by Murray in 1762
that the retail dealers are generally natives, and this evidently continued to be the case throughout the period.
One of the natural results would be the bringing of the
French commercial class largely under the influence of the
English, the latter practically monopolizing the wholesale
trade; and of such an influence we have many traces.[3]   It
is to be expected, of course, that we should find the townsmen more active in public appearances.   The addresses in
1763 on the subject of religion are evidently more especially from them; those from Montreal and Three Rivers expressly so represent themselves, though claiming also to
act on behalf of the country regions.   How correct the assumption of representation is we are left to determine for
ourselves, but it is safe to assert that there exists no
petition or memorial of any kind coming from the *habitants*
in the first instance, nor any indication of any right of
action being deputed by them to their so-called representa-

---

[1] See Haldimand's statement to Germaine, July 6, 1781, about the connection between
the traders of the town and the country and the influence of the latter over the peasantry. (Can. Arch., Q. 4, p. 40.)

[2] An ordinance was issued by Bigot, toward the close of the French régime, against
the country people moving to the towns.

[3] Especially in connection with the Quebec Act, 1774-5. See also Carleton to Shelburne, November 29, 1766. (Can. Arch., Q. 4, p. 40.) See above, p. 293, note.

tives.   The peasant was too ignorant and too unaccustomed to such measures.   But nevertheless we may conclude that, except on points manifestly only of urban application, the voice of the townsman is in the main expressive of general grievances and desires.   At the beginning of the period Haldimand expressly classes the shopkeeper among the general body of the inhabitants in their apparent indifference to the fate of the country.

B.   The Noblesse and the Clergy.

As said above, for full and vivid pictures of the different classes of the community we can go to Parkman.   All that is attempted here is to set forth such indications during our period as may seem to have a bearing on the problems of government.   And first in consideration must come the noblesse, the old secular leaders.   The earliest general representations we meet with in regard to them are found in the reports of the military commanders in 1762. Murray's picture is not a pleasant one (and it should be remembered that Murray is generally their determined champion, and was so regarded by them); it represents them as in general poor, extremely vain, arrogant toward the trading community, (though very ready to reap profits in the same way when opportunity offered),[1] and tyrannical with their vassals.[2]   The contemporary reports of Gage and Burton do not enter into characterizations, but agree with Murray's in stating that the English government will not be relished by the noblesse, and that any emigration will be from their ranks.   The vast extent of the seigniories (five or six miles front by six or nine deep), is enlarged upon by Burton; but these estates produced very little to their holders, and we have an apparently trustworthy statement to the effect that 128 of the seigniories

---

[1] It will be remembered that on account of the poverty of the class its members were allowed by the French government to engage in trade without losing caste.

[2] See Hey to Lord Chancellor, August 28, 1775, for statement of the low opinion he had formed of the noblesse in council.   Can. Arch., Q. 12, p. 203.

yielded an average of only £60 per year.[1] Certainly the poverty of the seigniorial families is a matter there can be no doubt of; we meet with constant references thereto throughout the period, it being frequently assumed that their means of livelihood had been taken away by the deprivation of public employment.[2] For it will be remembered that this class was from first to last under the French a military and administrative one,[3] though without any real influence on the government, which generally took the part of the *habitant* against them. They were not country gentlemen, most of them residing constantly in the towns and visiting their estates only for the purpose of receiving dues. Everything goes to show that their influence over the people was purely of military foundation, and that it fell to pieces when the military relation ceased.[4]

As shown by a report of Carleton[5] the most important part of the order left Canada at the capitulation or the conclusion of peace; those who remained being of a lower rank, of less property, and of less close connection with France. These latter are reported as comprising 126 male adults, some of whom have families. The first political manifestation which purports to be exclusively from them is the memorial of the seigniors of Quebec to the king, 1766, in defense of Murray,[6] signed by twenty-one names. The document is a strong expression of personal satisfaction with that official and his methods, beginning, however, with a comparison of the civil government with the military one they had first experienced in a manner very unfavorable to the

---

[1] Marriott puts the value of the best at £80 a year. (*Code of Laws.*) See above, p. 279, note, for reference in Carroll's *Journal* to poverty of the seigneurs.

[2] Masères states that 120 had lost office by the conquest, and Carleton writes to Townsend, November 17th, 1766, that they had been wholly dependent on the French crown. See also same to Shelbourne, March 2d, 1768. (Can. Arch., Q. 5-1, p. 382, and *Rep. Can. Arch.*, 1886, Note D.)

[3] Carleton to Townsend, Nov. 17, 1766. Can. Arch., Q. 3, p. 411.

[4] See Haldimand to Germaine, July 25th, 1778. Can. Arch., B. 42, p. 10.

[5] Nov., 1767. See *Rep. Can. Arch.*, 1888, p. 44.

[6] *Rep. Can. Arch.*, 1888, p. 19.

former.   It denounces the "Cabal" which the old subjects and a few deluded new subjects had formed against the governor and supplicates his restoration.   Of somewhat wider scope is the corresponding petition in the same year from the seigniors of Montreal, which, after asking for Murray's retention, goes on to complain of their own ex- clusion from office and of the expense of the required regis- tration of land (with thirty-nine signatures).   In November, 1767, Carleton writes [1] that as nothing had been done to attach the gentry to the British interest, and as they had lost all employment by the change, it could not be hoped that they would be very warm in its support.   "Therefore, all circumstances considered, while matters remain in their present state, the most we may hope for from the gentlemen who remain in the province is a passive neutrality on all occasions, with respectful submission to government and deference for the king's commission in whatever hand it may be lodged; these they almost to a man have persevered in since my arrival, notwithstanding much pains have been taken to engage them in parties by a few whose duty and whose office should have taught them better." [2]   One year later (November 20th, 1768), he speaks of their "decent and respectful obedience to the king's government hitherto," though frankly admitting that he has no doubt of their secret attachment to France, which "naturally has the affection of all the people." [3]

Of much greater importance than the noblesse, through their more deeply-seated influence over the people, were the Roman Catholic clergy.   Readers of Parkman will re- call the turgid rhetoric in which at the close of his "Old Régime" he sums up the vast share that had fallen to the Church from the very first in the founding and direction of the colony; and though during the period we are con-

---

[1] *Rep. Can. Arch.*, 1888, p. 41.

[2] See Carleton concerning the disapproval by the gentry of the verdict against the crown in the matter of duties, December 24th, 1767. (Can. Arch., Q. 5–1, p. 316).

[3] Can. Arch., Q. 5–2, p. 890.

sidering that influence was undoubtedly on the wane, (how much so will be seen in regard to the American invasion), still it was a factor that cannot be neglected. It would seem that the military period had been favourable to the preservation of the personal influence of the clergy, notwithstanding the indication referred to above of the loss of tractability on the part of the *habitant* in the matter of tithes. For they (as well as such other local magnates as were accessible), took in large measure not only during the military period but even probably in some degree till the Quebec Act, the place of the French local judiciary. Garneau says that all disputes were settled by the intermediation of the clergy and other local leaders,[1] and though his picture is undoubtedly overdrawn, every presumption is in favour of a considerable movement in this direction. It was to the clergy and to the old militia officers rather than to the noblesse that the peasant would naturally betake himself, if only for the reason that with them he felt more in sympathy as being largely of the same class. For the lower clergy then as now was largely drawn from the ranks of the peasantry. Murray, in his report of 1762, expressly states that the most prominent were French, the rest Canadians of the lower class. This is a division we should expect, and it is not surprising also to find indications of some jealousy and difference of view between the two sections. The Canadian born element would be much more easily reconciled to the new rule, and it is very probable that the moderate representations spoken of above, which refrain from laying stress on the preservation of the hierarchy, were inspired solely by this element, well aware that the continuance of that hierarchy meant in all probability the continuance of the domination of the foreign born priest. Gage, in his report from Montreal in 1762, speaks of this division of interest and of the necessity of detaching the Canadian clergy entirely

---

[1] *Hist. du Can.*, II, 386.   (Quebec, 1859.)

from France. The growth of a native priesthood with feelings not always in harmony with the old government of Church or State, had been a slow one, but that such an element was now firmly established there can be no doubt.[1] Up to the conquest the scale had been constantly turned in favour of the French-born element, which, according to Cramahé, regarded the Canadian clergy with contempt.[2] The policy of the new government may be seen from the statement in the same letter that the French clergy were then jealous of the Canadian as likely to get all the benefices, and that hence the French were in favour of a change which the Canadians were strongly interested to prevent.

Whichever element was uppermost however, and by whatever motives it may have been influenced, we have no indication of any but the most satisfactory behaviour throughout this period on the part of the Church in Canada. In June, on the conclusion of peace, a mandate was issued by the vicar general (the highest ecclesiastic remaining), recommending to the inhabitants submission and fidelity. In the autumn of the same year we meet the general addresses already spoken of,[3] which seem to have been called forth by the depleted state of the priesthood and by fear lest the lack of a bishop should leave it to die out. They are all probably inspired. One of these addresses is from the chapter of Quebec, and we must conclude that the moderation of the demands had met with the approval of the prevailing portion of the clergy. It expresses no anxiety for a continuance of priests from Europe, expressly saying on the contrary that those educated in the native seminaries would be more patriotic, more united, and less exposed to new opinion;[4] and that they

---

[1] See Haldimand to Germaine, September 14th, 1779. Can. Arch., B. 54, p. 177.

[2] Can. Arch., Q. 8, p. 160. To Hillsborough, July 5, 1772.

[3] Above, p. 284.

[4] The petition from Three Rivers dwells more fully on means of escaping French influence in preserving the clergy.

(the petitioners), would be satisfied with a merely titular bishop with full ecclesiastical jurisdiction, but without exterior dignity or compulsory means of support. It is fully evident that the petitioners are sincere, and that they aim only at the measures necessary to preserve their educational and spiritual position.

CHAPTER II.

THE BRITISH SETTLERS.

A.   Numbers, Origin, Occupations, Character.

The term "old subjects" was applied during this period and for long after to those inhabitants of the province who had been subjects of Great Britain before the conquest,— i. e., to the new English-speaking element that accompanied or followed the conqueror.   The numerical weight of this element would alone hardly entitle it to consideration, for at no time during the period did it in all probability embrace more than 500 or 600 male adults.   As late as 1779 Haldimand refers roughly to the non-Canadian population as 2,000 in number.   We know, however, that there was some exodus from the province in 1775-6, and it is probable that the maximum number of English-speaking inhabitants had been reached soon after the conclusion of peace.   For Carleton writes, November, 1767, that they are diminishing, being discouraged by the severe climate and the poverty of the country.[1]   But notwithstanding this insignificant numerical strength, the energy and the peculiar position of this element make it impossible to avoid reckoning with it.

Presumably these "old subjects" were subjects of Great Britain by birth.   But to what extent they had previously been resident in other parts of America, or what proportion of them was American born, it is not easy to determine. And the settlement of the point is of considerable interest in view of their connection later with the American revolutionists.   We are safe in concluding that the smaller portion only of them were in Canada previous to the conclusion of peace, and that this portion was the least

---

[1] *Report Canadian Archives*, 1888, p. 43.

respectable one, and composed mainly of those afterward spoken of with contempt by the provincial officials as sutlers and discharged soldiers [1]— a class mainly no doubt of European birth. As to the remaining and larger portion, the scattered references that we have lead to the conclusion that they were mainly born in the British Islands. But some of them had doubtless, for shorter or longer periods, been resident in the other colonies before coming to Quebec, and a few were American-born. Whether it was that the portion with previous colonial experience was more enterprising and free-spoken than the others, we find that it comes to stand for the whole in the official mind. Knox, in his "Justice and Policy of the Quebec Act," [2] evidently regards the British subjects in Canada as having all come from, or being all identified with, the other provinces; and this view may be regarded as the general one taken in England. We have, however, among the Haldimand papers a careful analysis of the British in the District of Montreal, 1765, in regard to birth and occupations, [3] from which we learn that of the 136 adult males there at that time, 98 were born in the British Isles, 23 in other parts of Europe, and 12 in the American colonies; nothing being said as to residence immediately before coming to Canada. But there are many indications that whether this analysis can be considered as representative of the whole body or not, the more politically influential of the new settlers were conversant with the social and governmental conditions of the other colonies to a degree which forces us to the conclusion that the knowledge must in most cases have been acquired by periods of considerable residence. In the first public appearance of the new element in the province under civil government — the presentment of the grand jury of October, 1764,— we find frequent references to the judicial

---

[1] The census report of 1765 mentioned below gives 43 of the 136 in the Montreal district as of this character.

[2] London, 1774.

[3] Can. Arch., B. 8, p. 96.

conditions of the other colonies such as would occur only to those who were recalling institutions (peculiar to the colonies), under which they had lived and to which they had become attached.[1] Similar evidence appears in their remonstrance against the judiciary ordinance of 1770,[2] and in some commercial representations concerning the English bankruptcy laws in 1767.[3] Further we have particular information in regard to individuals who later became noteworthy for open sympathy with the revolutionary cause, and find that they are nearly all of American birth or of American political education. A list "of the principal persons settled in the province who very zealously served the rebels in the winter 1775–6"[4] names 28 individuals, of whom only 7 are of non-American birth. In this list we find the names of many of the main leaders in the political movements just previous to the Quebec Act. It is evident in short that the most determined and outspoken section among the new settlers were American by birth or adoption, and it is probable that that portion was, in relation to the whole, a small one. This will be shown more fully later when I speak of political movements. That a distinction could be made, and was made by the provincial officials, is shown by a reference of Carleton to the scale of duties lately adopted as being approved by "both Canadian and English merchants, the colonists excepted."[5]

The new English-speaking population seems to have been practically all resident in the towns of Quebec and Montreal. Its main occupation was trade,— a trade which had the fur traffic for its backbone. Many of its members are asserted by their detractors to have come to Canada because they had failed everywhere else, but the fact that Canada offered exceptional advantages for the fur trade

---

[1] Can. Arch., Q. 2, pp. 233–63.

[2] Can. Arch., Q. 7, p. 95.

[3] Can. Arch., Q. 5–1, p. 248.

[4] Can. Arch., Q. 13, p. 106.

[5] Dec. 24, 1767. (Can. Arch., Q. 5–1, p. 300.) See also to Dartmouth, November 11, 1774. (Can. Arch., Q. 11, p. 11.)

affords a more creditable explanation. Many were mere
agents for English firms; some, especially of the discharged
soldiers, became small retailers of liquor. So averse were
they to land occupation, at least on the terms first offered,
that the lands set apart for the discharged soldiery were
in few cases taken up. But they took with considerable
avidity to the acquiring of seigniories when that form of
grant was re-established,[1] and Hillsborough, April 18,
1772, writes that he is pleased to find " that so great a
spirit of cultivation of the waste lands in the colony has
spread itself among His Majesty's natural born subjects."
There can be little doubt that by the end of the period they
had come into possession of a large proportion of the
seigneurial estates of the province;[2] but there is no probability that they at this time settled down on these estates
in any permanent manner. They undoubtedly continued to
be identified with the towns, and it is sufficiently correct
for all purposes to regard their connection with Canada as
caused and continued either by commercial interests[3] or by
situations held under government.

As to the character of this new element we are unfortunately dependent almost entirely upon the testimony of
its bitterest enemies. The causes of this enmity will be
more fully apparent later; the fact is that throughout the
whole period of civil government the provincial adminis-
trators and the " old subjects " were in direct and for the
most part bitter antagonism. The latter claimed that they
had come into the country in reliance on the Proclamation of
1763, which they considered contained a distinct promise
of the establishment in Canada of the forms of government
and the system of law that prevailed in the other colonies;
consequently they maintained a hostile attitude to the
system in operation, as purely provisional, and impatiently

---

[1] See elsewhere concerning land grants.
[2] See *Evidence*, Quebec Act Debates. Also Masères, especially with regard to English petitions and memorials for an Assembly, 1773.
[3] See Carleton, *Rep. Can. Arch.*, 1890, p. 1.

demanded the fulfillment of the asserted pledges. The governors on the other hand had speedily arrived at the conclusion that such changes would be most disadvantageous to the country, and would imperil its possession; and they consequently regarded with no favourable eye the turbulent little body which seemed to be aiming at the same licentiousness as (in the official opinion), prevailed in the other colonies. It is the same antagonism that we see contemporaneously in these other colonies, increased tenfold by the peculiar circumstances of the province. Race and social prejudices, and collisions between the civil and military elements, complicated the situation and intensified the opposition of the British trading community to the old French military system and its favorers. And in view of these facts we must take with caution the assertions of the governors, who, just as they erroneously looked upon the noblesse as the true representatives of the Canadians, seem to have indiscriminately classed together the whole old subject body as turbulent and republican, and bent on nothing but the oppressing of the French population and the acquiring of gain. That there were individual instances to which they could point in support of this view cannot be denied; nor can we doubt that the British element throughout the most of the period might well present to the harassed official an intolerant and unconciliatory attitude. But a scrutiny of the evidence will show that the constant official censure was to a large degree unjust and undiscerning, and that the British party in the Province of Quebec deserved very much more consideration from the authorities than it received. The matter is of importance from other grounds than those of historical justice. For there can be little doubt that the incorrect ideas that swayed the official mind on this point were one of the main agencies in the genesis of the Quebec Act.

Murray's expressions of dislike for his fellow-countrymen seem to date from the grand jury presentment of 1764, when he writes home of the "licentious fanatics trading here," whom nothing will satisfy except "the expulsion of the Canadians."[1]   The following March 3, he says that the merchants "are chiefly adventurers of mean educa- tion, either young beginners, or, if old traders, such as had failed in other countries; all have their fortunes to make and are little solicitous about the means."[2]   August 20, 1766, after he had left the province, he writes of the party which had procured his recall, that "most of them are followers of the army, of mean education, or soldiers disbanded at the reduction of the troops;" and adds, "I report them to be in general the most immoral collection of men I ever knew."[3]   This representation is evidently little to be regarded.   Carleton, though no particular friend of Murray, seems, however, to have at once assumed the same attitude toward the old subject, and probably with more confidence, as knowing that the home government was not at all likely to gratify their wishes.   As with Murray, his military training prejudiced him in favor of the old system and of the military noblesse, to both of which the English element was bitterly opposed.   Novem- ber 25, 1767,[4] he describes the old subjects as having " been mostly left here by accident, and are either dis- banded officers, soldiers, or followers of the army, who, not knowing how to dispose of themselves elsewhere, settled where they were left at the reduction; or else they are adventurers in trade, or such as could not remain at home, who set out to mend their fortunes at the opening of this new channel of commerce," and adds that they have for the most part not succeeded, and are abandoning the province.   March 28, 1770,[5] he writes in regard to the necessity he has been under of taking from the justices of

---

[1] Can. Arch., Q. 2, p. 233.

[2] Ib., p. 377.

[3] Can. Arch., B. 8, p. 1.

[4] *Rep. Can. Arch.*, 1888, p. 42.

[5] *Rep. Can. Arch.*, 1890, p. 1.

the peace their jurisdiction in civil cases, on account of the oppressive methods of many of them, and proceeds to explain what these methods were; saying that those who had failed in business sought the office in order to make it a means of extortion, and had therein very grievously taken advantage of the ignorance of the people.   This oppression seems to have been for a short time a real grievance, and has been considered one of the principal proofs of the evil character of the English element; but a closer examination will show that in that view it has been exaggerated.   For it was such as hardly could have been practiced by any but justices in the remoter parts of the province, or at least by those in the country districts, and I have shown above that very few of the English were settled outside of the towns.   So that it must have been confined to about a dozen individuals,[1] and cannot possibly be taken as any indication of the general character of the English-speaking settlers.   The matter is simply an instance of the careless grouping and indiscriminate judgments of the period, or possibly of intentional misrepresentation in order to prejudice the case of the old subject in the eyes of the home government.   That this result was attained may be seen in the writings of the pamphleteers who defended the Quebec Act, as well as in the arguments of its supporters in the Commons.

B.   Political Attitude.

What the political attitude of the English party was may be easily gathered from the foregoing.   Whether or not accustomed to the greater self-government of the American colonies we find the whole body strongly imbued with a certain degree of the American spirit and determined to lose no opportunity of pressing their claims for the establishment of English law and an Assembly.   They con-

---

[1] The list of justices of the peace for the whole province as first appointed, included only twenty-three names, of whom most were resident in the towns. See p. 312, note 1.

tended throughout that the promises of the Proclamation of 1763 on these points had been among the main inducements to the taking up of their residence in the province; and in season and out of season, without regard to the difficulties in the way either from the original constitution of the province or from the hazardous nature of the British hold on it, they pressed their demands on the home government and refused any tolerance to the existing provisional arrangements. So that at first sight it would appear (as has generally been represented), that in the pressing of these demands the party showed throughout a factious and intolerant spirit, and gave little evidence of political forethought, or of consideration either for the Canadians or for the difficult position of the administration. As to political forethought they must be judged mainly on a careful consideration of the later events, with regard to the question as to how far they were justified in their contention that the English system of law and government, so far as they claimed it, would not really be objectionable or injurious to the mass of the people. As to the intolerance and inconsiderateness of their attitude, we must guard as before against indiscriminate grouping; and it will be found moreover that the evidence on these heads is confined to the early years of the period. A comparison of the names appended to the various petitions and other public manifestations of the time with what appears later as to the individuals who espoused the revolutionary cause, shows that these manifestations were the voice really of that small section which, chiefly American-born, was most thoroughly permeated with American ideas, and which kept itself in touch with the movements on the other side of the border. The bulk of the party, English-born, slower of comprehension, and less used to American self-government, more or less acquiesced in the movements of the bolder spirits, partly on general principles of popular leadership, partly because they had a common ground in their desire for, and anticipation of English laws and governmental forms.[1] Hence, it is not surprising that we cannot trace any definite dividing line[2] between the English-born and the colonists until the actual resort to arms drove the leaders into the arms of the revolutionists. In connection with this it is interesting to note that the first public manifestation of the British party was the most violent and outspoken, supporting therein the idea that it was representative of the views of the American element when that element had in freshest remembrance the forms they were attached to and had hoped to bring with them into Canada. These hopes had been disappointed by the passing of the judiciary ordinance of September 17, 1764, which, though afterwards condemned by those who supported the continuance of the old system as having aimed at the complete overturning thereof, seemed to the English party a very partial and unsatisfactory measure. Accordingly, at the general quarter sessions of the justices of the peace held at Quebec in the following month, the fourteen English who were summoned (together with seven French), as a grand jury, seized the occasion to express in no measured tones their deep disappointment and disapproval.[3] The main presentment began (in direct contempt of court), by condemning the late ordinance in regard to the power

---

[1] It is not probable that the claim of general representative powers put forward in 1764 on behalf of the grand jury, (discussed below), was seriously entertained except by a few of the bolder spirits; but the attitude of protest and disappointment was evidently largely shared, even by those whose later actions were much more moderate. For in the evidence connected with an investigation in 1768 into the suspension by Murray of a public official, one of the charges against whom was that he had been prominent in this grand jury movement, we find a comparatively numerously signed letter of thanks to the jury from their English fellow-countrymen in Quebec, which states that the signers consider the jury "as yet the only body representative of this district," and that in regard to the digression from usual form in the proceedings, "the want of a General Assembly in the province sufficiently justifies your conduct to the public." (Can. Arch., Q. 5-2, pp. 629–69.)

[2] Though see Carleton's reference above to the difference of opinion in regard to customs duties. See also Carleton to Hillsborough, April 25, 1770, concerning the refusal of the majority of the old subjects to take the steps urged by the more violent concerning the judiciary ordinance of that year. (Can. Arch., Q. 7, p. 89.)

[3] Can. Arch., Q. 2, p. 242.

given to the justices and to the number and incapacity of these officials,[1] and expressed a determination never again under the system complained of, to act as jurors. It then proceeded to make the very remarkable claim on behalf of the signers as grand jurors that they "must be considered at present as the only body representative of the colony," and therefore "as British subjects have a right to be consulted before any ordinance that may affect the body they represent be passed into law;" furthermore demanding that "the public accounts should be laid before the grand jurors at least twice a year, to be examined and checked by them, and that they may be regularly settled every six months before them." This claim[2] shows that while considering the existing government as only provisional, they could not grasp the fact that as British subjects they were even under it to be excluded from some form of the self-government they had been accustomed to. The fourteen

---

[1] It is noteworthy that this condemnation was later abundantly justified by the complaints as to the ill-working of this provision and the revoking of it by the ordinance of 1770. Here we find the representatives of the English party strongly condemning at its initiation a measure the ill-working of which was afterwards used as a weapon of reproach against that party.

[2] Which they do not attempt to fortify with any precedent from the other colonies. though frequently bringing such on other points. I have been unable to find any direct connection between this incident and contemporary events in the other colonies, but the conclusion is irresistible that some such must have existed. By June, 1764, it was known in America that Grenville had given notice of the Stamp Act, and that a bill had been passed increasing customs duties. Before the end of the month Otis and others had formed a committee for intercolonial correspondence and resistance. Popular attention throughout the summer had become more and more concentrated on the subject, and in September the New York Assembly had boldly claimed for the people "that great badge of English liberty, the being taxed only with their own consent." (Bancroft, III, 89.) Of course, the Quebec movement was as yet fully taken up with a stage beyond which the other colonies had long passed. And we shall see later that it was not likely to get beyond that stage with the bulk of the party. Though it is to be noted that Cramahé writes in July, 1774, (to Dartmouth, Can. Arch., Q. 10, p. 79), that "His Majesty's subjects in this province, tho' collected from all parts of his extensive dominions, have in general, at least such as intend remaining in the country, adopted American ideas in regard to taxation, and a report transmitted from one of their correspondents in Britain that a duty upon spirits was intended to be raised here by authority of Parliament, was a principal cause of setting them upon petitions for an assembly." It connection with this see following pages in regard to the revenue trials and the Stamp Act.

English jurors alone also presented an additional article protesting against the admitting of Roman Catholics on juries or to the professions as "an open violation of our most sacred laws and liberties," and tending to the insecurity of the province.

The next appearance of these remonstrants is in the petition of the Quebec British traders against Murray in 1765, signed by twenty-one names,[1] the signers claiming to act on behalf of their fellow-subjects. The friction between the party and Murray seems to have steadily increased in the intervening year and finally had resulted in this representation, which was later thought to have procured the governor's recall. It began[2] by stating that the connection of most of the petitioners with the country dated "from the surrender of the colony," goes on to represent the conduct of the governor and the measures of government as oppressive and injurious, threatens removal from the country in case of non-redress, and ends by requesting the establishment of a house of representatives "to be chosen in this as in other Your Majesty's provinces, there being a number more than sufficient of loyal and well-affected Protestants, exclusive of military officers;" the Canadians to be "allowed to elect Protestants," without the burden of test oaths. The demand for an assembly reappears with more or less distinctness all through the period; though while Carleton remained in the province his decidedly discouraging attitude seems to have prevented any very united movement. But resentment at the withholding of representative institutions appears to be the main moving cause in a very determined stand by the English mercantile class after 1766 against the collection of the old French customs duties. In accordance with legal opinion as to the reversion to the crown of all sources of revenue possessed by the French government, the imperial authorities had in

---

[1] Eight of these were among the fourteen English jurors in 1764.
[2] *Rep. Can. Arch.*, 1888, p. 14.

1765 ordered the above collection, and July 21, 1766, a provincial proclamation was issued setting forth the duties and the ground on which they were claimed.[1] A few days later it is reported officially that the merchants "will not pay their duties unless otherwise compelled." Some of them were accordingly prosecuted in the Court of King's Bench before a jury composed entirely of English, and which the Chief Justice charged to bring in only a special verdict as to the facts, leaving to a higher court the point of law[2] as to whether the English crown had become by the conquest and cession entitled to the old French duties. But the jury, thoroughly in sympathy with the recalcitrant merchants, refused to be restricted in this way, and brought in a general verdict of acquittal. Another suit shortly afterwards had the same result, and all efforts to collect the duties seem then to have been dropped for two years.[3] In the fall of 1768, however, after an action in the British Common Pleas against Murray, in which the principle of the King's right to these duties was accepted without question, the commissioners of the treasury resolved to make another attempt, and instituted prosecutions anew. The issue was the same, however, though Masères (who was the prosecuting attorney), acknowledges that the jury " consisted of some of the most respectable inhabitants of Quebec, and of such as were most moderate in their principles and disposition." Writing in 1774 he says that it may be seen from these trials that these duties can never be collected in the Quebec courts; from which we may infer that no further attempt was made to collect them during the period.[4]

The ground of this determined resistance is nowhere clearly stated, but there can be little doubt that it was mainly inspired by some portion of the spirit then agitat-

---

[1] Can. Arch., Q. 2, p. 377.
[2] Called by him "very new and difficult."
[3] Can. Arch., Q. 3, pp. 254, 400.
[4] See Masères, *Commissions*, pp. 288–311.

ing the other colonies.   In a letter shortly before the later
trials Carleton states that the merchants based their opposition on the ground that the duties demanded were not
quite the same as the French;[1] but that the real question
was much broader is shown by the argument for the Crown
of Masères, the attorney general, (reported by himself).
In it he contends that "whatevor might have been asserted
to the contrary, in order to inflame the passions of the
people and prejudice the minds of the jury against these
duties, the king by them did not mean to exert any prerogative of imposing taxes by his own single authority and
without the consent either of a provincial Assembly or of
the General Assembly of the whole British Empire," and
that therefore the requisition did not endanger the public
liberty of the inhabitants and the privileges they claimed
"either as English in general or under the proclamation
of October, 1763, by which His Majesty had promised them
the enjoyment of the benefit of the laws of England."[2] The
attorney general is here attempting to remove the prejudice of a jury which was of the same class—the English
trading class,—as the accused, and it is evident that he
perceived that whatever the special plea put forward, the
opposition was founded on the general claim of being
English subjects, entitled to the operation of English laws
and principles.   It would seem also as if the spirit of opposition as expressed on the point had been steadily growing;
for Carleton had written, December 24, 1767, that he was
almost certain that a revenue would soon be raised from
the customs sufficient to meet all expenses of government,
and that "both Canadian and English merchants, the
colonists excepted," were willing to pay much higher
duties than those he was then proposing.[3]   Masères' description of the jury in the trials of 1769 shows that it

[1] Can. Arch., Q. 6, p. 65,—May 10, 1769.
[2] *Commissions*, pp. 304–5.
[3] Can. Arch., Q. 5–1, p. 316.

could not have been composed of these "colonists," and therefore we must conclude that either Carleton had deceived himself in 1767, or that the "colonist" spirit had on this point taken possession even of the "Canadian and English merchants."

This phase of the subject is the more interesting taken in connection with the undeniable acquiescence of the province in the Stamp Act shortly before.[1] For leaving out a very small circle no opposition to this Act sufficiently strong to send its voice down to us seems to have been made in Quebec or in Nova Scotia.[2] That it had been put regularly into operation is shown by the proclamation announcing its repeal, which says that "whereas many persons in publick office and others may at present have stampt paper and parchment that has not been made use of" they will be reimbursed for the same.[3] But no statement can be found of any revenue from the tax, and it is most probable that the "resistance passive" which Garneau attributes to the province[4] went far enough to reduce the receipts to a very small sum. That the section of the English party known as "the colonists" had made their voice heard against the act is shown by a reference of Carleton's, October 25th, 1766,[5] and by a statement of

---

[1] The Stamp Act was in force in Quebec apparently from November 1, 1765, to May 28, 1766.

[2] With regard to Nova Scotia some documents from a later period may here be referred to. In 4 *American Archives* (III. 619), we find a Whitehall memorandum dated September 1, 1775, that on that day His Majesty had graciously received an address from the House of Representatives of Nova Scotia, containing a declaration of entire submission to the supreme authority of the British Parliament and of readiness to pay taxes fixed by it, to be at its disposal. This loyal document, however, is followed (*Ib.* 780) by a letter from Halifax dated September 23, 1775, which says that the above address represents only about one-thousandth of the inhabitants of the province, and had been procured when most of the House of Representatives were absent; further, that owing to universal sympathy with the revolutionists no duties had been paid since August last, that some tons of tea arrived the day before had been thrown into the sea, and that the revolutionary forces at Boston had been continually supplied from Nova Scotia with fresh provisions.

[3] Can. Arch., Q. 5-2, p. 822.

[4] *Hist. Can.*, II, 399.

[5] Can. Arch., Q. 3, p. 259.

Murray, August 20th, 1766, (in regard to the Canadians), that "tho' stimulated to dispute it by some of the licentious traders from New York they cheerfully obeyed the Stamp Act, in hopes that their good behaviour would recommend them to the favour and protection of their sovereign." [1] Previously (February 14, 1776, while the act was yet unrepealed), the governor had reported that "His Majesty's subjects in this province have not followed the example of the neighbouring colonies, but have cheerfully submitted to the authority of the British legislature." [2] On the arrival of Carleton in September, 1766, an address presented to him from the combined English and French inhabitants of the city and district of Quebec expresses "the most profound and submissive reverence to the legislative authority of the British parliament, of which we lately gave a public and signal proof by an immediate and universal obedience to the Stamp Act." [3] Lastly, the argument which I have quoted from the attorney-general in the revenue trials of 1769 shows conclusively that the class he was trying to influence (i. e. the main, more moderate body of the English trading class), was not supposed to doubt, and therefore could not have made any fundamental objection to, the full legislative authority over the province of the British parliament.[4] This class then we may suppose to have acquiesced grumblingly in the Stamp Act, while the smaller section of American birth or training had no doubt vigorously protested against it. As to the Canadians, the compliant voice of the address to Carleton doubtless represents correctly the attitude of those affected; but there is no ground

---

[1] Can. Arch., B. 8, p. 1.

[2] Ibid., Q. 3, p. 26.

[3] Ibid., p. 344.

[4] Of course it must be remembered that as the province had no assembly the same objection could not be made to such a claim as in the other provinces (see p. 312, note 2). The matter therefore stands on a somewhat different footing. It seems, however, very probable that the Stamp Act agitation in the other colonies, and its success, had considerable influence in emboldening the Quebec merchants to the stout resistance later to the revenue duties.

to suppose that any attention was paid to the Act by the mass of the French Canadian people. But few of these could, in its brief life, have even become aware of its existence; for, as I have elsewhere shown, the *habitant* at this time very slightly availed himself of English legal forms or courts.

In the spring of 1770 the British element again appears in strong opposition to the government in regard to the ordinance of February 1, 1770, which on account of the oppressive conduct of some of the justices of the peace took away from the whole body all power in matters that affected private property, and instituted for the protection of creditors methods which were considered by the merchants as unsatisfactory and precarious and likely to affect the credit of the province. The memorial in which the objections of the merchant body were expressed is evidently what it purports to be, a document almost entirely dictated by commercial considerations; and though the action of the government was justifiable and the ordinance in question probably necessary, I cannot look upon this movement of its opponents as of the purely factious and oppressive origin attributed to it by Carleton. In the same year we have the outcome of a movement spoken of by Carleton in 1768,[1] in another petition for a general assembly, which they claim in part as promised in the proclamation of 1763, and in part because necessary to arrest the declining state of the province and make it really of benefit to the empire. The assembly is still contemplated as being composed only of Protestants, (nothing being said as to the qualifications of electors), the petitioners asserting as in 1765 that "there is now a sufficient number of your Majesty's Protestant subjects residing in and possessed of real property in this province, and who are otherwise qualified to be members of a general assembly;" which they pray shall therefore be

---

[1] He writes, January 20, that the agitation for an assembly which he thought had been dropped a year before, has been resumed, the leaders being "egged on by letters from home." (Q. 5-1, 370.)

called "in such manner as is used in those provinces in
America under your Majesty's government." (signed by 31
names).[1] Carleton left for England about the same time,
and this step was probably intended to counteract the
effect of his presence at home. For the following three
years quiet seems to have reigned in the province, the
British element applying itself energetically to the acquirement of landed property. As the home government, however, came more unmistakeably nearer to the adoption of
decisive measures in regard to Canadian affairs, the
political energies of the party revived, and as a consequence we have the very united and vigorous petitions of
1773 (October–January) for an assembly.[2] According to
Cramahé[3] the leaders of the old subjects sedulously attempted to induce the French to co-operate, and Masères
relates that the negotiations were broken off in consequence of a refusal of the English to insert in the joint
petition a specific request that the assembly might be composed of Protestants and Catholics alike, with more or less
of a preponderance secured to the latter.[4] The English then
proceeded alone, and petitions and memorials were forwarded to the home government about the beginning of
1774, signed there can be little doubt by almost every old
subject of any standing (outside the official circles), in the
province. The wording of these is in the main of the
same tenor as in the previous representations, but a very
noteworthy change appears in the reference to the nature
of the assembly asked for. In all the previous petitions it
had been requested to be called "in such manner as is used
in those provinces in America under your Majesty's government," coupled with the statement that there were
sufficient qualified Protestants in the province to constitute such a body. This evidently means the exclusion of

---

[1] Can. Arch., Q. 7, p. 359.
[2] Ibid., Q. 10. See also Masères, *Account.*
[3] Ibid., Q. 10, p. 22.
[4] See below, c. 5.

Catholics, who, however, were to be permitted to vote. But in the present petition the words are, " in such manner and of such constitution and form as shall seem best adapted to secure peace, welfare and good government." The explanation of this change is given by Masères,[1] agent for the party in London, who states that though the old subjects had formerly entertained hopes of an exclusively Protestant assembly, on hearing that Catholics had been admitted to that of Grenada,[2] and that the government contemplated the giving of the same privilege in Quebec, they had resolved to acquiesce in this indulgence, though unwilling to join with the French in asking for it. In other words, the party had become convinced that there was no hope of an exclusively Protestant assembly, and preferred a mixed one to none at all; probably relying on their influence over many sections of the French to secure a considerable if not the greater share of the power wielded by such a body. The petitioners make the statement that the granting of an assembly is the only sure means of conciliating the new subjects.[3]

In the matter of the laws to be established in the province we find that, as with regard to an assembly, the views of the British party became much more liberal toward the close of the period. The presentment of the grand jury quoted above shows that they were disposed at first to assume a most intolerant attitude, and (holding strictly to the wording of the treaty of cession), to enforce against the French Canadians the penal laws which were not enforced at home. But this we can consider the result of only a momentary access of irritation and disappointment, and as probably confined to a few individuals. For we find nothing of the kind later and have seen that all the petitions for an assembly contemplated the admission

---

[1] *Additional Proceedings, etc.*, p. 61.

[2] For conditions in Grenada see below, chapter V., B. b.

[3] This petition was supplemented by a corresponding one from the London merchants who were commercially connected with Canada.

of the French Canadians to the franchise.   It will also be shown later that the old subjects welcomed and eagerly availed themselves of the restoration of the French form of land tenure.   Representations in November, 1767 prove that a large part of them were opposed to the introduction of the English bankruptcy laws.   Masères, who had been an ardent British partisan throughout, and who became in 1774 the agent of the party in London, may be considered to represent pretty accurately their views on these points, and he expressly and frequently declares that the English inhabitants, aware of the uneasiness and confusion that an enforcement of the English laws of inheritance and landed property would have occasioned in the province, had always been willing that the French laws on these subjects should be continued.

I have thus brought my scrutiny of the "old subjects" down to the establishment of the new constitution and the bringing of the province within the range of the revolution.   The consideration of the attitude of the party in this crisis is reserved for another place.[2]   It will then be found that the division of feeling whose traces we have discovered beneath apparent unity, becomes at once very manifest, declaring itself in the same active opposition that was found in the other colonies between Tories and Revolutionists.

C.   Relations with the French Canadians.

Of social relations, which it is not within my province to go fully into, we do not meet many traces.   There are a few references to inter-marriage and other social connections between members of the noblesse on the one hand, and members of the English military or official circles on the other; but these could be in this brief time of but slight influence, politically speaking.   Little or no communication took place between the noblesse and the main body of the English — the commercial class, — the prevailing sentiments

---

[2] See below, chapter VI.

being more or less intense degrees of contempt or hatred.[1]
I have already referred to the fact that the bitter ani-
mosity between the English element and Murray was due
largely to the latter's partiality for the noblesse; and there
can be little doubt that the same state of things was
prevalent to some degree under Carleton.   But apart from
the aristocracy,— a small class, with constantly declining
influence,— we have considerable evidence of a very constant intercourse, daily increasing in influence on the
attitude of both sections, between the main body of the
English and the main body of the people.   This was based
in the first place on commercial relations, which gave the
few vigorous and enterprising English merchants, in
whose hands was the greatest part of the trade (probably
the entire wholesale and foreign trade), and who in the
later years also more directly affected the county districts
by the large acquirement of seigniories, an influence out of
all proportion to their numbers or weight with the government.   This development was aided by the appearance
of those new French leaders from the professional and
educated class of whom I have spoken above as becoming
rapidly imbued with English ideas of government.   There
can be no doubt that in the ten years during which civil
government had been in operation a very considerable
change had taken place in the social and political attitude
of the body of the people; and we must consider the main
factor therein to have been that part of the English element with which the people were brought into daily contact.

The first occasion on which we find representatives of
these two sections of the population acting together,— on the
grand jury of 1764,— is one in which the French part is exhibited in the light of a very easily hoodwinked or influenced section, which discovers the real nature of its
action only through later outside inspiration.   Early in 1766
we find in connection with some difficulties concerning the

---

[1] Murray to Shelbourne, August 20, 1766. Can. Arch., B. 8, p. 1.

quartering of troops at Montreal that the new attitude of the French in protesting against the billeting upon them seems to have been due to the instigation of the English civil element, which for some time past had been on extremely bad terms with the military.   The affair unmistakably shows among the French Canadians in that town an access of intelligence, or at least of knowledge of the non-military spirit of the English laws.[1]   The language of the memorial of the Quebec seigniors on behalf of Murray in 1766[2] proves that even then there was associated with the old subjects in their opposition to that governor a number of the new, who are said for the most part to be "slaves to their creditors."[3]   Of combined English and French movements we have, however, very few traces. We have seen above how the attempt at combined action failed in regard to an assembly in 1773, and it is probable that many other such fell through from similar causes. Shortly after Carleton's arrival he writes in connection with the Walker affair (an assault on an objectionable magistrate which was the outcome of friction at Montreal between the English civil and military elements), that the Canadians are being led by the English into the seditious practices of the other provinces in the belief that these are "agreeable to our laws and customs," and "are thereby induced to subscribe sentiments very different from their natural disposition."[4]   The degree of influence which the English element had acquired over the French in this short time is dwelt upon by Masères, who contends that in the event of an assembly being granted most of the French Canadian constituences would choose English representatives.   And in the account he gives of an approach by some of the leading French of the town of Quebec (of the professional class), to the English for the

---

[1] Can. Arch., Q. 3, pp. 122–70.

[2] *Rep. Can. Arch.*, 1888, p. 21.

[3] See above, p. 292, note 5, concerning meetings of French Canadians.

[4] Can. Arch., Q. 4, p. 40.

purpose of joint action towards an assembly, the French delegation is represented as admitting that even if the greater share of the assembly be granted to the numerical superiority of the French, the English will more than make up by their superior knowledge and capacity for public business.[1]

The vigor and modern character of the political methods resorted to by the British party may be seen by Carleton's reference to a memorial against the new judicial ordinance of 1770, in which he states that he was "really ashamed of the manner in which I was informed many of the king's old subjects had behaved, sending about handbills to invite the people to assemble in order to consult upon grievances, importuning, nay, insulting, many of the Canadians because they would not join them."[2] Similar methods are referred to with regard to the movement of protest against the Quebec Act, and the language used indicates a considerable degree of success. As early as November, 1774, (i. e., six months before the calling upon the people for armed service revealed their real attitude), Carleton writes of the upper classes of the Canadians that they "are not without fears, that some of their countrymen, under the awe of menacing creditors and others from ignorance, may have been induced" to join with the old subjects in their efforts against the "oppression and slavery imposed upon them [the Canadians; Carleton is quoting the representations made to the people], by those acts of parliament." These efforts will be discussed more fully in another place;[3] their success proves, among other things, that in this crisis at least the leadership of the people had fallen in very large measure to the more advanced section of the English party. At present it will be sufficient to point out that on the whole, if we except the ineradicable hostility between the

---

[1] Masères, *Additional Papers, etc.*, p. 21.

[2] Can. Arch., Q. 7, p. 89.

[3] Below, chapter VI.

noblesse and the commercial English element (an hostility which was not one of race), we certainly discover throughout the period no signs of irreconcilable discord and difference of view or interest between the main French and the main English population. It is true that the peculiar attitude of the government towards the English element imposed upon it the necessity of cultivating the body of the people more than otherwise perhaps would have been the case. But taking out the extremists on both sides we would probably find that the average opinions as to the disposition of government and the laws were by no means so wide apart as the makers of the Quebec Act supposed.

CHAPTER III.

THE PROVINCIAL GOVERNMENT.

A. General Status.

A full presentation of the conditions attendant on government in the province of Quebec throughout our period is essential to any accurate estimate of general policy then or later. It is therefore necessary to discuss some general problems that lay at the basis of authority, and to describe briefly the character and principles of administration previous to the Quebec Act.

The government of the province, not only during this period, but also under the Quebec Act down to 1791, may be described as that of a crown colony[1] without an assembly. As no other such government existed contemporaneously among the older continental colonies, or had existed since the first rude beginnings of government there, we cannot turn to these for illustration.[2] But a clear idea of the exact constitutional status of the province as it appeared to the highest legal authority of the time will be acquired from a study of Lord Mansfield's famous judgment of 1774 in regard to the island of Grenada.[3] Grenada and Quebec (together with East and West Florida), had been on precisely the same footing with regard to the conditions of acquirement and the constitutional documents that had issued concerning them. Both had been long settled French colonies, conquered by England about the same

---

[1] Using the classification of colonial governments into *crown*, *proprietary* and *popular*, according to the method by which the governor was appointed.

[2] We might perhaps except Georgia, 1751–4, during which time the province was governed directly by the crown. But as there was then also neither governor nor council, and as when in 1754 these were appointed, an assembly came with them into existence, it does not seem worth while to refer more directly to conditions there.

[3] Case of Campbell vs. Hall, 1774. Cowper's or Lofft's *Reports.*

time, and surrendered on conditions of capitulation very
nearly the same; they had been ceded permanently by the
same treaty under explicit statement of being affected by
the same stipulations;[1] and finally they had been grouped
together and made subject to precisely the same regulations
by the Proclamation of 1763.   This proclamation had been
followed in the case of each by commissions to governors,
couched (so far as the present point is affected), in almost
precisely the same terms.   The Grenada case turned on the
question whether the king, without the concurrence of
parliament, had power to make a legislative enactment
with regard to the Island subsequent to the date of the
above mentioned Proclamation of October 7, 1763, which
made known to all concerned, that as regarded the new
acquirements therein mentioned, he had "given express
power and direction to the governors of our said colonies
respectively, that as soon as the state and circumstances of
the said colony will admit thereof they shall with the
advice and consent of our said Council call and summon
general assemblies in such manner and form as is used in
the other colonies under our immediate government," and
that he had given power to the governors, with the consent
of the councils and of the assemblies as so constituted, to
legislate for the provinces concerned.   This is the material
instrument involved, though Lord Mansfield cites also
another subordinate proclamation of the same tenor, and the
commission to the governor by which he is given the power
spoken of; but whatever added force would come from this
last would also affect the province of Quebec to precisely
the same degree.   Lord Mansfield's conclusion is that,
while previous to the publication of these documents (i. e.,
previous to October 7th, 1763), the king alone, through the
legislative power over a conquered country given him by
the royal prerogative, could make any legislation concerning the recent conquests consistent with the constitution,

---

[1] See Houston, *Canadian Documents*, p. 64.

he had by the publication of these instruments divested
himself of this power, and had voluntarily and irrevocably
granted to the new provinces a constitution under which
the legislative power over them could be exercised only
by a provincial assembly or by the British parliament.   In
other words, the Proclamation of 1763 was a charter of
liberties granted to all who were or might become concerned with the regions in question, granted for the express
purpose (as stated in it), of inducing them to become so
concerned, and therefore, they having acted upon it, irrevocable without their own consent. The case in question
had reference to taxation; but evidently nothing depends
on this fact, for the decision of the chief justice is given
in general terms; "we are of the opinion that the King
. . . had precluded himself from an exercise of the legislative authority which he had before."

The conclusion from this is that the Proclamation of 1763
must be looked upon as the Constitution of Canada throughout the whole of this period, or up till the date at which
the imperial parliament first took legislative action concerning the country;[1] and the result is therefore reached
that government without an assembly (i. e., government as
it existed down till the Quebec Act), was constitutionally
invalid, all legislation by the governor and council alone
being constitutionally void.   This position cannot be
affected by any quibbling as to the exact terms of the
above mentioned instruments.   It is true that the words of
the Proclamation in regard to the calling of an assembly
are, "as soon as the state and circumstances of the said
colony will admit thereof," the governor and council being
apparently left judges as to when that might be; but we
do not find that any contention on this point was raised in
the Grenada case, or that Lord Mansfield, (who, it will be
remembered, was a strong assertor of royal prerogative and

---

[1] The Quebec Act (14 Geo. III, c. 83, Sec. 4.) practically recognizes this, in beginning with the express abrogation of the Proclamation and the subsequent commissions.

colonial subordination, and who therefore would undoubtedly have given full attention to any point which would
have enabled him to save the king's authority from this
decided check), took anything but a mere passing notice of
these words.   The words of the proclamation are "power
and *direction* to our governors:"[1] and that no argument can
be founded on the substitution, (probably unintentional
and in pursuance of official forms), for these in Murray's
commission of the phrase "power and *authority*," is shown
by an examination of the case of Nova Scotia some few
years previous,— an almost parallel case, the study of
which will I think strengthen my argument in every point.
The position of those settlers who in Nova Scotia claimed
the fulfillment of the promise of the full enjoyment of
English constitutional forms was, if anything, weaker than
in Quebec, for the fundamental proclamation under which
settlement had been invited, emanated not from the King-
in-council, but from the Board of Trade.[2]   It promised the
prospective settlers that a civil government should be established, "as soon as possible after their arrival, whereby
they will enjoy all the liberties, privileges and immunities
enjoyed by His Majesty's subjects in any other of the
colonies and plantations in America;" and the commission
of the governor, issued two months later, grants to him
"full power and authority, with the advice and consent of
our said council from time to time as need shall require, to
summon and call general assemblies . . .   according to
the usage of the rest of our colonies and plantations in
America."   In conjunction with such assemblies he and
the council were to have full power of legislation, granted
in precisely the same terms as are used in the commission
given to Murray.   And no provision is made, as none is
made in Murray's commission, for legislative action without such an assembly.   It will be noticed that the phrase

[1] The italicising is mine.

[2] March 7, 1749. See Houston, *Can. Documents*, p. 7.

used in the proclamation above, "as soon as possible after their arrival," is fully as indefinite as that quoted from the other documents, and that the determining of the possibility is apparently left to the governor. In this light he and his successor chose to understand it, and without taking any step towards an assembly proceeded to legislate with the council alone for six years. Finally, in 1755, the attention of the Board of Trade was called to this state of affairs, and it immediately submitted the validity of the laws so enacted to the British crown lawyers, the attorney-general at that time being the William Murray who afterward as Lord Mansfield delivered the judgment of 1774. The answer was that, "the governor and council alone are not authorized by His Majesty to make laws till there can be an Assembly,"— an opinion which was not supported by any arguments other than a reference to the king's order that government should be in accordance with the commission and instructions.[1] The Board of Trade immediately proceeded to compel the governor (notwithstanding his assurances that the legislative authority of the governor and council was not questioned in the province, and that very great difficulties would attend the calling of an assembly), to comply with the original promise, enjoining him moreover to see that one of the first legislative measures of the assembly should be the passing of an act of indemnity for proceedings taken under the laws previously enforced.[2]

There is no reason to suppose that the conclusion I have thus drawn from the highest legal opinion of the time is affected by later instructions to the governors. To Murray there was issued what Masères calls a "private instruction," granting to him and the council, power "to make such rules and regulations as shall appear to be necessary for the peace, order and good government, taking care that nothing be passed or done that shall in any wise tend to

---

[1] Houston, *Can. Documents*, p. 18.
[2] Ib., p. 17.

affect the life, limb or liberty of the subject, or to the imposing any duty or taxes." Carleton's commission in 1768
is accompanied by general instructions, of which the tenth
article is to the effect that, whereas he has been directed
by the commission "that so soon as the situation and circumstances of our said province will admit thereof, you
shall, with the advice of our Council, summon and call a
General Assembly," he is as soon as possible "to give all
possible attention to the carrying of this important object
into execution;" but that, "as it may be impossible for the
present to form such an establishment," he is in the meantime to make with the council alone such rules and regulations as shall be necessary, under the same restrictions as
were imposed on Murray. These instructions of course
emanated only from the executive power, and it is hardly
necessary to further contend that as such they were, according to Lord Mansfield, of no avail against the fundamental instruments discussed above. So long as the difficulties in the formation of an assembly were not so great
as to occasion the entire suspension of civil government,
the power of the Home executive to delegate legislative authority to the colonial one had no existence, for the simple reason that the former was not itself possessed of
any such authority. Difficulties such as existed in Quebec
had been pleaded by the government in Nova Scotia
thirteen years before in an exactly parallel case; but no
attention had been paid to the plea by the Crown lawyers
or the Board of Trade.

It is manifest, therefore, that the provincial legislation
throughout this period was *in toto* null and void. But this
does not quite dispose of the problems involved in the
matter; for, apart from the question of the legislative
competence of the Provincial government, the most
diverse opinions have been entertained with regard to the
laws legally subsisting throughout the period. The difficulty is with the civil laws only, it being universally

acknowledged that the criminal code accompanied the conqueror without further enactment. But it was also contended learnedly in many quarters, and it was the main article of faith with the English-speaking party in the province, that the fundamental imperial documents by which civil government had been established were adequate to, and had resulted in, the introduction of the English civil law, if not *in toto* at least in the same degree as that in which these laws were operative in the other colonies.[1] It may perhaps be contended that this was the view, not only of the "old subjects," but also in the early official world, and that the legislation whose validity has been discussed above was mainly intended only to provide administive machinery or applications for laws already established in bulk. The fundamental acts relied on for such an establishment were the capitulation of Montreal (and of the province), September 8th, 1760, the Treaty of Paris, February, 1763, and the Imperial Proclamation of October 7, 1763. It is necessary therefore to briefly consider these.[2]

The first of these documents is of a purely negative character, Amherst replying to the demand that the Canadians should continue to be governed according to the custom of Paris and the laws and usages of the colony, by the remark that they became subjects of the king. The

---

[1] The prevailing ideas in regard to the position of the colonies generally as to the introduction of English law, are probably expressed in Knox's *Justice and Policy of the Quebec Act*, 1774. He states that English colonists take with them such statute law only as, (of date previous to the starting of the colony), is applicable to their circumstances, or such of later date as expressly mentions the colonies. The result (he continues), is that the new colony is in most cases without laws, "and the magistrates usually adopt the usages of the neighbouring colonies, whose circumstances and situation bear a near resemblance to their own; and by the tacit consent of the people to their fitness they acquire the authority of laws; and things are conducted upon this (though somewhat arbitrary) footing, until a legislature is formed; and then the laws of the other colonies are taken as models; and with such alterations as circumstances render necessary, they are enacted the laws of the new colony." It is interesting to note that Knox adds that this was the procedure in Quebec, the old laws of the colony being adopted till the legislature could make new ones. If he refers to actual use this is practically correct; but by no means so with regard to the actual legislative steps taken in formal enactment. See below, chapter V, with regard to the province of Grenada.

[2] The pertinent parts are reprinted carefully in Houston, *Can. Documents*, pp. 32-74.

only bearing of the Treaty of Paris on the matter is an indirect one, Masères contending that the phrase with regard
to the toleration of the Catholic religion, "as far as the
laws of Great Britain permit," shows that it was the British
intention that these laws should be the fundamental rule
of government in the province.   The *intentions* of the crown
are to be considered presently; meanwhile it may be concluded that the Treaty of Paris, except with regard to the
criminal law, does not affect the legal point; unless indeed
it be considered necessary to combat the opinion that conquest and cession *ipso facto* make at once legal in the
conquered territory all the laws of the conqueror.   But it
should be enough on this point simply to refer again to the
opinion of Lord Mansfield (stated by him as a "maxim,"
the "justice and antiquity" of which were "incontrovert-
able "), that "the laws of a conquered country continue in
force till they are altered by the conqueror." [1]   The remaining question then is this.   Assuming as Lord Mansfield
does, that the king had up till the publication of the Proclamation of 1763 possessed general legislative power within
the limits of the constitution, were the English civil laws
introduced into Canada by that proclamation?

The proclamation declares that the king has by letters
patent under the great seal (i. e., by the governor's commission), "given express power and direction" to the governor to summon an assembly as soon as possible, in the
same manner as in the other royal provinces; that he has
granted to the governor, council and assembly, when thus
brought together, power, "to make constitute and ordain
laws, statutes and ordinances . . . as near as may be
agreeable to the Laws of England, and under such regula-

---

[1] In Grenada judgment. See also his letter to Grenville, December 24, 1764, *Grenville's Correspondence*, III, 476. Also reports of crown lawyers on Canada, 1766. There seems no need of further discussing this; the curious are referred further to *Blackstone*, I, 107; Clark, *Colonial Law*, p. 4; Bowyer, *Universal Public Law*, c. 16; Burge, *Commentaries on Colonial Laws*, I, 31; Halleck, *International Law*, p. 824; *Lower Canada Jurist*, II, App. 1. For these references I am indebted mainly to Lareau, *Hist. Droit. Can.*

tions and restrictions as are used in the other colonies;"
and that in the meantime "all persons inhabiting in or resorting to our said colonies may confide in our Royal Protection for the enjoyment of the benefit of the laws of
England." To which end power has been given to the
governor and council to establish courts of justice "for the
hearing and determining all causes as well criminal as
civil, according to law and equity, and as near as may be
agreeable to the laws of England." The first part of this
gives a power the conditions of the exercise of which were
never realized, and which thus has no bearing on the
present question; but the second part, which claims to
provide for the temporary non-realization of these conditions, and which directs the use of the laws of England "as
near as may be" while at the same time giving no authority to the provincial government directly to enact these
laws, would certainly seem to have been considered by its
authors at least as in itself sufficient to some extent for
their legalization or introduction. But even this would
appear not to have been the case. In response to an inquiry from Carleton concerning the putting into force in
Quebec of some English commercial law, the Earl of Hillsborough, then secretary of state, replies (March 6, 1768),
that as one of those who had drawn up the Proclamation
of 1763,[1] he could state "that it had never entered into our
idea to overturn the laws and customs of Canada in regard
to property, but that justice should be administered agreeably to them, according to the modes of administering
justice . . . in this Kingdom;" adding on the point in
question, that "it is impossible to conceive that it could
ever be His Majesty's intention, signified either by the
Proclamation or by the Ordinance for the establishment of
Courts of Judicature, to extend laws of that particular and

---

[1] He was then President of the Board of Trade. Horace Walpole refers to him at an
earlier period as "a young man of great honour and merit;" but his subsequent career
shows that he possessed little judgment or moderation.

municipal nature to the colony, even if the intention had been to have overturned the customs of Canada."[1] A further official indication of the intent of the proclamation is found, nearer the time of issue, in the report of the crown lawyers, April, 1766, on the legal condition of the province. This, after strongly advising that the local usages be left undisturbed, states as one of the main sources of disorder in the province, the alarm taken at the proclamation of 1763, "as if it were the Royal intention, by the judges and officers in that country, at once to abolish all the usages and customs of Canada with the rough hand of a conqueror rather than in the true spirit of a lawful sovereign."[2] Whatever this may imply it certainly refers to the Proclamation, not as introductive of any law or legal principle, but as at the most merely indicating an intention, to be more or less gently and gradually caried out. Finally Attorney-General Thurlow, in the Quebec Act debates 1774, refers to the document as a crude production, which "certainly gave no order whatever with respect to the Constitution of Canada," and asserts that it is an unheard-of and absurd tyranny to regard it "as importing English laws into a country already settled and habitually governed by other laws." "This proclamation . . . was not addressed to the Canadians; . . . I would ask from what expression it is, that either the Canadians can discover or English lawyers advance, that the laws of Canada were all absolutely repealed and that a new system of justice, as well as a new system of constitution, was by that instrument introduced."[3]

Authoritative legal and official statements therefore support the lay judgment in the opinion that the general and vague expressions of the proclamation could not be taken as adequate to the overturning in whole or part of the

---

[1] Can. Arch., Q. 5-1, p. 344.

[2] Smith, *History of Canada*, II, 27.

[3] Cavendish, *Report*, pp. 24-37.

ancient system of civil law, and the express introduction of English, either common or statute. The province could not be regarded in the light of a new colony, into which the settlers brought with them a certain part of the common law of the parent state; and hence it would seem that the introduction of common law could not be effected any more easily than that of statute. As to statute law, public promulgation has always been essential to validity; but no publication of any portion of that law was ever expressly made in the province.[1]

This discussion belongs, however, rather to the realm of legal theory than to that of practical constitutional investigation. For the validity of the legislation in question remained unchallenged either in the province or at home, and no hint of an indemnity for the acts committed thereunder is to be found in any of the discussions connected with the Quebec Act. We have official references now and then to individual ordinances as overstepping the legislative authority, and a few are disallowed by the home government apparently on this ground; but no general objection seems to have been made then or at any time thereafter to the exercise of the legislative power. Nor, stranger still, have modern writers on this period, even those occupying a legal standpoint, taken adequate note of these fundamental considerations; a neglect which must be my excuse for the extent to which I have gone into them.

---

[1] It is to be noticed in this connection that the general supposition among the English in the province in the earlier years, as to the introduction of English law, was based, not on the proclamation alone, but mainly on the ordinance of September 17, 1764; the inference being that this ordinance was considered necessary to the completing or enforcing of the work of the proclamation. Carleton writes to Shelburne, December 24, 1767, that the whole French constitution and system of law and custom "in one hour we overturned by the Ordinance, . . . and laws ill-adapted to the genius of the Can_ adians . . . unknown and unpublished, were introduced in their stead." It has been shown above, however, that this enactment was necessarily null and void, as an overstepping of the power of the legislator. See Lareau, *Hist. Droit. Can.*, II, 39–53, for discussion of this matter.

B.   General Administration.

It is of course not possible here to enter into any investigation of the constitutional functions at this period of colonial administrations in general, or of this one in particular.   My object is simply to indicate generally the lines and limits of practical conduct, with special reference to the peculiar conditions of the province.   Such a statement must be taken in close conjunction with the investigation of general policy to which the succeeding chapter is devoted, and especially with the analysis of Commissions and Instructions there attempted.

Murray's commission as governor (1764), invested him, apart from the Council, with the following powers and duties:

a. Keeping and using the public seal.

b. Administering required oaths to all other public functionaries.

c. A negative voice in both council and assembly and the power of adjourning, proroguing or dissolving the latter.

d. Appointment of ecclesiastical officers.

e. Pardoning or reprieving of legal offenders, so far as that power was delegated to colonial officials.

f. Certain military powers in time of war.

These seem to be the usual powers, and we need not delay on them, except to notice that the military authority granted Murray was purely a militia one (that is to say, of the extent usually granted), notwithstanding the fact that he represented with some force [1] the necessity of a different regulation on account of the peculiar position of Quebec. The representation was of avail later, for the supreme military command in the province (i. e., over the regular troops on all occasions, as well as over emergency forces in time of war), was practically joined to the civil in 1766,

---

[1] To Halifax, October 15, 1764.   (Can. Arch., Q. 2, p. 206.)

and formally so in 1770. Other changes were made later in the position of the governor, concerning which it is necessary to here make only the general statement that, with the military modification, the result was to place the English governor much more nearly in the place occupied by the old French one.

In regard to the council apart from the governor, and the relation between it and him, I find that during the most of the period, the conditions (defined in the governor's Instructions), were practically identical with the contemporary ones in the older crown colonies.[1] The phrase used constantly in regard to the relations between the council and the governor in the carrying on of joint duties, requires the governor to act with its "advice and consent." This position of the council is defined by Masères as one of "advice and control;" but how far the element of control really entered depended largely of course on circumstances and individuals. How far it could be eliminated under a strong hand may be conjectured from the fact that the governor was by his commission generally, if not always, invested with an unlimited veto power on all legislation, and that the carrying out of executive measures rested almost entirely with him. He had, moreover, on what he might choose to regard as emergencies, power of suspension from the council; besides being in the province the dispensor of general governmental favours, and in most cases the only effectual medium of access to the home administration.[2] An examination of the council

---

[1] See instructions to Sir H. Moore, governor of New York, issued November 27, 1765. Or for the Province of Georgia, about the same time. The latter province, in its late establishment as a crown colony, and the presence on its borders of far-reaching tribes of Indians, a source at once of danger and of profit, occupied in the southern system of colonies a position analagous to that of Quebec in the northern.

[2] How ineffective the "control" of the council practically proved in Quebec is tacitly acknowledged by Masères himself in his later recommendations of such changes in formation and maintenance as would protect it against the governor. In a close examination of the council records throughout the period, I have discovered only one instance where the official language (and I am not unmindful of the untrustworthiness in such

records leaves with us the impression on the whole of a
body so docile as to present no obstacle to the will of such
a man as Carleton.   Abridged as the latter's power really
was, he was able to rule more autocratically than even Murray.   But that this was not the intention of the home authorities may be conjectured from the changes in his instructions; and we shall see later how after the Quebec Act
a more decisive intervention was made in favour of the
council.

The council had no stated times or conditions of meeting,
the available members being apparently called together as
occasion arose.   The full list comprised twelve names, and
the *personnel* was subject to constant change, only three of
the original dozen remaining in the province at the close
of the period.   Temporary appointments had to be constantly made, and June 22, 1773, the lieutenant-governor
writes that no meetings had been held for the last three
months of 1772 for want of a quorum.   During the administration of Murray we have no details of the council proceedings.   This seems due to neglect on the part of the
colonial office in not requiring reports;[1] for references elsewhere leave no doubt as to the fact of meetings or the
keeping of minutes.   The first full report is in 1766, and

---

connections of official wordings), supports the theory as to the power of the council; and
in that instance, if control were really exercised, it can be shown to have been most
probably caused by exceptional circumstances.   Carleton's attitude toward his council
may be judged from his assertion of practical independence soon after his arrival, in regard to an instance where he had expressly convened only a portion of it. And it is to be
remarked that his conduct on that occasion was not censured by the home authorities.
(See Can. Arch., Q. 3, pp. 259-70.)   A few months later he dismissed two of the council on
his sole authority.   His representation of this matter also proved satisfactory to the
home government, which paid no attention to the plea of the aggrieved members, that
"the independence of His Majesty's council, not only of Quebec, but in every other
province, seems interested in this event." (Can. Arch., Q. 4, p. 40; pp. 198-239, 247.) This
is the only instance of the dismissal of councillors met with.   Murray's relations with
his advisors seem to have been amicable throughout.

[1] A neglect which I have frequently noted, and which I shall emphasize elsewhere as
steadily marking the home administration with regard to Canada down almost to the
Quebec Act.

from this time down we have regular accounts of proceedings.[1]

In comparing the English council down to the Quebec
Act with the council under the French régime, we find at
first sight a close resemblance in composition. The French
council in the last stage of its development, (i. e., from the
beginning of the 18th century), consisted, beside the governor, intendant, and bishop, of the same number of ordinary councillors (12), appointed, and apparently removable,
in the same way. If we regard the English governor as
representing the bishop, and the English chief justice and
governor as dividing between them most of the functions
of the intendant, (not indeed a very accurate supposition),
we may look upon the councils as practically identical in
composition. But in considering the respective spheres of
action, we discover very notable differences; differences
which for the general purposes of government made the
English council a very much more important body. In regard to legislative functions the French council had power
only in cases not provided for by the established *Coutume
de Paris*, the royal edicts, or the ordinances of the intendant
(the last especially affecting all parts of the life of the people); while in ordinary executive work its powers were again
much narrowed by the great range of the same official, whose
prerogatives were always jealously defended and exercised.
On the other hand, in judicial matters the French council
seems to have had a much wider sphere than the English,
and to have acted within it much more constantly and
vigorously. So much so indeed that there can be little
doubt that it was intended finally to be restricted, so far as
the peculiar circumstances of the colony should render ad-

---

[1] No definite instructions are found as occasioning this change, and it would seem
that none such are to be found contemporaneously in regard to the other colonies.
Carleton had doubtless, however, received directions of some kind before entering on
the government, and the 80th Article of his Instructions of 1768 require him, "upon all
occasions to send unto us . . . a particular account of all your proceedings and of
the conditions of affairs within your government." This direction does not appear
in the instructions of 1775 or 1778, though full minutes continued to be sent.

visable, to much the same sphere of activity as that allowed to the old parliaments of France. Within these limits it seems to have been a much more vigorous, though much less harmonious body than the English council, either of Quebec or of the older colonies. It met weekly, worked with dispatch, and made its influence daily felt in every part of the province. It was by no means under the control of the governor, and was always split up into two, and not unfrequently into three, factions; a want of harmony, however, which does not seem to have seriously affected the satisfactory execution of its main work.

In considering the actual legislation of the period we find the more important ordinances to be about forty in number, of which more than one-half were passed under Murray's administration, or in the first two years. The main subjects treated are as follows: The judiciary (9 ordinances); the currency (3); regulation of retail trade, including markets (14); relations of debtors and creditors (3); police regulations (3); registering of lands, etc. (1); highways (1); protection against fire (3). Measures of an exceptional character provided for the ratifying of the decrees of the courts of justice during the preceding military period, prevented anyone leaving the province without a government pass, forbade the selling of liquor to the Indians, made temporary provision for billetting troops in private houses, and imposed a fine for being more than three months absent from public worship. Much of the commercial legislation is decidedly paternal in tone. The ordinances of the first part of the period are as might be expected somewhat carelessly drawn. One has an *ex post facto* clause; another mixes together in the same enactment two apparently utterly unrelated regulations; a third describes and prohibits a serious offence without stating any penalty. In most cases fines are the only punishment, but in three ordinances (which are not noticed as repealed, and were therefore evidently considered as law through the whole period), the

penalties include imprisonment up to one month, though
the instructions debarred provincial legislation from affecting the liberty of the subject In three others (two of
which were disallowed, apparently on this ground), conviction could be secured by the oath of an informer, who
got half the fine. It is evident, in short, that the ap-
prentice work of the council was not guided by any particular directions from home. Such directions were,
however, issued to Carleton in 1768, and the legislation we
have subsequently is apparently devoid of such objectionable features. The minutes of council show the ordinances
to have been framed with very considerable care and deliberation,[1] following the lines of English parliamentary
practice. In most cases, however, the number of councillors present is merely a quorum or less than one-half the
whole.[2] The ordinances seems from the beginning to have
been published in both French and English, but it was not
till 1768 that the prior submission of the French translation
to the inspection of the council was made necessary before
publication. As to the occasion and manner of the initiation of legislation we have few particulars; but in one instance (February 16, 1768), we find an ordinance called
forth by the submission to the council through the chief
justice (an *ex-officio* member of it), of a presentment of the
grand jury in the supreme court; while in another case
(April 24, 1769), it seems to have been occasioned simply
by the representation of a Quebec magistrate.[3] Petitions
were no doubt very frequently the basis of action. The

---

[1] See (e. g.) the procedure in the case of the ordinance of February 1, 1770, for the reform of the judiciary. At a council meeting of August 18, 1769, a committee is appointed
to report concerning complaints on the subject. The report appears September 14, and
on being approved, the attorney general is ordered to prepare an ordinance embodying
its recommendations. The draft of this is submitted at the next meeting (January 10,
1770), is referred to a committee, and returned by it February 1st, with an amendment.
The amended ordinance is ordered to be translated into French, and on the translation
being approved of at the next meeting, (February 14), the two versions are ordered to be
immediately promulgated.

[2] The Quebec Act ordered that legislation should require a majority.

[3] See Can. Arch., Q. Minutes of council of above dates.

manner of publishing ordinances was at first by public reading in the towns on beat of drum, followed by printing in the Quebec *Gazette*. A few months later this was supplemented by an order that all curés should read to their congregation after Sunday services all government measures so published.

The multifarious forms of the council's executive activity can be as easily imagined as they would be tedious to enumerate. Its main and regular functions were the granting of lands, the establishment and maintenance of means of communication, the regulation of trade and manufactures, the appointment and supervision of judicial and local officials, the examination of public accounts, and the consideration of complaints against public officers. It acted in important matters by means of committees and much of its time was expended in the examination of petitions. General measures, aside from ordinances, were known as Proclamations or Advertisements, and seem at times to encroach on the properly legislative sphere; at least it is difficult to see the distinction between matters provided for in some of them and other matters which were clothed with the dignity of an ordinance.[1]

The judicial functions of the governor and council, (regulated by the governor's instructions), were the ordinary ones of the supreme colonial court of appeal, and do not require close discussion. I have spoken above of the corresponding powers of the French council as being very similarly exercised, but, through the greater range of appeal, as much more closely and constantly touching the people, even making allowance for the fact that the English council was not hampered by a parallel jurisdiction such as that of the intendant. The instances of judicial action on the part of the latter at any part of the

---

[1] None of these instruments appear after 1768. Many of them were simply the re-issue under the colonial seal, of general or special acts of the home executive.

period are few in number,[1] there being none under Murray's administration. Notwithstanding one dubious incident,[2] the council's judicial activity seems to have been beneficial. Its application of English constitutional principles, and the thoroughly English spirit of its procedure, are illustrated by a case in 1767 which seems at first sight a direct overstepping of its jurisdiction.[3] But that it was not given to vexatious or illegal interference with the courts is shown not only by the rarity of such cases, but also by the record of a couple of instances in which appeals were dismissed as not cognizable. Nevertheless, a general oversight seems to have been kept on the judiciary, especially in its lower stages. As a striking illustration we may notice here the action taken on receipt of well founded complaints against many of the justices of the peace of the District of Montreal in 1769, — complaints which a few months later were more fully met by an ordinance greatly curtailing the power of the justices.[4] In the meantime, and almost immediately on receipt of the complaints, a circular letter was addressed to the offending magistrates, in which the conduct complained of was censured in the strongest terms, and particular directions were given as to the method of amendment.

C.   Judiciary.   Civil Service.

The commission issued to Gov. Murray in 1763 granted him power, in conjunction with the council, " to erect,

---

[1] This is mainly due of course to the restriction of civil appeals to cases involving a high money value (£300).

[2] This was a case of the reversion by the council of a judgment of the court of common pleas. Appealed to the crown, (the only such appeal of the period), the Privy Council decided, (after a delay of four years), to uphold the original court. But to the consequent order the provincial council seems to have paid slight attention; for in 1774 we find an apparently well-founded complaint to Dartmouth from the original appellant in the case, to the effect that though the decision of the Privy Council had been transmitted to Quebec, the governor and council had taken advantage of a technical difficulty to refuse all reparation. The case seems from first to last a reversion and denial of justice. (See Can. Arch., Q. 10, pp. 94–104).

[3] See Can. Arch., Q. 4, p. 230.

[4] See full details in *Rep. Can. Arch.*, 1890, p. xvii, and following.

constitute and establish such and so many courts of judicature and public justice " as should be found necessary,
these courts being declared by the previous proclamation
of October, 1763, to be for the " hearing and determining
all causes as well criminal as civil according to law and
equity, and as near as may be agreeable to the laws of England." The institution of the judiciary in accordance with
the powers then given was through the provincial ordinance of September 17, 1764, which remained for the most
part the basis of the administration of justice throughout
the whole of the period. Its main provisions were:

1st. Establishment of a superior court, or Court of King's
Bench, presided over by a Chief Justice, " with power and
authority to hear and determine all criminal and civil
causes agreeable to the laws of England and to the Ordinances of the Province." To sit twice a year at Quebec,
with the addition of a court of assize and general goal delivery once a year at Montreal and Three Rivers. Appeal
could be made to governor and council.

2nd. Establishment of a Court of Common Pleas, to determine all cases concerning property above value of £10,
with appeal to King's Bench concerning £20 or upwards,
and to council directly for £300 or more. The judges "to
determine agreeably to equity, having regard nevertheless
to the laws of England, as far as the circumstances and
present situation of things will admit, until such time as
proper ordinances for the information of the people can be
established by the government and council agreeable to the
laws of England:" but "the French laws and customs to
be allowed and admitted in all causes where the cause of
action arose before October 1, 1764."

3rd. Establishment of justices of the peace in the different districts, with power to each in his own district "to
hear and finally determine in all causes and matters of
property" not exceeding £5, and to any two to do the same

up to £10.   Three were to be a quorum, with power of holding quarter sessions and determining up to £30, with appeal to the King's Bench, while two of the body were to sit weekly in rotation in the towns of Quebec and Montreal.

I have elsewhere spoken of the marked English character of this ordinance and of the manner in which it was received in the province.[1] There are no traces of reference to the old French judiciary, and apparently the only indications that the legislators were aware that the community for which they were legislating was not an English one, are the concessions as to the use of French procedure and law in causes begun before October 1, 1764,[2] the admission of French Canadians to juries in the King's Bench, (apparently not in the Common Pleas), and the admission of Canadian lawyers to practice in the Common Pleas, (apparently not in the King's Bench). I shall elsewhere detail the extension of these privileges by instructions from home; instructions which it will be remembered did not come into effect during Murray's administration. The only other judiciary enactment of importance under Murray is an ordinance of March 9, 1765, by which all juries were directed to be in future summoned from the province at large without regard to the vicinage of the action or crime.   This remarkable interference with one of the fundamental principles of the jury system seems to have been occasioned by temporary circumstances, and was remedied by Carleton very soon after his arrival in the province.[3]

---

[1] To what a large extent the legislators believed that they were introducing English law by this ordinance is shown by the amending one of November 6 following. For later opinions as to it, see Carleton, December 24, 1767, (Can. Arch., Q. 5–1, p. 316), and Reports of the Board of Trade, 1765, 1766, (Can. Arch., Q. 3, pp. 53, 171.)   See also above, p. 336 note.

[2] See also ordinance of November 6, 1764, for "quieting people in their possessions."

[3] Ordinance of January 27, 1766. This ordinance was approved. It should be considered in connection with that interference with the jury system in Massachusetts, which called forth the protest of the Massachusetts assembly July 8, 1769, against measures by which " the inestimable privilege of being tried by a jury from the vicinage . . . will be taken away from the party accused." (4 *Amer. Arch.*, I., 24.)

The instructions to Carleton of 1768 imply no change with reference to the judiciary, and taken literally would indeed intimate an intention of remaining closely by the English law and procedure. But that this was due simply to the careless following of old official forms is shown by later transactions. For not only was such an idea disregarded by the governor in his general policy, but the first important judiciary ordinance of his administration (February 1, 1770), is a direct abandoning of English institutions and a very considerable step toward the adoption of French. The ordinance was occasioned by that oppressive conduct on the part of justices of the peace in the district of Montreal which has been already mentioned, and had been prepared after an investigation by a committee of the council with the Chief Justice at its head, and an attempt to remedy matters by a letter of censure to the offending justices. There seems no reason to doubt the necessity and justice of the ordinance.[1] That of 1764 had given to the justices a power of final determination in matters of property far exceeding that ever exercised by similar magistrates in England (who, as the committee of council pointed out, were of a much more influential and disinterested class); and even this large power had been by some constantly overstepped and exercised in a most wantonly oppressive manner. Accordingly all jurisdiction (either singly or jointly), in matters of private property was now taken away and mainly transferred to the Common Pleas, the sittings of which were greatly extended and for which in such cases a definite line of procedure was laid down. The ordinance is also marked (as the old subjects complained), by the discretionary power granted to the judges. This, and the provision that the new jurisdiction given to the common pleas could be exercised by one judge (acting evidently in a summary manner), together with the prohibition of imprisonment and sale of lands in cases of debt,

---

[1] See *Rep. Can. Arch.*, 1890, pp. xvii-xx, 1-9.

are distinctly French features, and mark the measure as a considerable step towards the restoration of French procedure in civil matters. That this was intended is shown by Carleton's explanation when transmitting it home; he says plainly that its aims were the "reducing the justices of the peace to nearly the same power they have in England," and the "reviving part of the ancient mode of administering justice in the Province."[1] And that it was so regarded by the general public is evident from the vigorous and numerously signed memorials against it from the merchants of Quebec and Montreal; representations which cannot be disposed of, as Carleton tries to do, as merely the angry and hungry voice of the dispossessed justices.[2] For the objections raised are not against the depriving of these justices of their ill-used power, but against the unusual and inadequate character, (in the opinion of the memorialists), of the substituted procedure. The ordinance was approved by the home government without delay and without any remark on its inconsistency with the instructions of 1768. It was a fitting prelude to that article of the Quebec Act which enacted that "in all matters of controversy relative to property and civil right, resort shall be had to the laws of Canada as the rule for the decision of the same."[3]

I have discussed elsewhere the questions connected with the dispute regarding the validity in the province of French

[1] Can. Arch., Q. 7, pp. 7, 89. For ordinance see p. 12, and for British memorials, p. 95.

[2] It is to be repeated that the English party had protested strongly in 1764 against the great powers now taken from the justices.

[3] It should be noted that the only complaints that appear throughout the period on the part of the French Canadians with regard to the administration of justice, (apart from the matter of fees), are those remedied by this Ordinance. And the justices whose acts are complained of had not only been entrusted with powers greater than English law granted in the mother country, but had abused even these. No argument, therefore, can be drawn from the matter to show that the Canadians here displayed hostility to English law or judicial methods. But it must of course be conceded that the incident could not have had a favorable effect upon them; the effect probably was to confirm and continue the avoidance of the courts. The abuse had been fully removed, it should be clearly noted however, four years before the Quebec Act.

and English law; and it is well to bring here the consideration of the more practical and even more obscure problem
as to the laws actually *used* throughout the period. This
is one of the most important of the questions connected
with the introduction of English institutions; and it becomes of even more immediate interest from the standpoint
of the policy and effects of the Quebec Act. One of the
main bases of both the arguments for and the later oft-
expressed approval of that measure, was the belief that
the establishment thereby of the French civil law and procedure, as relieving the French Canadians from the griev-
ious oppression of a foreign code, would be and was most
effective in so inspiring them with gratitude as to keep
them loyal to the British connection. We shall see later
that they were not loyal; we have now to consider whether
the Quebec Act could really be expected to have the effect
attributed to it. And so far as the present matter is concerned, it will be found that the French Canadians were
not suffering from legal oppression in any sense, and that
therefore they could not and did not experience with the
Quebec Act any sudden or marked relief. Gratitude, or an
enlightened view of self-interest in connection with the
measure influenced only classes and individuals who did
not need the additional reason for preferring the imperial
to the revolutionary connection; the mass of the people
perceived no such change of conditions as to form an offset to other very clearly discerned and most unpopular
parts of the enactment.

That this is a totally different enquiry from the previous
one as to legal validity we very soon discover. For a slight
investigation shows that neither the governmental nor the
popular opinions (at least among the "old subjects"), as to
the laws which were strictly valid, very much affected the
action of the great body of litigants, and that throughout
the period the administration of civil justice was in a state
of compromise and (from the legal standpoint), hopeless con-

fusion.   Even the governmental opinion and practice on the point were sadly at variance, especially in the latter part of the period.   Neither Murray nor his advisers seem to have been troubled with any doubts as to the validity in the province of all English common and much English statute law, or of their own legislative competence, within certain limits as to penalties, to further apply that law to any extent that might seem desirable.   Whether they considered themselves, in the various specific ordinances, to be making English law valid by express enactment of it, or to be merely regulating the machinery by which the law, already in force through the fundamental documents on which the civil government rested, was to be put in operation, is not a matter of importance; I need only refer again to the language of the ordinance of September 17, 1764, in regard to the legal principles which were to guide the courts.[1] These provisions remained in force throughout the whole period, legally affected only by the slight compromises shortly to be mentioned; for even the ordinance of 1770, which was intended radically to amend that of 1764, and which was passed by a governor and council fully convinced that French civil law was about to be re-established, and fully in sympathy with the movement, makes no attempt whatever to anticipate events.   And it is also to be noticed that up to 1770 the justices of the peace had authority to exercise the very large civil power which it was the object of that ordinance to take from them, according to a form of commission unmistakably based on the English law, directing the recipient to act "according to the laws and customs of England, or form of the ordinances and statutes of England, and of our Province of Quebec."[2]

Even in these commissions, however, there are indications of that policy of compromise and withdrawal in regard to English law which was one of the guiding principles of

---

[1] See above, p. 345.

[2] See Masères, *Commissions*, pp. 135-8.

Carleton's executive administration; it is further manifest in many ways that Murray had also pursued this policy more or less from the very first. We find in the fundamental judiciary ordinance of 1764 provision made that in the court of Common Pleas the French laws and customs shall be admitted in all causes between French Canadians "where the cause of action arose before October 1, 1764;" and in an amending ordinance a few weeks later, entitled "An Ordinance for quieting people in their possessions," it is ordained that until August 10, 1765, the tenures of lands granted before the conquest and all rights of inheritance in the same, should remain as they had been under the French "unless they shall be altered by some declared and positive law." No such law was ever enacted, and thus it will be seen that even for those who maintained the validity of the provincial legislation, the legal side of the position assumed a very confusing and indefinite aspect.[1] Certainly the popular opinions as to the bounds of valid law were of the most diverse and clashing forms, and the indefiniteness and perplexity thus created was one of the chief grievances of the period. The confusion of opinion and practice on these points is referred to by Thurlow in the Quebec Act debates as beyond all description; another speaker asserts that this confusion had never been so great as at that time (1774).[2] Lord Lyttleton in his "Letter to the Earl of Chatham on the Quebec Bill," (1774), draws a striking picture of the almost anarchical state of things in the province,— a picture which is of interest mainly as showing how matters were presented to the English public.[3] For that it must be a greatly exaggerated one is

---

[1] See Carleton's evidence, 1774, as to the confusion in laws of property. (Cavendish, *Report.*)

[2] Which is to be expected from the increasing divergence between the practice and policy of government and its constitutional and legal bases of action.

[3] The letter is in defense of the Bill. It asserts that in Canada "the French laws prevailed alone till 1764, when the English laws got a footing. The governors and officers of justice [were] always doubtful which to take for their guide, sometimes preferring the English, sometimes the French laws, as each seemed applicable to the case before them.

shown by several reflections. It was in the first place the
interest of the government party, as upholding the Quebec
Act, to give a strong impression of the bad state of things
in Canada; the opposition on the other hand denied the
state of chaos represented. It will be remembered, moreover, that a state of things which to lawyers in England,
acquainted only with the imperfect and contradictory documents on which government had been constituted, and with
the complaints of partisans, might seem confused and
dangerous to the last degree, in the peculiar state of
Canada was not likely to prove so fatal. The condition of
things here described would seem certain to paralyse all
energy and prevent all progress in the province; but we
do not find in fact these results. Industry and enterprise
were undoubtedly much hampered; but yet the only department of commerce that did not largely increase was the
fur trade, and this was injured and impeded not so much
by the confusion of law that prevailed in Quebec as by the
want of all law in the regions outside its jurisdiction.

How then was the province preserved from the natural
consequences of the confusion and uncertainty that certainly did exist? Partly from the fact that on the basis of
a compromise system initiated by the government itself,
and more than connived at in the courts, litigation continued to be conducted chiefly according to the old laws;
mainly perhaps because the mass of the people resorted
but slightly to the established courts. I have shown above
that during the military period the French law and
customs seem to have been closely followed wherever they
could be discovered. A close study of the later period
leads to the conviction that, in at least all matters affecting private property (i. e., in almost all the matters in re-

One year a proclamation, another year an instruction to a governor, another year a local
ordinance, changed the principle and varied the course of their judiciary proceedings.
In this fluctuation no man knew by what right he could take or give, inherit or convey,
property ; or by what mode or rule he could bring his right to a trial." (Pamphlets, Can.
Archives, Vol. 62.)

gard to which nine-tenths of the people would be likely to
come into contact with the administration of civil justice),
these laws and customs continued to be given validity even
in the highest courts. Under the fundamental ordinances
quoted above, such validity could not be denied in a large
number of cases. In all cases, moreover, a large discretionary power could be used in the court of Common Pleas
through a liberal interpretation of the clauses directing its
action; and much scattered evidence could be brought forward to show that the law administered in this court was
French law wherever the use of English would have
seemed to work injustice. In regard to the court of King's
Bench, which was supposed to be adhering to English law
with special closeness and to be bound to reverse appealed
judgments founded on any other, we have the direct evidence of Chief Justice Hey before the Commons in 1774,
that in all suits respecting property Canadian law and
customs had been fully admitted by him, and that juries in
the court had always been in the habit of regarding these
customs as fully as juries in England regarded English
ones. Further, that in appeal cases, (to which the court
was practically confined), he had always determined by the
rules on which the case had been originally decided. In
what seems without doubt to be his report on the judicature in 1769,[1] after stating the legal changes that had been
worked by the supposed introduction of English law in
1764, he adds that "these things have not yet been practiced,"— a statement which would seem to refer to the
whole judicial administration. Masères testifies in 1774
that no inconvenience has as yet been occasioned in the
province by the English laws so far as they had been experienced through the decision of the courts; adding that
if these had been enforced in regard to landed property
great uneasiness and confusion would doubtless have re-

---

[1] Anonymous paper in Lower Canada Jurist, Vol. 1.

sulted.   This statement is in support of the more explicit
assertion in his report of 1769, that in the main with regard to landed property the Canadians had universally
adhered to their former laws and customs.   There is no reliable evidence to be set over against these statements,
made by men who for years had been intimately connected
with the administration of justice, and who had kept
up their relations with the province during the whole
period; we must conclude therefore that outside of strictly
commercial matters even the litigious among the French
Canadians were little if at all affected by English law.
That law was used of course in all matters confined to the
old subjects.   With regard to suits between litigants of
different nationalities it seems safe to assert that Canadian
land law and customs were given full validity,— a course
which would commend itself even to the English party
after the reversion in 1770 to the French methods of
tenure.   In commercial matters on the other hand the English law seems to have obtained without much demur; but
there is no reason to suppose that there was here any such
divergence of principle as to introduce many disagreeable
changes.

But, apart from the courts, it is evident that the question
of codes was not a burning one among the people at large,
for the reason that the main body had very little to do
with the administration of justice, civil or criminal.[1] Carleton writes to Shelbourne December 24, 1767,[2] that "The
people notwithstanding[3] continue to regulate their transactions by the ancient laws, tho' unknown and unauthor-
ized in the Supreme Courts, where most of their transactions
would be declared invalid." He adds that he has met only

---

[1] Carleton testified before the House of Commons in 1774 that there were very few
trials for offences on the part of the common people.

[2] Can. Arch., Q. 5–1, p. 316.

[3] That is, of the use or establishment of English law in the courts.   Carleton is writing
at the end of the period during which the Anglo-legal movement had been freshest and
strongest, and the last part of the statement is shown above to be incorrect.

one Canadian "who sees the great revolution [i. e., in law] in its full influence." This evidently means that the Canadians kept clear of the courts, making use of their former laws and customs through the aid of those persons who had in large measure arranged their difficulties during the military period.[1] Masères in 1774 says the greater part of the French Canadians remain ignorant of the extent of the changes and have proceeded in regard to their lands on the assumption that the ancient laws and usages were still in force. And as he goes on to say that no litigation has yet arisen to give occasion for decisions which would make them better informed, we must conclude that he means they had not in these matters resorted to the courts. In the Quebec Act debate Attorney-General Thurlow made the statement (uncontradicted), that "if any dispute arose there was no instance of the Canadians resorting to the English Courts of Justice, but they referred it among themselves."[2] These statements are supported by indirect evidence and justify us in concluding that the main body of French Canadian litigants had not resorted to the courts, but had used through private instrumentalities their old property laws and customs.

The main conclusion I have reached therefore is that, for the various reasons discussed above, the judicial conditions existing in Canada up to and at 1774 were not such as to cause the formal re-establishment of the old civil law by the Quebec Act to affect the mass of the people in any considerable degree. But nevertheless the situation was one of such confusion and uncertainty as made imperative some decided act of settlement. It may justly be urged that, even in the absence of material grievances, the very fact that the Canadians kept aloof from the courts showed

---

[1] See here also the evidence before Commons, 1774, to the effect that the noblesse kept out of the courts from pride, and resorted to arbitration.

[2] Cavendish, p. 31. Thurlow was speaking from a partizan standpoint, but he had gotten up Canadian affair thoroughly, having prepared an elaborate report after examination of all the available material.

a degree of dissatisfaction or distrust, if not dread, that called for immediate action. Moreover, that much friction and complaint existed cannot be denied. But a close examination of the manifestations of this will show that it was in large degree really political in origin, or that it was inspired not so much by oppression in the every day operation of law as by uncertainty with regard to the future. It is rather the apprehension of the educated and intelligent non-litigant[1] than the specific cry of the actually aggrieved. Where it is really the latter it will be found again that it is the expression of dissatisfaction with, not new law, actual or supposed, but new procedure. For there can be no doubt that this latter contrasted very unfavorably with the old in regard to the essential features of expense and expedition. So far as English features were at all responsible it is probable that the peasantry were kept from the English courts by these more evident changes and not by legal differences of which they were wholly ignorant.[2] In the letter quoted above, Carleton, after his strong statement as to the ignorance of the people in regard to the great legal changes and their avoidance of the courts, adds, "The present great and universal complaint[3] arises from the delay and heavy expense of justice," the courts having "introduced all the chicanery of Westminster into this impoverished Province." The judiciary under the old régime had been the most praiseworthy part of the administration, being effective, easy of access, and marked especially by expedition and inexpensive methods. It had been largely and beneficially inspired by the old French paternal attitude, the judges being always ready to interpose for settlement without the expense of a trial. In

---

[1] Neither noblesse nor clergy went into the courts.

[2] See especially on this point the evidence of the provincial officers before the Commons, 1774. (Cavendish, *Report.*)

[3] A good instance of the carelessness and exaggeration of the official language of the time. His own previous statement would show that such complaint must have been confined practically to the upper or educated classes.

all these points the change was decidedly for the worse, and taken in connection with the unfamiliar appearance of even the better parts of the new procedure, make it unnecessary to look further for the full explanation of whatever specific complaint or general apprehension is to be met with. With regard to seigneurial jurisdiction, it is not probable that the new régime had made any very noticeable difference. For though Parkman seems to think that the lower forms of that jurisdiction continued to be exercised in Canada down to the conquest, Carleton asserts that at that time there were hardly three feudal judges in the whole province.[1] And at all times there had been an appeal from the seigneurial to the royal courts in all matters involving more than one-half a crown. With regard to the reception and use by the Canadians of the most important feature of the changed procedure,— the jury,— we have the most conflicting statements; but Burke's opinion[2] that they had expressed no dislike of the new institution, directly or indirectly, seems thoroughly well-grounded.

As to the general civil service, I need delay here only on those features which would affect the popular estimation of the new régime. The great abuses of the later French administration might be expected to insure a favorable reception even of the very imperfect English one; but nevertheless we meet with considerable complaint. The main cause of this was the fact that the more important positions, being filled by patent from the home government, were practically independent of the provincial administration, and were almost always executed by deputy, the appointees renting them out to the highest bidder. The abuse is succinctly and strongly put by Murray in March, 1765. He writes: "The places of the greatest business in the province have been granted by patent to men of interest in England, who have hired them

[1] The statement is supported by strong contemporary evidence.
[2] Cavendish, *Report.*

to the best bidder, without considering the talents or circumstances of their representatives.   One man (e. g.) who
cannot read a word of French, holds five such offices." [1]
And in his defense at the close of his administration he attributes the difficulties of government largely to "the im-
proper choice and the number of the civil officers sent over
from England," not one of whom understood French, and
the compensation of whom depended entirely on their
fees.   Power of supervision and suspension was indeed
given to the governor, but that this was not sufficient for
the remedying of the evil is shown by Carleton's letter to
the treasury, January 12, 1775, just at the close of the old
order of things.   In this he speaks of the misfortunes
hitherto attendant on the Provincial government, in that
the inferior officers, "proud of the superior weight and influence of the Boards from whence their Commissions
issue," and relying for protection on their patrons, "almost lose every idea of that subordination so essential to
good order," and are in all measures of the colonial administration "for the most part cold and at best neutral." [2]
This was written in the belief that the operation of the
Quebec Act would remedy the evil; for though no direct
mention is made of the matter in that Act or in the instructions that accompanied it, Carleton refers later to the
clause in it "which vacated all commissions," as being "in
consequence of complaints;" it being thereby intended "to
put a stop to all deputations, and to compel all who had
offices here to reside and do their duty in person."   It is
evident that there was here a very serious abuse, capable
of paralyzing the best efforts of government.

Inseparably connected with the subject of the patent offices is the matter of fees in general.   For as Murray said
in 1766 the compensation to the deputies at least depended
entirely on what could be wrung from the people and the

---

[1] Can. Arch., Q. 2, p. 377.

[2] Can. Arch., Q. 11, p. 122.

government in this form. It is not necessary to suppose
that these fees were upon a scale of unheard of extortion;
indeed Carleton, their most determined opponent, expressly
states that they were not greater than in the other provinces,[1] and Murray declares that he was ordered by his instructions to establish them on that scale.[2] The hardship
consisted in the fact that a system which had been adapted
to the ability of the most prosperous of the other provinces
was suddenly fastened upon one utterly impoverished, and
with a people unused to such payments. The heaviness of
the burden is apparent in every direction. May 14, 1767,
Carleton writes, "Upon my arrival not a Canadian approached me that did not complain of the number of fees
demanded, and particularly of the exorbitant expenses
that attended the obtaining any redress by law;" adding
that the fees on the registering of land alone (a requirement which ultimately was not enforced, probably from
this reason), would have amounted to more than double the
current coin of the province. He encloses a copy of the
fees as fixed upon by Murray and the Council in 1765; — a
document of about twenty closely written pages of large
foolscap, the fees ranging all the way from £6 to 3d, and the
total number of official acts so to be remunerated being
about 350. The tendency of Murray's administration was
not to restrain such expenses,[3] but Carleton from the first
resolutely set his face against them, and one of his earliest
acts was to relinquish his own personal fees.[4] His vigorous
statements were not wholly disregarded by the home government, but no decided measures of alleviation were
adopted at any time within our present view. The heed-
less injustice which had ordered the fees to be established
on the same scale as in the other colonies seems indeed to
have been early repented of, for in the instructions of the

---

[1] To Shelbourne, May 14, 1767. (Can. Arch., Q. 4, p. 173.)

[2] Can. Arch., *Cal. Hald. Coll.*, p. 92.

[3] See *Advertisement* of the Council, Aug. 12, 1765. (Can. Arch., Q. 5-2, p. 812.)

[4] See *Rep. Can. Arch.*, 1890, p. xiii. Also Can. Arch., Q. 5-2, pp. 445-82.

Receiver General early in 1766 it is ordered that the salaries and profits of the inferior officials connected with the Provincial treasury shall be no greater than under the French government. In July, 1768, Hillsborough writes to Carleton in answer to his representations of abuses, that the king is determined to stop the evils connected both with the patent offices and with the fees in general; that the subject has been laid before the Board of Trade, and that in the meantime he is to make temporary regulations for the restraining of fees within bounds.[1] The new instructions of the same year contain, however, only the indefinite direction "to take especial care to regulate all salaries and fees belonging to places, or paid upon emergencies, that they be within the limits of moderation." It is most probably in pursuance of this recommendation that we find an entry in the public accounts for the first half of 1769, of a payment to the Chief Justice of £100 " in lieu of fees, at the rate of £200 per annum." In April, 1770, we hear of a committee which has " the fees of the public officers of this province under consideration;" but nothing seems to have been then effected, and for the remaining four years the matter, with all similar ones, awaited the expected radical change in constitution.

D. Finances.

It remains only to make a brief statement as to the finances of the provincial administration. It is in the consideration of the financial condition of Quebec as contrasted with that of the other Crown Provinces that we have brought home to us most vividly its peculiar and dependent position. In all the others, financial affairs were, through the Assemblies, in the hands of the people, and outside of the customs Great Britain had, normally, neither control nor expense. In Quebec on the other hand not only was the revenue (the word is here a misnomer), almost entirely fur-

---

[1] Can. Arch., Q. 5-2, p. 602.

nished and expended[1] by the home government directly, but the probability is that but a very small part of it had any connection with the province as a source. We have seen that the Quebec legislative authority was from the first expressly prohibited from "imposing any duty or tax;" and that the Council was more mindful of this injunction than of other such restraints is shown directly by entries in the Council minutes,[2] and by the fact that none of the ordinances disregard it. This restriction was to be in force only till an Assembly should form part of the legislature; but that it was intended even then to keep a large measure of control over the finances, and thus to prevent the growth of the obstacles which beset the royal path in the other provinces from this key to the situation having fallen entirely into colonial hands, is probably shown by the directions concerning legislation embodied in the instructions of 1768.[3]

It is evident that if my argument as to the legislative power subsequent to the Proclamation of 1763 be correct, revenue could be legally drawn from the province during the period only through the customs, or through such other special rights and prerogatives of the Crown as were attached to it under the French régime, and might be contended to have passed over unimpaired with the sovereignty of the country. I say *other* special rights, for it is clear from Lord Mansfield's judgment that the only customs duties that could be collected were those which had been found in force at the conquest,[4] and it seems equally certain that there is no radical distinction between these and such other dues as lands (e. g.) had hitherto been subject to. All together would seem to have been simply transferred in the same manner as other public property,

---

[1] At least after 1766, when the Receiver General was appointed.

[2] Can. Arch., Q. 3, pp. 160-70; Q. 8, p. 126.

[3] See below for general discussion, chapter V, section C.

[4] See resolution of Imperial Privy Council, Nov. 22, 1765, concerning requiring of old duties. (Can. Arch., Q. 2, p. 472.) See also below for suits against Murray in 1768.

and it is only on the impossible supposition that all French law and custom had been by the conquest and cession immediately abrogated that the right of the crown to them could be disputed. But these principles seem not to have been clear to the authorities at the time. Action in regard to the old land dues was no doubt hindered further by the confusion and uncertainty that prevailed as to the laws in general, and it seems certain that no revenue was derived from this source at any part of the period. The new rents from soccage lands, and the profits from the judiciary, we may also regard as not worth consideration. The fur trade monopoly in the northeast had been a considerable source of profit to the French government, and had passed unquestioned to the English; but it was leased through the whole of this period for £400 per annum.

The only remaining source of revenue was the customs, and it is to this quarter that we must look for any appreciable lightening of the burden of the English taxpayer. Unfortunately, though the references to duties are frequent, and though they received the careful attention of government from the first, we have no conclusive reports as to the amounts actually collected. On the conquest duties had been imposed by the commanding officer and levied until the establishment of the civil government; the rates required being slightly in excess of the old French ones, and the whole amount thus collected being stated as £11,000 sterling. In 1768 actions for recovery were brought against the governor in the British Court of Common Pleas, on the ground that the military government had no authority to impose duties; but on it being shown that these were substantially the same as those fixed by the French, the plaintiffs agreed to accept a verdict only for the excess. In accordance with this verdict we meet with various entries in the Quebec Council minutes in 1770 of orders for repayments of this excess to various other complainants, the sum repaid amounting in all to £2,000. So that it re-

sults that the duties levied during the first four years of
the occupation (when commerce was of course very much
depressed), would yield about £2,000 per annum. This
amount we should expect to be largely increased during
the later years; but there is no probability that anything
was collected under the civil government.[1] A Provincial
proclamation of May, 1765, seems to be intended to apply
the Imperial customs Act of the previous year; but as more
than a month later Murray reports that he is and will be
"entirely at a loss how to carry on the business of government without money,"[2] it seems to have effected no
change in the situation. In July of the same year the
home government took the finances of the province more
directly under control by the appointment of a receiver-
general, who was to be independent of the provincial administration, was to receive all moneys and warrant all ex-
penditures, and was to report directly to the Treasury.
His instructions[3] direct him to collect the old French
duties, and in doing so, "to strictly conform himself to the
ancient customs and usages of the said country before it
was conquered by His Majesty." Of the receipts the sur-
plus, after "defraying the expenses of civil officers and
contingencies of government in the Province," was to be
remitted home. The only result apparently of the new
official's efforts were the ineffectual actions against the
English traders which have been discussed above.[4]

From this consideration of the various possible sources
of provincial revenue, we may conclude that the amount
derived therefrom was so slight as to make very little difference to the Imperial treasury. As to the total expenses

---

[1] Murray writes to the Board of Trade, March 3, 1765, that he has long expected in vain
"the decision of the rum duties," and does not know "how government is to be carried
on here without a shilling. I am little solicitous about my own salary, the amount of
which is still unknown to me, but the indigence of the judge and other officers sent from
England is equally alarming and hurtful to the public." (Can. Arch., Q. 2, p. 377.)

[2] Can. Arch., Q. 2, p. 424.

[3] See Masères, *Commissions*, pp. 156–9.

[4] Pp. 313–16.

of the civil establishment we have no definite statements,
but from various references it may be concluded that they
were about the same as under the last years of the French
régime.[1] Masères states that the amount drawn yearly on
this account from the Imperial treasury was about £10,000.
In the "Returns on Public Income and Expenditure,"
(printed for House of Commons, 1869), Quebec is specially
mentioned only for the year 1768, when an item of £6,722
is set down for its civil establishment. The "Annual Register" and "Parliamentary History," which apparently aim
to give detailed financial statements from year to year, do
not afford any further light, no direct mention being made
of Quebec, although there are given regularly the estimates for the civil establishment, not only of Nova Scotia
and Georgia, but also of East and West Florida, which had
been granted civil constitutions at the same time and in
the same manner as Quebec. The only explanation seems
to be that (in accordance with the general neglect and
mismanagement of Canadian affairs), owing to the prominence of the military service in Quebec, the accounts
were included under military heads. The civil list established in 1775 (see Carleton's instructions), amounted to
about £18,000, and of this about £8,000 can be directly attributed to additional expenses caused by the enlarged
sphere of government under the Quebec Act. This then
brings us back to Masères' estimate.

---

[1] Murray states (*Report*, 1762), that in 1757 the total civil expenses of the French administration amounted to £11,158. The revenue of the same year (apparently drawn
mainly from the fur trade), was £13,961.

CHAPTER IV.

THE SPIRIT AND DEVELOPMENT OF ADMINISTRATION.

In the previous chapter I have attempted a description of the surface conditions of government in the Province of Quebec throughout our period,— such a description as might have been given by a contemporary, especially a contemporary official.   My object in the present chapter is to go behind the scenes, and examine the animating spirit under the official forms, with special reference to development in the bases of action.   In so doing regard will be had mainly and constantly to the Quebec Act as the centre of the inquiry, with the purpose of seeing what light, if any, may thus be thrown on its genesis and intent.

A.   The Colonial Governors.

My investigation here has therefore to do almost entirely with the Home or Imperial Administration.   But, as the chief of the influences brought to bear on that authority, it will be necessary first to consider the general spirit and policy of the heads of the colonial government.[1]   It is evident that a large discretion was necessarily always left to the Provincial Governor; but the normal limits of this discretion were at this time in the case of Quebec much extended from the fact that during the early part of the period the home government had no decided or consistent

These were, (a) Gen. *James Murray* (1725?—1794), younger son of a Scotch peer.   Brigadier with Wolfe at capture of Quebec and left in charge of the conquered province during the Military Period, he was Governor-in-Chief from Aug. 10, 1784, to Oct. 26, 1768, but left the country finally in June, 1766.

(b) Col. *Guy Carleton* (1724-1808), of an Irish family, was at the siege of Louisbourg and Quebec, and came to the province as Lieutenant-Governor, September, 1768.   He held that position until October, 1768, when he become governor-in-chief, so continuing till June, 1778, though absent from the province August 1st, 1770-September 18, 1774. Made Baron Dorchester and reappointed to Canadian Government, 1786.

policy, and that in the latter part the expectation of a speedy general constitutional settlement joined with other factors in causing a steady neglect of the immediate affairs of the province. It is therefore desirable to see in what ways and to what extent the actions of the Home Administration were based on the representations of the provincial authorities.

Gen. James Murray had been connected with Canada from the first hour of English rule there, and when put at the head of the new civil government had had almost five years' intimate knowledge of the country. If personal characteristics had prevented his fully profiting from his experience, there can be no doubt of his integrity, and of his strong desire to see justice done and the best interests of the country advanced. As has been shown above both he and the other military commanders seem from the first to have made every effort, consistently with the safety of the new possession, to reconcile the Canadians to the new rule. These same motives were no doubt as strongly present during his control of the civil government. That his success was not commensurate with his efforts, and that the two years of his civil administration were a period of constant turmoil, cannot, however, be denied; nor yet that the explanation must be largely found in his personal character, and in a want of tact and discernment which would have insured failure in a much less difficult situation. He was hasty in judgment and violent in temper, and his military training had prejudiced him in favour of the old Canadian military aristocracy, which he credited with more influence over the people than it had for a long time possessed. The same cause blinded him to the real character and importance of the new English-speaking commercial element. A light is thrown on Murray's character by some observations in his own defence just before the installment of civil government.[1] After refer-

---

[1] To Board of Trade, April 24, 1764.   (Can. Arch., Q. 2, p. 107.)

ring to the difficulties that have attended the military rule
owing to the character of the various sections of the population, and of the caution he has exercised in enforcing
martial law, "knowing how jealous the people of England
are of the military arm, upon all occasions, and how eagerly
they would have laid hold of the least shadow of blame," he
proceeds to speak of his mortification in being "too often
obliged to substitute reprimands from my own mouth in place
of fines and prisons, choosing to risk my own popularity
rather than give a handle to the factious. Hence, I find I have
been represented in England a man of a most violent, ungov-
ernable temper." Unfortunately for the entire validity of this
ingenuous defense, we find that the violent manifestations
of temper continued under the civil government; and we
cannot but conclude that there was too much ground for
the complaint made in the English petitions in 1765 of his
" rage and rudeness of language and demeanour.[1] In general, however, we find his attitude towards the French
Canadians to be one of forbearance and magnanimity,[2]
and the seigneurs came to look upon him as their special protector;[3] but that even they were not always safe
from his irritability may be seen in the memorial of the
Chevalier de Lery.[4] It must indeed be conceded that few
positions could have been more trying than Murray's at this
time.[5] He was left without revenue or clear instructions
to carry on government over a people who, rightly or
wrongly, he thought had conceived a slighting idea of his
position from the fact that he had been deprived of all
military command in the province; feeling himself moreover under compulsion to introduce an order of things
which he considered in the highest degree injurious and
unjust. But making all allowances for his difficulties, we

---

[1] *Rep. Can. Arch.*, 1888, p. 15.
[2] See letter to Justices of Montreal, Oct. 9, 1765. (Can. Arch., Q. 3, p. 90.)
[3] *Rep. Can. Arch.*, 1888, p. 9.
[4] Ibid., p. 31.
[5] See his defense, August 20th, 1766. (Can. Arch., B. 8, p. 1.)

must conclude that he was peculiarly ill-fitted to cope with them, and that his career in Canada cannot be considered to have been marked by much discernment or administrative ability.

Murray's own judgment and inclination were from the first strongly opposed to any radical changes in the civil law and constitution of the province. His views on this matter were probably closely connected with his strongly expressed opinion that the civil governor in Quebec ought also to have the chief military command. One of his first enactments was the Judiciary Ordinance of September 17, 1764, which, though evidently intended to give effect to the supposed Imperial policy of introducing the general body of the English law, was thought by the English extremists of the time to have given undue privileges to the French Canadian Catholics. In writing home in defense of this measure [1] Murray strongly recommends granting the Canadians "a few privileges which the laws of England deny the Roman Catholics at home." In the various and complicated disputes with the military authorities which soon follow, the governor appears in a comparatively favourable light as the upholder of civil law and the protector of the people against the military; though it is impossible to keep from feeling that his attitude was to some extent influenced by the strained nature of the personal relations then existing between himself and the military officers. Interesting hints as to his policy can be got from his defense against some anonymous charges made in 1765 or thereabouts, chiefly with reference to the military government. In this he says that it was a maxim of his "to shun addresses from the traders," and to consult the men of property in the colony (by whom he means the seigneurs,— the possessors of landed property), and that he had displeased the Protestants in trying to conciliate the Canadians to British rule. That his partiality for the noblesse

---

[1] Oct. 29, 1764. Can. Arch., Q. 2, p. 233.

went beyond the limits of justice and good government may be conjectured from the reference in their memorial in his defense to "the politeness and deference of this governor for persons of good birth,"[1] and from his own acknowledgment that he did "recommend to the magistrates at Montreal not to billet any of the soldiers upon the noblesse, unless in cases of the utmost necessity,"— a tenderness which he adds they had a right to expect from the regard paid to people of family in all countries. And he somewhat naively inquires, "Can there be a greater instance of the turbulent, levelling spirit of my accusers than this very complaint?"

Though recalled in apparent disgrace[2] Murray succeeded in vindicating himself from all the charges brought against him, and retained the office for two years longer. His recollections of his Canadian stay may be seen by a reference in a letter to Haldimand from one of the East Indian ports in 1775, in which he speaks of spending his life tranquilly now, differently from what he did in Canada.[3]

Colonel Guy Carleton had also had early experience in Canada, but it does not appear to have afforded him much idea of the real state of the country. He and Murray were of the same profession; and the integrity and earnest endeavour after good government which characterized the former can even more unhesitatingly be ascribed to the latter. To him also must be conceded a larger share of statesmanlike qualities than is exhibited by any other official in the early history of the country. Carleton was indeed, like Murray, first a military man, and his most striking services to Canada were perhaps military ones; but he

---

[1] *Rep. Can. Arch.*, 1888, p. 19.

[2] See concerning his reception, Can. Arch., B. 68, p. 157. He was recalled on the recommendation of the Board of Trade on account, as expressly stated, of the complaints of the merchants trading to and in the colony. The severe strictures of Hillsborough (quoted below. See also above, p. 344) may perhaps be explained by the fact that Hillsborough had been president of the Board when the Proclamation which he accused Murray of grossly misinterpreting had been drawn.

[3] Can. Arch., B. 6, p. 278.

was also a man of considerable civil experience, of wide statesmanlike views,[1] and of no small amount of discernment with regard to both men and events. He was for twenty years, intermittently, the chief figure in Canadian life; and his work here is consequently the main feature of what biographers agree in considering a somewhat distinguished career.

Personally he was a man of infinitely more dignity than Murray,— one who often left with his contemporaries the impression of a somewhat reserved and frigid nature. His self-control may be illustrated by the testimony of an eye witness to one of the most trying events of his life — the abandoning of Montreal to the Americans in 1776.[2] His attitude toward the revolution was a most unbending one, and is clearly shown in a letter to Dartmouth during the seige of Montreal,[3] in which he refers to the threatening communication of Montgomery in regard to alleged ill-treatment of American prisoners, and adds, "I shall treat all their threats with a silent contempt, and in this persevere, were I certain of falling into their hands the following week, not thinking myself at liberty to treat otherwise those who are traitors to the King, without His Majesty's express commands." Yet after the remnant of the American force had retreated from the walls of Quebec in the spring of 1776, leaving behind them many sick and wounded ("dispersed in the adjacent woods and parishes"), we find him issuing a proclamation to the local officials to make diligent search for such persons and to afford them all possible relief, reassuring them by the promise that as soon as their health should be restored they would

---

[1] For some acute general remarks on the tendencies of American government, see letter to Shelbourne, Jan. 20, 1768. (Can. Arch., Q. 5–1, p. 370.)

[2] Lt. Gov. Hamilton to Dartmouth, Aug. 29, 1776. (Can. Arch., Q. 12, p. 212.) Has been "exceedingly struck by the unmoved temper and firmness of the general. Though deserted by the most ungrateful race under the sun, though a general without troops, and at the eve of quitting Montreal to give entrance to lawless rebels his mind appeared unshaken . . . though undoubtedly wrung to the soul."

[3] Can. Arch., Q. 11, p. 267. (Oct. 28, 1775.)

be set at liberty.[1] In October, 1776, writing to Burgoyne in reference to a recent victory over the rebels, he says that inasmuch as it is over fellow subjects it is no ground for rejoicing. The attitude of Carleton in regard to Burgoyne's expedition throws further honorable light on his character. For though deeply mortified by the slight to himself in the transfer of the command on this occasion to Burgoyne, we have the latter's most emphatic testimony to his zealous and strenuous efforts to make the expedition a success.[2] The traits of Carleton's character which seem to have made most impression upon those who had to do with him in Canada were his justice and impartiality, testimony to these recurring from all quarters. Of a more even and balanced nature than Murray he made neither such bitter enemies nor such warm friends.

Carleton had the great advantage over Murray, so far as his relations with the home government were concerned, of coming to his government more fully and directly informed as to the trend of Imperial views in regard to Canada. The Board of Trade when advising Murray's recall had at length taken the state of the province into consideration, and had drawn up a paper of recommendations with which Carleton was of course conversant. Though nominally Murray's subordinate for the first two years, there was no official relation between the two, and apparently a strained personal one,— the natural consequence of the fact that Carleton really displaced Murray and was supposed to represent an opposite policy. The former has sometimes the air of censuring the conduct of his predecessor, and his first steps on arriving in the province were considered by some to have been dictated by hostility to Murray's friends in the Council. But however this may have been we find that Carleton did not escape the most

---

[1] A promise that was fulfilled, over 1,200 being sent home on parole. See Carleton to Germaine, Aug. 10, 1776. (Can. Arch., Q. 12, p. 135.) For the strongly favorable impression made on these troops by Carleton see *Journals* of the invaders.

[2] Burgoyne to Germaine, May 14, 1777. (Can. Arch., Q. 13, p. 107.)

disastrous part of his predecessor's policy,— the partiality
for and dependence upon the noblesse. The men, from
birth, character, and training, were essentially imbued with
the same prejudices and ideas of government, and Carleton was moreover in a degree bound to even greater consideration of the leading French families, from the fact
that he was likely to be entrusted with the carrying out of
the policy of preserving the institutions of which they
were supposed to be the main support. This supposition
he brought with him from England, and I have already
frequently referred to the fundamental error (as to the relations between noblesse and people), involved in it. It
was an error to which can be traced the main defects and
failures of his policy and of its outcome, the Quebec Act.
I have above credited Carleton with considerable pene-
tration and judicial ability in regard to men and events;
but in this matter his prejudices seem to have lulled his
judgment to sleep, and he remained contented with an estimate of the people derived from the small and unprogressive body which was nearest him, and which was now
every day becoming more and more detached from the
real life of the country. He was, moreover, scarcely more
just to the English element or more alive to its growing
influence over the Canadians than was Murray. His
personal stiffness and aristocratic bearing doubtless stood
constantly in his way; and as late as 1788, at the beginning of his second term of office, Mabane, one of the oldest
and most experienced of the ex-councillors, writes concerning Carleton's ignorance of men and things in the
province, his partiality and his unpopularity.[1] Hence perhaps it may well be doubted whether, though of much
broader views than Murray and infinitely superior to him
as an administrator, he was really very much better qualified for this particular period of government. His efforts
were fatally marred by his misconceptions of the situation.

---

[1] Can. Arch., B. 77. Mabane, it should be said, had had personal difficulties with
Carleton in the early days of the governorship.

Having, like Murray, from the first taken the Canadian noblesse under his protection, one of Carleton's first acts was to follow the example of the French government in providing for them to some extent from the public purse. He lost no time, moreover, in urging on the home government the advisability as a matter of policy of utilizing the services of the class in all departments of the public employ. The mistake as to their influence over the people he seems to have laboured under during the whole period, and it explains sufficiently, (without charging him with undue class or professional prejudice), the deference he always paid to their views and wishes. The first striking letter of Carleton on general policy that we meet with, is that of November 25, 1767,[1] in answer apparently to information as to a late important action of the Privy Council. In this he starts by saying that he takes it for granted "that the natural rights of men,[2] the British interests on this continent and the securing the King's dominion over this province must ever be the principal points in view in forming its civil constitution and body of laws;" proceeds to advise the attaching of the seigneurs to British interests, (as above), and finally, after a discussion of military requirements, expresses the opinion that all governmental steps should proceed on the assumption that the present predominance of the French-speaking population will not diminish, but increase and strengthen daily; so that, "barring a catastrophe shocking to think of, this country must to the end of time be peopled by the Canadian race," and any new stock transplanted will be sure to be "totally hid and imperceptible among them." Specific recommendations as to laws he does not enter into, but it is easy to see whither his premises will lead him. Hence we are not surprised to find him a month later recommending in the most definite and decided manner the almost entire reten-

---

[1] *Rep. Can. Arch.*, 1888, p. 41.
[2] The use of this phrase here is rather suggestive.

tion of French civil law and custom. In this very important letter (to Shelbourne, December 24, 1767,)[1] he reminds the minister that the Canadians "are not a migration of Britons, who brought with them the laws of England, but a populous and long-established colony," with its own laws and customs, forced to a conditional capitulation. "All this arrangement in one hour we overturned by the Ordinance of the 17th September, 1764, and laws ill-adapted to the genius of the Canadians, to the situation of the province, and to the interests of Great Britain, unknown and unpublished, were introduced in their stead; a sort of severity if I remember right, never before practiced by any conqueror even where the people without capitulation submitted to his will and discretion." Then, after implying that the above Ordinance is both contrary to the terms of the capitulation and beyond the provincial legislative power, and declaring that it "cannot long remain in force without a general confusion and discontent," he proceeds to advise its repeal and the gradual reinstating of the old Canadian laws almost in their entirety. In accordance with this advice he transmits a draft of an ordinance for doing this in regard to landed property. We see, therefore, that Carleton's mind was fully made up on this subject more than six years before the Quebec Act. His views seem if anything to have become only more firmly fixed during the following years. He frequently re-urges the attaching of the noblesse by employment or by other attentions, his confidence as to their influence over the people apparently remaining undisturbed. But the fact that he was absent from the province for the last four years of the period is to be especially noted; for these years were the most important part of it, being those in which political education would, (through the unavoidable influence of the events in the other colonies), be proceeding at the most rapid rate.

The conceptions and misconceptions of Carleton I have

---

[1] Can. Arch., Q. 5-1, p. 316.

considered especially noteworthy on account of the dependence the home administrations placed on him, and his
great influence in the moulding of the Quebec Act. We
have seen that he had the advantage of Murray in coming
to the government *en rapport* with the home administration; and so far as appears this perfect agreement and
confidence was maintained down till the last year of his
rule (when personal difficulties arose between himself and
the Secretary of State, Lord Germaine). The following of
the course of events leaves with us the conviction that the
colonial office depended on Carleton for practically all its
instruction on Canadian matters, and that all its steps were
guided by his recommendations. There have been more
successful officials in English colonial history, but never
one more thoroughly trusted. His military services in
1775 were confounded with his civil ones apparently, and
he retired from Canada with the reputation of a master in
all that concerned it. Accordingly we find that when in
1786 its affairs seemed to be again approaching a crisis
which could not be neglected, he was sent out, invested
with the new dignity of a peerage, to steer the ship of
state through the troubled waters of another change of
constitution.

B.   The Imperial Office.

With regard to Imperial policy I shall first notice for
a moment the general attitude of the successive home executives toward the political parties (or more accurately,
the different races), in the province. This is an enquiry that
will be resumed later in the attempt to determine how far
the Quebec Act was in accordance with previous measures,
and how far dictated by the supposed emergencies connected with the threatening stand of the other colonies.
Just now I confine myself to general expressions of policy,
contained in regular and confidential communications with
the provincial administration; communications which as of
a strictly private nature and made to the officials in the

full confidence of the home government, I can find no reason for taking at anything but their face value. At the outset it may be said that in small matters as in great the correspondence is of a nature to impress us strongly with the justice and humanity, if not with the far-sightedness, of the views entertained and advocated by one and all of the various secretaries in charge of the colonial department. The utmost attention is given to every symptom of discontent on the part of the people and the attachment of them by conciliatory and just treatment is constantly urged. Notwithstanding the energy of the English-speaking element in the colony in making themselves heard both there and at home, the authorities seem never to have lost sight of the fact that Canada was French and likely to remain French.[1] Early in the period the minister writes that dutiful behaviour will secure the French Canadians all the benefits of British government; and that these were not empty words is shewn by the instructions sent out in regard to the judiciary ordinance of September 17, 1764, as we gather them from the wording of the amending ordinance of July 1st, 1766.[2] The preamble of the latter states that his Majesty has signified by an additional instruction "that the welfare and happiness of his loving subjects in this province do require that the said ordinance should be altered and amended in several provisions of it which tend to restrain his Canadian subjects in the privileges they are entitled to enjoy in common with his natural-born subjects;" and it is accordingly enacted that Canadians shall be admitted equally with British-born on all juries and to the legal profession. In the following year the state of the provincial judiciary was taken up more seriously, and we get very important indications of the way in which the matter was viewed at

[1] See Carleton to Shelborne, Nov. 25, 1767, *Rep. Can. Arch.*, 1888, p. 42; also Cramahé to Dartmouth, December, 1773. (Can. Arch., Q. 10, p. 22.) See also debate in Commons on Quebec Act, 1774, for position taken by both government and opposition that the French Canadians must be the first consideration.

[2] For Ordinances see Can. Arch., Q. 5.

home, from the minutes of the Privy Council meeting of
August 28, 1767.[1] It was resolved that the government officials in the province should be instructed to report on the
existing defects, and "whether the Canadians in particular
are, or think themselves aggrieved according to the present
administration of justice, wherein and in what respect, together with their opinions of any alterations, additions, or
amendments that they can propose for the general benefit
of the said province." The proceedings here inaugurated
were interrupted and delayed by ministerial changes, but
the views of policy on which they were founded evidently
remained the same. In the spring of the following year,
Shelbourne was replaced in the secretaryship by Hillsborough, who retained it up till the eve of the Quebec Act.
His first letter to Quebec, dated March 6th, 1768, conveys
to Carleton, (who had been strongly advocating the retention of the French laws and customs), His Majesty's approval "of the humanity and tenderness you have shewn
with regard to the peculiar circumstances and situation of
His Majesty's new subjects;" and recommends him to take
measures to reconcile the new subjects to unavoidable delays in regard to a general settlement.[2] In the following
July he writes in the same strain, fully approving of all
the governor's recommendations (in regard to re-establishment of French law), and regretting the unavoidable delay
in the giving them force.[3] January 4, 1769,[4] he agrees with
Carleton's recommendation of the employing in the public
service of the French Canadians, but expresses the fear
that popular prejudices at home might make it difficult to
follow as regarded the military profession; in the following July[5] he says that there can be no doubt of the justice
and propriety of admitting Canadians to the Council. Jan-

---

[1] See below, chapter V for full report. (Can. Arch., Q. 4, p. 327.)
[2] Can. Arch., Q. 5–1, p. 344.
[3] Ibid., Q. 5–2, p. 602.
[4] Ibid., Q. 6, p. 3.
[5] Ibid., p. 67.

uary 11, 1772,[1] he transmits to Cramahé the new instructions in regard to the granting of lands, which he hopes
will "convince His Majesty's new subjects of the King's
gracious intention to adopt and preserve, in every case
where it can be legally done, the customs and usages that
subsisted in the colony before the reduction of it, and which
His Majesty observes they are very desirous to retain." This
is more than two years before the Quebec Act.

The attitude of the Imperial administrations toward the
new English-speaking element may be conjectured from
the opinion generally entertained at home, that the main
part of this was of American origin, and was inspired by
the same ideas and aims as the turbulent populace in the
other provinces. This idea, as is shown above, was probably mainly due to the intemperate attitude of the early
spokesmen of the party, and was evidently fostered both
by Murray and Carleton. The attitude of the Grand Jury
in 1764[2] was of course severely condemned at home, the
secretary transmitting His Majesty's highest disapproba-
tion of their "assuming to themselves authority similar to
that of a House of Representatives against the orders and
regulations of His Majesty's government established
there."[3] There are indications that possibly show that at
one time there was no desire on the part of the home government for any considerable increase in the number and
influence of the old subjects in the province, and we at
least have expressions which prove that none such was expected. The change in the land regulations was made to
accommodate the French, and apparently without any idea
that it would be welcome to the English settler. But yet
Hillsborough writes, April 18, 1772, in tones of satisfaction
at the apparent betaking of the English to the cultivation
of the land.[4]

---

[1] Can. Arch., Q. 8, p. 97.
[2] See above, pp. 311–13.
[3] Can. Arch., Q. 2, p. 464.
[4] Ibid., Q. 8, p. 124.

In regard to the movement in 1773 for an assembly the provincial government tried to adopt an amicable and neutral course in order to have the representations of the old subjects forwarded in a regular manner (i. e., through the authorities; which, however, seems not to have been done). Dartmouth writes, April 6th, 1774, approving of this course and stating his conviction "that the proposition has been stirred up to answer factious views; and the proceedings of the committee seem to have had no other object than to embarrass the measures now under consideration." [1] December 10th, 1774, he expresses the hope that the full operation of the Quebec Act, especially in regard to " the plan of judicature " intended, may satisfy all classes of subjects, and recommends to the governor to point out to the British " the attention that has been shown to their interests not only in the adopting of the English laws as far as was consistent with what was due to the just claims and moderate wishes of the Canadians, but in the opening to the British merchant by the extension of the province so many new channels of important commerce." [2]

On the whole we may sum up the policy of the government, Provincial and Imperial, towards the old subjects in in the words of Haldimand, who writes in October, 1779, that he and the Council agree in considering the Canadians the people of the country, to the 60,000 of whom regard was to be paid, rather than to the 2,000 others. [3] And the expressions of this disregard of the English-speaking element were the less unrestrained through the prejudices established mainly by the injurious misrepresentations of the Provincial officials.

In noting the Imperial policy in some of its special applications to Provincial affairs I shall leave out of sight for the moment those more important matters which when settled finally by the Quebec Act, became the centre of the

---

[1] Can. Arch., Q. 10, p. 42.
[2] Ibid., p. 125.
[3] Ibid., B. 54, p. 354.

contention that raged round that measure. These had reference to the boundaries of the province, to the position and possessions of the Roman Catholic Church within it, to the Provincial legislature, and to the civil law; and it appears better to disregard the chronological order to some degree in their case, so that the consideration of them may be brought as a part of the Quebec Act generally. Here, therefore, I have reference to such other parts of the general course of the home administration as throw light upon general policy. And the first and chief impression that is made upon us by the examination of these, in connection with the other less important parts of the progress of events, is that ignorance, neglect, and inconsistency were the prevailing conditions in the colonial office throughout as regarded the province of Quebec. This I have already reverted to; in connection with the Quebec Act it will be necessary to make some short inquiry into the causes of it.

The general character of what may be called constitutional documents calls first for notice. The main early ones have been already noticed in other connections;[1] they certainly give us no reason to suppose that the long line of colonial precedent established in the English administrative mind was departed from in the case of Canada, except in so far as would seem unavoidable in providing for security and order amongst a people totally ignorant of British methods of government and incapacitated by British law from participation in them. We have seen indeed that even the difficulties which thus lay on the surface and which might be expected to attract the notice of the most incapable and harrassed of ministers, *do* seem in these first measures to have been entirely disregarded; for the Proclamation of 1763, which unmistakably contemplates the early establishment of an assembly, seems to have been drawn up in utter ignorance or disregard of the peculiar conditions of the countries to which it gave a constitution. Not only does it show no special mark of regard for the

---

[1] See especially chapter III, section A.

original inhabitants of these new acquisitions, but it seems oblivious to their existence. So far as it goes, these acquisitions are considered, not as old and settled colonies of another race, but as totally unoccupied regions to which it was the duty of His Majesty's government to draw the speedy attention of His Majesty's loyal emigrants. The preamble to the proclamation states the ground of the measures therein taken to be the desire "that all our loving subjects as well of our Kingdoms as of our colonies in America, may avail themselves with all convenient speed of the great benefits and advantages which must accrue therefrom to their commerce, manufactures, and navigation," and the conviction that these measures "will greatly contribute to the speedy settling our said new governments;" it being further promised that, (italics are mine), "all persons *inhabiting in* or resorting to our said *colonies* may confide in our Royal protection for the enjoyment of the benefit of the laws of our realm of England,"— a promise made apparently without a suspicion that there could be any parties concerned who were not pining after the "enjoyment" in question. In view of this document we have little right to look for any great care or discrimination in the applying to the new government of the min governmental instruments. Nor on the other hand do we discover any marks of influence exerted upon the Imperial administration by the contemporary difficulties which were attending government under similar instruments in the old colonies. The conviction is forced upon us as we study the history of the first few years (down say till 1768), that the various executives must have been too busy with other matters to have had time to do more with regard to Canada than order the making out for it of new copies of the established forms.

The commission to Gov. Murray under which civil government was established in Canada, August 10th, 1764, is dated November 21, 1763, or about six weeks after the

Proclamation above referred to. What relation it bears to
the usual form of the document will best be discovered by direct comparison; and I have selected for this purpose the
almost contemporary commissions to Governor Cornwallis
of Nova Scotia in 1749, and to Sir Danvers Osborn of New
York in 1755.[1] Nova Scotia had, it will be remembered,
been ceded to Britain by the Treaty of Utrecht in 1713, and
the commission in question was issued in connection with
an attempt to hasten British settlement in the country and
to bring the civil government more fully into accord with
those of the older colonies. I have already quoted from it
above in the argument as to the unconstitutionality of government in Quebec without an assembly,[2] showing that the
commissions in that regard (and in regard to the nature of
the laws to be passed), were identical. The most of the
remainder is also practically identical, the only points
of difference being as to land grants and the construction of the Council. In regard to lands the conditions
are left to the discretion of Governor Cornwallis, acting
with advice of the Council, while Governor Murray is enjoined to follow in such grants the annexed royal instructions. In regard to the control of the governor over the
Council and general administration, Cornwallis is given
full power of appointment and suspension, while nothing
is said whatever on the subject in Murray's commission,
the matter being left to his instructions, by which he is
given practically the same power. On the whole we may
conclude, therefore, that the divergences between these
two commissions are not sufficient to weaken what I have
said above; the difference in regard to land grants being
easily explained by the necessity, (as dwelt upon in the
Proclamation of 1763), of special care in regard to Quebec
in this direction, owing to the danger of alienating the

---

[1] For first see Houston, *Can. Const. Doc.*, p. 9; for second, Masères, *Commissions.* All
these commissions are signed in the same way and by the same person.

[2] See pp. 329–30.

Indians and of injuring the fur trade. No hint is given of any alertness on the part of the English government in regard to the internal conditions of Canada, or of any idea of treating it differently from the other English colonies. But as it may perhaps be contended that Nova Scotia and Quebec were in somewhat the same condition owing to the presence in both of a large body of long-settled French, I will continue the comparison further, and will take up what seems to be a typical commission in the older colonies, viz., that granted to Sir Danvers Osborn, 1754, as governor of New York. We find that this commission is practically identical with that of Governor Cornwallis six years earlier; hence differing from Murray's only in the insertion of the provisions in regard to the Council (relegated to Murray's instructions), and in regard to land grants, where the same motive for divergence may be supposed to exist as in the other case.

To sum up, the commission to Murray in 1765 recognizes the peculiar position of Canada to the extent indicated by the following divergences from previous forms:

a. *In regard to the construction of the Assembly.* This in the earlier commissions is expressly directed to conform to the usages already prevalent in the colonies, but in Murray's is left to his discretion or to future instructions.

b. *In regard to the Governor's control over the Council.* This is provided for in the earlier cases by the commission, while in the case of Canada it is relegated to the instructions. The significance, (if there be any), would seem to be that Canada was intended to remain for the time more directly under the control and development of the English executive, a new instruction being a more easily wielded instrument than a new commission.

c. *In regard to Land Grants.* Here the divergence was manifestly suggested by features which were supposed not to exist to any extent worth considering in the case of the other provinces. In the case of Quebec the arrangement

was made entirely provisional, for an elaborate plan in regard to Indian government and land grants which might
affect the Indians, was intended at the time, and was actually sent out with the instructions under the Quebec Act.

These divergences are by no means unimportant, but it
will be readily conceded that, for the most part merely
negative, they would seem entirely inadequate, and by no
means in proportion to the changed conditions. They are
an indication not of settled policy, but of deferred action.
Hence I cannot agree with Masères, who points to the
similarity of the commissions to Sir Danvers Osborn and
to Murray as *in itself* proving that it had been from the
first His Majesty's intention to introduce English laws and
methods of government into Quebec, and thus to assimili-
tate it to the other colonies in North America. The only
conclusion we have a right to draw in connection with
other incomplete and contradictory testimony, is that the
attitude of the home government toward Canada at the beginning of the civil rule was a wholly uninformed and undecided one, and that the measures taken then were wholly
provisional.

No noteworthy changes are found in either of Carleton's
commissions (1766 and 1768); but this is not the case with his
instructions. By these the relation between the governor
and the Council continued to be (theoretically) regulated;
and we find that, instead of being left to nominate his own
Council subject to Imperial ratification, as had been the
case with Murray and Cornwallis, the names of the councill-
lors are inserted in the new instructions of 1768. Moreover, the home administration now expressly reserves to
itself the making of additions, the governor being given
power only of temporary appointment in emergency. In
regard to general civil service appointments Carleton's
power seems further restricted;[1] while as to suspension or

---

[1] It is worthy of notice that there is to be found in these instructions and commissions
a steady decrease of the appointing power of the colonial governor. While Gov. Corn-

removal, though the matter is vaguely worded, he is in all
cases obliged to immediately submit the matter to the judgment of the home Administration.   These changes are to
be considered in connection with the restoration to Carleton,
(practically in 1766, and formally in 1771), of that supreme
military authority which had been exercised by the governor during the military period, and which I have referred to above as a very material part of the approxima-
tion of the position of the English executive to that of the
French.   The restriction of the governor's civil power may
perhaps be considered in the same light.   This process of
check upon the governor will be seen more plainly in the
Quebec Act and its development; it is sufficient now to
have drawn attention to what, if we are to credit the Imperial course in these early years with any definite intentions, may reasonably be considered an entering upon the
path of later development.   The changes in question can

wallis in 1749 is given full power of appointment not only in regard to councillors, but
also for "all such other officers and ministers as you shall judge proper and necessary,"
the powers given to Osborn in New York (1755) and Murray in Quebec (1764), though
apparently as full with regard to the Council and to ecclesiastical officers, are less as
to the inferior officials. And as between them, we may perhaps see a first stage of restriction in the fact that the whole matter of the Council was relegated to Murray's instructions, and that in these two or three officers are named as *ex-officio* members of it.
The next stage is as noted above, the case of Carleton (1768) when, beside the great restriction concerning the Council, it is evident that the main posts in the civil service
have become patent offices in regard to which the governor has at most only temporary
and provisional powers. Of much interest in this connection are some remarks by Gov.
Pownall in the debate on the bill for regulating the government of Massachusetts Bay,
1774. (Parl. Hist., XVII, 1282-6.) He states that even in Massachusetts Bay, where by
the charter "the governor is obliged to take with him not simply the advice, but the
consent of the Council in the nomination of judges and other civil officers," the ultimate source of authority for all officers is the governor's commission; while "in those
governments which are established by the King's patent commissions the whole act of
appointment is in the governor. . . . He is the sole efficient; he may advise with the
Council, but he is not bound to take their consent; . . . he is not incompetent to the
act without their consent. His commission gives him full power to act, . . . ; if he
acts without the advice of his Council, he does indeed break through his instructions
and may incur His Majesty's displeasure; but yet the appointment is good to all intents and purposes. The first is the act of legal power derived from the commission;
the second is a matter prudential with which the mode of the act is properly and
wisely accompanied." I am not concerned now with the precise constitutional value of
these statements; for my present inquiry is into Imperial *policy* — manifestly to be
gathered as well from an instruction as from a commission.

hardly be explained indeed in any other way. Nor does the explanation clash with my general conclusion as to Imperial neglect and inconsistency; such instances of intermittent activity, unassociated with any harmonizing of the various conflicting elements, tend as yet only to make confusion more confounded.

We are not aided very much out of the maze by an examination of the few instances of special interposition on the part of the Imperial government in the conduct of affairs in the Province. These interferences, generally in the nature of disapproval or prohibition, are such as either mark the appearance in the colonial office of new brooms, (and the broom was very frequently changed),[1] or are

---

[1] It seems desirable to introduce here a statement (necessarily incomplete) as to the official relations of the Home and Provincial authorities. These we find to be somewhat complicated, the colonial governor being at all times obliged to keep up two and frequently three different lines of communication,— with the Secretary of State, the Board of Trade, and the Treasury. The first was the most regular and imperative channel, though partly so it would appear, only because a single and active official, not a Board, had to be dealt with; and on this correspondence, which it is safe to assume omits nothing of importance, this study is mainly based. Readers of Bancroft, however, know that the Board of Trade at this period was no effete institution, but that it had for some time been exerting itself in colonial affairs with unusual activity, and had drawn within its reach all departments of colonial business. (See Fitzmaurice, *Shelbourne*, I, 240-3.) It was apparently in full vigor at the opening of our period, (see its share in regard to the Proclamation of 1763), as Murray shortly discovered; for he writes privately to Halifax, Oct. 29, 1764, with reference to a severe check he had received from the Board for not communicating to it what he had written to the secretary. Murray's instructions of 1763 had rather obscurely directed him " upon all occasions to send to the Board only, a particular account of all your proceedings;" though in any matter requiring the King's immediate direction, he was to correspond with the Secretary of State only. But this vigor of the former seems to have suddenly and mysteriously declined, for Feb. 3, 1766, (Can. Arch., Q. 3, p. 122), Murray (who had since been careful to keep it fully supplied with information), complains of "the total silence to every remonstrance, reasoning and report, which hitherto I have had the honour to make to your Board, (from which I have had no letter that was not circular since the establishment of civil government here)." Shortly after a still more striking proof of the seeming decline of the Board of Trade is given by a letter to it from Shelbourne, Aug. 26, 1766, enclosing " an Order-in-Council of the 8th inst. revoking an order of 11th March, 1752, concerning the correspondence to be carried on between the Commissioners for Trade and Plantations and the governors of His Majesty's colonies, who are to correspond with the Secretary of State, sending duplicates to their Lordships. For the future also all measures relative to commerce and the colonies shall originate and be taken up in the ministerial executive offices of government, their Lordships acting as a Board of Advice upon such points only as shall be referred from His Majesty by Order-in-Council, or from the Lords of the Council, or a Committee of the Council, or from His Majesty by one of the principal

drawn forth by complaints which had the good fortune to be backed by special interest. I include here all actions with reference to provincial legislation; for though these would seem to form a part of the regular and necessary supervision, their rare occurrence throughout the period and the utter neglect of Ordinances which were direct oversteppings of the (supposed) Provincial legislative power preclude the idea of system or regularity.

We have seen above that the number of Provincial Ordinances was over 40; of these only six are noticed as repealed, four by an Order-in-Council of November 22, 1765, and two by a similar order of June 26, 1767. No direct statement of the grounds of repeal are to be found in any case, but in some we can discover them by an examination of the measures. We find one in regard to the retail liquor trade vetoed evidently on account of a very objectionable clause, which however, occurs also in another unrepealed

Secretaries of State; and the estimates for colonial service, and the direction and application of money granted thereupon (a business of late years transacted by your Lordships), is to be resumed into its proper channel." (*Calendar Home Office Papers*, 1766–9, No. 256.) This certainly seems to betoken a complete eclipse; an explanation is furnished in a letter from the Earl of Hillsborough to Mr. Geo. Grenville, Aug. 6, 1766, (*Grenville Correspondence*, III, 294.) Hillsborough had been president of the Board under the Grenville ministry, from Sept. 10, 1763, till the accession of Rockingham, July, 1765; he now informs Grenville that had he not been dismissed in 1765 he "could not have continued at the Board of Trade upon the footing I held it;" that he is now invited by Pitt to return to it, and has deliberated, "not whether I should come to the Board as it was constituted while you was minister, for I know I could not carry on the business in that manner; nor whether I should propose, what is certainly most desirable for the public, that it should be made an independent Department upon an extended plan, for I know the disposition of some too well to suppose that would be complied with, by parting with any power or patronage; but whether I could not contract the place so as that I might do the business in an easy manner to myself, and free from that very unpleasant and in some measure unbecoming attendance upon others which is the consequence of unexplained connections of departments in business, and always very disagreeable to that which is considered the inferior situation." Has finally decided to accept, "provided the Board should be altered from a Board of Representation to a Board of Report upon reference only; that the order to the governors in America to correspond with the Board of Trade only be rescinded; and that every executive business that has by degrees crept into the Board should revert to the proper offices, particularly all Treasury business; and that I should not be of the Cabinet (which was also offered to me)." (In corroboration of this see Fitzmaurice, *Shelbourne*, II, 1–3. Also for the earlier position and aspirations of the Board, *Ibid.*, I, 240.) Hillsborough

Ordinance of the same date. One, (on the currency), had been prepared in accordance with direct orders from home. Two others of the six related to the quartering of troops in the province and were repealed in consequence of a general Act of Parliament on the subject. The remaining one was in regard to the better observance of the Lord's day, and was evidently defective in neglecting to provide a penalty for one class of offences. On the whole no general conclusions as to principle or system can be drawn from the examination of the Imperial supervision of the Provincial legislation.

Nor do we get much more light from the examination of special executive interference, though here of course, we are not warranted in drawing the same inference of neglect. The general conduct of the Provincial government was constantly and largely influenced by the regular correspondence of the Secretary of State; but that correspondence was chiefly of a general and non-committal character, and a resolute governor like Carleton had no difficulty (especially in the frequent changes of the secretariat), in securing

---

resumed the position of president, and in 1768 becoming also Secretary of State for the colonies (now for the first time made a separate department), the two offices were filled by him till 1772. During this period therefore the range of the activity of the Board was a matter of choice with the Secretary and there seems to be only a personal significance in the communication to Carleton, (June 11, 1768), "that the examination of all laws and ordinances enacted in the colonies appertains to the Department of the Board of Trade," and (Sept. 2, 1772), that "the consideration of persons proper to be of His Majesty's Councils in the Plantations is more particularly within" the same Department. (Can. Arch., Q. 5-1, p. 419.) The Instructions to Carleton of 1768 and 1775 direct him to transmit to the Board, "for their information," duplicates of all reports; except (as it is worded in the 80th Article of the Instructions of 1768; in those of 1775 the sending of such reports is referred to only in general words), "in cases of a secret nature."

The third quarter to which the governor was responsible was the Treasury. The new regulations of 1766 referred to above shows that for some time the Board of Trade had had the control of all colonial finances; the proper channel to which they were now to return was the Treasury. In the Minutes of the Quebec Council of Jan. 22, 1767, we find a reference to a letter to Murray from the Secretary of the Treasury, dated Sept. 30, 1766, requiring him to forward the most minute account of the finances of the Province. In accordance with which from this time on regular financial reports seem to have been sent to that department; which had also in the Province thereafter an independent official,— the Receiver-General,— directly responsible to it alone.

I am indebted for valuable assistance in this matter of official conditions to the late article on *Hillsborough* in the *Dictionary of Nat. Biography.*

his position. We have a couple of instances of interference in behalf of officials who had incurred the displeasure
of Murray, but only one instance of the direct overturning of
Carleton's action.[1] A case of some constitutional interest
occurred in 1768, when Conway, the secretary, writes to
the governor directing him, in the case of a trial for murder
then pending, to grant the accused, if condemned, a free
pardon.[2] The accused was acquitted, and thus there was
no occasion for the carrying out of the injunction; but it
is of much interest in connection with a query addressed by
Hillsborough, March 2d, 1772,[3] to the crown lawyers[4] as to
whether there was any legal objection to the passing such
a pardon with the seal of the colony on a warrant to the
governor under His Majesty's signet and sign manual, The
reply (by Thurlow and Wedderburn), was that as the commission of the governor expressly restrained him in the
pardoning of murder they could not recommend it to His
Majesty to command that official, by warrant under the
signet and sign manual, to do that which by the constitution of his office under the great seal he had no legal
power to do.

A very significant interference finally is that of Hills
borough with Lieutenant Governor Cramahé in 1771 in regard to the proposition of New York for a consultation with Quebec and Pennsylvania on Indian trade affairs.
Cramahé seems to have returned at first a favorable
answer,[5] but on his reporting the proposal home, he was
informed that His Majesty did not approve of Indian congresses, "and the sending commissioners from the different
colonies for that purpose," and that therefore Quebec was

---

[1] In regard to the Indian trade.

[2] Murray's commission, like all colonial ones, especially excepted from his pardoning
power the crimes of treason and murder.

[3] It is probable that the greater scrupulosity of the later date is due to the character
of the then minister.

[4] *Calendar of Home Office Papers*, 1770-72.   No. 1146.

[5] He writes Oct. 31st, however, that Hillsborough's disapproval **had** arrived in time to
prevent his sending commissioners. (Can. Arch., Q. 8, p. 82.)

to take no further steps in the matter. Not satisfied with this Hillsborough wrote further a few months later that " it is His Majesty's pleasure that you do not for the future consent to any propositions for appointing commissioners to attend a congress on any occasion, unless such congress be authorized by particular directions from His Majesty, and His Majesty's pleasure first signified to you for that purpose." Here again, however, the matter is mainly perhaps of personal interest; for the action of Hillsborough is in perfect accord with his general attitude on American affairs.

CHAPTER VI.

THE QUEBEC ACT,[1]— ITS ORIGINS AND AIMS.

The Quebec Act of 1774 is the central point of my inquiry. It was the first intervention of the Imperial parliament in the affairs of the new province and constituted the definite settlement of government there that had been anxiously looked for during a whole decade. That settlement is of exceeding interest from almost every point of view; to the observer of religious development, whether or no he concurs in Lecky's opinion that it "marks an epoch in the history of religious liberty;"[2] to the investigator of political institutions, as an attempt to reconcile alien principles of government; or to the more practical student of politics, attracted by the effect of the measure both on the American Revolutionary crisis and on the later development of the vast regions which after the Revolution remained to the British crown. It is not necessary therefore to apologize for the somewhat extended discussion that I enter upon here; a discussion in which I shall have regard especially to the third of the above mentioned points of view,— the Act in its relations to the American Revolution.

Let us glance first at the ministerial steps leading up to the enactment, with a word as to the general causes of the delay of the settlement so long and urgently needed. I have throughout endeavored to show that the attitude of the home government towards Canadian affairs was for the earlier years one of the grossest neglect; and that when attention at last began to be given to the subject, and the

---

[1] See Appendix A for full reprint.

[2] *History of England*, IV, 299 (ed. 1892).

colonial officials had at length succeeded in impressing the
home official mind with the fact that Canada could not be disposed of by the mere making out for it of copies of the
forms which had done duty so long in the other colonies,
definite action was yet delayed in a manner that must have
been inexplicable in the province.[1] The main explanation is no doubt to be found in the shifting state of English politics at the time, and in the instability of administrations. Into these I cannot go as fully as would perhaps
be useful. It will be remembered that the downfall of
Whig ascendancy at the accession of George III in 1760,
was followed by what Lecky calls "ten years of weak governments and party anarchy."[2] Half a dozen different
ministries were formed and fell to pieces. From 1763 to
1772 no less than twelve changes took place in the office of
Secretary of State, six different individuals,— the Earls of
Egremont, Halifax, Shelbourne, Hillsborough, and Dartmouth, and the Hon. Henry Conway,— being in succession
at the head of colonial affairs. At length on the final downfall
of the Pitt-Grafton ministry early in 1770, Lord North succeeded in forming a Tory one which every day increased in strength, and which laid the foundation for a
Tory ascendancy of fifty years. It was not till this ministry had been firmly established that decided action in Canadian affairs became probable or perhaps possible.[3]

A glance through the political Memoirs, etc., which
exist in such abundance for this troubled period, does not

---

[1] As early as Feb. 21, 1764, Haldimand writes to Burton that party spirit in England
prevents definite arrangements being made for Canada. (Can. Arch., B. 9, p. 43.)

[2] *Hist. of Eng.*, I. 1.

[3] Knox, in his "Justice and Policy of the Quebec Act," (1774), says that from the conquest " the establishment of a proper mode of civil government therein was considered
by the then and by every subsequent administration as a matter of so great importance
and of so much difficulty that it became the object of almost constant deliberation." (p.
10.) The anti-colonial tract in support of the Act, attributed to Sir John Dalyrymple,
(" The Rights of Great Britain Asserted Against the Claims of America," 1776), correctly
says that the enquiry preliminary to the Act was begun under the Chatham Administration, and adds that in consequence a measure "was considered by the Board of Trade ; it
was certainly debated, if not adopted by the Cabinet as far back as the year 1767."
See below.

reveal many references to Canadian affairs.   Almon[1] is authority for the statement that the final blow to the long-tottering Rockingham ministry was administered by the violent opposition of the Chancellor, Lord Northington, to a proposed bill for the settlement of Canada.   This was in July, 1766, and that the measure had been under serious contemplation at least six months before is probable from a letter to Burke, (then the Prime Minister's secretary), of the January 9 previous.[2]   On June 2, 1767, we find what is apparently the result of the only interposition of either House of Parliament in Canadian affairs previous to the Quebec Act.[3]   The order of the day on that date in the House of Lords was the taking into consideration the papers laid before the House[4] on the previous Wednesday relating to the state of Quebec; and the House having gone into committee, reported the following resolutions: "That it appears to the committee that the Province of Quebec for a considerable time past has wanted, and does now stand in need of, further regulations and provisions relating to its civil government and religious establishment." This looks promising, but we hear nothing further of it, though on the 20th of the same month Shelbourne writes to Carleton that "the improvement of its [Quebec's] civil constitution, is under the most serious and deliberate consideration of His Majesty's servants, and principally of His Majesty's Privy Council."[5]   The following January (1768) one Marsh writes to Haldimand of the impossibility of getting the Ministry to attend to American affairs.[6] November 4, 1769, Hillsborough informs Carleton that the

---

[1] *Anecdotes of Chatham*, II, 76.   See also *Chatham Corresp.*, II, 434, and Albemarle's *Rockingham*, I, 350.   Lecky accepts Almon's statement without question, III, 64.

[2] Dr. Thos. Leland to Burke.   (Burke's *Correspondence*, Vol. 1.)   It is not impossible that the reference may be merely to the negotiations, not then completed, concerning the making good by France of the old paper money of the province.

[3] *Parliamentary History*, Vol. 16.

[4] At its own request of the previous May 20. (*Cal. Home Office Papers*, 1766–9. No. 492.)

[5] Can. Arch., Q. 4, p. 129.

[6] Can. Arch., B. 68, p. 263.

consideration of the affairs of Canada has been delayed by
the recess of Parliament, but that he has been assured that
it will be immediately taken up again;[1] January 2, 1771, he
writes again that a bill for the temporary giving of legislative power to the Council in Canada will be presented on
the opening of Parliament,[2] and the following July 3,[3] that
Quebec affairs have been submitted to the Privy Council.
But December 4, he informs him that the measures are not
yet ready, and that the matter being a delicate one will
probably be submitted to Parliament.[4] Lord North's government was firmly established by this time, and the delay
for eighteen months longer is probably due to the lingering of the final reports from the Crown lawyers. Finally,
May 4, 1774, Dartmouth writes to Lieutenant-Governor
Cramahé that on the previous Monday (May 2) he had presented the Quebec Bill to the House of Lords.

This session of Parliament it will be remembered was
mainly occupied with the three coercive measures in regard to the Province of Massachusetts Bay. These had
been introduced in the Commons almost simultaneously,
had met with a vigorous resistance, but had been pushed
through by the government with large majorities. It was
after they had been disposed of, and after most of the
members of both houses, fatigued by their close attendance, had left for the country that the Quebec Bill quietly
appeared in the House of Lords.[5] It was not introduced as

---

[1] Can. Arch., Q. 6, p. 121.

[2] Ibid., Q. 8, p. 1. The exact character of the contemplated measure seems also at
this time to have been known to the provincial officials; for April 30, Cramahé replies
that the prospect of a firm settlement was satisfactory to "all His Majesty's new subjects and the manner of doing it seems perfectly agreeable to their manner of thinking."
(Ibid., Q. 8, p. 45.)

[3] Ibid., Q. 8, p. 26.

[4] Ibid., p. 79. This seems to show that for a short time the ministry thought of settling Canadian affairs by executive act merely. According to Lord Mansfield's judgment of 1774 this was not, however, within the competence of the executive; and it was
probably from some misgiving on the point that it was decided to submit the matter
to Parliament. The Mansfield judgment was not delivered till November 28, six months
after the Quebec Bill had become law.

[5] See *Ann. Reg.*, 1774, p. 74. Also note in 4 *American Archives*, I, p. 214.

in any way connected with the previous American measures, and the government evidently anticipated no serious
opposition.	With very slight notice it passed the Lords on
the 17th of May, (apparently without a division), and on
the 18th was brought to the Commons.	But here it met
with an unexpectedly vigorous opposition, its opponents,
though few in numbers, stubbornly · fighting every clause.
Sir Thomas Mills, Receiver-General of the Province of
Quebec, writes to Haldimand, June 14, 1774,[1] that "we
have had as hard fighting and many more battles to establish government for Canada as there were to conquer it.
You would be astonished at the opposition made to the
bill; ten nights the House of Commons was kept till one
o'clock in the morning successively.	Every inch of the
ground was argued and every word disputed."

We are fortunate in possessing of the debate on this occasion a fuller report than of any other part of this Parlia-
ment.[2]	This is from the shorthand notes of Sir Henry
Cavendish, member of Lostwithiel, a supporter, (but not a
slavish one), of the government.	It will not be necessary
to go fully into the discussion, however, as it may easily
be imagined what line of battle would be assumed against
such a measure by an opposition with Burke and Fox at
its head.	Though the battle was spirited the opposition
seems soon to have become hopeless of effecting anything;
and its efforts were more remarkable for fighting every inch
than for serious or prolonged struggle at any one point.[3]
Lord North was on the whole conciliatory, showing no
special love for or interest in the measure, but yet evidently determined to push its main provisions through.
Very little indication is given that the bill was considered

---

[1] Can. Arch., B. 27, p. 374.

[2] Long known as the Unreported Parliament.	The earlier part is now supplied to us
from the same source as that for the debate on the Quebec Bill.	During this session
the order for the exclusion of strangers was enforced with unusual vigour.

[3] The chief contest was in the latter part of the discussion, on the matter of the jury
system.

to have any connection with the direct steps taken to repress America, the ministry taking no notice of the few
and obscure hints dropped to that effect. A peculiar
feature is the repetition by the Opposition of questions as
to the authorship of the measure, the Crown lawyers being
persistently taunted, (without drawing from them any vigorous disclaimer), with not being willing to father it, if
not at heart opposed to it. In this connection the letter of
Mills quoted from already is of great interest.[1] The writer
proceeds (from the point quoted above); "Much pain and
trouble it has cost me. The Bill was first put in my
hands containing ten sheets in folio, in my mind the
shorter it was the better. The limits, the religion, the
French law, and the Council,[2] they owe to me. My conscience, however, tells me that I was not only serving
justice and country, but also doing justice to the conquered." Of equal interest are his continuing words as to
the curious attitude of the ministry. "In the House of
Lords I had not much trouble, but great difficulty in keeping Lord North and the Ministry steady and firm in the
House of Commons. You would, however, have pitied
them, for they were teased and harrassed to death. They
were very negligent in studying the subject,[3] which of
course gave the others the best of the argument, and then
they had to combat against all the popular topics, viz., the
Popish religion, no juries, no assemblies, etc. Masères

[1] It is noticeable that June 8, 1769, the Secretary of the Board of Trade (Pownall)
writes to the Treasury requesting that Receiver-General Mills be allowed to remain
some time in England, as he can give useful information to the Lords of Trade respecting Quebec.

[2] The main points, it will be noticed, over which controversy raged then and after. It
will be seen later, however, that the origin of these was by no means so Minerva-like as
it appeared to Mr. Mills.

[3] Wedderbourne, the Solicitor-General, who had prepared a special report on Canadian
affairs and claimed to have thoroughly studied the subject, brought forward in the
argument as to the non granting of juries, the conduct of the juries of Quebec in the
revenue trials of 1766 and 1769, as proof that the Canadians were not fit for the institution. Whereas the juries on both occasions are expressly stated by Masères to have
been entirely English.

and Murray behaved infamously, Carleton and Hey exceedingly proper, steady and well." What degree of credit is to be given to any part of this self-inflated epistle it is impossible to enquire very closely. The animated character of the debate was kept till the close; the final word according to Cavendish being the vigorously expressed opinion of a thoroughly disgusted opponent that the speaker "should throw the Bill over the table, and somebody else should kick it out at the door."

Of considerable importance is it to observe the attenuated character of the House on this occasion. The total number of members at the time was 558, and the main divisions on this Bill were as follows: second reading, 105 to 29, final vote, 50 to 20. These numbers are undoubtedly much higher than during the actual debate, Cavendish noting on two occasions that only about 40 members were in the House. It is to be remembered that under these conditions the government support would belong to the most dependent, corrupt and unrepresentative part of this most corrupt and unrepresentative of Parliaments.[1] We need not follow the fortunes of the Bill through the slight opposition it met with, (from seven peers), on its return to the Lords, nor through the vigorous but unsuccessful attempt to repeal it in the following year. (Division in Commons, 174 to 86.) After a long labor and painful birth it had appeared for good or ill; it will now be necessary to examine its provisions more carefully, with a view to determining the ideas that inspired them and estimating their more immediate results.

B.   History of Main Provisions.

The phrase used by Mills above,—"The limits, the religion, the French law, and the Council,"—is a succinct statement of the main subject matters of the new enact-

---

[1] See statements of Lecky (Vol. III, pp. 171, 173) that in 1770 192 members of the Commons held places under government, and that it was computed in 1774 that fully half of the members for England and Wales represented a total of only 11,500 voters.

ment; and in discussing them I shall adopt the same order
both as logical and as the order of the Act itself.

a. *Boundaries.* First, therefore, as to the limits or bound--
aries of the newly defined Province. This part of the Act,
though the most short lived,[1] might probably be contended to
be the most noticeable and important with regard to the influence of the measure on the course of the American Revolution. The inclusion of the Western country within the
limits of Canada, in connection with other provisions, was
taken as indicative of a settled and long-meditated design on
the part of the English government to hinder the extension
of the self-governing colonies by attaching the vast unsettled
regions West and Southwest to the arbitrary government
which that Act seemed to establish.[2] There was the more
likelihood of suspicion or irritation upon this point because
of the fact that the final disposition of the western country
had been in suspense since the peace, and because the first
step of the imperial authorities with regard to it, in the Proclamation of 1763, had been by no means satisfact ry to the
older colonies. Modern writers have contended that the
settled purpose of hindering the extension of these colonies
by new and arbitrary measures, is clearly shown in that
proclamation, and shown thus for the first time; that in

---

[1] Repealed for the most part by the provisions of the Treaty of Versailles, 1783, the
Province of Quebec being then deprived of those parts which now form the states of
Ohio, Indiana, Michigan, Illinois, Wisconsin and part of Minnesota.

[2] The tenacity and attractiveness, (through its inherent probability), of this idea from
the colonial standpoint is easily understood. Its general vitality, moreover, is illustrated in the latest and best history of Canada from the native and Imperial standpoint (Kingsford's). The author, while vigorously defending the Quebec Act in the
main, and asserting that he can " discover no admissible ground for the acceptance "
of the belief that its main measures were due to the condition of things in the other
colonies, yet says of the extension to the west (for which otherwise he can find no explanation): " It is possible that the spirit of revolt dominant in the colonies may have
led to the desire of preventing the exercise of any pretension over the territory of the
Western provinces of Virginia and Pennsylvania [!]; and of opposing by legislation all extension beyond their admitted frontier." (V. 244.) The failure of this writer to find
other reasons may probably be explained from his accompanying assertion that west of
Montreal " at the period of conquest there was scarcely a white man established," and
from his disregard in this connection of the fur trade.

this light it was the first step in a new policy of tyrannical restriction of which the culmination was the Act of Parliament which in 1774 finally annexed the West to the unfree Province of Quebec.[1]

This contention is of course incompatible with the more ordinary view that the Quebec Act, in this as in its other provisions, was called out by the critical state of things in the older provinces in or about the years 1773-4; and before I go on to deal with the latter opinion it will be necessary to consider the variation.

It is manifest that if British colonial policy underwent such a decided change in the period 1760-3, we are justified in expecting to find evidence of that change in the confidential communications between the Imperial and the colonial authorities, or in the semi-official utterances of that

---

[1] The chief expression of this view will be found in Hinsdale, *Old Northwest*, c. 8. The writer considers that with the treaty of Paris, England, abandoning the old sea-to-sea colonial claims, made a decided change in her land policy; that while the Ohio grant of 1748 showed that "she had then no thought of preventing over-mountain settlements, or of limiting the expansion of the colonies in that direction," (p. 120), now, alarmed at their rapid growth, she took measures to permanently sever them from the western lands. This it is intimated was one of the main motives of the Proclamation of 1763. The writer, however, does not seem very decided upon the point, and concludes with the admission that on the whole, "in the years following the French war the Western policy of the British was not steady or consistent, but fitful and capricious; prompted by a solicitude for the Indian that was partly feigned and partly by a growing jealousy of the shore colonies." (p. 141.) Yet immediately after the half-abandoned position is resumed in the statement that "this policy of restriction culminated in 1774 in the Quebec Act," one of the main objects of which was "permanently to sever the West from the shore colonies and put it in train for being cut up, when the time should come, into independent governments that should have affiliations with the St. Lawrence basin rather than with the Atlantic slope." The irritated colonies, we are told, looked upon the new boundaries given to Quebec by the Act "as a final effort to wrest the West from them forever." Roosevelt (*Winning of the West*, I, c. 2), expresses the same ideas in a somewhat different form. Far-reaching as are the above views they do not attain that breadth of assertion which we find in an even more recent opinion, that from its conquest in 1760 Canada was regarded by the British government as a *point d' appui* "for the support of the ministerial policy in asserting British parliamentary supremacy over the colonies." (Review of *Life of John Patterson*, N. Y. Nation, July 19, 1894.) These opinions are illustrative of the latest phase of revolutionary study, that which centers round the comparatively fresh field of Western interests and advance. They are the result of hasty generalization from one-sided investigation, stimulated by the suspicions that contemporary events and the heated assertions of the revolutionary age itself tend naturally to engender. It is all the more necessary that they should be promptly confronted with the facts; which must be my justification for the detail with which I have considered the subject.

time or of the years intervening between it and the Revolution. It is to be presumed that the exponents of the idea of change have made search for such evidence, and fair to assume that they have brought forward all the evidence found. But what is presented as such practically amounts only to Hillsborough's representation in 1772 with regard to the intentions of those who drew up the Proclamation of 1763. It is not shown, or attempted to be shown, that Hillsborough's apparent interpretation of that document as containing a declaration of new policy, has more than the weight of his individual opinion; it is not shown that even Hillsborough ascribes any pecular influence to the acquisition of Canada. Yet herein is the whole matter. For it will be found on closer examination that the aim of the Board of Trade in that measure was precisely the same as had actuated it for years before; that the only change produced by the acquisition of Canada was the new and extensive field in which the old policy was to be applied.

It is assumed that the acquisition of Canada was the starting point or confirmation of the new policy. If this were so some trace of that view of the acquisition must surely appear in the state papers or political discussions with regard to it. Before going into the State correspondence let us glance for a moment at the circumstances attendant on the treaty of peace in 1763. From the day of the conquest of Canada in 1760 to that of its final cession, the question as to whether or not it should be retained by Great Britain, and what place, in the event of retention, it should occupy in the American system, was before the public, and keenly and thoroughly debated in the pamphlet and periodical literature. In this, if anywhere, we should expect to find traces of any new aspect that the possession of Canada might be supposed to give to American affairs; it is hardly possible that a new line of action based on that possession could be contemplated without foreshadowing or reflection of it in this quarter. An exhaustive ex-

amination of this material has not been possible; but the
close scrutiny of a very considerable portion [1] has failed to
furnish any evidence that Canada at any part of this period
appeared to the English public mind in the slightest degree
in the light of a weapon or base of hostile action against the
other colonies; nothing has been discovered to support the
belief that either the terms of peace or the following dispositions concerning the new Province, were influenced by
any but friendly and comparatively generous feelings toward those colonies.   The only evidences of illiberal feeling that can be produced are in the writings of those who
argue against the retention of Canada. [2]   The main points
of the very energetic argument for West Indian in preference to Canadian acquisition, were the alleged greater
commercial value of the former, and the danger that if the
older colonies were relieved of the menace of the French,
they would speedily become independent, troublesome, and
perhaps rebellious.   This was answered almost wholly by
the statement that the war 'had been undertaken and
carried on for the relief of the colonies through the expulsion or crippling of the French; that the colonists had
helped materially toward success, and that England therefore must in justice or generosity see that the French
should never again be a danger and hindrance.   It need
not be supposed of course that there was any losing sight
of the more domestic interests of Great Britain in this
matter; still less, however, can it be assumed that the in-

---

[1] That afforded by the Sparks Collection of Colonial Tracts in the Cornell University
Library, and by the similar collections in the Wisconsin State Historical Library, and
in the Canadian Archives.

[2] See especially, " Remarks on the Letter addressed to two Great Men. In a Letter to
the Author of that Piece." (London, 1760. Attributed to Edmund or William Burke.)
The vigorous reply to this: "The Interest of Great Britain considered, with regard to
her Colonies, and the acquisition of Canada and Guadaloupe,"—(London, 1760),— is at_
tributed to Franklin, and was one of the most influential of the pamphlets; the Ministry which took the course it contends for can scarcely be charged with hostile views.
A later pamphlet, ("An Examination of the Commercial Principles of the late Negotiation," etc., 1762), attributed to Edmund Burke, refers to the author of the foregoing one as
the chief advocate of the system which was proceeded upon in the negotiations for peace,
negotiations which had for their main object the possession of Canada.

terests of the colonies were neglected, or that underneath an apparent solicitude lay sinister designs. A striking feature of the contention is the readiness with which nearly all admit the greater commercial value of the West Indies, and the comparative worthlessness and lack of promise of Canada. The notable pamphlet entitled, "A Letter addressed to Two Great Men,"[1] declares that though "The possession of Canada is no view of Ambition," yet the ministry should make it "the *sine qua non* of the Peace, as the only method of guarding our invaluable possessions there from usurpations and encroachments" by the French. In a pamphlet presumably by Edmund Burke[2] it is shown with seeming conclusiveness that West Indian trade was far more important than North American. The writer complains further that the argument, (considered by him futile), for the retention of Canada on account of being necessary to the safety and prosperity of the colonies, had been so enforced upon the public mind "that Canada came at last to take an entire Possession of our Hearts and Understandings; and we were taught to believe that no cession was too great to purchase this inestimable security, this immoveable Barrier of all our Colonies." A pamphlet of 1762 in defence of the proposed treaty which bears strong marks of being inspired, rests the defence of the acquisition of Canada instead of Gaudaloupe wholly on the security of the old colonies; which, even if the defence be not an authorized one, shows that this was known to be the argument which would appeal most strongly to the constituency addressed.[3] Three years later a more elaborate

---

[1] "A Letter addressed to Two Great Men, on the prospects of Peace; and on the terms necessary to be insisted upon in the Negotiation," (London, 1760, 2nd edition. Jared Sparks collection. Attributed by Sparks to the Earl of Bath). Said by Lecky to have had "a very wide influence and circulation." (III, 291.)

[2] "An Examination of the Commercial Principles," etc.

[3] "A letter to the Earl of Bute on the Preliminaries of Peace. From neither a noble Lord; a candid member of Parliament; an impartial Briton, but an Englishman." (London, 1762.)

writer,[1] summing up in a judicial way the war and the peace, appeals to all parties to support him in the assertion that the chief sentiment of the nation throughout the period was, "That our colonies in North America merited the first and chief attention and care of their mother country," and that as they were in great danger from French encroachment, it was considered that, "nothing too great, nothing too expensive, nothing too hazardous could be undertaken for their relief."

This brief survey of the public expressions of the party writers with regard to the acquisition and use of Canada shows at least that whatever may have been the private motives of the Administration, the general political mind had at this time become impressed mainly with considerations as to the safety and advance of the colonies. An examination of the Parliamentary Debates on the preliminary Treaty in 1762 brings us a step further. No full report is to be found, but the abstract of the Parliamentary History gives the following resumé of " the principle arguments which were offered in favor of the Treaty in the Commons." "That the original object of the war was the security of our colonies upon the continent," and that therefore danger to them must once for 'all be guarded against; that such danger being afforded by the continued presence of France, to remove or contract her power was "the most capital advantage we can obtain, and is worth purchasing by almost any concessions;" that this moreover would have the advantage of " permitting our colonies on the continent to extend themselves without danger or molestation," thus increasing the range of British trade; that, however, such a colonial extension ought not to be regarded on commercial principles alone, for "extent of territory and a number of subjects are matters of as much

---

[1] " A full and free Inquiry into the Merits of the Peace; with some Strictures on the Spirit of Party." (London, 1765.)

consideration to a State attentive to the sources of real grandeur, as the mere advantage of traffic."[1] These were the motives and objects of the peace as set forth in a House which could not to any degree have been influenced in its expression by the fear or desire of the publicity given by the reporter; and they were endorsed by a vote in favor of the Treaty of 319 to 65.   In the whole series of Parliamentary debates from 1760 to 1774 I have met nothing any more fitted to support the idea that the retention of Canada should or could be regarded as an occasion or basis for an illiberal and restrictive policy toward the older colonies. Finally on this point of the general public spirit with regard to the retention of French Canada it should be noticed that this part of the British policy has escaped the suspicion of earlier prominent American writers, even of those of a marked bias.[2] Bancroft has traced carefully the genesis of the new applications of the colonial system, and has shown that they were evident some time before the conquest of Canada. With regard, however, to the retention of that country, he says that England "proudly accepted the counsels of magnaminity. . . . Promising herself wealth from colonial trade, she was occupied by the thought of filling the wilderness, instructing it with the products of her intelligence, and blessing it with free institutions."[3] Yet, he adds, at this very time the Board of Trade was intent on applying those new measures which for many years it had looked forward to.

---

[1] *Parliamentary History*, XV, 1271.

[2] The most candid and impressive of recent English historians of this period is doubtless Mr. Lecky. His conclusion on this matter is that, " The nation had learned to look with pride and sympathy upon the greater England which was growing up beyond the Atlantic, and there was a desire which was not ungenerous or ignoble to remove at any rate the one obstacle to its future happiness;" that it was felt " that the expulsion of the French from Canada was essential, not only to the political and commercial prosperity of the Northern colonies, but also to the security of their homes." (III, 294.) Nowhere in his lengthy discussion of the whole colonial difficulty does this historian give any indication of such a connection between the acquisition of Canada and the West and general colonial affairs as might be expressed in the idea that designs against the liberties of the colonies were in any degree based on the possession of these regions.

[3] *History of the United States*, Epoch I, c. 16.

Such is the degree of light thrown upon change of policy or the probability of it, by an examination of the circumstances attendant on the securing of the new acquisition to which the asserted change has been attributed. Let us now examine the early measures taken with regard to that acquisition. These are embraced in the Royal Proclamation of 1763, over which so much controversy has raged, and which, as before shown, was considered by many at the time, and has been held up since, as due, not to the motives which it expresses, but to those special anti-colonial ends to which the new policy was supposed to be addressing itself. In this document the preliminary, "Whereas we have taken into our Royal Consideration the extensive and valuable acquisitions in America; . . . and being desirous that all our loving subjects, as well of our Kingdoms, as of our colonies in America, may avail themselves with all convenient speed of the great benefits and advantages which must accrue therefrom to their commerce, manufactures and navigation," is followed by provisions for the establishment and delimitation of the four new governments of Quebec, East Florida, West Florida and Grenada, the general direction of their civil government, the bestowal of free lands upon those who had served in the war, and the disposition of the vast regions between the Mississippi and the bounds of the old colonies.   It is decreed that, "whereas it is just and reasonable, and essential to our interests and the security of our colonies, that the several nations or tribes of Indians with which we are connected, and who live under our protection, should not be molested or disturbed in the possession of such parts of our dominions or territories, as, not having been ceded to us, are reserved to them, or any of them, as their hunting-grounds," these regions are to be kept, "for the present and until our further pleasure be known," free from white encroachments of any kind, all persons already settled therein being enjoined to remove themselves. Further, "whereas

great frauds and abuses have been committed in the purchasing lands of the Indians, to the great prejudice of our
interests and the great dissatisfaction of the said Indians; in
order therefore to prevent such irregularities for the future,
and to the end that the Indians may be convinced of our justice and determined resolution to remove all reasonable
causes of discontent," all future purchases from the Indians
are to be made through the Colonial governments alone.
Trade with the savages is, under colonial license, to be free
"to all our subjects whatever."[1] It will be noticed that if this
document is to be regarded as specially hostile to the other
colonies, it must be concluded that not only are its real
reasons not avowed, but that the asserted motives of advantage to "all our loving subjects, as well of our Kingdoms as of our colonies in America," and of "the security
of our colonies," as necessitating more consideration for
the Indian, are directly and intentionally misleading. Even
the most confirmed supporter of this view, however, would
hardly expect to have the pretence kept up behind the
scenes, and would probably be ready to maintain that the
preliminary and accompanying secret discussions and correspondence would reveal evidence of the duplicity. It
will be striking at the root of the matter to proceed to the
application of this test.

But first a word with regard to that professed solicitude
for the Indian which has seemed so absurdly inadequate a
reason that it could be considered only the cloak of sinister
design. Without attempting to go into the history of
British treatment of the savages, (an honorable one, it is
usually admitted), it will be well to note the general attitude of the immediately preceding years and the relations
with the Indians which existed at the moment. It is not
necessary to rest the British case here wholly or mainly on

---

[1] This Proclamation has been several times printed. See Houston, *Canadian Constitutional Documents*, pp. 67-73; Franklin, *Works*, V. 75 (Bigelow ed.) ; Kingsford, *Hist.
of Can.*, V, 142-5; *Wis. Hist. Coll.*, XI, 46.

philanthropic grounds; the student of the period knows well that with the word "*Indian*" must be read the additional term "*Indian trade*," and that with this addition the Indian question assumed an important place in the general colonial trade system.   The fur trade had long been one of the chief bones of contention between the English and the French; it had been the mainstay of the French government in Canada, and it was natural that now, when French rivalry had just been removed and Canada had become a British province, it should assume a much greater and indeed disproportionate place in the official and public mind. It should be noticed that this trade was regarded as peculiarly a British one, (in contradistinction to colonial), and as one of the most important elements in the manufacturing monopoly of the mother country.[1]   No attempt is being made here to defend the general commercial or colonial system of Great Britain at this time; I simply wish to show that the action of the British government in regard to the Indians and the West was only, in the main, an application of that system, and does not require the assumption of any special change of policy or any new lines of hostility with regard to the colonies.   The slightest examination will show the vast importance attached to this matter throughout the period by the Imperial authorities, and the amount of care that was given to its regulation.[2]   But

[1] See Sir William Johnson to Lords of Trade, May 17, 1759, (N. Y. Col. Documents, VII, 375); he lays emphasis on the importance of the trade and on the fact that it was carried on wholly by the manufactures of Great Britain, all the produce being exported there.   In 1766 Franklin pointed out that the trade was wholly British, not colonial. (*Works*, III, 429, Bigelow ed.)

[2] When in 1766 Shelbourne, Secretary of State, issued general directions as to the policy of the Imperial government in American affairs and the points to which American officials were to give special attention, the first of the three divisions laid down was the management of the Indians and of the commerce with them. (*Cal. Home Office Papers* 1766-9, No. 348.)   And in 1775 the same statesman used in the House of Lords the following language: "The peltry or skin trade is a matter which I presume to affirm is of the last importance to the trade and commerce of the colonies and this country. The regulation of this business has cost His Majesty's ministers more time and trouble than any one matter I know of." (*Parl. Hist.*, XVIII, 671)́. For important aspects of the trade see also, Turner, *Indian Trade in Wisconsin*, and Moore, in *Mag. Am. History*, Sept., 1892.

apart from this there was another side to the matter, of special colonial importance,— the necessity in regard to the security of the colonies of the maintenance of general amicable relations with the Indians. The two aspects are indeed not to be separated in actual fact; for it will be readily seen that the general relations with the Indians were closely and inextricably bound up with the trade, and that anything which affected either one was likely to have the most essential bearing on the other.

The rivalry between English and French for the alliance of the Indians was not over with the peace; throughout the whole period down to the Revolution the home government was justly apprehensive of tampering with the Indians on the part of the French and Spanish traders from Louisiana.[1] To considerations as to dangers to the older colonies from this quarter was added the natural apprehension that French intrigues among the savages would be directed toward the recovery of Canada. Those best acquainted with the tribes had given warning even before the end of the war of the deep dissatisfaction and unrest even among the allied ones; the warning was justified and all the fears of the government confirmed by the great Pontiac outbreak in the spring of 1763. This was at its height in June of that year, exposing the colonies to ravage and danger such as they had never before experienced; it is evident that it might well have had a decided influence with regard to the Proclamation of the following October. All the professions of concern for the interests and contentment of the Indians which that document contains have therefore every probability of sincerity; there is no reasonable ground for surprise at the stress laid on this matter.

But that the measures of the Proclamation with regard to the Western country had long been in contemplation,

---

[1] See Hillsborough to Carleton, Nov. 4, 1769. (Can. Arch., Q. 6, p. 121.) This danger would of course increase with any lessening of or impediment to the trade from the British side.

and that the treatment of the Indian and his alleged grievances in it can be ascribed neither to the Pontiac outbreak
nor to any general change of policy in connection with the
acquisition of Canada, is conclusively shown by the fact
that steps of this kind had been contemplated, or seriously
debated, from at least the very beginning of the war.
March 15, 1756, the Board of Trade had enjoined on the
New York government to take measures for granting full
satisfaction to the Indians for the white encroachment of
which they complained, and which was one of the principal causes of the decline of British interest among them.[1]
During the war the French made effectual use of these encroachments in arousing the fears of the Indians, and the
British government was obliged to strain every nerve to
pacify them. Such efforts were, however, largely thwarted
through the interested action of the Colonial authorities,
and there seems every reason to believe that the alleged
land sales by the Indians were frequently obtained by
fraud. This certainly was the firm conviction both of the
home government and its colonial representatives, and it
was this conviction that lead to the measure of 1763 for
making such sales a public and not private matter. In
1759 Sir William Johnson strongly represents to the Board
the discontent of the Indians, and the damage thereby done
to the Indian trade; declaring that "The Indians ought to
be redressed and satisfied in all their reasonable and well-
founded complaints of enormous and unrighteously obtained patents of their lands."[2] In 1761 the legislature of
New York undertook to make new grants in the neigh-
bourhood of Lake George; the Board of Trade, having considered the matter, reported adversely thereon to the gov-

[1] N. Y. Col. Documents, VII. 77. For this and most of the other references down to
1761 I am indebted to Mr. Kingsford, who has clearly represented the conditions of this
matter during these years. (*History of Canada*, V.,135-8.) It is to be noted that the
letter of the Board to Chief-Justice DeLancy of N. Y., in 1756, refers to the policy the
Board was then urging as one that had been put in action in 1699.

[2] N. Y. Col. Documents, VII., 375.

ernment (Nov. 11, 1761). This report represented that the proposed grants were dangerous to the security of the colonies, the chief cause of the former hostility of the Indians having been "the cruelty and injustice with which they had been treated with respect to their hunting-grounds, in open violation of those solemn compacts by which they had yielded to us the Dominion but not the property of those Lands;" that as they had since been made allies by partial relief, and now, having acted faithfully, "impatiently wait for full redress and reformation," "under these circumstances and in this situation the granting of lands hitherto unsettled and establishing colonies upon the Frontiers before the claims of the Indians are ascertained appears to be a measure of the most dangerous tendency." It was accordingly recommended that an immediate stop should be made to the proposed settlements "until the event of the war is determined and such measures taken thereupon with respect to our Indian allies as shall be thought expedient."[1] This report was approved by the King-in-Council (Nov. 23, 1761), and instructions for colonial officers in accordance therewith were ordered to be prepared. These, drawn up by the Board of Trade, appear the following Dec. 2.[2] On the ground that the "peace and security of Our Colonies and Plantations upon the Continent of North America does greatly depend upon the amity and alliance" with the contiguous Indians, and that this amity and alliance are endangered through the alleged unjust treatment of the Indians in regard to their lands, the Imperial government, resolved to protect the Indians in "their just Rights and Possessions and to keep inviolable the Treaties and Compacts which have been entered into with them," ordains practically the same measures as were taken two years later in the Proclamation of 1763.

---

[1] N. Y. Col. Documents, VII. 472.

[2] Ibid., VII. 477. "Draft of an Instruction for the Governors of Nova Scotia, New Hampshire, Virginia, New York, North Carolina, South Carolina, and Georgia, forbidding them to grant lands or make settlements which may interfere with the Indians bordering on those Colonies." Apparently sent out at once.

We see therefore that the action in 1763 with regard to the Western lands, instead of being indicative of a change of policy occasioned by the acquisition of Canada, was merely the re-enunciation in a more general and important form of the principles which had been acted upon at a time when it was still hotly debated whether Canada should be retained at all or not; that it was indeed merely the logical following up of opinions which are evidently the controlling ones at least as early as 1756. Instead of their being evidence, or ground for reasonable suspicion, that the solicitude with regard to the Indians was in whole or part assumed and the cloak of other motives, we find that this solicitude, (the selfish commercial meaning of which is shown above), had been a predominant motive from the beginning of the war, and that it is unmixed, in the most secret and confidential transactions of the government, with any indication of ulterior designs.

The above inquiry has been into the origins of that part of the Proclamation which deals generally with the disposition of the West. With regard to the limits of Canada a somewhat different question is presented. For in this respect the Proclamation differed essentially from the Quebec Act; the former confining the Province to a very narrow area, and the latter including within it the whole sweep of the West between the Ohio and the Mississippi. The idea of a continuity of policy between the two measures, on the part of those who regard both as parts of the same new hostility which had been acted on since the conquest of Canada, rests on the assumption that the prohibition of settlement and the confirmation of Indian possession were only preliminary either to the erection of new governments exclusive of the other colonies, or to that incorporation with Quebec which was accomplished in 1774. I take the same view as to continuity of policy; with the difference that I regard both measures simply as parts of the old colonial system that had been applied practically throughout the century. It will be necessary therefore to trace carefully this side of the matter, with the purpose of opposing both the view noted above, and that older one which sees no connection on this point between the measures, but regards the Quebec Act as especially called forth by the difficulties with the older colonies at and just before the time of its appearance.

And first it should be noted that Canada, as ceded to England by France in 1763, was assigned no definite limits. The term used in the treaty of Paris [1] is "Canada with all its dependencies," and the boundary fixed between British and French territory in North America was, so far as Canada could be affected, simply the Mississippi River. Nor does any further indication of limits seem to have been given in any way by the French; for in a letter published shortly after the conquest [2] the Marquis de Vaudreuil, (the French governor who had signed the capitulation), states that he had "traced out no limits whatever" for the surrendered territory. General Murray in his official report of 1762, says that it is "impossible to ascertain exactly what part of North America the French styled Canada, no chart or map whatever having fallen into our hands, or public record of any kind to show what they understood by it." Hence the British Government might consider itself to have a comparatively free hand in the defining of the new Province, having regard to the fixed boundaries and well-established claims of the adjacent Colonies, [3] to the Mississippi

---

[1] Articles IV, V, VII. (Chalmer's *Treaties*, London, 1790).

[2] Annual Register, 1761, p. 267.

[3] The degree to which these latter were likely to be considered as restrictive may be inferred from the following statement of a recent American text-book with regard to early charter claims in the West. "Those charters had all lapsed, and the only colonies in 1750 of which the charter limits reached beyond the Appalachian mountains were Connecticut and Pennsylvania." (Hart, *Formation of the Union*, p. 3.) Roosevelt (*Winning of the West*, I, 37), after stating that the claims of the colonies in the West were heeded by the British no more than by the French, adds in regards to these claims, "The mere statement of the facts is enough to show the intrinsic worthlessness of the titles." Winsor (*The Mississippi Basin*, p. 447), has pointed out that the drawing by the treaty of 1763 of the Mississippi as a line of demarcation between the English and the

as the Eastern boundary of Louisiana, and to the somewhat indefinite regions granted to the Hudson Bay Company.[1] But how this freedom might be affected by popular opinion as to the legitimate limits of the new Province, will be seen from the fact that Canada had always been claimed by the French to extend over almost the whole extent of the vast territory through which her traders had carried on the fur-trade,[2] and that the non-inclusion of these regions down till the Quebec Act was a prominent subject of complaint among all classes of the inhabitants.[3]

Very soon after the treaty the British Government proceeded to consider the difficult question of the disposition of the outlying regions in America. The Board of Trade having recommended (in a renewal of the considerations of 1761, pointed out above), that the Western territory outside

French, meant " a distinct abandonment upon the part of the British government of the old sea-to-sea claims of the early English charters." Yet these had been the only basis of the Western claims of the colonies; it could hardly be expected that Great Britain would feel bound to pay any further attention to them. And not with any more reason can it be contended that the disregard of them in later measures showed any special hostility or injustice. I am concerned here however only with the degree to which the home government might consider its action in the settlement of the new acquisitions to be impeded by the old grants. That the view as to the entire lapse of the charter rights was consistently maintained by the Imperial authorities, will be seen from an examination of the negotiations for the treaty of peace in 1783. (Dip. Corr. of the Revolution; Hinsdale, Old Northwest, pp. 178-9). There is no record apparently of any objection made by Virginia to the proposed Walpole or Vandalia cession (1768-75) on the ground of her charter claims. (Monograph by Mr. Alden, elsewhere referred to).

1 These latter were not definitely ascertained till the Imperial Act of 1889, which settled the northern boundary of the Province of Ontario.— Houston, Canadian Constitutional Documents, p. 6.

2 The address of thanks for the Quebec Act from the French Canadians of Montreal, 1774, refers to it as having restored the Province to " ses anciennes limites."

3 See especially French and English petitions and memorials of 1773 and 1774. (Can. Arch., Q. 9, 10.) Also in Masères. Also Carleton to Shelbourne January 3, 1767, (Can. Arch., Q. 4, p. 50) and Dartmouth to Carleton December 10, 1774. (Ibid., Q. 10, p. 125). Garneau echoes these complaints in the assertion that " D'abord l'Angleterre voulut repudier tout ce qui était Francais et enlever meme aux habitants les advantages naturels qu'offrait à leurs enfants l'etendue du pays." (Hist. Can., II, 289.) With regard to the narrowing of the Province in 1763, it may perhaps be supposed that the Government was influenced by some idea of consistency in regard to its own past attitude in the disputes with the French over boundaries in North America. When the great extension of the Quebec Act was under debate the Opposition taunted the administration with the change of base on this point, asking what would be the result should the French ever be in a position to reclaim Canada.

of Canada (a term they use in a restricted but indefinite sense), and the other colonies should not be subject to grants of land or to settlement, the King communicates his approbation of this suggestion, but adds that it would be necessary to put the region under some civil government, in order that it might not seem to be abandoned or become a refuge for malefactors ;[1] and that it would probably be best to attach it to the Government of Quebec. In reply August 5, 1763,[2] the Board agrees that a government is necessary, but objects to its being that of any one existing province, especially of Quebec, for three reasons:—(1) that if included within the limits of Canada the Indians might thereby conclude that the English title to the country came only from the late French cession, (2) that the annexing of it to any one province would give that province an undue advantage in the Indian trade, and (3) that as government in that region could probably be carried on only with the aid of the greater part of the military forces in America, its annexation to Quebec would require, to prevent constant disputes between the civil and military authorities, that the Governor of Canada should be virtually Commander-in-Chief.[3] Accordingly the Board suggests instead that the region should be governed by the Commander-in-Chief under his military commission, and that pending the receipt of information necessary to the drawing up of his instructions, a Proclamation should be issued declaring the territory reserved for trade and the Indians. These recommendations were adopted, and with the others noted above formed the basis of the Proclamation of Oct. 7, following. This, so far as it relates to Quebec under this head, begins by clearly defining the limits of the new

---

[1] See last clause of the Proclamation.

[2] Can. Arch., Q. 1, p. 110.

[3] This last objection should perhaps be especially noted, in considering whether aims hostile to the civil rights of the other colonies were being entertained on the basis of the acquisition of Canada. If so, it could hardly seem objectionable that the Governor of Canada should be Commander-in-Chief.

" Government of Quebec," reducing it to a rectangular district of not more than 100,000 square miles extending along
both sides of the middle St. Lawrence from the mouth of
the river St. John to the point where the St. Lawrence was
intersected by the 45th degree of N. Latitude. As thus fixed
the boundaries remained till the Quebec Act, the Province
so constituted forming but a small part of the region over
which the French Government in Canada had claimed
sovereignty. The eastern portion cut off was placed under
the Government of Newfoundland.

There seems to be no reason for doubting that on this
point as on the others the Proclamation is what it appears
to be, and that the motives which dictated it are to be
fully gathered from the foregoing representations of the
Board of Trade. That the measures referring directly to
Quebec can scarcely be regarded as unfriendly to the
colonies is shown by the fact that they arose partly from
a desire to prevent Quebec from having an undue advantage in the Indian fur-trade. It was not regarded as a
complete settlement, and was intended to be supplemented
by steps which should properly provide for the temporary
government of the region. But as it proved, neither time
nor energy was available till 1774 for further arrangement,
and even the instructions to the Commander-in-Chief,
spoken of by the Board of Trade, seem never to have been
issued.[1] On the eve of the passing of the Quebec Act,
(long after its main features had been decided upon), Dartmouth, then Secretary of State, writes to Lt. Gov.
Cramahé that "there is no longer any hope of perfecting
that plan of policy in respect to the interior country
which was in contemplation when the Proclamation of 1763

---

[1] Knox (*Justice & Policy of the Quebec Act*, Lond. 1774), states in an authoritative
manner that it had been intended to defray the expense of the system contemplated by
a tax on the Indian trade, and that the plan was abandoned because it was not judged expedient to lay this tax, while the American budget was already sufficiently burdened.
See also Franklin, *Works*, V. 38.

was issued." [1] The details of the plan, (referred to as drawn
up by the Board of Trade in 1764), we learn from the instructions to Carleton of 1775, [2] it being incorporated therein as
some guide in his future dealings with the Indian trade.
The main feature is the institution of a semi-military
government, (i. e. by civil officials relying on the military
for constant support), administered in a summary manner
by a superintendent and deputies; government having
almost for its sole object the regulation of the fur-trade,
and no consciousness being shown of the existence in the
region of any permanent white settlers. The Superintendent was indeed appointed; but being left without sufficient power the result was unsatisfactory, and he was
superseded by 1768, each province then having authority to
frame regulations for its own traders. [3] The fur-trade,
subject from the want of effective government to a variety
of injurious impediments, became every year more and
more disorganized and unproductive, and complaints as to
the insecurity of life and property throughout the trading
grounds increased every day in volume and vehemence.
It was soon seen that some more effective measures must
be taken for the control of the region. Dartmouth in the
letter just quoted, after speaking of the difficulty of carrying out the plan of policy at first intended, proceeds:—
"Many circumstances with regard to the inhabitancy of
parts of that country were then unknown, and there are a
variety of other considerations that do, at least in my
judgment, induce a doubt both of the justice and propriety of restraining the colony to the narrow limits
prescribed in that Proclamation." [4] The main "circumstance" here spoken of was probably the discovery that
white settlers had spread themselves too widely and fixed

---

[1] Can. Arch., Q. 9, p. 157.

[2] Can. Arch., *Instructions, 1763-87.*

[3] Hillsborough to Carleton, June 11, 1768 (Can. Arch., Q. 5-1, p. 419). Franklin's letters
show the expense of the system as one of the chief reasons for change.

[4] See also same to Carleton Dec. 10, 1774. (Can. Arch., Q. 10, p. 125.)

themselves too firmly throughout the region to make it
possible to eject them (as was ordered by the Proclamation of 1763), or to prevent their further increase.[1] Every
year only multiplied the evidence that the Western country
was fast and irretrievably losing its character as a mere
Indian hunting-ground, and that settled civil government
could not long be delayed.[2]

As to the dangerous and almost anarchial state of things
throughout the West during the whole of this period we
have abundant evidence. The official reports are full of
complaints of the unsettled and inadequate state of government and of the impossibility of carrying on the fur-
trade without constant friction and disorder.[3] I cannot
better state the situation than by quoting from the well-
expressed report of a committee of the Quebec Council,
April 24, 1769,[4] drawn up as the result of an investigation
called forth by complaints of the traders.[5] This was after
all pretence of control through a general superintendent
had been withdrawn and each Province had been given
power to frame regulations for its own traders. It begins
by representing the great inconvenience and injury of the
" situation and present condition of the places where this
trade is carried on, and in which all regulations, whether
made by this or any other Province, must of consequence
have their operative influence. They are at present, as we
understand, the subject of no civil jurisdiction whatever,
without any internal principles of government within them-

---

[1] See Murray to Halifax March 9, 1764, where he speaks of these settlements as " certainly noble ones." (Can. Arch., Q. 2, p. 78.) See also Houston, *Can. Const. Doc.*, p. 108,
note 2.

[2] See petition for such a government, from inhabitants of the Illinois, June 27, 1773.
Cal. Hald. Coll., p. 203. Also Dartmouth to Gage concerning same. *Ibid.*, p. 232. This
was an old French settlement; it was not to be expected that English settlers would be
less forward in opposition to military government.

[3] Advocate–General Marriott asserted in 1774 that for want of a good government since
the Conquest, the trade was then only one-third of what it had been under the French.
Code of Laws.

[4] Can. Arch., Q. 6, p. 83.

[5] For these complains see *Minutes* of the Quebec Council, Jan. 15 and March 2, 1768.
They were directed mainly against the Provincial regulations then in being.

selves, nor annexed for the purposes of civil government
to any Province which has; so that we are at a loss to conceive how any province in particular or all the separate jurisdictions in America combined, can form a system. . . .
and give it binding effect upon persons casually residing in a
country not liable to receive a law from them, or enforce
obedience to it when formed." The inevitable result of the
situation here outlined is briefly referred to by Dartmouth
in a letter to Gen. Gage, of March 3, 1773, in which the
latter is ordered to bring to England every thing required
to explain "as well the causes as the effects of those abuses
and disorders which in some of your former dispatches you
say had prevailed to a great degree of enormity in that
country."[1] The report of the Quebec Council proceeds to
maintain that matters could not be remedied without Imperial action in the annexing of the whole of the trade region
to some one of the existing civil governments, and contends that no plan of concerted colonial action, (such as
New York shortly after proposed), could be satisfactory.
There were the usual difficulties of the time in regard to
such co-operation; but over and above these, it was made
almost impossible by the fact that Quebec, the province
most concerned, was in a radically different governmental
and industrial position from its neighbors. In 1771 New
York proposed a scheme of joint action by Pennsylvania,
Quebec, and itself, which Quebec refused to accede to; Lt.
Gov. Cramahé writing home on the subject, Oct. 31, 1771,
that "the interest of the two Provinces [Quebec and New
York] differ too widely to expect they will ever perfectly
agree upon regulations."[2]

---

[1] *Cal. Hald. Coll.*, p. 232.

[2] Can. Arch., Q. 8, p. 82. This is the occasion of the significant interference of Hillsborough against American Congresses which have I spoken of above (p. 389.) Cramahé,
though recognizing earlier the peculiar interests of Quebec, seems to have been willing
at first, through despair of other remedies, to join in discussing common measures.
January, 1772, we find the Quebec Council in receipt of a more definite proposal for joint
action from New York, and rejecting the same on the grounds, (1), that the Quebec government had no authority to take the financial measures involved, and (2), that the steps

It will then be seen that it might well appear to the home administration that no other step was open than the annexing of the territory to some existing civil government. To have kept it separate would have meant merely the continuance of a military or semi-military control, sure to be productive of even greater friction with the other Provinces and their traders, of increasing damage to the trade, and of more serious discontent on the part of the various small settled communities. And having reached this conclusion it was almost inevitable that the Imperial authorities should choose for this purpose the Province with which the region had been earliest and most closely associated, and to which it was believed by so many to belong,— that of Quebec.[1] The report of the Quebec Council quoted above, had been transmitted home; its main conclusion was the setting forth with considerable force the pre-eminent claims of Quebec to this acquisition. Whatever influence the state of affairs in the other Provinces exerted in this regard, we meet no trace of such influence in the confidential communications between the British and Canadian authorities. We have no reason to suspect the candour of Dartmouth in the letter above quoted, addressed as it was in the regular course of private correspondence

---

proposed would be detrimental to the Provincial trade. We have here mainly no doubt jealousy of the more powerful neighbor and apprehension at the inroads she was making in a branch of trade which had so long been Quebec's chief stay. Apart from the prohibition of the Minister, (which it is noteworthy, is not referred to), the Quebec Government had probably confidence that the old advantages would soon be restored to the Province by Imperial action. No further intercourse with the other colonies appears on the subject before the Quebec Act. How far the bearing on this matter of the provisions of the Quebec Act was instrumental in affecting the Revolutionary attitude of New York and Pennsylvania, as rousing their commercial anger and jealousy, would probably be worth a closer investigation. At least we have here no inconsiderable element in the general and profound dislike of the measure among the older Northern colonies. See the commercial aspect of the *Remonstrance* of the N. Y. Legislature, March 25, 1775. (Parl. Hist., XVIII, 650.)

[1] To attach it to any one other Province would be objectionable (we may reasonably assume the authorities to have felt), because of the various conflicting colonial claims in the West, sure to be aroused to the greatest activity by such a measure. Whereas the Government could, consistently with the Treaty, disregard all, and put the matter on another basis by givin it to Quebec. This would be at least a plausible line of argument.

to an official of long standing and known discretion. If other matters had been of weight in the Imperial councils there would seem to have been no reason for the careful concealment, and no possibility of the unintentional neglect, of them in this quarter.

On the other hand, although it is true that before the actual appearance of the Quebec Act we have no indication that the extension of the Province made by it had any connection whatever with the contemporary difficulties of government in the other colonies, and although it must be conceded that apart from such reference the Imperial authorities seem to have ample justification for that extension, yet it is undeniable that the considerations which excited the fears of the Continental Congress were put forward by supporters (as well as by opponents), of the measure, both in Parliament and outside. But this was not prominently done, at least at first; so incidentally indeed that in the whole of the spirited debates in both the Commons and Lords on the Quebec Bill in May and June, 1774, such references appear in the mouths of only two supporters of the Bill, and their utterances are apparently not specifically noticed by the opposition. One of these more candid or incautious speakers was Solicitor-General Wedderbourne, who stated in the Commons that one of the objects of the measure was to deter Englishmen from settling in Canada, and that one of the great advantages of the extension of territory would be that the other inhabitants of North America "will have little temptation to stretch themselves northwards."[1] He added moreover, "I think this limitation of the boundary (i. e. of the older colonies) will be a better mode than any restriction laid upon govern-

[1] Cavendish, *Report*, p. 58. Wedderbourne was at this time one of the pillars of the Government in the Commons. But he was not responsible for the present Bill, and though in his official capacity supporting it as a whole, he plainly intimated that it had not his entire approval. The statement had been immediately preceded by the remark that he did not think that any temptation should be held out to natives of England to emigrate.

ment. In the grant of lands we ought to confine the inhabitants to keep them according to the ancient policy of the country along the line of the sea and river."

This statement as I have said seems to have excited no comment from either side of the House; [1] an oversight on the part of the opposition which is the more remarkable from the fact that several of their speakers hint darkly at "the secret designs" of the Bill, and taunt the Ministry with concealing their real motives, [2]—hints and taunts which elicited no reply. Lord North, the leader of the House, upheld the extension as made simply in the interests of the fisheries in the East and of security to life and trade in the West; though it will be seen that the preamble of the Act refers only for the Western territory to the need of civil government for the "several colonies and settlements." The enacting clause pays special attention to the northern and western boundaries of Pennsylvania as "granted by the Charter," beside making the provision "that nothing herein contained . . . shall in any wise affect the boundaries of any other colony;" but there is no reference to the Western claims of any of the Provinces. As first introduced the clause read very differently,—"all the said territories, islands and countries, extending southward to the banks of the river Ohio, Westward to the banks of the Mississippi . . . not within the limits of any other British colony, as allowed and confirmed by the Crown." A petition against this indefiniteness was presented by the Pennsylvania proprietories, and Burke also objected in behalf of New York. Lord North professed every readiness to pay regard to both settled and unsettled boundaries, while declaring that the original intent had been to leave the fixing of more precise southern bounds to later local agreement; and on Burke's motion, representing that otherwise

---

[1] The chance reporters from whom the Parliamentary History of the period was compiled, seem also not to have heard it or to have not thought it worth while noting.

[2] *Cavendish*, pp. 1, 37, 85, 214 — pagings which refer to the beginnings of the speeches in which the references occur.

the Colonies would in this matter be left at the mercy of the executive, the established clause was substituted for the above.

When with this and other Amendments the bill went back to the Lords it was received by a small but spirited opposition, headed by Chatham. Its principal defender was Lord Lyttleton, who referred to the idea put forward by Chatham that Canada would at a future day be used as a proper instrument to quell British America, with the remark that he was not apprehensive of this, but that if the Americans were determined to persist in their rebellious course he saw no reason why Canada, with the rest of the Empire, should not be so employed; and that in such an event he regarded it as happy that the local situation of the Canadians was such that they might form some check to the "fierce fanatic spirits" of the other Provinces.[1] This however illiberal, does not apparently refer to this situation as one resulting from the provisions of the Quebec Act. Whatever the inference, this and the statement of Wedderbourne quoted above are the strongest suggestions of hidden motives on this point, that, so far as I have discovered, appear at this time in the mouths of supporters of the Government. In the close tracing of the preliminary steps through the ten years preceding the Act I have met with no other evidence fitted in any degree to support the belief that the extension by it of the boundaries of Quebec was dictated by hostility to the growth and liberties of the other colonies other than that which may perhaps be said to mark every part of the colonial system. And whether these statements are fitted to support that belief will appear very doubtful to those who have entered into the spirit of that colonial system. Even if it should be established that they were not merely private and incidental utterances, but were really expressive of definite ideas and motives on the part of the originators of the Quebec Act, it will yet remain to be

---

[1] *Parliamentary History.* Vol. 17, p. 1402 *et seq.*

shown that they betoken a different standpoint than that occupied by the Board of Trade for some time back. Closely connected with that view of the interests of Great Britain which for a long time had inspired the hostility to colonial manufactures, for example, was a strongly rooted preference of shore to inland colonies; a preference based on the belief that the farther the colonists removed themselves from the ocean and the mother country, the more inevitably would they be led to manufacturing enterprises and the less easy would it be for Great Britain to restrain this activity. It was simply another aspect of the trade considerations which led to such emphasis being placed upon the conciliation of the savages; it cannot be shown to imply any new development of anti-colonial policy, or any insidious scheme of building up in the West new communities of alien social and governmental constitution, with the aim of being later used as instruments against the growth and liberties of the older colonies. By the ordinary colonial views of the older illiberal school the attitude of Wedderbourne and Lyttelton can I think be sufficiently explained.

And not their views alone; but also such parts of the Imperial policy in regard to the West as cannot be attributed to real solicitude for the Indian and for the safety of the colonies. For if I have been successful in presenting my point of view in the above, it will be already evident what position I take with regard to continuity of policy throughout this period in respect to the Western lands. I see no reason to agree with Hinsdale even in the more moderate assertion that " the Western policy of the British was not steady or consistent, but fitful and capricious;"[1] it seems to me that no inconsistency is to be detected between the policy that dictated the Proclamation of 1763,— a policy that was manifest as early at least as 1756,— and that which was expressed in the Quebec Act of 1774. It has been one

[1] *Old Northwest*, p. 141.

of my objects throughout this investigation to show the long course of weakness, ignorance, and procrastination that stretches between the acquisition of Canada and the final settlement of its constitution. These qualities are not entirely absent in the treatment of the matter under discussion; but that treatment nevertheless presents more consistency and firmness than we find in almost any other part of the dealing with the situation. The frequent changes of Ministry and Secretary seem to have affected the peculiar sphere of the Board of Trade less than any other part of the administration; simply, it is to be contended, because that Board was now acting on long established principles, applied to the new conditions as a matter of course, and only slowly giving way to the inevitable western changes. These are the principles of the old colonial-commercial policy; and no better expression of them can perhaps be found than in the words of the Board of Trade itself in 1768, in its adverse report with regard to the proposed new settlements at Detroit and in the Illinois country.[1] The significant part of this is as follows:

"The proposition of forming inland colonies in America is, we humbly conceive, entirely new. It adopts principles in respect to American settlements different from what has hitherto been the policy of this kingdom, and leads to a system which, if pursued through all its consequences, is, in the present state of that country, of the greatest importance.

The great object of colonizing upon the continent of

---

[1] Franklin's answer to Hillsborough, 1772 (*Works*, V. 55, Bigelow edition, 1887). For the report itself see its quotation by Hillsborough (*Ibid.* V. 5–12). For very interesting record of the progress of the scheme to which this was the death-blow, see letters of Franklin to his son, Sept. 27, 1766—March 13, 1768 (*Ibid.*, 138–45). This reference I owe to the unpublished monograph on western settlements of Mr. G. H. Alden of the University of Wisconsin. It exhibits Shelbourne, Secretary of State for the Southern Department when the scheme was first advanced (by Franklin and others), as decidedly favorable to it, together perhaps with some other officials. But Shelbourne was evidently in this as in some other matters, in advance of his time (see Fitzmaurice, *Shelbourne*, II, 31); the Board of Trade seems not to have wavered in its position, and Shelbourne's retirement in January 1768 in favor of Hillsborough, the chief representative of the opposite view, may perhaps not unreasonably be regarded as helped on by his heterodox liberalism. It is apparently the first vigorous shaking of the older policy; but that policy is still triumphant.

North America has been to improve and extend the commerce, navigation, and manufactures of this kingdom, upon which its strength and security depend.

1. By promoting the advantageous fishery carried on upon the northern coast.

2. By encouraging the growth and culture of naval stores and of raw materials, to be transported hither in exchange for perfect manufactures and other merchandise.

3. By securing a supply of lumber, provisions, and other necessaries, for the support of our establishments in the American islands.

In order to answer these salutary purposes, it has been the policy of this kingdom to confine her settlements as much as possible to the sea-coast, and not to extend them to places inaccessible to shipping, and consequently more out of the reach of commerce; a plan which at the same time that it secured the attainment of these commercial objects, had the further political advantage of guarding against all interfering of foreign powers, and of enabling this kingdom to keep up a superior naval force in those seas, by the actual possession of such rivers and harbours as were proper stations for fleets in time of war.

Such, may it please your Majesty, have been the considerations inducing that plan of policy hitherto pursued in the settlement of your Majesty's American colonies, with which the private interest and sagacity of the settlers coöperated from the first establishments formed upon that continent. It was upon these principles, and with these views, that government undertook the settlement of Nova Scotia in 1749; and it was from a view of the advantages represented to arise from it in these different articles that it was so liberally supported by the aid of Parliament.

The same motives, though operating in a less degree, and applying to fewer subjects, did as we humbly conceive, induce the forming the colonies of Georgia, East Florida, and West Florida, to the south, and the making those provincial arrangements in the proclamation of 1763, by which the interior country was left to the possession of the Indians."

Here we have, it will be seen, not only the constant reference throughout to a policy which is considered as of long standing, but the definite statement that this policy was directly acted upon by the government on an important occasion as early as 1749, and that it was operative in the arrangments of 1763. It is true that Hillsborough, while quoting this statement with the fullest approbation, has just before spoken of " that principle which was adopted by this Board and approved and confirmed by his Majesty, immediately after the treaty of Paris, viz. : the confining the western extent of settlements to such a distance from the sea-coast as that, etc. ;" but it is evident either that this is due to a confusion and heedlessness quite characteristic of the writer, or that it is a mere misuse of language, by the " principle " affirmed there being really meant only the new application of an old principle to conditions which had now for the first time fully presented themselves. In Franklin's reply to Hillsborough he accepts without question the definition of policy, and in proceeding to refer to the grant on the Ohio which had been approved in 1748, brings this forward, not to show that that policy was not then in operation, but on the contrary, going on the assumption that it *was* then in force, to show that the region in question did not come within its operation, because not in fact and not considered " without the reach of the trade and commerce of this kingdom." [1] It is clear that Franklin's argument on this matter is entirely without point unless it proceeds on such a basis. If the Board of Trade were not to be supposed to be animated by the principle in question as a general one, their action could show nothing with regard to the application of it to the region included within the grant of 1748.

But we have, it is said, evidence of inconsistency or different policy in the treatment of the more southern portion of the West in 1772 through the approval of the establishment of a new colony south of the Ohio, to be known as Vandalia. The inner history of this matter will show, however, that it cannot properly be so regarded. For whether or not this region was, as Franklin contends in the argument noted above, regarded as on a different basis

---

[1] *Works*, V. 32.

as early as 1748, it is very clear that it had so established itself by 1772. As early as 1764, Franklin tells us,[1] government contemplated the placing of it in a different position, as a part of the plan then under consideration for the regulation of the Indian trade; aiming by its purchase from the Indians to "establish with their consent, a respectable boundary line, beyond which his Majesty's subjects should not be permitted to settle." The negotiations then entered upon with the Indians were however delayed, and meanwhile, between 1765 and 1768 large numbers of settlers came into the region and brought about a critical state of things with the Indians. This hastened the action of the authorities, and the purchase was finally completed by the treaty of Fort Stanwix in November, 1768. That the home government had reconciled itself fully to settlement here and had made the purchase with such settlement in view, is shown (as was pointed out by Franklin),[2] by the reference in the Board of Trade Report quoted above to "the liberty that the inhabitants of the middle colonies will have (in consequence of the proposed boundary line with the Indians) of gradually establishing themselves backwards."[3] And yet it is this same Report, it will be remembered, which is drawn up for the purpose of making that strong re-statement of general colonial policy which has been quoted from above. So that for the Fort Stanwix region there would seem to be no question that Franklin is correct in stating[4] that "the true reason for purchasing the lands comprised within that boundary were to avoid an Indian rupture, and give an opportunity to the king's subjects quietly and lawfully to settle thereon." Or, as he strongly puts it, that the proclamation which had reserved lands for the use of the Indians had lost its force with re-

---

[1] *Works*, V. 38.

[2] *Ibid.*, V. 55-6.

[3] *Ibid.*, V. 10.

[4] *Ibid.*, p. 43.

gard to that portion of these lands which the Indians by selling had shown they had no use for.[1]

In 1768 therefore, government, while strongly re-enunciating the general Western policy, had just as clearly acknowledged that this policy was not to be applied to the region south of the Ohio.[2] This latter territory was now definitely deprived of that character which, in the ministerial mind, still remained attached to the more northern country, viz.: appropriation to the Indian as a hunting ground. Between 1768 and 1772 settlement continued to pour into the Ohio country to such an extent as to show beyond doubt that this character had departed for all time.[3] So that in 1772, when the Walpole matter came up for final determination, it was not difficult for Franklin to make a triumphant case against the belated views of Hillsborough. The commercial policy had here yielded finally to the force

[1] A hasty reading of this part of Franklin's paper might possibly give the impression that he minimizes or loses sight of the general principles of policy which inspired the Proclamation of 1763, and that he regards it as mainly intended to pacify and protect the Indians. Such a view I should regard either as an error, or as the misleading emphasis of a partizan brief. But I do not think Franklin is chargeable in either respect; for in a previous part of his paper (V. 32) he plainly declares that the definition of the policy of the Board in 1763 as laid down by Hillsborough, he will not "presume to controvert." And as I have shown above, his later argument is evidently based on the acceptance of the principles of the Report of 1768. In what he says as to the cessation of the force of the Proclamation through purchase from the Indians he has reference of course only to the lands south of the Ohio,—a region to which, he labors throughout to show, the principles of the established policy did not properly extend. Franklin was too good a debater to prejudice his case by going out of his way unnecessarily. And hence the reference to Mr. Grenville (V. 37) as having, with regard to the Proclamation, "always admitted that the design of it was totally accomplished as soon as the country was purchased from the natives," I can regard as quoted purely with reference to the country that had been purchased in 1768, and as not giving, or purporting to give, Grenville's views with regard to the policy or intent of the Proclamation as a whole. When the "admission" was made does not appear; the language would seem to show that it was subsequent to the purchase. But it will be remembered that the Grenville government had entered into negotiations for such a purchase (with regard only to the region south of the Ohio), as early as 1764. (*Franklin*, V. 38).

[2] It is probable that the unimportance of this latter territory with regard to the fur trade was of strong influence in bringing about this attitude. Franklin says that the Indians were willing to sell because they had no use for the lands "either for residence or hunting." (V. 37).

[3] Franklin asserted in 1772 that it was certain that at least 30,000 settlers were then there. (*Works*, V. 74.]

of circumstances, and the words in which the grant (Vandalia) was finally recommended by the Committee of Council must be looked upon as intended to show the reasons for this departure from what was still however the established policy.   As stated by Franklin [1] these reasons were as follows:

"1. That the lands in question had been for some time past and were then in an actual state of settling, numbers of families to a very considerable amount removing thither from his said Majesty's other colonies.

"2. That the lands in question did not lie beyond all advantageous intercourse with the kingdom of Great Britain."

It is evident therefore that the grant of 1772 is neither a mark of inconsistency nor a sign of the overthrow of the old commercial-colonial policy with regard to the West.   If circumstances had forced this step south of the Ohio, the Quebec Act two years later showed that there had been no such change with regard to the rest of the country.   Though even this latter it would seem could not be regarded as purely as before as a mere fur region; it has been shown above that the modifying of the first ideas with regard to its disposition was doubtless partly due to the discovery that a degree of settlement had gone on even within it which could not be entirely disregarded. [2]   It was not disregarded, but it was regarded as slightly as possible by the attachment of the whole region to Quebec.

A very notable pamphleteer of the year 1774 [3] forcibly sums up this matter.   After stating that the Proclamation of 1763 was intended to be followed up a general plan of regulation for the Indian trade, he affirms, (as noted above),

---

[1] *Works*, X. 355.

[2] The preamble of the Quebec Act speaks of the several French colonies and settlements which by the Proclamation were left without civil government; (a petition for it had been received from at least one of them).   Nothing is said of new settlement; but Dartmouth's letters show that it must have been known that it had steadily proceeded.

[3] "The Justice and Policy of the late Act of Parliament for making some effectual provision for the Government of the Province of Quebec asserted and proved; and the conduct of Administration respecting that Province stated and vindicated."   By Wm. Knox.   Lond. 1774.   Though unable to prove it, I believe this to have been inspired.

that the events of the year following proved fatal to the
doing of this, as it was not thought expedient to lay that
tax upon the trade by which the expense was to be deferred.
"This was the reason that so large a part of the ceded territory in America was left without government, and that
the new province of Quebec contained so small a portion of
ancient Canada." The small French settlements in the
region, he continues, were left under the military government of the posts, "as most likely to prevent an increase
of inhabitants." But in the parts contiguous to the old
colonies immigrants flocked in and forced the Indians to
fall back; and as these new settlements were without civil
jurisdiction and were every day increasing, "the case was
judged to be without other remedy than that of following
the emigrants with government and erecting a new Province between the Alleghany mountains and the river Ohio
for that purpose." But to prevent a recurrence of the
necessity it was resolved, (and done by the Quebec Act),
to put the whole remaining region under the jurisdiction
of the Government of Quebec, "with the avowed purpose
of excluding all further settlement therein, and for the
establishment of uniform regulation for the Indian trade."
The Province of Quebec was preferred, "because the
access by water is much easier from Quebec to such parts
of this country as are the most likely to be intruded upon
than from any other colony." Only under one uniform
government could the Indian be protected, and thus be
prevented "the quarrels and murders which are every day
happening and which are the certain consequence of a
fraudulent commerce." There seems no reason to doubt
the substantial correctness of these assertions; especially
when we find the Government despatching to Carleton with
his new commission in 1775, as a guide in his dealings with
the Indians and the Western trade, the identical regulations
which had been drawn up by the Board of Trade in 1764.[1]

---

[1] Can. Arch., *Instructions to Governors.* Appendix to Carleton's Instructions, 1775.

The writer is evidently speaking from the standpoint of the illiberal commercial-colonial policy; but it will be seen that he is apparently ignorant of any but trade motives for this part of the recent measure, and that he regards it as dictated by precisely the same policy as that which had produced the Proclamation of 1763. And this policy, I repeat in conclusion, was caused neither by the acquisition of Canada nor by the colonial troubles of the seventies. It was only a new application of that principle of commercial monopoly which, as Burke says, runs through twenty-nine Acts "from the year 1660 to the unfortunate period of 1764;" there is no ground whatever for connecting it, in origin or maintenance, with the special troubles in the other colonies, or with any sinister designs against these latter. A connection which, I need scarcely again observe, certainly cannot be made if the continuity of policy as between 1763 and 1774 be conceded.

But while defending the originators of the Quebec Act from the heavier reproach brought against them on this point, I do not wish to be understood as in the least defending the Western policy of the measure in itself. Disastrous as the Quebec Act proved, no part of it I think was more shortsighted or more disastrous than this treatment of the Western lands. Following up the Proclamation of 1763, it seemed an attempt to indefinitely maintain in the great heart of the continent, when apparently thrown open for Anglo–American expansion, the policy of monopoly and re striction against which the colonies on the coast were chafing so sorely. It was natural that the latter should imagine themselves threatened and impeded more malignly and seriously than could have proven to be the case; it was on this side, I have little doubt, that the Quebec Act figured most prominently amongst the colonial grievances. Great Britain might well seem to have become "the most active foe of the English race in Amer-

---

[1] Roosevelt, *Winning of the West*, I. 36. Though I have quoted this expression, I by no means agree fully with the way in which it is used by this writer. He attributes to

ica."[1] In this light I am inclined to emphasize strongly
the importance of the Act in alarming and embittering the
colonists.[1] They were not likely to stop and reflect that
though the policy of the mother country apparently
remained the same, that policy had already broken
down in one important section of the new territory before the
inrush of the pioneers, and that there was no probability
that it would be any more permanent with regard to the
remaining portions.

b. *Religion.* The second important provision of the Quebec
Act was that noted one by which it was enacted that the professors of the Catholic faith within the Province "may have,
hold, and enjoy the free exercise of the religion of the Church
of Rome, subject to the King's supremacy, . . . and that
the clergy of the established Church may hold, receive, and
enjoy their accustomed dues and rights," in regard to such
professors. At the same time the adherents of that Church
were relieved from the oath of Supremacy established by
Elizabeth on condition of taking a simple oath of allegiance. These are the provisions which move Lecky to describe the Act as marking an "epoch in the history of religious liberty," and which at the time moved the Continental Congress to express its astonishment that a British
Parliament "should ever consent to establish in that country
a religion that has deluged your island in blood, and dispersed impiety, bigotry, persecution, murder, and rebellion
through every part of the world." We must examine these
provisions in the light of the attitude of the Home and Provincial governments to the church throughout the period;

England a too conscious and special hostility, and dates it from the close of the
war. His error seems mainly due to the apparent deficiency in grasp of the subject
and consistency of view which is shown in the assertion elsewhere that the interests of
Quebec, "did not conflict with those of our people or touch them in any way, and she
had little to do with our national history and nothing whatever to do with the history
of the West." (I. 28.)

[1] See in regard to this the *Remonstrance* of the N. Y. Legislature, Mar. 25, 1775, to the
British Parliament on the subject of the Quebec Act. It is taken up almost wholly with
this side of the measure. (*Parl. Hist.* XVIII, 650.)

and we shall find that on the one hand the framers of the Act had no purpose of "establishing" the Roman Catholic Church, and that on the other, the measure is by no means so notable from the standpoint of religious liberty as it has appeared.

The prominence of the religious element in Canada, and the position the Roman Catholic Church had so long occupied in secular matters as well, made the treatment of that church, and its future position, one of the most important and pressing of the problems that confronted the new Government. The conquerors were pledged by the Capitulation to full toleration of the Roman Catholic worship; though that instrument, promising to all religious communities the continued enjoyment of their property, had distinctly refused to assure the tithes or other dues of the secular clergy.[1] The pledge of toleration was incorporated in the IV. Art. of the treaty of Paris in 1763 by the following clause: "His Britannic Majesty on his side agrees to grant the liberty of the Catholic religion to the inhabitants of Canada; he will consequently give the most precise and effectual orders, that his new Roman Catholic subjects may profess the worship of their religion, according to the rites of the Roman Catholic Church, as far as the laws of Great Britain permit." This is identically the same stipulation, (in slightly different words), as that in the Treaty of Utrecht fifty years before;[2] but it will be noticed that strictly interpreted it does not seem at first sight to be the same concession as that made in the Articles of Capitulation. It is impossible to delay on the questions as to how far the strict interpretation of the then existing laws would have interfered with "the liberty of the Catholic religion," or how far those laws were at that time enforced at home or were

---

[1] Capitulation of Montreal, Art. 27, 34. Houston, *Can. Const. Documents*, pp. 45, 47.

[2] See Lecky, *History of England in the 18th Century*, I, as to the general resemblance of these treaties. See also Marriot, *Code of Laws*. It is rather curious that, though directly comparing the treaties, Mr. Lecky fails to see that the earlier one contains precisely the provision which he refers to as marking, fifty years later, an epoch of religious liberty.

valid in America.[1] Of rigid construction there was no real
question in the case of Canada, and it will appear later that
there is no evidence of the slightest attempt on the part of
the British government throughout the period to interfere
with full religious liberty, or with the establishments necessary for its effective maintenance. But that the above
phrase, "as far as the laws of Great Britain permit," was
by no means an unconsidered one, but was intended at least
at first to have a very definite significance, is clearly shown
by a very important communication from the Earl of Egremont, Secretary of State, to Murray, on the occasion of
the latter's appointment to the new civil Government in
Quebec (Aug. 13th, 1763).[2] The new governor is instructed
in this that information has been received which causes a
suspicion that the French have hopes of using the religious
liberty promised the Canadians for the retaining through
the clergy of their hold upon the people, and that he is
therefore to be on his guard against any such attempts.
The King, (the Minister continues), has no intention of restraining the Canadians in the free exercise of their religion,
but the condition *as far as the laws of Great Britain permit*
must always be remembered; these laws prohibiting absolutely "all Popish Hierarchy in any of the dominions belonging to the Crown of Great Britain." "This matter was
clearly understood in the negotiations of the Definitive
Treaty. The French Minister proposed to insert the words
comme ci devant, in order that the Romish religion should
continue to be exercised in the same manner as under their
Government; and they did not give up the point until they
were plainly told that it would only be deceiving them to
admit these words, for the King had no power to tolerate

---

[1] It is perhaps worth noting that among the list of convicted criminals in Great Britain
in 1771 is found the name of one John Baptist Maloney, who was sentenced to perpetual
imprisonment for the crime of exercising the office of a Popish priest. He was afterwards pardoned on condition of leaving the country. *Calendar of Home Office Papers*
1770-2, No. 376.

[2] Can. Arch., Q. I. p. 117.

that religion in any other manner than *as far as the laws of Great Britain permit.* These laws must be your guide in any disputes that may arise on the subject." It is clear from this that the French Government desired the words *comme ci devant* to be inserted instead of the phrase in question, and that the object of that phrase was merely to deprive the Catholic religion of any legal status or hierarchy in the Province. Taken in this connection it will be seen that the Treaty was really intended to grant all that had been promised in the Capitulation.[1] And the principles thus clearly stated at the start, we find adhered to throughout the period with more vigor and consistency than can be discovered in any other part of the Canadian policy.

In the above letter Egremont goes on to advise Murray to give public notice that no new foreign priests would be allowed to remain in the country without Governmental permission, and also to require all ecclesiastics to take the oath of allegiance. The following October 25, Murray writes as to the general subject of religious policy, on the occasion of the transmission home of religious petitions,[2] which he reports as due to anxiety on the part of the Canadians as to the continuance of the priesthood. If this, he says, be provided for, they would part with the hierarchy without much reluctance; and he suggests a plan for having priests educated in Provincial seminaries as heretofore, and ordained abroad at the public expense,— a plan which

---

[1] As to the opinion that the laws did not prohibit the free exercise of the Roman Catholic religion, and that it was at the discretion of the crown whether Catholics in the newly acquired colonies should be admitted to office and honors, see Att.-General Yorke's opinion concerning the position in regard to office of the Catholics in Grenada. (*Cal. Home Office Papers*, 1776-9, No. 403.) This opinion is further of great interest in view of the question as to the formation of an Assembly in Canada, and the admission of Roman Catholics to it. It states clearly that the statute requiring the transubstantiation test oath does not apply to the new possessions, and that his Majesty is the only judge in regard to the use of such. This should be considered in connection with the opinion of Lecky as to the importance of the Quebec Act in religious history. On the general question as to the position of Catholics see further, opinion of Thurlow and Wedderbourne, (*Cal. Home Office Papers*, 1770-2, Nos. 659, 713); Report of Wedderbourne, 1772 (Christie, *History of Lower Canada*, I. c. 2); Marriott, *Code of Laws.*

[2] See above, p. 284.

he thinks "the most feasible means of procuring a national clergy, without continuing a Bishop," and likely to give "universal satisfaction and make the Canadians in time forget their former connexions.[1]" To these suggestions Halifax (Jan. 14, 1764)[2] makes the guarded reply that he hopes soon to transmit definite directions on "that very important and difficult matter." We meet nothing further directly on this point, but that Murray's suggestions were not taken is shown by the fact that a Bishop for the province was allowed to be ordained in France in 1766, (the permission seems to have been given as early as 1764), and to proceed to Quebec in the same year; continuing there at the head of the church for the remainder of the period. There is some mystery about this transaction, and Masères asserts that the Bishop had only a verbal permission to assume authority, and that he was supposed to have promised to confine himself to the necessary and inoffensive duties of the office, (which promise, he adds, was not kept). The English government, according to Masères, was brought thus to "connive" at this evasion of the laws under the opinion that the step was necessary to secure to the Canadians the enjoyment of their religion without giving loopholes for the creeping in of foreign influences. But that this was regarded as only a temporary step is shown by a Board of Trade report on the state of Quebec, May 16, 1766, in which the "unsettled state of eclesiastical affairs " is designated as the first of the matters requiring attention.[3] In Oct., 1767, Carleton recommends the appointment of a coadjutor in order to obviate the necessity of having the Bishop consecrated abroad; a recommendation which the Secretary approved (March 6, 1768),[4] but which was referred with others to the shortly expected regulations about religious matters in general. In 1772 however, the matter came

---

[1] Can. Arch., Q.1, p. 251.
[2] Ibid., Q. 2, p. 5.
[3] Ibid., Q. 3, p. 53.
[4] Ibid., Q. 5-1, p. 344.

up again in the absence of Carleton, and, like the appointment
of the Bishop, seems to have been temporarily settled by
another connivance, (in this case only of the Provincial government), at an evasion of the laws; the Lt. Governor
writing (July 25, 1772), that as the Bishop had lately obtained
" the requisite power for consecrating the coadjutor whom
Gov. Carleton had pitched upon, I agreed to his perform-
ing the ceremony, but in a private way, because it was not
the act of government, and to avoid giving a handle to
busy and troublesome people." [1] To which Hillsborough
replied, Sept. 2, 1772: "Your having permitted the person styling himself Bishop of Quebec to consecrate a
coadjutor in consequence of power which you say he had
received for that purpose, and which I presume must therefore mean from some foreign ecclesiastical authority, appears to me to be a matter of the highest importance, and
the more so as I do not find upon the fullest examination
that any authority whatever has at any time been given by
His Majesty for the exercise within the colony of any
powers of Episcopacy in matters relative to the religion of
the Church of Rome." [2] Hillsborough was shortly after replaced by Dartmouth, and the latter writes Dec. 9, 1772 in
a similar strain, declining to give any countenance to the
late consecration of the coadjutor, and making the matter
depend on the deliberations of the Privy Council then pending; though he adds that he will not undertake to say that
the exercise of some Episcopal authority may not be necessary to *the toleration* granted. [3]

During the whole of the period the power of appointment to benefices resided in the Governor alone, having
been first granted to Murray, in 1763. The instructions to
Carleton in 1768 direct him "not to admit of any ecclesiastical jurisdiction of the See of Rome or any other ecclesias-

1 Can. Arch., Q. 8, p. 160.
2 Ibid., Q. 8, p. 166.
3 Ibid., p. 220.

tical jurisdiction whatever,"— an instruction which would
seem to be in direct opposition to the continuance of the
functions of a French ordained Bishop. Another article
ordered him to provide for the gradual settlement of Protestant clergymen; and it was no doubt as a following up
of this that in July 1768 a mandate was issued to him to
appoint under commission two such to the parishes of
Quebec and Three Rivers, to enjoy the same during life,
"with all rights, dues, profits and privileges thereunto
belonging in as full and ample manner as the ministers of
churches in any of our colonies in America."[1] But Carleton, viewing this as a "stile of office" due to carelessness,
remonstrated against it as extending, in the opinion of the
Provincial lawyers, "to dispossess the people of their private churches and their clergy of their tithes and all parochial dues," and gave the clergymen simply licenses to
preach, with a right to such dues only as should arise
from Protestants under the laws relating to the Church of
England.[2] This action was apparently approved of by the
home Government, the Secretary writing that there had
been no intention of authorizing the general demand of
tithes,[3] as had been shown by the attachment of a stipend
out of the general revenue.

On the verge of the Quebec Act, Dec. 1st, 1773, Dartmouth writes that the coming settlement will give all satisfaction to the new subjects on the head of religion, but
on such a basis that all foreign jurisdiction shall be abolished and the Province itself made equal to the supplying
of all the essentials to free worship in the true spirit of
the treaty.[4] The settlement thus foreshadowed — that of
the Quebec Act,— viewed in the light of the policy thus
clearly maintained down to its enactment, cannot be said to
depart from it, the Article (5th) which provides for "the free

---

[1] Masères, *Commissions*, p, 148–52.
[2] Can. Arch., Q. 5–2, p, 726–730.
[3] Ibid., Q. 5–2, p, 756.
[4] Ibid., Q. 9, p., 157.

exercise of the religion of the Church of Rome," expressly adding, "subject to the King's supremacy declared and established by an Act made in the first year of the reign of Queen Elizabeth." Nor can it be regarded as "establishing" the Roman Catholic Church in any sense in which the Church of England was not also established. For the only new privilege bestowed on the Roman Catholic clergy is comprised in the phrase, "the clergy of the said Church may hold, receive, and enjoy their accustomed dues and rights in respect to such persons only as shall profess the said religion,"— a phrase which has always been interpreted as implying the re-establishment of compulsory tithes; while the next article goes on to make provision for the applying "of the rest of the said accustomed dues and rights" (i. e. the tithes of Protestants), to the support and encouragement of the Protestant religion. And that the intent of the framers of the Act did not reach even to thus equalizing the two Churches is clearly shown by the ensuing instructions to Carleton 1775. The 20th Article enjoins him to remember "that it is a toleration of the free exercise of the religion of the Church of Rome only to which they [the new subjects] are entitled, but not to the powers and privileges of it as an established Church, which belongs only to the Protestant Church of England." The 21st Article further forbids all appeals to or correspondence with any foreign ecclesiastical jurisdiction, makes government license essential in every case to the exercise of Episcopal or parochial functions, and conditions the holding of all benefices on good behavior. I cannot here enter fully into the legal question of the peculiar relative positions thus apparently granted the two churches; it must be left with the remark that it is the very evident intention of the Administration, as shown in the Governor's instructions and elsewhere, to make the Church of England *theoretically* the Established Church for the whole Province, and effectually so wherever the field was not already in

possession of or could be gradually secured from, the
Church of Rome. Thus provision is made that a Protestant minister should be appointed to any parish in which
the majority of the inhabitants should solicit it, and that
the appointee should receive "all tithes payable in such
parish;" as also that all rents and profits of vacant benefices should be applied to the support of a Protestant
clergy.[1] Any introduction of, or correspondence with, foreign ecclesiastical jurisdictions, was strictly prohibited, no
Episcopal or Vicarial powers being allowed to be exercised by Roman Catholics except such as were indispens-
ably necessary to the free exercise of religion. And even
these were to be exercised only by Governmental license
"during our will and pleasure," in correspondence with
"the spirit and provisions of the Quebec Act;" such license
being made essential to all ordination or holding of
benefices. Benefices were to be conferred only on Canadians born, and the Governor and Council had power of
suspension in case of criminal offenses or of treason.

These provisions show in brief that the determination to
allow none but strictly *religious* privileges to the Church of
Rome in the Province, which had been insisted upon in the
Treaty of Paris, was not less strongly incorporated in the
Quebec Act and its accompaniments; and therefore, that
instead of that Act being the complete surrender to the
Church of Rome it appeared to Protestant contemporaries
and has often been represented since, that Church was
granted no new privileges beyond the *securing* to it of support *from its own adherents*. It was a change that affected
only these adherents, changing for them a voluntary into
a compulsory burden; a change the political results of
which will be elsewhere discussed.[2] Briefly it seems prac-

---

[1] It will be seen that both of these provisions discriminate in favor of the Church of
England against the Church of Rome; the latter not being allowed under any circumstances to take tithes from Protestants or to receive anything from vacant benefices,
which remained wholly at the disposal of the Protestant executive.

[2] See below, Chapter VI. A.

tically accurate to put the matter thus: The tithe was by the Act attached to all land as a state exaction, that portion of it paid by adherents of the Roman Catholic Church being applied to the support of the Roman Catholic clergy, the remainder, at the discretion of the Government, to the support of a Protestant clergy. But the ensuing instructions to the Governor, (apparently without authorization in the Act),[1] further divert to the benefit of the Protestant Church *all* the profits of vacant benefices, and *all* the tithes of parishes where the majority of the inhabitants were or should become Protestant.

What light do the debates on the Act throw on these arrangements? On the whole they lead to no conclusion opposed to those drawn from the examination of the earlier policy. But they do not increase our estimation of the care or the clear-sightedness of the framers of the bill. As first introduced the religious enactment embraced only the 5th Art. of the final Act, no mention thus being made of the Protestant Church, and no limitation being placed on the clause "subject to the King's supremacy." Considerable battle raged around the question as to whether or no the Roman Catholic Church was really established. Lord North maintained that no more was done than was required by the Treaty with regard to the free exercise of the faith, and that Papal authority in the Province would certainly not be permitted;[2] the Solicitor General stated that he could see no more in the bill than a toleration, with the clergy made dependent on the State rather than on the people.[3] In answer to the charge that nothing had been done for the Protestant Church Lord North brought into the committee the amendment in favor of that Church which forms Art. VI of the Act, characterizing this as an establishment. Some further debate took place as to the

---

[1] It would seem as if Wedderbourne the Solicitor General was responsible for at least the latter clause. See Cavendish, *Report*, p. 218.

[2] *Cavendish.* p. 10.

[3] *Ibid.*, p. 54.

royal supremacy[1] and at the next sitting the Government
brought in the amendment which forms Art. VII, and
which apparently goes far to nullify the "supremacy"
clause of Art. V. This however was undoubtedly considered as necessary to full toleration and as not diminishing
the hold of government over the Church,[2] and was agreed
to without a division.[3] It is probable that the conciliatory
and hazy attitude of the Government on this part of the
bill was due to a consciousness of the strong position of
the opposition from a popular standpoint. This aspect of
the situation was wittily referred to by Barré in a passing
reference[4] to the rumored impending dissolution of Parliament. "People may say" he remarked, "upon its dissolution as they did after the death of King Charles, that by
some papers found after its decease, there is great reason
to suspect that it died in the profession of the Roman
Catholic religion." A privy councillor retorted that the
parallel at least held good in the circumstance that the dying
Parliament, like the dying Catholic, was "attended by a
number of troublesome people, disposed to put many
troublesome questions."

The above examination will cause it to appear very
doubtful if the position of the Church was really much improved by the enactment, supposing the latter to be
rigidly applied. Apart from the effects with regard to
the attitude of the people referred to above, there were
new elements indeed of positive disadvantage. The

---

[1] In which occurred one of the most violent attacks on the "secret designs" of the bill
that we meet with. The assailant was Barré, who pointed to the indulgences given the
Roman Catholics as confirming his suspicions, and warned the Government that "if you
are about to raise a Popish army to serve in the colonies,—from this time all hope of
peace in America will be destroyed. . . . I smelt out this business from the beginning." Thurlow, who followed the irate Colonel, took no notice whatever of the
insinuation. *Cavendish*, p. 228.

[2] As shown above by the later instructions to the Governor.

[3] *Cavendish*, pp. 250-1. When the Bill went back to the Lords this last amendment
however received the especially hostile notice of Lord Chatham, who declared it offensive as an attack on the Great Charter or the Bill of Rights. Lord Lyttleton replied
forcibly that full toleration could not exist without the clause.

[4] *Ibid.*, p. 239.

clergy were now legally assured of support; but that support, we are frequently told,[1] had been, since the conquest, quite as assured by the voluntary contributions of a pious people, over the recalcitrant of whom might still be exercised, in the generally hazy state of the ecclesiastical powers, a great share of the many-sided authority so abundantly wielded under the old régime. Now however the Quebec Act had strictly and narrowly defined the real position and power of the Church; it had stripped it of nearly every vestige of its old temporal prestige, and of every right of pretension to any but a strictly religious status. Further, this Act had in all probability actually diminished the revenues of the Church; for it had deprived it entirely not only of all right to dues from benefices unfilled, (and the filling of vacancies was in the hands of a Government ordered to lose no opportunity of securing the advancement of the Protestant religion,[2] to whose benefit the receipts from such vacancies were to be appropriated), but also of all right to dues from any parish in which a majority of Protestants might become settled. It must therefore appear that the apprehensions of the Continental Congress as to the establishment of the Popish worship were unfounded; that the position and prospects of the Church through the new legislation, especially when viewed in that connection with the previous policy and the accompanying instructions which shows its intent and the spirit in which it would be administered, were not such as to give evidence of an exceptional liberality which could be explained only by sinister designs against the other colonies.[3]

---

[1] Expressly and frequently asserted in Quebec Act debate. These statements must be considered very cautiously it is true; but yet there seems no reason to believe that the Church had not been sufficiently supported through the period.

[2] For the intent of the Government on this point see *Cavendish*, p. 219.

[3] The above examination of the intentions and early measures of the British Government with regard to the Roman Catholic Church in Canada should be considered in connection with the later position assumed by that Church. This later position has no sufficient support in the Quebec Act, but has been acquired since, in direct opposition to some of its most important provisions, as a very important part of that long course of

Further light will be thrown on this matter by considering the parallel course of the Imperial authorities in the Island of Granada. This, with some neighboring islands, conquered in 1762, had been ceded to Great Britain in 1763 "in full right . . . with the same stipulations in favor of the inhabitants . . . inserted in the IV. Art. for those of Canada."[1] The Royal Proclamation of October, 1763, had named the Government of Granada as the fourth of the new Governments to which that Proclamation was intended to apply; and civil commissions were made out for it similar to those in the case of Quebec. But its later fortunes had diverged markedly from those of the latter Province, in that the Assembly promised by the proclamation and directed by the commissions was actually called together and constituted in 1765, at which time "none of the French Roman Catholic inhabitants claimed a right or even expressed a desire of becoming members, either of the Council or Assembly."[2] This body, evidently entirely English-speaking in composition, acting on the same assumptions as to the introduction of English law as the same party in Quebec,[3] proceeded at once to pass "an Act for regulating

revived French development of which the Quebec Act was the basis. In other words the assumptions from which that measure proceeded, and the position in which it placed the Province with reference to the new English element, were made by the Church the starting-point of a brilliant course of aggrandizement; that Church becoming therein identified with the revived national feelings and forces whose growth bore it in turn triumphantly forward. A full comment on this is of course impossible ; but it will be instructive to notice the words of the most authoritative of modern French Canadian constitutional writers. " La réserve de la suprématie spirituelle du roi d'Angleterre semble avoir été mise dans le statut de 1774 et les instructions royales qui suivirent pour la forme. Elle resta lettre morte. Les représentants du pouvoir comprirent que toute tentative pour l'imposer à la colonie resterait sans succés. L'acte constitutionnell [in 1791], n'en parle pas." (Lareau, *Hist. Droit Canadien*, II. 140). It was at the period of the war of 1812 that the preponderating position of the Church was finally and firmly secured. By that time it had again in reality taken possession of the once almost emancipated French Canadian, and could make its own terms with the government which seemed so dependent upon his loyalty.

[1] Treaty of Paris, Art. IX.

[2] Edwards, *History of the British Colonies in the West Indies*, I, p. 62 (Phila., 1806).

[3] See the almost contemporary action of the Grand Jury in Quebec, especially with regard to the protest against the privileges granted to Roman Catholics. The "old subject" element in the Provinces is identical in spirit and aims, with the difference

the elections of the general Assembly of Grenada and the
Grenadines, and for the better ascertaining of the electors
and elected," which required all members of the Assembly
to subscribe the Declaration against Transubstantiation,[1]
(no such restriction being placed on the franchise evidently). On the protest of the French inhabitants,[2] the
Board of Trade intervened against this and other Acts of
the same body, by a Report made March 4, 1768, in which
they condemn the above Act as tending "to give disgust
and dissatisfaction to your Majesty's new subjects," and
state that the test there required "is not (as we conceive)
extended to the colonies by any Act of Parliament, and is
a qualification the enforcing of which is entirely left to
your Majesty's discretion." This recommendation is evidently based on the opinion of Attorney-General Yorke, to
whom the case had been referred,[3] and as the result the
following year the Governor of the Island received royal
instructions to admit Roman Catholics into both Council
and Assembly as well as into the commission of the peace,
without the taking of the test oath against transubstantiation.[4] This, through the unbending attitude of the Protestant party, gave rise to such bitter political contests that

---

that in Grenada it proved more uncompromising and intolerant. This distinction is
doubtless due to the facts, (1) that representative Government had been put in force in
Grenada and thereby the direct control of the executive greatly lessened, (2) that in
Grenada the British were relatively a much stronger element. In 1771 the white population of the Island was about 1,600, (the slave population being nearly 40,000), of which,
considering the analogy of Quebec, a very considerable section must in 1775 have been
English speaking. (*Edwards*, I. 74).

[1] See an anonymous Pamphlet entitled "Observations upon the Report made by the
Board of Trade against the Grenada Laws." (W. Flexney, London, 1770). This is ably
written, from the standpoint of the British party in the Province, and contains the
Board of Trade Report almost in full apparently. I have not been able to find it elsewhere.

[2] *Cal. Home Office Papers*, 1766-9, No. 403.

[3] *Ibid.* It is uncertain from this entry whether the date assigned, (Jan. 12, 1767), is
that of the reference or that of the advice. The form of the statement of the case would
seem to show that the referrers were decidedly leaning to the opinions maintained in Mr.
Yorke's answer. The reference is endorsed, "your opinion on this case is much wanted."
See note above on this opinion, p. 435.

[4] Edwards, *West Indies*, I. 62. Southey, *West Indies*, II. 395.

representative government remained practically suspended
throughout the rest of the century. Yet the Crown persistently refused to revoke the objectionable instructions,
notwithstanding the strong constitutional arguments
brought against them.[1] As to the general treatment of the
Roman Catholic Church in Grenada, we find as in Canada,
that the treaty engagement of full toleration was liberally
carried out; and it would seem moreover that it was not
till 1783 that any step was taken to interfere with the established interests of the Church of Rome or to further
those of the Church of England, the act of that date still
providing "some allowance . . . for the benefit of the
tolerated Romish clergy."[2] It is thus evident that the liberal
attitude of the Imperial government with regard to the
Roman Catholic Church was not peculiar to Quebec, but
that it had been initiated earlier and extended further in
a non-continental Province,—one which could not be supposed as ever likely to be in a position to affect political
conditions among the older colonies,—than in that one
where the policy was regarded as inspired by deep hostility to those English-American political institutions with
which the Protestant church was supposed to be especially
identified.

The only conclusion we can draw therefore on this point,
is the one to which we have been led by our examination
of the earlier policy; namely that in the measures of 1774
with regard to the Roman Catholic Church in Canada the
home government was influenced mainly or solely by the

---

[1] For these see the pamphlet of 1770 referred to above. There would seem to be no doubt,
notwithstanding the opinion of Mr. Yorke, that the action of the Crown in this matter
was, constitutionally, altogether indefensible, and indirectly so declared by the Mansfield judgment of 1774. And it is well to note here what I shall probably refer to again;
that the consciousness of this may in all likelihood be discerned behind the refusal to
take similiar action, even through Parliament, in the case of Quebec before or at the
time of the Quebec Act. It is rather curious that no pertinent reference to the Granada
case is found in the Quebec Act debates; though that the action of the Government was
carefully observed in Quebec itself is to be seen from the petition of the English-
speaking party there in 1773.

[2] Edwards, *West Indies*, I, 72.

necessity of maintaining its treaty obligations, and by the
desire to protect a conquered and docile people from the
intolerance of a political party which it believed to be
identified in spirit and aim with the objectionable elements
in the older colonies.   That this latter was a subsidiary
and minor motive, and that, on the other hand, there was
no general spirit of religious liberality in action, is shown
by the fact that the general liberal attitude and the particular measures alike, were confined to those provinces
with regard to which treaty obligations existed.   The
" case" submitted to Yorke in 1767 begins with a distinct
statement that " in the Leeward Island, Barbadoes and
Jamaicas, they do not admit a person to be of the Council,
Assembly, or a justice of the Peace" except on subscription
to the declaration against transubstantiation; yet nothing
in the way of alleviation was done or hinted at in regard
to these cases.   I can therefore see no sufficient ground
for Lecky's reference to the Quebec Act as marking " an
epoch in the history of religious liberty."   It is true that
by that Act, as in the Grenada instructions, more was
given than was called for by the Treaty obligations; but
those additional privileges were far more political than
religious in their origin and intent.   In the case of Quebec,
full political privileges were denied expressly on religious
grounds.

As to the measure of toleration accorded throughout the
period to the Roman Catholic worship, there can be no
doubt that it was complete.   The faithful and even generous observance of the Treaty on this point is frequently
acknowledged in the native petitions and calls forth the
censure of the Protestant element. Further, whatever may
have been the suggestions of individuals, no encroachments were made on the property or privileges of the
Church during the period.   Masères expressly asserts that
the churches and chapels were left entirely in the hands
of the Catholics (town Protestants borrowing them on

Sunday for an hour), their priests in possession of the glebe lands and parsonages, and all old ceremonies and even processions continued without molestation.[1] And though the assertions of the same writer as to the pomp and importance gradually assumed by the Bishop and the use by him of excommunication, etc., seem[2] undoubtedly an exaggeration, it is evident that the confidence of the clergy and people in the good faith of the conquerors and in their liberal interpretation of the privileges promised, steadily increased. The genuineness of religious toleration is sufficiently proved by the fact that the only complaints in regard to the matter that we meet with are the protests of the noblesse against their own exclusion from public employments through the oaths required of all officials. The requirement of these subsisted unaltered through the whole period, they being given a prominent place in Carleton's instructions of 1768. But considerable latitude must have been allowed with regard to them in the case of minor officials, for we find several of the smaller offices in the possession of French Canadian Catholics. We have also seen above that Catholics were admitted throughout the period on juries and to the practise of the law,— an indulgence violently condemned by the English grand jurors of 1764, as contrary to the constitution. Outside of these few exceptions however, the religious oaths excluded the French Canadians from all civil and military employments, including the Council and the possible Assembly. The real importance of this exclusion is with regard to its influence (elsewhere discussed), upon the establishment of representative institutions.

---

[1] Carleton distinctly confirms this by saying that the Bishop had of his own will lessened the number. (Can. Arch., Q. 6, p. 54). Some interesting testimony on this matter will be found in the introductory memor to the *Life of John Carroll*, (Md. Hist. Soc., 1876, pp. 30–34). It is there asserted that Carroll's mission in 1776 to the Canadian clergy failed because of their entire satisfaction with the treatment of the Church by the British authorities; a conspicuous instance of the latter's attitude being afforded by the statement of the Canadian clergy that the "government actually furnished a military escort to accompany the grand procession on the festival of Corpus Christi."

[2] See letter of Carleton just referred to.

Though not of much interest to us now, a prominent part of the problem connected with the treatment of the Church of Rome in the Province had reference to the communities of regular clergy, and especially the Jesuits. These communities however were not an essential part of the religious organization, and had not the hold upon the people which would make their fate a matter of national concern.[1]   Nor was Great Britain's attitute toward the Jesuits different than that of contemporary powers, Catholic and Protestant.   Their great power under the old régime has been graphically described by Parkman; but it had been declining for some time previous to the conquest, and at this time the vigor and possessions of the Society were much inferior to those of the Sulpitians or Recollets at Montreal,—an order which was much more favourably looked upon by the government from the first.   The 34th Art. of the capitulation of Montreal would seem indeed (unless it is to be construed in connection with the preceding one), to promise the possession of their property to all the communities; but, though the Order was not suppressed till 1773, it is evident that the home Government from the first looked upon the possessions of the Jesuits as its own. At the beginning of the civil government Murray was directed to prevent further additions to it or to the other orders,—a direction which was repeated more positively later and strictly followed through the whole period. In the instructions to the Receiver-General in 1766 he is ordered, "whereas the lands of several religious societies in the said Province, particularly those of the Society of Jesus, are, or will become, part of His Majesty's revenue," to endeavour by peaceful agreement to get these into his present charge in order to prevent any losses thereto.   In 1767 Shelbourne writes[2] that the property of the Jesuits, (which has been represented as producing £4,000 per annum), "must become on their demise a very considerable

---

[1] See Murray's Report, 1762.
[2] To Carleton, November 14.   (Can. Arch., Q. 4, p. 298.)

revenue to the Province, in case His Majesty should be pleased to cede it for that purpose." To which Carleton replies [1] that the order he is convinced is in reality poor, their lands yielding very little and their total income being given by themselves as 22,658 livres, from which they have 19 persons to support. All the legal opinions of the time supported the view that the property held by the Jesuits had become legally vested in the Crown; and in the instructions to Carleton of 1775 it is declared that the Society is "suppressed and dissolved and no longer continued as a body corporate and politic, and all their rights, possessions and property shall be vested in us for such purposes as we may hereafter think fit to direct and appoint." But the remaining members of the order in Canada were to be supported out of this property for the rest of their lives, and it was not till the death of the last one in 1800, that the lands actually came into full use as part of the state revenue.

c. *Civil Law.* The third feature of the Quebec Act which requires our consideration is that one which is described in the Declaration of Independence as the "abolishing the free system of English law." It is expressed in that clause of Art. VIII which directs that "in all matters of controversy relative to property and civil rights resort shall be had to the laws [and customs] of Canada as the rule for the decision of the same , . . until they shall be varied or altered by any Ordinance that shall from time to time be passed in the said Province." This provision was modified by Art. IX, directing that all royal land grants, past or future, in free and common soccage, should be exempt from its operation, and by the provision of Art. X, that the execution and administration of wills should proceed, at discretion, according to either English or French law

A reference to the former discussion as to the adminis-

[1] Can. Arch., Q. 5-2, p. 590; Q. 6, p. 109.

tration of justice in the Province throughout the period[1] will be sufficient to show the inaccuracy of the word "abolishing" in regard to the effect of this clause; further on I shall examine the above modifying provisions in the light of later instructions and enactments, with a view to determining how far English law was now abandoned or excluded.   My object at present is to scrutinize this provision in the light of previous policy, with regard especially to that origin in and reference to the momentary relations with the other colonies so freely asserted by the revolutionary leaders.   It is evident that these leaders held the same views concerning the intent and legal effect of the Proclamation of 1763 and the accompanying documents as did the English-speaking party in Canada.   In the general treatment of the matter above there was quoted that remarkable statement from Hillsborough of the absence of any intention of the overturning of French law on the part of the framers of these documents.   This emphatic testimony is supported from other sources, and must be taken at least to show that, even at the beginning, there was no deliberate, intelligent purpose of suddenly substituting English for French law.   The acts of omission or commission from which such an inference was drawn may be much more reasonably explained as evidences only of ignorance, neglect, and indecision.   But this state of affairs cannot be held to have continued longer than the first two years of civil government (1764-6).   The administration in the province had soon become convinced that any violent assimilation of the laws and customs of Canada to those of the other provinces was radically unjust and impolitic, if not also impossible.   This conviction we find expressed in protests to the home government, and in increasingly liberal interpretations of the documents by which the Provincial officials felt themselves trammelled.   Murray writes March 3, 1765, to the Board of Trade concerning the great

---

1 See above, Chapter III, Section C.

difficulties which occur "in establishing the English laws in this colony," and proceeds to a general description of the state of the colony "where the English laws are to be established," in which he displays a marked sympathy with the French and a strong distaste for the task which he thinks has been laid upon him.[1] This representation does not seem to have been effectual in eliciting any definite or different explanation of the Proclamation of 1763, or any general statement of policy which would have let the provincial government feel at liberty to change its aims; but it was probably taken into account in the new instruction in the spring of 1766 by which the slight indulgences granted the Canadians in the Judiciary Ordinance of Sept., 1764, were approved and extended.   Doubtless also it had a strong influence in stirring up the home authorities to the beginning of the first serious investigation into the problems of civil government in Canada,— an investigation which as I have elsewhere shown came to a definite head in 1767, but which did not bear full fruit till 1774.   For the present, however, the provincial government seems to have been still left in the dark, and it is evident indeed that down to the new administration in September, 1766, there had been received in the Province no definite intimation of any radical change in the views and aims of the home executive.[2]

But that before this date such a change had to a large extent occurred we learn from other sources.   Or rather we should say that the home authorities had before this time, whether by the representations of the Colonial officials, by the introduction of new blood, or by other causes, been awakened out of the ignorance and neglect which had allowed the main documents relating to the Province to be couched in the most vague and misleading language, and the mi-

[1] Can. Arch., Q. 2, p. 377.

[2] See Can. Arch., Q. 3, p. 249.   Also the Commission of Chief-Justice Hey, Sept., 1766. (Masères, *Commissions*, pp. 124-8).   The failure to fully inform the Provincial Government is probably to be explained in part by the fact that it had been resolved to recall Murray.

nor documents to be made out mainly on the lines of
official routine established through dealings with the other
colonies. The letter from Murray which I have quoted
above is dated March 3, 1765, and on the September 2 following we find the first indication of attention to the subjects
there suggested in the shape of a Board of Trade report
to the Privy Council, signed by four names, the first being
that of the Lord Dartmouth who as Colonial Secretary engi-
neered the Quebec Bill nine years later. Unfortunately we
have not any full copy or satisfactory abstract of this, and
are obliged to depend for our somewhat vague information
as to its recommendations on a supplementary Report of
the Crown lawyers (Yorke and De Gray), of April 14, 1766.
This latter[1] states as one of the main sources of disorder in
the Province, the alarm taken at the construction put upon
the Proclamation of 1763, "as if it were the Royal intention, by the judges and officers in that country, at once to
abolish all the usages and customs of Canada with the
rough hand of a conqueror rather than in the true spirit of
a lawful sovereign,"[2] and refers to the Report of the Board
as ably applying itself to the remedying of this grievance.
Then, after discussing the subject of the constitution of the
courts, they proceed to consider the proposal in the
report, "that in all cases where rights or claims are
founded on events prior to the conquest of Canada, the
several courts shall be governed in their proceedings by
the French usages and customs which have hitherto prevailed in respect to such property;" approving of it as far as
it goes, but proceeding to maintain that in *all* matters affecting the possession or transfer of real property, "it would
be oppressive to disturb, without much and wise deliberation, and the aid of laws hereafter to be enacted in the
Province, the local customs and usages now prevailing

---

[1] Smith, *History of Canada*, II., 27-38 (Quebec, 1815).

[2] A reference which it will be noticed does not go so far as to deny that abolition in
some degree or manner was intended by the Proclamation, or that the terms of it would
not admit of such an interpretation.

there.[1]" This it will be seen, is a very decided advance on the Board of Trade's first plan, which, though of a very indefinite scope, manifestly had still lingering behind it the idea which lay at the base of the earlier documents, viz.: that Canada was eventually to become thoroughly an English province ruled by English law. That the advance was not unfavorably received by the Board may be inferred from a communication from it to the Privy Council June 24, 1766, transmitting a "draught of particular instructions for the Governor of His Majesty's Province of Quebec, for the establishing of courts of judicature in that Province," which they state to be drawn up according to their previous report, *supplemented by the suggestion of the Crown lawyers*.[2] These instructions do not immediately appear, nor do we find anything further as to the Quebec judicature or laws till June 20, 1767, when Shelbourne writes to Carleton that the improvement of the Quebec civil constitution "is under the most serious and deliberate consideration," especially of the Privy Council; the main problem being, "how far it is practicable and convenient to blend the English with the French laws in order to form such a system as shall at once be equitable and convenient both for His Majesty's old and new subjects, in order to the whole being confirmed and finally established by authority of Parliament."[3] The *deliberate* character at least of the course taken is fully established by the next document we meet. This is a Privy Council resolution of August 28, 1767, adopting the report of the Committee appointed to consider the draught of instructions submitted by the Board of Trade June 24th, 1766.[4] The report was to the effect that the doc-

---

[1] It will be remembered that in their use of the term "customs and usages" the English lawyers have no doubt in mind in great part what occupied a position corresponding to that of the common law of England. The word *now* should be noticed here also, in connection with the argument above as to the practical maintenance of the French law. This was in 1766, and certainly no disturbance of that law occurred later.

[2] Can. Arch., Q. 3, p. 171.

[3] Can. Arch., Q. 4, p. 129.

[4] Can. Arch., Q. 4, p. 327.

ument submitted by the Board of Trade was too general and too unsupported by specific proofs of grievances to be approved without further information; especially as no explicit complaint had of late been received from the Colonial officials; and that therefore full reports and recommendations as to the alleged judicial defects should first be obtained from these officials, "it being unwise and dangerous to the Province to frame or reform laws in the dark." In accordance with these proceedings Shelbourne in the following December directed Carleton to institute a specific investigation, and an Under-Secretary was at the same time commissioned to go out and join in the same.[1] And having thus decently shelved the subject, the Home Government, busy with other matters, awaited with great equanimity the appearance of the reports.

But before the news of this step had been received by Carleton, he had with characteristic energy and decision made up his mind as to the solution of the matter, and December 24, 1767 had sent to Shelburne an abridgement of the civil laws of Canada in use at the conquest, with recommendation that for the present they should be continued almost entire, to be altered by future Ordinances as might seem fit. As a beginning or model he submitted for approval a draft of a proposed Ordinance, for "continuing and confirming the laws and customs that prevailed in the Province in the time of the French Judicature, concerning the tenure, inheritance, and alienation of land."[2] The answer to this was the letter from Hillsborough of March 6, 1768, quoted from above,[3] which states that the proposed Ordinance has been approved by the King, though it is to be held in reserve pending a general settlement, and which therefore shows conclusively that more than six years before the Quebec Act, the Home Government, uninfluenced,

---

[1] For his instructions, see Can. Arch., Q 4, p. 331.
[2] Can. Arch., Q. 5-1, pp. 316–343.
[3] P. 387.

so far as we can discover, by anything except the repre·
sentations made as to the state of the Province, had resolved to go at least as far as that Act went. But there
were still the reports ordered to wait for,[1] and meanwhile
the stationary condition of affairs[2] is shown in the Instructions of Carleton, August, 1768, which, though going into
minute directions as to forms of legislation, make no reference to the all-important question as to how far that
legislation should be based on English or on French codes.

The investigation ordered was entered upon vigorously
by the provincial Government. It is significant to note the
anticipation of that government as to the result, (even before the receipt of the letter of March 6th from Hillsborough), as shown by a Minute of Council of March 28, 1768,
to the effect that a committee was appointed on that day to
take from the old French laws such extracts "as may appear to them necessary to make a part of the future regulations of the Province."[3] The reports were transmitted
in September, 1769, the main one embodying Carleton's views,
and minor ones giving the dissenting opinions of the Chief-
Justice and Attorney General. Though the original documents are not to be found, we have other means[4] of arriving
pretty accurately at the contents. Carleton recommended
that the whole body of the French civil law as it had existed
before the Conquest should be restored, to be changed explicitly by fresh Ordinances as might seem necessary; consequently that no English civil law should be in force except such as might later be expressly introduced in this manner. Masères and Hey on the contrary thought that the Cana-

---

[1] Thought the more necessary probably in order to be able to make a good case for a
measure which was likely to be vigorously opposed.

[2] Possibly, however, only the old neglect.

[3] Can. Arch., Q. 5-1, p. 435.

[4] Evidence before Commons in the Quebec Act Debate; Correspondence of Carleton;
writings of Masères. There is very strong reason for believing that the paper in the
Lower Canada Jurist, Vol. I., attributed to Chief-Justice Hey, is his report on this occasion. His views are, however, very clearly stated by him in the evidence referred to
above. See especially *Cavendish*, pp 156-7.

dians would be contented and the best interests of the Province secured, by the continuance or adoption of the English law and procedure as a general basis, and the special revival of the French law in regard to landed property and inheritance; the general aim being the gradual assimilation of the Province to the other English possessions in America.[1]

The home authorities did not allow themselves to be hurried. The next step, almost two years later, is an Order-in-Council of June 14, 1771, transmitting the Provincial reports and all other papers concerning Quebec to the crown lawyers,[2] and ordering them to return separate and detailed reports as a basis for legislation. Meanwhile, however, as if to palliate the delay of the full settlement, there was issued (July 2d, 1771), a new instruction in regard to land grants, by which a very noteworthy step was taken toward the return to French law. The Proclamation of October, 1763, had conferred on the governor and Council "full power and authority" to grant lands, "upon such terms . . as have been appointed and settled in other colonies," and in accordance with such special instructions as might thereafter be given. These special instructions were issued to Murray when appointed Governor in 1764, and directed the grants to be made in free and common soccage, according to English forms, to be held by an oath of fealty and a quit-rent of two shillings sterling per 100 acres; the grants to be in restricted quantities and on the usual conditions of cultivation, and a special caution being added against following the example of some of the other colonies in making excessive allotments to individuals unable to fully cultivate. Under these regulations the amount actually granted was very small, not exceeding 14,000 acres

---

[1] Special attention is directed to these recommendations by Masères and Hey, which will be found in detail in their evidence in 1774 before the Commons. They represent, in my opinion, by far the better settlement.

[2] Attorney-General Thurlow, Solicitor-General Wedderbourne, and Advocate-General Marriott.

in all, according to the statements of Carleton and Masères;[1] which is apparently accounted for by the fact that the terms were deemed severe and unprofitable, especially in comparison with those of the French grants.[2] The Minutes of Council show that the lands which had been awarded on much easier terms to discharged soldiers, had been but little availed of.[3] The expense of the necessary registration was a considerable obstacle, and in the later years the government seems to have delayed completing grants from the anticipation of new instructions.[4] Such a change had been urged by Carleton two years before, in a communication in which he had described the old French form of grant, and had strongly presented the advisability of reverting to it thereafter except at the eastern extremity of the province, where he considered it advisable that old subjects only should be encouraged to settle.[5] His reasons for this advice are not very clearly given, and would seem to have been largely military (in the advantage of renewing in some way the obligation of military service as a condition of tenure), but we are safe in concluding that among them was a conviction that the English forms were not conducive to the settlement of the country. The action is on a line with the constant tendency shown by Carleton to revert wherever possible, to the French forms. Though the proposal was looked upon favorably by the home government,[6] no effective action was taken thereon till July 2d, 1771, on which date the "additional instruction" spoken of above was issued, by which it was ordered that for the future lands should be granted "in fief or seigneurie, as hath been practiced heretofore, antecedent to the Conquest," according to the old French forms, but with the omission of the judi-

---

[1] The former in official correspondence April 15, 1767 (Can. Arch., Q. 4, p. 152); the latter in *Quebec Commissions*, p. 182.

[2] See Cramahé to Hillsborough, Can. Arch., Q. 8, p. 142.

[3] Ibid., Q. 4, p. 230; Q. 8, p. 116.

[4] Minutes of Council, April 18, 1770. Ibid., Q. 7, p. 129.

[5] To Shelbourne, April 12, 1768. Can. Arch., Q. 5–2, p. 477.

[6] Hillsborough to Carleton July 9, 1768. Can. Arch., Q. 5–2, p. 602.

cial powers thereto anciently belonging. The ground of the change is stated in the preamble to be representations that the former terms "have been found to be inconvenient and inadequate; and that it is more for our advantage and for the benefit of our subjects . . . if the ancient mode of granting lands . . . was to be adopted." This radical and deliberate change of policy bears very striking testimony to the genuineness of the decision as to the full restoration in the Province of French law and custom. In this light it was regarded in Quebec, Cramahé informing Hillsborough [1] that the French Canadians looked on the change "as a fresh proof of his Majesty's gracious intention to continue to them, so far as it can be done, their ancient usages and customs." [2]

But though such a decisive step had been taken, nothing further was attempted until the reception of the final reports from the Crown lawyers. These need not be considered in detail, their main provisions, following the rec-

---

[1] May 5, 1772. Can. Arch., Q. 8, p. 142.

[2] He continues: "His old subjects are no less pleased with this method of granting lands, for upon the terms at first required, they could never have settled them to advantage." The effects of the change on land occupation were certainly immediate and striking. Before the end of 1771 we find before the Quebec Council petitions for land under the new forms amounting to an aggregate of 60,000 acres (Can. Arch., Q. 8, p. 116), and in little more than a year from the publication of the new instructions no less than 56 petitions had been received for immense tracts (averaging probably not less than 100 square miles in extent), most of which are expressly asked for *en seigneurie* and all of which are undoubtedly so meant. Most of the petitioners, it is to be noted, were of the English speaking element. Apart from the questions of the intrinsic merit and suitability of the English and French tenures it will be seen that two reasons must have existed for this preference of the English investors for the French form. The first was the fact that the aristocracy of the Province was founded on the feudal possession of the land; the second, that it must have been at this time very clear that, whatever should be the ultimate form of government, the French laws and customs were bound to prevail in regard to landed property. It will be seen on the other hand, that this great success of the first step in the return to French institutions must have largely tended to confirm the intentions of the Home Government in that regard. Though it is to be noted that the Quebec Act of 1774 seems to attempt to regain in this matter some of the ground lost in 1771; for while the instruction of the latter date make no provision whatever for the further use of the English form of grant or tenure, the IXth Art. of the Act is especially inserted for the legalization and protection of "free and common soccage." In connection with the later history of this matter of feudal tenures see Houston, *Can. Const. Doc.*, p. 109, note 12.

ommendations of Carleton, being embodied in the Quebec Act. They were elaborate and able documents, marked by an enlightened spirit of justice and generosity toward the French Canadians. That the Act of which they were the basis was not the best settlement of the question is to be attributed rather to the misleading prejudices and short-sightedness of those to whom the Crown lawyers looked for information than to the integrity and ability of the latter.

Having now reached the Act itself, it is necessary to note briefly what light is thrown upon this part of our enquiry by the circumstances attending its passage. We find on the general point so little discussion that it is evident the opposition felt that the fundamental position of the government was too strong to be assailed. But later, after letting the provisions through the Committee with only an incoherent protest, their energies revived on the favorable subject of trial by jury, and an amendment providing for optional juries formed the rallying point for the most vigorous effort of the whole debate. The position of the government seems on the whole even here the stronger and more consistent; though it is difficult to escape a suspicion, (not upheld however by any specific evidence), that it was animated somewhat by the remembrance of the obstacle the jury system had proved to government in the revenue cases of 1766 and 1769.[1] It was contended that the system was incompatible with the French law and custom now granted;[2] that the bill as only fixing the laws and customs, did not exclude juries, the whole constitution of the judiciary and the procedure being reserved to His Majesty;[3] and that the

---

[1] See above, p. 396, note 3, for the misconception on this point.

[2] To which the fiery and significant retort was made: "In God's name, what can be the views and what the operations of that bill with which juries are incompatible? What can be the purposes and designs to be answered by this bill? I have no pleasure in thinking of them; I have too much decency to name them." (*Cavendish*, p. 26.)

[3] In which connection it is very noteworthy that the words *as the rule* in the clause, 'in all matter of controversy relative to property and civil rights, resort shall be had to the laws of Canada, as the rule for the decision of the same," are asserted by one speaker, (*Cavendish*, p. 282. The statement or the inference from it, was not contro-

present arrangement was intended only as a basis or starting point for future Provincial legislation, it being unwise
for the Imperial legislature to attempt such particular
changes as could properly be made only as they were
called for and by those upon the spot.   This is evidently
a strong position, and if at all upheld by later actions
should go far toward freeing the government even from
the suspicion I have referred to above.[1]

That the profession of an intent of bringing in English
law through Provincial enactment was sincere was shown
by the action supplementary to the Quebec Act.   In the
Instructions to Carleton in 1775 for his guidance, especially

---

verted), not to have formed a part of the original bill, but to have been inserted after
its presentation to the Commons. This change was characterized by him as a "concession," which, as not binding procedure to the French forms, left the way open for the
later institution of the jury system. As a curious and somewhat perplexing offset to
this however, it is to be noticed that the original bill is asserted by another opposition
speaker, (*Cavendish*, p. 19), not to have said whether the laws of Canada or of England
were to be resorted to. This must mean that the clause in question had been entirely
omitted, which would be incompatible with the above statement as to the absence of a
part of it. In the lack of the original draft no light can be thrown on this. It will be
remembered that the clause in question must have been considered by many what it can
reasonably be contended to be, in large degree superfluous, so far as the establishment
of the French civil law was concerned. That is, the revoking in the previous clause of
all the acts of government by which the English law was contended to have been introduced, would alone, under the operation of the Capitulation and Treaty, leave the field
in most respects fully in possession of the former code.

[1] It seems worth while to note here more fully a rather remarkable incident in the history of the jury system in the Province during the previous period. March 9, 1765, a
Provincial ordinance was passed directing that for the future all juries should be summoned from the Province at large without regard to the vicinage of the action or
crime. This remarkable abrogation of one of the fundamental principles of the system
seems to have been occasioned by temporary circumstances; and that it was sanctioned
by the Home administration is shown by the fact that in the following November a
Royal order was issued providing for an exception to it. No later direct reference to it
can be found; but that some instruction must have been sent in connection with the ex-
cepting Ordinance is shown by the appearance on Jan. 27, 1766, of a Provincial ordinance
repealing that of 1765. This is stated in the Council Minutes to be in accordance with
the precedent of the exception taken. The repealing ordinance takes occasion to speak
expressly of the general advisability of the facts being ascertained "by the oathes of
good and lawful men of the neighborhood of the places where they had happened,
according to the ancient and wholesome rules of the common law of England." The
dates here should be compared with those of the English administrations and the whole
matter considered in connection with the latter more flagrant overriding of the same
principle in the case of the other colonies.

in future legislation, he is enjoined by the 12th Art. that while, in accordance with the spirit and intention of the Quebec Act, the Canadians "should have the benefit and use of their own laws, usages, and customs, in all controversies respecting titles of land and the tenure, descent, alienation, incumbrance, and settlement of real estate, and the distribution of the personal property of persons dying intestate," on the other hand the council should consider, in adopting regulations to this end, "whether the laws of England may not be, if not altogether, at least in part, the rule for the decision in all cases of personal actions grounded upon debts, promises, contracts, and agreements, whether of a mercantile or other nature, and also of wrongs proper to be compensated in damages," especially where old subjects are concerned. Viewed in connection with the 13th Art., which recommends the taking of measures to secure to the Province the benefits of the principle of Habeas Corpus,[1] this shows that the administration cannot be justly accused of being willing that the Government should revert entirely to the old principles and forms. It is apparently intended rather that only so much of the old law should be retained as could in any way be contended for as essentially bound up with the securing to the French Canadians that full enjoyment of their property which had been promised in the Capitulation and Treaty. That this limit was not adhered to was due in part to a necessary development of what was now done; in part to the confirming and extending of the main policy of the Quebec Act during and after the revolutionary war.

d. *Legislative Assembly.* We have now reached the last

---

[1] The address of Congress to the people of England, Sept. 5, 1775, especially complains that the English in Canada were "deprived of trial by jury and when imprisoned cannot claim the benefit of the habeas corpus act." The recommendation made by the Home government as to the Habeas Corpus was acted on in 1785 by a Provincial Ordinance modelled on the Act of Charles II. The jury system had been extended to civil cases to some extent by an ordinance of the previous year (Smith, *Hist. Can.* II, 169, 176). The delay in the case of both was owing probably in main part to the intervening American war.

important feature of the Quebec Act,—that withholding of a representative legislative assembly which was evidently considered by the revolutionary fathers as the main feature of the "arbitrary government" they viewed with such apprehension. That such an apprehension on this ground was most natural and reasonable cannot be denied; on the other hand it will appear from our examination that the skirts of the legislators can on this point be even more effectually cleared of guilt than on the others.   I have already shown that the fundamental proclamation of 1763 and the later documents by which the civil government was established, promise and presuppose the early institution of a representative body, no notice being taken of the religious difficulties that lay in the way.   The whole of the matter at this early stage is one of the strongest proofs of the unconsidered and hasty character of the first steps taken with regard to Canada.   In considering the latter phases of it our chief interest lies in the gradual development of English governmental opinion on the point, and in the tracing of the causes which led to the determination of 1774 against representative institutions.

The matter seems to have been first seriously taken up by the Board of Trade in that report of September 2, 1765,[1] which I have noticed above as recommending a faint degree of return to the old laws.   In regard to an assembly we find in it, as is to be expected,[2] a decidedly favorable tone. It states that " the situation and circumstances of the colony have not hitherto been thought to admit of a House of Representatives." but that the only objection they can find is the difficulty in regard to admitting Catholics as members; a difficulty however which they think might be obviated by such a division of electoral districts as would enable the Catholic electors to choose resident Protestants, there be-

---

[1] Can. Arch., B. 8, p. 12.

[2] For it is to be remarked that the more the English system was abandoned and the French reverted to, the more remote and unfitted would the idea of an Assembly become m

ing no law denying the franchise to Roman Catholics.[1] Such a settlement they think would "give great satisfaction to your Majesty's new, as well as natural-born subjects; every object of civil government which the limited powers of the governor and Council cannot extend would be fully answered, and above all that essential and important one of establishing by an equal taxation a permanent and constitutional revenue." This does not seem to us a very liberal provision, but probably in the then state of the laws and of public feeling in England and the colonies, it was thought the extreme limit that could be granted. The statement as to revenue brings to our notice a strong and constant ground for the establishment of representative institutions,— the relief that could thereby be most easily afforded to the English taxpayer.

The general course of events subsequent to this report I have considered elsewhere, and it would seem that the recommendations concerning an Assembly were regarded as of subordinate interest, no reference whatever being apparently made to them. The language of the later instructions to Murray and Carleton, and the narrow legislative power to which the Government and Council continued to be restricted, show however that the idea of settled Government without an Assembly had not yet seriously entered the mind of the home authorities. Indeed the careful directions concerning legislation with an Assembly at a time when it was recognized that the future constitution of the Province must be settled soon by Parliamentary enactment would indicate that the calling of an Assembly before that settlement was considered not improbable. The instructions issued to Carleton in 1768 give minute directions for the framing of legislation "when an Assembly shall be summoned and met in such manner as you in your discretion shall think most proper, or as shall be hereafter di-

---

[1] Note that this is the idea finally adopted by the British party in Canada.

rected and appointed." They go on however to make more general provisions of such a character as to show that, while there was apparently no thought of withholding an Assembly, the relations with such bodies in the other colonies had inspired the determination to take special precautions in regard to new establishments. A significant article directs that in all enactments, "for the levying of money or imposing fines, forfeiture or penalties, express mention be made that the same is granted or reserved to us . . . for the public uses of the Province and the support of the Government thereof, . . . and that a clause be inserted declaring that the money arising by the operation of the said law or Ordinances shall be accounted for unto us in this Kingdom and to our Commission of the Treasury or our High Treasurer for the time being, and audited by our Auditor General."[4] The 11th Article puts restrictions on legislation of an unusual nature or affecting British commerce, such laws not to go into operation till approved by the Home Government. The 12th, stated in the preamble to be occasioned by the practices of some of the other Provinces, makes provision against the evading, through temporary laws, etc., of the control of the home authorities. The 14th is concerned with the prevention of the assumption of too great privileges by members of the Assembly or Council, (said also to be occasioned by experiences with the other Provinces), and the prevention of self-adjournment of the Assembly, together with a very noticeable clause granting the Council "the like power of framing money bills as the Assembly."

The special import of these provisions will be noticed later. Following up the main inquiry, we find in the Canada Report of Solicitor-General Wedderburn, December, 1772, the next important reference to the subject, and the one which

---

[4] It is to be noted that a clause of the same tenor as this though not in quite the same language is in the instructions of 1765 to Sir H. Moore, of New York (Colonial Office Records, London).

sets forth most clearly the main ostensible grounds on which the Assembly was finally withheld. His conclusion is that it is at present wholly inexpedient to establish the institution in Quebec; for, although admitting that legislation could be properly attended to only by such a body, he considers the difficulties in its formation too great to be overcome. Into such an Assembly the Roman Catholic French Canadians, in the capacity both of electors and of members, must or must not be admitted. To admit them as members would be a dangerous and unconstitutional experiment, and would lead to inexhaustible dissensions between them and the old subjects;[1] while to exclude them would cause a feeling of inequality, and a fear of being exposed to injustice. On the other hand the question of the franchise was involved in equal difficulties; for the denial of it to the Canadians would leave the Assembly no more representative than a Council, while to extend it to them indiscriminately as landholders would be offensive to the upper class among them, and not beneficial to the lower.[2]

---

[1] It will of course at once occur to the reader that in Granada, seven years before, the experiment had been tried. But, as is shown above (pp. 444-7), the results had not been of a kind to encourage a repetition of it; for government there had been from that date involved thereby in the greatest difficulties, through just such "inexhaustible dissensions" as Wedderbourne must now have had in mind. The conditions further of Canada and Grenada were very different, the difference being of a kind to cause even greater difficulties to be apprehended in the former. The temper of the English party had already been shown. They were however but a very small factor as compared with the mass of the French Canadians; and the British government had therefore to bear in mind not only inevitable dissensions between the two races, but also the imperilling of the safety of the new Province with a discontented English element and a popular House almost entirely French. In Grenada there could be very little danger, and if trouble did arise it would be confined to the Island and could scarcely have dangerous connec tions outside. The use of the word *unconstitutional* by Wedderbourne shows also perhaps that he had in mind the vigorous attacks made, (it is true on somewhat different grounds), on the Administration for the step in Grenada.

[2] In this latter sentence we see the weak point of an otherwise cogent statement. But it is to be remembered that Wedderbourne was preparing his report on information furnished by Carleton, one of the main features of whose policy was to represent the great importance of attaching the noblesse and maintaining them in their imagined influence over the lower classes. The idea as to the privilege of the suffrage not benefiting the people was based on representations as to the ignorance and political incapacity of the latter, and the probability that under representative institutions they would only fall into the hands of demagogues or of English creditors.

On these grounds Wedderbourne advises that instead of an assembly, the legislative power should be granted with important restraints to a Council considerably enlarged and made more independent of the Governor.

For these opinions the provincial officials were no doubt mainly responsible. Carleton was strongly set against an Assembly, as not adapted to the province and as not desired by the Canadians. Masères also seems to consider a very liberally framed Council the best plan, (a purely Protestant Assembly being manifestly impossible), for some years to come. The latter's advice on this matter to the British party in Quebec is of much interest. Just before the Quebec Bill was introduced he writes to the representatives of the party, (whose agent he was), that he is not yet sure of the sentiments of the Ministry on the point, but conjectures that they are of opinion that the province is not yet ripe for an assembly and are therefore inclined to establish instead a nominated Council with larger powers; that his own opinion is that such a Council would be better for the Province for several years to come than an assembly into which "Papists" should be admitted; that the only objection he sees to a Protestant Assembly is the danger of offending the more numerous Catholics; but that if this difficulty be got over by some compromise, (as by granting the suffrage to the French Canadians), he would be very glad to see an assembly granted, "as indeed I suppose it would in that case be." He proceeds then to advise, as in his opinion likely to be more helpful in the procuring of their object than any other step, that the petitioners should declare that they "conceive the British Parliament to have a complete legislative authority over the Province of Quebec, and that such authority will continue after the establishment of an assembly," and that they are willing "that every member of such future assemblies should be required to recognize the said supreme authority in every article whatsoever both of legislation and taxation in the plainest and strongest terms before he is permitted to take his seat." Such a declaration he thinks, "would greatly tend to remove the prejudices now subsisting in the minds of many people in England against the erection of new houses of assembly in America, arising from the conduct of the assembly in Boston and in other of the American Provinces in totally denying the supreme authority of Parliament."[1] Masères it will be remembered was at this time on the English Exchequer Bench, and probably in a position to know as accurately as any outsider could the attitude of the authorities on a subject in which he was so much interested. His was by all odds the keenest intellect prominently concerned in Canadian affairs at the time, and though occasionally his writings show signs of haste and want of balance as well as some intolerance and narrow legal habits of thought, a close study of the period will I think lead to the conclusion that he possessed a more accurate knowledge of Canadian conditions, and clearer and more far-sighted views as to the policy that should be adopted in regard to them, than any of his contemporaries. Though, as we see above, upholding the supreme authority of the British Parliament, (his legal training made any other view almost impossible to him), he belonged in many respects to the more liberal and advanced school of thinkers on colonial Government.[2] Certainly his writings prove that he would have been one of the last to have countenanced any plan of aiming to restrict colonial liberty through the instrumentality of a despotism in Canada. The advice here given to the Quebec leaders shows indeed that he was of opinion that the Ministry was strongly prejudiced against Colonial legislatures. That this was correct there can be no thought of denying. But it is further shown here, as by many other references, that the Ministry was also of opinion that the unquestioned suprem-

---

[1] *Proceedings*, etc., pp. 35-8.

[2] See his *Freeholder*.

acy of the British Parliament could be secured in the Act of settlement. In this advice Masères, as the counsel of a political party, is merely recommending the further reassuring of the Ministry by docile professions. In none of his writings, even in those of much later date than the Quebec Act, is there any reference to the possibility of that Act, (of which he was one of the most determined opponents), being dictated as regarded the withholding of an assembly, by the motives which had been attributed by the colonists. On the very eve of the new settlement we find him of the opinion that the only serious objections to such a body in the mind of the authorities, were on the one hand the danger of allowing full weight to the overwhelming French Catholic majority, and on the other the difficulty of making a Protestant Assembly palatable to that majority.

Our most important source of information on this point, however, outside the Ministerial correspondence, is the debate on the Act itself in the House of Commons. And the main impression which its study leaves with us is that the opposition was very careful *not* to press for an immediate Assembly, and that the Ministry was very careful to base the withholding of it purely on the ground, (1) that it would be unjust to exclude the French Roman Catholics from it, and (2) that it would be unsafe to admit them. Att. Gen. Thurlow asserted without contradiction that no one had claimed that it was at present fit to give an Assembly to Canada; and later in the debate, Fox admitted that he would not explicitly assert that it was expedient at that time to call one. Lord Beauchamp, a Government supporter, affirmed that no member had advocated the appointment of a Council because of the conduct of the popular assemblies in America, or had ventured to say that it would always be inexpedient to give the latter. Almost the last word on the subject was the following from Lord North: " That it is desirable to give the Canadians a con-

stitution in every respect like the constitution of Great
Britain, I will not say; but I earnestly hope that they will,
in the course of time, enjoy as much of our laws and as
much of our constitution, as may be beneficial for that
country, and safe for this. But that time is not yet come."
It is evident on the whole that the opposition could not offer a
solution of the difficulties that seemed to lie in the road, and
that the Government, whatever secret motives may have
influenced it, was quite able to defend its position by pointing to these difficulties. The hints of the opposition as to
the Bill giving evidence of secret hostility to liberty, were
rather in reference to other features than to the more
complicated and less assailable point of the withholding
of representative institutions.

It would be more correct to say that the Quebec Act *deferred*
than that it *denied* an Assembly; for the wording used is,
"whereas it is at present inexpedient;" as Lord North stated
it, " That this establishment is not to be considered perpetual, is admitted in the bill itself." There was not at any time
any serious question of the permanent refusal to the Canadians of representative institutions; and the references to the
period of tutelage and probation that should elapse before the
granting of such institutions seem to presuppose a short one.
It is indeed impossible to conceive that any administration
could have expected that the country would long be satis-
factorily governed by a Legislature which had no money
powers whatever, beyond levying and applying of municipal rates, and which was expressly prohibited from making effective, even for a day, any enactment which imposed
a greater punishment than fine or imprisonment for three
months. In fact the action taken in this particular must
simply be looked upon as the shelving of a difficult subject,— as a continuation of the policy of delay and compromise which had marked all previous dealings with Canada. The Government had the positive assurances of
Carleton, to whom it looked mainly for information, that

the Canadians did not want an Assembly, would indeed prefer not to have it; and the small English party was thought as yet to have a weight in the country too small to require much attention. The period during which an Assembly was to be delayed was of course not clear to the mind of anyone; but it is possible that the Ministry wished first to have settled the difficulties to which the Assemblies in the other provinces were giving rise. In so far then it is probably true that the framers of the new constitution were affected as to this point by the general situation of things in America; but there seems to be no ground for going any further. The Ministry was encouraged to delay representative institutions because it had assured itself that the great body of the French Canadian people had no desire for these institutions, and could be safely and perhaps beneficially left without them for a few years to come; but there is no reason to suppose that this delay was intended as the first step of a system of oppression which was ultimately to extend to the other colonies through the instrumentality of the docile slaves that had been secured in Canada. It is undeniable indeed that as early as 1768 the Imperial authorities, while of the opinion that an Assembly should be constituted as soon as possible, had resolved to take stringent measures for the restricting of the money power of the same, and the keeping of it in unquestioned subordination to the British Parliament. But this is a phase of the subject which does not concern us here. It was simply the application to Canada, in a strictly constitutional way, of the general claims which gave rise to the American Revolution. I am not interested here to enquire whether the Imperial government went as far in Canada as it attempted to go elsewhere; the question is rather, did it go farther? Did it attempt to take advantage of the political ignorance and docility of a long enslaved people for the purpose of upholding, in direct opposition to all the free principles of English government, a set of conditions which might continue to be or might become, a menace and check to the other colonies?

With regard then to the origins of the Quebec Act it need only be added that the above examination must at least show that if that Act were in any important degree due to the causes assigned it by colonial suspicion, the government which orignated and pushed it through must have taken unusual pains to keep its reasons and its purposes hidden. But why should such concealment have been thought necessary with regard to the whole or any part of the enactment? This same government had just carried through three Bills[3] of the most stringent and repressive nature, striking, to the popular view, heavier blows at American freedom and growth than anything contained in the Quebec Act, and had found itself in these measures backed by a consistent and overwhelming support, both in Parliament and throughout the country. Why should it now have scrupled to say that it was also taking measures of precaution in Canada? The government of that day was not an enlightened one, and would have been content to secure popular support, without looking to the future; it might well have concluded, for example, that the preserving of the vast regions of the West from the encroachments of the rebellious colonies would prove a popular measure. Rather than concealed indeed, we might expect to see this motive, if occupying a prominent position in the Government mind, put forward with prominence. We might expect to find it used to explain and defend the more doubtful parts of the measure, and especially that apparent establishing of the Roman Catholic Church which so aroused the horror of the Continental Congress, and which was almost as unpopular in England as in America. On the other hand, if the *secret* design hinted at by the opposition and believed in by the colonists

---

[3] With regard to Massachusetts.

had existed, it is not to be supposed that it would have been alluded to by such able and prominent members of the party as Wedderbourne and Lyttleton. As to the more decided utterances in the Debates for the repeal of the act in 1775, both of the Opposition and of the Government,[1] they must be regarded as after thoughts. The Opposition was undoubedly inspired by the objections with which the Act had been met in America, and the Government was alarmed and exasperated by the increasing menaces there to Imperial control, and ready to use or threaten to use, any instrument that lay ready to its hand.

C. *Application of the Act.*

In connection with the Act should be noted the instructions that accompanied the new commissions under it, and some later official developments. The new instructions with regard to legislation had now a more definite basis in the elimination of the confusing element of a possible Assembly, and we find the following changes: (1) A restriction of the legislative period to the months of January, February, March and April; apparently for reasons connected with the climate and the communication with Eng land. (2) Suspension till royal approval of some classes of ordinances, with [a prohibition of any commercial ordinance by which the inhabitants should be put on a more advantageous footing than any other of His Majesty's subjects, "either of this Kingdom or of the Plantations."[2] Prohibition of all religious legislation.

A clause with regard to the procedure of the new Council[3] had consequences of some interest which lead us a little beyond our period. It was the first part of the 2nd Article of the above instructions, and read: "It is further our will

---

[1] Lord North here openly avowed his intention of arming the Canadians if necessary, for the purpose of reducing the refractory colonies to obedience.—*Parliamentary History*, Vol. 18, p. 680.

[2] This is perhaps worth noticing with regard to the question of the hostility of the measure toward the other colonies.

[3] This consisted of 23 members, 8 being French Canadians.

and pleasure that any five of the said Council shall constitute a board of Council for transacting all business in which
their advice and consent may be requisite, Acts of Legislation only excepted, (in which case you are not to act
without a majority of the whole)." No clear statement is made anywhere as to a quorum.[1] This very indefinite provision Carleton promptly availed himself of as
might have been expected from his action in 1766,[2] and June
27, 1778, he sends home the Minutes of the Board of Council[3]
for the preceding eight months. These minutes do not appear in the State Papers, but we have the similar ones from
Haldimand, October 24, 1779, for the period from November 1,
1778, to September 25, 1779.[4] An examination of these
latter shows that this "Board of Council" consisted of five
members beside the Governor and Lieut.-Governor, all of
whom were also members of the Legislative Council; that
it refers to itself as a "Board," and holds meetings in 1778
on the 7th, 9th, and 30th November, and in 1779 on the 10th,
11th, and 17th May, the 7th and 12th June, and the 15th
July,[5] the Governor being present at all but two meetings.

We have here evidently a *quasi* Cabinet, without Parliamentary responsibility, invested apparently with all
the executive powers of the Council though meeting so
infrequently as to be but a slight check on the Governor.[6]
But though the wording of the instruction under which it

---

[1] In the debate in the Commons the Quebec Bill had been attacked for the absence of
any such provision; which was replied to by Lord North by an assertion (*Cavendish*, p.
241), that it was intended, as shown by the words "the major part," that the quorum
should be a majority of the smallest number (17) of which the Council should consist.
But this clause had reference only to legislation, and the answer looks like an astute
evasion of the point at issue.

[2] In regard to his then treatment of the Council, see p. 338, note 2.

[3] Referred to by the Council Clerk as the "Privy Council."

[4] These are referred to simply as the "Minutes of His Majesty's Council," the "Journal
of the Legislative Council" for the corresponding session being sent at the same time.

[5] The corresponding "Journal of the Legislative Council" is for the session 11th-16th
January, 1779.

[6] Who had the choice of the members. It looks as if, under Haldimand at least, this
"Board" was used only as a pretense of complying with the constitutional requirements
as to the "advice and consent" of the Council.

was instituted would seem fully to admit of this interpretation, (indeed it is difficult to avoid the conclusion that it
was so intended, and had been procured to that end by the direct efforts of Carleton), it did not go unquestioned in the Colony. Early in the spring of 1778 we find Chief Justice Livius,
(a somewhat hot-headed personage, who persisted in raising other disagreeable questions and was a couple of
months later suspended from his office by Carleton), dis-
puting the constitutionality of the new institution, and demanding, (April 12, 1778), definite written information as to
Carleton's order "selecting and appointing five members of
His Majesty's Council to act as a Council to the exclusion of
every other member." The information desired was refused,
as was also permission to read the minutes of the Privy
Council. Nothing further on the head appears in the Colonial
correspondence; but that Livius successfully presented his
point to the home authorities is shown by an additional
and very definite instruction issued to Haldimand, (who had
without new instructions succeeded Carleton in the Chief
Governorship), on the 29th of the following March.
This, after citing the portion of the 2nd Art. of Carleton's
instructions above quoted, proceeds as follows:— "And
whereas it is highly fitting and expedient that no misrepresentation of our Royal will and pleasure in this instance
should continue or obtain, we do hereby direct and require
that this article shall not be understood to delegate authority to you our Governor to select or appoint any such
persons by name as you shall think fit to make such
Quorum, terming the same a Privy Council, or to excuse
you from summoning to Council all such thereunto belonging as are within a convenient distance. On the contrary
that you do take especial care to preserve the constitution
of your said Province free from innovation in this respect;"
to which end the Governor is to communicate this additional instruction to the said Council. And by a second

additional direction of the same date, evidently intended
to reinforce the effect of the first, he is commanded not to
fail [1] in promptly communicating to the Council, "to the
end that they may jointly with you . . . carry our intentions effectually into execution," all instructions on subjects
concerning which their advice and consent were made
requisite. The tone and import of these orders are unmistakeable; but the inner history is by no means clear, nor
can the home administration escape from some suspicion of
inconsistency or at least obscurity of policy. The representation of the original instruction as intended only to
give directons concerning a quorum seems a hardly tenable
position; as said already the entirely new forms and terms
used, taken in connection with previous events, might
well lead to the conviction that the new terms and forms
were intentional and intended to provide for new things.
Though on the other hand it is hardly conceivable that
there was a fully formed intention of allowing an institution to become established which would practically have
the effect of taking away all executive voice from the
Council and reducing it to a purely legislative capacity.
Whatever the inner history, the effect is clear; the Council as a whole was restored to its old executive sphere
with effective intimation that that sphere was not to be
monopolized (at least openly), by the governor. And it
must be acknowledged that this final action of the home
executive does not support the charge that it was aiming to assimilate the Provincial government as much as possible to the old French absolute form. Members of Council
had to be residents of the colony,— a provision which
seems a distinct intervention in the interests of self-government. The same conclusion seems fairly to be drawn
from the repetition in the Governor's instruction of 1775

---

[1] A less emphatic injunction to the same effect had always been a part of the instructions, but Haldimand had disregarded it.

of the 35th Article of those of 1768, ordering that "every orthodox minister within your government be one of the vestry in his respective parish;" a direction which must be construed in connection with a consideration of the contemporaneous position of vestries in England.

The immediate results of the Quebec Act with regard to the official abuses which had been so complained of, were not very gratifying. The vacating of all commissions by it was intended, Carleton says, "to put a stop to all deputations, and to compel all who had offices here to reside and do their duty in person;" but August 10th, 1776, he complains that the same abuse had been introduced again in a great measure by royal mandamuses, (one person being thus granted five offices), and that into these "still slide . . . a string of terms, authorities, fees, perquisites and all that dirty train."[1] And in regard to the accompanying and still greater evil of excessive fees he writes later, (June, 1778), that although "the King had been pleased bountifully to augment the salaries of his servants in this Province that they might live comfortably in their respective stations without oppressing his people," yet the matter has become worse than ever, there existing in the Province "no rule or regulation for fees of offices, but each man for himself as guided by his own desire of gain, which of late has broken out with greater keeness than ever before."[2]   These minor developments are possibly worth more attention than I can here give to them. For they bear strongly on the general conclusion as to the Quebec Act to which my investigation has led me, viz.: that the return to the old institutions in the degree thus accomplished, was a step neither warranted by the necessities of the moment nor by any principles of sound policy; but that the French Canadians would have been satisfied with a part of what the Act gave, accompanied with a full

1 Can. Arch., Q. 12, p. 119.
2 Ibid., B. 37, p. 192.

remedy of the really pressing evils in the uncertainty of the law and the abuses of its administration. The remedy for these abuses did not depend on the return to the old institutions; on the contrary we have seen that that return was not accompanied by it. Still less do we find it followed by the expected improvement with regard to the confusion and uncertainty of the law. The immediate and continued result was in accordance with the mixture of aim and motive. To show this it is necessary only to refer to any respectable history of the period. It was not till 1777 that the civil courts were re-established in Quebec; we are informed by a writer who is almost contemporary, and who had had exceptional means of knowing the exact legal conditions, that an official investigation in 1787 disclosed "such a scene of anarchy and confusion in the laws and in the administration of them by the courts as no English province ever before laboured under; English judges followed English law; French judges followed French law; some of them followed no particular law, but decided according to what appeared to be the equity of the case."[1] Christie writes of the year 1790, that it was complained that although the Quebec Act had been sixteen years in force, "the courts had not yet decided whether the whole of the French laws or what part of them composed the custom of Canada, as they sometimes admitted and sometimes rejected whole codes of French law."[2] Garneau[3] groups together the whole period from 1760 to 1786 as marked by the same "excès de tyrannie et de désordres," and states that the investigation into the judiciary by Dorchester in 1786 showed the utmost uncertainty and confusion. More modern writers[4] accept this condition of affairs

[1] Smith, *History of Canada*, II. 175.

[2] *History of Lower Canada*, I, 67.

[3] *Hist. du Canada*, III. 57. The statement is apparently endorsed by Lareau, *Hist. Droit Canadian*, II., 168.

[4] See for example Kingsford and Bourinot.

without dispute.   It is only intended here to point out that
the Quebec Act has thus no defence, in at least this first
stage of its life, from the standpoint of good government
in the Province.   This should be kept in mind as we pass
to the special consideration of some of its more immediate
disastrous effects, and as we reflect more generally upon
its remoter results in the history of British North America.

CHAPTER VI.

THE QUEBEC ACT AND THE AMERICAN REVOLUTION.

A.   The Revolution in the Province of Quebec.

In the frequent extolling by British and Canadian writers of the *policy* of the Quebec Act, the reference is of course to the supposed effect of that Act in confirming the loyalty of the French Canadians at the revolutionary crisis, and thus in preserving the newly-acquired territories from the grasp of the revolutionary movement.   If the conclusions of the last chapter be well taken, it will be seen that, whatever the outcome of the measure, the inference as to policy is largely mistaken; that in other words, if the results were as stated, it would seem a rare and happy instance of immediate temporal reward for disinterested well-doing.   It is not meant to deny that in the generally threatening conditions in America the firm attachment of the new subjects must have appeared to the home government as a very desirable thing; nor that the conviction of this desirability was probably a considerable factor in confirming the final conclusions as to their treatment.   Such a motive would be of necessity strongly present in the case of such an unknown quantity as the new acquisition of a segment of another nationality; I have simply tried to show that it was not accentuated by the contemporary existence of other colonial problems to the extent of appreciably affecting the policy adopted toward the new subjects.

But further, I am obliged to take exception to the position of the upholders of the Act for other and stronger reasons.   The credit for political sagacity assigned to the authors of that measure must be impugned not only on the ground that their work had little if any reference to the circumtances on which the credit is given, but also for the conclusive reason that the immediate results of the Act were precisely the opposite of what had been anticipated and have ever since been assumed. It is the object of this chapter to show that not only was the Quebec Act not effectual in keeping the mass of the Canadians loyal, but that what effect it did have was in exactly the opposite direction. And before proceeding to this it should be noticed that in anticipating or extolling the results of the new settlement on the French Canadians there is curiously left out of sight by the upholders of the Act, any consideration of its effects either on the British in Canada or on the older colonies. Yet it is evident that for the true estimate of its policy, wisdom, or results there must be an accurate balancing. In view of the accompanying measures of the Government of the day in regard to the other colonies directly it is not surprising to find any thought of this entirely absent at the time. We however have no excuse for now neglecting it.

The question of the influence, direct or indirect, in general or in particular parts of the country, of the new settlement of Quebec affairs on revolutionary development in the other colonies, is one of an interest so great and so closely connected with my work that I can only express my regret at being unable at present to investigate it thoroughly. It must be left with a reference to the general classing of the Act with those of the same session in regard to Massachusetts Bay,[2] and to the emphasis so placed upon the measure in the early steps of the Continental Congress. One remarkable bit of private testimony in connection therewith might also be mentioned. In the Dartmouth Papers we find a letter from one Joseph Reed to the Earl of Dartmouth, Secretary of State, dated Philadelphia, Sept. 25, 1774, and giving an account of the alarming proceedings of the Congress then sitting there. The writer proceeds:— "But what shall I say to your

---

[2] This has been universal among American writers. See Roosevelt, *Winning of the West*, I., for a more emphatic and recent position; and in connection the treatment above of Quebec boundaries, Chapter V, section B, a.

Lordship of the appearances in this country; what seemed a little time since to be a spark which with prudence and wisdom might have been extinguished, is now a flame that threatens ruin both to parent and child. The spirit of the people gradually rose when it might have been expected to decline, till the Quebec Act added fuel to the fire; then all those deliberate measures of petitioning previous to any opposition was laid aside as inadequate to the apprehended danger and mischief, and now the people are generally ripe for the execution of any plan the Congress advises, should it be war itself."[1] Without delaying further on the direct influence in the revolting colonies of the general feeling with regard to the Quebec settlement, it may be pointed out that the attitude of that section of the British party in the Province itself which I have above distinguished as closely in sympathy with what became the revolutionary element, is a fairly correct index to the general feeling. That element in Quebec had, in the circumstances of the province, no legitimate or immediate share in the general colonial quarrel; its grievance was the Quebec Act purely; yet we find this a grievance of strength sufficient to drive it almost immediately into secret and as soon as possible into open revolt.

In noting these consequences of the new settlement with regard to the English-speaking party in Quebec, we have first to observe its efficacy in openly separating the more advanced and more moderate section.[2] The first step of

---

[1] Hist. MSS. Commission, Report XI. Appendix, V. p. 362. I am indebted for the reference to the *Report* for 1890 of the Canadian Archivist, p. XXI. It will be noticed that the writer selects from the various obnoxious measures of the late Parliamentary session, the Act in regard to Quebec, without any mention apparently of the more directly threatening ones concerning Massachusetts Bay. His thought may probably be more distinctly seen in a later horrified reference to "The idea of bringing down the Canadians and savages upon the English Colonies." Of the writer I know nothing surely; but he is possibly the same person to whom the Congressional *Diary* of Richard Smith makes reference March 1, 1776, as the "Secretary to Gen. Washington," and as having his salary then raised by Congress on account of important naval duties. (See *Amer. Hist. Review*, April, 1896, p. 507.)

[2] See above c. 3, for analysis of the English party.

the party was the drawing up of protests against the Act; in which mild proceeding however all apparently did not take part. For Carleton writes Nov. 11, 1774 to Dartmouth, that the more respectable part of the English at Quebec, "notwithstanding many letters received from home advising them to pursue a different course," had presented a dutiful and submissive address; but that in Montreal, "whether the minds of the latter are of a more turbulent turn, or that they caught the fire from some colonists settled among them, or in reality letters were received from the General Congress, as reported, I know not, certain it is however that shortly after the said Congress had published in all the American papers their approbation of the Suffolk Co. resolves in the Massachusetts, a report was spread at Montreal that letters of importance had been received from the General Congress," and public meetings were held by the British there for the consideration of grievances. Thence the infection had spread to Quebec where the same course was pursued, though "several discrete persons" at both places had declined taking part. Since then there had been several "town-meetings as they are pleased to style them," though he speaks doubtfully, "as they have taken uncommon pains to keep their whole proceedings from my knowledge." He describes these town-meetings and reports as all "breathing that same spirit, so plentifully gone forth through the neighbouring Provinces," and speaks of the necessity of government guarding zealously "against the consequences of an infection, imported daily, warmly recommended, and spread abroad by the Colonists here, and indeed by some from Europe, not less violent than the Americans." [1]

The immediate outcome of these proceedings were numerously signed petitions against the Act, addressed to the King and to both Houses of Parliament. There can be no

[1] Can. Arch., Q. 11, p. 11.

doubt that the leaders here and from this time on were constantly in more or less direct communication with the American Revolutionists and were aiming to keep as closely in touch with their efforts as possible. The letters spoken of above by Carleton undoubtedly did represent some such connection, and a few days later (Nov. 18, 1774)[1] Carleton transmits a copy of one which had fallen into his hands, and which probably was the communication referred to. And as it speaks of itself as being "our first public correspondence with the town of Quebec,"[2] it will be worth while to refer more fully to it. It is dated Boston, Oct. 10, 1774, and is a moderate and dignified letter of thanks by one David Jeffries, on behalf of the "Committee of Donations" of Boston, for a contribution (apparently of wheat)[3] "to relieve the distressed poor of this oppressed town," and is addressed to "the Gentlemen of Quebec" through a trading firm named Minot, originally from Massachusetts. It speaks of the necessity of the union of all parts of the continent against oppression, and of the satisfaction afforded by the sympathy of the town of Quebec; refers to the policy of Great Britain in "creating divisions amongst them and using them as engines to beat down and destroy the liberties of each other, that so all may be an easy prey to tyranny and despotic power,"— a policy to which "the eyes of the colonists are opened;" and expresses the hope of the continued support of "our friends in Canada," with whom the writers will think themselves "happy in keeping up a brotherly correspondence." This letter is anterior to any action of Congress in regard to Canada, and the communication now opened was constantly kept up.[4] The Amer-

[1] Can. Arch., Q. 11, p. 103.

[2] Ibid., Q. 11, p. 105. This expression does not by any means exclude, (rather indeed implies) previous correspondence with individuals.

[3] Sent the previous 6th September. Congress had met for the first time at Philadelphia the day before.

[4] In the following November we find the Massachusetts Provincial Congress appointing a committee (of which John Hancock and Samuel Adams are members), for the devising of means of keeping up a correspondence with Montreal and Quebec. John Brown was later appointed the agent of this committee.

ican portion of the party together with a few of European
birth, (nearly all apparently at Montreal), undoubtedly from
this time became active partizans of the Revolutionary
cause, which they publicly embraced on the appearance of
the American invading force.　January 12, 1775, Carleton
writes that the British subjects are "still exerting their
utmost endeavors to kindle in the Canadians the spirit that
reigns in the Province of the Massachusetts,"[1] and the following March 13,[2] that some of them "continue suggesting
into the minds of the Canadians an abhorrence for the form
of government intended by the Act.of last session," and
that they have translated the letter of Congress and actually imported 200 or 300 copies of it.

I need not go into details of the intrigues carried on and
of the various methods of communication employed.　The
point of main interest here is that the final split in the
party becomes now very evident.　An attempt was made at
Montreal to have delegates elected to the Congress of 1775,
and notwithstanding Mr. John Brown's explanation of the
cause of its failure,[3] there can be no doubt that the great
body of the English were decidedly opposed to the step on
general grounds, and that the leading American element
found itself at this point finally separated from its former
constituency.　We find in short that the main body of the
"old subjects" remained, in spite of the Quebec Act,
heartily loyal to English rule during this crisis; that their
attitude was the same as that of the Tories, (the later
United Empire Loyalists), in the other Provinces.　They
were probably willing to go farther in opposition to the
government than their brethren in some of the other Prov-

[1] Can. Arch., Q. 11, p. 110. See also anonymous letter from Montreal, Jan. 18, 1775. [4
Amer. Arch., I, 1164].

[2] Can. Arch., Q. 11, p. 129.

[3] This was to the effect that the English in Quebec could not join the non-importation
agreement, as in that case the French would immediately monopolize the Indian fu
trade.　(John Brown to Boston Com. of Correspondence, March 29, 1775, 4 *Amer. Arch.*,
II. 243.)

inces, for they were under more irritating conditions;[1] but they were not willing to go to the length of taking up arms.[2] As to Quebec city we have very decisive evidence. I have above estimated the total male adult British population as hardly 600 in number and it will be a liberal allowance to grant the town of Quebec at this juncture half of these.[3] But the official returns of the number of the defending force includes, November 16, 1775,. "200 British militia,"[4] and May 1st, 1776, "277 British militia."[5]   And that the efforts of these were not luke-warm is abundantly shown by letters of the officers engaged.[6]   Carleton himself testifies that their conduct was such as could hardly have been expected from men unused to arms.[7]   It is, on the whole, safe to say that after the Spring of 1776 the British party in Canada was seemingly united in upholding the British cause. Almost the entire American element had departed with their retreating countrymen,[8] and the remainder of the party had apparently become reconciled to government and had been taken for a time into its full confidence.   We find

[1] And hence did go to the verge of sedition, and at first probably were somewhat luke-warm in the defense of the Province.

[2] Their attitude at Montreal is probably accurately represented by a paper in the *Hald. Coll.*, (*Rep. Can. Arch.*, 1888, p. 918,) which purports to be a proposal of terms of capitulation to Montgomery, and which is signed by English and French names. It stipulates for the free possession and enjoyment of rights and religion, non-interference of soldiers with the inhabitants, and *that they should not be obliged to take up arms against the mother country.*   Accompanying this is another document, unsigned, which protests against the terms of the capitulation as a treaty between two enemies, (whereas it ought to be a fraternal union), and expresses a desire for such a union with the other colonies.   There can be no doubt that this latter is the voice of the few revolutionary sympathizers.   Carleton writes Oct. 25, 1775, that on the attack on Montreal by the rebels a few of the inhabitants, "mostly colonists," had refused to take part in the defence. From which we are justified in concluding that the most of the English element had taken part.

[3] Montreal was the chief trading centre.

[4] Can. Arch., Q. 1, p. 344.

[5] Ibid., Q. 12, p. 25.

[6] See of Col. Caldwell in *Transactions* Lit. and Hist. Soc. of Quebec.   New Series, Part 8; and of Col. McLean, in Can. Arch., Q. 12, p. 39.

[7] Can. Arch., Q. 12, p. 7.   To Germaine May 14, 1776.

[8] The list of revolutionists sent home by Carleton May, 1777, contains 27 names and is apparently intended as a full one.   Ibid., Q. 13, p. 106.

intrigues it is true carried on through the whole war; but these were conducted in the main through the re-visits of those who had departed with the Americans, and were directed solely toward securing a hold upon the French Canadians. November 20, 1776, Carleton transmits loyal addresses from the British subjects of Quebec, and expresses himself as so well satisfied of the sincerity of the signers that there is "reason to hope that this part of His Majesty's Dominions may with proper arrangements be made the firm support of the British interests on this continent."[1] But although they had refused to go the full length desired by their more violent early leaders, the English-speaking party continued unanimously opposed to the Quebec Act, and maintained a more or less vigorous agitation against it down to its partial repeal in 1791. We hear of hostile petitions presented in 1778, and again in 1784, and an examination of the language of these shows that the position of the main body continued to be pretty much as represented by Masères. With the introduction of the Loyalist element at the close of the war the party gained immensely in weight, and attention to its representations could no longer be delayed.

But my main purpose in this chapter is to enquire into the results of the Quebec Act on the French Canadians. The generally accepted view that they were fully satisfied with the Act and thereby strongly attached to the British connection, is one which, without examination of evidence, proceeds naturally from the belief that the measure was based wholly or mainly upon their expressed desires. I have shown above that this was not the case, for the reason that the self-constituted interpreters of these desires had drawn their conclusions from very narrow and mistaken observation and very one-sided information. It is not surprising therefore to find that the results did not at all correspond with the expectations of the promoters of the measure.

---

[1] Can. Arch., Q. 12, p. 238.

Overwhelming evidence shows that the French Canadians were not faithful to British rule at this crisis, and that they were least faithful at the time when the Quebec Act might be supposed to have had most influence. Further evidence, equally strong, if not so great in quantity, shows that the effect of the Act on the mass of the people was one of alienation rather than conciliation.[1]

It will be well to enquire first if there is any ground to expect these results, rather than those which have been so long assumed with such apparent reason. What do we know or what can we reasonably conclude as to the opinions of the mass of the people on the points which formed the main subject-matter of the Quebec Act? Of the four main provisions which I have discussed above, two,— the extension of the boundaries of the province and the decision against

---

[1] As to the first of these statements — the hostility to British connection as shown by support of the invading revolutionists,— I do not assume any attitude of discovery. The evidence when really looked at is too overwhelming to have altogether escaped the observer. The latest and strongest expression of the truth I find in Kingsford's *History of Canada*, (V. 439,— published since my investigation was made), who says in regard to Montgomery's appearance: — "It was a rare case when the Canadians showed disfavor to the invaders; many joined their ranks." As will be seen later Mr. Kingsford however is mistaken in representing this attitude of the Canadians as only temporary. And that some more detailed and circumstantial statement is necessary to affect the general error, is shown by the wide extent of its assertion and its constant repetition. Lecky says in regard to the American invasion: "The Canadians remained loyal to England ... The contagion of New England republicanism had not penetrated to Canada;" the people "were especially indignant at the invasion." (IV, 215). In a text book of the University of Toronto it is asserted that, "While the American War of Independence was in progress the French Canadian people remained faithful to their allegiance and resisted all the efforts of the Americans to induce them to revolt against the English." (Bourinot, *The Constitutional Hist. of Canada*. The statement is repeated with emphasis in the same writer's *Parliamentary Procedure and Practice*, Revised ed. 1892, p. 13.) It is needless to say that French Canadian writers have loudly and unanimously maintained the same position. A good example of the assertions of even the more enlightened and impartial of these is the following from Lareau (*Hist. Droit Can.* II, 148): "Cette concession [i. e. the Quebec Act] de la part de l'Angleterre eut sa récompense; pendant que les colonies anglaises brisaient le lien colonial, le Canada, comptant sur la justice du vainqueur resta fidèle au drapeau britannique." It seems therefore the function of such a special study as this to do what the general historian of course cannot, viz., so circumstantially to present the truth as to place it forever beyond cavil.

The second of the above statements,—as to the alienating effect of the Act,—has not I think been heretofore made, much less enforced.

an Assembly,—we may conclude to have been practically matter of indifference to the average *habitant*. The previous complaints as to the narrowing of the province had sprung from the greed of the trader or the historical pride of the educated; it was expressly testified by the most trustworthy of the witnesses before the Commons in 1774, that the mass of the Canadians neither knew nor cared anything about an Assembly, and that the few who did dreaded its establishment as likely to bring the Province into difficulties with the mother country. With regard to the third provision,—the reputed establishment of the Roman Catholic Church,—there is every ground for believing that the French Canadian would see in it only a dreaded and objectionable feature,— the re-establishment of the compulsory tithe. As early as 1762 Murray asserts that the people "under sanction of the capitulation every day take an opportunity to dispute the tithes with their curés;"[1] and in the following year (as already pointed out), general petitions support his assertion that the people are not anxious for the continuance of the hierarchy, but will be content with the preservation of the priesthood as a devotional and educational body. Every year of British rule, there can be little doubt, increased this attitude of independence in regard to the once all-powerful church. It will be well in this connection to recall De Tocqueville's remarks in discussing the isolation of the peasant in Old France at this time. He points out[2] that the clergy were the only members of the superior classes left in the country, and that the curé would thus have become the master of the rural population "s'il n'avait été rattache lui-même d'une facon si étroite et si visible à la hiérarchie politique; en possédant plusieurs des priviléges de celle-ci il avait inspiré en partie la haine qu'elle faisait naître;" a position which he emphasizes in a note which points out an ex-

---

[1] Can. Arch., B. 7, p. 1. See above, chapter 2.

[2] *Ancien Régime*, B. II, c. 12, with note.

ample from the year 1767 "de la manière dont les droits pécuniaires de clergé lui aliénaient les coeurs de ceux que leur isolement aurait du rapprocher de lui." As I have elsewhere pointed out, there is no good reason for regarding the Canadian *habitant* as so far removed from the state of mind of the peasant in Old Fràrce as has been generally ` assumed. With regard to the civil code provisions of the Act (in connection with which must be considered the previous reversion to the old forms of land tenure), it must be concluded that at the most the re-establishment of the old French civil law, in view of the fact that the peasant had never discontinued its use,[1] could have had very little effect on the average French Canadian. And when he considered that the tithe had been made compulsory, and that the seigneurial method of land grant was again in full operation, it would be strange if he should not feel some apprehension with regard to the reappearance of other old oppressive relations connected with the land. I have shown above that there is every reason to believe that the relations between the seigneur and the *habitant*, even early in the English period, were practically identical with those in old France, and that no part of the changed conditions had been so early and fully appreciated by the latter as their release from their former military and judicial subjection. In their ignorance of the real scope of the new measure they would naturally be apprehensive of the reviving of this old burden; and it is evident that before as after its enactment its English opponents took full advantage of their fears and ignorance.

Very little direct evidence has been found on this point, and still less that is free from suspicion. The British party, of course, before and after the Act, represented it as undesired and resented by the mass of the people. This contention is not to be regarded as weakened by the fact that a memorial and petition in favor of its main provis-

---

[1] See above, pp. 352-7.

ions were presented in their name to Parliament while deliberating on the measure.[1] For Masères' statement that these are not really representative may be easily conceded in view of the fact that of the fifteen signatures, most are those of members of the noblesse.[2] A movement of more importance and interest has been already referred to in the account of the English proceedings prior to the Act; it culminated in an offer from some French leaders in Quebec to join in the English petition for an Assembly provided that this should contain a request for the admission of Catholics to the House.[3] On the rejection by the English of this condition the matter dropped. As indicating the attitude of a section probably larger in number and certainly more nearly in accord with popular feeling than the noblesse, this incident is of great interest;[4] but it is still of little value in the determination of the question as to the views of the mass of the people on the points at issue. The very contradictory evidence given before the Commons in 1774 by the Provincial officials is no more helpful; it being evident that Masères and Lotbinière represent a small advanced portion of the traders and professional men, (perhaps also of the noblesse), and that Hey and Carleton speak for the clergy and the bulk of the noblesse. With regard to the first reception of the Act by the people we have equally

---

[1] For these see Masères, *Account of the Proceedings*, pp. 111-31.

[2] See on this point, Carleton's evidence before Commons. 1774. Also English petitions for an Assembly, Dec., 1773 (Can. Arch., Q. 10, p. 26). A curious letter in 1776 from one M. Pelissier to the President of Congress describes the signers of the French petition as "quelques adulateurs [i. e. of Carleton] et quelqes ignorans fanatiques des anciennes coutumes." (4 *Amer. Arch.* IV., 596.)

[3] See Masères, *Account of the Proceedings*, pp. 3-40.

[4] It is noteworthy also as indicative of the rise of a new set of native leaders (distinct from noblesse and clergy). The lawyers and others of the lay educated class who had rapidly acquired some insight into English political ideas are evidently taking the place that had been opened up to them by the substitution for the feudal régime of the freer spirit of the English institutions. The new attitude is probably represented by the evidence of M. Lotbinière before the Commons in 1774; and the desire for forms of English self-government was undoubtedly inspired by the hope of thus giving effect to the great numerical preponderance of the French.

conflicting statements.   It was not to go into force till May,
1775, and it is doubtful whether it was published in the
province during 1774; so that statements as to public opinion during the latter year probably can have reference only
to the few who beforehand would become intelligently acquainted with its provisions.   September 20, 1774, Carleton
writes to Gage of the "joy and gratitude and fidelity" of the
Canadians in consequence of the late Act,[1] and three days
later he reports to Dartmouth the great satisfaction of all
classes of the French Canadians.[2] Nov. 11th[3] he again speaks
of their gratitude and represents their uneasiness at the
measures which the old subjects are taking against the Act.
But it is noticeable that he here refers to the noblesse and
clergy as being apprehensive that some of the Canadians
through ignorance and from their trade relations with the
English, may be enticed to join the latter in their movements; especialy as they are being told that the late Acts
will reduce them to a state of slavery and oppression.   At
the same time he sends addresses, (three, from Montreal,
Quebec, and Three Rivers),[4] expressing the gratitude of
French Canadians; addresses which beyond much doubt are
from precisely the same quarter as the petitions immediately preceding the Act.   The one from Quebec speaks
apologetically of fellow-countrymen who " par des circon-
stances malheureuses " may have been drawn into common
action with the English discontents.   February 4, 1775,[5]
Carleton writes further to Gage that " all that have spoke
or wrote to me upon the subject express the most grateful
sense of what has been done for them; " but at the same
time uses language in regard to the *habitants* which seems
to show that he is beginning to perceive that the satisfaction and gratitude does not extend to them.   And the indi-

---

1 Can. Arch., Q. 10, p. 123.

2 Ibid., Q. 10, p. 120.

3 Ibid., Q. 11, p. 11.

4 Ibid., pp. 17–23.

5 Ibid., p. 290.

cations of this soon became so unmistakeable that even his obstinate prepossessions could no longer resist.

Of the suspicious attitude which in all probability the average French Canadian had maintained in regard to the re-establishment of old oppressive institutions the English discontents had been quick to take advantage, magnifying the provisions which might seem likely to operate for the revival of old burdens. We find Carleton writing November 11th, 1774,[1] that the people are being told the most extravagant stories of the arbitrary power put into the hands of the Governor and noblesse; and the French addresses of thanks of the same month (quoted from above), evidently imply that these representations were already perceived to have had effect. The most emphatic testimony on this matter comes from Masères.[2] Though prejudiced, and dependent for information on those who were more so, still his assertions here are so amply supported by other evidence and by later events that we cannot neglect them. He gives a letter to him from some of the English in the province[3] which asserts in the most positive terms that "great numbers throughout the Province have offered to join us in petitioning for the continuance of English laws, and disavowing their consent and knowledge of the petition which was sent home last year in their names, though signed only by a few persons in the province;" but that they have been prevented from so joining by the intervention of their superiors, who told them that if they did so they would be deprived of their religion. More reliable proof of the attitude of the *habitant* is furnished in the fears entertained by those who best knew them. These are shown in a letter which was circulated among them by the clergy in December, 1774, and January, 1775, attempting to reas-

---

[1] Can. Arch., Q. 11, p. 11.

[2] See *Additional Papers.*

[3] For letters of this tenor and probably from the same source, see Almon's *Remembrancer*, II (1776), pp. 130-44.

sure them on those provisions of the Act which were supposed to have alarmed them.[1]

The new constitution went into force in the Spring of
1775 and the hostility of the people to it seems to have
steadily increased. Two curiously roundabout and discon-
nected pieces of evidence deserve perhaps especial notice.
One is an official intimation from St. John's Island, of October 13, 1775, to the effect that private letters have been
received there from Quebec with the information that "the
Canadians have absolutely refused to join us, assigning for
reason that the English law is taken away from them, and
that as the King has broken his word, they have a right
to do the same." [2] The other is a letter of June 20, 1775,
from two New Hampshire agents to Revolutionary leaders in
that Province, reporting the information as to the disposition of the Canadians that has been gathered by Indian
scouts. This is to the effect that the Canadians are waiting anxiously for the appearance of the Colonial forces;
"they determine not to take their old law again, if we will
but joyn with them, they will joyn with us." [3] In August,
1775 Chief-Justice Hey writes from Quebec to the Lord
Chancellor that His Lordship would be astonished to learn
"that an Act passed for the express purpose of gratifying
the Canadians and which was supposed to comprehend all
that they either wished or wanted, is become the first object of their discontent and dislike;" the general wish being for English laws in peace and English officers in war.[4]
Thomas Gamble of the provincial commissariat department
writes from Quebec September 6, 1775, to the Deputy
Quartermaster General in emphatic language concerning

---

[1] Anoymous, but said by Masères to be supposed to have been written by one of the
Quebec Clergy. See Masères, *Account of the Proceedings*, pp. 264-75.

[2] Gov. Legge to Gen. Howe, *Hist. Mss. Comm. 11th Report*, App. V., p. 388.

[3] *N. H. Prov. Papers*, VII, 525.

[4] Can. Arch., Q. 12, p. 203. Evidence stronger than this it would be difficult to
imagine. For it will be remembered that Hey, who now laments the failure of the
Act, had in large measure supported Carleton in the representations on which it was
founded.

the ill-disposition of the people. "In short, the Quebec Bill is of no use; on the contrary the Canadians talk of that damned absurd word liberty." [1]

It is only however when we come to the test of Canadian feeling which was afforded by the revolutionary invasion of 1775–76 that we reach firm ground in this matter. Previous to that event we have no definite references to French Canadian opinion in regard to the troubles in the other colonies. About the quarrel on its merits the average Canadian knew nothing [2] and cared little if anything. On the other hand the revolutionists had from the beginning seen the importance of Canada, and begun to guard against danger from that quarter. [3] I have already narrated the earliest trace that appears of connection between the revolutionists and the English party in Quebec. A few days later, (October 26, 1774), the first Continental Congress, having drawn up those Addresses to the people of Great Britain and to the individual colonies in which the Quebec Act figured prominently as a grievance, adopted one also "to the inhabitants of the 'Province of Quebec.'" This is a skillfully drawn paper, largely occupied with an explanation of those principles of English constitutional liberty of which the Canadians had been defrauded by the Quebec Act; adjuring them to disregard religious differences, (for "the transcendent nature of freedom elevates above all such low-minded infirmities,") [4] and by choosing delegates to the ensuing Congress to join in heartily with the other colon-

---

[1] 4 *Amer. Arch.*, III, 963.

[2] See Masères' *Freeholder*, written for their instruction on this assumption.

[3] I have not found anywhere any connected statement of the early steps of Congress and other revolutionary authorities in regard to Canada, and have therefore attempted briefly to supply it.

[4] The address to the people of Great Britain, which had referred to the Roman Catholic religion as having "deluged your island in blood, and dispersed impiety, bigotry, persecution, murder, and rebellion throughout every part of the world," had been adopted five days before. It is probable that the elevating nature of freedom has rarely operated with greater celerity. The good work went on apparently; for the Instructions of Congress to the Commissioners sent to Canada in 1776 ordered them to assure the clergy of "the full, perfect, and peaceable possession and enjoyment of all their estates." (4 *Amer. Arch.*, V, p. 411.)

ies, who had determined to "consider the violation of your rights by the act for altering the government of your Province, as a violation of our own."[1] Of this diplomatic document a translation was ordered to be made, and 2,000 copies to be struck off for distribution in Quebec by means of the delegates from the bordering Provinces. That it had been disseminated in Canada at least as early as March of the following year is shown by. Carleton's correspondence;[2] and that a revolutionary agent had already by that time met with much success is shown by the letters of John Brown.[3] Definite information of the results first appears from the official side in a letter of secret intelligence to Carleton from Montreal of May 6, 1775, stating that on May 4th most of the English residents of the town had assembled and been "harangued" by a "New Englander," the object of the meeting being supposed to be, "to choose two deputies to send to the Congress to be held at Philadelphia on the 10th of next May." On the following day the same agent reports that the attempt had failed, through the backing out of the most of the English.[4] August 14, 1775, Carleton writes to Dartmouth of the continued efforts of the Congress to corrupt the Canadians, and encloses a copy of new letters from it and from the New York Legislature.

But before this, Congress had resolved to make a military demonstration against Canada for the double purpose of seizing the important points, and of establishing connections between the revolutionary forces and the disaffected Canadians. The first movement was one by Arnold by way of Lake Champlain in May, 1775, and on news of it Carleton called on the noblesse for assistance in raising the militia. The result was a sudden and complete shattering

---

[1] *Journals of Congress*, I, 40-5.
[2] Can. Arch., Q. 11, p. 129.
[3] See especially 4 *Amer. Arch.*, II. 243, where Brown speaks of the peasantry having been worked upon, "chiefly *in terrorem;*" by which must be meant misrepresentation as to the Quebec Act.

See above, p. 485.

of the expectations based on the Quebec Act. Carleton had wished to see revived the old feudal military conditions, and seems to have believed that under the new settlement they did again exist; and his attitude, in connection with the consequent efforts of the noblesse, at once confirmed the fears of the people as to the meditated re-establishment of all the obnoxious powers and privileges of their old masters. This conviction the latter seem to have done their best to foster; for Chief Justice Hey writes to the Lord Chancellor in August, 1775, of the just offense given to the people by the elation of the noblesse over the supposed restoration of their old privileges.[1] After speaking further of the misrepresentations which had been made to the Canadians by the English as to the results of the Act, Hey remarks that as the restraint of the sharp authority by which they had once been controlled was now removed, they break out "in every shape of contempt and detestation of those whom they used to behold with terror, and who gave them, I believe, too many occasions to express it."

Nothing is more certain than that the *habitants* universally resisted from the first every means of influence that the seigneurs brought to bear upon them, maintaining firmly that the latter had no military authority and that all they could demand of their tenantry was the payment of seigneurial dues. In some cases the noblesse did not escape physical violence.[2] As early as June 7, Carleton writes to Dartmouth of the utter failure of the noblesse to induce either the Canadians or the Indians to take up arms. The minds of the people he says, are poisoned with lies,

---

[1] Can. Arch., Q. 12, p. 203. See also Burgoyne to Germaine, May 14, 1777. (Ibid., Q. 13, 107) for opinion that the attitude of the Canadians is largely due to the unpopularity of the seigneurs. We find it further asserted in a private letter of the time from Montreal, that though the people were in general averse to being commanded by the noblesse, they say they will go anywhere under British officers. (July 10, 1775. 4 *Amer. Arch.*, II, 1623.)

[2] For circumstantial accounts of several of these occurrences see letters from Quebec in Masères, *Additional Papers*, pp. 71–83. Also on the general attitude of the Canadians. *Ibid.*, pp. 91–111, 147–52. These letters of course (as well as Masères' comments on them) are partisan, and for that reason I have not brought them forward more prominently; but in view of other evidence, I have no doubt as to their practical truth and accuracy.

and the clergy and noblesse have lost much of their old influence.[1] The 20th of the following month one of the military officers at Quebec writes to a brother officer that not a single Canadian had yet been raised and that there was no hope of forming a militia.[2] August 14 Carleton informs Dartmouth that though the militia has been organized in some of the parishes, "the difficulty I have found in proceeding so far convinces me until their minds change, it will be inadvisable to attempt assembling any number of them, except it become absolutely necessary to try that measure for the defence of the Province, and that there is no other resource whatever."[3]

The Americans had now temporarily retired, leaving it fully understood that they would return shortly in greater force; and from this time on Carleton strained every nerve, with the aid of martial law, to organize a defence. His official correspondence furnishes us with the best information we can look for of the actual conduct of the people in this emergency. And we cannot hesitate to accept this evidence at its full import, when we consider that it is the disappointed confession of a man who had constantly represented that people in another light, and who was mainly responsible for the measures which were now proving so ineffectual. As of precisely the same nature we give with his also the reports of Cramahé, who commanded at Quebec while Carleton was defending Montreal. September 21, 1775, the former writes from Quebec that "no means have been left untried to bring the Canadian peasantry to a sense of their duty and engage them to take up arms in defence of the Province, but all to no purpose," though the better classes had done their utmost "to reclaim their infatuated countrymen;" and that Canadians are actually serving with

---

[1] Can. Arch., Q. 11, p. 164. This is apparently Carleton's first perception or at least confession of the latter fact. It is significant that two days later he proclaimed martial law throughout the Province.

[2] *Rep. Can. Arch.*, 1885, p. 177.

[3] Can. Arch., Q. 11, p. 222.

the Americans in every quarter.[1] On the same day Carleton writes from Montreal to the same effect, adding that "the rebels have been more successful with them [the *habitants*] and have assembled them in great numbers, . . . and with the assistance of the Canadians have invested the forts."[2] October 25, 1775, he reports that an attack made on the town by the rebels, of whom two-thirds were Canadians, had been repulsed, and that the success had had for a moment a good effect on the minds of the inhabitants of the surrounding country, who on the eve of the assault had resisted the orders to have all ladders in the suburbs brought in. Taking advantage of this effect, he says he had assembled some 900 militia (various other detachments coming in had been attacked and forced to disperse by other parishes, the seigneurs who had raised them being taken prisoners), but that these are now disappearing thirty and forty a night.[3] November 5, 1775, he complains that his efforts have been frustrated by "the corruption and I may add by the stupid baseness of the Canadian peasantry, who have not only deserted their duty, but numbers of them have taken arms against the Crown."[5] A few days later Cramahé sends news from Quebec, (then invested by Montgomery), of the inadequacy of the defending forces, the militia he has having with difficulty been brought to mount guard; adding that the rebels have on their side the Canadian peasantry.[6] Not long after he says that the enemy without is not so formidable as that within, and that even if the town be kept 20 battalions will be needed to re-capture the country.[4] On the 22nd November Carleton, (who had returned to Quebec on the fall of Montreal), writes of the "blind perverseness" and "unprecedented defection" of the people, "without even pretending the least cause of complaint." However with the defeat of

---

[1] Can. Arch., Q. 11, p. 249.
[2] Ibid., p. 261.
[3] Ibid., p. 267.

[4] Ibid., p. 324.
[5] Ibid., p. 274.
[6] Ibid., p. 285.

Montgomery and the retreat of Arnold the Canadians assumed a less menacing attitude (a change largely due no doubt to the cantonment among them by Carleton of troops), and the Governor writes in September, 1776, that "there is nothing to fear from them in prosperity and nothing to hope for in distress, the multitude being influenced by hope of gain or fear of punishment."[1]

Such is a small portion of the testimony of the main officers as to the conduct of the Canadians in the hour of greatest danger; it is abundantly supported from the side of the defenders by the scattered statements of inferior officials, civil and military, which my space will not allow me to dwell upon. I cannot, however, refrain from again reverting to the testimony of Chief-Justice Hey, who all this time had been quietly and judicially watching the progress of events from Quebec; as well as adding that of a French Canadian witness. August 28, 1775, Hey writes (to the Lord Chancellor)[2] that the behavior of the Canadians had greatly changed the views he had formerly entertained of them and that he is now convinced their former good conduct was due only to fear, and that no dependence can be placed on them, for they are either terrified or corrupted. The 11th September following he adds that hardly a Canadian will take up arms; on the 17th that "not one hundred except in the towns of Montreal and Quebec are with us." The French Canadian to whom I have referred is M. Badeau, a notary of Three Rivers, who from that very favorable point of observation watched with royalist sympathies the progress of the invasion, and who has left the result for us in a "Journal des operations de l'armée americaine."[3] From this I take the following entries: — September 7th, 1775,—Carleton "partit pour Montreal et eut la douleur de voir que plus il s'avançait par en haut, plus il trou-

---

[1] Can. Arch., Q. 12, p. 188.
[2] His letters are in journal form.
[3] *Collections* Quebec Hist. Society, 3d series, Montreal, 1871.

vait les habitants opposés à ses dessins."—Sept. 8th:
A draft being ordered from St. John, the "paroisses
de Chambly s'étant mis du coté des Bostonnais firent an-
noncer dans toutes les autres paroisses de ne point pren-
dre les armes contre les Bostonnais, que ces gens là vena-
ient pour nous tirer d'oppression, le peuple canadien cré-
dule quand il ne faut point, donna dans le sentiment des
paroisses de Chambly et presque toute le gouvernement des
Trois-Rivières refusa de marcher à l'exception de quelques
volontaires" from three parishes.—Sept. 12: News has
been received that a detachment of 67 recruits which had
set out for Montreal under two seigneurs has been stopped
by "les habitants de la paroisse de Chicut," and the seigneurs made prisoners.[1]—February 29, 1776: The American
detachment in the town of Trois-Rivières having ordered a
new election of militia officers, one part of the inhabitants
objected to the captain nominated on the ground that "il a
le coeur Anglais et qu'il a recu de commission du Gen.
Carleton."—April 30: A list of 16 names has been given
to the Americans as comprising all the royalists in the
town.—May 4: The passing of some American troops. "Il
n'est pas possible exprimer combien la canaille triomphe
de la passée de ces gens là; il semble que chaque brigade
leur apporte une fortune."

If any corroboration of testimony such as the above is
needed it will be found in the reports which come to us
from the continental forces,— in the letters of commanding
officers and the journals of less prominent persons. August
14, 1775, John Brown had written that the Canadians, "wish
and long for nothing more than to see us with an army
penetrate their country. They engage to supply us with
everything in their power."[2] The following September 6,
Ethan Allen reports the conclusion of an Indian alliance

---

[1] Full accounts of this (most probably) and other similar occurrences will be found in
Masères, and in Almon's *Remembrancer* for 1775.

[2] To Gov. Trumbull, 4 *Amer. Arch.*, II, 138.

in presence "of a large auditory of Canadians who approved of the league, and manifested friendship to the colonies, and testified their good-will on account of the advance of the army into Canada."[1] Schuyler informs the New York Congress September 29, that "The Canadians were friendly to us and join us in great numbers."[2] November 3rd an anonymous report comes from the River Sorel that the Canadians there have armed and been embodied in favor of the Americans to the number of more than 1000,[3] About the same time Arnold reports to Washington his most kindly and hospitable reception by the people.[4] That the American observers were not deceived through their too sanguine expectations may be inferred from letters of Schuyler to Washington in which the belief is expressed that the Canadians would join Carleton if reverses overtook the invaders;[5] as also by a caution from Montgomery about the same time.[6] But the latter reports again from Montreal November 24, that "I can have as many Canadians as I know how to maintain; at least I think so, while affairs wear so promising a prospect."[7] The expedition of Montgomery went on to its disastrous culmination, and on the following January 11, Arnold still asserts that "The disposition of the Canadians is very favorable," though they "are timorous and want encouragement."[8] Gen. Wooster's report is however that "there is but little confidence to be placed in the Canadians; — they are fond of being of the strongest party."[9] February 27 Arnold in-

---

[1] To Gen. Schuyler. 4 *Amer. Arch.*, III, 742.

[2] *Ibid.*, III, 841.

[3] *Ibid.*, p. 1343. This seems confirmed by a letter of the same date from Montgomery to Schuyler. *Ibid.* III, 1392.

[4] All the *Journals* of the Arnold expedition speak in the same tone. Though it is to be noticed that several of them speak also of the exceedingly high prices charged by the Canadians for provisions. See especially those of Wild, Dearborne, and Thayer.

[5] 4 *Amer. Arch.*, III, 1373.

[6] To Schuyler, December 5. *Ibid.*, IV, 1392.

[7] *Ibid.*, p. 1695.

[8] To Congress. *Ibid.*, IV. 627.

[9] *Ibid.*, p. 668. On the previous January 2, Arnold had reported his force as including 400 Canadians. *Ibid.*, p, 670.

forms Washington, (apparently referring to the Canadians, though there is obscurity,) that he has received a rein-forcement of 400 men, and that many are daily coming in.[1] An officer posted at Trois Rivières writes March 24, 1766, that he has been placed in charge of the business of re-placing in that District, (comprising 17 parishes,) the mili-tia officers appointed by Carleton with others in the Conti-nental interest, and that he finds that though the Canadians are sometimes shy, "in general they seem to be fond of hold-ing commissions under Congress;" that about thirty such officers have been elected in the District and that late Canadian recruits number 500.[2] In March the Commission-ers of Congress, (Franklin, Chase, and Carroll), set out for Canada. On their arrival they found a surprising change in the attitude of the Canadians; but while dwelling on the fact and its causes they still think it possible "to regain the affections of the people, to attach them firmly to our cause."[3] Gen. Thomas informs Congress May 7, that the French had become so much disaffected that it was now very difficult to get supplies from them;[4] and a few days later Arnold writes from Sorel that he is "convinced they are in general our bitter enemies."[5] But still on the follow-ing June 1, the more sanguine Sullivan reports "the lower and some of the higher class of French people in our favor," and that he had that day been offered 600 men from three parishes.[6] June 5th he writes to Washington of the despair of the people at the leaving of the Americans and

[1] 4 Amer. Arch., IV, p. 674.

[2] Ibid., V. 481. The new officers were chosen by popular election, and it is re-ported that in some parishes there have been several candidates and high party feeling. "I receive information that bribery and corruption is already beginning to creep into their elections. At some the disputes run so high that I am obliged to interfere." That similar elections took place in the District of Montreal is showu by a letter of Gen. Wooster. 5 Amer. Arch., I. 12.

[3] See letters of the Commissioners of Congress, May 1 and 8, 1776. Lossing, Schuyler II. 48-50. See also an important letter from Col. Hazen to Schuyler. Ibid., pp. 46-7.

[4] 4 Amer. Arch., VI. 451.

[5] Ibid., p. 580.

[6] Ibid., p. 679.

of their joy at his arrival.   "It really was affecting to see the
banks of the Sorel lined with men, women and children, leap-
ing and clapping their hands from joy to see me arrive. . . .
Our affairs have taken a strange turn, . . . The Canadians
are flocking by hundreds to take a part with us. . . . I really
find by the present behaviour . . . that the only reason of
their disaffection was because our exertions were so feeble
that they doubted much of our success, and even of our
ability to protect them . . . ; a vast majority will be for us,
and perhaps as many, according to their numbers, are
really in our favor as in some other colonies upon the
Continent; many of them are with Gen. Thompson in this
expedition and great numbers are here, ready equipped,
waiting my orders." [1] And even after the final break-up had
come Sullivan reports that "the Canadians were in general
very kind to them upon their retreat, and gave them every
assistance in their power." [2] That Canadians remained en-
rolled in considerable numbers till the end is shown by the
General Orders of July 21, 1776, directing the march to
Albany of "the Regiment of Canadians with all the Canadian families, now at Ticonderoga." [3]

From the above testimony it is very evident not only
that the Canadians had overwhelmingly declared in favor
of the invaders from the first down till the disaster at
Quebec, but that even after that event a considerable number clung to the colonial cause and were still ready at any
moment to attach themselves to any enterprise of vigor
sufficient to give any promise of success.   The ordinary
judgment with regard to their conduct both from the British
who saw in their neutrality even only the basest ingratitude, and from the Americans who experienced a very
considerable change in the later months of disaster, is not
sufficient or satisfactory.   According to this the people

---

[1] 4 *Amer. Arch.*, VI. 921. These extravagant assertions are answered by Washington
with a caution against fickleness and treachery. (*Ibid.*, p. 927.)

[2] *Ibid.*, VI. 1037.

[3] 5 *Amer. Arch.*, I. 656.

were moved mainly by fear and the desire of being on the stronger side; they embraced or acquiesced in that cause which was for the moment locally predominent.[1] But to say that the Canadians were a timid race is to disregard wholly the facts of their military origin and training, and especially the strong testimony from both sides to their valor and conduct under the most disheartening circumstances in the last war. Nor is it sufficient to say that they had no interest in, as no knowledge of, the present colonial quarrel; that they had been growing prosperous, had devoted themselves wholly to the repairing of the ravages of the old struggle, and were now anxious only to be left in peace. The inevitable result of such a temper would have been the offering to the invader of their peace, if not active opposition, at least a stolid and hostile indifference; from which, as we have seen, their real conduct could not have been further removed. And this furthermore, takes no account of the strong influences that were brought to bear on the people from the British side. The chief of these were the strenuous measures resorted to by the clergy. Admitting all I have said as to the decreasing command of the popular mind by the church, it must still be admitted that for an *indifferent* community, the extreme step of refusing absolution to any one who had joined the invaders, might be supposed to have been a most powerful deterrent. Yet we are told that every priest in the country except one had taken this course.[2] That the step was en-

---

[1] Frequent assertions of this kind are to be found, especially from the British side. As early as September 6, 1775, Ethan Allen reports that the Canadians "keep under arms throughout most of their parishes, and are now anxiously watching the scale of power." (4 *Amer. Arch.*, III. 742).

[2] See Col. Hazen to Antill, April 20, 1776. Can. Arch., B. 27, p. 398. See also letter of Col. Caldwell (British), in *Transactions* Quebec Lit. and Hist. Society, New Series, Pt. 8 (1871). Also Jones, *Expedition to Canada*, p. 33. For the general attitude of the clergy see *Journal of Chas. Carroll*, (Md. Hist. Society, 1876), Introd. Mem., pp. 30-4. This shows that their faithfulness was based not only on the general British treatment and the Quebec Act, but also on strong and well founded suspicion of the tolerance of the colonists. Later however, after the conclusion of the French alliance, there are indications in Gov. Haldimand's correspondence of disaffection even here.

tirely without efficacy can not be supposed; no doubt it
did much to prevent a more open and general rising.[1] That
any defection occurred in the face of it must be taken as
the strongest proof that the Canadians were neither timid
nor indifferent, but that they conceived themselves to have
strong ground for discontent and apprehension.   Their
national feeling was not yet involved, for there was as yet
no open connection between the revolution and France.   In
the entire absence of evidence of the existence before the
Quebec Act of such discontent or apprehension as would
now explain their conduct, we are driven for that explanation to the Act itself.   It seems not too much to say that,
supplemented as it was by the misrepresentation of its opponents, and still more by the most ill-advised attempt
to establish through it the old military position of the
noblesse, it drove the people into the arms of the revolutionists.

But it is further necessary to show that the defection of
the Canadians at this crisis was not the momentary effect
of sudden panic or of a passing wave of popular feeling.[2]
Active misrepresentation might go far to explain such;
though only on the hypothesis that the English agitators
and the colonial emissaries had suddenly acquired an influence very much greater than the natural leaders of the
people.   The Quebec Act went into force May 1, 1775, and
was superseded on the following June 9 by a condition of

---

[1] See "Journal of the Principal Occurrences during the Siege of Quebec . . ; collected from some old MSS originally written by an officer during the Period of the gallant
Defense made by Sir Guy Carleton." (London, 1824.) This refers to the action of the
clergy in refusing the sacraments, especially extreme unction, as "a most potent spell,"
and therein finds the cause for the fact asserted [incorrect] that only about 300 Canadians joined the invaders.

[2] This seems to be the position taken by Mr. Kingsford, who has stated clearly the
first defection, but who later (V. 486), says: "It is simply a duty to record that this
feeling passed rapidly away, and never again obtained activity. During the period of
the whole struggle, the French Canadians remained attached to the British government,
and no encouragement was given for a second invasion of the Province." This positive
assertion however is not to be reconciled with facts which are stated in a later volume
(VII. pp. 11-14; 30).

martial law that continued about eighteen months; consequently before 1777 the people were not in a position to
judge of or be influenced by it except as a matter of speculation. But misrepresentation as to it ought certainly to
have been dispelled long before that time[1]; from the spring
of 1775 the government was in a position to do the worst
that could have been apprehended. Nevertheless we find
still in existence throughout the war a strong popular leaning toward the continental cause. There was of course no
occasion or opportunity for open demonstrations; we must
judge by the reports of the provincial officials. The value
of these is emphasized by the fact that the conclusions arrived at were not hastily formed or insufficiently grounded,
but were the result of the most careful examination by the
best methods available into the real sentiments of the *body
of the people*, not as before of the few who had thrust themselves forward as their spokesmen. A vigorous investigation was set on foot by Carleton and continued by his
successor Haldimand, and in the autumn months of 1776
we meet with frequent examinations by the judicial authorities of suspected persons and of intercepted emissaries
from the revolted colonies. These were continued all
through the period down to the conclusion of peace (and
therefore long after the civil government had been re-established). It will be impossible to go into them fully, but
the calendaring of the Haldimand Collection by the Canadian
Archivist[2] will afford an easy and accurate index to their
contents. Further, we find that after the retreat of the

---

[1] It will be remembered however that this point is not material to my main inquiry.
That is directed, not toward the practical working and effect of the Act, but with reference to the question as to whether the measures it embodied were as necessary and
politic at this juncture as they have always been represented by its upholders. The
matter may be summed up in the questions: Were the French Canadians laboring
under such grievances as to make welcome the measures adopted for their relief, and to
cause these measures to have over them the expected influence? In view of the acknowledged effect of the Quebec Act on the minds of the American revolutionists, was it
nevertheless justified as a matter of policy by its effect on the French Canadians?

[2] See *Rep. Can. Arch.*, 1888, pp. 892-942, and *ibid.*, 1890, p. 130.

Americans, Carleton had caused troops to be cantoned through the parishes, and had thus kept himself informed of the state of public feeling. Riedèsel, who was in command of the German auxiliaries, writes to Haldimand November 29, 1787, that Carleton had given him a commission to learn the sentiments and conduct of the *habitants* in the districts in which the German ·troops were quartered in 1776; that he (Riedèsel) had procured the information from the captains of militia, the curés, and the commanders of the troops, had sent the same to Carleton, and had received his thanks therefor. He adds that he has still duplicates and will send them to Haldimand if desired.[1] And that the latter availed himself of this means, is shown by a second letter to him of Riedèsel in the following April, stating that as desired he has traversed the parishes of his own district several times, and has compared information got from the militia captains, from the curés, and from the German commanders, and that he sends as a result the adjoined lists of names. In the Canadian Archives we find further a collection of papers marked "Instructions to Captain Breckenridge, sent to find out the people that harboured the rebel spies, with the report of his proceedings in 1780."[2]

These facts mark the care exercised by the Government in at least their later reports. The various depositions show that emissaries from Congress and disaffected persons within the province were constant in their activity among the people through the whole period; and the frequent bitter references of Haldimand to the impossibility he finds in catching or tracing these firebrands[3] is sufficient proof in itself of the more than passive sympathy of the people. The salient points of the official reports will

---

[1] Calendar Hald. Coll., p. 390. See here also for the letters of the following April, spoken of below. It will be seen that Riedésel uses the words "lists," showing how minute the enquiry and information was.

[2] *Report Can. Arch.* for 1888, p. 906.

[3] Cal. Hald. Coll., pp. 272, 236. (Early in the period Carleton complains that the emissaries of Congress can travel with more ease and safety than the King's messengers.) .

be best noted in brief extracts chronologically arranged.[1]
May 9th, 1776, Carleton sends home the Ordinances that
had just been passed in the first legislative meeting in
the Province under the new constitution, and adds that
these "have been framed upon the principle of securing
the dependence of this Province upon Great Britain, of
suppressing that spirit of licentiousness and independence that has pervaded all the British Colonies upon this
continent, and was making, through the endeavors of a
turbulent faction here, a most amazing progress in this
country." In the same month he writes to Burgoyne that
"these people have been governed with too loose a rein
for many years, and have imbibed too much of the American spirit of licentiousness and independence to be suddenly restored to a proper and desirable subordination."
This letter was in answer to complaints from Burgoyne
concerning the difficulty he found in procuring enough Canadians to perform the necessary batteaux service for his
expedition;—a difficulty to the serious nature of which
we have various further references, the Canadians even
when started deserting at every opportunity and frequently
refusing obedience. In the spring of 1778 Carleton was replaced in the Governorship by Haldimand, and the first
official communication of the latter (July 25, 1778), is to the
effect that beyond the upper classes and clergy "the Canadians are not to be depended upon especially if a French
War breaks out."[2] In October of the same year he writes
of the caution he is exercising, "not to make demands that
from exciting murmurs might lead to a declaration of sentiments which the French Alliance with the rebels has undoubtedly raised in numbers of them, who in regard of the
rebellion were unquestionably attached to Government, and
renewed in the others;—the symptoms of which change in

[1] For exact references see the *Reports Can. Arch.*, as above.
[2] This and the immediately following letters are from the Haldimand Collection. See *Calendar*, in *Reports Can. Arch.*, under dates.

the Canadians is everywhere manifest." June 7th, 1779, he
states that "the Canadian inhabitants both above and below" had "become adherent to the united cause of France
and the Americans." By "above" he seems to mean in
the Western region, for the letter is written in connection
with the failure in that quarter of an important expedition
under Hamilton against Vincennes and other posts; writing
to Germaine in the following year.[1] Hamilton speaks bitterly
of the unlooked for treachery and unexampled ingratitude
of the Canadians. The testimony shows therefore the widespread nature of the dissafection.[2] June 18, 1779, Haldimand writes further in regard to the French alliance and
the proclamation to the Canadians of d'Estaing, commander
of the French fleet, that "any considerable misfortune happening to me just now would raise the whole country in
arms against us; and this opinion is not founded upon distant and precarious information, but upon a precise information of the general disposition of the inhabitants."[3] October 25, 1779, he says that he believes the appearance of the
enemy "would be followed by the revolt of a great part
of the province."[4]

---

[1] Can. Arch., Q. 18, p. 9.

[2] There seems to be no question that the French Canadians scattered through the
northwestern regions favored the revolutionary cause more or less actively throughout
the war. See on this Roosevelt, *Winning of the West*, I, and Hinsdale, *Old Northwest*,
pp. 150–9. In regard to the expedition of George Rogers Clark the latter says, "It is
perfectly clear that had they [the French Canadians] taken the side of the British, Clark
could never have done his work." (p. 159.)

[3] This latter statement is to be carefully noted. For the sources of information see
above.

[4] As part of the investigation of this matter from another standpoint it may be worth
seeing how much help the government actually received from the French Canadians in
the defense of the Province. The material we have is sufficient to show that, the statement of Hey above was almost literally true; that outside the noblesse, not more than
100 actually bore arms in any sort of fashion at any time during the period. Nov. 16,
1775 the number of Canadian militia at Quebec is officially given as 300, May 1, 1766, as
508; there is no likelihood that it ever exceeded this latter figure. Outside of
the town of Quebec there were practically none in arms. May 6, 1779, Haldimand
writes to an officer (apparently in answer to an offer of service), that the raising of 200
or 300 Canadians at that time would be a much more difficult operation than he (the
officer) imagined; from which and other indications we may conclude that very few if

The above examination has been directed solely to the conduct of the mass of the people, *bourgeois*[1] and *habitant*. The clergy and the noblesse remained faithful, though unmistakable indications of wavering were to be perceived even amongst them after the conclusion of the French all-

---

any Canadians of the class we refer to were then in arms. Among the military papers we have complete commissariat returns giving the description and number, monthly, of the different classes to whom rations were issued, and from these I have extracted the numbers set down as "Canadians" from Nov., 1778, to the end of 1780. This most probably includes those upon corvée service, which was performed during the summer months. In these months the average amounts to from 500 to 600; outside of them to not more than 50. This is for the whole Province and apparently for all classes of Canadians. It shows that even fewer were under service in the later years than in those I have more fully considered, and warrants the conclusion that outside of the actual service given by about 150 noblesse and by about the same number of the better class of bourgeois, the people (embracing 15,000 able bodied men), contributed practically nothing toward the defense of the Province.

[1] I have referred above to the *bourgeoisie* generally as apparently not sufficiently differentiated from the *habitants* to justify a close separate examination. In the main this may also be concluded of their conduct at this crisis; but an exception must be made with regard to a few of the better situated. The approving notices of the government class with the noblesse and clergy the better sort of the "bourgeoisie" or "citizens." But that these references are really applicable only to a very small number,—the government vision here, as in the representations previous to the Quebec Act, being cognizant only of those whose position brought them into prominence,—is abundantly proved by the exact statements given of the number of French Canadians who took part in the defence of Montreal and Quebec. The population of the towns together must have been about 20,000 (in 1765 was 14,700), of which eight-tenths would come under the class we are considering. Yet we find that not more than 500 Canadians *of all classes* took part in the defence of Quebec, and Carleton writes from Montreal (then closely invested by Montgomery), Oct. 28, 1775, that the walls are defenceless, and it is doubtful if a guard for the gates could be procured from the militia. Later he writes from Quebec that though it could hold out if the townsmen could be depended upon, there are so many traitors within that a successful defence is very doubtful. Jan. 11, 1776, Arnold reports from before Quebec that he has been assured that more than one-half of the inhabitants would willingly open the gates. July 25, 1778, Haldimand classes "some part of the bourgeoisie in the towns" with the noblesse and clergy as not included in his statement that the Canadians were not to be depended upon. But in September of the following year he complains of the unlooked for ingratitide of even the better sort. On the whole there seems to be no ground for supposing that in this crisis any more than in their general attitude, the body of the inhabitants of the towns differed essentially in sentiment from those of the country; though it is evident that in the narrow compass of the towns, directly under the official eye, it would be impossible for disaffection to be so openly shown as in the open unrestraint of the widespread country settlements. It is safe to conclude that the section of the bourgeoisie which showed decided attachment to the cause of Government was made up mainly of those closely connected in various ways with the official or higher classes, or of those who were more or less directly influenced by English commercial relations.

iance. This was to be expected however; and it will be remembered that the same national instinct would be operative with the mass of the people also after that event. I have spoken above of the strenuous efforts of the clergy in the early years in behalf of the established government. The noblesse seem at the same time to have enlisted for the defence of the Province almost to a man. As late as October, 1780, Haldimand writes that " the Quebec Act alone has prevented or can in any degree prevent the emissaries of France and the rebellious colonies from succeeding in their efforts to withdraw the Canadian clergy and noblesse from their allegiance to the crown of Great Britain."[1] This may be correct for the time at which it was written (after the French alliance), but there is no reason to suppose it so for the earlier more critical years. The hereditary feeling of hostility to the British colonies was very vivid among the noblesse, the leaders of the old border wars. They were also naturally prejudiced against the forms of government and the constitution of society prevailing throughout these colonies; institutions which had now become all the more distasteful from their supposed influence in the lately-developed independent attitude of the Canadian peasantry. The noblesse had been well treated by the English authorities in Quebec; the aristocratic governors had deferred constantly to them in all matters, and had steadily held out hopes of employment and the restoration of old privileges; in no particular whatever could they look for the same degree of favor or influence from a connection with the doubtful cause of the rebellious colonies. Previous to the French alliance, no influence whatever can be discovered which was likely to incline them in the least toward the continental cause; all the material conditions and every instinct of caste and education operated to range them on the imperial side. After the French alliance, the British hold was too firmly established

---

[1] Can. Arch., B. 54, p. 354.

in the Province for their defection to have made any difference. At no time as I have shown, could they have thrown into the scale the weight of more than their own small number. Indeed there is strong reason to believe that if they had embraced the colonial cause, that fact alone would have done much to place the mass of the people on the opposing side.

As to the clergy the same course of argument applies, with the addition of the fact that the church in Canada was convinced of the intolerant temper of the colonists in regard to their religion, and was well aware that at the most it could not hope in that connection for as much as it had enjoyed in Quebec from the conquest. There is no reason whatever to believe that in any event would the clergy in those earlier years have refrained from active opposition to the continental cause.

It must therefore be concluded that the Quebec Act had added no element of strength to the British cause in the Province; that on the contrary, while it had confirmed the allegiance of those whose allegiance needed no confirmation, it had been the main cause of the disaffection of those who otherwise would have been at least quiescent.

B.   The Failure of the American Expeditions.

If the conclusion reached above be correct, we are confronted with a difficulty in the utter failure of the expedition. It might not unreasonably be concluded that such a failure bears strongly against the position I have taken; that if the Canadians were thus so favorably disposed toward the invaders, the utmost vigor and ability on the part of the few British defenders would have been wholly inadequate to the prevention of the definite attachment of the Province to the Revolutionary cause. To answer this objection it will be necessary to view the enterprise from the American side to see if any other factors enter into the situation. Such I think will be found to be the case; it will be found that not only did the revolutionists fail to make any effective use of the Canadian alliance, but that by the mismanagement and misconduct of both officers and men, the Canadians were from the first impressed with the incapacity of their would-be emancipators, and were gradually driven by actual ill-treatment to neutrality if not to hostility. The favorable moment was let slip and did not return. With the spring of 1776 not only was the British force strengthened to a degree which enforced caution upon the most hostile of the peasantry, but by that time that peasantry had had its revolutionary fervour cooled by treatment as arbitrary and injurious as anything that could be expected from the dreaded revival of the conditions of the old régime. The evidence on this point leaves us wondering, not at the cooling off of the Canadians, but at the retention by them of any degree of respect for or sympathy with the revolutionary cause. That a very considerable degree was retained is shown above, and the fact testifies to the strength of the original feeling; but until the Franco-American alliance it did not again in all probability reach sufficient vigor to afford any likelihood of active manifestation.

It is not my intention to enter upon any full consideration of the invasion of Canada by the Revolutionary forces in 1775-6; full accounts already exist for all parts of this enterprise except for that Canadian side which it is here attempted to supply. The general causes assigned for the failure of the movement are well-known, and it is assumed that sufficient explanation thereof is given under the heads of such apparently unavoidable drawbacks as disease among the troops, short terms of enlistment, lack of ready money. Even if these difficulties had existed in the degree usually stated, it would be rash to assume that the responsibility of the authorities for the disaster is thereby much reduced. But the extent of these obstacles can be shown to have been greatly exaggerated. The degree of disease among the troops would have been found a comparatively small factor if disease alone had interfered with their efficiency; the lack of specie was at no time a fatal defect.   It seems very evident that Congress never made efforts adequate to the degree of importance attached to the enterprise by leading military authorities.[1]   What that degree was is shown by many emphatic utterances.   Washington, in his Instructions to Arnold, September 14, 1775, especially impresses upon him that the command is "of the utmost importance to the interest and liberties of America," and that upon it the safety of the whole continent may depend; further adjuring him solemnly to pay every regard to the attitude of the Canadians, "bearing in mind that if they are averse to it, [i. e., the expedition], and will not coöperate, or at least willingly acquiesce, it must fail of success.   In this case you are by no means to prosecute the attempt.   The expense of the expedition and the disappointment are not to be put in competition with the dangerous consequences which may ensue from irritating them against us, and detaching them from that neutrality which they have adopted.[2]   "In the following October, R. H. Lee writes to Washington of the expedition: "The ministerial dependence on Canada is so great that no object can be of greater importance to North America than to defeat them there.   It appears to me that we must have that country with us this winter, cost what it may.[3]

---

[1] It has been impossible for me to enter on a close examination of the responsibility of Congress with regard to its earlier insufficient support of the expedition. A severe view will be found expressed in very pointed terms in Lossing's *Schuyler* (II. 55-7). Congress is there charged with general ignorance as to the military operations, and especially with a failure to apprehend the great importance of the Canadian ones. Its efforts were spasmodic and its promises rarely fulfilled; it replied to reports of the desperate condition of things with indefinite resolutions which sounded like mockery. In the dread of a standing army it had adopted the ruinous policy of short enlistments; persisting in this even when the evil effects had been fully felt. While appreciating the difficulties of the situation, it seems to me that there are very strong grounds for these reproaches. With regard to enlistment, Richard Smith makes the following diary entry of proceedings in Congress January 19, 1776: "A motion that the new troops be inlisted for 3 years or as long as the war shall continue was opposed by the Northern Colonies and carried in the negative." (*Amer. Hist. Rev.*, April, 1896, p. 494.)

[2] 4 *Amer. Arch.*, III., 765.

[3] 4 *Amer. Arch.*, III. 1137.

And four days later [1] Washington impresses upon Schuyler, who was about to lead the western part of the force,
that "The more I reflect upon the importance of your expedition, the greater is my concern lest it should sink
under insuperable difficulties.   I look upon the interests
and salvation of our bleeding country, in a great degree
to depend upon your success." To Arnold in the following
January he states that "To whomsover it [i. e., Quebec and
in consequence Canada], belongs, in their favour probably
will the balance turn.   If it is in ours, success, I think,
will most certainly crown our virtuous struggles; if it is in
theirs, the contest at least will be doubtful, hazardous,
and bloody." [2] That Congress shared in this opinion at a
later stage at least is shown by a letter from the President
to Gen. Thomas, May 24, 1776, in which it is stated that
Canada is "an object of the last importance to the welfare
of the United Colonies.   Should our troops retire before
the Enemy and entirely evacuate that Province, it is not
in human wisdom to foretell the consequences." [3] On the
same day Congress forwarded to the Commissioners in
Canada all the hard money it had been able to procure; [4]
sending in addition about three weeks later $20,000 in
specie and $190,000 in paper.   These funds might earlier
have had an important effect that now was impossible; that
the main obstacle was not now at least of a financial character may be seen from the statement to Congress by the
Commissioners at Montreal, in May, that though there was
plenty wheat and flour in the country, "it was with difficulty that either could be procured a few days ago, for
ready money." [5] It cannot be questioned of course that the
money problem was present from the first, and that it had
an important bearing.   The journals of the Arnold expedi-

---

[1] 4 *Amer. Arch.* p. 1196 (Oct. 26, 1776).
[2] *Ibid.*, IV. 874.
[3] *Ibid.*, VI. 558.
[4] *Ibid.*, p. 580.
[5] *Ibid.*, p. 587.

tion show that however friendly the Canadians had been at
the first contact, they were even then thriftily endeavoring
to turn an honest penny from the necessities of the troops;[1]
insisting in some cases on the immediate payment of hard
cash. But this dislike of paper money is easy to understand quite apart from any special distrust of the Americans, if we remember the ruinous experiences of the Province with it under the French régime, and the losses
thus experienced since the war in spite of all the efforts of the English Government.[2] However friendly in
feeling, the Canadians were not anxious to run much risk
either of person or property. But that they did risk something, and that the failure of ready money alone would not
have seemed to them a fatal drawback, is very evident. The
American force could not have existed in amity a month
if the Canadians had not accepted promises, written and
spoken, in lieu of hard cash; it was not until even these
promises had failed and past ones had been disgracefully
repudiated, that in combination with other matters, the
financial element became serious. February 21, 1776,
Wooster informs the President of Congress that he
should soon, in the absence of specie, be forced to " lay
the country under contribution; there is no other alternative. We have not by us one half money enough to answer
the pressing demands of the country people to whom we
are indebted."[3] About a week later (March 4), Arnold issued
a Proclamation giving paper money currency, " declaring
those enemies who refuse it." " Many (he says), received
it willingly, but the greater part were averse to taking
it."[4] The supply even of paper was however apparently
soon exhausted, and we hear of the inhabitants being
forced to accept receipts for services or supplies in the

1 See especially Wild's *Journal* (Nov. 5, 1775), Dearborne's (Nov. 6), Thayer's (Nov. 5).
2 See on this subject the paper by Mr. Breckenridge in the Chicago *Journal of Political Economy* June, 1893, pp. 406—31.
3 4 *Amer. Arch.*, IV. 1470.
4 Arnold to Deane, *Ibid.*, V. 549.

form of "certificates not legible, with only one half a signature, and of consequence rejected by the Quarter-Master
General." [1] The situation is probably accurately enough
described by the Commissioners to Canada in their statement May 1st, that, "The general apprehension that we
shall be driven out of the Province as soon as the King's
troops can arrive concurs with the frequent breaches of
promises the inhabitants had experienced, in determining
them to trust our people no further." [2] A week later they
report that £14,000 is owed in the colony, and that with
the payment of this and some ready money, together with
a change in the ill-conduct of the expedition in other respects, "it may be possible to regain the affections of the
people, ... in which case the currency of our paper
money will, we think, follow as a certain consequence." [3]
It is evident, therefore, that, in the opinion of those best
qualified to judge, the absence of ready money was but a
comparatively minor difficulty; that if the Canadians were
otherwise well treated it would present no more difficulties than in the other Provinces.

To what ill treatment then had the Canadians otherwise
been subjected? What misfortunes had they experienced
from the American occupation, other than the lack of
prompt payment for supplies voluntarily furnished? The
evidence for the answer of this question is entirely sufficient,
and undoubtedly shows that at least in the latter part of
the expedition, they had been treated, not with the forbearance and tact so strongly recommended by Washington,
not even as neutrals from whom nothing was to be expected,
but rather, in spite of their abundant evidence of good
will, as irreconcilable enemies.

One of the earliest explicit statements on this point that
I find is contained in a letter from Col. Moses Hazen to Gen.

---

[1] Hazen to Schuyler, April 1st, 1776. Lossing, *Schuyler*, II. 467.
[2] To Congress, May 1st, 1776. 4 *Amer. Arch.*, V. 1166. It is to be noted that it is here
clearly shown that up to this time the inhabitants had trusted the invaders.
[3] May 8, 1776. *Ibid.*, p. 1237.

Schuyler, April 1, 1776.[1] After making some strong statements about the changed attitude of the Canadians, he proceeds to give reasons therefor: "Their clergy have been neglected and sometimes ill-used; . . . . the peasanty in general have been ill-used; they have in some instances been dragooned, with the point of the bayonet, to furnish wood for the garrison at a lower rate than the current price;" half of the imperfect certificates given in payment being moreover later dishonored by the Quarter-Master General. Hazen encloses as evidence of his representations a letter from one Captain Goforth of the Continental force, commanding at Three Rivers, detailing outrages committed by the troops on their march to Quebec.[2] "A priest's house (Goforth writes), has been entered with great violence, and his watch plundered from him. At another house they ran in debt about 20sh. and because the man wanted to be paid, run him through the neck with a bayonet. Women and children have been terrified, and forced, with the point of the bayonet, to furnish horses for private soldiers without any prospect of pay." That these complaints are accepted as just by Schuyler, or that he had abundant other evidence, is shown by his statement to Washington shortly after, that "The licentiousness of our troops, both in Canada and in this quarter, is not easily to be described; nor have all my efforts been able to put a stop to those scandalous excesses."[3] He had previously expressed to Congress his apprehension "that the imprudent conduct of our troops would create a disgust to our cause in Canada; it even hurts it in this colony."[4] These representations are thoroughly supported by the investigations of the Commissioners of Congress, whose statements as to the non-

---

[1] 4 *Amer. Arch.*, V. 869. Reprinted in Lossing's *Schuyler*, II. 46-7.

[2] *Ibid*, V. 871. The letter is undated but cannot be later than March. It will be noticed that from the reference to the march to Quebec, this seems to show a high degree of lawlessness and violence in the troops early in the expedition, when there was little or no excuse through the pressure of want.

[3] 4 *Amer. Arch.*, V. 1098. (From Fort George, April 27, 1776.)

[4] To President, April 12. (*Ibid.*, p. 868.) The colony referred to is New York.

fulfillment of pecuniary obligations to the inhabitants have been already referred to. May 8th they write from Montreal that the Canadians " have been provoked by the violences of our military, in exacting provisions and services from them without pay, — a conduct towards a people who suffered us to enter their country as friends that the most urgent necessity can scarce excuse, since it has contributed much to the changing their good dispositions toward us into enmity, and makes them wish our departure."[1] Congress did not need this report to be convinced of the truth of the charge, for we find it on April 23 resolving, " That the Commissioners of Congress to Canada be desired to publish an address to the people of Canada, signifying that Congress has been informed of injuries offered by our people to some of them, expressing our resentment at such misconduct." Matters, however, evidently did not improve; for May 10, 1776, Gen. Sullivan writes to Washington that " the licentiousness of some of the troops that are gone on has been such that few of the inhabitants have escaped abuse either in their persons or property. . . . Court-martials are vain where officers connive at the depredations of the men."[2] In the following June Washington expresses his conviction that "many of our misfortunes [in Canada] are to be attributed to a want of discipline and a proper regard to the conduct of the soldiery."[3] A few days later (June 21, 1776), an investigation was ordered by Congress. The report of the investigating committee on the following July 30, placed as the first of the causes of the failure the short terms of enlistment, which had made the men

---

[1] 4 *Amer. Arch.*, V. 1237.

[2] *Ibid.*, VI, 413. Sullivan writes from Albany on his way to Canada, and evidently is inspired by the traces of depredations he has come across. This is in New York therefor; but it may well be imagined that conduct would not improve in the enemy's country. The statement of Sullivan probably throws light on an entry in the Diary of Richard Smith (*Amer. Hist. Rev.*, April, 1896, pp. 510). Under date March 8, 1776 it is here noted that "Accounts transmitted from Canada by Col. Hazen of the damages done to him by our soldiers who had destroyed or damaged his house at St. Johns and killed his cattle &c. were referred to a committee."

[3] To Sullivan. *Ibid.*, p. 927.

"disorderly and disobedient to their officers," and had precipitated the commanders "into measures which their prudence might have postponed, could they have relied on a longer continuance of their troops in service."[1]

There would seem therefore abundant ground for the conclusion that the colonial forces had conducted themselves in such a manner as to expose to serious maltreatment even the most friendly portion of the Canadian people. The conviction will be strengthened by a glance at some evidence with regard to the general character and conduct of the rank and file of the troops; evidence which shows clearly that the invading force as a whole was, throughout the latter part of the expedition at least, afflicted with a degree of disorganization and disaffection fitted to deprive it of all claim to respect on the part of the Canadians, and to make misconduct inevitable. Very much allowance is of course to be made for the unavoidable defects that attach to a militia, and that were bound to be magnified in troops enlisted and serving under the conditions of the early part of the war. The fatal use of the short enlistment plan was something for which Congress was responsible; the lack of harmony and union as between troops of different colonies was certainly to be looked for.[2]

---

[1] *Journal of Congress*, v. 289. I have thought it necessary for my purpose to detail some of the more striking evidence on this point. But that the conduct in question has not been without recognition even from partial writers, is shown by Bancroft's statement that, "The Canadian peasantry had been forced to furnish wood and other articles at less than the market price, or for certificates, and felt themselves outraged by the arbitrariness of the military occupation." (IV, 376.)

[2] An indication of the existence and nature of this difficulty in the matter I am treating is afforded by the following Resolution of the General Assembly of Connecticut, Oct., 1775. (*Col. Records of Conn.*, XV, 136.) "This Assembly being informed that certain questions and disputes had arose amongst the troops lately raised by this colony . . . . and now employed against the ministerial forces in Canada, which disputes, unless prevented, may be attended with unhappy consequences. Therefore it is hereby re solved by this Assembly that all the Troops . . . . lately raised by this Colony . . . are and shall be subject to the rules, orders, regulations and discipline of the Congress of the Twelve United Colonies during the time of their inlistment." See also as to Montgomery's difficulties, Lossing, *Schuyler*, I. 426–7. Under date Dec. 18, 1775, a British officer in Quebec writes that news has just been received that "the besiegers were greatly dis-

These features are found in all the early operations of the Continental troops, and the special difficulties and disasters of the Canadian expedition were sure to make them more manifest and injurious. But that in this expedition there was also displayed other and more serious and fundamental defects in the character and bearing of the men is hardly to be denied. The impartial observer is forced to the conclusion that the word mercenary would not on the whole be an unjust appellation. It will be remembered that the word occurs in the exceedingly strong language used by Washington himself at this time about the force under his command. He writes to Congress in the latter part of 1775 that "Such a dearth of public spirit and such a want of virtue . . . . I never saw before; . . . . such a mercenary spirit pervades the whole [force] that I should not be at all surprised at any disaster that may happen."[1] And if this could be said of the troops assembling for defence in the heart of the country, we cannot be surprised to discover the same unsatisfactory condition in offensive operations of such magnitude and difficulty as those in Canada.

That the spirit in the Canadian expedition was unsatisfactory in the extreme from the beginning is shown clearly in Montgomery's statements.   October 31, 1775, he writes: "The New England troops are the worst stuff imaginable for soldiers. They are homesick; their regiments have melted away, and yet not a man dead of any distemper. There is such an equality among them, that the officers have no authority, and there are very few among them in whose spirit I have confidence. The privates are all gen-

---

satisfied with their General's proceedings, and that their body of men appears backwood in doing the duty required of them." ("Journal of principal occurrences during the seige of Quebec." Edited by Shortt, London, 1824.) Col. Trumbull (as quoted below), in describing the remains of the expedition as he encountered it on the retreat, says that there was "neither order, subordination, or harmony; the officers as well as men of one colony, insulting and quarrelling with those of another." (*Reminiscences,* p. 302.)

[1] Sparks, *Washington,* III, 178.

erals, but not soldiers; and so jealous that it is impossible, though a man risk his person, to escape the imputation of jealousy."[1] The most strenuous efforts were found necessary to induce the troops to enter at all upon the enterprise; it seems most probable that, but for the general belief in the weakness of the enemy and the warm support of the French-Canadians, it would have been found impossible. The force steadily diminished; on the 20th of November, Schuyler writes to Congress that "The most scandalous inattention to the public stores prevails in every part of the army. . . . . The only attention that engrosses the minds of the soldiery is how to get home the soonest possible."[2] With this temper it was to be expected that the force would diminish even more rapidly under disaster. On the receipt of the news of the failure of Montgomery's attack on Quebec, Gen. Wooster writes to Schuyler from Montreal: "Many of the troops insist upon going home, the times of enlistment being out. Some indeed have run away without a pass or Dismissal, expressly against orders. I have just been informed that a Capt. Pratt of the 2nd Battalion of Yorkers has led off his Company for St. Johns."[3]

There is some direct testimony as to the behaviour of the troops at Quebec in the journals of survivors. In that of Henry we have under date December 12 an account of the sacking by the troops of the house of a prominent Canadian near the town, and the evil results on the soldiery. "Though our Company was composed of freeholders, or the sons of such, bred at home under the strictures of re-

---

[1] To Schuyler, from St. Johns. See Lossing, *Schuyler*, I. 427. The justice of these and similar complaints, Lossing says, "impartial history, enlightened by facts, fully concedes."

[2] Lossing's *Schuyler*, I. 466. It is but fair to say that a more favourable impression is given by other statements in this letter, which however in their isolation do not seem on the whole to effect my general conclusion. In the *Diary* of Richard Smith (*Amer. Hist. Rev.*, Jan., 1896, p. 296) we have the following entry of Dec. 18, 1775: "Montgomery's soldiers very disobedient and many of them come Home without Leave."

[3] Jan. 5, 1776. (*New Hampshire Prov. Papers*, VII. 720.)

ligion and morality, yet when the reins of decorum were loosed, and the honourable feeling weakened, it became impossible to administer restraint. The person of a tory, or his property, became fair game, and this at the denunciation of a base domestic villain."[1] This writer indeed takes pains to assert expressly that only Tories were plundered, and that the peasantry were especially protected and respected; but the mass of adverse evidence forbids us to consider the statement of weight further than with regard to his own company. In Caleb Haskell's *Journal*[2] we have a glimpse of the attitude of the time-expired troops. Under date Jan. 30-1, he tells how the writer's Company, "looking upon ourselves as free men," in that their time of enlistment had expired, were tried and punished by Court-Martial for disobedience to orders, and how, "finding that arbitrary rule prevailed," they had finally concluded to remain and serve (which they did until the beginning of May, decamping then at a critical moment). Some interesting particulars are further found in these journals of the conduct of those who were taken prisoners on the occasion of the assault. Ebenezer Wild tells us under date January 3-4, (i. e., on the third and fourth days of captivity), that Carleton having sent for a list of the names of the prisoners, especially of those who were old countrymen, "they, [i. e., presumably, the old countrymen; in all probability meaning thereby those born in the British Islands], chiefly enlisted in the King's service."[3] More particular information is given by Capt. Simeon Thayer[4] who says that the old countrymen were threatened by Carleton with being sent to England and tried as traitors. In the lists given by Thayer with regard to the American losses in the assault on Quebec, we find the following figures for all ranks:— killed, 35; wounded, 33; prisoners, 372; enlisted, 94.

[1] *Account of the Campaign against Quebec* (Albany, 1877), p. 98.
[2] Newburyport, 1881. (Pamphlet.)
[3] *Proceedings Mass. Hist. Society*, April, 1886.
[4] *Collections R. I. Hist. Society*, VI (Providence, 1867). App. to *Journal*.

We see therefore that fully 25 per cent. of the prisoners at Quebec took service with their late enemies, apparently without much delay. If these comprised only "old countrymen," it is an interesting fact with regard to the composition of the troops. But we have little ground for confidence as to the firmness even of the acknowledged colonists. Col. J. Trumbull, (Acting Adjutant General with Gage), writes to his father, Governor Trumbull of Connecticut, on July 12, 1776,[1] of encountering the remnants of the Canadian expedition "ruined by sickness, fatigue, and desertion, and void of every idea of discipline or subordination." Of the 10,000 men of the previous spring, 6,000 are left; of the other 4,000, "the enemy has cost us perhaps one, sickness another thousand, and the others God alone knows in what manner they are disposed of. Among the few we have remaining, there is neither order, subordination, or harmony; the officers as well as men of one colony, insulting and quarreling with those of another." About the same time Lt. Ebenezer Elmer says of the same troops, "The whole of their conduct at Canada since the death of the gallant Montgomery seems nothing but a scene of confusion, cowardice, negligence and bad conduct."[2] In an account of the naval operations on Lake George in October, 1776, Trumbull further describes the dangerous influence exerted by Carleton over the prisoners then taken by him. These had all been allowed to return home on condition of not bearing arms again till they were exchanged; when encountered by Trumbull on the homeward march "all (he says) were warm in their acknowledgment of the kindness with which they had been treated and which appeared to me to have made a very dangerous impression." He therefore "placed the boats containing the prisoners under the guns of a battery and gave orders that no one

---

[1] Trumbull, *Reminiscences*, p. 302. (Appendix.).

[2] *Proceedings New Jersey Hist. Society*, II, 132. This is written at the Mohawk river, in the relief expedition of Gen. Sullivan. It is a significant fact that this very detailed journal is very largely taken up with Court-martial proceedings.

should be permitted to land, and no intercourse take place with the troops on shore until orders should be received from Gen. Gage."[1]   When the situation had been presented to Gage the latter ordered that the troops should return home immediately without being allowed to land.   This seems to show not only the ease with which the prisoners had been shaken in their patriotism, but also a very great lack of confidence in the main force.   A glimpse of the genesis of these forces in the spring of 1776 is to be obtained from a letter of one Capt. James Osgood to the Chairman of the New Hampshire Committee of Safety.   He informs him that he has enlisted for Canada about 60 good men; adding "I have had a great number Deserted after paying them the Bounty and part of advance pay to support their families."[2]

I shall add but little on this general point.   An account by an officer of the American force of the final withdrawal from Quebec seems to show that this closing act was by no means creditable; the writer describes it as a "disgraceful retreat," marked by the "utmost precipitation;" he himself "meeting the roads full of people, shamefully flying from an enemy that appeared by no means superior to our strength."[3]   The commissioners to Canada write to Congress May 17, 1776:   "We want words to describe the confusion which prevails through every department relating to the army," and point out "the unfeeling flight and return at this juncture of all the soldiers and the greater part of the officers who were entitled to be discharged."[4]   On May 27, after dwelling on the distressed condition of the army, they tell of the plundering of the baggage "by those whose times were out, and have since left Canada.   We are informed by Capt. Allen *that the men who, from pretended indisposition, had been exempted from do-*

---

[1] *Reminiscences*, p. 34.

[2] *New Hampshire State Papers* VIII, 164.

[3] 4 *Amer. Arch.*, VI. 398.

[4] *Ibid.*, p. 587.

ing duty, were the foremost in the flight, and carried off such burdens on their backs as hearty and stout men would labour under." [1]

In view of these facts we must at least concur in the words of Washington, already quoted, "I am convinced many of our misfortunes are to be attributed to a want of discipline and a proper regard to the conduct of the soldiery." Nor can we demur from the belief expressed by the President of Congress that "there has been very gross misconduct in the management of our affairs in Canada." [2] I am not interested here to point out that this misconduct on the part of the troops was supplemented by gross mismanagement on the part of the leaders, from Congress down; as stated before it is not my purpose to write a history of the expedition, or seek the full explanation of its failure. That purpose is rather to show that the revolutionary cause, as expressed in this movement, could in no sense attract the French-Canadians; that on the contrary, this contact with that cause must in every respect have acted strongly to repress the zeal of the ardent among them, to bring doubt to the most sanguine, to anger and antagonize not only the indifferent but even the amicably inclined. Herein is the explanation of the failure to secure for the movement that effective aid from the strong predilections of the Canadian people which had been confidently and justly expected. It is an explanation which is consistent with the existence of such a predilection in a high degree; in it I am confident, is comprised in the main the explanation of the non-inclusion of the Province of Quebec (and of consequence all Canada), in the regions destined to form the United States. It is, I think, not to be doubted that had the favorable attitude of the Canadians been carefully cultivated, had the *personnel* of the invading force been of

---

[1] Introductory Memoir to Carroll's *Journal*, p. 38. (Maryland Hist. Soc., 1876.) The italics seem to be the commissioners'.

[2] To Washington, June 21, 1776. (4 *Amer. Arch.*, VI, 1009.)

higher grade, had the means been furnished, both to enable that army to avoid all arbitrary conduct, and to avail itself more thoroughly of the French Canadian assistance, the campaign would have ended in an altogether different manner.   Even if the disaster at Quebec had still been experienced, it would not have had the demoralizing effect it did have; the invaders would have been still strongly sustained by a friendly people until adequate reinforcements had arrived.   It is useless to contend that the French Canadians were a timid race, and of little help to whatever cause they might embrace; students of the previous war find them in it, as throughout their whole history, displaying under the most discouraging circumstances, in very high degree the qualities of regular troops.[1]   It is inconceivable that in fifteen years they could have so degenerated.   They embraced about 15,000 able-bodied men, practically all trained to arms; here was certainly a factor that, well managed, might indeed prove the decisive one.   At the very least we are justified in concluding that with this aid organized and kept effective, the American force could have maintained itself in the country until the French alliance had formed a basis for more decisive operations. That alliance alone, when it did come, was sufficient to stir again to the depths the whole Canadian people, including even the classes which before had immovably supported the British cause; it is surely not too much to say that if the total withdrawal of the Continental forces had not enabled the British to get a firm control of the country, and to take all possible measures of precaution against new attacks or uprisings, the province would have presented a most favorable field of effort; a field the French would have been only too eager to occupy.

---

[1] See above, p. 283, for Carleton's testimony (that of an antagonist), as to their conduct.

CONCLUSION.

The latter part of the foregoing study has had for its central point the relations of the Province of Quebec with the American Revolution, as gathered about the Quebec Act of 1774 and the revolutionary invasion of the Province in 1775–6. I have attempted to examine the Quebec Act in the light of its origins and environment, and thus to show, at this great crisis for America and for English colonial empire, the nature and degree of the connections, conscious and unconscious, existing in the British administrative mind between the new fortunes of Canada and the West and the conditions and problems of the older colonies. And from the side of the Revolution especially I have followed up that crisis until the parting of the ways has (as we see it now), fully declared itself; until the British North America of the future has been clearly differentiated from the British North America of the past. How unnecessary and indeed surprising that differentiation was, and how it came about, the last chapter has been intended to show.

In addition to these two important aspects of the Revolutionary connections of the Quebec Act, reference has also been briefly made to the effect of the Act in the hastening or aggravating of the difficulties with the other colonies. This however I have not been able to fully enquire into. Closer investigation will, I feel sure, show that the disastrous influence of the measure upon the colonial temper was as great as that of the more direct attacks upon colonial institutions. It would seem as if this most unfortunate of enactments had been specially under the patronage of some malign genius; for the unfortunate nature of its provisions is equalled by the unhappy moment of its appearance. We cannot wonder at its evil influence on the colonial troubles, nor at the misconceptions of the irritated colonists. It was most natural to suppose that it had a vital connection with the coercive measures in whose company it appeared; it needed but a slight degree of suspicion to invest it with the most sinister aspect. Rather than being surprised at the ideas of the Revolutionary fathers in regard to it, I have been surprised instead at finding that their suspicions are so utterly without foundation. The reasonableness of these suspicions and the impress that they have left on later historical writing, though not the only reasons for the care with which I have traced the origins of the Act, seem to me alone sufficient to justify that care. I have attempted to show that it had a natural and altogether explainable genesis apart altogether from the special difficulties in the other colonies; that practically no evidence seems to exist that any one of its objectionable provisions was, in origin or development, appreciably affected by these difficulties. The matter has been treated not merely negatively; it has been shown also that these provisions had been fully determined upon years before the events occurred to which their origin has been supposed to be due, and upon grounds, entirely apart from them, which might well seem amply sufficient to justify such action.

I may possibly be accused of viewing this matter with too particular an eye for the exact date; it may be said that colonial difficulties had existed and been steadily growing from 1764 down. It should perhaps be sufficient to reply that these difficulties previous to the close of 1773 had not called forth or seemed likely to call forth, any seriously repressive measures on the part of the home government; that still less is it to be supposed that they could possibly have evoked such deeply laid and carefully concealed plans of hostile far-reaching action as the Canadian and Western measures have been ascribed to. It is indeed I think undeniable that the belief in such plans, at that day or since, has been held or at least advanced only in

connection with the idea that the provisions of the Quebec
Bill were subsequent in origin to the more serious and
aggravated phase of colonial difficulties that may be said
to date from the latter part of 1773.[1]   But a more conclusive
line of answer to this objection will probably be furnished
in a reference to the lack of continuity in the Imperial
executive as between 1764 and 1774, in connection with a
real continuity in Canadian policy, so far as can be discerned, from the very beginning of serious attention to
Canadian matters. I have shown above that all the important provisions of the Act, except that in regard to an Assembly, had been fully discussed and to all appearances practically decided upon, not only before the formal establishment
of the Tory Ministry of 1770, but also before the termination
of the Chatham influence in 1768.   That is, if the Quebec Act
had been passed in 1768 or even in 1767, it would, so far as
we can judge, have been mainly identical with the measure of
1774.   It was in July 1766 that the Chatham ministry was
formed, and Shelbourne placed in charge of the Colonial
Office; yet in September, 1766, we find Carleton the new
Quebec governor, fresh from conference with the home
executive, entering upon a strong pro-French administration in the Province, and evidently fully confident from the
first of the support of the home government along lines of
action which ended logically in the Quebec Act of 1774.   A
reference to the pages in which I have described above the
origins of the Act will show the Chatham administration
to all appearance fully committed to three of the four important provisions which make up its substance.[2]   The extension of the bounds of the province was, I have contended, simply the following out of the long-established

---

[1] As bearing on this as well as on the estimation as to the effect of the Act, it may be
worth while to note a curious British opinion of a few years later. In the debate in the
House of Lords on the Quebec Government Bill of 1791, Lord Abingdon referred to the
Quebec Act as one of the most unfortunate in the statute book, in that it "laid the
foundation-stone of division between the North American colonies and this country."
(*Parl. Hist.* XXIX, p. 659.)

[2] See pp. 411-31; 432-36; 450-56.

colonial-commercial policy; the action in regard to the
Church of Rome was merely the attempt to fulfill (with a
certain degree of political liberality), the engagements of
the treaty of 1763, and was not in excess of the previous
steady attitude of the government toward that Church; the
advisability of reversion to French law at least in part had
been officially recommended by the crown lawyers and by the
Board of Trade as early as the spring of 1766, and its likelihood had been officially intimated by Shelbourne to Carleton
in June 1767; in regard to an Assembly we find even Fox admitting in 1774 that he would not assert that it was expedient
that one should be then granted. It is thus clear that the
party (so far as we can hold by party lines in this
chaotic period), which in the main stood for the more
liberal and advanced colonial policy, was practically
committed to the same Canadian policy as their opponents. But neither the most distrustful colonist of the
revolutionary period nor the most pronounced Anglophobist
of our later historical literature, would be likely to ascribe
to Fox or Burke or Shelbourne that line of far-reaching and
insidious hostility to colonial freedom and growth which
has been ascribed to the authors of the Quebec Bill. The
fact that party lines were more closely drawn when the bill
actually came before Parliament must be ascribed mainly
to the irresponsible position of an opposition,— an opposition too which was acting more as individuals than as a unit; [1]
especially as the debates show that that opposition, instead
of fighting specific provisions or pointing out better ones,
confined its efforts mainly to generalities, or to such favorable points of popular agitation as Popish establishment
and the absence of trial by jury. And in these debates the
position that the French Canadians alone were to be considered and the neglect or disregard of the English element and prospects, was almost as marked on the opposition
as on the governmental side. The whole consideration of

---

[1] See Fitzmaurice, *Shelbourne*, II., 310.

this phase of the matter must therefore I think support my conclusion as to the lack of connection between the Canadian measures and the strained relations with the older colonies.

But it is not only in this light that my study centres about the Quebec Act. That measure has two aspects with regard to which we must consider it:— (1) the temporary and long-past one, now of purely historical interest, of its various connections with the American Revolutionary crisis; and (2) the permanent living one, of strong interest to every student of institutions, and of vital interest to every modern Canadian, of its effects on the after history of British North America,— of its place in the development of that great commonwealth which the Dominion of Canada seems destined to become. If it does become such, it will only be after surmounting, mayhap at great cost, those most serious obstacles which, placed in its path by that Imperial policy of which the Quebec Act of 1774 was the controlling basis, have grown steadily with its growth. They are the obstacles presented to Anglo-Saxon domination and to political unity in modern Canada through the continued and magnified existence there of an alien and hostile nationality, rooted in and bound up with an alien and hostile ecclesiastical domination.[1]

This opinion is my apology for the care with which I have dwelt upon the more purely institutional aspects of the period. I have tried to present a full statement of the social and political conditions of the province during the early years of the British occupation, in the belief that it is only by their study that we can claim to pass judgment upon their treatment. The misfortune for the country of the non-assimilation of French and English through these 130 years of common political existence in British North America has of course been frequently dwelt upon; but it has usually been in a tone of resignation to those mysterious dispensations of Providence which made the Quebec

---

[1] See Goldwin Smith, *Canada and the Canadian Question*. Chapter 2.

Act an unavoidable necessity, and would have made any
other course then, or any counter course since, disastrous
and impossible. What else could have been done, we are
asked,— usually with extravagant laudation of the humanity and generosity of the British government in thus pur-
suing the only path open to it. It has been one of my objects to try and show that something else, something very
different, *could* have been done; that the policy that was
adopted with such far-reaching and disastrous consequences,
was precisely also the one that was the most dangerous with regard to the conditions of the moment. It is no
part of the historian's (and certainly not of the special
investigator's) task to enter upon constructive work, to
replace everything that he has pulled down; and therefore
I do not feel called upon to go into particulars with
regard to the possible legislation of 1774. But I do
not wish to evade the problem; it should be manifest
from the above examination that the alternative course
was simply to set the new English Province firmly and
definitively upon an *English* instead of a *French* path of
development. As shown above, the way was clearly
pointed out by other advisers as well qualified to speak as
those whose advice was taken in 1774. I know that in this
our age of highly-defined and all-pervading nationality,
this apparently light hearted and reckless treading upon
the holy ground of national development may bring down
upon me the severest censures. But my critics will remember that we are dealing with another age, one in which
nationality was not the breath of the political nostril; one
in which new and alien acquisitions were absorbed and
assimilated as an every day process.[1] And I hope I shall

---

[1] The contemporary history of the French colony of Louisiana is a case in point, and
will I think support my argument in every respect. Ceded to Spain in 1762, the new
rule began in 1766 with infinitely worse prospects than that of the English in Canada; for
the Spanish were driven away by a revolt of the colonists in 1768, and after re-establish-
ing themselves by overwhelming force in the following year, began their régime anew
by taking summary vengeance upon the colonial leaders. It had moreover been under-

not be further reproached with a slavish respect for legal enactment, in attaching the importance I do to the measures, actual and possible of 1774.   An enactment which determines the ecclesiastical conditions and the whole civil code of a people is surely not to be spoken of lightly; but I regard it only as the first step in a progress which under its pressure became the inevitable one; as the opening of an easy and secure path and the providing of encouraging and helpful guides in a journey for which no other route or guide was available.

It may seem that it is to place too much emphasis on the effect of the Quebec Act even to represent it as the first step in a development which it made inevitable.   The matter is one which I do not feel at liberty to stop and discuss fully here; but some considerations must be briefly referred to.   The main one has regard to the probably different history of early English colonization in the Province if the British government in 1774 had not so avowedly and definitely handed it over to a French future.   In the discussions in

---

stood at the time of cession that in deference to the express wish of Louis XV., the colony would be allowed to retain its old laws and usages; but after the insurrection the Spanish government proceeded to thoroughly assimilate it in law and governmental forms to the other Spanish colonies in America. The degree of success attained in the face of circumstances so much more discouraging than those which existed in Canada, is shown in the statement by Gayarré, (*Louisiana under Spanish Domination*, p. 310), that when in 1791 the fourth Spanish governor ended his administration, "He left Louisiana entirely reconciled to the Spanish domination, which had been gradually endeared to the inhabitants by the enlightened and wise deportment of almost every officer who had ruled over them." Yet the colony had remained thoroughly French in stock; for in 1800 a distinguished Louisianian official states in a memoir intended for Napoleon I, that "Almost all the Louisianians are born French or are of French origin." Napoleon in that year re-acquired the colony for France; and when in 1803 the United States were negotiating for its purchase, he was informed by M. Barbé Marbois (later the author of a *History of Louisiana*), that "These colonists have lost the recollection of France." When in the same year the French officials took possession of the province they were received with suspicion rather than enthusiasm. M. Marbois reports: "Every one will be astonished to learn that a people of French descent have received without emotion and without any apparent interest a French magistrate. . . . . Nothing has been able to diminish the alarm which his mission causes. His proclamations have been heard with sadness, and by the greater part of the inhabitants with the same indifference as the beat of the drum is listened to when it announces the escape of a slave or a sale at auction." (*Gayarré*, p. 582.) There was here of course an additional element in the apprehensions as to the French attitude with regard to slavery; but in view of the evi-

Parliament and out with regard to that measure, both before and after its enactment, we find that its advocates insist with strong self-righteousness that in Canada it is the French Canadian only who is to be considered; that the small English section there has scarcely a right to be heard; that Canada (as Carleton had urged), was French and destined to remain French; that it was probably for the interest of Great Britain to discountenance any large English admixture. This view I have shown above was no doubt largely due to the incorrect ideas which Murray and Carleton had fostered with regard to the origin and character of the English already in the Province. Whatever its full explanation the tone is unmistakable. It may be considered a part of the striking inadequacy of the prevailing British mind at that time to the Imperial position that had so wonderfully come to the nation; an inadequacy which was being most generally shown in the petty legality and short-sighted selfishness which were marking all the rela-

---

dence as to the temper of the colony before that question could have arisen, it does not seem that it can be assumed to have much to do with the point at issue.

Lack of space prevents my following the development of the colony in its more complex history as a part of the United States. What the nature of that development has been however may I think be correctly inferred from the fact that even by 1823 we are told of " the adoption of that people into the great American family having now superadded many features of the English jurisprudence to those already stamped upon the institutions of Louisiana by the French and Spanish." (North American Review, XVII, 244.) When in 1820 Edward Livingstone was appointed by the General Assembly of Louisiana to draw up a report on a new criminal code, one of the objects of the same was laid down as being, " To abrogate the reference which now exists to a foreign law for the definition of offences and the mode of prosecuting them." (Ibid.) Before 1839 we find that the success achieved in the Americanizing of the territory is such as to attract the envious attention of the English element which in Quebec was at that moment struggling with the culmination of the long period of increasingly bitter hostility there between the French and English. Lord Durham tells us (Report on Canada, 1839) that they [the English] "talk frequently and loudly of what has occurred in Louisiana, where . . . the end . . . of securing an English predominance over a French population has undoubtedly been attained;" and in his final recommendations as to remedying the Canadian troubles he points out that "The influence of perfectly equal and popular institutions in the effacing distinctions of race without disorder or oppression and with little more than the ordinary animosities of party in a free country, is memorably exemplified in the history of the State of Louisiana, the laws and population of which were French at the time of its cession to the American Union."

tions with the older colonies. What I wish especially to call attention to here is the effect that this attitude and its results already in Quebec, must have had at the close of the war upon those who were compelled to seek refuge from the victorious colonists in other parts of the British dominions. These United Empire Loyalists were of the same temper, I have shown above, as the English already resident in Quebec; even if the Quebec Act did not fill them with the same lively apprehension of tyranny that it aroused in these and in the revolting colonists, it must yet have been in a high degree obnoxious. The immediate effect is doubtless to a very considerable degree expressed in the fact that of the 50,000 Loyalists (approximately), who settled in the remaining British Provinces during and within a few years after the war, only about one-quarter chose the oldest and presumably much the most attractive part of the country. And of those who did choose the Province of Quebec, practically none it would seem, elected to settle amongst the French Canadians (where previous to the new constitution a large amount of land had been eagerly taken possession of by their compatriots), but went instead into the untrodden wilderness. It is true that by so doing they did not escape the dominion of the new order of things, for they remained subject to the Quebec Act till 1791; but they could hope thereby to reduce the necessary evil to a minimum (as proved the case), and to build up with greater prospects of success the active opposition to it that they at once entered upon.

What would have been the consequences at the time of this migration of the existence in Quebec of a constitution, not indeed wholly English either in fact or promise, but with an English admixture sufficient to afford a working basis and a guarantee with regard to the line of development? It can scarcely be doubted that the English immigration into the Province would have been so largely increased that the balance of population would thereby have been at

once in considerable degree redressed. As a result a security would have been thereby provided that all the
English conditions that had already obtained would have
been upheld with accelerating influence, and that development would have proceeded mainly along that line. The
large degree of influence that had been so rapidly gained
by the few English over the French Canadian masses in the
period 1763–1774, would probably have steadily increased;
the new French Canadian native leaders, who had already
shown a very considerable degree of knowledge of and apti-
tude for English conditions, would have coelesced more
and more with the English element; the whole history of
Quebec and Canada would in short have run a different
course. As it was, we find that the Quebec Act bestows
on the Province, even from the French standpoint, only
misfortune; that under it the law is uncertain and its administration almost anarchy; [1] that the English and French
elements enter with the addition to the numbers of the former after the war, on a period of bitter political strife;
that finally in 1791 the British government, while pacify-
ing the main body of the English discontents by forming
them into a new Province, at the same time continues and
confirms thereby the policy of 1774, with apparently a
more conscious purpose of such a use of the French nationality as might perhaps be justly expressed in the maxim
divide et impera. It was a development of the Quebec Act
policy that was largely due to the intervening revolutionary war; but such a development was possible
only on the basis of that Act and the results of its
seventeen years' operation. It denotes the unaccountable
persistence in the British mind of the idea as to the efficacy of the measure in preserving the Province from
the grasp of the revolutionists, and a determination to
guard against similar danger in the future by keeping to
and developing this line of action. As Lord Durham ex-

---

[1] See above, pp. 477–9.

pressed it in 1839, "the system of Government pursued in
Lower Canada has been based on the policy of perpetuat-
ing that very separation of the races, and encouraging
these very notions of conflicting nationalities which it
ought to have been the first and chief care of Government
to check and extinguish. From the period of the conquest to the present time the conduct of the Government
has aggravated the evil, and the origin of the present extreme disorder may be found in the institutions by which
the character of the colony was determined."[1]   The "extreme disorder" referred to was the result of the fact
that by the act of 1791 the way was left clear within the
province of Quebec for that period of embittered resistance
on the part of the small English minority which was to
end in civil war, and in the vain attempt of 1840 to undo the
work of the previous sixty-six years by stifling the French
majority in a reunion with the English mass of Upper
Canada.   What degree of responsibility for this crisis
of race hostility rested on the policy definitely inaugurated in 1774 and confirmed in 1791, is forcibly shown
above in the words of the special Imperial Commissioner
who was sent out in 1839 to deal with that crisis.   His report further points out how from the Conquest "the continued negligence of the British Government left the
mass of the people without any of the institutions which
would have elevated them in freedom and civilization.   It
has left them without the education and without the
institutions of local self-government, that would have
assimilated their character and habits, in the easiest and
best way, to those of the empire of which they became a
part."[2]   The evil policy of 1774 was, he adds, adhered to
in 1791, when "instead of availing itself of the means
which the extent and nature of the province afforded for
the gradual introduction of such an English population into

---

[1] *Report*, p. 27.
[2] *Ibid.*, p. 12.

the various parts as might have easily placed the French in a minority, the Government deliberately constituted the French into a majority, and recognized and strengthened their distinct national character. Had the sounder policy of making the province English in all its institutions been adopted from the first and steadily persevered in, the French would probably have been speedily outnumbered, and the beneficial operation of the free institutions of England would never have been impeded by the animosities of origin." [1] And as noticed above he points to the history of Louisiana as an example of what might and should have been done.

It therefore does not seem an extreme view to regard the great difficulties that have beset English rule in Canada, as well as the grave problems that still confront the Dominion, as a natural and logical development from the policy of the Quebec Act. And if I am mistaken in my opinion of the comparative ease and completeness with which these difficulties and problems could have been avoided, and with which from the time of the conquest the province could have been started on the path of assimilation to English conditions, it must be admitted that I err in good company, both of that time and of this. In the tract reputedly Franklin's, entitled, "The Interest of Great Britain considered, with regard to her colonies, and the acquisition of Canada and Gaudaloupe," the following opinion is expressed of the future of the new province: " Those who are Protestant among the French will probably choose to remain under the British government, [2] many will choose to remove if they can be allowed to sell their lands, improvements and effects; the rest in that thinly settled country will in less than one-half a century, from the crowds of English settling round and among them, be blended and incorporated with our people both in language and manners." Lord

---

[1] *Report*, p. 29.

[2] See p. 288 above for the facts as to emigration.

Durham's opinion of the policy that should have been followed, and of the degree of success that might have been attained from the first, has already been quoted. So convinced was he of its necessity and practicability that he strongly urged the adoption of that policy even at the late date at which he wrote. " Without effecting the change so rapidly or so roughly as to shock the feelings and trample on the welfare of the existing generation, it must henceforth " he declared, " be the first and steady purpose of the British Government to establish an English population with English laws and language in this Province, and to trust its government to none but a decidedly English Legislature." [1] In his view this apparently harsh policy was the truest mercy to the French Canadians, " isolated in the midst of an Anglo-Saxon world." For, " it is but to determine whether the small number of French who now inhabit Lower Canada shall be made English under a Government which can protect them, or whether the process shall be delayed until a much larger number shall have to undergo, at the rude hands of its uncontrolled rivals the extinction of a nationality strengthened and embittered by continuance." [2] Finally on this point I will quote the words of the most prominent of modern students of Canadian history and prospects, — Goldwin Smith. To Anglicize Quebec at the Conquest he declares " would not have been hard. Her French inhabitants of the upper class had, for the most part, quitted her after the conquest and sailed with their property for France. There remained only 70,000 peasants, to whom their language was not so dear as it was to a member of the Institute, who knew not the difference between codes so long as they got justice, and among whom, harsh and abrupt change being avoided, the British tongue and law might have been gradually and painlessly introduced." [3]

---

[1] *Report*, p. 128.
[2] *Ibid.*, p. 130.
[3] *Canada and the Canadian Question*, p. 81.

Apart from speculation or the consideration of national or natural rights, my judgment of the Quebec Act and my opinion as to alternative measures must rest upon the facts which I have brought forward. I have tried to show that in ten years of British civil rule, the French Canadian had advanced steadily in the comprehension of English principles of society and government, and had lived in prosperity and fair contentment;[1] that by 1774 he was ready for a compromise civil code which might have left him the principles of the regulation of landed property to which he was most wedded, and yet have proclaimed itself as an *English* code, the starting point of English accumulation. This would have established a system which with regard to land would not from the very beginning have been without analogy in England itself at that period, and which on all other important sides, including procedure, would have been exclusively English in spirit, substance and development. With this aspect the Province could not have presented to English-speaking immigrants at the close of the American war the forbidding features that it did present under French law. This does not seem a visionary outcome with regard to the most difficult of the matters involved, the Civil Code. The grant of representative institutions and the fostering of local self-government would naturally accompany the English legal aspect. Connected with settlement there might have been, and would almost necessarily have been, an avoidance of those other features of the Quebec Act settlement which I have shown above were objectionable to the mass of the people, and the only discoverable causes of their disloyalty in the American invasion. With a system distinctly and avowedly English in spirit and main substance there would have

---

[1] How speedily the Quebec Act had operated for the undoing of this work may be judged from Pitt's declaration in 1791 in regard to the separation into two Provinces by the Constitutional Act, that "he had made the division of the province essential, because he could not otherwise reconcile their clashing interests" [i. e. of the English and French elements]. *Parl. Hist.* XXIX, 404.

been no room for those fears as to reversion to the old
feudal order which so aroused the peasantry, and consequently no field of labor for the revolutionary agitator;
in the absence of the so-called establishing of the Church
there would have been lacking that most distasteful re-fast-
ening upon them of compulsory tithes. In other words,
without any conceivable antagonizing on other grounds of
the ordinary French Canadian, there would have been
avoided all those aspects of the Act by which alone can be
explained the hostile attitude of the *habitant* during the war;
while the greatest of all steps would have been taken for
the preserving of the future from the perils of racial hostility and alien institutions. The various lines along which
Anglicising might for the future have proceeded can be as
easily imagined as described; the way of every one was
effectually barred by the Quebec Act.

APPENDIX I.

THE QUEBEC ACT, 1774.[1]

An act for making more effectual Provision for the Government of the Province of Quebec in North America.

Whereas his Majesty, by his Royal Proclamation, bearing date the seventh Day of *October*, in the third Year of his Reign, thought fit to declare the Provisions which had been made in respect to certain Countries, Territories and Islands in *America*, ceded to his Majesty by the definitive Treaty of Peace, concluded at *Paris* on the tenth Day of *February*, one thousand seven hundred and sixty-three: And whereas, by the Arrangements made by the said Royal Proclamation, a very large Extent of Country, within which there were several Colonies and Settlements of the Subjects of *France*, who claimed to remain therein under the Faith of the said Treaty, was left without any Provision being made for the Administration of Civil Government therein; and certain Parts of the Territory of *Canada*, where sedentary Fisheries had been established and carried on by the Subjects of *France*, Inhabitants of the said Province of *Canada*, under Grants and Concessions from the Government thereof, were annexed to the Government of *Newfoundland*, and thereby subjected to regulations inconsistent with the Nature of such Fisheries: May it therefore please your most Excellent Majesty that it may be enacted; and be it enacted by the King's most Excellent Majesty, by

---

[1] 14 Geo. III., Cap. 83. In full from British *Statutes at Large* (London, 1776), xii., pp. 184–187.

and with the Advice and Consent of the Lords Spiritual and Temporal, and Commons, in this present Parliament assembled, and by the Authority of the same, That all the Territories, Islands and Countries in *North America*, belonging to the Crown of *Great Britain*, bounded on the South by a Line from the Bay of *Chaleurs*, along the High Lands which divide the Rivers that empty themselves into the River *Saint Lawrence* from those which fall into the Sea, to a point in forty-five Degrees of Northern Latitude, on the Eastern bank of the River *Connecticut*, keeping the same Latitude directly West, through the Lake *Champlain*, until, in the same Latitude, it meets the River *Saint Lawrence;* from thence up the Eastern Bank of the said River to the Lake *Ontario;* thence through the Lake *Ontario*, and the River commonly called *Niagara;* and thence along by the Eastern and the South-eastern Bank of Lake *Erie*, following the said Bank, until the same shall be intersected by the Northern Boundary, granted by the Charter of the Province of *Pennsylvania*, in case the same shall be so intersected; and from thence along the said Northern and Western Boundaries of the said Province, until the said Western Boundary strike the *Ohio:* But in case the said Bank of the said Lake shall not be found to be so intersected, then following the said Bank until it shall arrive at that Point of the said Bank which shall be nearest to the North-western Angle of the said Province of *Pennsylvania*, and thence by a right line, to the said North-western Angle of the said Province; and thence along the Western Boundary of the said Province, until it strike the River *Ohio;* and along the Bank of the said River, Westward, to the Banks of the *Mississippi*, and Northward to the Southern Boundary of the Territory granted to the Merchants Adventurers of *England*, trading to *Hudson's Bay;* and also all such Territories, Islands, and Countries, which have, since the tenth of February, one thousand seven hundred and sixty-three, been made Part of the Government of *Newfoundland*, be, and they are hereby, during his Majesty's Pleasure, annexed to, and made Part and Parcel of, the Province of *Quebec*, as created and established by the said Royal Proclamation of the seventh of *October*, one thousand seven hundred and sixty-three.

II.   Provided always, That nothing herein contained, relative to the Boundary of the Province of *Quebec*, shall in anywise affect the Boundaries of any other Colony.

III.   Provided always, and be it enacted, That nothing in this Act contained shall extend, or be construed to extend, to make void, or to vary or alter any Right, Title, or Possession, derived under any Grant, Conveyance, or otherwise howsoever, of or to any Lands within the said Province, or the Provinces thereto adjoining; but that the same shall remain and be in Force, and have Effect, as if this Act had never been made.

IV.   And whereas the Provisions, made by the said Proclamation, in respect to the Civil Government of the said Province of *Quebec*, and the Powers and Authorities given to the Governor and other Civil Officers of the said Province, by the Grants and Commissions issued in consequence thereof, have been found, upon Experience, to be inapplicable to the State and Circumstances of the said Province, the Inhabitants whereof amounted, at the Conquest, to above sixty-five thousand Persons professing the Religion of the Church of *Rome*, and enjoying an established Form of Constitution and System of Laws, by which their Persons and Property had been protected, governed, and ordered, for a long Series of Years, from the first Establishment of the said Province of *Canada;* be it therefore further enactéd by the Authority aforesaid, That the said Proclamation, so far as the same relates to the said Province of *Quebec*, and the Commission under the Authority whereof the Government of the said Province is at present administered, and

all and every the Ordinance and Ordinances made by the
Governor and Council of Quebec for the time being, relative
to the Civil Government and Administration of Justice in
the said Province, and all Commissions to Judges and other
Officers thereof, be, and the same are hereby revoked, annulled, and made void, from and after the first Day of *May*,
one thousand seven hundred and seventy-five.

V.   And, for the more perfect Security and Ease of the
Minds of the Inhabitants of the said Province, it is hereby
declared, That his Majesty's Subjects, professing the Religion of the Church of *Rome* of and in the said Province of
Quebec, may have, hold, and enjoy, the free Exercise of the
Religion of the Church of *Rome*, subject to the King's
Supremacy, declared and established by an Act, made in
the first year of the Reign of Queen *Elizabeth*, over all the
Dominions and Countries which then did, or thereafter
should belong, to the Imperial Crown of this Realm; and
that the Clergy of the said Church may hold, receive, and
enjoy, their accustomed Dues and Rights, with respect to
such Persons only as shall profess the said Religion.

VI.   Provided nevertheless, That it shall be lawful for his
Majesty, his Heirs or Successors, to make such Provision
out of the rest of the said accustomed Dues and Rights,
for the Encouragement of the Protestant Religion, and for
the Maintenance and Support of a Protestant Clergy
within the said Province, as he or they shall, from Time to
Time, think necessary and expedient.

VII.   Provided always, and be it enacted, That no Person,
professing the Religion of the Church of *Rome*, and residing in the said Province, shall be obliged to take the Oath required by the said Statute passed in the first Year of the
Reign of Queen *Elizabeth*, or any other Oaths substituted
by any other Act in the place thereof; but that every such

Person who, by the said Statute, is required to take the Oath therein mentioned, shall be obliged, and is hereby required, to take and subscribe the following Oath before the Governor, or such other Person in such Court of Record as his Majesty shall appoint, who are hereby authorized to administer the same; *videlicet,*

I A. B. do sincerely promise and swear, That I will be faithful, and bear true Allegiance to his Majesty King George, and him will defend to the utmost of my Power, against all traitorous Conspiracies, and Attempts whatsoever, which shall be made against his Person, Crown, and Dignity; and I will do my utmost Endeavour to disclose and make known to his Majesty, his Heirs and Successors, all Treasons, and traitorous Conspiracies, and Attempts, which I shall know to be against him, or any of them; and all this I do swear without any Equivocation, mental Evasion, or secret Reservation, and renouncing all Pardons and Dispensations from any Power or Person whomsoever to the contrary.   *So help me God.*

And every such person, who shall neglect or refuse to take the said Oath before mentioned, shall incur and be liable to the same Penalties, Forfeitures, Disabilities, and Incapacities, as he would have incurred and been liable to for neglecting or refusing to take the Oath required by the said Statute passed in the first Year of the Reign of Queen Elizabeth.

VIII.   And be it further enacted by the Authority aforesaid, That all his Majesty's *Canadian* Subjects within the Province of *Quebec,* the Religious Orders and Communities only excepted, may also hold and enjoy their Property and Possessions, together with all Customs and Usages relative thereto, and all other their Civil Rights, in as large, ample, and beneficial Manner, as if the said Proclamation, Commissions, Ordinances, and other Acts and Instruments, had not been made, and as may consist with their Allegiance to his Majesty, and Subjection to the Crown and Parliament of *Great Britain;* and that in all Matters of Controversy, relative to Property and Civil Rights, Resort shall be had to the Laws of *Canada,* as the Rule for the Decision of the same; and all Causes that shall hereafter be instituted in any of the Courts of Justice, to be appointed within and for the said Province by his Majesty, his Heirs and Successors, shall, with respect to such Property and Rights, be determined agreeably to the said Laws and Customs of *Canada*, until they shall be varied or altered by any Ordinances that shall, from Time to Time, be passed in the said Province by the Governor, Lieutenant Governor, or Commander in Chief, for the time being, by and with the Advice and Consent of the Legislative Council of the same, to be appointed in Manner herein-after mentioned.

IX.   Provided always, That nothing in this Act contained shall extend, or be construed to extend, to any Lands that have been granted by his Majesty, or shall hereafter be granted by his Majesty, his Heirs and Successors, to be holden in free and common Soccage.

X.   Provided also, That it shall and may be lawful to and for every Person that is owner of any Lands, Goods, or Credits, in the said Province, and that has a right to alienate the said Lands, Goods, or Credits, in his or her Lifetime, by Deed of Sale, Gift, or otherwise, to devise or bequeath the same at his or her Death, by his or her last Will and Testament; any Law, Usage, or Custom, heretofore or now prevailing in the Province, to the contrary hereof in any-wise notwithstanding; such will being executed either according to the Laws of *Canada*, or according to the Forms prescribed by the Laws of *England*.

XI.   And whereas the Certainty and Lenity of the Criminal Law of *England*, and the Benefits and Advantages resulting from the Use of it, have been sensibly felt by the Inhabitants, from an Experience of more than nine years, during which it has been uniformly administered; be it therefore further enacted by the Authority aforesaid, that the same shall continue to be administered, and shall be observed as Law in the Province of *Quebec*, as well in the Description and Quality of the Offence as in the Method of

Prosecution and Trial; and the Punishments and Forfeitures thereby inflicted to the Exclusion of every other Rule of Criminal Law, or Mode of Proceeding thereon, which did or might prevail in the said Province before the Year of our Lord one thousand seven hundred and sixty-four; any Thing in this Act to the contrary thereof in any respect notwithstanding; subject nevertheless to such Alterations and Amendments as the Governor, Lieutenant-governor, or Commander-in-Chief for the Time being, by and with the Advice and Consent of the legislative Council of the said Province, hereafter to be appointed, shall, from Time to Time, cause to be made therein, in Manner herein-after directed.

XII.   And whereas it may be necessary to ordain many Regulations for the future Welfare and good Government of the Province of *Quebec*, the Occasions of which cannot now be foreseen, nor, without much Delay and Inconvenience, be provided for, without intrusting that Authority, for a certain time, and under proper restrictions, to Persons resident there: And whereas it is at present inexpedient to call an Assembly; be it therefore enacted by the Authority aforesaid, that it shall and may be lawful for his Majesty, his Heirs and Successors, by Warrant under his or their Signet or Sign Manual, and with the Advice of the Privy Council, to constitute and appoint a Council for the Affairs of the Province of *Quebec*, to consist of such Persons resident there, not exceeding twenty-three, nor less than seventeen, as his Majesty, his Heirs and Successors, shall be pleased to appoint; and, upon the Death, Removal, or Absence of any of the Members of the said Council, in like Manner to constitute and appoint such and so many other Person or Persons as shall be necessary to supply the Vacancy or Vacancies; which Council, so appointed and nominated, or the Major Part thereof, shall have Power and Authority to make Ordinances for the Peace, Welfare, and good Government, of the said Province, with the Consent of his Majesty's Governor, or, in his Absence, of the Lieutenant-governor, or Commander-in-Chief for the time being.

XIII. Provided always, That nothing in this Act contained shall extend to authorize or empower the said legislative Council to lay any Taxes or Duties within the said Province, such Rates and Taxes only excepted as the Inhabitants of any Town or District within the said Province may be authorized by the said Council to assess, levy, and apply, within the said Town or District, for the purpose of making Roads, erecting and repairing publick Buildings, or for any other Purpose respecting the local Convenience and Oeconomy of such Town or District.

XIV. Provided also, and be it enacted by the Authority aforesaid, That every Ordinance so to be made, shall, within six months, be transmitted by the Governor, or, in his absence, by the Lieutenant-governor, or Commander-in-Chief for the time being, and laid before his Majesty for his Royal Approbation; and if his Majesty shall think fit to disallow thereof, the same shall cease and be void from the Time that his Majesty's Order in Council thereupon shall be promulgated at *Quebec*.

XV. Provided also, that no Ordinance touching Religion, or by which any Punishment may be inflicted greater than Fine or Imprisonment for three Months, shall be of any Force or Effect, until the same shall have received his Majesty's Approbation.

XVI. Provided also, That no Ordinance shall be passed at any Meeting of the Council where less than a Majority of the whole Council is present, or at any Time except between the first Day of *January* and the first day of *May*, unless upon some urgent Occasion, and in such Case every Member thereof resident at *Quebec*, or within fifty miles thereof, shall be personally summoned by the Governor, or, in his Absence, by the Lieutenant-governor, or Commander in Chief for the Time being, to attend the same.

XVII.   And be it further enacted by the Authority afore-said, That nothing herein contained shall extend, or be construed to extend, to prevent or hinder his Majesty, his Heirs or Successors, by his or their Letters Patent under the Great Seal of *Great Britain*, from erecting, constituting, and appointing, such Courts of Criminal, Civil, and Eccle-siastical Jurisdiction within and for the said Province of Quebec, and appointing, from Time to Time, the Judges and Officers thereof, as his Majesty, his Heirs and Success-ors, shall think necessary and proper for the Circum-stances of the said Province.

XVIII.   Provided always, and it is hereby enacted, that nothing in this Act contained shall extend, or be construed to extend, to repeal or make void, within the said Province of Quebec, any Act or Acts of the Parliament of *Great Britain* heretofore made, for prohibiting, restraining, or regulating, the Trade or Commerce of his Majesty's Col-onies and Plantations in *America;* but that all and every the said Acts, and also all Acts of Parliament heretofore made concerning or respecting the said Colonies and Plan-tations, shall be, and are hereby declared to be, in Force, within the said Province of *Quebec*, and every Part thereof.

THE QUEBEC REVENUE ACT, 1774.[1]

An Act to establish a fund towards further defraying the charges of the Administration of Justice, and support of the Civil Government within the Province of Quebec in America.

Whereas certain duties were imposed by the Authority of his Most Christian Majesty upon Wine, Rum, Brandy, *eau*

----

[1] 14 Geo. III., Cap. 88.   In full from British *Statutes at Large*, London, 1776.

de vie de liqueur, imported into the Province of *Canada*, now called the Province of *Quebec*, and also a duty of three pounds *per centum ad valorem* upon all dry Goods imported into and exported from the said Province, which Duties subsisted at the Time of the Surrender of the said Province to your Majesty's Forces in the late War: And whereas it is expedient that the said Duties should cease and be discontinued, and that in Lieu and in Stead thereof other Duties should be raised by the authority of Parliament for making a more adequate Provision for defraying the Charge of the Administration of Justice and the Support of Civil Government in the said Province: We, your Majesty's most dutiful and loyal Subjects, the Commons of *Great Britain* in Parliament assembled, do most humbly beseech your Majesty that it may be enacted; and be it enacted by the King's most Excellent Majesty, by and with the Advice and consent of the Lords Spiritual and Temporal and Commons, in this present Parliament assembled, and by the Authority of the same: That from and after the fifth Day of *April*, one thousand seven hundred and seventy-five, all the duties which were imposed upon Rum, Brandy, *eau de vie de liqueur*, within the said Province, and also of three pounds *per centum ad valorem* on dried goods imported into or exported from the said Province under the Authority of his most Christian Majesty, shall be and are hereby discontinued; and that in Lieu and in Stead thereof there shall from and after the said fifth Day of April, one thousand seven hundred and seventy-five be raised, levied, collected, and paid unto his Majesty, his Heirs and Successors, for and upon the respective Goods hereinafter mentioned, which shall be imported or brought into any Part of the said Province, over and above all other Duties now payable in the said Province, by any Act or Acts of Parliament, the several Rates and Duties following: that is to say,

For every Gallon of Brandy, or other Spirits, of the Manufacture of *Great Britain*, Three-pence.

For every Gallon of Rum, or other Spirits, which shall be imported or brought from any of his Majesty's Sugar Colonies in the *West Indies*, Six-pence.

For every Gallon of Rum, or other Spirits which shall be imported or brought from any other of his Majesty's Colonies or Dominions in *America*, Nine-pence.

For every Gallon of Foreign Brandy, or other Spirits of Foreign Manufac-ture imported or brought from *Great Britain*, one Shilling.

For every Gallon of Rum or Spirits of the Produce or Manufacture of any of the Colonies or Plantations in *America*, not in the Possession or under the Dominion of his Majesty imported from any other Place except *Great Britain*, one Shilling.

For every Gallon of Molasses and Syrups which shall be imported or brought into the said Province in Ships or Vessels belonging to his Majesty's subjects in *Great Britain* or *Ireland*, or to his Majesty's subjects in the said Province, Three-pence.

For every Gallon of Molasses and Syrups, which shall be imported or brought into the said Province in any other Ships or Vessels in which the same may be legally imported, Six-pence; and after those Rates for any greater or less Quantity of such Goods respectively.

II. And it is hereby further enacted by the Authority aforesaid, That the said Rates and Duties charged by this Act shall be deemed, and are hereby declared, to be Sterl-ing Money of *Great Britain*, and shall be collected, re-covered, and paid, to the Amount of the Value of which such nominal Sums bear in *Great Britain;* and that such Monies may be received and taken according to the Propor-tion and Value of five Shillings and Sixpence the Ounce in Silver; and that the said Duties hereinbefore granted shall be raised, levied, collected, paid, and recovered, in the same Manner and Form, and by such Rules, Ways and Means, and under such Penalties and Forfeitures, except in such Cases where any Alteration is made by this Act, as any other Duties payable to his Majesty upon Goods imported into any *British* Colony or Plantation in *America* are or shall be raised, levied, collected, paid, and recovered, by any Act or Acts of Parliament, as fully and effectually, to all Intents and Purposes, as if the several Clauses, Powers, Directions, Penalties, and Forfeitures relating thereto, were particularly repeated and again enacted in the Body of this present Act: and that all the Monies that shall arise by the said Duties (except the necessary Charges of raising, col-

lecting, levying, recovering, answering, paying, and ac-
counting for the same) shall be paid by the Collector of his
Majesty's Customs, into the hands of his Majesty's Receiver-General in the said Province for the Time being, and
shall be applied in the first place in making a more certain
and adequate Provision towards defraying the Expenses of
the Administration of Justice and of the Support of Civil
Government in the said Province; and that the Lord High
Treasurer, or Commissioners of his Majesty's Treasury, or
any three or more of them for the Time being, shall be, and
is, or are hereby impowered, from Time to Time, by any
Warrant or Warrants under his or their Hand or Hands, to
cause such Money to be applied out of the said Produce of
the said Duties, towards defraying the said Expenses; and
that the Residue of the said Duties shall remain and be reserved in the hands of the said Receiver-General, for the
future Disposition of Parliament.

III. And it is hereby further enacted by the Authority
aforesaid that if any Goods chargeable with any of the said
Duties herein-before mentioned shall be brought into the
said Province by Land Carriage, the same shall pass and be
carried through the Port of *Saint John's*, near the River
Sorrel, or if such Goods shall be brought into the said
Province by any inland Navigation other than upon the
River *Saint Lawrence*, the same shall pass and be carried
upon the said River *Sorrel* by the said Port, and shall be
there entered with, and the said respective Rates and Duties
paid for the same, to such Officer or Officers of his Majesty's
Customs as shall be there appointed for that Purpose; and
if any such Goods coming by Land Carriage or inland Navigation, as aforesaid, shall pass by or beyond the said place
before named, without Entry or Payment of the said Rates
and Duties, or shall be brought into any Part of the said
Province by or through any other Place whatsoever, the
said Goods shall be forfeited; and every Person who shall

be assisting, or otherwise concerned in the bringing or removing such Goods, or to whose Hands the same shall come,
knowing that they were brought or removed contrary to
this Act, shall forfeit treble the Value of such Goods, to be
estimated and computed according to the best Price that
each respective Commodity bears in the Town of *Quebec*, at
the Time such Offence shall be committed; and all the Horses,
Cattle, Boats, Vessels, and other Carriages whatsoever,
made use of in the Removal, Carriage, or Conveyance of such
Goods, shall also be forfeited and lost, and shall and may be
seized by any Officer of his Majesty's Customs, and prosecuted as hereinafter mentioned.

IV. And it is hereby further enacted by the Authority
aforesaid, That the said Penalties and Forfeitures by this
Act inflicted, shall be sued for and prosecuted in any Court
of Admiralty, or Vice-Admiralty, having jurisdiction within
the said Province, and the same shall and may be recovered
and divided in the same Manner and Form, and by the same
Rules and Regulations in all Respects as other Penalties and
Forfeitures for Offences against the Laws relating to the
Customs and Trade of his Majesty's Colonies in *America*
shall or may, by any Act or Acts of Parliament be sued for,
prosecuted, recovered and divided.

V. And be it further enacted by the Authority aforesaid,
That there shall from and after the fifth Day of *April*, one
thousand seven hundred and seventy-five, be raised, levied,
collected and paid unto his Majesty's Receiver-General of
the said Province for the Use of his Majesty, his Heirs and
Successors, a Duty of one Pound sixteen Shillings, Sterling
Money of *Great Britain*, for every License that shall be
granted by the Governor, Lieutenant-Governor, or Commander-in-Chief of the said Province to any Person or
Persons for keeping a House or any other place of publick
Entertainment, or for the retailing Wine, Brandy, Rum, or

any other Spirituous Liquors within the said Province; and any Person keeping any such House or place of Entertainment, or retailing any such Liquors without such License shall forfeit and pay the Sum of ten Pounds for every such Offence, upon Conviction thereof; one Moiety to such Person as shall inform or prosecute for the same, and the other Moiety shall be paid into the Hands of the Receiver-General of the Province for the Use of his Majesty.

VI.   Provided always, That nothing herein contained shall extend or be construed to extend to discontinue, determine, or make void any Part of the territorial or casual Revenues, Fines, Rents, or Profits whatsoever, which were reserved to, and belonged to his Most Christian Majesty, before and at the Time of the Conquest and Surrender thereof to his Majesty, the King of Great Britain; but that the same and every one of them, shall remain and be continued to be levied, collected, and paid in the same Manner as if this Act had never been made; anything therein contained to the contrary notwithstanding.

VII.   And be it further enacted by the Authority aforesaid, That if any Action or Suit shall be commenced against any Person or Persons for any thing done in pursuance of this Act, and if it shall appear to the Court or Judge where or before whom the same shall be tried, that such Action or Suit is brought for any thing that was done in pursuance of, and by the Authority of this Act, the Defendant or Defendants shall be indemnified and acquitted for the same; and if such Defendant or Defendants shall be so acquitted; or if the Plaintiff shall discontinue such Action or Suit, such Court or Judge shall award to the Defendant or Defendants Treble Costs.

APPENDIX II.

AUTHORITIES.

No attempt is made here to furnish a complete bibliography. I have tried to make use of all the material that might bear on the subject; to give a full catalogue of the books consulted would scarcely be possible, and would certainly appear pedantic. In the following list I include in the main therefore, only titles to which reference has actually been made. The arrangement is alphabetical:

ALBEMARLE (Earl of). *Memoirs of the Marquis of Rockingham and his Contemporaries.* (2 v. London, 1852.)

ALMON (J.). *Anecdotes of the Life of Mr. Pitt, Earl of Chatham.* (London, 1793.)

ALMON (J.). *The Remembrancer: A Repository of Passing Events.* (J. Dodsley, London, 1774, 1775, 1776.)

FORCE (Editor), *American Archives.* (Fourth Series, 1774–6, 6 vols.— Washington, 1837–46. Fifth Series, 1776–83, 3 vols.—Washington, 1848–53.)

ASHLEY (W. J.). *Lectures on Canadian Constitutional History.* (University of Toronto.)

BANCROFT (George). *History of the United States.* (Author's last revision. 6 v. New York, 1884–5.)

BOURINOT (J. G.). *Manual of the Constitutional History of Canada.* (Montreal, 1888.)

BOURINOT, (J. G.). *Parliamentary Procedure and Practice in Canada.* (Montreal, 1892.)

BURKE (Edmund). *Correspondence.* (8 v. London, 1852.)

British Statutes at Large. (London, 1776.)

Calendar of Home Office Papers of the Reign of George III. (1760–5; 1766–9; 1770–2. London, 1878–81.) Published under direction of the Master of the Rolls.

CANADIAN ARCHIVES. Furnishing the substance of the greater part of the study. The material therefor is collected in the following series of copies of British State Papers:

 a. *State Papers and Correspondence concerning the Province of*

Quebec, 1760-80. [The MS. copies of the more important documents have been compared with the originals or original duplicates in the Record and Colonial Offices, London. The series is calendared as Q in the Reports of the Canadian Archivist, beginning with that for 1890. It includes the complete official correspondence between the Secretaries of State for the Southern Department and the Colonies, the Board of Trade, and the Colonial officials, together with copies of the more important papers belonging more properly to the Privy Council and the Treasury. With all documents concerned.]

b. *The Haldimand Papers.* [A copy in 232 MS. volumes of the collection (deposited in the British Museum) of official and other matter accumulated by General Haldimand, long and prominently connected with Quebec, and Governor-in-Chief 1778-83. This series has been calendared as B in the Reports of the Canadian Archivist (1884-9), and has been used mainly through that guidance.]

CARROLL (John). *Life of.* (Md. Hist. Soc. 1876.)

CHATHAM (Earl of). *Correspondence.* Edited by Taylor and Pringle. (London, 1838. 4 vol.)

CHRISTIE (Robert). *History of the late Province of Lower Canada.* (Montreal, 1866. 6 v.)

CLARK (Charles). *A Summary of Colonial Law, etc.* (London, 1834).

Collections of the Rhode Island Historical Society. (Providence, 1827-85.)

Connecticut, The Public Records of the Colony of. [Referred to as *Col. Records of Conn.*] (Hartford, 1850-90.)

STEPHENS (Editor), *Dictionary of National Biography.* Vol. XXVI. Article *Hill, Wills.* (London.)

DURHAM (Earl of). *The Report on the Affairs of British North America.* (London, J. W. Southgate.)

EDWARDS (Bryan). *The History, Civil and Commercial, of the British Colonies in the West Indies.* (4 v. Phila., 1806.)

FITZMAURICE (Lord Edmund). *Life of William, Earl of Shelburne.* (3 v. London, 1876.)

FRANKLIN (Benjamin). *Complete Works.* Compiled and edited by John Bigelow. (10 v. New York and London, 1887-8).

GARNEAU (F.X.). *Histoire du Canada depuis la decouverte jusqu'à nos jours.* (2 v. Quebec, 1845-6.)

GAYARRÉ. *Louisiana under Spanish Domination.* (New York, 1854.)

Grenville Papers. (London, 1852.)

HART (A. B.). *Formation of the Union, 1750-1829.* (New York, 1892.)

HENRY (J. J.). *Account of the Campaign against Quebec.* (Albany, 1877.)

HINSDALE (B. A.) *The Old Northwest.* (New York, 1888.)

Historical Manuscripts Commission, Reports of. (London,—Eyre and Spottiswoode.)

HOUSTON (William). *Documents illustrative of Canadian Constitutional History.* (Toronto, 1891).

JONES (C. H.). *Campaign for the Conquest of Canada*, 1775-6. (Phila., 1882.)

Journals of the survivors of Arnold's Expedition against Quebec, 1775-6. [These can be easily referred to through the names and dates given in the text. A full list, with exact titles and references for finding, will be found in the *Proceedings Mass. Hist. Soc.* 2nd Series II (1885-6), pp. 265-7. Another list with further bibliographical infortion is furnished as a Preface to Thayer's *Journal*, in *Coll. Rhode Island Hist. Soc.* (Providence, 1867) pp. IV-VII].

Journal of the Principal Occurrences During the Siege of Quebec . . . ; collected from some old MSS. originally written by an officer during the period of the gallant defense made by Sir Guy Carleton. With Preface and notes by W. T. P. Shortt. (London, 1824.)

Journal of Charles Carroll of Carrollton, during his visit to Canada in 1776. Edited by Brantz Meyer. (Md. Hist. Soc. Papers. Centennial Memorial volume, 1876.)

Journal of Congress. Vols. I. II. (Phila. 1777.)

KINGSFORD (W). *The History of Canada.* (8 volumes published. Toronto, 1887-95.)

LAREAU (Edmund). *Histoire du Droit Canadien.* (2 v. Montreal, 1888-9.)

LECKY (W. E. H.). *A History of England in the Eighteenth Century.* (8 v. London, 1892.)

LOSSING (B. J.), *Life of General Philip Schuyler.* (2 v. New York, 1873.)

Lower Canada Jurist. Vol. I.

MARRIOTT (James). *Plan of a Code of Laws for the Province of Quebec.* (London, 1774.)

MASÈRES (Francis), [Attorney-General of the Province of Quebec, 1766-9. The most acute and voluminous of contemporary writers on Canadian affairs. Hasty, prejudiced, religiously intolerant, and much given to legal discussions; but on the whole an invaluable witness. A careful study has led me to an agreement with many of his main statements and conclusions.]

  (a) *A collection of several commissions, and other public instruments proceeding from his Majesty's Royal Authority, and other papers relating to the state of the Province of Quebec.* (London, 1772.)

(b) *An account of the Proceedings of the British and other inhabitants of Quebec.* (London, 1775.)

(c) *Additional papers concerning Quebec.* (London, 1776.)

(d) *The Canadian Freeholder.* 3 vols. (London, 1767.)

New York, Documents relating to the Colonial History of the State of. (Albany.)

New Hampshire Provincial Papers.

New Hampshire State Papers.

Official Returns on Public Income and Expenditure. Ordered to be printed by the House of Commons, 1869.

Proceedings Massachusetts Historical Society. (Boston, 1879–95.)

Proceedings New Jersey Historical Society. (Newark, 1845–77.)

Parliamentary History. Vols. XV, XVI, XVII, XVIII, XXIX. (London, T. C. Hansard, 1813.)

QUEBEC Literary and Historical Society, Publications of.

   a. *Historical Documents.* Series 1–5, Quebec, 1840–77.)

   b. *Transactions.* (Quebec, 1837–62.)

   c. *Transactions.* (New series, Quebec, 1863–86.)

Quebec, Ordinances made for the Province of, by the Governor and Council of the said Province since the Establishment of the Civil Government. (Brown and Gillmore, Quebec, 1767.) [Compared with State Paper copies.]

Quebec, Ordinances of, 1767–8. [MS. in Toronto Public Library with no place or date affixed.]

Quebec, Report of the Debate in the Commons on the Bill for the Government of, 1774. From notes of Sir Henry Cavendish, member for Lostwithiel. Edited by Wright. (London, 1839.) [Referred to as *Cavendish* or *Report.*]

ROOSEVELT (Theodore). *Winning of the West.* (3 v. New York, 1889–94.)

SMITH (Goldwin), *Canada and the Canadian Question.* (Toronto, 1891.)

SMITH (Richard). *Diary of, 1775–6.* (In American Hist. Review, January and April, 1896.)

SMITH (William). *History of Canada from its First Discovery to 1791.* (2 v. Quebec, 1815.)

SOUTHEY (Captain Thomas). *Chronological History of the West Indies.* (3 v. London, 1827.)

SPARKS (Editor.) *Writings of George [Washington.* (12 v. Boston, 1855.)

TRUMBULL (Colonel). *Reminiscences.* (New Haven, 1841.)

TURNER (F. J). *Character and Influence of the Indian Trade in Wisconsin.* (Johns Hopkins University Studies. Ninth Series XI–XII.)

562   BULLETIN OF THE UNIVERSITY OF WISCONSIN.

TRACTS AND PAMPHLETS, COLONIAL AND POLITICAL. [The following are of special importance in this connection.]

A Letter Addressed to Two Great Men, on the Prospects of Peace; and on the Terms Necessary to be Insisted Upon in the Negotiation. (London, 1760. 2d edition.) [Anonymous. Attributed by Sparks to Earl of Bute.]

Remarks on the Letter addressed to two Great Men. In a letter to the Author of that Piece. (London, 1760.) [Anonymous. Attributed sometimes to Edmund or to William Burke.]

The Interest of Great Britain Considered with regard to her Colonies, and the acquisition of Canada and Gaudaloupe. (London, 1760.) [Anonymous. Attributed by Sparks to Franklin.]

An examination of the Commercial Principals of the late negotiation between Great Britain and France in 1761. (London, 1762.) [Anonymous. Attributed to Edmund Burke.]

A letter to the Earl of Bute on the Preliminaries of Peace. From neither a noble lord, a candid Member of Parliament, or an impartial Briton, but an Englishman. (London, 1762.) [Anonymous.]

A full and free Inquiry into the Merits of the peace; with some strictures on the Spirit of Party. (London, 1765.) [Anonymous.]

Observations upon the Report made by the Board of Trade against the Grenada Laws. (W. Flexney, London, 1770.) [Anonymous.]

History and Policy of the Quebec Act Asserted and Proved. By William Knox. (London, 1774.)

Letter to the Earl of Chatham on the Quebec Bill. By Sir William Meredith. (London, 1774.)

The Rights of Great Britain Asserted Against the Claims of America. By Sir John Dalyrymple. (London, 1776.)

Answer to Sir William Meredith's Letter to the Earl of Chatham. [Anonymous.] (London, 1774.)

An appeal to the Public; stating and considering the objections to the Quebec Bill. [Anonymous.] (2nd Edition, London, 1774.)

WALPOLE (Horace). *Letters.* Edited by Peter Cunningham. (9 v. London, 1861.)

WINSOR (Justin.) *The Mississippi Basin.* (Boston and New York, 1895.)

ld keep on writing to me

lay in June. Across Man-
wedish liner, the *Grips-*
renço Marques, Mozam-
on June 11, many of my
they looked at towering
e. Reluctant to leave the
rought up, many of the
d up the gangplank.
rted by a steward to my
nan a pink-faced, jovial
fr. Taguchi, aren't you?"
he pillow? I'm sorry, but
l to see it before you.
ou, to have such a good

the pillow, and picked

ered to you through the
portunity to send you a
about to leave for your
dge that your friends in
ppiness and our reunion,

w life and a completely
you. My present concern
rough my letters might
ently pray that my fears
awful war ends, I intend
f my country. But I will
eart for your happiness.
ind may again enjoy the
be able to resume our

hat you will always be in
at your friendship and
my thoughts.

THREE UNFORGETTABLE LETTERS

by *Taguchi Shu*

ON DECEMBER 7, 1941, when the report was flashed over the air that Japan had made a sudden attack on Pearl Harbor, I was engaging in jovial conversation with intimate American friends in my apartment in New York City. The report came like a bolt from the blue and suddenly made these dear friends enemies and me an enemy of theirs, and I could not grasp the fantastic idea at all. Rather the fateful war that had then been set into motion appeared to me like an affair involving entirely distant worlds, with no relation to me.

A short time afterwards I was placed under detention at Ellis Island as an enemy national. Whether the war between my country and America had ever occurred to me as an actuality or not, when at last I found myself incarcerated, it dawned upon me like a blast of icy wind that my status now was that of an enemy national. With this realization, I was overcome by indescribable feelings of loneliness, insecurity, and despair.

There at Ellis Island more than two hundred of my fellow countrymen were detained with me. Each had his own world of worries, but over all there hovered demoralizing insecurity. As for me, isolated as I was from the outer world, it was wretchedness itself to gaze out of windows covered with meshed steel wires from morning to night, to see before my very eyes the massive and towering figure of Manhattan in whose gay streets I had spent so many pleasurable moments. More than by a feeling of uncertainty and

1

hopelessness, I was crushed by the reality of my
from the world I loved so dearly.

It was at such a time that a letter came—a l
heart and made my feelings soar:

My Dear Shu:

After some time and effort, I have at last asce
not illegal to write letters to an enemy national
to write this. My purpose of course is to try to
spiritual comfort I can, for your sudden chan
and the sudden shock may have thrown you in
spair, and also to show you that your Americ
merely fair-weather friends. Friendship should
ship maintained only in fair weather. People nee
when it rains. If friendship means merely going
movies together, the word "friend" is just a w
And if anybody needed a friend now you need
if the whole world should become one's enemy a
with discouragement and despair, I know by e
mere knowledge that one has a friend—even
heart is true, supplies one with strength, courage,

I believe without one iota of doubt that th
check this letter and the Americans who surro
people who have the right concept and consci
equality, justice, and freedom, and are people
upon the individual with prejudice. It is becaus
lieve they will not prevent a letter written wit
from reaching you.

From the very first, I have never considered
lawful for one to entertain friendly affections f
their respective countries are at war with each
to draw a clear line of distinction between ind
and racial prejudice and national movements—
and wisdom of American democracy. I have ne
this fact.

I have so little spare time now. Even if I were
to write to you my conscience does not permit
typewriter during office hours. . . . It is a joy t
that by many small efforts I am contributing i
cause of my country. Such being the case, I do n

my friend, not knowing that I had left, wo
only to get letters back undelivered.

The time for embarkation came—a hot
hattan on the New Jersey side was the
holm, which was to take us as far as Lo
bique, in southern Africa. We boarded he
fellow countrymen breathing a deep sigh a
Manhattan for what might be the last tim
country where they had been born and
teen-agers had tears in their eyes as they tr

After the baggage inspection, I was esc
stateroom. No sooner had I entered it
man came in. He was the purser. "You're
he asked. "Have you seen the letter under
because of censorship regulations we ha
You're a very fortunate man, I can tell y
friend."

I immediately rushed to my cot, lifte
up the letter. It said:

My Dear Shu:

In the hope that this note will be deli
kindness of the purser, I am taking this o
few words of farewell. Now that you are
country, I want you to go with the knowl
America are ceaselessly praying for your h
which we hope will not be too far away.

When you return to your country, a n
different environment will no doubt meet
is that the thought conveyed to you t
bring or cause you unhappiness, and I fe
are unfounded. Until the day this sad and
to devote my heart and soul to the cause
continue to pray from the bottom of my
When this war has ended and when man
blessings of peace and freedom, we shal
friendship.

Whatever fate may unfold, I assure you
my heart. Remember always, please, t
your trust have greatly enriched my life an

May God bless you and keep you until the day we meet again. I shall live for the day when I hear from you again.

Your American friend,

X

For a while I stood still. My eyes felt very warm. How could this letter come to me when the sailing of the *Gripsholm* had not been made public? Probably it was here that my friend demonstrated his great intelligence, ingenuity, and effort. Often the need to develop one's mind to the maximum if it is to be useful at all had been a subject of X's conversation.

Four years passed like a dream.

As a newsreel war correspondent, I had a busy, restless life. Lugging a camera, I went from one war theater to another—to Rabaul, which was under relentless air attacks all the while I was there, to Singapore, to Java, to the Philippines. My last two years at the war front were spent in the Philippines, where I tasted, as combat cameraman, the bitter hardships and tragedies of defeat. The sufferings I had to undergo were indescribable. Completely surrounded in the mountains of northern Luzon, subjected to daily torrents of bombs from the air, severe shelling from the ground, the situation of the army was hopeless. All avenues of escape were closed. Food supplies hardly existed. Sickness and starvation were taking a fearful toll. The dead and the dying were all around me. The living were too emaciated, too weak, even to look after themselves. I lost hope—how often I cannot say.

In these moments of despair, there was something that gave me the will and the desire to survive. It was the indelible memory of friendship, the warm sentiments which overflowed in the letters I received from my friend. Even in the chaos that followed the successive defeats, when morale was very low and the sense of human values had all but disappeared, when hopelessness and despair gripped the lives of the men around me, I did not lose myself. Those unforgettable letters sustained me. Though the whole world may seem to be blacked out and everyone appears to be an enemy, the mere knowledge that one has a true friend makes him feel that there are millions pulling for him.

In June, 1946, after nearly a year in a prisoner-of-war camp, I returned to my country. The cities were a mass of ruins. The people who walked the streets, their minds and discipline shaken by the defeat, aroused in me a feeling of desolation. Long absent from my country, I felt, when I stood among the ruins and among these people, as if I were alone, isolated, in a human desert.

One day, shortly after my repatriation, a friend informed me that an American officer who had come to Japan with the first wave of the army of occupation had been making frequent inquiries about me. Curious to know what I was wanted for, I paid the officer a call. He was a courteous, gray-haired gentleman with friendly eyes, a disarming smile, and gentle speech. Just one look at him was enough to make one feel that he was a friend. When I told him that I was the person he had been inquiring about, he politely gave me a chair and immediately started to talk.

He took out some letters from a drawer of his desk. They were addressed to him from many of my American friends inquiring after me. Letters from an American newsreel cameraman, and from other acquaintances, were there. Among the stack was one whose handwriting attracted my notice. It was the one I wanted to see most, even though it was addressed to the officer.

Dear Major——:

I have no words to thank you for your kind reply to the letter I wrote you immediately after the end of the war. I am deeply grateful, for I know you did this favor despite the pressure of your army duties.

I need not tell you how anxious I am to hear more about him in greater detail. Even though news about him may be of the worst, it would be preferable to know about it.

I am writing this letter with such care as to dispense with unnecessary details, because it may be censored by persons who would have no interest whatever in what is of great concern to us, and I certainly do not want them to waste their valuable time.

It would be one of the mean tricks of fate that such a worthy subject as Shu should be deprived of life. However, I hope, for the sake of himself and his family, that he is still alive. And if it be the will of God that he lives, I know that he is contributing to the building of a peaceful world.

May I thank you again for your kind and considerate letter.

The fact that you understand how I feel certainly gives me great hope, courage, and assurance.

Sincerely yours,

X

Tears welled in my eyes and vision became blurred. This letter deepened and strengthened all the more the faith to which I had long continued to hold fast—faith in the fact that friendship is the greatest treasure anyone could have.

How wonderful to think that during the four horrible war years, when country fought country, when our peoples burned with enmity and hatred, when a great gap—the field of battle—was created between us as a no man's land, there was someone on the other side of the lines who always thought and prayed for me: and when the guns became silent and peace returned, that someone would snatch the first opportunity to establish contact. It teaches one the greatness and goodness of friendship: it gives humanity limitless hope.

THE ADMIRAL THAT DAVY JONES
DIDN'T WANT

by Yokoi Toshiyuki

To AN OLD-FASHIONED sea captain like myself, it was my duty to go down with my ship. But what was I to do when it sent me back up?

No matter how many years I spent at sea, I never got over the cranky-child feeling of foreboding which engulfed me the first time I gazed down into the impenetrable blue-green depths, from which all life in the beginning came, in which it still begins, and in which I knew mine would eventually end—to begin again into what? My past, my future, and for an unbearably long time, my present. That's probably why it's a rare seaman who swims for pleasure.

A ship is a psychiatrist's couch and gazing into the tidal throb of the great mother sea is like staring at a tranquilizing metronome, ticking time backwards, reflecting the past in its motion. And as an Admiral of the Imperial Japanese Navy, I might just as well have been flat on my back in a clinic instead of on my bridge, surrounded by eight other aircraft carriers, five battleships, thirteen cruisers, and twenty-eight destroyers. We were the First Imperial Task Fleet, out searching for United States Task Force 58 that lulling warm night of June 18, 1944.

My mind drifted back to December 7, 1941, when it had all started. It would be a modern war—complicated logistics, not living off the land as the Army had done for a decade in China. The generals wouldn't realize this. The Navy had supplies for only six months of full-scale warfare ready at hand and sources of production were insufficient to appreciably extend it. Now three and a half years had passed, full-scale naval warfare had been avoided as much as possible, but the Navy was at the bottom of the supply barrel, and even the generals realized it.

The coming battle was the frantic poker player's last bet, his *whole* pile against his opponent's. And I could tell that it was a very long shot. The odds were too uneven.

It was a "sucker bet," but there was no other way out.

Even so, both sides were opening the game cautiously. On February 11, 1944, our Japanese naval patrols located an American Task Force of over seventeen carriers. Against this we were moving our First Task Fleet, including my small carrier *Hiyo*. For months the two Task Forces had cat-and-moused one another around the Pacific.

Now, on June 18, our fleet was cruising some four hundred miles due west of the Marianas. We were completely undetected, we were sure of it; sure also we would sight the American fleet before it sighted us, and destroy it. Fighting morale was at fever pitch from the Supreme Commander right down to the lowest mess hand.

Vice-Admiral Ozawa was in command of the fleet—an acknowledged expert in torpedo warfare, but in my opinion, inexperienced in full-scale naval operations. Ozawa was probably the most courageous officer in the Imperial Navy. He was a man who interpreted Horatio Nelson in terms of the Samurai Code and lived accordingly. His physical stature, over six feet, was massive for a Japanese, and may have overshadowed any weak points in his professional career. A nation which built a modern war machine on a feudal framework still preferred for its heroes those who looked like heroes.

Ozawa started the operation by breaking the first cardinal rule of warfare: he divided his force into three tactical units, each built around a core of three aircraft carriers. With the force extended in full line, thirty miles between each division, the plan was for the whole fleet to sweep the sea in search of the enemy. Ozawa banked heavily on what he considered "the proven superiority" of Japanese naval aircraft; he wanted to extend their effective range by pivoting his operation on the main air base in the Marianas, thus giving him the added advantage of heavier land-based bombers. "I will pound the American fleet with carrier-based planes, land-based bombers, and the guns of my surface vessels. I will give them no time to counterattack."

But I was not as confident as Ozawa. Most of my twenty years of active service had been spent as a pilot. I had no illusions about what it took to make a first-class aviator, and I had fewer illusions about the fact that my men just didn't have it.

To me, a pilot needed the full Naval Air Training curriculum and at least two years of active duty aboard a carrier. My men were Jerry-trained wartime substitutes run through poorly equipped schools where ideological fervor filled the gaps in technical training. And few had as much as four months aboard a carrier—weeks or months of inactive, fuel-conserving ready-room time was the substitute for on-the-spot practical experience.

Yet, somehow to my amazement, these men got their planes safely off the flight deck and, often as not, even got them back down—at least, in broad daylight, on calm seas, and without the tension and distraction of being under fire.

With these, Ozawa was out to challenge the most experienced naval airmen in the world, also vastly superior in number to our own forces. Either advantage in itself would have balanced out the scales, but both advantages on one side put the odds vastly in favor of the Americans.

Still, I realized the Japanese held one joker: the Americans were probably totally unaware of this Japanese weakness. And to play this card right, the Imperial Task Fleet had no alternative but to move in close, even to within visual sighting range of Task Force 58 —to give the green airmen every advantage of surface support and minimize the chances of air-to-air contact.

I spoke to Ozawa, offering my own plan before the fleet had even set out, but I was brushed aside. It wasn't according to the books, Ozawa said. Ozawa epitomized the British military historian General J. F. C. Fuller's assessment of the Japanese tacticians who "on the one hand had . . . displayed a low cunning of incredible stupidity, and on the other had a lack of imagination of unbelievable profundity."

There would be a long-range attack, taking fullest advantage of the superiority of the Japanese aircraft—ignoring the fact that a plane is no better than its pilot.

At 0300, June 19, I despondently sent off my first scout aircraft.

The sun rose clear and sharp in the morning haze by 0630. Intelligence reports started to flow in. The American Task Force had deployed wide, west of the Marianas, and was coming in fast towards the center of the Japanese fleet.

"Do they know we're here?" That was the vital question. The American vanguard was already within Admiral Ozawa's calculated range of attack.

The *Hiyo*'s deck came alive. Semaphore men flagged the first planes off, and I held my breath as successive fighters and torpedo planes made their run, drop, peel-off, and climb departures.

By 0830, Task Force 58 was within three hundred miles of Imperial Task Fleet One. The last of the attacking force of 260 Japanese aircraft faded below the eastern horizon. At 1000 hours a second group of eighty-two followed them. All available aircraft were now airborne and not a single American plane had been sighted. Ozawa was jubilant. We had taken the Americans by surprise.

I sighed in relief. If the attacking Japanese air fleet could whittle down the U.S. carrier strength, then Japan had a chance. I looked up at the golden disc riding higher in the late morning haze, then over at its silken counterpart flying from my mast. "The fate of the thousand-year empire," I mused, "hangs on the outcome of the next few thousand seconds."

In the intelligence center of the flagship, total silence hung like an arrested breath. A thousand seconds passed like as many years. Then the staccato chirp of the complicated Japanese Morse code, "Attacked . . . static . . . enemy carriers . . . battleships . . ." then total silence like one tortured, asthmatic gasp.

A second radio contact, this time with the second air group. They reported total failure in making any contact with enemy units. They were giving up the hunt and returning. One squadron reported the necessity of detouring to Guam for refueling.

Noon arrived and still no further report came from the first air group. I was puzzled. I gazed into the calm blue sea and felt it beckon. This kind of warfare was new to me. I wondered how Ozawa was taking it; no books ever spilled any ink over fighting like this— no news from one side, from the other no contact.

Lunch was a nervous torture. The rice was cold and I almost gagged on it. Then the code room called down—a message. I raced up the ladderway to have my worst forebodings borne out. The fifty planes which had landed at Guam had been ambushed on the ground by an enemy they hadn't been able to find. Only one was able to take off.

I returned to the bridge and gazed deep into the blue again. Then a flicker of motion caught the corner of my eye and I looked over toward the eastern horizon. The first air group was returning, under total radio silence—but not in any recognizable formation.

One by one.

One hundred two planes limped in—102 out of 342.

In the ready-room the American strategy took shape in retrospect. They had concentrated on defending their carriers. They had set their battleships out as bait and when the slow Japanese torpedo bombers began their approach run from twenty miles out, the American fighter cover moved in from over the rear-placed carriers and swarmed over the Japanese. Few torpedo bombers survived the first attack to reach their targets. Only minor hits were reported, scored on two battleships, and the carriers went unscathed.

Ozawa's plan might just as well have been drawn up for him by Washington.

By now my *Hiyo* was some thirty miles in the vanguard of the Japanese fleet. I looked back in utter despair and where beyond the horizon I imagined the flagship should be I saw great columns of black smoke. Minutes later the code room received a message from the cruiser *Yahagi* notifying our division of the sinking of the carrier *Shokaku* and instructing me to take on its planes.

As the *Hiyo* approached the rendezvous point where the *Shokaku* should have been, I saw nothing but wreckage and thick floating oil. Not far beyond, the newest carrier in the Imperial Navy, flagship of Vice-Admiral Ozawa, the 45,000 ton *Taiho,* lay at a 50-degree list under a mourning canopy of black smoke. Immediately after the *Taiho* had sent off all its planes with the first attack group, she had taken a torpedo in her port bow from an American sub. As it was not considered serious enough to cripple the carrier, no one was unduly alarmed; hours later it was found that the shock had split the seams of the main gasoline storage tank and the vapors were playing havoc between decks.

At 1432 hours, as the 30,000-ton *Hiyo* hove to within a mile of the stricken flagship, I was thrown violently against the bulkhead by shock waves as the *Taiho* rolled over on its port side and exploded.

The next morning, June 20, the remaining units rendezvoused with their tankers for refueling. At 1045 they were still linked to the tankers by the great serpentine fuel lines when the message came in, "Two enemy capital ships, one cruiser, several destroyers sighted ‚ . . 20 degrees . . . five hundred miles off Peleliu . . ."

The expected American counterattack, but Imperial Fleet Head-quarters, now aboard the carrier *Zuikaku,* seemed to ignore the warning completely.

Minutes later the radio room reported picking up the air-to-surface radiophone of approaching American planes. I ordered General Quarters sounded and watched the former cocky overconfidence of my green crews give way to tenseness.

All day we waited. Had they been only scout planes? Had they missed sighting the Japanese fleet altogether? An hour before sunset, approximately six miles to port, over the haze and what I imagined should be Carrier Division Three, anti-aircraft puffs appeared. I ordered all aircraft up and climbed into the anti-aircraft fire control tower. The last plane had barely cleared the *Hiyo* flight deck when silver specks appeared overhead in the dying sunlight, elevation about 9,000 feet. Far from the ring formation, the *Hiyo* was covered by four destroyers and they immediately commenced fire. Futile at such range, I thought, but as if to accommodate them, the silver specks peeled off and arced downward.

I ordered hard a-starboard and full anti-aircraft barrage. The first column of water spewed into the air one hundred yards to port —right where I would have been. Others blossomed around me, but the *Hiyo* took no hits. The barrage was perfect and deflected all the later attacking planes that had any chance to correct for the *Hiyo's* evasive action.

The last dive bomber peeled over, broke through the canopy of tiny man-made clouds, corrected its dive and released. It was a certain miss, but a close one, the way it was arced. Then, angling in, it hit the tip of a mast and was deflected downwards right into the control tower where I stood.

When the smoke cleared, the navigating officer lay dead at my feet, but I could barely make out the body through the curtain of blood that covered my eyes. I wiped the blood away; my left eye was gone, I could feel the sting of shrapnel all over me. A voice nearby cried out, "Torpedo planes, off to port." Six squat Grumman Avengers sped in on the last stages of their 5-degree downhill approach dive. The *Hiyo's* guns put up a withering barrage. Two Grummans disappeared. A third seemed discouraged by the barrage and released its torpedo out of range.

A fourth seemed favored by the gods. He kept coming in—500 meters . . . 400 . . . 300 . . . then he disappeared in a brilliant yellow puff, but a long black sausage appeared below the billow and dropped perfectly into the water—a sight I have never been able to forget, a perfect release, a feat I have held in admiration ever since.

At this range it was too late to evade. A white streak slashed towards the *Hiyo*. I felt towards my very self. There was a tremor from port, somewhere near the engine room. White steam poured from the funnel. All motion stopped. The sudden cessation of the noises I had grown so accustomed to was like a deafening rush of wind. Even the guns stopped. I staggered off, half-blind, for the bridge. Two more torpedo streaks appeared to port. Both hit astern, one in communications and one below the volatile oil tanks. Gasoline flowed out through cracked seams and ignited. Heavy firefighting equipment failed; hand pumps were useless. Flaming oil flowed toward the magazine.

I ordered all available men to carry the wounded onto the flight deck. The flag-officer struck the Imperial battle flag and took down the Imperial portrait and important documents for removal to a destroyer. The wounded were placed on rafts and put over the side. All hands were mustered on deck to abandon ship. As they came up and took their stations, I made a brief farewell speech and all cheered, "Banzai! Ten thousand years' life to the Emperor!"

As they filed over the side, someone near me struck up the old sea chanty, "Seafaring may we lay our bodies deep . . ."

The last officer left the deck. I saluted as smartly as my smarting wounds allowed, then sat down on an empty shell box and lit a cigarette. My blind left eye began to throb. With my good eye, I watched my men pull away, then stared down at the approaching deep. It would soon no longer be impenetrable for me.

The refrain, "lay our bodies deep," carried over the water. The last thing I remember thinking to myself was, "Now is the end . . . And the beginning?"

The deep blue momentarily veered away as the bow of the *Hiyo* lunged up, paused, and with a great sigh of escaping air, slipped silently back into the blue. I vividly remember the rushing water, the debris swirling past, the strange world of dancing corpses, boxes, pirouetting wreckage, approaching sleep. Then, a jolt from below froze all motion, dangling wreckage and corpses in eternity—a sharp pain in my left side—bubbles, swirling—and oblivion.

A wave slapped my face and brought me back into consciousness. Above were stars. Somewhere beyond the mass of wreckage the underwater explosion of the magazine had thrown me free to the surface. I could hear the soft refrain, "Seafaring may we lay our bodies deep . . ."

But the hands that pulled me out said, "Not yet, Admiral."

HOMECOMING 1945

by *Akiyama Isa*

No ONE was at the station to meet him. He hadn't expected anyone, of course; still he looked around hopefully at the milling crowds for a familiar face. Instead he saw the empty, hulking, roofless remains of the station, the shaky walls propped up by boards, and next to the ruins of the building, the hastily constructed plywood barracks that served as the station now.

A black quivering mass of flies papered the plywood walls. He watched the lazily sunning insects, trying to ignore the knowledge of what had made them suddenly so well-fed, but it was hard to suppress a shudder.

Suddenly stepping to the walls, he took his military cap off and began slapping and cutting viciously at the flies. Mockingly the flies escaped out of his reach only to swarm back again.

People were gathering to watch him. He dusted off his cap and put it on, tightened the army pack on his shoulders, and walked away. He did not understand himself why he had so furiously attacked the flies. It was a foolish gesture and he felt ashamed.

There were no buses. He started down the road towards his home on foot. The road stretched out in front of him wider than he remembered it, for the houses on both sides had been explosively cleared; nothing remained but rubble: stones, bricks, tiles, pieces of corrugated tin, broken crockery.

Here and there water spigots jutted nakedly. He turned his head quickly away from the sight of scorched tree trunks, but there was

16

something humorous in the half porcelain bathtub and part of a toilet exposed to the public gaze.

The pack on his shoulder grew heavy, but he plodded on. All around him there was an awful stillness, the quiet which follows a gigantic upheaval. It seemed to him that he was alone in the vast dreamlike devastation surrounding him. Then he saw a three-sided lean-to pieced together from corrugated tin and half-burnt planks that had been rescued from the debris. A woman in rags sat on the earthen floor inside, looking out at the road.

He called out, "Do you happen to know anything about the people near Nikitsu?" The woman gazed at him blankly. He repeated his question as he approached nearer. Then he saw that one half of her face had been kneaded and twisted like soft dough.

The woman remained silent, staring straight ahead, expressionless. She was beyond hearing or seeing, she was merely waiting for release. He mumbled an apology and walked on past her hut.

By the familiar curve of the road, he knew at last his home was near. He had prepared himself for what he would find and yet he was in no way prepared. Ever since that dreadful day one month ago when official confirmation reached him, he had read and listened to every scrap of information he could pick up in the news and from the rumors. Every moment on the troop train had been spent in preparing himself. But even now he did not want to believe.

He found the location of his house; the stone lantern, leaning tipsily, was still standing in the garden. The foundation stones faintly marked the floor plan. He walked through—this had been the family room, this was his parents' room, this the dining room, the kitchen, his sister's room.

He put down his pack slowly and tried to think what he should do next. The numb remains of what had once been his home was proof that the official report was true. No one in his family or in the neighborhood could have survived.

The compounded feelings of bitterness, anguish, and loss swirled through him until he was unable to think at all. Aimlessly he kicked at a battered saucepan lying near his foot. Something glittered in the heap of rubble beneath the pan.

He stooped to look. The glitter came from a small *juzu*, a rosary made of crystal beads. With trembling fingers he picked it up, marveling that a string of beads had remained intact in the midst of all that wreckage. He knew the *juzu;* it was from the one his mother used in her morning devotions to Buddha. He could see vividly his mother's serene face as she sat quietly before the small family altar softly intoning the sutra.

Very awkwardly he tried to slip the *juzu* around his clasped hands as he had done when he was a child, but the weakened string gave way and the beads scattered to the ground.

Like a person coming out of ether, he was gripped by the pain of grief. He saw what had been whole a moment ago disintegrate in an instant at the touch of his hands. He threw himself on the ground and wept.

Gradually he became calmer. He sat up and wiped his face with his shirtsleeves. His utter hopelessness and resentment and sorrow seemed to recede from him with the flow of tears.

Then he bent, carefully picking up the scattered crystal beads. The beads could be restrung and made whole again. The links unifying individuals with one another were frail and transitory, constantly being strained and broken, but faith could relink all into one again. He wrapped the salvaged beads in his handkerchief and put it in his pocket. Then he shouldered his pack and walked away toward the heart of the city slowly, with steady steps.

THESE TEN YEARS

A STORY OF SEVEN EX-SOLDIERS

by Kon Hidemi

AUGUST 15, 1945: The Emperor for the first time addressed his people over a nation-wide radio hook-up; Japan for the first time admitted a victorious enemy to its shores. The news of Japan's unconditional surrender, however, did not reach the ears of a great many Japanese soldiers, particularly those who had fled deep into the mountain jungles of the Philippines.

In the wilderness on both sides of the Canganyan Highway, the soldiers were scattered and isolated from their units and headquarters. In a secret lair in Canganyan, General Yamashita, the "Tiger of Malaya," and his staff awaited the final act, without any hope of reversing the tide of the war. In fact, it was not like war at all. To live for the day was the best one could expect. The one-sided situation brought U.S. tanks and airplanes everywhere, on and over the all-encompassing battlefields. Looking down at the star-marked tanks on the highways, the beaten soldiers would murmur, *"Chikusho—*beasts! They're probably eating good food!"

These same men thrust from their thoughts the fact that when they were found they would fall victim to the tanks' flame throwers, as they had seen many comrades incinerated—it was food they talked of. The soldiers that lived through tonight never thought of tomorrow. The simple fact that they were living was enough.

Naturally, food was scarce. Or rather, there was no food in any real sense. Anything edible was devoured. Lizard was a top-grade à-la-carte item; even this soon became hard to find. Corporal Kihara and the six other soldiers were always faced with imminent starvation.

The seven soldiers, however, somehow managed to live on—thanks to Corporal Kihara's talent. Before he was drafted, he had a criminal record. In the army he had a peculiar MOS (Military Occupational Specialty)—stealing; when the war was lost he became a hero because his specialty now saved his comrades' lives. Whenever he came back from hunting he always carried something that joyfully surprised the other six men. Unhulled rice was one of his most surprising offerings.

The farmers' houses were empty—all the food stocks had either been taken away by the farmers or looted by the withdrawing Japanese soldiers. Nevertheless, Corporal Kihara could smell out secret hoarding places. With looted boxes of K-rations in his hands, he looked like an angel.

Human beings can live if only they have fire, rice, and salt. Luckily the men had kept aside a little salt when they were separated from the main force. For the other two necessities—rice and fire—they depended solely on Corporal Kihara. In addition to being an excellent thief, he was a master fire-maker. Without him the seven soldiers could not have survived more than a week, while others around them were dying of fatigue and hunger.

The tiny nipa-house in which the seven hid themselves was located in a narrow crevasse between steep mountain sides. Low-flying P38s would fly past but never strafe the house or any of the seven soldiers, so they used to look up and whistle at the planes, assured of perfect safety.

Among them was Odaira who was formerly a journalist. He hated the war the most. Every time he sighed "We're finished," Pfc. Nara retorted, "That's what an intellectual believes. That's defeatism. You're trying to discourage us!"

Nara was every inch a soldier. Each morning he got up and led the others to recite the Emperor's Commandments to Soldiers. He seemed firmly to believe in the day when he would recapture Manila. Looking at the enemy tanks and airplanes, seeing no counterattack from our side, he still denied reality. Strangely enough, however, the other six were more influenced by Nara than by Odaira. Whenever Nara shouted "Get up—all of you!" they simply followed his words and bowed in the direction of Japan, as they used to in the routine life of the barracks.

Pfc. Takeuchi held a special position because of his young age.

Whenever the others were involved in a discussion, he always stayed silent. When he did speak, he associated himself with the general point of view. Whenever the seven tried to decide a matter by voting, he was always the last in casting his vote. Consequently, he gave the impression of deciding everything.

"He is another Kihara—but intellectual," criticized Odaira, whose opinion was always voted against by the others. Odaira insisted that the Japanese Army would give up very soon, making further food conservation unnecessary. Nara and Narazaki vehemently opposed this. In such cases, Takeuchi always agreed with Nara, though he himself ate up his own reserves, thus tacitly backing Odaira's prediction.

One day as usual Kihara went food hunting. In a few minutes he hurried back and told them breathlessly, "I saw a white-flagged car carrying officers down the highway." This seemed to fit in with a mysterious silence they had noticed the last few days. No airplane roared. No artillery blasted. They had, in fact, been wondering if a cease-fire was in order. They were excited at the news.

Confused, they looked at Odaira for his opinion.

"There's nothing to say. The war is over," he said.

Even Nara could think of no reply. As no tanks passed by, Narazaki suggested they send out a scout to find out what had happened. Pvt. Taguchi voiced agreement.

"I will go," Pfc. Tobo offered. But everyone shook his head disapprovingly to the half-starved private. Narazaki spoke out, "You must stay here and conserve your strength. I'll take the job."

He went down the mountain side with Pfc. Odaira—to learn of Japan's unconditional surrender five days after it happened. The news—the first authentic information they had received in the past six months—made Nara cry.

Every one of the seven belonged to a different unit whose fate nobody knew. They had lived thus far only by relying on their own unity—dividing scanty food among them. But now that the war was over there seemed little reason for them to keep on doing so. In the American camp, they could sleep with arms and feet stretched without the worry of food hunting and P38s. Odaira gave his usual optimistic forecast.

"You beast!" Nara shouted, "Can't you realize we'll be chained by the enemy?" He could have hit Odaira, if he had had the strength.

Nevertheless, when the sun went up next morning, all seven descended the mountain for the first time to an open road. Truck after truck with American drivers rolled past carrying full loads of Japanese soldiers. The seven waved at them. But nobody answered them back.

"Goddamit! They behave like total strangers!" They spat on the ground.

The seven soldiers were finally picked up by a truck that passed by. For the first time in eight months they went out of the Canganyan Valley, emerging on flat land under the glaring sun. As they passed by, they were threateningly stared at by the natives who had already come back.

At the northwest end of the highway stood a temporary camp headquarters. With the help of Nisei enlisted men, several American officers had already started assigning POW work to the Japanese soldiers who silently waited in a long queue in front of the camp. At the gate of the camp, the seven soldiers were separated according to the units to which they had once belonged. Tobo and Taguchi were hospitalized, their conditions had grown worse on their way to the camp.

A minute before they bade farewell to each other, Narazaki said, "If we ever get to Japan safely, how about meeting every August 15 for a dinner together?"

"You idiot! How can you say such a thing—you're a prisoner of war. You'll never go back to Japan," Nara retorted, almost shouting.

They were separated before they could argue further or agree on a place to meet, encamped in different groups, not knowing each other's whereabouts.

Odaira became editor of a mimeographed newspaper for the camp POWs. Pfc. Nara did not know this, but one day he was startled to find in the POW paper the news of the repatriation ships he had never expected. In the camp, he was treated in a way that seemed, by comparison, almost heavenly. The letters POW painted on his back and pants did not bother him in the least. Labor was light. Making latrines for GIs, sticking in fence poles and other light work, could hardly be called "labor." Without any strict watch and with the small quantity of porridge which seemed rather appropriate for undernourished men, he—as the men around him —were quite satisfied.

As the living grew better, each man became, however, more anxious to know about the homeland. The news trickled in slowly. Knowledge was painful. Almost all the cities were reduced to ashes. Nagasaki and Hiroshima were wiped out by hell bombs. Then the men knew they'd had better luck than the people at home.

Soon, Japanese repatriation ships anchored in Manila Bay, where capsized ships still lay with their red bellies sticking out of the water.

It was 1946—when Generals Homma and Yamashita were sentenced to death—that Nara finally landed in Kagoshima. He was shocked to see the shattered homeland, aghast at the horrible sight of Hiroshima as the train passed by. He went straight to Kawachi, his home town, which looked almost strange to his eyes after eight years in the Army. To his surprise, his mother and sister-in-law were safe in his house. His brother was working in the pig-bristle factory, already an expert brushmaker.

Nevertheless, life for Nara was miserable. To feed an extra mouth was difficult in those days. Demobilized Nara Hachiro turned out to be an unwelcome guest. Nara dreamed of the Philippine mountains where he could depend on Kihara's loot. No fresh fruits or vegetables were available. Potatoes and pumpkins were staple foods. Even these were in short supply, hunted by many Osaka citizens who daily swarmed to the Kawachi area. Nara Hachiro became acutely aware of how desperately the rural areas were hit by food shortages. Daily the newspaper spread photos of beggarlike citizens under the burned tin-plate shacks.

On the lightless roads there roamed vagrant dogs looking for things to eat or at least bite. Gang robberies became a common affair. The homeland he had so longed for in the Philippines now became a place where there was nothing to admire.

Nara wanted to go to Osaka for a job, but how could he find a job in a destroyed city of debris and ashes? He finally decided to stay on in his house, no matter how his brother and sister-in-law might show their disgust with him.

Hachiro tried to help and went out into the rice fields early each morning. His brother liked this and spoke more friendly, "To tell you the truth, farming was best during wartime. Rice was so precious. Everyone respected us. But no hands, you know, after you were drafted. I was also mobilized into the factory. Nobody could take care of the fields. . . ."

In the fields Nara Hachiro felt strangely easy. But day after day the monotonous life in the farmhouse grew more vacant and dry. He had seen a world that no one in his family could ever even dream of. In the Philippines he used to look at the natives toiling in the rice fields, planting tobacco seeds, and bearing so many children. He thought they were foolish. But now, looking at his brother's way of living, he could hardly find any difference.

"I saw a colored movie in Manila. That was beautiful . . . ," he began one night.

"You mean, they have a better culture than ours?" the brother asked.

"Yeah, direct from America."

"But in the south . . . you can't stand heat . . . don't you ever go crazy with a climate that never changes?"

"It's hot. But the movie theaters and hotels have air-conditioning. When it's hot, it's better to get inside the movie house . . . you get pretty cool," he explained.

"Yeah? With what do they make it cool?" The brother was curious.

"Electricity of course."

Then the sister-in-law burst into laughter, "My goodness, electricity is for warming things up. How can you cool things with electricity?"

Hachiro avoided answering. He thought his sister-in-law was ignorant. But he himself also knew little of how all such technical contradictions could be worked out.

Odaira Shuntaro succeeded in securing his old job, thanks to the city editor who had been bureau chief in the Philippines. But back in the office he found that men who were once his juniors were already at the "desks" exercising control over the younger men. It was as if an old veteran non-com were at the mercy of green young officers. Moreover, the men at the desk seemed to embarrass him by showing an air of constraint.

After four years in the Army, he was accustomed to organization. He himself did not regard the matter with as much concern as others did. He was rather happy with the simple fact that he could return to his old job. Settling himself in the company's dormitory in Yoyogi, he felt there need be nothing to worry about.

In contrast to the days before Odaira was drafted, the newspaper business seemed to be growing into a full-fledged profession. According to editorial policy the reporters could now write anything. In the dark days—in wartime—however, they had been simply messenger boys who carried around the stinking official announcements of the General Staff Headquarters or of the Information Bureau. No evening editions. No more than two pages. But the several thousand employees of the company were a great financial burden.

When Odaira Shuntaro landed at Kagoshima, he could see everywhere flowers in full bloom. But the towns and cities had been reduced to ruins that extended as far as the eye could see. Human beings had become lost, but nature was in full bloom. Shuntaro could still believe that eventually life would rise again from these ashes.

But now Odaira had become very realistic, and therefore very pessimistic. Back in the newspaper office, where things went along most realistically, he did not realize that his once flexible way of thinking had changed into almost a stiff-necked tenacity. In the year the war ended, people seemed simply to give up in the face of the hardships that came from a scarcity of food and housing. In 1946 the Higashikuni Cabinet was succeeded by the Shidehara Cabinet, which ignored the mounting inflation. People began to criticize the government, particularly after April when the new Constitution restored freedom of speech. People took advantage of privileges obtained through the sacrifice of others.

Among governmental officials and newspapermen, there was speculation that a riot might occur in the autumn. They pointed to various signs that seemed similar to conditions and situations in Russia and Germany just before the revolutions.

Shuntaro daily frequented the black-market area near Shimbashi to have a sip of *kasutori,* a Japanese calvados. People paid little attention to the taste of things. Anything drinkable was welcomed. *Kasutori*—with its strong after-effect—charmed people who had little money to spend. Mostly moonshined by Koreans in Japan, it was extremely dangerous. Odaira knew this, yet as evening came on, he could not stand a minute without a glass of *kasutori.*

One night, he was staggering out of the narrow lane of the market, when he was suddenly accosted. "That's Odaira, isn't it?"

At first glance he thought a black-marketeer was approaching him. It crossed his mind that the figure was a thief carrying loot on his back. But that sun-tanned face with elephant eyes quickly reminded him of someone familiar.

"Oh, Takeuchi!" Shuntaro shouted.

Takeuchi was wearing a pair of khaki pants, a patched-up shirt, and a combat cap—a complete black-marketeer's uniform.

"How's everything?" Odaira asked.

"I'm selling frying pans here. Good sales, though," said Takeuchi with a big smile that made him look younger. Bachelor that Odaira was, he could not understand why so many people would buy frying pans.

Looking at Odaira Shuntaro's bewildered face, Takeuchi explained rather proudly, "These are made very cheap by a former munitions plant." A former armament plant became a frying pan factory! A most becoming outcome of a defeated economy, Shuntaro thought. But he also wondered how long Takeuchi could continue selling frying pans, for sooner or later the public would have enough of them.

"Say, how about a drink?" Shuntaro asked.

"A *kasutori?*" Takeuchi responded very quickly.

"Until good drinks appear, *kasutori* will be the best. Then, you'll give up selling frying pans?" Odaira asked as a glass was placed on the counter.

"Naturally, why not? So long as they sell, I'll work at it. That's all," Takeuchi said matter-of-factly. He used to follow the majority. In whatever circumstances he might be, Shuntaro thought, Takeuchi would never change his character. He was a man who could nonchalantly accept even these confused and tired days.

"I guess someday you'll be a big shot," Shuntaro said.

"Hah, hah! Here, again, you're fortune telling. You used to tell us the future of the war. Now we're in peace. For that prediction I'd like to buy a drink," Takeuchi said, wiping his mouth with his dirty right hand.

"A *kasutori?*"

"No, of course not. Say, by the way, I sent a letter to Nara Hachiro—"

"Where's he now?" Shuntaro asked, reaching for his glass.

"Farming in Kawachi. I told him he'll never be satisfied with farming. I think I can teach him how to sell these frying pans. He is an honest fellow, you know. If I tell him to sell, he will sell as I say. . . ."

"Okay, then, when you two fellows sell everything, let's have a big drink," Odaira said.

The bill was on the table. Takeuchi, however, made no motion to pick it up despite his talk about big sales. Finally, in disgust, Shuntaro picked up the bill. When he paid, Takeuchi simply said, as if he had not noticed it before, "Sorry, I'll buy next time."

In May 1946, Yoshida Shigeru formed his Cabinet. The much feared riot did not occur—not because Yoshida's policy was appropriate, but because the people knew riots would never bring forth food and better living. On the other hand, several violent incidents occurred between labor and management. Following the first authorized May Day, a so-called "Food May Day" was held on May 18.

As Shuntaro went out to cover the story, he was surprised to see the furious way the crowds were shouting in front of the Premier's residence. "Come out, Yoshida!" "We want Yoshida!" And some 250,000 people cried "Down with the Yoshida Cabinet!" as they passed by the Diet building.

Odaira remembered the wartime days when the military hierarchy allowed no criticism. People were trained to follow the imperative order blindly. In postwar days, people's reactions led them to oppose anything imperative. Once trained to obey orders, people easily accepted the order of the Occupation Forces without question.

The Occupation Forces least expected such peaceful and obedient behavior, as they knew well the stubborn resistance of the Japanese armies over the previous four years. But they knew little about the Japanese psychology of obediently accepting orders, even those of the conqueror. The so-called 2:1 (February First) Strike in 1947, therefore, was quickly subdued by a word from MacArthur's Headquarters. People's dissatisfaction, however, was bound to explode somewhere, sometime. Japan was an unstable country where there was no assurance even of being able to live. The general public, therefore, became easy victims of the Communist campaigns. Legal strikes occurred as a daily routine. Strikes, thefts, and robberies filled almost every page of the dailies. Minor crimes such as pickpocketing and stealing were virtually ignored by editors who were too busy following up the big stories. Even police and justice authorities could not spare enough time for minor crimes. Under such circumstances, all Tokyo citizens were terror-stricken when they heard of a bank robbery that resulted in the death of eleven bank clerks.

A middle-aged man walked into the Shiinamachi Branch of the Teikoku Bank one dull day in January, 1947. Somehow he persuaded all the clerks to take a drink of poisoned "medicine," then calmly walked out with 110,000 yen.

This was a crime big enough for all the newspapers to follow, but Odaira Shuntaro picked up a small and strange crime story. From a Metropolitan Police detective he heard of a thief who stole only from foreigners. As the crimes were repeated, the police authorities were increasingly criticized.

In those days, most of the fashionable foreign-style houses in Tokyo had been procured for the use of VIPs, high-ranking officers and their families. The elusive burglar was reported to have succeeded in sneaking into even the most strictly guarded houses. When he broke into a Major-General's house in Azabu, however, he committed the serious mistake of making a noise that awoke the General, who came downstairs with a Colt automatic in his hand.

The General fired two shots as the figure jumped over a high concrete wall. No fingerprints were found. Nothing was left behind. The story itself was interesting, at least to Shuntaro's journalistic sense. In the story Odaira wrote he also added that the Metropolitan Police Board would be harshly criticized unless they could nab a thief who preyed on and baffled the Occupation Forces.

The story when it appeared in the paper received a surprising response. In the Occupation days, people use to look at the foreigners as "special personages" who rode in comfortable off-limits Japanese railway cars while Japanese were sardine-packed into dirty, crowded coaches. The Occupationaires gave the general public a feeling of oppression. The story, therefore, created a modern Robin Hood who invaded the "Occupation houses" when everyone feared even to talk about his feelings.

The editor, however, called in Odaira and warned, "Watch out, Odaira. The newspaper section of GHQ seems to be displeased with your story." Shuntaro nodded but did not try to comment or express an opinion.

The story was a scoop. The other reporters congratulated Shuntaro. But he was not pleased with their flattering words, as he knew well he would not be able to write good stories any more if GHQ were watching him.

While he was in this dismal mood, a letter arrived from Takeuchi, written in a clumsy square hand. It was an invitation to a party which Nara would also attend. Shuntaro, however, could not make up his mind, remembering how Takeuchi had stuck him with the bill, but on the designated day, he received a telephone call from Takeuchi, who assured him "strictly no charge." Shuntaro then decided to go.

At Yaeko's House in Suitengu, Odaira was glad to find, besides Takeuchi and Nara, former Cpl. Narazaki, Pfc. Tobo, and Cpl. Kihara, who had saved his comrades' lives by "surprise presents" in the Philippine days. Yaeko's House was actually a high-class restaurant disguised as an ordinary house—a black-market restaurant-sake shop, a product of MacArthur's "Dry Days." Odaira was dumbfounded not only by the house but also by beautiful Yaeko, the hostess. Clad in a fashionable kimono that would have been hard to find even in prewar days, she was entirely out of place, even with Takeuchi, who was also wearing a brand-new suit, giving no hint that he had ever worn an old khaki black-marketeer's uniform.

"Now that Odaira-san is here, let's start the party," Nara said with the dignity of a master of ceremonies, his sun-tanned, rough farmer's face beaming.

Ushered into the next room, the guests were again astonished at the gorgeous set-up of the table.

"Takeuchi had always been smart in grabbing a chance," Narazaki murmured. "But I never dreamed he could do this much."

"No, no. I haven't done anything yet. I simply wanted to ask your assistance for my future and show my thanks for the past," Takeuchi replied. "You see, I once bumped into Odaira-san in a Shimbashi black-market. That's the hardest time I ever experienced. I didn't have dough enough to buy drinks. Odaira-san bought a drink for me. I never forgot his kindness. Ever since I've wanted to do something to repay him. Right now I'm selling tiles for foreign-style toilets. Mr. Kihara is working for me as a repairman. With your assistance, I'm planning to be a more useful man in this society." Takeuchi's speech finally came to an end.

As he poked his chopsticks into one of the dishes, Odaira could not but remember the days in the Philippines when he had least dreamed of such a day. The soldier who once dreamed of Manila's recapture by the Japanese Army was now making handsome money supplying tiles, riding high on the current building boom.

"Kihara, you were always good at everything. But I didn't know you were with Takeuchi," Odaira said. Kihara simply smiled off the remark, while Takeuchi took over.

"Yes, Kihara is good at repairing foreign-style toilets. He can even climb up to high footholds when we have to measure the number of tiles necessary for the outer decoration of the building. But he is too good at everything. That's his trouble. He can't stick to the same job for long."

"You mean your talent kills you?" Odaira turned to Kihara. "And what are you doing now?"

Kihara still did not answer. Takeuchi again began to speak in a boss-like way. "This fellow is now mad for photography. He's really good at it. I wonder if your newspaper company could hire him. . . ."

Then Tobo, who had been silent, said, "Narazaki-san . . . you were our commander. . . ."

"Ya . . . a very bad one," Narazaki said, as if in scorn of himself. And he explained he was working as a salesman. With his poor eloquence, he was apparently making little money. Everyone remembered how he had insisted on the uselessness of fighting when he brought back the definite news of Japan's complete surrender.

Tobo said he was teaching at a primary school in a small town on the northern tip of Honshu. "In my town, people are so poor that I can't just be a teacher to the school kids. . . . I registered in the Communist Party because I know I have to work for the poor," he said, full of the passion of a young man.

Hearing his old buddies' remarks, Odaira noticed the maids who were serving sake to the guests. Their hands and fingers were extremely white—different from those of ordinary maids. "What kind of house is this?" Odaira whispered to Nara.

"Oh, this house?" Nara made a forced smile, saying, "Ah . . . a sort of a company dormitory."

That was enough. It seemed rather stupid to ask who the mistress was. Takeuchi had done really well taking advantage of the disorder. Odaira could not help wondering at these strangely changing times that caused such tremendous shifts in people's fortunes.

"Say, how about a picture?" Takeuchi asked Kihara, who brought out a German-made camera—too-expensive a camera for the hobby of a latrine repairman. Kihara took pictures of the guests from various angles.

The editorial room of Odaira's office was always filled with confusion and shouting, as if reflecting the world's movement. Social chaos gave birth to many like Takeuchi while igniting political consciousness among the young who tried to mold chaos into revolutionary movement.

The strikes that had occurred recently seemed to Odaira to indicate something different from the ones that had driven the workers to walk out because of a desperate need for higher wages to meet the cost of living. Now the strikes reflected political colors.

On July 5, 1949, Mr. Shimoyama, President of the National Railways, was found dead on railway tracks in the southern outskirts of Tokyo. The police authorities sought clues in the then-prevailing dangerous atmosphere among the railway workers' union, but the vague announcements of the police led all the newspapers into confusion. It was thought that the president might have committed suicide—from the excessive strain of negotiating with the union. The newspapers were divided in their opinions. And the controversial views never crystallized into a conclusion. There appeared nothing to prove the truth.

While this case remained wrapped in mystery, the second incident happened. On July 15, a driverless and empty train suddenly plunged down the tracks and went off the rails near Mitaka Station into some private houses, killing ten persons and seriously injuring seven. A witness reported to the police that he heard a railway worker shout just after the train started to run, "Watch this! Revenge on those who fired us!" Certain suspects were arrested, but no concrete evidence was produced.

The next month, another train was derailed in Matsukawa. After the train was overturned, the police frantically looked for evidence only after the spot was completely trampled by the crowds that thronged around it.

In all these incidents there was one common element: none of the arrested confessed to anything the police were seeking. No one admitted any knowledge of the incidents—of the first run-away train, the second derailment, the resulting deaths. All took advantage of the right to keep silent to any questions that might tend to incriminate them. This otherwise "most humane" right given by the new Constitution baffled the police in their effort to find the truth. Without scientific investigation methods far more advanced, there was little chance of solving the mysteries and the general public grew impatient.

Whatever the truth might have been, the Communist Party and its followers objected loudly to the official attitude that openly suggested that secret party movements were behind the incidents. But, whether true or not, the authority's announcements gave the public an impression of treacherous and villainous behavior on the part of the Communist Party.

The Party that was liberated by MacArthur and secured over 2,140,000 votes for six seats in the Diet in the 1946 General Election increasingly lost popularity in a series of bloody incidents. Odaira could well imagine Tobo's perplexed state of mind, since Tobo had enthusiastically engaged in Party activities in a lonely mountain town as a fresh Party member, apparently driven by an urge for justice in the midst of a disorderly society.

The Party line, however, underwent no changes until May Day of 1952.

In the meantime, Odaira was busy answering phones and assigning cub-reporters. One day, Narazaki came into his room. As an automobile salesman, he had been trying hard to sell cars to Odaira's newspaper company. But he succeeded only in making contracts for a few motorcycles. He was not talented as a salesman, lacking the necessary eloquence and smooth appearance—the last things Narazaki ever could attain.

"It's not so hard to sell cars, but the trouble is how to get paid," Narazaki said half-musingly.

"Even this office?" Odaira asked.

"No," Narazaki said quickly. "Your company has a good reputation. So I don't worry about payment; in this case, it's the competition that's tough."

Narazaki confessed that he was a "grade C" salesman receiving instructions from a younger man who handled the actual negotiations. Consequently, he had to be satisfied with a minor share of commissions.

"But anyway, I have to thank Takeuchi. He bought several station wagons from me." Narazaki sighed. "I really owe a lot to him."

"That's good that Takeuchi will buy. He's got a knack of getting ahead of the others," Odaira said.

"Yeah, the guy who makes money always makes money wherever he goes," Narazaki murmured, and got up to leave.

Narazaki looked too downcast for Odaira to let him go that way.

"Say, Narazaki, how about a drink?" Odaira asked.

They went to the black-market area behind Yurakucho Station. "They built the restaurants first," Narazaki mumbled to himself. "Say, about a restaurant, I've been trying to bring that Kihara to his senses. You see, he's no good."

"But, that camera, you remember? That was a very expensive one. If a person sold it, he could build a little house," Odaira said, his cheeks rosy-hued after two glasses of synthetic sake. "Anyway, it costs one or two hundred thousand yen." Odaira stared at his partner.

"Yeah?" Narazaki suddenly changed his tone, "Then . . ." He paused a moment and said, "I hate to say this. But I wonder if he has resumed his 'special line of work.' " Narazaki seemed really puzzled. "He saved our lives in the Philippine mountains, but he shouldn't do that here in Tokyo," he said, raising his voice.

Odaira laughed. But soon his journalistic sense reminded him of something. He dared not tell it to Narazaki. Instead he asked, "Narazaki, are you still associating with him?"

"Yeah. That stupid Nara wants to marry Kihara's sister," Narazaki replied.

"How is he living?"

"Not magnificently. Kihara's always playing around, but still he lives far better than I do. He says he can sell his pictures."

Odaira did not ask any more questions. But Narazaki continued, "You know Kihara's sister-in-law? She's been working in Takeuchi's restaurant. She has a very bad reputation. Even Takeuchi doesn't think much of her. But that poor Nara is crazy about her, though I told him to give up such a woman—a thousand times!" Odaira simply nodded, as Narazaki went on, "Kihara says nothing. But she looks hopelessly ugly even after living in Tokyo so long. Only a farmer like Nara could see anything in her."

"That's too bad," Odaira said.

"You think so, too?" Narazaki said half-questioning.

"I don't know her. So, I can say nothing about the marriage. But Kihara's sister must be like Kihara, I think. What does she say?"

"Oh, she's willing, of course. But we know she can't be a good wife for Nara."

As they talked on they finally shook hands and said, "Let's wise him up!" They said farewell in front of Yurakucho Station.

Despite severe food shortages, housing problems, and high commodity prices, certain privileged and wealthy classes lived fantastically well. Bribing became a daily affair between Government officials and the seekers of special privileges. One of such scandals was finally exposed; it was a great surprise to most of the people when they first learned that the Showa Denko Company extended its "hands" to Cabinet members. Even Premier Ashida Hitoshi was suspected of receiving excessive "party contributions" from Hinohara Setsuzo, the President of Denko. Ashida expelled the implicated men from the cabinet. Though surprised, the general public showed some slight indignation. Some people even sent letters to the editor: "Those who were exposed are just the unlucky ones. There are many who don't get caught . . ."

In September, 1950, *Lady Chatterley's Lover* was indicted as an "obscene publication." Literary circles protested en masse, on the ground that there were thousands of other erotic or pornographic publications wrongly set loose by the postwar liberalism.

Moral delinquency permeated almost all ranks and walks of society. Politicians and businessmen tried to approach the powerful officials of the Economic and Scientific Section of SCAP, which held almost unlimited authority over economic affairs in defeated Japan. Takeuchi, of course, used every possible means of taking a part in, and winning, the bidding for contracts for the construction and remodeling of buildings. Odaira made a secret check through his own men: Takeuchi had done so much that once indicted he would have little chance of being acquitted. Takeuchi was safe only because the police authorities were too busy catching up with crimes of greater magnitude.

Under such circumstances, the Communist Party had a great advantage in its anti-government campaign. The Party obtained twenty-five seats in the general election after the collapse of the

Ashida Cabinet. The third Yoshida Cabinet was formed. The revolutionary force was becoming a serious threat to the conservative
camp when suddenly in June, 1950, war broke out in Korea.

The Korean war lasted a long time and brought with it a great
inflationary boom through the magic of *tokuju,* Special Procure-
ment. This was a heavenly manna that artificially resurrected the
otherwise suffocated Japanese economy.

America also tried to reverse its policy towards Japan. The puni-
tive policy was now shifted to a baby-sitting policy so that Japan
could be kept comfortably in the buggy of the Western camp. The
constitutional renunciation of war was to be found a failure, and
made virtually a dead letter.

All these sudden changes were so dazzling that Odaira almost forgot Taguchi, one of his old pals. Odaira phoned Takeuchi, but
it was Nara who answered the phone. "I sent a post card to you.
Taguchi died in a sanatorium near Kamakura. He died miserably.
Had he informed us earlier, we'd have done something if we only
knew a little earlier . . ."

Odaira Shuntaro went to Zushi to attend the funeral ceremony of
Taguchi. He found Nara and Narazaki already helping.

Taguchi's father complained meekly, "If only we could have
bought butter—or something nourishing." For Taguchi, stricken
with tuberculosis, there had been no nourishment or medicine. His
death had been like the melting away of a candle.

After the ceremony all three kept silent, feeling a strange vacancy
of mind. Finally Nara said, "How about dropping in at our place in
Suitengu for a drink?"

But neither Odaira nor Narazaki accepted the offer.

Instead, Odaira hurried back to the office. He called in a junior
reporter who covered the Metropolitan Police Board.

"Say, about that Jesse James, Jr.—guess you should track it down
again."

"Is there any new angle?" the reporter asked.

"Positively, it's one of my friends," Odaira said.

"Your friend? Oh, no."

"Yes. I haven't got any concrete evidence yet. But this guy can
climb up a high fence quite easily. You said the thief usually enters
through a washroom. This guy is an expert repairman of flush
toilets," Odaira calmly explained.

"Well, you think I should track him?"

"Yes. Somehow I am in debt to him, I mean I was. But now I can't help it. He's too slimy and going too far. I've just been to a friend's funeral and really felt I shouldn't let a crooked friend run around loose in this society while an honest but weak and poor guy simply dies away. If he comes back to his senses—maybe after serving a term—I will shake his hands, of course," Odaira said rather emotionally.

Giving a detailed description of Kihara, Odaira added, "Try to make him give himself up, if you can."

A few days later, the reporter came back to report on the progress of the Jesse James, Jr., case. He found several suspicious points, but they weren't enough to indict Kihara, who seemed to have committed a series of almost perfect crimes.

"Unless he strikes again, we can't nab him," the reporter concluded.

"A lucky fellow!" Odaira sighed.

But he wasn't. Kihara's luck came to an end. He moved into the Yokohama area. Though he succeeded in sneaking into a foreigner's residence, he got caught on a barbed-wire fence. While he desperately tried to get loose, a bullet from a pistol got him in the leg.

"I should have stopped him earlier!" Odaira clenched his fists with belated regret, but felt strangely relieved that he had not caught Kihara with his own hands.

Kihara's arrest was worth a three-column spread in every newspaper. One day, Odaira received a letter from Narazaki:

The news really upset me. Kihara was Jesse James, Jr.! I now remember so well how we praised his stealing ability. It saved us. But actually I'm relieved to hear about his arrest. His stealing habit should be punished under the present situation. I've been thinking for a long time that he might be the fellow. How many times have I thought of informing the police about him! Now he's been arrested! I know we owe our lives to him, but I feel "justice has longer arms than our poor sentiments."

Odaira chuckled. Narazaki's line of thinking was practically the same as his own. He was greatly encouraged to have such an honest, righteous, and warm man courageously fighting against the disorder of the present society.

Then he remembered Nara, who was so taken with Kihara's sister, Asako. When Nara visited his office, he disclosed an amazing story. He was going to open a bar in the Ginza. Odaira couldn't help thinking that Nara—the farmer—would be a sure victim of some sharp practice or other.

"Are you serious about this crazy idea?" Odaira asked.

"Sure, of course. I bet the business'll be a success, if you bring in lots of friends." Nara seemed completely certain that his venture would succeed.

"The Ginza is no place we can afford to go," Odaira said, giving up the idea of dissuading him.

"Don't think that way. Soon beer will be on the market. Foreign liquors, too. From now on bars should not be limited. I'll try not to limit the customers to the wealthy class."

Odaira was suddenly aware of the contradiction that prevailed almost everywhere in society. After the disorganization of the Zaibatsu and the promulgation of the Anti-Monopoly Law and the Economic Decentralization Law, the peers and nobles lost their powers and became the "has-been" families. Their houses and mansions were bought up by the upstarts and black-marketeers—a complete social upheaval.

Of the seven warriors who had shared their scanty food in the deep mountains of the Philippines, Taguchi had died, Kihara had been arrested, leaving only five in the whirl of the confused society. Even the remaining five were now living entirely different kinds of lives.

One night, Odaira was invited to the foreign correspondents' club, where he could drink beer to his heart's content. Here there was none of the arrogance often found among the "conquerors." Equality and liberty prevailed. Odaira treasured this atmosphere that he could hardly find in any other place.

As he passed by Yurakucho Station, he saw gaily attired "angels of the street" swarming around the station. They looked like flowers blooming on a scorched land.

Totally devastated Japan had quickly absorbed the fashions of the world. Girls were using American cosmetics and wearing costumes straight out of *Vogue* regardless of their dimensions and coloring. He remembered a "Letter to the Editor" that had come in that morning. It severely criticized the recent stylishness of the Japanese girls on the ground that there were so many war-suffering people even among the victors. The letter was full of bitter words against frivolity and flippancy. That much was understandable. But Odaira could hardly think it entirely wrong that Japanese girls wanted to cast off the wartime *mompei*—the dull-looking pantaloons.

"As soon as the girls become prettier, the men start working harder"—that old rule, Odaira thought, could be applied to everyone but that lone wolf Narazaki—though he had looked busier in his most recent visits. Then one sunny afternoon in a coffee shop near his office, Odaira eliminated Nara as an exception to the rule. A very modern girl was sitting beside Narazaki, who abruptly asked, "Haven't you met this girl before?"

Odaira struggled with his memory.

Then Narazaki startled both Odaira and the girl by saying, "She was Mrs. Taguchi, don't you remember?"

The girl blushed. Odaira quickly flashed back to the day of Taguchi's funeral. Yes, there was a girl who was wearing a black mourning kimono.

Narazaki told all about his new bride. She was formerly a nurse in the sanatorium where Taguchi died. Competing with several rivals, Taguchi succeeded in winning her hand, probably because of his naïveté.

"We've already started living together," Narazaki frankly confessed.

Odaira simply said, "Congratulations." The couple looked completely unbalanced—at one end, the rugged simplicity of Narazaki; at the other, the modern winsomeness of Katsuko.

In the early postwar days there was no one who could openly criticize MacArthur and his policy. Naturally, there was no such freedom under the Occupation administration. But a powerful additional inhibition was also operative—Japanese nature was accustomed to obeying blindly the ruler's words. MacArthur did not understand this blindly obedient nature. He seemed to believe that Japan was full of militaristic nationals. When he realized his misconception, he tried to alter his policy. The general public, however, was scarcely aware of changes taking place far above them. They were simply following the orders that came out of the Daiichi Building through the Japanese Government, always carefully muffled with showers of beautiful modifiers.

The people, therefore, were completely stunned when they were confronted with the unexpected news that MacArthur—the almighty five-star general—had been fired by Truman. After MacArthur's departure, there sprang up an interesting phenomenon—an increasing anti-Americanism. Japanese began publicly criticizing the foreign nationals who had been strutting through their country. The citizens of Kyoto and Osaka attacked their municipal authorities on account of local regulations that prohibited Japanese drivers to pass Occupation vehicles.

This tendency was given further impetus by the Communist Party. They claimed that the democracy the Americans had brought to Japan was suspect; it provided liberty and freedom only between the Japanese but not between Japanese and Americans.

The leaders who had been previously purged by MacArthur in June, 1950, went underground, whence they apparently maintained command over their followers. "Red" students started riots on the campuses. Professors could not control their students. Some professors even tried to get on the bandwagon by making themselves look "pink," if not completely "Red." The Teachers Union of Japan started to make political announcements, while the core Communists prepared operation "Y" for armed uprisings. Pistols were smuggled in from "nowhere." Flame bottles were secretly prepared for military operations. "The Communist Party that should be loved by the people" had disappeared.

In the late afternoon of May Day, 1952, Odaira was on his way to the Ministry of Education to cover a story on the 6-3-3 System. His car was passing near the north entrance of the Hibiya Park when the driver pointed toward the Imperial Plaza and shouted, "Look, Odaira-san, something must be up!"

A cloud of dust was rising high, suggesting some serious trouble.

"Let's go back. To Babasakimon, if we can," Odaira ordered, though he began to doubt whether the car could get through the crowds that were swarming around. The car, however, somehow managed to get through. Every window of the Daiichi and Meiji Buildings was full of American faces looking down curiously.

A photographer was coming back from the Plaza. His torn shirt and bloody face clearly reflected the seriousness of the trouble. Then a group of students gathered around the American cars parked alongside the road. The cars were turned over and set afire one by one.

"That's outrageous," the driver yelled.

As Odaira looked around, most of the Occupation cars parked around the Hibiya-Babasakimon area had either smashed windows or were being turned over and set afire. From the direction of the Plaza could be heard the sound of flame bottles exploding. A rescue squad of policemen were running from Hibiya. The students scattered as the policemen tried to grab them.

"It's getting too dangerous. Let's go back," Odaira said. At that moment he saw a pale young man staggering toward the car. He could not see the man's face, which was covered with dust and blood stains. But Odaira noticed something.

"Tobo! Here!" he shouted with a little suppressed voice, gesturing to the half-opened door. The man collapsed on the floor.

"Let's go back!" Odaira said, as he closed the door.

"Where to? The office?" the driver gasped.

"No! To the Ginza! Quick!" An idea flickered in Odaira's mind.

Parking the car in front of a bar in West Ginza, Odaira carried Tobo to the rear entrance. "Nara! Are you there?" he shouted.

Down the staircase came Asako, clad in pajamas.

"Asako-san, is he out? Well, this fellow is our mutual friend. He's hurt. Could you do something to help him?"

Tobo's face was ashen when he was laid down on the tatami in the attic. Tired and excited, Tobo looked seriously hurt.

"What happened?" Asako asked.

"Oh, he just got messed up in the May Day celebrations. He'll be all right with an hour of sleep," Odaira answered.

"Is he also a friend of my husband?" she asked. "He looks so courageous for his age, doesn't he, Odaira-san?" She was intently looking down at Tobo's closed eyes. Odaira looked away from her heaving bosom, lifting almost out of her pink pajamas.

Soon Tobo opened his eyes, looked mysteriously around, and tried to raise his head.

"No, no. You should be a good boy and be quiet!" Asako patted Tobo's shoulder.

"Where am I?" Tobo meekly asked.

"You're in Nara's house. This is Mrs. Nara," Odaira explained.

Tobo smiled a wry smile, as if he were ashamed of being helped by a "running dog" of capitalism and "a poison seller of capitalism."

"I must go." He raised his upper body.

"Where to?" Odaira tried to push him down.

"To the Imperial Plaza, of course."

"Nonsense, May Day is over," Odaira said, almost harshly.

"I won't be defeated! War isn't over," Tobo murmured and collapsed.

Odaira left the bar, asking Asako to keep an eye on Tobo. When he came back to his desk, however, he received a telephone call from Asako, who told him that Tobo had left the bar saying he would give himself up.

That day, he learned later, about five thousand policemen had been involved in hand-to-hand fighting with five to six thousand members of the All Japan Student Association, the Daily Workers' Union, and the Korean Federation in Japan. Many people had been seriously injured. The police had used tear gas, which finally dispersed the rioters.

Odaira, however, could never trace the whereabouts of Tobo. Possibly he was among the rioters arrested. He was shocked at what happened that day. But there was another person who was further —and in an unexpected fashion—shocked by the effect of the May Day riot. It was Nara Hachiro.

A few days later he came to Odaira's office and explained with tears in his eyes. His wife, Asako, had been unfaithful since their marriage. But on May Day she had kissed Tobo when he could not move. "That's why Tobo left our house," he said. "I'm deeply sorry for what my wife has done to my old friend."

Odaira could remember Asako looking down at Tobo's closed eyes. Now in front of him was Nara also with closed wet eyes, murmuring that he would divorce his wife.

"If I should keep on with this life, I would be most miserable," Nara sighed. "Anyway, I will think it over," he said and left.

Takeuchi Renpei seemed to be most prosperous. Amid the deflation, buildings were being constructed one after another. His business, naturally, increased.

Odaira received an invitation to a party from Takeuchi. When he arrived at the restaurant in Tsukiji, he found Nara, Narazaki, and Takeuchi already sitting around a large table.

"Tonight is the Old Comrades Get-Together Party and also the farewell to Nara. He is going back to his farm," Takeuchi declared.

Nara bowed twice or thrice to every toast.

"That's good," Odaira said and quickly reflected whether his remark was fit for an occasion where Nara had divorced his wife and was going back to farming.

"Well, I think farming is the best job I can do," Nara said, almost delightedly.

"But it took lots of money and time before you realized it," Takeuchi jokingly teased him.

"Yet, you're lucky, you drank lots of liquor when I was simply sipping that atomic-bomb bootleg," Odaira joined the kidding.

"Well, I'll never drink foreign liquor again in my life," Nara replied seriously.

"Say, let's stop talking. Let's drink!" Takeuchi shouted and gestured to the Geisha girls, suggesting they pour more sake for everyone.

Taguchi dead; Kihara and Tobo in the custody of the police, though for different charges; Nara now going back to where he came from.

Ten years had passed so quickly—or so slowly, in a sense—Odaira was musing, when suddenly Takeuchi said: "Let's the three of us find a bride for Odaira! Otherwise he will be simply drinking sake until he passes away!"

"Never mind my business! You've two or three mistresses. That'll cover my share. I don't need any dame around me!" Odaira shouted, but was soon ashamed as every Geisha looked curiously at him.

He poured himself some sake and gulped it down—trying vaguely to swallow something that he should forget.

REVENGE

by Mishima Yukio

IN WALKING THROUGH, say, a bright, sunny seaside resort, one passes at times a house that exudes a strangely dark quality. The sensation is inexplicable, but somehow it creeps up on you. The house itself may be in perfect condition, nothing dilapidated about it or the least bit out of place—it may even be bright-looking, but the darkness is there, emanating every moment from within.

The Kondo place is such. There is not a thing broken or neglected about the house. All the locks are new and shiny. A well-kept lawn, with a neat white fence encircling it, and yet there hovers about it a lonely, ominous aura of some sinister secret locked within.

Two name plates hang on the gate. One says *Kondo Torao,* and on the other *Masaki Natsu* is written in small, quivering ideographs, as if to hide behind the first.

The household consists of five. These are Kondo Torao, the master of the house, and his wife Ritsuko. They have no children. Torao's mother, Yae, lives with them on a small inheritance left by her husband.

Then there are Masaki Natsu, Yae's late husband's widowed sister, and her daughter Haruko. They had kept a separate household until recently—a small apartment—but since they had almost used up what little money Natsu's husband had left, they had to depend on what Haruko brought home by teaching kindergarten in a nearby Catholic Church. They have come to live with the Kondos to save room rent.

Torao himself commutes to work in Tokyo from this seaside resort. He comes home at exactly the same time every evening. Then the family gathers in the dining room for supper.

They are sitting around their late supper table. The dead calm that comes every evening is particularly bad tonight, the air humid and close. The dining room is not lit very bright. The entire house is dark for that matter. They are saving on their electricity bills. Broiled fish and salad served individually are on the table.

"Mother bought this fish from the fishermen directly," says Ritsuko. She is always the first to open the nightly conversation.

"Bargained! Bought them very cheap," the old lady says proudly. "If you know how, you can always buy things cheap."

Torao hardly ever joins in the conversation of the women. A former lieutenant in the Army, he is very well built, but his face is pale and his rimless glasses add coldness to his features.

Natsu, too, eats in silence. She and her daughter look exactly alike, even to their anemic complexions. Natsu's care-worn lines add sharpness to her thin face.

The conversation lags. The sound of evening waves reaches their ears. The family has a queer habit. Whenever conversation lags, all stop eating and listen. They cock their ears as though expecting to hear something. This doesn't happen too often in the daytime, but is particularly noticeable at night.

And this is one of those times. As they listen, they suddenly hear a noise in the kitchen. They all turn their heads that way, their faces slightly pale.

"It's only a rat," says Yae.

"Yes, it's a rat—it must be," adds Natsu, and laughs all by herself, artificially and too long.

Suddenly Ritsu puts her chopsticks down, and starts to speak, determined to get something off her chest. "I've got to say it. I thought I'd wait until supper was over," she says, without looking at anyone in particular, holding the edge of the table. "I went swimming today. Alone. And I saw him. . . . Genbu. He was standing quite close, glaring at me."

The four of them stare at Ritsuko.

"But that's impossible, how could he be here in this town?"

"You don't know what he looks like in the first place."

"But I did see him," Ritsuko insists. "He was about sixty, strongly built, about five feet seven in height, not clean shaven. He had on an open-collared shirt, and khaki trousers. I think he had on a pair of *geta*."

"Oh! I know," says Yae, calmed. "That is the description of Genbu that Yamaguchi-san gave in his letter. You just happened to see a man who fits that description. If Genbu leaves his home town, Yamaguchi-san will send us a telegram." She looks around, she pauses. "The more I think about it, the more I am grateful that we happened to know Yamaguchi-san, living in the same town as Genbu."

The entire family is dependent upon this Yamaguchi for their peace of mind. Yamaguchi is obligated to Yae's husband, who had been an official in the Ministry of Internal Affairs before he died. Yamaguchi is an old man, now retired to his home town, the same as Genbu's. Yae wrote to him, asked him to write back a detailed report on Genbu. Yae used Natsu Masaki's name because she did not want the name of Kondo to be known in connection with this affair. To keep Yamaguchi's goodwill, Yae often sends money and presents out of her meager funds. Yamaguchi, to break the monotony of his retired life, writes back long letters. He also promised that as soon as there is a sign of Genbu leaving town, he will notify the Kondos by telegram.

"It's only your imagination," Yae says, meaning to comfort Ritsu.

"But I still think it was Genbu. I felt it in my bones." Ritsu is stubborn. "We'd better be very careful tonight."

"Yes, we'd better, whether it was Genbu or not." Yae looks at Torao. "You see that everything is locked. Make sure of the garden and all." Then she falls into a half monologue. "But we are in some fix, aren't we? We can't go to the police. If we do, and tell everything—terribly embarrassing for Torao. Might even affect his future."

Torao continues to keep silent, sullen. He is the only one eating now, but he is doing so mechanically, merely putting his food into his mouth. He too is highly upset. His forehead is covered with perspiration, but he doesn't even wipe it. His wife takes a handkerchief and daubs it for him.

Dinner over, they move to the porch to cool off. A whiff of a breeze comes in from an open window.

"How nice and cool," Yae exclaims, a bit exaggeratedly.

"By the way, I remember now that I had a similar experience not long after we had that first letter from Genbu," Natsu starts again, returning to the topic. "I saw him in my dream. The face of Genbu whom I've never met—it was so vivid. I remember it very well."

"It was your imagination, too," Yae answers her, not altogether unhappy that Natsu has returned to the topic everyone fears. "I do the same thing, every night, almost. Even now. It must be the same with you, Torao. Especially as you knew Genbu's son."

"We should have our ground covered with small pebbles," Ritsuko exclaims brightly, thinking her idea excellent. "Then we can hear the slightest footsteps. With the sand we can hardly hear anything."

"And where do we get the money for such a thing," Yae says. "Luckily, we can trust Yamaguchi. But even now I often wake up in the middle of the night, suddenly. It's been eight years. Eight long years have we been living in this same state. Not a day of peace."

Yae and Ritsu exchange glances, and in those glances are eight years of continuous worry and fear. For eight long years, when nighttime comes the family gathers into one room, locks up everything, shuts out the outside world. Every night a nightmare attacks some member of the family; a huge Genbu standing at his or her head, holding an axe up ready to bring down . . .

"I suppose it will have to come someday," Yae sighs.

"What would have to come?" someone asks.

"I said, Genbu will come someday. Torao might just as well be prepared. I am. Of course, I am not young. I have only a short life left. But poor Ritsu and Haruko, they are so young yet."

Ritsu and Haruko are in the kitchen, washing dishes. In the silence, the rustle of the paper in Torao's hand is a roar.

The door bell suddenly peals.

The three look at each other quickly. The two in the kitchen rush to where the three sit. The five of them stand around the table. None speaks a word. No one has ever called at this late hour before.

Torao turns his body, wondering whether to go to the door or not. Yae stops him, and whispers to him low, "It's best not to resist. I'll go to the door."

Yae turns on the light in the guest room, then at the front door. In the dining room, the three women surround Torao. Torao's face shows deathly pallor. Natsu holds her daughter's hand tight.

The tension heightens when they hear the voice at the front door.

"Masaki-san, telegram," the interloper calls.

"To me, why, who . . ." Natsu starts to the door.

"Auntie, it must be from Yamaguchi," Ritsu says. "He can't use the name Kondo, you know."

The four hear Yae walk from the front door, through the guest room into the dining room. The expression of high joy on her face is in odd contrast to that of fear on the rest of them as they rush to her side.

"*Kuratani Genbu died—Yamaguchi,*" she reads aloud, and falls to a chair. She closes her eyes, leaving the four to their joy. She seems infinitely tired.

"I am so glad," she says at last. "Now, I can burn those letters I kept for the police, in case . . ." She gets up, opens a box on a chest of drawers, takes out a bundle of envelopes. Out of one of them she draws a letter, brown with age. She reads aloud:

"To Kondo Torao:
"You have come back to Japan, after putting the blame for a war crime on your subordinate—my loving son. How could you do it? I, his father, will avenge him. My hate for you will not stop until I kill you and your whole family.

Signed in blood.
Kuratani Genbu"

Yae, after reading, puts the letter with the rest. She stands up, places a pan over a hot plate and puts the bundle into it. Long before the letters' brown papers catch fire, all can smell the evil odor of the burning blood on the paper, turning darker brown.

The papers catch fire fast. As the last flames die down and the pan holds only gray ashes, the family is thrown into new, fresh fear.

"You can't put too much store in that telegram," Haruko says. "Maybe Genbu himself sent it to make us drop our guard!"

UNDERGROUND ESCAPE

by Tsuji Masanobu

FROM THE RADIO came the halting voice of the Emperor.

"To bear the unbearable, to suffer the insufferable . . . Lose not again your trust both at home and abroad . . . We are with you, our subjects . . ."

Thus, everything ended. In the basement of the Bangkok headquarters, suppressed cries rose from the ranks of men standing at attention with bowed heads.

As I listened, I told myself, "I have no excuse. I have committed a sin for which ten thousand deaths cannot atone. It would be *bushido* to apologize by committing *hara-kiri*. However, the Imperial wish is that we disarm unconditionally and abide by the orders of the Allied Powers. To obey is the duty of a subject. It is not the wish of His Majesty that we, by our actions, should lose again our 'trust both at home and abroad.' "

I felt as if my very bowels were being torn into shreds. In the midst of this intense suffering, with cheeks still wet with tears, I attended the final conference in the Commander's room. At this meeting, a certain high-ranking general said, "How can we bear to hand over our swords now hanging at our waists? We should return to Japan armed as we are and should be disarmed there. Unless we can do that, I'll cut the enemy to pieces or cut open my stomach."

Was there no one to refute the rantings of this officer? Unable to stand it, I said quietly, "The Imperial Rescript asks us to bear the unbearable. If there is anyone who does not agree with His Majesty's wish, I see nothing wrong in his cutting up the enemy or com-

48

mitting *hara-kiri* on his own initiative. But it would be a mistake to have the attitude of the entire army decided by the emotions of one individual. We must strive to send every last youth back home safely. Please go ahead and cut open your stomach in front of Loyalty Shrine."

It was a struggle for me to say what I did before a large gathering, especially to a superior officer who had looked after me and cared for me for so long; however, I felt there was no other way out of the difficulty.

Deputy Chief-of-Staff Hamada, who had listened with quiet composure from beginning to end, said detachedly, "Tsuji, I have one thing to ask of you. Japan must suffer for the next ten or twenty years. If possible, I'd like you to go underground in China and open up a new way for the future of Asia. I know a Taiwanese who is head of a group of pirates. If you want to go to Taiwan, I'll introduce you to him."

I answered, "Taiwan's not too bad. But, I'll try my hardest to go underground in Thailand, becoming a priest."

And my resolution was complete.

There had been distributed to the Southeast Asia Army a number of "special volunteers," seventeen-year-olds who had been hand-picked and educated to become "special attack corps," the so-called Kamikaze, chosen for duties in the Navy, Army and Air Force from which there would be no return. Now, without any planes to fly, they had been parceled out among various ground detachments as so-called "strategic forces," to be used as spies and subversive agents. There were around fifty of these youths in Bangkok.

I spoke to these youngsters, none now older than twenty-two or -three, telling them I intended to go underground in Thailand by becoming a Buddhist priest. When they heard this, eight of these young men came and asked to go with me. All had been real priests in civilian life. I decided to choose two or three of the best, but all insisted on joining me. On their youthful faces was written the firm resolve to work for the reconstruction of their country with the same spirit they had subjected their bodies to in the rigid military training they had recently completed.

They were set on joining me in going underground. I had been with them for only a few lectures, yet for some reason I felt toward them a deep confidence and immeasurable love. When the majority of the older men had only one thought in mind—to return to Japan as soon as possible—here were youngsters competing for the right to stay in Thailand.

"All right. I'm asking you all to stay and die with me. We might have to stay underground for ten years, maybe twenty, but I want all of you to give your lives as foundation stones in the establishment of true Thai-Japanese friendship."

I, too, resolved that I would be ready to die with these youths, more like my own young sons or my own young brothers.

The memory of the Deputy War Minister came to my mind. He had been a Commander of the Army Air Force in the Philippines. There he had thrown hundreds of youthful "special attack corps" fliers into the teeth of death. But once the situation developed in favor of the enemy, he defied the orders of Commander Yamashita, abandoned his men, and fled to Taiwan.

I pledged to myself, "No matter what happens, I'll throw away this body of mine with these youngsters."

I immediately investigated the family backgrounds of these youths. I found that Probationary Sub-Lieutenant Tada was the only son of a widowed mother and already the head of a temple. I felt that I would have to send Tada home. I spoke to him of Karmic fate and said, "I want you to go home and get in touch with the families of the other seven men. Then I want you to start on the reformation of the religious world of Japan."

He did not utter a word of dissatisfaction and replied, "I deeply regret that I cannot be accepted. But I feel that what you tell me is also my task. I shall return as you order."

I next visited the Embassy. I found the Ambassador weighted down by the swift changes of the past few days. Suffering was written all over his face, but he greeted me in a quiet voice. "I'm very sorry. The future Japan must win back the trust of the world through her moral principles. Let us work toward the rebirth of a nation that will not contain even a single criminal."

"Today's situation is the result of the sins of us military men," I answered. "In the hope of atoning for even a part of this great sin, I want to stay in Thailand together with seven young men as foundation stones in the erection of a lasting friendship between Thailand and Japan. Could your excellency not ask for the understanding of the Thai leaders for this venture?"

"Very good. As my last service to my country, I shall immediately ask for permission for your venture from the Thai Minister of Education and the Prime Minister. I know you will do your best."

The British forces had not as yet arrived in Thailand. Although I had not heard of my being designated as a war crimes suspect, I was fully ready to meet such a fate. If the British Army were to start a search for me, I knew that I would be causing undue trouble to the Ambassador. Although he was a civil servant, the Ambassador did not pause and think of his own position. I felt that he showed himself to be a true patriot by granting my request.

If this man had become an Army leader, he would surely have been like General Nogi. I could not but feel admiration for Ambassador Yamamoto when I compared his soft-spoken determination with the arrogance of the high-ranking officers who took full advantage of the power of their military uniforms. Ambassador Yamamoto had showed himself ready to give up everything out of his deep concern for his country.

I felt that Ambassador Yamamoto was a true diplomat and true patriot. I shook hands firmly with him and soon left. In all probability, this was a final farewell. I could not halt the streams of tears that flowed down my cheeks.

Priestly garb for eight men were prepared. The costumer was Maruyama Kamito of the Hikari Mission, a priest of the Nichiren Sect, and the dressing room was an inner suite in the Thailand Hotel.

Taking care not to disturb my Army colleagues, who were deep in slumber, I tip-toed out of my room. Just as I reached the car that I had readied in secret, I noticed Sub-Lieutenants Akutsu and Shirakura waiting, shoulders fallen in despondency.

"Thanks very much for everything. Please take good care of yourself," I mumbled.

We exchanged our final farewells. Thirty years of military life had come to an end. The lonely sentinel presented arms as I slipped out of the headquarters gate. The street lights reflected on the polished bayonet affixed to his rifle.

Good-by Army life, good-by comrades.

This was the beginning of an underground trek that spanned three countries and 7,500 miles. The path was to lead through hell, with countless deadly barriers along the way.

The first mile-post was the small ossuary for the remains of Japanese erected in the compounds of Ryab Temple, mercilessly destroyed by bombings. I got out of the car at the rear gate and peeped through the hedge, but saw no one. I wondered for a moment whether I had made a mistake, when one of the disciples, who had moved the night before, woke up and opened the half-door for me. He was tired and more asleep than awake as, rubbing his eyes, he said, "Good morning, master."

Nonetheless, his greeting was cheerful.

The disciples, suddenly raised by their master, were frantically folding up their bedding. I met the guardian of the ossuary, the old priest Chino.

"I am Aoki. I hope you will be kind enough to teach me."

The ossuary was composed of two towers, thirty-six feet high and sixteen-feet square at the base. It contained the remains of Japanese who had died in Bangkok over the past fifty years and the votive tablets of 120 war heroes who had died in Thailand and French Indo-China.

Before taking up my chopsticks for the first meal of my new life, I had to chant three times; *"Homage to the Sutra of the Lotus of Good Law."* I felt awkward. I told myself that this would not do, I would have to learn to become a priest completely.

After the meal, the old priest Chino poured hot water into his bowl, stuck his fingers in, and washed the clinging rice from the sides. Then he placed the bowl to his lips and drank. Somehow I could not bring myself to follow his example and picked loose the remaining rice with my chopsticks and then drank down the water.

As soon as the morning meal was over, we lined up in front of the ossuary and, with young Kubo leading us, began chanting sutras. While we repeated the sutras together, with wooden and metal gongs keeping time, I found myself being captivated by the rhythm, learning much more rapidly than I had expected.

I realized the truth of the old saying, "Children near the temple chant unstudied sutras." In one week's time, I had learned the entire Prajna Paramita Sutra. I felt that I would find salvation here for my wounded soul. To chant sutras before this image morning and night seemed to me more a comfort than a regimen or strict training.

There was no light or water in the ossuary. Our only drinking water was rain caught from the roof through a trough into a large vat. In the back yard was a twelve-foot-square pond. It had not been cleaned out for years and was covered with greenish growth and smelled. However, after a day's training, it was our custom to strip to the skin and bathe in this pond. Our greatest pleasure was to surround a lone candle after supper and talk together for two or three hours until bedtime on the future of Japan.

For breakfast, we had *miso* soup and pickles; for lunch and supper, cooked dehydrated vegetables, with perhaps a piece of salt fish. Fresh fish bought in town was a rare luxury. Five yen worth of bananas were first offered before Buddha and then became dessert. Laundry was done by each man. I realized fully how extravagant and spoiled my past twenty years had been—twenty years during which orderlies had waited on me hand and foot. After a week's time I was able to put on by myself the priestly robes of Thailand.

As the monsoon season gradually drew to a close, we began suffering from lack of water. Up until this time we had relied upon the frequent tropical squalls. Mosquito larvae began hatching in our drinking water. The time had come for us to buy our water from the old Chinese who came daily, at one yen for two pails of water carried on a yoke. The water smelled odd. I followed the water seller and to my surprise found that he was getting the water from a puddle formed in a bomb crater. A dead dog was floating in the pond.

In the face of the approach of the British forces, resident Japanese had problems in obtaining their identification certificates. Thai Government and police officers must have felt that their turn to boast had now arrived. Long queues of Japanese lined in front of Thai Government offices, waiting. When their turns came I saw these Japanese, bereft of the backing of their country, rubbing their hands in pitiful pleas before Thai officials.

Finally our turn came. We were asked birthplace, age and occupation, then had to sign our names to our affidavits. I took from my Dhuta bag the ink horn and brush that I had carried with me always, either on battlefields or in a quieter life. But, I was handed a pen and told to sign my name in Romanized Japanese. I did not know what to do, when Kubo said he would sign in my stead.

"A Buddhist monk does not know English," he explained, and I was able to pass the first barrier.

I noticed a Japanese, wearing dark glasses, standing by looking at me. He came close to me and prodded me in my ribs with his finger. It was Ishida, a classmate of mine in the military academy. He had come to Thailand several years previously as a member of a Japanese firm and engaged in underground activity. He was a specialist in gathering information. We spoke to each other with our eyes, putting heart and soul into them. I realized that he also sought to remain in Thailand and work underground.

We were then taken to the room of the Chief of the Religious Education Bureau to be interviewed personally. Beads of perspiration formed in my armpits and wet my robe. As the supposed head of a group of student priests recently arrived from Burma, I was first to be questioned. In the center of the room sat the Bureau Chief, like a judge at a trial. On both sides were seated members of the bureau. All eyes were turned upon me as I entered the room; I felt that they could see through my disguise. If caught, there was nothing I could do. I calmed myself.

"What sect do you belong to?"

"The Shinshu Sect."

"How many years have you been a priest?"

"Twenty years in Japan and roughly two years in Burma. I have only recently arrived in Thailand and am not as yet used to the Thai robes."

"Do you also beat drums?"

"No, it is only the Nichiren Sect that beats drums."

"What is the significance behind the beating of drums?"

"Oh" (and I felt cold sweat suddenly flow down my sides), "that is to chase away enemies of Buddha."

"For what purpose and for how long do you desire to study in Thailand?"

"I would like to stay for about ten years and become a link in bringing about eternal friendship between Japan and Thailand through Buddhism. If you will only allow me to stay in your country . . ."

"Good. Please study hard and strive for the friendship of Thailand and Japan."

This one sentence was like gospel from heaven. I had passed my first test. They had watched with suspicious eyes the clumsy way I had worn my robe. Yet in this way I passed safely.

The remaining seven pupils who were next on the inquisition stand succeeded in passing their tests, thanks to the impression left by my answers. I was more fatigued than I had ever felt on any battlefield. I slept soundly for the first time since taking off my Army uniform. The snoring of my seven disciples was also loud. How great must have been the anxiety of these young men over the examination. Undoubtedly, they could not have encountered in all the examinations in the past one that worried them so much. I wrote,

> *ominous the clouds that darkly whelm the eastern skies.*
> *a hundred devils daily trod our homeland hills,*
> *gallons the searing tears that wet this yellow robe*
> *but a while must I sit within this crucible, steeling my soul.*

At the beginning of October, the Free Thai Cabinet changed the name of Thailand to Siam and began suppressing the Japanese. I could feel the stealthy approach of danger. Kubo came frantically to me, his face sallow with fear. "A terrible thing has happened. This morning, when the Chief Abbot got into contact secretly with the Chief of the Thai Bureau of Religion, he was told all Japanese priests would be arrested without notice on October twenty-ninth."

I felt my heart thump. The Chinese vernacular press had for some time reported rumors that Japanese Army officers had gone underground in disguise. British authorities had changed their attitude and had decided all Japanese priests were to be detained and questioned until their true identities were established.

I knew if placed in a concentration camp, I'd soon be recognized by some Japanese. There was too strict a surveillance for any possibility of my escaping the country. I felt that the end had come. However, it was by heaven's grace that I had been able to learn one week in advance when the British planned a surprise raid on us.

That evening a group of uniformed Japanese officers and noncom's appeared at the ossuary. "The senior aide-de-camp has ordered us to take home all the remains of Japanese officers and men deposited here."

It was evident that they were afraid of being involved in my affairs. I went to where two of the men were getting the remains ready to take home and asked, "What has happened? Why do you have to take away all of the remains so suddenly?"

"Something quite unexpected has taken place. Last night the British headquarters sent over an urgent order demanding Staff-Officer Tsuji's immediate appearance. The Chief-of-Staff told the British that Staff-Officer Tsuji left a note and disappeared on August 16 and that Tsuji, judging from his character, had probably committed suicide. We are taking back these remains for the purpose of making a clean cut between the Army and this temple."

Everything was now clear to me. The worst had come. There had not been a single letter either from my commanders or from my colleagues. If I had not taken the initiative to ask, I would have remained completely at a loss to explain this new development. It was certain that everybody was afraid of having anything to do with me.

"All right. Such being the case, I won't rely on anybody. Nor must I cause anybody trouble. If the British only knew that disguised as a priest, I am living right next to their headquarters, they'd come to get me. I'll fight to the last with my sword, until the rivets holding the blade to the haft break."

And I steeled myself to meet my doom.

Never since my desertion had I felt as oppressed and as stifled as I did now, but my indomitable will to fight flared up within me. In the bloody fighting in North Burma, the units defending the fortifications at La-Meng had fought even after they had lost arms and legs and not a single man surrendered: it was a fight to the end. I resolved to stay underground in spite of all dangers. I thought the Imperial Rescript terminating the war undoubtedly a true Rescript, but so was the Imperial Rescript declaring war. If one Rescript is obeyed the other is automatically disobeyed. In such an age as now the only thing to do, I felt, was to throw away all thoughts of self and to choose, on one's own initiative, the path one believed right for the eternal future of Japan. From the standpoint of the British Army, it was natural to hunt the corners of the earth for me. Churchill had said, "Undaunted in defeat, magnanimous in victory, liberal in peace, and resolute in war." Were Churchill in my place, he would undoubtedly have done what I did.

When the time came to see off the remains of the 150-odd war dead which I had faced in my morning and evening prayers each day for over two months, I was filled with sadness and a sense of impending tragedy. As long as they had rested in the ossuary, I felt the spirits of the dead, for whom I prayed, watched over me. But now I had lost my last support. I was completely alone in a hostile world. The tragic determination that filled my heart seemed to freeze the blood in my body. How easy life had been in the great organization of the Army, with supports both above and below, to right and left of me. Even when I stood at the head of my troops with the gold braid of a staff officer slung over my shoulder, a hail of bullets falling all about me, life was easier than this utter sense of aloneness that now oppressed me.

All the strength I had I poured into the performance of the religious rites that evening.

I felt as if I were a fish caught in a far-flung net that was slowly being drawn in—in toward the enemy. The net seemed too high for me to jump over and too strong for me to attempt a bodily breakthrough. I am ashamed to admit it, but I couldn't sleep a wink that night. I even felt a sense of uneasiness at the sound of Lao Tai's walking stick as he went his nightly round of inspection. At the same time, the sound reassured me; it was good to know that someone was watching. I often mistook the light of passing automobiles for the flashlights of men come to arrest me.

The morning sun of October 28 shone red through my window. It seemed to bless and encourage me.

I left the temple alone, filling my heart with prayer. I picked up a *samlor* and hurried toward Surion Avenue. I passed through a number of check points as a Thai priest. I entered the Chungking headquarters.

The youth who had received me the other day greeted me with a smile and led me into a waiting room. After a short while, a difficult-looking youth swept into the room. In written exchanges, I learned that he was Section Chief Kuo. A little later Chief Secretary Cheng turned up for work. He was no more than thirty years of age. Thin and rather pale, he was nonetheless handsome. Who would have imagined such a youth as being the representative of Lieutenant-General Hsieh, responsible for the 1,500,000 Chinese in Thailand.

With the big paws of the country monk, I gripped the delicate hands of this youth in a grasp of steel. I could not help noticing the slight blush that colored his face. For roughly an hour we conversed by written exchanges. He, being a native of Canton, could not understand my broken attempts to speak the official language of Peking.

My real name, my career, my part in the East Asia Federation Movement, the memorial service for Generalissimo Chiang Kaishek's mother and my relations with Tai Li, I wrote down everything that I could.

"I want to go to Chungking, meet General Tai Li and Generalissimo Chiang Kai-shek, open the way for Japanese collaboration with China. If this is impossible, please arrest me immediately and hand me over to the British authorities. I am not a man to fear for my life and run away."

The two youths nodded as they read and I noticed their faces gradually color with excitement. Their eyes were shining. When I had finished, Cheng then wrote, "Please wait. We want to hold a conference," and then left the room.

I wondered whether it would be good news or bad. I waited for thirty minutes and when the two came back, both were smiling. I shouted silently to myself, *You've made it.*

Cheng wrote with delicate fingers just two words: "Very good."

He told me then to arrange everything with Section Chief Kuo. To think of these youths, still not quite thirty, negotiating on more than an equal basis with both Thai and British authorities filled me with envy. At their age, I was still a Lieutenant in the War University. If they had been Japanese bureaucrats, just what measures would they have been able to take? In all probability the best they could answer would have been, "We'll ask Tokyo. Just wait a while!"

Filled with emotion and excitement, but putting on a serene exterior, I returned in a *samlor* to the temple. With my arrest scheduled for the next day, I had succeeded in planning an escape less than twenty-four hours before the action could be carried out.

British sentinels were stationed at night a short distance from the front gate of our temple. Inside the temple gate, plain-clothes Thai police began to appear constantly. It was not an easy job to get through this barrier. On the afternoon of October 28, I hurriedly cleared up all my personal matters. I felt that neither the British nor the Thai authorities (except ex-Prime Minister Apaiyon) knew as yet that the priest Norinobu Aoki was in actuality Staff Officer Tsuji. The best thing to do was to make out that Aoki had committed suicide. Then, Chino, Kobiki and the seven youths would not be held responsible or be grilled. I shut myself into my own room and wrote my last letters.

In a wooden box, inscribed, *Articles belonging to the late Colonel Masanobu Tsuji of the Japanese Army,* I placed my sword and my blood-stained binoculars. Then I wrapped the box in a yellow robe and handed it to my disciples to be placed in the custody of the Chief Abbot of Mahatat Temple. I saw my yellow-robed disciples off with clasped hands until the dusk swallowed them from sight.

I slung a carpet bag over my shoulder, the bag in front and the blankets behind; then, dressed in the white shirt and trousers of a typical Chinese, I slipped into the dark from my room. I stopped for a moment in front of the main temple and offered a silent prayer. Then, like a thief, I walked silently toward the main gate.

It was exactly nine o'clock, October 28, 1945.

The main gate, to describe it more accurately, was the front approach to the adjoining Ryab Temple. Left half-destroyed by bombing, it was now overgrown with grass and weeds. Because of the infrequent worshipers, it had become the nightly gathering place of thieves. In one corner of the approach was an old poplar tree. It was a suitable spot to hide. Cowering behind the tree trunk, I waited for the promised car, but only machine-gun carriers came and went.

Every thirty minutes, patrols passed by and every hour the helmeted and armed sentinels were relieved. The muzzles of their guns were always pointed toward the Japanese temple. The watch that I had bought for my escape showed one o'clock. The street outside emptied itself of passers-by. I could hear drunken British soldiers shouting with loud voices as they chased Thai girls.

Two o'clock passed. Three o'clock. The streets became completely lifeless. Only the sentinels were alive and awake. Four o'clock came. My arms and face had become a swollen mass of pain from the countless mosquito bites. I thought that all would end when daybreak came. I wondered if my luck had all run out.

Wait, I told myself. The defense detachment at La Meng did not surrender. I decided to say my final prayers. Turning toward the northeast, I bowed my head in deep prayer. With the rosary given to me by my mother in my hand, I said in a small voice the *introibo,* the praise of Buddha and the Prajna Paramita Sutra. When I finished and looked up toward the gate, a miracle had taken place. Both the sentinels were seated on the sidewalk, wrapped in deep sleep. The gods and Buddha had not failed me. Hot tears rolled down my cold face.

The eastern skies began to lighten almost imperceptibly. Early rising Chinese passed by in threes and fours, carrying bundles of vegetables, headed toward the direction of the market. I adjusted the carpet bag and the blankets slung over my shoulders and started walking unhurriedly. I passed the gate. The two sentinels still slept, their heads supported by their rifles.

I coughed as if to clear my throat and stamped more firmly on the ground to make steps heard. I leisurely passed the sentinels. The sentinels, wakened by my footsteps, glanced upward a second, then as if satisfied at seeing a Chinese, went back again to sleep. I felt a big burden roll off my shoulders.

I mixed with the hurrying Chinese vendors and reached an intersection where a Thai policeman stood on duty. I put my luggage down beside the police officer and waited for a *samlor*. Before the Thai policeman could suspect anything, a rickshaw passed by. It was clearly a rickshaw reserved for Chinese. "Surion Avenue. Ten Bahts, hurry, hurry," I said in Thai.

The rickshaw man who had been on the lookout for a passenger put down the shafts of the rickshaw. My Thai language studies had been justified. The rickshaw man must have been pleased to find such a good passenger. The regular fare to Surion Avenue was five Bahts. I promised him ten. Completely happy, the rickshaw driver sped on, overtaking several *samlor*. On the way, told to stop by several British and Thai police, he shouted back in an energetic voice, "This passenger Chinaman," and sped on.

There was little traffic along the streets and the rickshaw man out-did himself for speed. At 5:45 A.M., I entered the headquarters of the Chinese underground movement. The hunted bird had finally found refuge in the bosom of an Oriental. The sun rose to the East, as if to brighten my future path. The Chinese headquarters showed no unpleasantness at the arrival of such an early guest and I was shown into the waiting room. Ten young men were sleeping on the office desks and the sofa. They made room for me on this sofa. I had intended to stay awake, but before I knew it I was dead asleep on the divan. I had passed through my first death barrier. (After 7,500 miles of travel and three years in disguise—part as a military advisor to Chiang Kai-shek while still a wanted man by the British—Tsuji began the last leg homeward.)

One of my daily worries was how my fatherless children were faring. I often wondered how my wife could keep the home fires burning in a home that did not exist. I did not know even where my family was or how they had managed to live through the past several years. They did not have a single cent in savings and had not a single yen of income. I often thought that perhaps they had already starved to death. The whole family might have ended their lives in mass suicide. I was able to forget my family and sacrifice thirty years for the sake of my Emperor and my country, lulled by the sense of security of the guarantees given me by the state. Time and time again I had chided myself for the lack of will power shown in my attachment to my family. However, this was a human failing, a human weakness, a human sadness.

In August of the year before, the Chungking Government had guaranteed me contact with my people in Japan. Since then I had not heard anything further. Yet, as I had not had any bad dreams, I tried to comfort myself with the thought that my family must still be alive somewhere in Japan.

I had no idea when I would be able to return to Japan. I was a criminal who knew not when or where he might be called upon to give up his life. I decided to write down the actions I had performed in my forty years and leave this record to my children so that they would not repeat the same mistakes. I began with my childhood memories, and completed five volumes by the end of January, 1947: "My First Aspirations," "My First Taste of War," "Bitter Battles," "Good Battles" and "Evil Battles." I spent seventy-odd days on this autobiography of more than 400,000 words. It was a book of confessions and at the same time a book of precepts for my offspring. I wrapped and sealed the document and sent it to my family in the care of Staff Officer Chao, who was leaving for Tokyo in the company of Major-General Wang. In the 400,000 words were the spirit of martyrdom for my country and my concept of humanity. I read over this document written in blood and tears and prayed, "My children, proceed with courage and with justice."

My whole heart went with this document.

At the beginning of March, I was lying in my semi-dark room that had once belonged to the maid, sick with a high fever from overwork and fatigue. Suddenly, Staff Officer Liu called on me and said: "Congratulations. A letter has come for you from your home."

I thought that I was having a hallucination as I stared at the letter which had already been opened and censored. It was written in pencil in childish characters, but I immediately recognized my eldest son's handwriting. "Please forgive these long years of unfilial neglect. We are all healthy and well. Eiko is going to Shimizutani. I have quit school and through the kind efforts of Mr. Kawamichi am working in the Kimura Food Store. Mother is doing dressmaking . . ."

My wife and children were alive! The gods and Buddha had protected the children of this sinful father and the wife of a sinful husband. My wife and children had suffered and persevered through desperate effort. My wife was working during the day in a clothing factory, treading a sewing machine, at nights attending a dressmaking school. She had gritted her teeth, had suffered all manner of shame, had brought up my five children.

My son had quit high school midway and had found work in a bakery shop. My heart went out to my eldest son, who was helping his younger sisters through school. I wonder how my eldest daughter felt as she studied at the alma mater of her own mother—a girls' school that had welcomed her with warm sympathy. My wife, it seemed, had not written a letter, being absent at the mill. However, my father-in-law's letter hinted at the difficult life my family was leading.

Whatever the case, they were all alive. They had all been allowed to live. I was the husband of an innocent wife and the father of innocent children—at whom people pointed their fingers and whispered in contempt. I could only thank the gods and apologize to my wife. I wanted to say, "Please bear a little while longer." Yet I did not know whether I would be able to meet them again. In the first half of my life, during which I had forgotten my family and my children, I had taken too great an interest in the state, I had been too conceited in my own position. I now forgot my 102-degree temperature, raised my body and prayed toward the East. Hot tears dropped unchecked upon the letter from my child.

As Manchuria greeted its second winter of Nationalist control, the Chief-of-Staff, General Chen Cheng, was transferred there to take over the command of the Chinese Nationalist forces. He boasted that he would occupy and maintain by armed force the whole of Manchuria. However, the war turned daily in his disfavor.

Studying the general situation, I advised boldly and bluntly the policy of a northern and southern "dynasty" in opposition, saying, "Abandon Manchuria, hold on for a time to North China, but withdraw all the rest of the Nationalist forces to the south bank of the Yangtze and consolidate your positions there." However, this advice was greeted with resentment.

Men in positions of responsibility, from the Second Section Chief down, did not even try to transmit my suggestions to the Generalissimo, fearful of the gravity of the situation. They were endlessly absorbed in the disgraceful scene of discussing the local withdrawal from Kirin and Changchun in Manchuria, without ever reaching a decision. I felt deeply the lack of capable men in the Defense Department. I realized that there was no way left to save the Chinese Nationalist Government. There was no longer any reason why the Defense Department should continue to feed me.

Awaiting the completion of "An Evaluation of the Material War Potential of the Soviet Union," I presented formally in February my resignation, only to be told, "The British are still looking for you. If you go home, you will surely be caught and sent to the gallows. Bear for a while and wait."

"I am very grateful for your thoughtful consideration of my future," I told the Department. "Since I was appointed to serve in the Defense Department, I have with sincerity produced material and data only to see these, time and time again, put aside unused. Even if I were not wanted in Japan as a war criminal, I could bear this and stay. I cannot remain a day longer in China if my purpose is only to escape capture. Whether I am arrested or not, I leave to fate. In my native home I have an old mother close to eighty years of age, sick in bed. If just because I am afraid for my own life I am unable to be at my mother's side at her death, knowing beforehand as I do now that she no longer knows whether she will live through each day, how can I continue my life, knowing I have failed to carry out these filial duties? If I should be arrested upon my return home, I shall make no pleas in my own defense but shall go to the gallows with a smile on my lips. This is the only natural way in which I can atone for the sin of defeat."

This was the gist of an appeal I made directly to the Chief of Staff. Finally, at the end of April, permission came for my return home. "You will be allowed a two-month vacation. We would like you to come back once again and help us out."

I doubted whether they really desired the return of an old and tough colonel of a defeated army.

Already aboard the ship were some three hundred Japanese compatriots from Taiwan. A motley crowd of war-crimes suspects, professors from Taipeh University, detained technicians, artisans and merchants. They were returning to Japan, having lost all hope in the face of the worsening plight of the Chinese Nationalists. The whole group was filled with pessimism over the future of the Kuomintang.

General Chen I, who had been appointed Governor of Taiwan

immediately after the war to take over from the Japanese there, was unable to restrain or control his officials and soldiers from wrong-doing. The smoldering resentment of the Taiwanese natives festered until it could no longer be held down, and it exploded in the February 28 incident of 1948, followed by the massacre of Taiwanese and Japanese by the Nationalists in retaliation. The blood of the tens of thousands who were shot filled the Taiwanese with lasting hatred for the Kuomintang. There even appeared among the population a desire to shake off the rule of the Chinese Nationalist Government and link hands and fate with Japan. On the departure of the group from Taiwan, Taiwanese police, hiding from the sharp eyes of Chinese Nationalist officers, afforded every convenience to the Japanese and showed toward them a protective attitude. After the end of the war, the Taiwanese had dreamed of the arrival of a magnificent army from their homeland to take the place of the Japanese forces. They experienced bitter disappointment on greeting a pack of starving wolves, carrying earthen pots and wearing straw sandals. Then came a wave of rapacious government officials who deprived them of their homes, looted their belongings, and brazenly accepted bribes. *Fapi,* unbacked by gold or silver bullion, flooded the country. Resentment developed into opposition and eventually a bloody struggle. Here, too, the Kuomintang revealed the figure of a tottering and corrupt regime heading for oblivion.

Our ship left Shanghai on the evening of May 16. I watched from the deck the fading outline of Shanghai, doomed once again to be wrapped in the flames of war. Those who stood on the pier waving good-by, and those who waved back from the decks, were all filled with an indescribable feeling. When the ship passed the entrance to Woosung Harbor, I recalled to mind the old battlefields of the First Shanghai Incident, sixteen years before, on which I had lost sixteen subordinates.

My quarters were situated in the ship's hold near the stern of the vessel. We were packed in like so much freight, allowed only a square meter of space per person. I could not even stretch out my legs. The person next to me was a young fellow by the name of Nagai. A student of the Tungwen University of Shanghai, he claimed to be the nephew of the novelist Nagai Sanjin (Kafu). He himself was of the literary type. Yasuda of the Domei News Agency was also aboard. He was on his way home with a baby, not yet weaned, whose mother was a Russian girl he had since divorced.

The child's name was Shepherd and soon became the darling of the ship. The hold, packed indiscriminately with men and women, was filled with nauseating odors, and ruled over by selfishness. I wondered if this ship's hold were the epitome of defeated Japan.

The group of Japanese soldiers, who had been detained as war-crimes suspects, were known as the Kiangwan Unit. Among these men was Major-General Fukuyama, who had been a classmate of mine in the Army University. He played *go* from morning to night, rubbing his bald head. He did not even guess that this pseudo-university professor could be his classmate. Of course my disguise was so designed as not to allow him to recognize me, although we met face to face on several occasions. After this experience I gained confidence and felt that at this rate I would not be discovered. Kadoya Hiroshi was the commander of the entire group of repatriates. I had known him several years earlier while at Supreme Headquarters in Nanking but he, too, failed to recognize me. My work clothes were black with the coal tar painted over the ship's bottom. No matter how one could have looked at me they would not think me a university professor.

After two or three days' journey northward, the boat touched at Tsingtao. Here again, a customs inspection more strict than at Shanghai was held. The looting and stealing by the military police were worse than at Shanghai. The Tsingtao group of Japanese repatriates, mostly women and girls, did not have the strength to repack their luggage which had been ripped apart mercilessly. Somebody suggested that we help the women. Roughly twenty of the strongest volunteered and in a cloud of dust blown up by a strong wind, we helped these pitiful compatriots. A mountain of luggage was immediately loaded aboard ship and, tired though we were, we experienced the pleasure of having been able to help our neighbors.

Leaving the pier, we heard a Japanese voice from among the Chinese police standing on the wharf. "Please take good care of yourself. Do write, won't you? There isn't a single decent person among the Chinese dogs. Japanese are really good people."

What a surprise this was! The mystery soon cleared up, the voice had come from a Taiwanese police officer. This youth had been employed by the Japanese Navy and had crossed over to Tsingtao. After the war he had become a Chinese Nationalist police officer.

From the pier, packages of cigarettes were thrown aboard ship. One Chinese watched with a sour face this exchange of friendly gestures between the Japanese and the Taiwanese. He seemed to be the officer in command, but he could do nothing.

After ten days our vessel finally entered the harbor of Sasebo. Our quarantine ended, instructions concerning our processing after landing were shouted through megaphones by repatriation officials and former Army officers. I was impatient with the innumerable delays. I was seized with the desire to step as soon as possible on the soil of Japan. Every second seemed an eternity.

On the morning of May 26, we finally landed.

As I took my first step upon the soil of Japan, I, unnoticed by the others, quietly picked up a handful of earth and smelled its sweetness. It was the first smell of my motherland in six years. Could my longing for and love of the soil of my motherland be this strong?

Though the country was defeated, the hills and the streams were still left, together with the Emperor.

Impoverished as this soil may be, it was our earth, it was our land.

By no means was it Stalin's land.

Withered and dried though these hills and streams might be, they were our mountains and they were our rivers.

By no means were they Truman's.

We must make this land green once again, with our blood, our sweat and our love.

If fertilizer is needed, then shall I not hesitate to grind to powder these old bones.

CAPTURED BY AMERICANS

by Fuji Seii

THE JAPANESE traditional Boys' Festival, May 5, is the anniversary of my repatriation from Australia and my release from one and a half years as a prisoner of war. I make it a rule to celebrate my health and luck, and to summon up memories of the past war.

Whenever May 5 comes and the carp pennants are floating on the breezes of my homeland, I feel eager to find a chance to get in touch with those who saved my life, the crew of an American submarine. I don't know their names. The only name I still remember is Captain Hess, but I'm not even sure that this was the real name of the submarine skipper. I might have been told false names for security reasons.

The only way I have of identifying myself to the crew members who may chance to read this story is that I was a sort of artist who drew many portraits and cartoons of them. I signed them Fuji, and reminded them all that it was the same pronunciation as the mountain. We prisoners were three—a lieutenant, nicknamed Tojo because he so closely resembled the war leader, a sergeant called Snafoo, who looked very strong even though he couldn't have been more than twenty-two, and myself.

This is the story of my adventure, told in the hopes that one of the readers may happen to be of the crew who saved us, and will look me up that I may thank him for being alive and happy today.

It was October 16, 1944, when our ship was torpedoed. The ship was part of an Army convoy en route to Borneo from Manila. I had just finished my turn at the anti-submarine watch and was about to descend the hatch to my quarters when a dazzling flash illuminated through the blinding rainstorm one of the crammed troopships off to port. Nishikawa, who was at my side, and I dashed to the hand-rail and saw, to our horror, the white wake of a second torpedo headed straight for our ship.

There was no time for evasive action despite our shouted alarm. The blast of the torpedo in our sister ship was still ringing in our ears when we felt the sickening death shudder of our own craft. I was in the water before I knew it and no sooner had I caught hold of a life raft than the silhouette of our ship disappeared beneath the waves. There were nine other soldiers at the raft, and we barely survived the sucking power of the sinking ship. The rain was so heavy that even breathing was difficult. Two days and nights the storm continued unabated, and all that time we clung to the sides of the small raft. It was too small to hold us all and one seriously wounded soldier died the second morning.

On the third night the storm passed and the water became as calm and as smooth as a pond. We realized that we were completely exhausted and fatigue forced us at last into the sleep we had been fighting off for fear of drowning. At one time we all climbed up onto the raft together, vainly seeking a place to sleep. Our combined weight sank the raft and it bobbed up again yards away. We swam frantically to regain it and unsuccessfully tried the same thing again and again.

I am not sure that we were all fully awake. We talked of how the others had fared. Someone ventured that rescue ships had saved all the others. Another claimed our ship had not sunk, but that we had been blown overboard by the blast and that it had continued on its way. The men spoke as in dreams, but we believed one another in our own befuddlement. Then Lieutenant Shimazu cried out, "How foolish I am to think that we are here. Why, an M.P. launch has just visited us and it took me to Headquarters to report on the damage to the ship." He added that he had just come back on the same motor launch and he had just come from Manila. We believed him and flapped and kicked our legs frantically, urging the raft on in the direction that Lieutenant Shimazu said was Manila. How long we continued, I cannot tell, but when no land appeared and darkness fell, we stopped and agreed to wait till morning.

Morning came, but nothing could be seen but sea and sky and

puffy white clouds. The day dragged on and at night two of the soldiers went mad and swam away from the float, laughing and sobbing in the dark. Their voices didn't last long.

By the fourth night everyone seemed devoid of sense. We argued ferociously which way to go. A cloud bank appeared on the horizon and we all thought it land. We all saw the white sails of fishing boats and believed with Shimazu that it was Manila. Then we saw a small canoe coming toward us. We could see figures rowing. Though it was still bright, they were seen only in silhouette. When we shouted, waving our hands, they also responded to us with raised hands. Excited with joy, we bellowed for help. But alas, when the boat approached us at about fifty or eighty meters, it suddenly disappeared. At the same time the white sails which we had seen running on the horizon turned out to be an illusion.

It was not a serious disappointment for us, because soon after that we saw another boat, full of soldiers. We thought there would be no more chance to live if we missed this boat or if it disappeared. The boat approached us. We could hear shouting. We rowed the raft with the last of our strength. No sooner had we reached the boat than I fell down and fainted.

When I woke up after about ten hours' sleep, I found the soldiers in the boat still rowing. Nobody looked happy. Only the creaking of the oars echoed in the star-scattered night. Soon I realized that the people of the boat who saved us had also suffered shipwreck.

While days passed, we became uneasy and undisciplined. We drank salty water to wet our throats. I knew it could not do any good, but we could not help doing so. Sometimes we rowed. Sometimes we put an oar straight up, tying our clothes as a sail for our boat. This did not last long because we became uneasy, afraid the wind would change from day to night. Then we gave up everything, leaving our boat to run along with the tide. It was natural that my body, soaked in the sea for three days and nights, was badly burned by the southern sun.

The sixth evening presented a wonderfully beautiful scene. It was a magnificent sunset which I still remember vividly. By that time everybody was so tired that no one tried to stand up. At first we used to talk about the time when we would land or be saved by a ship. But the last day of our life in the sea we uttered very few words, and just lay down in the boat.

It was October 22, 1944.

A soldier found something on the horizon of the scarlet-colored sea. A rescue ship?

Up from despair, we shouted and waved our hands, even though our voices could not reach the ship. The ship, glittering in the reflection of the setting sun, was coming straight toward us. How we admired the triumphantly approaching ship! The drowning man will catch even at a piece of straw. I loudly recited what my parents used to pray in front of the Shinto shrine. I did not know what to do. The ship was still coming straight, raising white foam by its bow. But wait, it was not a ship, but a submarine. The submarine approached until I could see the complete shape. No, it was not a Japanese submarine.

The submarine suddenly stopped near our boat with a blow of steam. (I thought it was steam, but maybe I was wrong.) A pair of steel plates which looked like radar were twinkling to and fro. Abruptly a manhole burst open and a bunch of sailors jumped up with tommy guns and pistols. Some of them dashed to the deck gun and loaded swiftly.

Our boat was floating toward the submarine. I thought we would be soon killed. I could see even the bore of the gun which was directed at us. Then, I realized I was thirsty.

A soldier murmured, "I can't die until I get a sip of water."

There was a tense moment. Nobody breathed, expecting a blast in the next instant. How could I die and why should I die after the week's struggle against death? I could not help shouting "water" in English. "Give me water!" Nishikawa followed me.

An officer, who turned out to be the captain of the submarine, whispered something to a crewman. "Is there anybody who can speak English?" was the first voice I heard from the enemy. I noticed warm sympathy in the voice of the crewman. A few minutes later, Lieutenant Shimazu, Sergeant Nishikawa, and I were on the deck of the submarine.

Shimazu and I, in broken English, asked them to give us water, because we'd had no water for a week. We just wanted water, even if we were to be killed.

The captain, who looked kind and generous, ordered something to a crewman who saluted and disappeared into the conning tower. Soon, two men emerged with two big cans of water and one big sack of canned foods. They threw them down into the boat.

I did not feel it was war. What I saw was nothing but peaceful and godly acts of Christianity. The captain told us to stay; we were captured. I said good-by to the soldiers who remained in the boat and told them to report us dead and not to expect us to come back alive. We had been taught all prisoners would be killed. Even if we were not killed, it was the most shameful thing to become a prisoner of war. The submarine began to move, leaving the rest of the soldiers in the boat alive, set free.

The captain led us to the bridge. I stepped into the door, and smelled—it was the smell of humans which I had forgotten for a long time. I had forgotten human life, especially since I had become a soldier. Smoke of cigarettes, music, the soft atmosphere of people—I felt I heard falling down from me the crashing sound of chains which had tightly held me in a life-long yoke. It was paradise even though everything in there was a weapon. How sweet the water was! I drank seven cups straight.

My story seems to have come to its end. The entire crew of the submarine was very kind. I cannot forget the two weeks' life in the submarine. The captain, whose name was Hess, was a gentleman who treated us nicely. He promised us to return what we had in our pockets, a watch, pencils and other things. I still have the watch, which is no longer usable because it had soaked in the sea for a week, but I keep it as a memento.

The gunner was kind and I felt as if he were my elder brother. I met him at the mess room usually, where a Spanish cook became one of my best friends. I taught him some Japanese and he was very glad when he found that *bread* in Japanese was *pan* because its pronunciation was very similar in his language.

They showed us no hostility or cruelty. A Swedish sailor told me that he became an American because he loved democracy. Nobody forced us to learn democracy, but I noticed they loved and enjoyed it.

The submarine anchored at Perth, Australia. We were sent to Brisbane by airplane. It was a nice trip, though we were afraid what would happen next. In Brisbane we joined the camp for Japanese prisoners of war. I was repatriated to Japan on May 5, the Japanese traditional Boys' Festival day. Since then, I have been happily working. Recently I married.

I want to show a picture of my wedding to the crew of the submarine. I am afraid they may not be able to recognize me, because I was so sunburnt and thin at that time. And my hair was longer.

I also fear that I may not recognize them because they had handsome mustaches then and now must have returned to well-shaven
faces and civilian suits. But still I am very eager to correspond with
them.

The signature attached to this story of mine is the one I signed
my drawings with. Perhaps it will help friends and former captor-
saviors to recognize me. I hope so.

BANSHU PLAIN

by Miyamoto Yuriko

Nuiko was out by the gate. The instant she saw Hiroko coming, she beckoned, she beckoned to her urgently.

"What . . . ?"

"Hey, hurry up!"

Hiroko entered the house wonderingly. Nuiko put her arm around Hiroko's shoulders as if to hurry her up the stoop. Inside a newspaper lay on the floor mat. Nuiko opened it and pointed out an article: "What do you think of that?"

Hiroko, with obvious but uncommitted emotion, read the news. It was reported in the paper that the Public Peace Law of Japan would be abolished in a few days in accordance with the Potsdam Declaration and that all political prisoners being held under this law were to be set free in the near future.

"Then, Jukichi will be back sooner than expected. Oh, how wonderful!" said Hiroko's aunt cheerfully, coming out of the kitchen wiping her hands. "By now, they should have received the newspaper at the station in Iwakuni and your mother must be glad, too."

Hiroko, however, found herself incapable of acknowledging her aunt's open expressions of joy, not even with a smile. "We cannot say anything until we see more how things go." Hiroko sounded so tormented that Nuiko, her cousin, took a second look at her in surprise. Hiroko, still standing, stared intensely into the newspaper. "In such a place as a prison . . . well, things are very different from what we imagine. Jukichi has been punished not only by the Public Peace Law. . . . He has been tortured in many ways. . . ."

Hiroko's heart was wrenched by the news that the political offenders of the Public Peace Law would soon be released.

Jukichi had been arrested after the exposure of the spies whom the Secret Police had infiltrated into the Party. It just so happened that one of the suspected spies had a physical peculiarity, and in some way due to it, met an unnatural but accidental death. Since the case involved the Communist Party, the trial seemed to be a vendetta pure and simple. When Hiroko learned of the charges and followed the proceedings at the court for the first time, it appeared to her eyes and ears that the state had used its powers in too wily a manner to care about the justice or dignity expected of it. Justice was not judged by common sense, but by a quite opposite spirit of arbitrariness. Jukichi was treated most cruelly. He alone, among the several defendants, was sentenced to life imprisonment, though the charges against all, the responsibility placed on them, were the same; he differed only in having been in the party a shorter time. Next to one name were written as many charges as seemingly could be enumerated. Hiroko felt painfully that each charge was an iron link in the chain which resounded heavily at Jukichi's every step, every movement. She looked upon the incident as a natural event of social history. She did not find anything wrong in what Jukichi and his comrades had done. It was the spies, the actions of authorities who maintained their positions by the intrigues of spies —that was a criminal way to conduct a political struggle and showed immoral decadence. Hiroko could not understand: why was it that those who were young and unselfishly absorbed in improving society in accordance with the natural process of history; why should they be penalized?

To be found guilty even under such transparently unreasonable law, was for those like Jukichi's mother something bad and fearful. How many times had Hiroko during these past ten or more years had to soothe her and struggle to make her keep faith in her son.

Right there, reading that the political prisoners punished under the Public Peace Law would be set free, Hiroko knew in her heart that here was for her the last and most unendurable torture. Immediately after the acceptance of the Potsdam Declaration, Hiroko had been struck with sheer joy. Quivering with anticipation, she tried to picture the inner thoughts with which Jukichi received the news. Constantly running through her head were such thoughts as "When is he coming? I wonder when he is coming. How wonderful it would be to go meet him in Abashiri, and come home together by sea."

Time passed. After a month or so, she began to doubt the Declaration would ever be put into practice with such a questionable government in power. Could the Public Peace Law be abrogated, really? When? How? All the progressive people in Japan, who had been tortured for so long, had the same doubt as she. By the tens of millions, they looked to the future, suspiciously, dry-eyed.

The instant it became known which door would be opened in that wall that was the Public Peace Law, Hiroko felt like a mother calling for her child, not rescued and about to be left in a flaming house. "Jukichi? . . . Jukichi? . . . Others are coming out. . . . What about Jukichi?"

Hiroko, however, had no one to whom she could unburden her anxiety. The flame which in her mind was driving her beloved husband into intolerable danger did not show itself to anyone else.

Hiroko, the newspaper still in her hand, went listlessly back to her room and sat down at her favorite place. Both her aunt and Nuiko, not knowing what to say, first one then the other quietly slipped away.

After an hour or so, Hiroko called from where she was still sitting. "Nuiko, are you in?"

"Yes, I am. Is there something you want?"

"Could you please go to the post office for me?" Hiroko handed Nuiko two letters marked with red ink for registry and special delivery. "Anyway, I think the best way is to ask Mr. Tsukamoto and Mr. Nagata. Depending on developments, I might even have Mr. Nagata go to Hokkaido to prevent injustice being slipped over on us. You agree with me, don't you?" Hiroko asked.

All the family were familiar with Mr. Tsukamoto, Jukichi's close friend since childhood. Mr. Nagata, a lawyer, has steadily dealt with the troublesome paperwork for many years. Hiroko wrote them about the news, asking them to investigate how Jukichi was actually going to be treated. She told Mr. Nagata to draw money for the trip from Mr. Tsukamoto, if he felt it necessary to go to

Abashiri. For her absence from Tokyo, she had managed to put aside some money for any emergency that might arise while she was away.

Nuiko went right out. Hiroko thought over what else should be done now. For the several years Jukichi had been on trial, Hiroko, knowing little about the law, had judged and acted according to common sense, relying on her insight and imagination. Jukichi perhaps never realized how many of the inconveniences he had to put up with were brought about by her frequent oversights and errors.

Hiroko slept in an eight-mat room by herself. Though it was a few days short of October, she had to use a mosquito net in her room. The late moon rose. The *daimyo* bamboos cast shadows on the *shoji* through the outer windows of the veranda.

In Tabata, there used to be a small restaurant called "House of the Spontaneous Smile." On a wall panel opening on the inner courtyard was a sumi-ink painting of bamboo which was said to have been drawn by Taikan while intoxicated.

Every year, a meeting of *haiku* poets was held there to reminisce upon Akutagawa Ryunosuke. Jukichi, as his first major research, had brought to light the change in the thinking of Japanese intellectuals as shown by the literature and, most particularly, the suicide death of Akutagawa.

Hiroko had read that treatise of Jukichi's in a magazine she found on a table in a small hotel in a foreign country. What was the Hiroko of those days doing then? Did she ever imagine that Jukichi, whom she has thus come to know, would become so thoroughly entangled in her life as this? Who can say that Jukichi, then throwing the entire energy of his youth into his research and writing, himself imagined that in another three years he would be cast into prison sentenced to life.

Then again, Jukichi might have known that something like this would happen and had resolutely prepared himself and had gone ahead and married her anyway.

Watching the shadow-play pictures cast by the *daimyo* bamboo leaves stirred faintly by every wisp of breeze, reminded Hiroko, lying in bed with her eyes wide open, called up the memories of the dusty trial court shining in that late April sunlight. At 10 A.M. of the very day the appeal was to have been judged, Tokyo was alarmed by a formation of small planes. Hiroko got a call from Mr. Nagata, who had been in the court since before the appointed time.

He said on the phone that the trial would be postponed. She took off the steel helmet which had been lying heavy on her shoulders and got out of her new *mompe* coveralls. By and by, the air-raid alarm was down-graded to standby. Then the second call told that the court had suddenly decided to open and that she should come immediately.

"How spiteful they are! Surely they know the family can't make it in time," said Hiroko.

"Anyhow, please come as soon as possible. I'll try hard to delay the opening," Mr. Nagata answered.

It took Hiroko an hour to get from her house to the court. She had to walk a ways, take a street car and walk again. There was no other shorter way. She was out of breath when she rushed into the third-floor court room.

The hearing had already been opened and the slender-faced chief judge of the triumvirate was reading aloud from some paper. Jukichi was sitting in the first row of seats. Two guards, who had usually sat apart from him, were close by on either side on the same bench that day. Hiroko sat behind Mr. Nagata. They were the sole audience in the deserted court.

The paper the chief judge was reading was the summary of the review and the sentence. Hiroko felt strange about the whole thing. For what purpose had there been the preliminary examinations or the trials? She found that the analysis and description of the event which Jukichi and his comrades had been trying to clarify with their reasoning and an objective examination of the situation, differed very little from the one-sided reasoning of the prosecution that had been written twelve years before. A slight difference could be noted, though, in less use of vilifications and in the fact that the event was judged an accident, though considered formerly to have been premeditated. Whatever efforts Jukichi made, however reasonable his statements might be, the court had decided beforehand. The sentence was a manifestation of judicial obstinacy.

Hiroko's amazement was renewed, though she knew she made it out too simple, at the fact that a fifty-year-old husband and father, an educated man, could stand there without the slightest hesitation, reading out the most unreasonable judgment.

The chief judge finished reading. Then pausing a minute and raising his voice, he read that Jukichi would be sentenced to life imprisonment. He continued and rattled on in a most business-like way that Jukichi could further appeal within a week if he were dissatisfied with the judgment. All the members of the court stood up at once. So did Jukichi. Hiroko, unconsciously standing up, caught sight of Mr. Nagata's honest white face which had turned an unusually deep red.

All of them followed at the chief judge's heels into the anteroom. Jukichi, leaving, turned to Hiroko and smiled. It was his usual smile. He widened his mouth to knit the edges of it in a hint of cynicism. It was the smile she knew so well. It drew from her a smile. But hers was only a momentary one, and weaving between the benches, she headed straight for him. The guards on either side kept walking, as if to separate them, urging him on. All of Hiroko's movements and her facial expression revealed her concern. Jukichi accepted and understood this; he smiled another smile—one to soothe her. Then turning around and speaking so that either Hiroko or the lawyer could take it, "Well, then, see you the day after tomorrow, again." With his manacled hands, he put on a braided hat and went out. That was a Saturday.

Hiroko could not picture how she herself had looked then, though for the rest of her life she would never forget how Mr. Nagata's face had turned so violently red, or how Jukichi, face smooth and pale from years of illness and being cut off from sunlight, with his gentle but indomitable black eyes, smiled almost humorously.

Those eyes and that smile of Jukichi were formed in the play of *daimyo* bamboo shadows upon the autumn mosquito net—as they were on the small pillow covered in white, and across the palms of Hiroko's hands. Jukichi's hair, which had not yet been cut short, fell long and disheveled over his forehead and gave her a delightful feeling when she ran the fingers of memory through it. How many years have passed since her fingers actually touched it?

There is the word "cruelty," so is there the fact of cruelty. If Jukichi and his comrades were not released from prison, while others are set free with the abolition of the Public Peace Law . . . this is cruel . . . too cruel. . . .

I wonder if cruelty itself is not but power used in such a way that harsh treatment cannot be considered to be impossible.

She sat up in her burning bed, passion billowing forth from her longing for Jukichi, swelled by resistance to the cruelty of power.

In none of the few-minute meetings over the past twelve years had Jukichi shown confusion or suffering on his face. Seeing that face, Hiroko would be refreshed, forget her agony. One summer when he met her in the reception room he had been suffering from dysentery and didn't even have enough strength left to sit up on a chair. He came in his nightgown and sank in a heap on the chair. From across the table, his hair, which had fallen out almost completely, was but a thin suggestive wraith of a hairline and random wisps, exactly as an artist would draw a ghost. Hiroko, blinking, stared with wide-open eyes. Even then when he was perhaps dying, he still had that smile, which was her salvation. When she looked at that smile, Hiroko spontaneously returned it, and her round face reflected the ripple of excitement which stirred within.

Hiroko, however, knew that night must come for her. She knew too that night undifferentiated from the interminable night-like day, also was Jukichi's plight. Enduring the variety of days and nights, she began to feel that she and Jukichi had become a mysterious ship. Night and day meant to her, not an aimless lapping of waves against their ship asea, but a tidal flow of time which would never ebb; a transition of history.

. . . . . .

After leaving Himeji, Hiroko spent a day getting on and off trucks, walking hurriedly along leaning on some cart or other. And now she was on a wagon, her tired feet dangling down like a child's.

To both sides of the highway spread the broad Banshu Plain illuminated by the diaphanous setting-sun of autumn. Mountains were seen in the westward distance where Mt. Rokko would be. Beautiful light white clouds floating across the sky soothed Hiroko as she gazed at them from the cart.

On such an autumn afternoon Hiroko was unexpectedly on an old wagon on her way east through the Banshu Plain. She was going forward to Jukichi. . . . This expectation made the slowness of the old-fashioned cart seem very comfortable. Banshu Plain has a unique undulation, different from that of Tokyo's Kanto Plain or that around Nasuno along the far northern Tohoku Line where Hiroko used to live. These fertile fields were plowed light to blend with the remote mountains of Hanshin which though high and steep rise calmly in the evening sky. Here and there were dazzling pools like shallow lakes.

Their baggage on the cart with Hiroko, two young men were

following along the highway. Once accustomed to walking, they put their suit jackets over their arms and began to whistle.

Both are cheerful youths with beautiful teeth. They often joke and smile. They speak in Korean. All the other Koreans Hiroko has seen on her trip were moving west, in the direction of the channel and home; only these two are going toward the east.

They seemed to have something good waiting for them at their destination; they jested and ran after each other like frolicking puppies; they sang songs at intervals. Still, they didn't go away from the cart.

The autumnal sun, combed by the breeze, melted Banshu mountains, fields, small town and trees into a golden glow. The wagon was moving towards their destination along the solitary highway very slowly. The clatter of the wheels, *"katori, katori . . ."* unexpectedly harmonized with the gaiety of the young men. All was in harmony with Hiroko's heart, filled as it was with various memories. Such would never happen to her again, to be carried so along the highway like this. Hedges of a small town, rusty remains of large factories standing beyond the pine wood of Akashi—Hiroko stared at them. She felt in all sincerity that the whole of Japan was moving forward like her slow cart.

DAMOI—HOMEWARD BOUND

by *Yamamoto Tomomi*

THE STATION was a turmoil of prisoners. They arrived from camps scattered all over the environs of Karaganda. Flying red and white placards and flags, with pictures of Stalin held high, the repatriates seemed in high spirits. But everyone seemed to be seriously ill. I could see some walking toward the station supported by their comrades. The biggest group was from Camp Number 6.

On the grassy space by the railway station a platform had been erected. The democrats from each camp would get up on the platform and swear to "work for the reconstruction of a democratic Japan" and to "overthrow the reactionary Ashida Government." In the background Soviet political officers stood by, egging the men on, a prisoner's band played the "International" and the "Red Flag."

It was already dark when we got on our car, the sixteenth in the long train. We were thankful that our group of internees was able to be together. Major Egin personally came to the car to bid us farewell. I felt my heart go out to him and, for a moment, the bitter memories of Karaganda days dimmed. But on August 8 our train finally began its homeward journey.

Our *damoi* (going-home) train was composed of fifty-odd cars. White and red placards were nailed to the outer walls and pictures of Stalin, decorated with bunting, gave our train a festive look. Inside each car were placed large, medium and small buckets—one of each. They were for storing and carrying drinking water and food.

As utensils we were each provided with a tin can and one tin mug.

One of the cars was devoted to the headquarters of the "Democratic Committee." It housed the democratic leaders and an orchestra composed of young and ardent prisoners. We were given copies of the "Short History of the Communist Party" and were told to elect a leader for our car. The idea was to put finishing touches to our political education before our embarkation for Japan.

The heat of summer had already passed and we could feel autumn in the air. As we traveled north, even the days were cool, the nights quite cold. With the exception of those placed in the several cars reserved for the seriously ill, we were not provided with mattresses or blankets, and there were two or three nights we could not sleep for the cold.

Our *damoi* train sped eastward, carrying its miserable freight of 1,300-odd sick and crippled prisoners of war, the slag from the Soviet Union's vast crucible of prison labor. Though our bodies were worn, our limbs torn and our flesh weakened, our hearts burned with hope and joy. We told ourselves we were returning, returning home after a long exile. The wheels sang a jubilant song. How different it was from our westward trip three years before. The train whistle had sounded so devastatingly lonely at that time.

Three years of hard labor had changed our appearance. Our cheeks had flattened, our eye sockets deepened. Our faces were tanned ebony black from the fierce sun of Kazakhstan. I looked at my calloused hands. In the deep, dirt-engrained lines, I read a story of toil and suffering.

Just as we had changed, Siberia had also been transformed in the three years. The attire of the Soviet people had greatly improved. There were few who went about bare-footed. New buildings had been built by the tracks, new coal mines opened up. The railroad bed had been improved, the tracks properly ballasted and made firm. Perhaps for this reason, our train swayed less and traveled at a greater speed than three years previously.

All along the tracks we saw Japanese prison camps, Japanese soldiers waved at us. Placards bearing "democratic" slogans decorated the entrances to these compounds. I realized that the Japanese prisoner of war had contributed the greater part of the improvements I saw on all sides.

Hours on end I watched the countryside speed by—past Irkutsk

—Lake Baikal, a shimmering beauty of deep blue, with large steamers plying its surface—Ulan Ude, the hillsides dotted with army camps and masses of tanks parked side by side.

Everywhere I saw signs of the eternal fear that hovers over the Soviet Union. Tunnels and bridges were guarded by soldiers with machine guns. Each line of the doubled-tracked Trans-Siberian Railway crossed bridges that were set miles apart—obviously to minimize damage from possible bombing. If the spans had been set together, they could be blown up by one lucky shot. Spaced as they were, two hits would be necessary. These reminders of the evil of the Soviet *vlast* dampened my enjoyment of the beauty of the countryside. The glory of the stretching taiga, the rolling meadows in the river valleys, and the pastoral patches of farmland scattered here and there seemed tainted, and I would turn away my eyes in sorrow.

Traffic on the Trans-Siberian Railway had greatly increased. Trains were traveling westward at ten- or fifteen-minute intervals. At first the hellish screech of passing trains woke me from my sleep; after the third or fourth day I became used to the sound. The majority of the trains were composed of boxcars or flatcars piled high with coal, ores, lumber and limestone. There were also oil tankers and refrigerators. Once or twice we saw large cannons being transported west. Often we came across prison trains, with their miserable load of human freight. Once we stopped in a siding just opposite one of these. From a barred window peered a beautiful young girl. She asked for a smoke. I tossed her one *papiros* from the twenty-day ration that had been given us on our departure. She told me that she had been a clerk in a Moscow department store and had been arrested for having stolen a blouse from the counter. Now she was being sent to some place in Siberia to serve out a seven-year prison term. She envied our freedom and wished us good luck. Even today the memory of that face haunts my mind.

Just west of Chita we came across a gang of Japanese prisoners working on the railway track, packing gravel under the ties. They told us that they had gone as far as Nahotka for repatriation but had been sent back as "reactionaries," not ready to be returned to Japan. They warned us that we should throw away our homemade mahjong sets and our chessboards. Otherwise, they said, we too would be regarded as "reactionaries" and be detained in Russia. As soon as our train started to move, we threw away all our baubles that would mark us as still "bourgeois" in the tastes of our captors.

At the junction of the Molotov Line, running to Manchouli on the Manchurian-Soviet border, and the Trans-Siberian Railway, we were taken to a typical delousing station for our bath. There we met a group of Japanese "democrats" on their way home from some district conference of "democratic leaders." They came aboard our train and, to our surprise, showered us with invectives. They did not like the way we went around in our undershirts during the day. They did not like our use of the post-position -san (Mr.) in addressing our friends. They called us "reactionary" and lacking in "democratic training," even criticized the way we sang the "International." To them we were lukewarm prisoners, not fully converted to their own brand of militant Communism.

I was completely surprised by the fanatic zeal of these youngsters, each man hardly out of his teens. I realized that the indoctrination of prisoners in eastern Siberia had been carried out with an intensity that I had not dreamed possible. It was evident that unless we were careful we would be marked as "reactionaries" and possibly detained at Nahotka. I resolved to be on guard.

Eighteen days after our departure from Karaganda, we reached Nahotka on the afternoon of August 26. I saw the sea and breathed deep of the salt air. With deep emotion I told myself that just beyond the ocean lay Japan and home. At last I was being sent home. I had traveled safely five thousand miles across Siberia. My heart swelled with joy and relief.

Upon alighting from the train, we were formed into ranks of five abreast and led to Camp Number 1. This, I learned, was the receiving center for prisoners arriving in Nahotka from the interior. To my surprise I found Japanese prisoners guarding the compound, not a single Soviet soldier in evidence. In fact, the whole camp was run and managed by Japanese. Leaders of the "Democratic Committee" welcomed us from the platform of an open-air theater. We were then allotted our quarters.

The camp was a village of tents set up on a sandy beach; inside, two-tiered platforms served as our bunks; our latrine a wooden pier built out into the sea. The food served to us was plentiful and nourishing, although it was the same kasha and black bread that we had eaten during our stay in the Soviet Union. I realized that the Soviet Union was making a last-minute effort to fatten us up for delivery to the Japanese Government.

No work was required of us. However, we would be called out to carry rocks from a nearby quarry to build up a sea wall against high waves blown shoreward during storms. We were called upon to sing the "International" and other Communist songs as we marched to the quarry and back. Discipline, Communist discipline, was a *must*, and we had to close ranks and keep in step as we marched. Our only guards were Japanese members of the camp staff.

On our way we met other groups of prisoners, singing in the same lusty manner. They belonged to Camp Number 2, the next step in our processing. Here the prisoner had his clothing checked. Here also was he given his last bath prior to his return to Japan. The next and last step was Camp Number 3, where each prisoner went through a rigid "customs" inspection. In short, he was stripped of whatever money he had and all printed matter and written notes. I also learned that there was a Camp Number 4, where the seriously sick were interned. The prisoners in this camp awaited the arrival of hospital ships from Japan.

I will always remember the thrill that I got when I first saw a Japanese ship enter the harbor. It loomed in the haze in the distance and gradually approached land, then stayed four hours and again left for Japan. I told myself that I, too, would be on a ship within a week or so.

We were next moved to Camp Number 2. Here the barracks were made of lumber and seemed more substantial than Camp Number 1, but we found ourselves troubled by fleas, bedbugs and clouds of black flies that hung thick on the ceilings during the day and tormented us at night. The finishing touches to our political indoctrination were continued—lectures, discussion meetings, *Nihon Shimbun* reading circles where we read aloud this Communist Japanese-language newspaper, song practices, demonstrations, plays and motion pictures. We hardly had any time for rest.

The leaders of the "democratic movement" told us that the Japanese Government was not interested in seeing Japanese prisoners returned. Since repatriation in May of that year, only twelve or thirteen ships had been sent to Nahotka. In addition, although the ships could carry five thousand men on one trip, the Japanese Government was limiting prisoners to two thousand. Thus, only 25,000 could be repatriated monthly. In June so many prisoners had piled up in Nahotka, many had to sleep outside on the cold ground.

Some had been transferred, as a result, to interior camps to await their turn. The reason for this unwillingness of the Japanese Government to accept prisoners for repatriation was due to the critical food shortage in Japan, the problem of unemployment, and the lack of preparations to greet repatriates.

This explanation aroused us to anger and added fuel to the fire of anti-Ashida sentiment, which the "Democratic Committee" sought to instill in the prisoners of war. Until we boarded our repatriation ship, we believed this lie and cursed the Japanese Government.

One day, I was present at a discussion meeting sponsored by the "actives" of Camp Number 2. The talk drifted to the plans each of the prisoners had for his return to Japan. With the best of intention, I told the group that I wanted to go to the United States to see what "democracy" was like there. One of the leaders of the group asked me whether I believed America to be democratic.

"Of course, I do," I replied. "America was an ally of the Soviet Union and fought in the democratic camp against the Nazis and the Japanese militarists. Now that I have seen 'democracy' in the Soviet Union, I hope to see 'democracy' in the United States."

A hush fell over the group. The leader looked at me and said, "Comrade Yamamoto, are you in your right senses? You seem to harbor dangerous bourgeois thoughts. Only the Soviet Union is a true democratic country. The United States is a country of imperialistic aggression."

I answered, with more heat than I had intended, "Democracy is equality. I believe that we should hear both sides of the story and see both sides of the world. I do not believe that the Soviet Union has a monopoly on democracy."

The leader, white with anger, warned, "Comrade Yamamoto, you are a reactionary. You are not ready to go home. You still need to be taught discipline and Communist theory."

I shrugged my shoulders and left the group. By next morning I had forgotten the incident. Two days later our group was called out for transfer to Camp Number 3, the next step in our processing for repatriation. At the gate the names of the men in our group were read out. I eagerly waited for my name. The last man left the gate, but my name had not been mentioned. I became frantic and went to the Japanese reading the list. He checked and told me that I had not been included. I felt as if struck by a huge hammer.

Like lightning, I went to the headquarters of the "democratic move-ment." The man who had warned me the previous day was sitting in a corner, looking at me triumphantly. I told the committee chairman I had been left out from the list of men going to Camp Number 3.

He answered, "We know. You need to study a little longer in the Soviet Union. You are reactionary and will have to have some of those bourgeois thoughts pounded out of you. Tomorrow morn-ing you will be taken to Camp Number 5 with a few other people and there set to work."

I spent a sleepless night, gigantic waves of misery rolling into my heart. I had come this far and now I was going back to a labor camp. I dared not venture a guess as to how long I would be kept.

The next morning, I was called out to the front gate. There were four other men beside me. We were all "reactionaries," unfit to be sent home. Led by one of the Japanese members of the camp man-agement, we headed for the hills behind Nahotka. Time and time again, I looked toward the sea and cried in my heart at missing my chance to go home.

Camp Number 5 turned out to be a neat compound of wooden barracks, painted a clean white. I was handed over to the Japanese camp authorities with the explanation that I needed "correction" for mistaken thinking. To my surprise, I immediately ran into friends that I had known in Camp Number 3 in Alma Ata. To my greater surprise, I learned that the bulk of the 1,300 men, left in that camp when we departed for Karaganda, were still in Na-hotka. The group had arrived early in June and only the seriously sick had been sent home. I saw Nagayama, who had been in my platoon. "Nagayama-san," I called and like a slap in the face came his answer, "Comrade Yamamoto! Only reactionaries use the word -san."

I was surprised at the subtle change that had come over him. He was no longer the affable youngster I knew in Alma Ata. He was a rabid Communist. I found this true of all the others. I felt alone in my complete misery.

For one whole year I was to live in an atmosphere of intense suspicion and fear. It was for me an amazing, though trying, lesson in the formation and the workings of a police-state psychology. A man was first driven into desperation. This was a simple task. Any prisoner, living for months within sight of men returning home, would gradually lose all hope. It was agony for me to watch the repatriation ships steam into the harbor and leave with their load of happy prisoners. It was agony also to think that just beyond the blue barrier of the sea lay Japan and home. When something is held too long just beyond a man's reach, he loses all hope of ever grasping it. This was how it was with the prisoners in Camp Number 5.

Then we were set to work, harder than ever before. My bad heart for some reason or other had become completely normal. My pulse no longer acted up. Perhaps this was because I was at sea level. Whatever the case, I was sent out to work on neighboring farms and on the port facilities of a planned gigantic harbor. Named in the honor of Zhdanov, Deputy Prime Minister of the Soviet Union, the port, upon completion, was to outrival nearby Vladivostok.

The work we had done in Alma Ata or Karaganda was nothing compared to that forced on us at Nahotka. Pay, food, fear of punishment were no longer incentives. The prize at stake was our return to Japan. If we wanted to go home, we had to be good "democrats." To be good "democrats" meant that we had to show a frenzied anxiety to work to our bones in building up the Soviet Union. The fear of being branded as "reactionaries" and of being transported back to Karaganda was the lash that whipped us to superhuman efforts. The norms accomplished were fantastic, but the Japanese camp leaders never seemed satisfied.

At the same time our political indoctrination was stepped up. On our way to and from work, a man read articles from the *Nihon Shimbun* to us as we marched. During intermissions, we sat around in circles and had more Communist doctrine pounded into us. During the actual working hours, we dared not rest nor talk with others. Even a slight letup was interpreted as shirking and a demonstration of a reactionary trend. We were afraid even to voice our utterly human longing to go home to Japan.

Upon our return to the camp, we underwent further indoctrination, attending lectures and plays. The theme was always hatred. Everything was a "struggle," a "fight." We were always combatting imagined "enemies of Communism" in our midst, in our own hearts, and in Japan.

"You are the vanguards of a revolutionary army. You are training to land in the face of the enemy when you return to Japan.

You must overthrow the present Government, abolish the Emperor system, throw out the American tyrants, and establish a people's republic"—day in day out, the same theme of hatred was pounded into us. We were preparing for a "struggle to reconstruct Japan into a democratic nation." We were preparing for a showdown battle with the "new Fascist ruling class of Japan and their puppet police." We were training to become reinforcements for the Japanese Communist Party in its "fight to liberate the Japanese people from foreign domination." Thus, a new Fascism arose in our own camp. We were required to be militant in our bearing and attitude. We marched to work as if we were on a parade ground. Our language became terse and military. A completely new idiom was concocted as vehicles for the new chauvinism bourgeoning in our midst.

We had to show conformity and agreement with the slogans mouthed at political meetings. By the fervor of our *shikari* (so it is) and *soda* (that's so), which we shouted at our speakers, was measured our political loyalty to Communism.

The plays that were shown us, put on by the "actives," harped on this same hate motif. They were well-acted, with a passion rare even on the legitimate stage. They moved the spectator strangely and implanted rancor deep within his heart.

I, too, found myself influenced by the atmosphere in which I lived. I knew that I had to be regarded as an "active" if ever I was to see Japan again. I realized too that I had to try doubly hard; for there was already a black mark against me. I took part in the plays, the discussion meetings and the kangaroo courts that periodically took place to denounce our erstwhile leaders. These kangaroo courts, which were called "popular trials," illustrated most aptly the underlying mob psychology that makes Communism a potent danger. Any laxity on the part of our camp leaders was the signal for a "popular trial." We would haul a leader before a mass meeting, criticize him for staying in the camp while others went out to work. This, we charged, was "anti-democratic." A true active showed his fervor for Communism by his deeds. We would strip leaders of their powers, brand them as "reactionaries," and relegate them to the ranks of the common prisoner.

In this way there were several changes in the Japanese camp *vlast*. In time I came to be recognized as one of the leaders. However, I well knew the temper of the mob. I absolutely declined to take any position of authority and continued until the last as a common worker, though a recognized "active." As a result, I saved myself the ignominy of being hauled before a "people's court" and being taken down by the mob.

Winter came to Nahotka and the ships from Japan stopped coming. It was a dreary and bitter winter. Day in day out our work continued, though heavy snows blanketed the roads and covered our work site. Spring arrived and once again I picked up hope as reports of the resumption of repatriation filtered into our camp. Then the ships came and, from our work sites along the harbor, we watched column after column of prisoners from the interior of Soviet Russia march the two and a half miles from the cluster of repatriation camps to the embarkation point.

Summer came and passed. With each passing month, my hopes of ever returning to Japan became dimmer and dimmer. The first signs of autumn were on us when we heard the news that the repatriation camps in Nahotka would be closed. I knew then that I would never see Japan again. Everything seemed to darken before my eyes. I resigned myself to a lifetime in the Soviet Union. With my knowledge of the Russian language, I told myself, I would be able to make out somehow. Perhaps they would free me after a time. Perhaps, in due course, I could settle down and marry some Russian woman. These thoughts ran daily through my mind.

One day, in the second week in September, we were suddenly ordered to prepare for our departure. It was then that the great news was given to us. We were at last going home. It was a happy moment when we moved to Camp Number 1, part of which was being dismantled. We were told that we were among the last leaving; the camp management would also leave on the next ship or so. Our ordinary work clothes were changed for us in Camp Number 2. Then we were sent to the last barrier, Camp Number 3. This, too, was safely passed.

The *Takasago Maru* lay docked at the pier that we had helped build. As we lined up on the wharf, our leaders called on us to sing our Communist songs. As the Soviet officers counted us aboard, we marched up the gangplank singing at the top of our voices. Nurses waited on deck to greet us. Their kind words brought tears to my eyes, but I wiped them away. The evil spell of the Soviet Union was still upon me—I could not show any human feeling.

For three hours our ship waited at the dock, although every prisoner had come aboard. We were waiting for a truckload of lepers, Japanese prisoners of war who had caught the dread disease in Siberia. They finally arrived. The sailors swabbed with disinfectant the decks where the lepers had passed. Then, with a shrill whistle, the *Takasago Maru* began moving. I was on my way home after three full years and eight months of captivity.

The ship pulled away.

I was free.

THE SAD SAMURAI

by John Fujii

HIS NAME is Watanabe.

He was the admiral of a dry-land fleet in the final stages of the Burma retreat who is now making a living selling soap.

Or he was a lieutenant who spent the first half of the war in a Manila hospital with malaria and the last half on Palau Island, a virtual prisoner of war.

Or he was a Domei war correspondent, attached to the Army, that spent the war years following one division from one theater to another only to miss the final battle. He eventually heard his first shot of the war six months after the surrender when Vietminh guerrillas exchanged small-arms fire with a French patrol just outside his Saigon camp.

These are the ex-samurai who meet by chance at Shinjuku station between trains, jostle each other on the crowded Ginza, or sit on adjoining stools at a cheap sake shop.

These are the sad samurai who have surrendered their swords. These are the modern "Ronin" looking for a cause. These are the bewildered souls that try to forget prison camp to *pachinko's* pinball jangle and a *shochu*-gin jag.

You meet them everywhere in Japan.

There is the general who asks you to write a letter in English to a business firm in Bombay. He has a nominal desk job in a concern managed by a former subordinate. The last time you remember him was as a tired old man sitting disconsolately in the bleak prison yard at Singapore's Changi and before that with the epaulets of a staff officer attached to Field Marshal Terauchi's Southern Army headquarters.

There is the Nisei interpreter from Hawaii who served eight years of his twenty-year term as a war criminal and is now selling advertisements for an English-language newspaper.

The Army lieutenant who never heard a shot fired in anger—who spent the war in a hospital and on a by-passed Pacific atoll—makes a visit to the capital just once a year, to pay his respects to his fallen comrades at Yasukuni Shrine and then retires to his Shizuoka farm because Tokyo is too foreign.

These are the men who appear out of nowhere and then drift back into the crowd at Shinjuku or Asakusa.

Many of the former professional soldiers have made their readjustments to peacetime living. A former admiral is president of a thriving export-import firm; a former staff officer is managing director of an amusement company, while a former Air Force major represents his industrial concern in the New York office; still another staff officer, noted for his spectacular underground escape from arrest as a war crimes suspect, has been elected to the National Diet from his home province.

Others have found their niche in postwar society, holding down positions commensurate with their experience and ability. In Japan nearly everyone is an ex-samurai since universal conscription marshaled every able-bodied Japanese into uniform at one time or another.

Some have drifted into the twilight of society: the men who make a living on the edge of human decency and legalized rackets. But these are the handful who refuse to cope with the changed times. There are others who brood in their native village, futilely awaiting a day of retribution.

Perhaps the most unfortunate are the "men in white," the war cripples who solicit contributions in the trains and trolleys and who line the approaches to Yasukuni Shrine. They are the human pariahs of modern Japan, the men who are unable to make a living and are forced to swallow pride and dignity to ask for alms from their more fortunate comrades.

Their pensions are meager in inflationary Japan, and hospital space inadequate, so that they are spewed out into a society that tries to forget them. But the conscience of a mother who has lost her son in battle, of a former soldier who remembers how he was spared from injury, and of a general public who sympathizes —keep these "sad samurai" from starvation.

LOVE IN THE ANNAM JUNGLE

by *Oka Masamichi*

THE SKY over Saigon was clear as it always is, and the streets sizzled in the shadeless 95-degree heat. I felt dizzy in this heat, but I picked my way along under the tall acacia trees, feeling unusually conscious of the heavy sword and bayonet at my side. Roy, who walked with me, did not say much. The heat was too much even for him, I guess. Roy was Vietnamese, a member of a secret organization whose aim was the independence of Vietnam from France. He spoke some English, but his Japanese was more fluent. He and I were on our way to his headquarters.

Until then, I had little interest in the independence movement in Vietnam, but Roy had urged that, as a memento of my last days in Saigon, I meet its leader. I had allowed his urging to get the better of me.

He took me through a small store and stopped before a room in the back. "Here it is," he said and led me inside. In the room were over ten Vietnamese, on the four walls maps of all sorts. Roy spoke in Vietnamese to the one who sat at the center. I could not understand, but I perceived that he was talking about me. I could see right away that this man was the leader. He got up slowly from the chair, then extended his hand to me. "Glad you came," it sounded to me, with the expressive gestures of the French. We talked about this and that for a while. He seemed to know a great deal about me. Then, suddenly, he asked, "What is your opinion of our independence movement?"

The leader's question baffled me. I was merely a passer-by, and naturally enough could not answer such a question put to me in all seriousness. When the leader saw that I could not answer, he began to explain to me about the movement. He said that the French rule of Vietnam had now come to its end, that "the people of Vietnam are ready to revolt against the French exploitations." He spoke these words with heated eagerness, pounding the table with his fist. "In order to win this independence, we must have the cooperation and help of the Japanese. I presume you are willing to give us that cooperation."

There was no room for yes nor no. I saw for the first time that I had been deceived by Roy. I noticed that the others, who hadn't said a single word, had surrounded me. If I refused, I knew what to expect. I looked at Roy; he evaded my eyes, and kept his lowered, but presently he bowed his head and murmured, "Please, help us."

I was a lieutenant of dentistry in the Japanese Army. Roy was a native of Saigon. He and I were friends, but there was a certain limitation to our friendship. I had never expected him to deceive me like this.

With the termination of the war, I had received orders to head for Phnom Penh whence I was to board a ship for Japan. I had intended to go to an airport in Saigon to fly to Phnom Penh. On the day before, Roy had given a farewell party for me, at which time he urged me to see his leader. I accepted the offer, merely thinking that he wanted to show off to me his wide circle of acquaintances. And this was the result.

The leader and his aides looked somewhat menacing, and yet I saw that there was a feeling of entreaty, too. But I, on my part, faced the moment of deciding the course of my entire future. There was only one way to stay alive, and that was to cooperate with them, to take part in their independence movement. There ensued a heavy silence, at the end of which I opened my mouth. "All right. I will cooperate."

My answer loosened the tension immediately, and I said inwardly, "All right I'll show them what I can do. I'm young and strong. It may not prove insignificant for me to take part in this revolution."

The time was the end of August in the year the war ended. Saigon at that time was tense, on the eve of revolution. By day there were demonstrations, big and small, and at night shots were heard every-where in the streets. All the young people were concerned with this independence movement, either directly, or indirectly, or so it seemed. But this promising situation did not last long. The Allies who had ability and power arrived, replacing the Japanese Army who had neither. The leaders of the independence move-ment and their comrades gradually left Saigon and took cover in the jungle. I had been under close watch while in Saigon, and finally left the city with the leader. After many days we reached the jungle in Tay Ninh district, and here my days as a soldier in Ho Chi-min's Army and my war against the jungle started.

In the jungle I met a girl, or rather re-encountered her. Many had run to the jungle with their families; there were many women and children. There were also young women who had come into the Ho Army on their own. Nyun was one of these. She spoke excel-lent Japanese, having worked during the war for a Japanese firm in Saigon, where I had seen her once or twice. The unexpected reap-pearance of Nyun threw a bright light into the life in the jungle which was naturally dark and oppressive. She looked lovelier than when I had seen her in Saigon and her nineteen-year-old body was full of energy. I found myself drawn to her. Her duties were inter-preter and KP. I suppose she too had a special feeling for me from before. We met alone, often, and these rendezvous increased as days went by.

By this time we Japanese became busy. Our duties were public relations with the Japanese Army, to go to them and ask for the arms and ammunition for which they had no further use. I left the jungle once with this mission to go near Saigon to see battalion and company commanders and negotiate with them for the release of their arms and ammunition. Of course they had no more use for them, but that did not mean they should give them to the Ho Army. The mission was not an easy one. Some of them sympathized with me, but refused. Some of them bawled me out, told me to go back to Japan, while others wanted to know why I chose such a hard task. My mission was not a success.

Then the communists gave me still harder orders. They told me to take some poison with me to the Japanese and rob them of their arms. I, a Japanese, could not take this order—that must have been obvious. I perceived an underlying motive behind this order. It came from Hee, the commander of a company. He was in love with Nyun, and wanted to do away with me by impressing upon me an order I could not possibly take.

He was raving mad and threatened me with the point of his bayonet. "Why refuse my order?" he demanded.

"I can't deceive and kill fellow Japanese," I said flatly.

"I did not say for you to kill them," he lied. "I merely wanted you to bring back their arms."

"But I still don't want to deceive them." I was adamant.

He put me in confinement for non-compliance. "I'll give you two days to think it over," Hee said, before he closed the door on me. "In two days you choose either obedience or death."

I was locked up in a hut built in the jungle. I did not sleep that night. Hee might really kill me on the pretense that I had disrupted military law and order. But I had one hope: Nyun.

Nyun did not betray me. She and some Vietminh soldiers whom I did not know freed me after a short skirmish with the guards. When she first found out that there was little chance for me to come out alive, she went to the neighboring company, met a company commander by the name of Tom, and begged him for help. I was deeply touched when I learned that she had gone in the dead of night through the jungle to save my life. I took her hand and wept on it. Commander Tom, who had given her the soldiers who helped release me, welcomed me into his company. Nyun, of course, went with me. She and I were married shortly after that. In the communist camp, marriages are free.

Among the Vietnamese there is a religious organization called Kao Dai. It has a membership of some two million and, besides being a religious group, is a political and ideological organization. The Kao Dai had an army of about five thousand men which immediately after the war sided with the Vietminh, waving the flag of independence, but shortly afterward it succumbed to French propaganda and went over to their camp.

By the time the rumor spread that Kao Dai was acting suspicious, the gap between Kao Dai and Vietminh was too deep and wide to be mended. We Japanese faced a predicament, for my company and Kao Dai were closely situated and naturally the Japanese in their group were friendly with the Japanese in our company. We hated to see the gap grow between us.

Just at this crucial time Captain Okada of our company was killed while on a scouting mission. He was a typical old samurai and we—that is, the fifteen Japanese in our company—were deeply attached to this man. His death shocked us profoundly, for it was rumored that he was killed by the Vietminh and not by Kao Dai, as the Vietminh would have us believe. We Japanese knew how he was loved and respected by the Kao Dai themselves. The Kao Dai liked us Japanese and we could see no reason for their killing Captain Okada. The rumor was further strengthened by the suspicious character of the Vietminh, who looked with deep skepticism on the continued friendship that existed between the Japanese of the Kao Dai group and Japanese in the Vietminh. The Vietminh had thought Captain Okada was the leader of this alliance.

We Japanese began to wonder if we might not follow in Captain Okada's footsteps. We had often overheard the Vietminh whisper that "the Japanese are only to be used." The Vietminh, a people long oppressed by a foreign power and naturally distrustful of any foreigners, including the Japanese from whom they sought help, could not, we felt, be relied on.

Not long after the Okada incident Japanese, one by one, began escaping from the Vietminh. Some said that from this jungle in the Tay Ninh district one could cut across Cambodia and get into Thailand; others suggested the northern route to Hanoi, saying once there, one could find some kind of hideout; still others thought to run into China proper through Indo-China. Not one said he would surrender to the French. We all believed the rumor that, having come from a communist camp, we would never be allowed to live if we returned to the French side.

I did not join these Japanese in their escape. For one thing, I had Nyun; for another, I knew there were French armies in the north and felt sure that it was impossible to enter Hanoi or China proper.

One by one all the Japanese left except me. About this time there was a reorganization in our army and the company I belonged to came to be called the 11th Branch Company, I the sole Japanese soldier in it. Later, rumors seeped through to us that most of the Japanese who had tried to escape had been killed by the French or had died of jungle diseases, while those fortunate enough to escape disease, death or the French were forced to return to the company. They were all emaciated, and easily fell prey to desperation, for there was little hope for them in the jungle, and they could not surrender themselves to the French. I was at the time bedridden by malaria, but I kept telling the returnees not to lose hope, that we would all find some way to live. But my encouragement brought little result, for one day all of them took a group of Vietminh and attacked a company of French trucks, meeting wholesale destruction. It was a suicidal act.

From this time on I made up my mind to forget that I was a Japanese. I even changed my name to a Vietminh name, An Torun, and decided to live the life of a Vietminh in every respect. My wife agreed with me wholeheartedly, saying "You are not a Japanese who once occupied the French Indies. But please don't forget that you are a soldier of a defeated nation." She often repeated these words, urging me not to look for promotion. There is no rank in the communist army, so there are no officers or non-coms. She urged me not to want to become a company or a battalion commander with responsibilities. "I know how you feel, but please cooperate," she pleaded. "It is foolish to be ostracized by them because of trivial matters."

So I joined the Vietminh in their morning ceremony of the raising of the independence flag.

A year or two of the life in the jungle passed peacefully and uneventfully. To escape French attacks the communists penetrated deep into the jungle. Other than occasional contacts with French reconnaissance planes and scouting parties, there was hardly any fighting in the area.

The communist Vietminh worked their own vegetable gardens, planted rice, hunted. The staple food was rice, and most of it came from the south, but the shipments were disrupted often, and often we suffered its scarcity. There were many days when we lived on yams and tapioca. Our shelter was a leaky hut and we were soaked to the bone when it rained. When out of food, we lay around on empty stomachs.

Our baby was born in a hut built of grass and bamboo. We were overjoyed at the sound of the baby's cry, on a bed made of bamboo shoots, for it seemed to us a miracle that a strong, healthy baby could be born to a woman who lived on rice and salt and hardly any other nourishment. The baby was a girl, our girl.

We named her Kon Choku. In this district it was a custom not to name a baby until it was a year or so old, but to give it a pet name of some animal. Kon Choku meant "little mouse."

The Germans in the company loved her, and sang "Schön" to her. These Germans had been prisoners of the French in Africa during World War II and had been brought to the French Indies to fight against communists. They then became the prisoners of the communists. In this jungle army there were, besides these Germans, some French who had surrendered to the communists; Spanish, Belgians, and Poles who had fought under the German flag during the war and who had been French prisoners and had followed the German prisoners' fate. These Europeans had no resistance against malaria and many of them died. The Germans had an innate hatred for the French and fought against them bravely.

Kon Choku brought forth that thing called human love long forgotten in the hearts of these men who had become despondent in the jungle. Some days she was never returned to us, going from one hand to the next. The Vietminh fought over her.

Nyun and I were beside ourselves with joy in having Kon Choku, but we were in the depths of poverty, the kind of poverty neither of us had ever experienced before. As for our clothing, I had only one black suit rationed to me by the communists. Nyun had two, one of which was tattered beyond mending. Of course when I had first come into the jungle I had had some Japanese Army clothes, but these had long since been exchanged for food.

Kon Choku never knew a toy. She only had a stick to hold in her tiny hand. My wife got an empty medicine box from the dispensary and put a coin in it for Choku to rattle. She liked the sound it made, and shook it for all it was worth, clucking happily. It was the only toy Nyun and I were able to give her, she who was the only source of joy and happiness in our otherwise grim lives.

One morning when she was about ten months old I was awakened early by an unusual cry. I jumped out of bed and took her in my arms, but she would not stop crying. She looked frightened by something, her pulse was fast, her breathing hard. Soon she began to have spasms. I ran to the dispensary, and got the chief. He was a chief, all right, but with very little medical knowledge. He looked at Choku, and merely shook his head.

"Anyway, we'll give her a shot of camphor," he said. It seemed to take some effect, for her spasms stopped, but there was still no life in her face. I was seized with a strong premonition that she would die. Her pulse became faint, her breathing weakened.

"Choku, Choku, don't die," my wife hugged her, her face wet

with tears. She kept repeating Choku's name, but Choku never opened her eyes again. It all happened so quickly. Who took her life away? What in the name of fate snuffed out the life of so small a creature with no resistance?

Choku had had acute meningitis. She was buried in the jungle. I asked to let Choku take with her to heaven the only toy she ever had. The teeth marks of Choku on the box stayed in my mind a long time.

We had not been attacked by the French in a long time. Except when the communists sent out guerillas, there was hardly any fighting between us and the Franco-Vietnamese Armies. For one thing our base was too deep in the jungle; for another our defense too well organized. Every road, no matter how narrow, was studded with land mines and any road wide enough to pass on was barred with huge trees placed crisscross. The entrances of these roads into the jungle were heavily guarded and even if the French tried to attack, they would have been no match for the communists who knew the jungle inside and out.

But the long lull did not mean that the French had forgotten us. They sometimes sent native scouts or dropped incendiaries from the sky. One day, after these bombings from the sky had continued an unusually long number of days, we heard an explosion quite distant from our barracks. It sounded like one of our land mines.

"Enemy?"

It was the enemy. After four long years the enemy had finally caught up with us. Without knowing how big a force we faced, nor what their intentions were, the fighting began. Whether it was because they were surprised by our land mines, or that they found our guards, we did not know, but they kept up the machine guns for a long time. There was a certain amount of disorder on our part because we hadn't seen any fighting in a long time, but considering it all, and due mostly to the training that was kept up, the soldiers took to their stations very quickly, while the non-combat groups took to shelter.

The sound of the machine guns came closer. We could hear our rifle shots mingle with those of the machine guns. Perhaps our soldiers had met the enemy. Fighting continued through the night. If we held on to our position we knew from experience that the

French would never come closer than absolutely necessary. And we also knew that they left with the dawn.

It was not due entirely to this French attack, but our company was forced to leave the jungle where we had lived nearly five years. We headed south. The most immediate reason was the lack of food. Our first plan to raise our own food did not work and we could not fight starvation and malnutrition as forcefully as we fought our human enemy. We had come to the limit of our physical endurance. The soldiers were actually living corpses—cheeks sunken, eyes bulging, legs like rakes, with flat torsos topping them. It was unanimously agreed that we should quit the jungle.

On July 19, 1951, we left the jungle of Tay Ninh for the district of Tan An, about one hundred kilometers northwest of Saigon and the biggest rice area in the district. The way was long and a march with women and children would be difficult. If we could manage to cover six to seven kilos a day, it would still take us a good half month to reach our destination.

The march started with the combat groups in the front and the non-combatants following. The entire group was barefooted; we carried enough food to last twenty days. From the third day we started on night marches, which were far more difficult. We could not even talk loud, for we were marching through enemy territory. The jungle is dark even in the daytime and at night it was pitch dark. Poison snakes and poison ants were everywhere. Then there were those horrible ticks that lived on the leaves. If bit by one even an adult ran a temperature the next day. Leeches are grotesque things. The ones in this area were about an inch long and lived in wet ground. If one stood on one spot any length of time, leeches crawled up, fastened to a leg, and sucked blood.

My rice rotted. Wet from the rain and steamed by the jungle heat, it mildewed. Then it turned yellow and rotted from inside. There is nothing you can do with it when it gets to that stage.

After we had marched about twenty days, the jungle thinned out and our vista brightened; before us was a river, one of the branch streams of the great Mekong. It was a deep river and the stream was fast. On the bank were many cutters that our comrades in the south had prepared for us.

"Boats!"

Everyone suddenly came to life. Boats were the height of civilization for us at the time, for we could go forward without the painful use of our legs. There were some children who now saw boats for the first time.

Beyond this river was the Dank Kup Moy district. Once across Nyun came down with dengue fever. The march had to be continued; I took her by the hand and carried our meager belongings hanging on both ends of a pole, resting on my shoulder. On the second day after we had entered Dang Kup Moy, it rained all day. It was raining when we started our march at night. I didn't mind getting wet so much as the slipperiness of the road. Nyun was half-dazed with a high fever and every time one of us fell the other did, too. Getting up was hard enough for me, but I had to pick her up with me. Her breathing was hard and only the sound of it, heard through the rain, assured me that she was still alive. The water became deeper and deeper and soon it came up to our knees.

After a while we finally reached a high plateau. We took a much needed rest. The rain stopped, the moon came out, but we could still hear the water gushing all around the lower sections that surrounded the enemy's plane emplacements.

Nyun rested on my lap still as death. I could feel her high fever through her clothes onto my flesh. She would not answer me. After some rest, we resumed our march. Where we stayed was too high, we made too easy targets for the enemy.

We finally reached our destination after such hardships as we had never before experienced, and there we took up a sort of colonial troops' life. Food rations became much better, and both Nyun and I improved in health rapidly.

There was a woman by the name of Min who lived near us. She told us that she had made a number of trips to Saigon, going through some very vigilant French guards. We did not know why she took such risks to go to Saigon, but we decided to ask her to contact Nyun's parents, which had been impossible when we were in the jungle.

On her first trip Min could not find Nyun's parents, but on her second we gave her the address of some rich relatives of Nyun's. She found them and brought back with her presents from Nyun's parents: materials for Nyun, a hat for the baby—we now had our second child—and a shirt for me.

When we found that Nyun's parents were well in Saigon, I decided to send Nyun to them. I could not leave the communist army, but Nyun was a woman, and she had a baby. The communists were fair to women and children. When I spoke to Nyun about my thought, she was at first against it. But after I talked to her, explaining that to continue as we were the three of us might die, but separated one of us should be able to stay alive, she finally consented to go.

"After about a month, I'll come back," she said, explaining that she intended to leave the baby with her parents and come back to me. I was vigorously against this idea. I felt strongly that mother and child should not be separated. She said then that she would just try to visit me in about a month.

So Nyun left. I thought back to those six years we had spent together, never separated a day. I gave her little comfort, we spoke different languages, and yet, in spite of it all, she loved me deeply. The memories of our six years were filled with sadness, rather than the sweetness of love.

A month after she left I went to the Munition Headquarters in Cholon to wait for her. But unluckily I came down with malaria and had to be hospitalized. I begged them to let me stay until Nyun came, but they brought me back to Dang Kup Moy and put me in the hospital. About ten days later a letter came from Nyun with six hundred piastres in cash, some clothes, sweets and razor blades. The presents were not much, but her deep love expressed in them was almost painful. Her love for me, involving the risk, danger and hardships of walking all the way from Saigon to this hidden jungle retreat, cut into my heart.

"My loving Nyun," I wept while bedridden with malaria, reading, "I left the baby and came here but missed you. The money— six hundred piastres—is not very much, but please take it. I am sorry I was late as I could not get the passport in time. It is very difficult to obtain a passport from French Army territory into the free territory and the French sentinels are very difficult to deal with. Please take care of yourself. I will wait for you for any number of years."

The letter had evidently been written from Cholon. It also said that when she parted with Min, she had sent by her the sum of one thousand piastres, a blanket and a mosquito net. I had not received them; I showed the letter to Min, saying that I would like at least to have the mosquito net. Min said she knew nothing about any of these things. Naturally I believed my wife. Filled with hatred for this woman, I sued her and with all the evidence against her, I won the suit.

Shortly after this I received another letter, saying that Nyun intended to come to Cholon again. I applied for a leave and went there. Again I missed her. But I wanted to see her so much this time, that thinking she was only late, I continued to wait for her even though my leave was up. I sat around doing nothing for over a month. My company kept sending for me to come back. One day a Dispensary Chief of my company saw me at Cholon and bawled me out. "Why can't you obey military regulations?" he demanded.

I had missed Nyun twice, but I reluctantly went back to my company in Dang Kup Moy. Then a letter came from Nyun. She was in Cholon, where I had waited for her over a month. Such is the irony of fate!

Not long after this I was released from the Vietminh communist army. It was not an order, but more or less permission, for I had applied for the release myself. The idea had been Nyun's. Her second letter advised me to apply for the release, to put in an application that since I was not well I could not be of much service, and therefore should be let out of the army, so as not be a burden to the communists. Nyun had always been my guide and advisor in all the things dealing with the communists.

This time, too, I followed her advice. I received the notice of release much quicker than I had expected. While in Cholon waiting for Nyun, I had become friendly with an officer of the Cholon outfit. When I became a civilian, I immediately went to this man, Lee, and he introduced me to a big farmer, who owned three water buffaloes. I obtained a job as a farm hand—in a mixed territory of both French and Vietminh forces. Lee often came to see me. One time he confessed that he wanted to surrender to the French and wanted me to go with him. He wanted to go to Cambodia.

But it takes some preparations to surrender to the French. Besides, who knows but what we might be killed for once having belonged to the communists. We were thus discussing surrendering to the French on our way from a hospital where I was being treated for beriberi when we were caught in the midst of the biggest aerial attack we had ever experiencd. We saw paratroopers jump from the planes and land less than a mile from where we crouched on the ground. The sight of countless white parachutes raining down from the blue sky was very impressive. The big air attack signified the beginning of the long awaited French offensive.

One day in May, 1953, not very long after this big attack, I sat in the sugar plant in Hippoa talking to a battalion commander of Vietnam Government forces. Lee and I had finally surrendered to the French, or rather we had sneaked into French territory in the dark of the night.

We got into a boat, rowed by the daughter of Haai house, crossed the river and entered Hippoa. Lee was afraid of being caught as a revolutionist, and ran away. I immediately reported to the police. The feelings toward the Japanese were unexpectedly good in the police office as well as in the town. The battalion officer of the government forces welcomed me with open arms.

"We have no intention of hurting the Japanese at all. If you like, you can stay with us," he said. "I have a deep concern and respect for the Japanese spirit. If you know *kendo* and jujutsu, we would like to have you teach us."

Before me were bottles of a beer I had not seen in years, American cigarettes which I saw for the first time. The battalion officer further said he would help me find Nyun and my baby and repeatedly urged me to stay with the government forces. "Please understand that it is not our desire to fight against our own brothers. The sadness of killing our own people is beyond your imagination. The source of this tragedy is that we are a weak people," he explained. "This weakness allowed the independence group to seek help from the communists, while we stand with the U.S.A. We fight our own people, but it's like eating our own flesh. The underlying motive of the two camps is one and the same, a strong independent government."

There sounded through all this the pathos of a weak nation. The Commander begged me to stay, but I left him and went on to Saigon. It had been eight years since I had left this town, where I had been persuaded to join the Vietminh at the point of a gun. Of course I was under the watch of the Government Army. I was questioned on my enlistment in the communist army, my activities since, my plans for the future.

I had nothing to hide. The group that questioned me belonged to the French Army and was called 2-0 Company. It was a sort of gendarme, a secret police. They seemed not to know what to do with me because I was a foreigner of a non-friendly nation. Presently they moved me up to Supreme Headquarters. I was questioned again, but the French officer who questioned me, a lieutenant, asked "Where do you want to go from here?"

I told him that I wanted to look for my wife and he consented, saying he would look for my wife with me. He put me in a jeep and took me to MacMahon Street immediately. But I did not know Nyun's house. All I knew was that it was on that endless street. In the first place I never dreamed that I would be looking for it like this, and I was unprepared for any real search; naturally we did not find it. The lieutenant's kindness was in vain.

As I had no one who claimed me, I was allowed to stay in the French Army barracks. I was not allowed to go out. I stayed in the barracks every day, having nothing to do. Vietnam non-coms and their wives felt sorry for me, tried to look for Nyun themselves, but also in vain. What worried me most was that, being a foreigner with no one to claim me, I might be sent back to Japan. Thus I spent about one month in despondency. I was treated well, but I lost weight daily.

One day I was given two days' leave. I had a feeling that this was my last chance. If I could not find Nyun this time, I felt sure I would be sent back to Japan. With a white suit that was given to me by a Vietnamese and a pair of shoes such as I had not worn for years, and which almost killed me, I went back and forth on MacMahon Street. Whenever I saw a woman about Nyun's age, I ran after her, or turned back and followed her, scrutinizing her face to make sure she was not Nyun.

Whenever I found a group of people together, I went up to them and asked them about Nyun, but they all shook their heads. At last my feet began to bleed, and I took off my shoes, and went barefooted. Is it possible that I shall never see her again? I asked myself. I regretted having surrendered to the French indiscreetly. Had I stayed in Cholon I might have had a better chance of finding her again.

The next day I wandered out into the streets of Saigon again. The town of Saigon was the same as it had been eight years before. On both sides of the well-paved streets, under the green trees, walked men in white open-collar shirts, women in Annamese costumes, with not-a-care-in-the-world looks. A woman peddler passed by, calling out something in a high voice. Foreign cars, Renaults and Citroens dashed by.

I started to go to MacMahon Street again, then changed my mind. I headed for Buniyan Market. I remembered suddenly that Nyun had written that she was in a textile business, selling materials. Buniyan Market is in the most crowded part of the town and Malays, French, Annamese, Chinese and Indians walked its alleys. I almost passed out from fatigue. I, a foreigner, was looking for one woman among the 150,000 people of Saigon.

"Where are you going?" I was suddenly called from behind, and I turned. A woman stood smiling at me. Who was she? "Where are you going, An Torun?"

Then I remembered. Right after we went into the jungle and before we married, this woman had been staying with Nyun. She was the first acquaintance I met since coming to Saigon.

"Nyun—I'm looking for Nyun. Do you know?" I stuttered.

She probably thought I looked queer, for she looked at me for some minutes, before she spoke again. "Your wife is in the market," she said. "Come with me," and she started to walk before me. I was so excited I could not say anything. Presently the woman stopped. Before me was a small dress material shop, and a woman stood in front of it. It was Nyun!

We faced each other without uttering a word. She stood there wide-eyed. Then an expression something like fright ran through her eyes for a fraction of a second, but immediately her poised, cool, assured look that I had been used to seeing for so long was back, and she gave me a loving glance.

"You are back," she said and smiled.

BLACK-OUT

by Koyama Itoko

TERUYO saw the clouds breaking as she finished breakfast, and now the sun shone brightly. Its welcome warmth reminded her that spring was just around the corner. She heard someone shake the front door roughly and shout "Hello." She got up and went to the door. As she opened it, a man quickly thrust a ball of rubber bands under her nose.

"Don't want any," she said, just as quickly, and locked the door without giving him a chance to open his mouth. He walked away and she heard him muttering to himself. On a nice day like this, after rain for four or five days at a stretch, there were usually many peddlers and junk men.

"Look, plum blossoms! One, two, there's another." She heard Ichiro's young voice as he played with the little girl next door.

Teruyo sat on the porch where the sun beamed in, and brushed her husband's everyday clothes. Thinking a slight stoop gives one a refined look, she brushed and straightened the wrinkles caused by it rather reluctantly; she smiled when she found a soiled handkerchief, a stub of rubber off a pencil, and two pinballs. When she opened the handkerchief she smelled the faint odor of her husband. She looked around quickly and brought it close to her face. She liked her husband's smell. It had an odor quite indescribable, sweet and sour, slightly "greenish," but with a vigor of life, with a faint sweetness of chestnut flower. She could smell her husband's body from his hand-

110

kerchief. As she pressed it against her face and drew in a breath, a deep feeling of happiness enwrapped her whole being. Her eyes half closed, her head slightly to one side, she soaked herself in her husband's odor.

"*Gomen nasai.*"

She came to with a start, and turned crimson to her neck. She remembered suddenly that she was busy today. She had a pile of washing, umbrellas to dry, and rain shoes to wash. She quickly rolled up the handkerchief and pushed it under the trousers as if to hide it from someone, before she stood up.

A man over thirty, dressed in an old-style dark suit, was standing there. She didn't know him. He had a bundle in one hand, and she said to herself, "Another peddler?"

"Is this the house of Yamada?"

"Yes."

The man's deeply tanned face relaxed a bit. Then he started to search his pockets for something.

"Who is it, please?"

"My name's Sato, and I'm from Sanshu."

Never heard of him, she thought—"Sanshu?"

"No, you don't know me. I was only asked to—" The man brought out an envelope of good quality, but which was all wrinkled.

"Oh!"

"I was asked to deliver this to the master of this house. The man who asked me, his name is Yoshida, was with me on the boat," he said. "I repatriated from Java— Yes, a late repatriate . . . Yoshida, he said he was from Sumatra. The master here, I heard, was on Sumatra, too."

"Yes, that's right."

As he talked, Teruyo became a little cautious. About half a year ago, she remembered . . . there was a man who had said he had repatriated from the south, and she had been swindled in a big way. His talk had sounded straight enough to convince her, had given her the impression that her husband was obligated to him, that he had been taken care of by him on the boat. So, she had fed him a good lunch, and had given him train fare home. She had been highly reprimanded when her husband came home that night. But this man, he didn't look the kind . . . he looked too naïve. She thought hard and quickly.

"I am only related to the family here. I was asked to mind the house today. I—er—I don't know anything—"

What if Ichiro should run in, yelling "Mommie," but he was safely outside the fence. The man believed her and, nodding, said, "I went to his office first, but they said he was away for a few days and gave me this address. It happened to be quite close to where I am staying, so I came here.

"I am going back home on the next train. I don't come to Tokyo often, so I didn't want to take it back with me."

His talk lacked the smoothness of a swindler. His eyes were simple, didn't look as though the head behind them were capable of any false design. Teruyo relaxed her guard a little.

"That's very nice of you."

"I should've sent it earlier, but it was way in the bottom of my trunk and I forgot all about it. Well then, I am leaving it with you."

Teruyo dropped her eyes to the envelope awkwardly. Something made her hesitate.

"I don't know—I don't know whether I should keep a thing like this or not."

"Of course, I know how you feel. But neither can I keep it forever, and I can't very well throw it away, you know. It's only a letter. Just give it to the master, and I'm sure it will be all right. Goodby, then."

The man picked up his bundle and turned to go. "He is not a bad man," she thought. "He brought this thing purely out of kindness." She glanced absently at the name in Roman spelling in faded ink. Then she noticed. "Oh! But look. The name of the company is right, but this name is not. How is this read? It begins with J."

"What!" he exclaimed, turning back. Then he said simply.

"The name is Yamada Yaichi, isn't it? Then that's how it's spelled. In Malaya, the 'Y' sound is spelled with J. They write Jamada Jaichi."

Teruyo turned the envelope over. She read "Rahima" in Roman spelling.

"Is 'Rahima' a person's name?"

"I think so."

Teruyo's curiosity was suddenly aroused. "Is it a man's name?"

"I think it's more common in women," he answered.

"From a woman—to my—I mean, to the master here. From a woman in Sumatra? On what business, I wonder, at this late date?"

"Oh, there are plenty of them like that. I don't know much about Sumatra, but in Java—I had three letters to deliver, all from women. The ones who don't forget and write at this late date usually have children. They usually send photographs of their children."

"Children?"

"Women there are lighthearted. I had one myself, but soon as I left I forgot her. You can make them easy, but forget them easy, too. But when they have children, then they are different. The memories become deeper, I guess. The letters I brought were all to my friends, so I know well. The two of them had a child each. Both of them looked very much Japanese—they were nice kids."

"Then the master here also had someone like that too?"

"Don't know about that. Yoshida said something, but I don't remember."

"And where is he now?"

"Yoshida? You got me there. He and I parted at Shimizu Port. "Well, I must go. I guess you better not say anything to the madame here. Once some awful trouble broke out—of course I only heard about it afterwards. To tell you the truth, I don't enjoy this kind of errand myself. But can't very well throw the darn thing away, you know. Sometimes they enclose a tiny precious stone. But really, it was a good thing it was you today, and not his wife. I must hurry now. Good-by."

And he was gone. Teruyo, as though in a trance, heard him open the door, step out, and shut it but did nothing. Even after his footsteps were heard no more, she stood there dumfounded.

When she came to, she realized she was holding the letter in her hand. She felt something like a sting on the tips of her fingers, and threw the letter to the floor. But she picked it up again like a child commanded to do so, and returned to the porch with it.

The sun was still shining, but it did not look the same to her. How it could change so in a matter of five or seven minutes, she didn't know. Was the sky blue or black? The sunshine stung her eyes. She started to pick up the things she'd left; his clothes, rubber stub, pinballs, and all. They felt different, surfaces rough, or cold or crude. They all felt bad to her hands. She pulled out the handkerchief from under the trousers. She put it to her face absent-mindedly—it was a habit with her. The odor was still there, sweet and sour, the odor of chestnut blossoms. She swallowed bitter saliva. She swallowed again and again, but something stuck in her throat and wouldn't go down. She felt nauseous. She stepped to the edge of the porch, but nothing came up. She felt a chill in the pit of her stomach.

Teruyo never once doubted her husband. He was a quiet man, an introvert, extremely kind. Their premarital private detective check showed that he had never had any relations with women. Just as Teruyo's parents feared, he was awkward and was at a loss at their nuptial bed. That's the kind of man he was. It was during the war when they were married, and like everyone else, they didn't have much of a honeymoon. He soon got used to married life, and he had learned to love enough to satisfy Teruyo. The half year together before he was called to duty was spent without even noticing the scarcity of everyday necessities, or the severity of life in wartime, so happy and content they were with each other. To this day she couldn't remember without blushing the last night she had with him before he left—neither of them slept a wink. She was sure she conceived Ichiro that night.

He wrote to her even from the boat, and many times after he got to the front line. Even as the war became more severe, and mail had a hard time getting through, she continued to hear from him. She wrote to him when Ichiro came, and he sent a pair of rubber-soled shoes by return mail. When the war ended, he was on the first boat back. To get back that soon, he must have gone to considerable trouble. So, all told, he was away only about two years.

After he returned, there seemed no outward change in him except that he loved her more deeply, and was kinder. He often talked about boats that were sunk, and automobiles that were overturned. "Sure thankful that I am back alive. After all, Japan is best."

She once heard him talk thus in his sleep. He seemed genuinely happy when tending to their little garden. "He needn't become so domestic, so young," she even thought to herself.

And this Yaichi of all persons. Teruyo could not possibly make herself imagine the other woman. How, when, could a thing like that happen? She had kept all the letters Yaichi wrote to her. She didn't have to get them out. She remembered them all, each and every one of them by heart. How could he write letters like that to his wife with one hand, and hold Rahima with the other. No, no, not Yaichi! She didn't know about other men, but not her Yaichi.

Try as she may, she could not picture her husband holding another woman in his arms.

Then what is this letter left by a man in dark, ominous clothes. The letter which gave her such a feeling of apprehension. It was sealed tight. Why? He said it happens quite often. He said when a woman writes at this late date, she often has a child. Teruyo put the letter against the light. The letter papers, folded, filled the entire envelope, but the half of it felt hard and was darker.

"Is it a picture?" she wondered. "Feels like it. But why should I believe that man whom I've never met before, a man who appeared suddenly, and disappeared just as suddenly as the peddlers and the swindler. I am the one that knows Yaichi better than anyone else. That man never even saw Yaichi once. Yes, everything will be clear if I open this letter." Teruyo brought out a pair of scissors, and started to put them to one corner of the envelope, and stopped. Until now she had never opened anything addressed to her husband, no matter how trivial it may have seemed. But that was not what made her stop.

She suddenly had the premonition that if she opened it some dark, ominous thing would jump out of it, and would spread its wings throughout this house. After all, was not everything happy and peaceful until that dark messenger came? Teruyo threw the scissors to the floor.

Ichiro came in and started to chatter something, but she answered him absentmindedly. She couldn't remember, afterwards, just how she spent that day. She ate lunch with Ichiro mechanically, and just sat all day by the pile of washing she'd got out to do in the morning.

She hardly slept that night. She dreamed often of being chased by someone, woke up many times. Sometimes she heard someone at the door, that husky voice saying *gomen nasai,* and then she would really wake up. Then, remembering it was the middle of the night, she would say to herself that no one would come at this time of night, and try to go back to sleep.

And then it was morning, and Ichiro was sleeping by her side as usual. Teruyo sat up, fluffing her hair, listened absently to the distant rumble of the train. When she came to fully, she realized that her nightgown was soaking wet and stuck to her skin, and she felt as if she had taken a bath with her clothes on. The face of the dark-clothed messenger and the letter flashed in her mind. It was then she realized who it was that had chased her all night in her dream. An instant later she felt that she had had dreams like this many times before, that this sort of thing happened quite often, and that it really was nothing, nothing at all to worry about. Teruyo got up, and still in her nightgown, went into her husband's room. She opened his drawer. The white envelope was still there.

"Then it really did happen."

The letter was there, where she had placed it the day before. Then the memories of what happened yesterday welled in her mind, clearly and definitely, with great impact. She wondered if she were going to spend today as miserably as she had spent yesterday. Each day would increase her mistrust and jealousy of her husband, increase her own unhappiness. Would the days continue like this until her husband came home? What would she do when he did come home? She started to drop her thin nightgown off her shoulders, then leaned against the desk, as if falling.

The next day, she could not stay in the house any longer. She felt like crying aloud. She feared she would go crazy. She took Ichiro, nonchalant and happy, oblivious of his mother's inner turmoil, and called on her sister. Her sister lived beyond Omori. It took them almost an hour to get there, by train and bus. Teruyo's sister was nine years her senior, but having had no children, did not show it. Her chief worry was in her husband, a doctor, who was forever chasing women.

"Well, hello. Long time no see," her sister exclaimed.

She was sitting in a room littered with magazines, reading. She wore a sober expression. Ichiro went out to play on the lawn with a young nurse.

"You know those question and answer columns in the newspapers? Their advice is sometimes impossible. Just because it's other people's affairs, their answers are quite irresponsible. Private detectives are much more dependable."

"Are you having trouble again?" Teruyo interjected.

"Oh yes, same as ever. Yaichi-san is different, I know, but most men—you can't trust them one minute. Once they are out of the house, they let go of themselves like birds out of a cage, By the way, you don't look your usual gay self. What's the matter?"

"I don't know. I can't eat anything these last few days."

"Maybe you are going to have your next one. It's about time, isn't it?"

"No, it's not that."

"Then let my hubby give you a check."

"Is he out on a call?"

"So he said last night, but it turned out to be some 'urgent' sick woman. I gave him a pretty bad time last night, so I think he will come home all right tonight."

"What do you do at times like that?"

"What do I do? You mean when he is up to something? I go after him thoroughly, check everything, and leave no stone unturned."

"And when you do find out everything, doesn't it make you feel worse?"

"Yes, but if I don't, that would be worse yet. I show him all the proof, how he slept with a certain woman on such and such a night, at such and such a place. With a two-faced husband like mine, that's the only way to deal with him."

"But I rather feel that even if there were something, I'd feel happier not to know anything. You know, innocence is bliss!"

"Not with me. I've got to know everything once I get suspicious, or I'd never feel rested—it would get on my nerves."

"Yes, it does, doesn't it?" Teruyo mumbled inaudibly.

"You, who always brag about Yaichi-san, what's wrong with you? It couldn't be that he is up to something, is it?"

"That's what I can't be sure of."

"If something is wrong, I'll look into it for you. I know a real good private snoop. He is a bit expensive, but real good. If it's someone at the office it won't take more than two or three days."

The more eager her sister became, the more reluctant Teruyo was to confide in her, and she found herself holding rigidly, like a soldier defending a fort, to her belief in Yaichi—denying everything, everything.

"No, I don't think it's anything at all, I am sure of it. It's . . . it's some mistake, it must be. It couldn't be—I know."

But, once back home, she couldn't help going directly to the desk drawer. She felt herself spinning round and round in a circle.

When Yaichi finally returned, it was night.

"*Okaeri nasai,*" she greeted as she met him at the door. When she saw his lively self, with his usual half smile on his right cheek, her mind was suddenly made up. After all these days of indecision . . . she tried to remain calm till then, but found her hands shaking involuntarily, from time to time.

The lights went out just as he finished changing into his home clothes.

"Are we still having black-outs in Tokyo? They say we don't have enough water in the power dams, but what we really lack is brains in our statesmen, not water."

Teruyo emptied a kettle of hot water into the wash basin. Yaichi, after he washed up, took the candle into Ichiro's room to have a look at his son's sleeping face. Teruyo, sitting in the dark in the dining room, heard him murmur something to the child.

"What's the matter. Did something happen?" he asked as he came back in. "Why so quiet?"

He was out of the bedroom and had put the candle and a stick of sweet cake on the table.

"Got a knife?" he asked.

"Yes, here . . ."

Teruyo gave it to him, and poured some tea into his cup. Her throat was dry, but she could not bring herself to drink with him. Not just now. Her husband looked inquiringly at her over the flickering flame of the candle.

"There's a letter for you from Sumatra," she whispered, half hoping he wouldn't hear and it could be forgotten.

"Yes?"

Just then the light went on.

There was only an expression of simple curiosity on his face. Teruyo took out the white envelope. Yaichi looked close at the addressed side, cocked his head, and turned it to the other side. His brows pricked and his face turned pale. His cheek muscles pulled crookedly to one side and tightened. These, Teruyo did not miss.

The candlelight dimmed. Her husband's fingers went to one corner of the envelope, then stopped an instant. Teruyo reached out, grabbed the other corner and pulled. She felt a slight resistance, but not much. Taking the letter in her right hand, she put it over the candle flame. Yaichi started to say something, but without turning she put up her free hand to stop him, holding it up as if to ward off something. Dainty whiffs of smoke hugged the envelope. The candlelight dwarfed to a tiny speck, almost went out . . . then at the next instant, the envelope burst into flame, illuminating the entire room.

"Teruyo!"

Teruyo, tightened her lips, hung on to the envelope until it almost burned her finger tips. She inhaled deeply then blew out the flame.

As if that were the signal, the light went out again.

No one lit the candle.

"I thought this was the best way. I couldn't think of any other way," Teruyo murmured low in the dark.

There was no sound of any movement. The room was as if empty.

After a while, Teruyo noticed that her hand was being held. She felt the hold tighten slowly to a firm, warm grip.

THE AFFAIR OF THE ARABESQUE INLAY

by Ishikawa Tatsuzo

Dear Sir:

Reference is made to your latest inquiry after our investigation into the present whereabouts and recent activities of one Mr. Wu Kao-chih.

We hereby take great pleasure to inform you of the results of our inquiries to date.

It is also sincerely requested that you would kindly understand that our report as yet includes certain insufficiencies primarily due to the difficulty in establishing the present whereabouts of the person involved.

Yours Sincerely

(signed:) T. Torii
Chief of Torii Detective Agency

Encl: Report to date. T.T.

Mr. Wu Kao-chih, of Chinese nationality; born Nanking, 1918. Father alleged to have been a noted trader by the name of Wu Hsiung-ta.

Mr. Wu Kao-chih studied economics in a university in Shanghai. Later he was brought to Japan by his father. Here he studied economics at Waseda University, as evidenced by the students' enrollment records of said University.

In 1937, the Lukowkiao Incident set off the Sino-Japanese War.

However, Mr. Wu did not return home until 1938, upon his formal graduation from Waseda University.

After the war, early in 1946, he again came to Japan, allegedly making a quick fortune at smuggling and such activities by taking full advantage of his nationality.

In June, 1951, upon the signing of the San Francisco peace treaty, and resumption of Japanese authority over the affairs of Third Nationals and the subsequent decline in his business, he returned to China.

His subsequent whereabouts are unknown, except for August, 1953, when Yumiko Ueda, with whom he had maintained a special relationship while he was in Japan, received by mail an expensive English-made jewelry box. The parcel noted the origin as Nanking.

To our regret, further details are not available.

Judging from several old photos he left in Japan, he would seem to be five feet five inches or so in height, tending toward plumpness, of a gay disposition, and of Southern Chinese racial type.

According to information gathered from his acquaintances in Japan, we have drawn up an outline of his life and character as follows: During his entire three years in Japan as a student of the Economics Department of Waseda University, he rented a room in the home of Mr. Arai Yasuhiro, then a director of the Japan-Formosa Spinning Company. Regarding him, widow Arai recalls, "Mr. Wu Kao-chih was a very steady student and pro-Japanese." She also said, "My husband was a good friend of the senior Mr. Wu. We invited young Wu to our house. Brought up in a good family, he was very polite and modest. But he also had progressive ideas—thinking that China should throw off her old ways and rebuild a new China which could cope with progress and the rest of the world."

Mrs. Arai's impression coincides with those of Wu's classmates. He remained a bachelor, and was strictly against the Chinese custom of early marriage.

In the Spring of 1938, upon his graduation from Waseda University, he returned to a China under Japanese military occupation. Further records of him from that date until 1946, when he revisited Japan, are unavailable due to lack of means of investigation from here. However, consolidating data from the testimonials of Ueda Yumiko and other people, the history we have reconstructed for him during the period in question is an extremely tragic one.

In December, 1937, the Japanese Army was pressing close to Nanking city from the east. Mr. Wu Kao-chih, then in Tokyo, had received no word from his family since November. After the fierce fighting on December 12 and 13, Nanking surrendered. The Japanese Army issued the formal declaration of the occupation of Nanking on December 17. Mr. Wu desperately wanted to know of his father, mother and sisters. He did all he could to find some means of returning home, but the severe restrictions which then prevailed allowed him no chance of exit from Japan—legal or illegal.

Late in March, 1938, he somehow managed to return to his homeland. In Nanking, he found only ashes and rubble where his father's office had been. His father's house was demolished. All possessions had been looted. No trace of his parents or sisters was found. He was told that tens of thousand of Nanking citizens had been massacred by the Japanese Army; then the corpses were buried in mass graves outside the city walls.

For almost half a year, Mr. Wu wandered around trying to locate —or at least to learn the whereabouts of the bodies of—his family. During that fruitless search, Mr. Wu's attitude toward life seems to have undergone a complete change. So, too, did his personal character.

From that time until his return to Japan in 1946, his activities are unknown. He is believed to have availed himself of the opportunities offered by the confusion of the war and to have established his financial position solidly. In 1946 Mr. Wu came to Japan, alone. First, settling himself in the so-called Nanking Street, of Chinatown, Yokohama, he started trading. Soon he moved to Tokyo, pocketing large profits through the importation of American luxury goods, Taiwan sugar and bananas. Black-marketing gasoline seems to have brought considerable money into his pockets.

He bought a fine house in Denen Chofu, hired secretaries, maids, drove a Cadillac—himself, no chauffeur. At night he frequented cabarets in the Ginza with his friends.

It was about February of 1950 that Ueda Yumiko got to know Mr. Wu. Yumiko was then thirty-two, had been working at Cabaret Tokyo from January 1950.

Ueda Yumiko was born on a farm in Kumagaya, Saitama Prefecture, the second daughter. Her father, Ueda Harukichi, died of illness in 1944. After finishing girls' high school in Kumagaya, she came to Tokyo to be a student nurse at the Central Red Cross Hospital. Later she became a nurse in the First National Hospital, where she worked for three years.

The relationship between Mr. Wu Kao-chih and Ueda Yumiko became regularized in 1950. Mr. Wu bought a house in Taka-bancho, for Yumiko and her child, providing a maid. But this relationship was brought to its conclusion as described in the following.

Our investigator interviewed Ueda Yumiko, who is now living at her brother's farm in Kumagaya. She told our investigator, "I first met him in the cabaret where I worked. He always brought a few friends with him. His Japanese and his manner were so natural that I could hardly believe he was a foreigner. He was a fine, clean-cut gentleman, generous with his money. He was perhaps at his most prosperous at that time. I overheard it said that he could make several hundred thousand yen selling an imported car to a Japanese."

One night one or two months after they first met, Wu was drinking sake at the cabaret. He looked at his watch, and murmured that he didn't realize it was so late. Yumiko unconsciously looked at her wrist watch and said, "Oh, it's just nine-sixteen."

Wu looked at her wrist—then stared at the watch as if to check its movement. "What are you gazing at?" Yumiko says she asked.

"It's very beautiful. May I see it closer?" he said and took her hand.

"No, it's only a cheap one, I'm ashamed," she reportedly answered.

"No, it's not at all cheap. It's a rather rare watch. Do you mind if I see its back?" He was unusually insistent, she recalls.

Yumiko took the watch off her wrist and handed it to Wu. He turned it over, closely examining the inlaid arabesque design of a little red flower. Then he returned it to her without a word.

Half an hour later, just before they left, Mr. Wu whispered into Yumiko's ear, "Yumiko-san, couldn't you sell me that watch for five thousand yen?"

Surprised, Yumiko hesitated.

"Maybe five thousand yen is too cheap? Will seven or eight thousand yen do? I must have that watch," he insisted.

"Why? It's just an old watch. You can buy any brand-new one you see," Yumiko said.

"Please think it over. I don't mind paying even ten thousand yen for it." And he left.

The next day, he came to the cabaret alone—which was unusual. He asked her about the watch. She sold it, agreeing to eight thousand yen—but when later she opened the envelope he had given her, she found ten one-thousand-yen notes.

Placing the watch in his vest pocket, Mr. Wu asked her: "Where did you buy this, Yumiko-san?"

"I was given it."

"Is that so? Well, may I ask who gave it to you?"

"It's a keep-sake of my dead parents."

"A keep-sake? Was your mother wearing this?"

"It was from my father."

"That's not true. This is a woman's watch."

"Yes, that's right."

"Let me guess. It must be your lover who bought this for you."

"Oh, it's such a trifle, let's forget it." She tried to change the subject, but Wu turned serious and started to tell her a story. He had a very intimate friend—a crazy collector of timepieces—whose collection included over fourteen or fifteen hundred old and new, Western and Oriental, watches and clocks. Wu had allegedly picked up some slight knowledge of watches from his friend. Wu told her that the watch was an extremely novel piece—not made in Switzerland, England, or America. Nor did it look Japanese. The design on the back side seemed Chinese, but the face was in the European style.

He wanted to know where it came from. Otherwise, he said, he could provide no clue to his friend's research—that was the general outline of Mr. Wu's story. Yumiko was taken in by the story. She confessed, "In fact, I don't know the details of its origin. I got it from a relative of mine who had been a soldier. It often goes out of order— It isn't a good watch—"

"Is that so? . . . a soldier gave it to you . . . I wish . . . well, if I could see him sometime . . . That soldier couldn't have been to, say . . . well, Korea? . . . Manchuria? . . . Singapore? Perhaps China? . . . I wonder . . ."

"Yes, he's been to China. During the war. And he returned— wounded in battle."

"Ah, I see . . . China!" He raised his voice a little. He smiled. His eyes glistened strangely.

After this Wu came to Yumiko's cabaret as often as twice a week.

In addition to the usual tips, he began leaving special pocket money in her hands. Yumiko was naturally impressed by the fact that Mr. Wu was a bachelor, living in a big mansion.

Not long after, she was invited to accompany him on a business trip to the Osaka-Kobe area. It was a five-day trip with stopovers at the Takarazuka Hot-Spring and Kyoto Hotels. At this time they entered into their special relationship. Yumiko confessed to him that she had a child. Mr. Wu bought clothing material and other presents for the child. According to Yumiko, Mr. Wu Kao-chih was not of a demanding nature, never trying to monopolize her.

About a month after that trip Mr. Wu bought a new, though small, modern house in Takabancho. Yumiko moved from her shabby room in Asakusa-Tabaramachi, with her child, and hired a maid. In short, she became a mistress to Mr. Wu Kao-chih, a Chinese living in Japan.

Every month, she received fifty thousand yen as living expenses, besides occasional presents and extra money he gave her whenever he visited the house. Yumiko's life became comfortable. She quit the cabaret, but was still able to save over twenty thousand yen a month. Then one night Mr. Wu Kao-chih resumed the long-forgotten talk about her watch. It came as a great surprise to Yumiko, who had believed that Wu was interested in the watch for his collector friend.

It was a lie—a pious means to an end.

It seems that watch had, without any doubt, belonged to Wu's mother. His father had bought it for her on their twentieth wedding anniversary. The design, specially ordered by his father, precluded there being another like it in the world. Wu wanted to locate the person who had had the watch previously. Whoever gave it to Yumiko might know something about his parents and sisters, missing since the occupation of Nanking.

Mr. Wu also told Yumiko that he had to see the soldier who had given the watch to her. His real purpose in revisiting post-war Japan was not to make money but to find Japanese who knew the fate of his parents and sisters. He "had a hunch that some Japanese should know," he said, his face suddenly gone white.

Yumiko had no reason to refuse to cooperate with him, particularly as she was being provided for so generously, but a chill went down her back when she thought of how Wu had, as the ancient saying puts it, "attained the fact by sure steps."

She was thankful for all he had done for her and her child, whatever his real intention might have been. Yet she could not disclose the truth. What would happen if that soldier was the very person who had killed Wu's family? The soldier was none other than the father of her own child.

Yumiko confessed to our investigator that she had "only hatred and no obligation at all toward that soldier," but still she was unwilling to disclose his identity to Wu. Nevertheless, her past finally yielded to the power of her present. He was the father of her daughter; still, he was never her formal husband. On the other hand, though only a mistress, Yumiko felt a love and obligation toward Wu, sentiment that finally made her confess the name of her former lover.

Haneda Otojiro, registered domicile Odawara City, Kanagawa Prefecture. After finishing middle school, worked for Hakone Tozan Railway and at other jobs. In 1935, entered the army as a Private Second Class. In August, 1937, at the outbreak of the Sino-Japanese incident, went to China. By the time of the fall of Nanking, he was a corporal. In July, 1938, Cpl. Haneda received a wound in a guerilla mop-up—bone fractures of the left thigh and knee joint. Hospitalized in the army's Nanking Hospital, later returned to Japan. In the First Army Hospital met Ueda Yumiko, then assigned as a nurse.

After about a year, he was released from the hospital with a slightly crippled leg. Soon after, rented a room in Tokyo, where both lived together. In spring 1941, Yumiko gave birth to a girl.

Not long after the daughter's birth, Haneda left Tokyo for Odawara—with the excuse that he could find a better job there. Six months passed without a word. In the spring of 1942 Yumiko received a letter telling her that he had to marry another girl as the inevitable result of certain circumstances. In the letter was enclosed a three-hundred-yen check. Yumiko tried every way to locate Haneda, but failed.

As to the watch, Yumiko told Mr. Wu that she had received it while she was nursing Haneda in the First Army Hospital. He said that he bought it in a curio shop in Shanghai. Mr. Wu did not believe the story of Haneda. Rather he suspected that former-Corporal Haneda had been among the troops occupying Nanking.

It might be said to be the instinct of a son whose parents had been killed.

No sooner had Mr. Wu obtained the name of Haneda from Yumiko than he went straight to Odawara city. In five days he succeeded in locating Haneda. He seems to have spent a considerable amount of money in checking over the whole town through five Chinese residents of that city.

Haneda Otojiro was not living in Odawara. But Mr. Wu did locate Haneda's brother, who revealed Haneda's whereabouts as near Okachimachi, back in Tokyo. Haneda was dealing in black-market goods of the American occupation forces. He was living in a four-room house near Ueno, with wife and employees—but no children.

Mr. Wu was not so hasty as to call on Haneda at his house. He went to the shop Haneda was operating. First approaching as a customer, Mr. Wu was soon selling him imported articles—at prices considerably below market. Haneda was delighted. Haneda soon began to treat Mr. Wu as a trusted friend. Haneda did not see through Mr. Wu, who passed as a Japanese called Iwamoto Yoshizo.

They were soon on quite familiar terms. One night at a sake party Mr. Wu, alias Iwamoto, asked Haneda, "By the way, this may sound odd, but, don't you by any chance know a girl named Ueda Yumiko?"

Haneda was startled. "Anything happened to Yumiko?" he asked.

"No, nothing. But is she your wife?"

"No. Not my wife. But I lived with her for a while."

"Did you?—and, uh, you had a child, didn't you?"

"Yes, I did. Is . . . my child is all right?"

"Seems so. Seven or eight now, isn't she?"

"Maybe, eight or nine, by now. How on earth do you come to know them?"

"No, no, I don't really know them. Only, well, one of my friends is taking care of them. A few days ago—I was in his house—we talked about the Okachimachi Market. This woman suddenly asked me if I knew a man in the market called Haneda. I was surprised. She seems to have been working in the Cabaret Tokyo in the Ginza. But then I think she had already quit the place," said Wu, alias Iwamoto.

Soon after Haneda Otojiro went to the Cabaret Tokyo to find

Yumiko. He was directed to her new home. Luckily, Mr. Wu was not there.

The moment Yumiko faced Haneda, an old, almost forgotten, burning rancor welled up in her heart. She kept him standing on the stone floor of the entrance hall, never asking him to step inside.

"Halloo, Yumiko. It's been long time—"

"What brought you here? I really wonder how you could even dare to come," she sputtered in rage.

"Of course, I have no face to come to you like this, but—I just wanted to see my child."

"Your child? Huh! You wouldn't really like to face the child you deserted, would you? You'd better leave."

"Don't talk like that. That time, well, I was in a tight squeeze. I apologize——" Haneda tried all the excuses and explanations he could muster. "You see," he said. "Well, as a matter of fact, I have given you so much trouble in bringing up the child—but if you agree, I would like to send her to the university—with my money. I mean, I am getting along fairly well now." He also added that he had no child with his present wife, who was willing to adopt his child by the former affair.

Yumiko was furious at his selfishness. She threatened him with a pair of *geta* she grabbed from the stone floor. He left without further argument. Yumiko did not say anything to Mr. Wu, as she feared giving him the wrong notion that she was continuing her old affair.

She received an anonymous parcel, obviously from Haneda, who, though, did not put his address on it—there was one hundred thousand yen inside. Unable to return it, she kept the money in the drawer of her wardrobe. A few days later a messenger brought a basket of fruit. She ignored the basket and returned the money with it.

Haneda Otojiro tried to get his child back through various means —money, presents—all of which failed. In consequence he apparently began to consider some drastic action to achieve his end. But it took another month before he could finally carry it out.

In the meantime, Mr. Wu was handling Haneda in his way. Practically all of Haneda's business now depended on "Iwamoto Yoshizo." It was precisely the way Mr. Wu had approached Yumiko, made her his own, and explored the secret of the watch—the way only a persistent Chinese could pursue.

One night "Iwamoto" took Haneda to Atami and got him drunk. Making sure that he was tight enough, Iwamoto—alias Mr. Wu Kao-chih—asked, "You always wear khaki pants. You've been in the army?"

"Of course. —Who's asking me? I am a corporal—decorated—the Order of the Golden Kite—" Haneda said in drunken pride.

"Well then—you were crippled in the leg—an honorable wound?"

"That's right—mortar shell got me. Almost lost a leg——"

"Where did you go? South?"

"Central China. From there as far as Nanking. Had a real rough time . . ."

"Central China? Then you were there in the early stage of the war?"

"Sure, just after it broke out. I went there in August. First, Shanghai, then to Changshu, Wusieh. . . ."

"Nanking?"

"Yeah, Nanking. I climbed up that front wall . . . must have been twenty feet, high . . . straight up."

"No, higher than that?"

"You know Nanking, Iwamoto-san?"

"Sure, been there many times. You see, I was an interpreter. I'm pretty good at Chinese," Wu said.

"Really?"

"True. It was terrible, Nanking. We killed a lot. Fifty or sixty thousand. . . ."

"Ah, far more than that. We just couldn't figure out how to dispose of all those corpses. I myself must have got ten, maybe fifteen," Haneda confessed.

"Yeah? Even I got five or six," Wu said, pouring sake into Haneda's glass. "You been near the Military Academy?"

"Sure. That building was turned into a headquarters—later."

"Back of that building, there was hill commanding a good view, remember?"

"The big mansions, I remember, I remember. Our unit cleared that area."

"There were some people left behind, I think."

"Just old men and women. They begged and begged—mercy—it was really funny."

"Get any loot?"

"Sure, loads. We couldn't carry it around, though we could take anything. We threw it all away. And then, anyway, I was sent back wounded around then."

"Then you didn't bring back anything?"

"Nothing—except a little watch I took—"

"A watch? That'd be a good souvenir. Where'd you get it?"

"Let me see—an old woman. She had a good watch . . . from an old woman. I tried to take it . . . She wouldn't let me have it. Then an old man told her to let it go. He spoke some Japanese . . ."

"Yes . . . and then you . . ."

"I guess so . . . anyway, they're dead. We were busy mopping up, you see, so I locked 'em up in a room and threw in a hand-grenade . . . I went away, busy . . . I don't know what happened . . . besides, who cares? Just some old Chinese . . ." Haneda was so tight that he probably didn't even remember his words the next day.

Wu finally knew the murderer of his parents. Yet that night he slept in the same room with Haneda, as if nothing had happened.

Mr. Wu Kao-chih, however, began scheming to kill Haneda. Yumiko tried to persuade him to hold his hand, but Wu did not listen. He cold-bloodedly checked every possibility of murdering Haneda—or in his words, avenging his parents. Take him mountain climbing and push him off a cliff; drugs; fake auto-accident; push him from an express train. Every possible murder-method Wu thought over and re-checked, and rejected. On the other hand, he kept Haneda in a good mood, still supplying him with goods at cheap prices.

Then, a tragedy took place. On October 3, 1950, Yachiyo, the daughter of Yumiko, mysteriously disappeared on her way home from school. That evening Yumiko reported her daughter presumably kidnapped to the police and a search was begun.

The police went to Haneda's house only to find no trace of the girl. Haneda set up a firm alibi and was instantly cleared. Three days passed without news of the missing girl.

Yumiko lost her composure. Mr. Wu seemed to have been of help, at least in public, as her friends report. But he did not try to deal directly with Haneda. "Mr. Wu Kao-chih, protector of the missing girl," knew such action would spoil his hopes of revenge. Yumiko was no longer normal—sleepless nights, days of worry. On the third night, when Mr. Wu was away, she dashed out of the house. How she got there she could not remember, but later that night she was standing in front of Haneda's house in Ueno.

She knocked at the door. Haneda came out. She pounced on him, screaming, "Give me back Yachiyo. Give her back!" Haneda called the nearby police box. The police officer came, listened to the trouble, but hesitated to get involved in some family squabble between a man and woman who had once lived together, someplace else. It was out of his jurisdiction, he claimed, and put Yumiko into a taxi, telling her to go home.

She didn't. She came back to Haneda's again, went inside the garden. She set fire to several places around and under the house. Flames spread; the fire enveloped the whole four-room house.

Neighbors were alarmed. Yumiko was seen crazily jumping around the flaming house, shouting, again and again, "Give me back my Yachiyo." She was caught by the police.

Haneda's wife narrowly escaped. But Haneda himself was found the next morning, a burned body among the ashes and rubble.

In the afternoon an employee of Haneda's shop came to the Ueno police station to give himself up, bringing Yachiyo with him. He had been ordered by Haneda to kidnap the girl and take her to Odawara. Hiding there for several days, he had read of the tragedy in the newspaper.

In February, 1951, Ueda Yumiko was sentenced to serve five years in Toyotama Penitentiary. Mr. Wu arranged to send Yachiyo to Yumiko's brother in the country.

In May, 1951, Mr. Wu Kao-chih disposed of all his business affairs and his properties. In June, he left Japan. A few days before taking a CAT plane for Hongkong he paid a visit to Yumiko in the Penitentiary. "I guess, I owe you so much," he said. "You did the thing in my behalf. Because of you, I did not become a murderer. Yet my parents have been avenged."

He handed her a one-million-yen time-deposit certificate and an ivory signature seal with which to claim it, and said, "I am leaving Japan for good. When you are released, please use this money for yourself and Yachiyo-san. I'll be wishing for your happiness, from a faraway land."

Then he left.

In February, 1953, her lawyer arranged her release on bond using part of the money Mr. Wu had left. Yumiko went back to her brother's where Yachiyo was staying. In August of that year, a beautiful London-made jewelry box was delivered from Mr. Wu. There was no sender's address, just the postmark "Nanking." No further news has come from Mr. Wu, since then. But Ueda Yumiko is living peacefully, helping out on her brother's farm.

In that jewelry box lies the seal Mr. Wu had specially made for Yumiko—an ivory seal, with the arabesque design of a little red flower inlaid in the top.

BLACK MARKET BLUES

by Koh Haruto

OHIZUMI met Jack Kurosawa in front of Shimbashi Station and the two walked toward Tamura-cho. The streets were full of Christmas decorations; there were many show windows that had big and small Santas. It was only three days until Christmas.

"Don't worry. I've heard that there's never been a miss so far," Jack assured Ohizumi, looking at him from under his hunting cap.

"I don't know anything about this fellow Buchanan we are about to see," Ohizumi said bluntly. "I put my trust in you, you know that."

Ohizumi had never had any previous dealings with Buchanan. He had not wanted to come to Tokyo with the dangerous dollars in his pocket. His wife Takako did not want him to, either. Ohizumi did all his buying and selling of dollars at his hideout in Kamakura. Those who wanted to sell or buy came to him, and he did his business sitting down, but these last few days he was rushed with dollars. He'd got rid of most of them, but the five thousand he had taken yesterday gave him a big headache. He could not refuse the money because of some obligations from the past. He felt, when he bought the money, that he would have a hard time with it. Sure enough, he could not get rid of it in one day. It was too close to Christmas, and though everyone wanted dollars, no one had enough yen for them.

"It's such a big amount, you know," Jack said, keeping his voice down. "Buchanan is about the only person who can buy such an amount so close to Christmas." Ohizumi felt that Jack was trying to make him feel obligated to him, which annoyed him. He intended to give Jack about fifty thousand commission if the deal went through. He knew, of course, that after Christmas there would be no sale of dollars. He nodded to Jack, looking sharply right and left from behind the gold-rimmed glasses that he used for disguise. Outwardly his easy manner and big shoulders made him look like a boxer, but he was constantly conscious of the five thousand dollars in his pocket.

"I know it's the way with this business. When it comes in like this, I have a hard time getting rid of it," Ohizumi had to confess. "I've got to find more new outlets."

Ohizumi intended making this his last deal. After Christmas, through New Year's, he intended to take Takako to Osaka and hide there for a while. Jack didn't know this, so he answered him lightheartedly. "After we get there, if you feel it isn't safe, we can always leave without doing any business," he said. "There is the Radio Japan Building. It's not so far now."

Ohizumi could hardly hear Jack for the noise on the street. Ohizumi intended doing just that, leaving the office if he smelled anything. The money was not all his; a part of it belonged to Moriwaki, his partner in this business.

They turned the corner and entered a street that was like the bottom of a gorge, then stopped in front of a six-story building with granite stone steps. They walked up to the third floor—they did not use the elevator—and knocked on a door. Beside the door hung a small wooden plaque with Buchanan's name in Japanese. Ohizumi did not fail to note the position of the elevator before he reached that door.

Inside, they were shown to some chairs by a tall blonde who disappeared into the next room. "Let's sit down," Jack said and buried himself in a big chair.

Ohizumi followed suit, and asked, "What kind of a fellow is this Buchanan?" He said it as if wondering about it himself, and not as a question. "What does he do?" This was more like a question.

"I really don't know," Jack said.

Ohizumi had asked the same thing before on the way here and got the same answer. At that time Ohizumi had thought Jack wanted to keep his client's business a secret—not say too much about him—but Ohizumi understood now that Jack really did not know. He made sure of the two exits—one that they had just used and the other through which the blonde had disappeared.

There are those who run away after getting the money, and those who point a gun, he thought. "Did you do your business in this room, too?" he asked Jack.

"Yes, I waited a long time then, too," Jack answered. "Not even a cup of tea. I don't even remember what Buchanan looks like. Come to think of it, I don't even know that it was him," he muttered between puffs of his cigarette.

The fact that Buchanan was willing to buy five thousand dollars told Ohizumi that he was not just an ordinary black market dollar dealer. Ohizumi looked at his watch. It was past three. If he was robbed of this money, he would be finished. He had never been robbed before, but he knew of many who had. One of them committed suicide. It was a distasteful business, but the takes were big. Even after dividing the share with Moriwaki, there should be one thousand yen in it for him.

Twenty minutes passed. He'd finished three cigarettes. "He makes us wait, doesn't he?" Ohizumi said quietly, but he was restless inside.

"What do you want to do?" Jack asked. Ohizumi knew he couldn't say much; they might be listening in the next room.

Ohizumi looked at his watch again. Thirty minutes had passed, but still no Buchanan. To Ohizumi, Buchanan was "first time," but to Buchanan too, Ohizumi was "first time." There was no reason for him not suspecting that Ohizumi might be a cop. Ohizumi was beginning to feel a choking sensation. "It's a bad business, this black market." He tried to think of Takako to calm his nerves.

He'd met Takako in one of the new cabarets. The mouth that dimpled when she smiled was terribly sexy. He had divorced his former wife who had two children by him because she would not come in with him on his black market dealings. Takako told him to quit as soon as he made enough money to start a bar. Most of what he'd made in the past was spent in divorcing his first wife, in marrying Takako, and in buying his hideout in Kamakura. He'd had to start all over again at the beginning of this year—but now, at the end of the year, he had made just about enough to start a bar. I'll quit this time for sure, he thought.

Wonder what she is doing now. She didn't want me to come to Tokyo today. I didn't either, for that matter. Ohizumi was thinking these things when the door to the next room suddenly opened.

Ohizumi got up and took a few steps backward, his eyes glued to the big man that walked in with a package under his arm. From past experience Ohizumi felt that it was going to be all right, but it was best to be on guard.

"Did you bring the stuff?" Buchanan asked in broken Japanese, looking at Jack searchingly.

"This fellow has it," Jack answered. He had also gotten to his feet. "This is the one I told you about over the telephone a while ago."

Buchanan shifted his searching gaze from Jack to Ohizumi.

"I have it here," Ohizumi patted his breast pocket. Buchanan put the package on the table. Ohizumi saw at once that it was in thousand-yen notes, for the package, two million yen, would be about one foot four inches square. As these calculations flashed through his mind, Ohizumi's nimble hand unbuttoned his coat and brought out the envelope containing the dollars. Jack stood watching.

Ohizumi put the dollars on the table. It was a breath-taking moment. Their glances imparted fire. Ohizumi did not think anything. He only followed the other's motions. Everything, even his life, depended on this moment, but he did not even think of that.

The deal was over. Ohizumi divided the thousand-yen notes into two, put one into the envelope, and the other into his grip.

Buchanan did not say anything unnecessary. Ohizumi wondered if Buchanan was a German. He did not seem like an American, nor Australian. He imparted a heavy feeling. Ohizumi walked to the door, thinking, Best not to show my back to him.

After getting out of the building, he hurried to the station. He felt the fears that he had not been aware of when he exchanged the money with Buchanan. It's best to return to Kamakura as quickly as possible, he thought. This is the last deal in dollars, the last business of the year for me.

He felt elated when he entered the second-class car of the Yokosuka line. But when he reached home a foreigner was waiting for him. He had brought eight thousand dollars. Ohizumi took it against his better judgment. Maybe it was because the deal with Buchanan had gone off so smoothly, maybe because he had been at the business for years.

Takako was furious. "You said yesterday with that five thousand dollars that you were through."

Ohizumi could not answer back. He felt the error too keenly himself. "It was your fault, Nancy," he answered, using his pet name for her. "You should have sent him back and not let him wait for me."

"All the money we saved to open a bar," she said in tears. "The day after tomorrow is Christmas Eve. Tomorrow I wanted to go shopping with you on the Ginza."

He had invested more than two million yen in this deal. He remembered Jack's advice. But the price had been so cheap. If successful, the profit would be terrific.

"I'll get rid of it tomorrow. Think, we'll net five hundred thousand. We need all the money we can get to start a bar, you know that."

"I know, yes," Takako answered but not cheerfully. "I know the more, the better. But I'm worried."

"Don't worry, I'll get rid of it," he said, trying his best to make Takako feel at ease. "We'll clean up everything the day after tomorrow, celebrate the Eve in Ginza, and leave for Osaka. We'll start the preparations for the bar after we come back, if the coast is clear."

Next day, Ohizumi sat alone in his living room, thinking. The night before he had succeeded in making Takako believe that everything would be all right, but he himself did not really know where to turn to get rid of the eight thousand dollars. He couldn't ask Jack any more. He thought of his co-worker in Yokosuka, but knew he could not handle such a big amount. Then he remembered Peter Nemuro, a boxer by profession. Peter had once traded dollars, but although quick with his fists, he had not been so with his brain; he had suffered one big loss after another and finally quit. He might know of someone. Ohizumi called him in Tokyo by phone. Peter, after hearing that Ohizumi could not talk over the phone, agreed to come to Kamakura immediately.

When Peter came, and listened to Ohizumi, he advised him to go to Jack. Ohizumi told him in detail about his deal with Buchanan. "I think Jack was right. There's only two days to Christmas, you know," he said, and folded his arms.

Then he thought of Fukumoto, who was once a member of the boxing club Peter belonged to.

"Can you contact him right away?" Ohizumi asked quickly, and added, "Can't lose any time, you know."

Peter left after promising to contact Fukumoto immediately. Ohizumi gave him five thousand yen and assurance that there would be more after the deal went through.

The arrangement was made that day for Ohizumi to meet Fukumoto at a tea shop called the Milano off the Ginza. Ohizumi's identification was a brown overcoat and gold-rimmed glasses and Fukumoto, he was told, was a small, pale-faced fellow.

Ohizumi called Moriwaki, his partner, and told him he would call on him about noon the next day, and told him to wait for him. Moriwaki had invested five hundred thousand, and after the deal was over Ohizumi intended to clear the account with him, and wash his hands of the whole nasty business.

When Ohizumi went to the Milano the next day, a small, pale-faced fellow got up from the corner booth. Ohizumi walked up to him.

"Glad to meet you," said the pale-faced fellow and smiled. He was well-mannered, which gave Ohizumi the feeling he was not quite dependable. Then to his mind came the face of Takako who had said with a dark expression just before he left, "I have a bad feeling this morning. Somehow, I don't want you to go today."

He shook off his sense of foreboding and immediately started to talk business. "Is it you who wants to trade?" he asked.

"No, it's not me," Fukumoto answered quickly. "As soon as Peter called me last night, I contacted several and came across a fellow named Seki who said he would buy."

"I see. Where is this fellow Seki?"

"I contacted him just before I came here," Fukumoto continued. "Made arrangements for you to make a deal at the place called Kagetsu in Tsukiji."

Ohizumi wondered why Fukumoto would not take him to Seki's house. He also wondered why he had to wait until three that afternoon. He would have to call Moriwaki and extend the hour of appointment with him.

"It's big money, you know," Fukumoto said. At present market prices what Ohizumi had was equivalent to three million yen. "I suppose Seki has to get the money ready."

"All right then," Ohizumi said. "I'll meet you there with Seki at three. You sure he'll be there?"

"Oh, sure," Fukumoto said.

From there he went to Moriwaki and told him to accompany him to Tsukiji that afternoon. Moriwaki was skeptical about the way Ohizumi did his business, and said for him to divide his money. Ohizumi replied he did not have time, that he had to get rid of it before Christmas. And all the time he was talking to Moriwaki, he was thinking of Takako, and the prospective bar he was going to operate with her. With her looks it was a cinch men would flock to her bar like bees to flowers. What made him think so much about his new bar was probably his appointment in Tsukiji. About three years earlier at the height of his business he had frequented a place called Kiki-no-ya, the House of Chrysanthemum, in the red light district. He had become chummy with a geisha called Kikuharu, Spring Chrysanthemum. That was before he met Takako. Fond memories of those days came back to him and he only half-heard what Moriwaki was trying to say to him. "Well then, let's meet this fellow Seki," Moriwaki said in the end. "If anything smells bad, all we have to say is we didn't bring the money. Where are we meeting him?"

"That's the funny thing. It's close to Kiku-no-ya."

"Really?" Moriwaki was also amused. "That's very interesting." Moriwaki and Ohizumi both laughed knowingly.

After a quick lunch they left Moriwaki's apartment early. They went straight to Tsukiji to have a look at the place first. Moriwaki carried the money, for they thought it best that Ohizumi should go there alone without anything on him. They first went to a small tea shop where there was a phone. Ohizumi took down the phone number and told Moriwaki to come to Kagetsu as soon as he called.

Ohizumi then went to Kagetsu. The house had a black fence on the street side, which shut out the street noise. Once inside, Ohizumi had the illusion that he had come far, far away from the Ginza. The girl who met him at the entrance hall took him to a room with an expensive-looking *tokonoma*, with all its usual hanging scrolls, flower arrangement and art objects. She asked him to wait. She sat on the *tatami* at the exit, her finger tips touching the *tatami* as she bowed, got up, slipped out, got down on her knees again to close the sliding partition. Her quiet graceful manners, typical of *machiai* or tea house and high-class Japanese restaurant waitresses, reminded him again of the time he used to come to these places often. Then he was dealing in cigarettes and food stuffs, sending out his assistants with two or three truck loads every day. His biggest clients were these *machiai* places and high-class restaurants.

While Ohizumi sat thinking of these things, the partition opened and Fukumoto came in. "Seki was waiting for you, but he said you might be late and he went to the theater," he explained as he sat down. Ohizumi thought it odd. He knew he was not very late. He thought afterward that this was when he should have smelled something, when he should have quit the place.

"Did you bring the money with you this time?" Fukumoto asked.

"I don't have it with me now," Ohizumi said. "But my partner has it—he's waiting for my call in a nearby tea shop."

"Well then, please call him," Fukumoto said getting to his feet again. "I'll send for Seki at the theater." He left the room.

Ohizumi called Moriwaki, and told him to come. In the meantime, the waitress carried in cakes and fruit and put them on the table. Moriwaki came immediately, and Fukumoto joined them, saying Seki would come right away. Ohizumi thought it odd again; for he knew that though it takes a little time to call a person out from a theater, this was taking a little too long. Just then the partition at Ohizumi's back opened wide, and three big foreigners came in. Ohizumi and the others jumped to their feet. One of the three foreigners, a red-faced giant of a fellow, pointed a gun at them.

"We're C.I.D.s," he barked. "Put up your hands."

Ohizumi was quiet. He slowly put his hands up, and scrutinized Fukumoto sharply. Fukumoto was pale. Ohizumi wondered if this was Fukumoto's doing.

"Why are you carrying dollars?" the red face continued. "We're going to question you."

Ohizumi thought then that they were fakes. The investigations were always carried out at headquarters, not at a place like this. He thought of all these things while watching one of the three men search Moriwaki, and take out the eight thousand dollars he had in his pocket. He gritted his teeth— Ohizumi would not have let him have it that easy; he would have jumped out of the window before he let these fakes have it.

"It's our business if we carry dollars," Ohizumi yelled. "We carry any amount for our business. If you want to investigate, take us to your headquarters."

"We'll take you to headquarters," the big fellow said, with a mocking smile. "Walk," he said, and pointed the gun at the three Japanese.

Seki did not show up till the end.

After they were shoved into a car, the three foreigners stopped another taxi. This fact assured Ohizumi that they were fakes; if they had been C.I.D.s, they would have been there with a jeep. Inside, alone in the car, Ohizumi put his big hands around Fukumoto's neck. "How dare you fool us like this?" Ohizumi said between his teeth.

"I don't know, I don't know anything," Fukumoto wailed and cried like a baby.

"Then it's Seki, Fukumoto was only a decoy," Ohizumi decided.

The car with the three foreigners was following their car, but the distance between the two got greater and greater, and finally it disappeared.

"Turn the car back to Kagetsu," Ohizumi ordered. But the people at Kagetsu did not know Seki, said he had never been there before.

Ohizumi turned again to Fukumoto, but he only sobbed, "I only did it so I might make some extra money for the New Year."

Fukumoto knew the apartment where Seki lived, but when they went there Seki had already moved out. They learned then that Seki was a Chinese by the name of Sai. Ohizumi, for the first time, ate dirt—and hard.

Just as he came out of the Ikuta Building, Ohizumi was stopped by a policeman.

"I want to ask you something," he said. Ohizumi did his best to suppress his fear and remain calm. Could Fukumoto, whom he had just left, have reported him? It couldn't be.

"What do you want," Ohizumi said slowly.

"Not here," said the policeman, "Please come to headquarters." The policeman was extremely polite, with a faint smile flickering around his mouth all the time. Ohizumi was glad he did not have any dollars on him. In his pocket were a few yen notes, and an I.O.U. he'd just had Fukumoto write out for the money he'd been robbed of by the fake C.I.D.s. He wanted to report the robbery but to do that was to chance being arrested himself.

"I am not doing anything," he said, his eyes darting sharply right and left, remembering to keep a smile. "I don't know what you want, but ask me here, if you want."

"It won't take you long," said the young policeman, still polite. "I only want you to come with me for a little while."

The policeman was asking him, not ordering him. Perhaps it is nothing to worry about, Ohizumi told himself. Because of his past job during the war—he was once a private secretary of a minister— he had many friends everywhere. If anything went wrong, he could ask their help, though he wasn't quite sure about getting it.

"If you are not going to tell me why, I don't have to go," Ohizumi said firmly. "I am busy. Besides if you want to arrest me, you'll have to take the proper procedure."

The policeman seemed to think it best not to rile him. He said gently, "Were you not robbed of some dollars by some fake C.I.D.s?"

So that's it, it was Fukumoto. He reported because he couldn't pay. The reason he was robbed was because Fukumoto was a fool and was now trying to get him this way— I'll kill him! He mulled these things over in his mind quickly.

"Don't know anything about fake C.I.D.s," he barked. "I'm busy, don't you see? I can't be bothered. I live in Kamakura, and come to Tokyo only to do business."

"We know you live in Kamakura," the policeman said. "Do you come to Tokyo every day these days?" The policeman's manner remained calm and polite. Cold sweat came over Ohizumi; so they were following him. "There were others who were robbed besides you," the policeman continued, unmindful of Ohizumi's fear. "One of them reported and the fake C.I.D.s were picked up. They confessed everything. We checked with the *machiai* house in Tsukiji about you."

Ohizumi thought for a moment to give up to the police, and then changed his mind quickly. What's wrong with me these days? he thought. If I complain, I'm only confirming that I traded in dollars.

Conversation dragged on for a while but in the end the policeman gave up, and said, "I'll report to my chief that you would not come. That's all I can do for now," and they parted.

Clad in a dull, yolk-colored overcoat of English material, Ohizumi looked the prosperous businessman, but since the fake C.I.D. incident, his money was all gone, and he was having a hard time figuring out how he was going to pay his bills. He walked into the Lilac tea shop, where he had once carried out million-yen deals.

"Has Akiyama been here?" he asked the head waiter.

"No," he answered without changing expression, and whispered something to a waitress.

She came up to Ohizumi and said in a low voice, "Mr. Akiyama called and said he would be here about four," and left to fill his order.

"Wonder what he wants." Ohizumi looked at his watch. Forty minutes more until four. He drank his coffee, and left the tea shop to kill time, leaving word that he would be back.

When he got back, Akiyama was waiting for him. "I've news for you," Akiyama said as soon as he saw Ohizumi. Akiyama was excited. "Kamioka is here in Tokyo. He's driving a big car. One of the only three such cars in Japan now, the latest model Chrysler."

Kamioka was in the textile black market, but Ohizumi had loaned him money a couple of times before. "He went to Kobe, didn't he?" Ohizumi asked. "I think of him once in a while. He was a quiet fellow," he added.

"Said he wanted to see you," Akiyama went on. "He will be here at two tomorrow. I thought sure he was having a hard time," said Akiyama.

"Yeah, he was kind of slow, as I remember him," Ohizumi said. "Is he an auto broker?"

"No, I think he's in this," and Akiyama made a gesture of giving a shot to his knee.

"Maybe I'll borrow some money from him," Ohizumi said, thinking back to the days when he was able to lend one or two million yen to his friends easily. Now his position had been reversed.

"Kamioka wants me to go to Kobe with him, and I think I will," Akiyama said. "He said he'd find me clients. I've got to deal with foreigners in my line of business. Why don't you go, too?"

"If I were young like you—" Ohizumi said. He didn't know what Takako would say.

Akiyama smiled at that. Ohizumi, who once couldn't be without a woman one night, had stopped going to bars and cabarets after he had married Takako. After the baby, Tamako, was born, he went home early every night

Ohizumi met Kamioka at the Lilac the next day. He looked quite dapper in his gray overcoat and soft hat. When he had gone home the night before, he'd told Takako about being stopped by the police and about Kamioka, and told her that he might borrow some money from him. Takako was pleased, and they both forgot about the nasty business of the police, talking for hours about opening the bar.

"Let's go out," Kamioka said, after the greetings were over. "I've got my car outside."

The car they got into passed the front of the Piccadilly Theater and crossed the bridge. Kamioka came close to Ohizumi, and said low, "Heard about your mishap at Tsukiji. It was a darn shame."

"Yeah, a rotten business," Ohizumi said. "The place made me a bit careless. And I got stopped by police yesterday, too. One bad thing after another. I want to quit this business and start a bar with my wife," he said in the end. "I want to help your work a few days, to make enough to start this bar."

Kamioka put his hand into his pocket and drew out a newspaper bundle. "Please use this," he said. "I have lots of money now."

"I will borrow it then," Ohizumi said. He felt the money from outside, and thought it contained about a million yen. "I am going to use this money to help you, and make some capital for the bar. I have a hunch the police are after me, so I don't want to take too many chances, and also, I want to quit it in two or three days."

"Okay," Kamioka said cheerfully. "I'll make the contacts for you right away. My name's George Mizuki, remember."

Their business was risky. They made a lot at a time, but they lost big, too. Once Ohizumi was followed by the police and he had to throw into a gutter drugs worth five hundred thousand yen. At one time a loss of three million yen meant nothing to him. Now everything was different. It had become hard work to make fifty thousand.

When he went home, Takako met him with a letter from the policeman he'd met that day in Tokyo. It said that the police would not inconvenience him in any way, and therefore wished him to come to police headquarters.

In the course of the following few days, he was followed constantly by the police. In three days he made enough money to start the bar and was busy getting things into shape.

One day after he had been to see Fukumoto to get the money the latter was paying him bit by bit, he was walking toward the Lilac to meet Sedo, his new partner in the bar business whom Akiyama had introduced him to. He was told that Sedo's wife had worked in a bar, and that Sedo was once a manager in a hotel in Atami. He neared Sukiyabashi Bridge, and turned back, from sheer habit, only to see the same old policeman. Cold sweat came over him.

"You did not come after all," the policeman said, smiling. "We waited for you."

"But don't you see," Ohizumi had calmed by this time, "as I told you the last time, I had nothing to do with it."

"There are Japanese, Koreans, and Chinese who were robbed just like you," the young policeman said quietly. "The total money stolen was fifteen million yen. The fake C.I.D. men were caught, but we need witnesses to confirm the crime. I'll see that no harm will come to you. Please come with me."

"But I am busy," Ohizumi answered bluntly.

"I know that, but the American court requires witnesses." The policeman was half pleading. "Those who were robbed all say the same thing you do."

"If you make it so that I was robbed of yen," Ohizumi said, "then I'll come with you."

"That's all right," the policeman was quick to agree. "All you have to say is that you were robbed by the men in Tsukiji."

"If you fool me, I'll never forgive you," Ohizumi threatened.

"Sure thing," the policeman assured. "I won't cause you any trouble."

Ohizumi got into a taxi with him. When they arrived at headquarters and saw the officer in charge, Ohizumi was told that the man who reported the robbery was a Japanese, a former Navy Officer. He was robbed of eight hundred dollars, but when the fake C.I.D.s got in the jeep, he took the number and reported. They arrested a C.I.D. First Lieutenant, by the name of Burton, and another C.I.D. Sergeant by the name of Michael.

"Burton has confessed," the officer told Ohizumi. "They asked us to investigate, and your name came up."

"I thought it was kind of funny," Ohizumi admitted. "But I could do nothing at the point of a gun."

"They are going to have a trial next Thursday," the officer continued, "And we want you to appear as a witness."

"I am busy with my business," Ohizumi told the officer.

"We know that, but according to the American procedures they cannot establish a crime unless supported by witnesses," the officer explained. "We had about three appearing, but they all backed down at the crucial time. We want you to please have courage and be a witness."

The officer pleaded with him. Ohizumi thought of Takako and the newborn baby. After all, the dollars robbed from him would not return, and he did not want any part in a trial. But at the same time he did not want to be labeled a coward. The police had been following him for the last few days, and must know of his activities in dope peddling. It might be wiser to listen to their wish now.

"The policeman who brought me here said you would fix it so that I was robbed of yen and not dollars," Ohizumi said. "I'll be the witness with that agreement."

"Yes, that's all right. We'll do that," the officer said, an expression of relief coming over him.

"I have my wife and a baby to think of, you know," Ohizumi said. "I don't want to be pinched, on top of being robbed."

"I don't blame you a bit," the officer said, smiling. "The court martial will be held not very far from here. You can go see the officer of the judicial affairs across the street from there and work it out with him."

Ohizumi knew that it was bad to deal in black market dollars. But it was not only men like him who dealt in them. There were many politicians who bought dollars in large amounts. If the military law officer would agree to Ohizumi's proposition, he had decided to be their witness, to prevent more Japanese being robbed by men like Burton and Michael.

He spent the rest of the day on the business of his new bar. He doubled the money he borrowed from Kamioka in three days and returned the million he had borrowed. For the new bar, Sedo would put in two million yen, just twice Ohizumi's amount. The profit would be divided into four and six. Ohizumi also agreed to register the bar under Sedo's wife's name, in order to be prepared for any unforeseen outcome of the military trial.

The next day he went to see the judiciary officer to get his agreement.

On the day of the trial he went to the place as directed. He got off the elevator on the fourth floor, and started to walk down the hall. He met a huge man—a face he had not forgotten. Seeing Ohizumi, the man growled to him in broken Japanese. "If you testify, I'll do this to you," and he drew his open hand across his throat. "You'll be sent to Okinawa, maybe."

According to American law, until a crime is established against a person, that man can go about as a free man. No wonder no one was willing to testify.

Ohizumi only smiled. He had given up the dollar black market. He'd already got the money to start his bar. He had returned the money to Kamioka, too. If anything should happen to him, Takako and his baby could live on the profit from the bar.

He entered the waiting room. There were two Chinese, a man and a woman, both young. They had dark expressions on their faces. Burton came in, this time with another tall fellow Ohizumi remembered. This must be Michael. They both threatened in their broken Japanese, while an MP looked on expressionless.

The time came and they entered the court room. When he sat down in the witness chair, he forgot about Takako and his baby. He forgot about the new bar he was about to open. He only remembered the mortifying feeling he went through when he was robbed by the two men he was about to testify against.

"These are the men," he yelled. "These are the ones who robbed me of three million yen," he said, renewing the fear and remorse he felt when the money was taken from him.

About a month later, he heard Burton and Michael had been sent back to their country. He was paid for the four days he spent testifying at the court.

His new bar was opened near Kyobashi. It was christened the Pearl, but Sedo and his wife would not give him his share of the profit.

It was registered under Sedo's wife's name, so there was nothing Ohizumi could do about it.

Ohizumi gave it all up. He just wasn't cut out for the rackets. There was an honest job open in a lumber company and he made an appointment with the personnel director.

PLEASE NOT A WORD TO ANYBODY

by *Mizuki Yoko*

I DON'T REMEMBER when Mrs. Komori first came to our neighborhood or when she moved away, but I do remember how I was attracted by her native manners. We never once passed on the street with just a casual nod of the head. We always exchanged gossip, oh, twenty and thirty minutes at times, sometimes much longer, talking about this and that, mostly that . . .

Then I began to see less and less of her and when I did see her I noticed that she had lost some of her immaculateness.

Just before I saw her last, I noticed she spent more and more time in the vacant lot in front of the local shrine, playing absent-mindedly with her two small children, or pushing the carriage to and fro intently.

"The old lady Yano died recently," she said one day.

"What? When?"

"About ten days ago," she said in a low voice. "But, please, not a word to anybody. It's sort of a secret."

"But why?" I asked, curious.

"Well, you remember she never joined any of the neighborhood donations. We thought it best not to bother anybody."

The old lady Yano was Mrs. Komori's landlady. She was a notoriously mean woman, not just stingy, but downright mean. There is always one like her in every community. She never once put money into any neighborhood collection for sick donations or bereavements, saying she needed special consideration herself although

149

everyone knew she had quite a bit of money hoarded away. She had let the Komoris have the room, called Western style because it had a wooden floor instead of one of *tatami*, with the understanding that they move out when the baby came. But when the baby did come, and it took to the old lady, she became friendly and said they could postpone moving until the baby entered school.

Once, quite some time ago, when I first came back from the country, to which I had evacuated from the threats of air raids, I went to get old lady Yano's bag and money for the rice ration. She was sitting in her dark three-mat room in the center of the house, the only room she kept for herself since renting out all of her rooms. An old velvet scarf, in vogue years ago, was wrapped tightly around her head; she sat before a chest of drawers, the like of which can only now be found in some antique shop—you know the kind, black, inlaid sparingly with mother-of-pearl. What aroused my curiosity further was the money bag she had—a black leather thing, the kind my mother used to call an "opera bag," and that I used to see only in pictures carried by grand old dames of the Meiji or Taisho eras. This bag and the lute that stood against the inlaid chest impressed me and stayed in my mind a long time.

"Who was she before?" I asked myself many times. I knew nothing of her background, for she had moved to our neighborhood while I was in the country.

What I heard about her later was that her husband was at one time a fairly well-known journalist and had owned a small paper in the country, but her married life had not been very happy as her husband had a woman on the side. They never had any children and after her husband died, the girl she raised, adopted from a distant relative, ran away with a lover. Old lady Yano later adopted a grown-up youth, and the neighbors remember how happily she took this adopted son's new bride around to introduce her to them; they felt sorry for her when the young couple felt the old lady was a burden, left her alone in the big old house, and went away to live in the country where he got a job as a teacher in a small college.

But the sympathy was short-lived. Old lady Yano rented out all of her rooms. Everyone knew she had more money than she could spend, yet she was never friendly with neighbors.

She had died of cerebral hemorrhage. Mrs. Komori sent a telegram to the adopted son and did everything she could to help. She was appalled, however, when the son came with his wife and had no sooner arrived than he put the old lady into a coffin and took her away to be cremated. They didn't even see to it that her body was bathed, let alone changed her clothes into the customary white kimono, traveling hat and straw-sandaled costume to prepare her for the long journey to the other world. The kimono for the dead is always sewn by three people, so Mrs. Komori would have known had a third person been called on to help.

"These young people nowadays." The tenants all shook their heads.

The young couple announced that the house was now theirs and they were going to move in; they wanted all the tenants to move out as soon as possible. The tenants protested that it was next to impossible to find another place with only a few days' notice. The couple moved in anyway, and immediately started to complain that their children quarrelled with the Komoris' and that the Komoris made too much noise.

"So, the only thing to do is to spend the daytime like this, to keep the children separated," Mrs. Komori smiled faintly. "But I don't mind this nearly so much as their suspicious nature."

The couple were sure that the old lady had some money put away somewhere and they had started to search. They lifted the *tatami*, they took down the ceilings and panels, but no money was found.

"The way they look at us, I'm sure they suspect us." Mrs. Komori put on an expression of sheer perplexity.

"It is funny, isn't it, that there is not a yen anywhere?" I put in, equally perplexed.

"But you see," Mrs. Komori came close to me and said almost in a whisper, "I saw her get the money out one time from a money bag she kept inside her kimono, between herself and the *obisashi*. She kept it there all the time, day and night. There was a lot of money in it. They should have at least changed her clothes when they put her into the coffin. I must find some place to move to." She smiled again faintly. "Come to think of it, she wasn't such a bad woman."

I never saw Mrs. Komori after that.

UPS AND DOWNS

by Shibaki Yoshiko

A LITTER of two-month-old pups, three in all, had just been fed their supper of ground meat and rice gruel. Their tummies full, they became lively and climbed all over her lap.

"No, no. Not till you get your mouths and ears wiped," and she cleaned gruel from their long ears and around their mouths.

Saeko was raising them to make some money, but she had a genuine love for them, too, so that she wished to sell them to some nice people who would take good care of them. She thought of her many friends, not entirely without envy, who had married well. She herself was happy, if not too well off, as she would have been were it not for the war.

Her husband, a college professor, did not bring much money home. She had married him out of a girlish craving for a man who might gain fame through his intellect, rather than through physical prowess. But now, looking at the house under construction next door, the speed with which the man next door made his wealth— he was a taxi driver who only a few years ago had opened a small repair shop, and was now building a garage—and comparing it with her own house, she thought that being the wife of a taxi driver wouldn't be so bad. She wondered, at the rate they were going, when she would ever get a new house. That is why she had taken up puppy raising, to help ease the domestic finances. She was aware that to own a pedigreed dog had become a fad among social and well-to-do people. As a prospective buyer of one of her pups she thought of Kuri Reiko, her old school chum.

Reiko, daughter of a well-known Doctor of Law, was married to the son of another prominent business man. Two or three years after the war had ended, Saeko's graduating class got together. It was the first time in years. They had met regularly up till the first few years of the war. In the chaotic social conditions that followed the end of the war, social get-togethers were rare. For one thing, no one knew where anybody else was. But as things gradually returned to normal, the girls came together to talk over the hard times they had had. They came, most of them dressed in drab clothes, but not minding it at all. Among this drably dressed group Saeko remembered how Reiko shone. She looked radiant, not only because of her natural beauty, but because she was dressed immaculately. Everyone looked at her with envy. She had come to the meeting in her own private car. Somehow, Reiko always had, even from their school days, a natural charm which prevented other women from being jealous of her good fortune. Maybe it was because she was not haughty, though she was proud. Reiko told the girls gathered there that her husband was doing very well.

But Saeko had since heard Reiko's husband was not doing so well, that they had sold their house in Tokyo and retired to their villa in Chiba prefecture.

"It must be a nice little villa by the sea," dreamed Saeko. "Just the home for one of my puppies."

The pups had played themselves out, and were now sound asleep, piled up on top of each other.

Her small son came running into the house. "A policeman followed me from the school, and he is now standing outside, Mummy," he told her.

Her heart made a small jump as she heard the word "police," and went to the door, wondering what he could want of her.

"You are Mrs. Suzaka, the wife of Suzaka Keitaro?" the young policeman asked her politely.

"Yes, that's right." Her voice shook a little as she heard her husband's name mentioned by the police.

"Do you know a woman by the name of Kuri Reiko?"

"Yes, I know her," she answered, relieved, but wondering at the odd coincidence. "What has happened to Mrs. Kuri?"

"She's been arrested, but she's being released," he said. "She has to be released in custody of someone, and she mentioned your husband's name."

"But isn't there some mistake?" Saeko said, unable to believe her ears. "She is not the type to be arrested. She comes from a very good family."

"Yes, of course," the young policeman admitted, and looked ill-at-ease.

"Tell me," Saiko persisted. "What has she done?"

"I don't know the details," the policeman said. "I was sent here by my chief, but I heard it was a light offense."

"Well, I'll go to the police station," Saeko said firmly. "I have to first make sure."

The policeman thanked her and went away.

The atmosphere of the police station was oppressive, even to Saeko with her clear conscience. She could not enter into it as light-heartedly as she would a post office. When she sat before the officer in charge of Kuri Reiko, she had the feeling that she herself was being questioned, though the officer was very polite. She noticed the sharp difference between his manner and the cold arrogant manners of the pre-war police of the Imperial Government. The officer asked her about her relationship with Reiko, and about Reiko herself.

"Well, then it is true that she's from a good family, as she insisted she was," the officer said in the end. "Come to think, she does have that air about her."

"I have not seen her for two or three years," Saeko asked. "What has she done?"

"Shoplifting," he answered. "Her second offense."

Saeko turned pale. She was astounded, it was the last thing she had expected.

"She did it twice in the same shop, a second-hand clothes shop. The owner wants her indicted, but being a wife and a mother, we decided to release her in the custody of some socially responsible person. She would not tell us the names of her own people."

Presently a haggard-looking woman was brought before Saeko. She wore a skirt too short for her and a faded sweater. Saeko could not recognize the woman at first. Then, as the contours of her face became clear, she saw the woman was Reiko and she could hardly believe her eyes.

The officer gave a short lecture and said, after the brief procedure to effect Reiko's release, "Please take her home and have your husband give her a good talk."

Once outside, Saeko took Reiko to a nearby noodle shop. After a bowl of hot noodles, faint color reappeared in Reiko's pale cheeks and she smiled for the first time. "Thank you very much," she murmured. "I have not eaten for three days."

"For three days?" Saeko was appalled.

"Yes, three solid days. You see, it was my only way to show my resistance. They called me a thief. I am not. How could I do such a thing, and disgrace my family and my parents' name? You know that, you know I am not that kind." She said these things in one breath, and her eyes shone in her otherwise dull face with outrage.

"Yes, yes, I know," Saeko said, trying to comfort her. "Tell me about it."

"I don't know where to begin," said Reiko, looking lost.

"The last I heard about you, you had moved to Chiba," Saeko said, by way of helping her. She refrained from telling Reiko that she had been considering her as one of the prospective buyers of her puppies.

"That was such a long time ago," Reiko said dreamily. Actually it had been only three or four years.

Then Reiko began to explain. The last time she and Saeko had been together was during the time when her husband Kuri began to fail in his business. They had to sell their house in Tokyo. Immediately after the war ended, Kuri, who made use of his grandfather's connection with the pre-war, government-subsidized South Manchurian Railway Company, supplied materials to the Japanese government railways. It was still the time when things were scarce and everything he touched made money. But as things returned to normal and pre-war companies got back on their feet, the competition became too keen. As a last hope, he put everything into selling the railroad a patent. He spent a great deal of money bribing officials, dreaming that once he succeeded, his company would grow tenfold. He failed and lost everything.

Reiko took her two small children and went to Chiba. Kuri went to Tokyo every day to find some capital. He used to bring home men Reiko never saw before, men whose looks made her distrust them immediately, but her husband asked her to entertain them, and she used to sell her kimonos and obis to do it.

Some of her husband's friends tried to find him a job, but he would not let go of his desire to have a business of his own. "My life is through if I have to be tied to somebody with a meager salary," he used to say. He told Reiko that he was sure to make good once more, and she believed him; and, believing him, did not hesitate to sell her clothes. Saeko remembered that Reiko's trousseau was the talk of her friends. Reiko sold her kimonos one by one.

"At first, it was fun to get cash for a kimono, a kimono I was tired of, or that I was too old for, I was not a bit sorry to sell," Reiko said. "The children were still small so I kept my maid. You see, I did not know what it is to economize," she said, laughing to cover her embarrassment.

She didn't know when Kuri did it, but after about two years in Chiba, she found out that the villa there had been mortgaged, and they had to move back to Tokyo. They found a small room in the suburbs of Tokyo, not far from where Saeko lived. She gave up her maid, but she was the type that could not call on her relatives without taking a present, even if she had to sell one of her obis to raise the money. It was the training she'd received from her grandmother, who had gone to Peers' school. But no matter where she went, she met only criticism of her husband. Some even suggested that she get a divorce, though no one offered to take in her and her two small children.

She herself had no ability to earn a living. She had been trained to be a wife and a mother. Piano, flower arrangement, tea ceremony and dress-making studied when a girl were all useless as a means of earning a livelihood. Her only hope was in Kuri. Kuri kept saying that he would make good once more and she blindly believed him. She was disappointed in him and no longer loved him, but she continued to believe, as he believed, that he would make a comeback. It was the kind of belief that only they could understand. They had to have it because it was all they had.

About three months before, Kuri wanted to take a trip to Osaka in a desperate effort to find a backer. He had no money to buy a ticket, and as he told her that he was certain of the success of this trip, she took her last kimono and *haori* coat to the second-hand kimono shop she always dealt with.

"This kimono and this *haori* I don't want to sell," she told the shopkeeper. "I want to borrow some money with them. As soon as my husband makes some money, I will come back to get them, so please do not put them on sale until then."

"That's all right," said the shopkeeper, and gave her the money.

The kimono and *haori* she left at the shop were old; they were her mother's last present before she died. Reiko recalled the sadness she felt when she lost her mother. She consoled herself with the idea that they would be returned to her as soon as Kuri came back from Osaka. But in spite of this sacrifice on her part, Kuri returned empty-handed.

"What are we going to do?" she asked her husband. "We have nothing to eat."

"Go to some relative or a friend and borrow some money," he ordered.

"I have nothing to wear to go out."

"I'll make some money soon."

"Have you made any at all lately?"

"This time for sure," Kuri smiled. "The House of Kuri has a large piece of land in Aoyama cemetery. We don't need that big space. I am going to sell a part of it."

"What a thing to say," and she loathed her husband as she never did before, for even thinking such a thing.

She had to go some place to borrow some money, and to do so she needed clothes to wear. She went to the second-hand kimono shop, and asked the shop owner to let her have the kimono and *haori* for just one day. He refused and would not listen to all her pleadings. In the end, taking advantage of another client that came in, she made for the kimono and *haori* and started to go out. The shopkeeper grabbed her, took her kimono and *haori* from her, and knocked her down in the scuffle. She almost died of shame. She was furious when she thought of the money the shopkeeper had made through her kimonos during the past three years. She thought she would not hesitate to sell the family cemetery, even her life, to avenge this.

Kuri continued to dream of the great business he would again transact. "I am going to try once more," he said, and left the house without saying where he was going.

Kuri did not return. She spent a week as if dead. Then one night after a heavy snowfall she went out into the street. When she passed the front of the secondhand kimono shop, she saw her own kimono in the window, for sale. It looked so forlorn to her, it seemed as if it were pleading with her, begging her, to take it away from the store. She went to it, absentmindedly, and held it tight to her breast. That was all she did.

"Did you tell all that at the police station?" Saeko asked.

"Of course I did," she said flatly. "But they would not release me unless someone with good social standing claimed me. I am sorry I made use of your husband, but I could not let this be known among my relatives."

They both looked up at the clock at the same time; they were both thinking of the children who must be waiting for their return.

"Please take something to your children." Saeko gave her some money, unobtrusively.

"Thank you for everything." Reiko bowed low, without looking at the money as she hesitantly accepted. "I shall never forget."

Saeko watched her walk toward the station and stood there until she disappeared into the crowd.

THE ONLY ONE

by Nakamoto Takako

SEIKO ran into Sumiko's all excited, jabbering rapidly. It was about their mutual friend, one of the Tachikawa set, Rose. She had married a GI and was to leave for America soon.

"She's some sharp one, that Rose, ain't she?" finished Seiko, very much affected by the news about Rose. Sumiko didn't seem to care at all, though. Stretched out on her double bed, she just continued all through Seiko's tale to smoke and look up at the sky through the open window. Merely "humphing" intermittently, she felt that Rose was taking a big gamble with her future.

"We are 'only ones' and that's just as good as being married," she offered.

"No, it's not," Seiko answered angrily. "Being married and being an 'only one' are two entirely different things." She crushed her cigarette with her manicured fingers. "Don't be a fool," she continued. "Marriage is the only thing; we can't just go on like this forever."

Sumiko, in her cool and contemptuous manner, saw that Seiko was being terribly stubborn and stupid about the whole thing.

"Gosh, how I wish John would marry me and take me to America. Wouldn't you like that too, Sumiko?"

Sumiko just stared at the ceiling and Seiko, seemingly ignored, started pacing the room impatiently. "This room depresses me," Seiko said. "Let's get out of here and go see that amateur play in the village."

Sumiko, too, wanted to escape from the tenseness of the room. "Yes, let's. My Robert isn't coming tonight." She got up and dressed quickly.

Outside the air was balmy as they walked towards the village theatre. It was a fine spring night and the little village of Nishitama had almost completely covered all of the old scars of the war now six years past.

The theatre was small and packed with people—its air was heavy. The first play of the usual multi-featured program had already started. It was "The Son" by Osanai Kaoru. On stage under the dim lights the story was approaching its climax. Father, the policeman, stood face to face with his own son, whom he sought in the name of the law. As a first attempt by an all amateur cast, the play was effectively done.

The play ended and the lights went on. The audience was quick to notice the presence of Sumiko and Seiko. Whispers of *pon-pon* and *pon-suke* echoed around them, but they were used to this and managed to ignore it with a studied callousness. There were a hundred and fifty more girls like them in the village, and nobody knew where they had come from.

The curtain went up for the second play. A young bride and her mother-in-law were arguing about some minor kitchen matters. "You're nothing but a daughter-in-law," the old matriarch screamed. "You keep your place."

Sumiko bit her lip. Memories flashed into her mind, and she saw herself again as a young bride suffering those same agonies ten years before.

"Get out of here," she heard the old matriarch again. "How dare you answer me back!"

Sumiko bit her lip harder. She fought an urge to leap onto the stage and slap the mother-in-law in the face, as she had wanted to do so many times so long ago. Tears welled in her eyes and rolled down her cheeks. She let out a soft whimper. Crying at a cheap amateur show like this, she said to herself, but the tears kept coming, threatening to turn into sobs. Suddenly the curtain was down, the lights were on, and she was aware that the people around her were staring in amazement, and she heard them whisper, "Imagine! A *pon-pon* crying."

She paid no attention, but Seiko did. She pulled at Sumiko hard and insisted, "Let's get out of here."

Outside the heavy scent of flowers and new leaves filled the air, and the great change from the mustiness of the crowded theatre left them gasping. The scent and sounds seeped deep into Sumiko and moved her to new tears. She wanted to go off and cry alone. Seiko was angry.

"You sure made some scene, didn't you?" she rasped. "They were all looking at us. How could you cry at such a crummy, low-down ham show anyway?"

"I couldn't help it. I tried to stop."

"Sentimentality doesn't become our type. Now, me, you couldn't get a drop of tear out of me even if you shook me upside down. Seeing you cry just makes me sick."

Sumiko felt as if she had broken some unwritten law of her set. Seiko stamped off furiously, her heels clicking sharply in the still night.

Sumiko walked on slowly, taking out-of-the-way deserted roads. She was trying to calm her nerves, but the thickly scented air only seemed to open old memories, and in her loneliness the feelings she had fought down these ten long years gushed out and took hold of her.

"Alone, all alone," she cried to herself bitterly.

As the little scooter came out of the night and stopped by the side of the house it sounded like the wings of a huge bird. Then Robert's face smiled through the window into the room. Sumiko was stretched out on the bed, but didn't get up.

Usually, she welcomed him with a hug and kiss, as she had learned from American movies. She knew if she didn't she would lose him, and with him her meal ticket. But today she just didn't seem to care. Ever since that night of the village play, she had felt accursed. She had been living, heart and soul, back in those dark days in that northern village where she had grown up. Remembering the hopes and aspirations of the young girl she had once been and looking at herself in her present state left her dispirited.

Seeing that she wasn't going to get up, Robert rushed into the room and with the extravagant physical demonstrativeness she felt so typical of Americans, he came towards her. He spread out his hairy arms to take her to him. She shook her head and fended him off. Robert winced and shrugged his shoulders. He took her hands and asked, "What's the matter, baby?"

"Nothing. I just don't feel so good."

She put her hand up to her temple, closed her eyes and turned her head to the side. But Robert put both his hands on her shoulders and sought her lips with his. He kissed her face, took her in his arms and pressed her close to him. Sumiko felt suffocated, and the smell of his body nauseated her.

Sumiko had black hair and black eyes and her face was yellow. Robert's skin, though sun-tanned, glowed pink like all those who eat meat regularly, and his body was covered with fine hair the color of corn. She had held many men like him these last several years, but today, for the first time, the foreign smell stuck in her nose. Their bodies were close, but the waters of the Pacific separated them. Sumiko closed her eyes and resigned herself to what she knew must follow.

Robert sought only to satisfy his own selfish desires and seemed to disregard her feelings altogether. But then it was his natural right. As an "only one" she was in no position to resist the desires of Robert. It was her lot always to submit to him, even though afterward she felt completely empty and drained. His emotions, pent up these last few days in the confines of a tiny cockpit, allowed only to press buttons and pull switches on his bomb runs over Korea, had suddenly found an outlet in Sumiko.

Finally, he rose and dressed. His wallet came out of his pocket and a roll of bills appeared on the table. It was the greater part of his pay, about fifty thousand yen. He sat at the edge of the bed and lit a cigarette. Sumiko did not rejoice over the money as she usually did; she put it away and went back to bed.

Fifteen minutes later they were walking along the banks of the Tama River. Unable to stand the silence, she had suggested a walk and Robert had agreed. He was a happy-go-lucky sort, a sergeant in the Air Force who had been a clerk in a cannery firm at home. He was over six feet tall and Sumiko, of average Japanese height, did not even reach his shoulders. Such combinations, though, were not uncommon in this neighborhood. They had already passed several similar couples and a few "butterflies," as the "only ones" called them, dressed in bright sweaters and skirts, flitting by in contrast and seeming defiance to the peaceful scene or rolling hills and dark forests which surrounded them. They passed a young Japanese farmboy, pulling a cart loaded with honey buckets. There was the same familiar accusing glare as he looked at Sumiko. She had heard that to oppose the invasion of her kind of girls, the village had started a young people's movement. In the young farmer's eyes, behind his glare, glowed his dream of some day seeing tractors and combines running the fields of Musashino Valley.

They reached the river bank where the Tama divided, the larger branch flowing on to the great concrete and dirt channel that led it on to the great metropolis of Tokyo. In the shallow water of the other branch, the natural bed of the once great river, she saw some youngsters fishing. As she gazed at them, completely un- conscious of Robert lying stretched out on the grass, the scene changed in her mind to the dirty little creek that flowed by her house and she saw herself chasing *medaka* fish with her brother.

The little brook that ran through the *buraku*, the *Eta* ghetto, where she grew up was dirty and covered with oil. The bottom was filled with garbage and the corpses of small animals. Sumiko hated to play in the dirty creek and wanted to go to the clear-water brook nearer to town, but her brother would not go because many town children played there. The wings of revolt that fluttered in Sumiko's heart were too small to make the flight alone.

She went to the town high school, boarding at a distant relative's home, and tasted for the first time the free and happy existence away from the *buraku*. She decided to go far away from home when she finished high school and far, far away from the stifling *buraku*. She hated the outcast blood that flowed in her veins, hated the *buraku* with its stinking animal hides that hung in every back- yard. The movement to liberate the people of the *buraku* that had started right after World War I had penetrated her district by that time, but she remained indifferent to it. She knew that cen- turies of prejudice could not be wiped out in a few generations.

The day after her graduation she went to Tokyo and joined her brother who had a job in a munitions factory. The war in China, which had started while she was in high school, developed into the Pacific war shortly after her arrival. Noboru, her brother, was soon drafted.

In the home where she now boarded was a young son who was active in a leftist literary group. Sumiko had no great intellect and no desire to take part in their activities, but among those who came to the house was one Wakabayashi Kazuo, a college student.

She was attracted to his clean, naïve ways, and he to her passionate eyes and sensuous red lips.

Once the group was arrested and imprisoned for weeks. She didn't know why, but she took food and magazines to them. After their release, Kazuo came not only with the group but sometimes alone to see her. Often they would go to the Rokugo Bridge across the Tama River far below where Sumiko now sat with Robert. Air raid drills were commonplace and there was a feeling of urgency which caused them to draw closer.

The moment finally came, and Sumiko remembered how she wept alone, hiding from everybody. Her heart leapt with joy a few days later when she received a letter from Kazuo summoning her to his family home. His mother had consented to their marriage, and Sumiko rushed to her new life in a home bound with ancient traditions.

Sumiko wanted to return to Tokyo after the ceremony, but Kazuo wanted her to stay with his aged mother during his absence in service. His mother, old and proud, had dreamed of Kazuo taking a wife from a home of equal status, and had only consented to this marriage because she was convinced Kazuo would never return alive from the war. Even at that she was prostrate with shock when the post-marriage investigations revealed that she was an *Eta*, a pariah. To this day Sumiko shuddered with rage when she thought back to those dark days after Kazuo left, just as she had the night at the play.

"It certainly was a good thing that there was no child. Our blood must be kept clean or the curse of our ancestors would be upon us," her mother-in-law would confide in her favorite niece, loud enough for Sumiko to hear. She had wanted this niece for Kazuo's bride. The particular ancestor, for whom the mother-in-law wanted the family's blood kept clean, Sumiko was always reminded, was some vague figure famous in Japan's dim past.

"That's right," the niece would agree sweetly, "the important thing is the purity of the blood."

Sumiko would shake with rage and pound her head against the stone wall, cursing her own birth. Hot-headed, strong-willed Sumiko could not endure this long and she fled to her own home. The mother-in-law must have considered it good riddance, for she never came after her. But to one who despised her origin, the *buraku* was not the right place to start life again. While she spent her restless days under her father's roof, the war came to an end. With it, as if shaken by a violent earthquake, the world tumbled around her. Sumiko could not stay any longer shut up in the *buraku,* holding the picture of Kazuo.

She fled to Tokyo, the only place on earth where she felt she could spread the wings of freedom and revolt that had been held down so long. She was startled at but not afraid of Tokyo, with its streets filled with tall, blue-eyed GIs. She tried to get a job at a factory where she had worked before, but it had shut down when the war ended. She got a job as a bar girl, lowering herself to that only, she often thought, to spite her mother-in-law. She did not realize of course that it was a very perverted sense of triumph.

With their warped sense of newly gained freedom, the girls in the quarters where she lived sold themselves right and left for small luxuries. These things were scarce, she granted, but she remained faithful to Kazuo, dreaming of the day he would come back to her, thin and wan as she saw the repatriates at the stations.

"Don't be old-fashioned!" the girls would say. "What's the sense of waiting for someone you don't even know is still alive?"

But she feared her faith was not true one night after she had been tricked into a deal with an American by her best friend. That night, she remembered vividly, she went back to her room and rolled over and over on the *tatami,* crying and laughing. When she got over her hysteria, she calmly burned Kazuo's picture.

"I can't face him anymore," she cried bitterly.

The way after that was preordained, and she followed it. Thickly but well made-up, she picked her own customers and became an expert at the game. Her spirit of revolt would not allow the various social leeches to take nearly half her rightful earnings.

Four years after the war she visited her brother who, like many of his people, had gone into the black market after his return. She learned that Kazuo was back. He had been to her home seeking her, but they knew nothing of her. He had become very active in the Communist movement and fallen out of touch with Noboru.

Sumiko felt a stab at her heart. "It's too late, too late. I can't face him."

Robert came upon the scene soon after.

A tear rolled down her cheek, her entire conscience embodied in it. Since the night of the play, she had been existing almost as a living corpse. She could fight the accusing and hateful glances of her own people by glaring at them in return or merely ignoring and pretending not to see them, but she could not fight back or run away from the accusing voices in her own heart. She had gone into this life to spite her mother-in-law and the world, but wasn't there some other way out?

The days passed and with them her depressed feeling worsened. Robert continued to come and continued to release his pent-up emotions on Sumiko. Her long periods of dejection displeased him. She could neither muster the necessary feelings to hold him fast nor get up enough nerve to part with him altogether, for she had no other means of livelihood.

Robert was away and Seiko dropped in, dressed in a bright printed skirt and loud make-up. Sumiko looked up at her and sighed enviously. Seiko was so full of life. At one time, Seiko had been a housemaid in Yokohama. She had learned enough pidgin English to get along, but could neither read nor write, which caused her quite a bit of trouble in keeping in touch with her boyfriend. In Yokohama, however, there were students who wrote English letters for the girls for a small fee, and Seiko patronized these as frequently as she did fortunetellers.

"I just had my fortune read," Seiko snapped. "He made me sick. You know what he said?" Her ill-humor showed openly on her face. " 'You're not a bad girl,' he said, 'but you are too flighty. You should try to settle down.' Yeah, that's what he said," she pouted. "Imagine, he thought I was a butterfly. So I got mad and told him, 'Don't make me sick. You may not know it, but I am an 'only one.' "

"Sure!" Sumiko said simply. She did not say more. Seiko seemed to think that there was all the difference in the world between a butterfly and an only one.

"Wouldn't you get mad too," Seiko continued, "if you were taken for a butterfly?"

"But if we couldn't be an only one, we would have to become a butterfly."

"Oh, no, not I, never! I am going to get married and go to America. John always says so."

Sumiko envied Seiko. She was still capable of having dreams, of thinking of America as a fairyland where there were no problems. Sumiko had seen too many cases where girls, blinded by this dream, had been smashed by a sudden change of heart, an unsympathetic chaplain, or harsh immigration laws. They had fallen still deeper into petty crimes and greater vices or had committed suicide. Sumiko had no more dreams.

"You have no interest in what I am talking about, no sympathy," Seiko cried. "I can't imagine John having a change of heart. I won't."

But for all her enthusiasm Seiko revealed between puffs on her cigarette that all was not serene and peaceful within her. Sumiko perceived that Seiko and John were not getting along as well as Seiko would have her believe. To lose their present men would mean for both the loss of their livelihood. Perhaps that's all the more why Seiko clung so fast to her dream, though even she must have realized that the dream was without foundation.

Sumiko had been playing a game of solitaire, a game of fortune-telling. Now, with a casual flip, the ominous ace of spades stared up at her. Seiko came closer to the table and stared at it.

"Whose is it?" she yelled.

"Nobody's in particular," Sumiko answered coolly. "It could be yours and it could be mine. Whoever it is, we might as well face it. Neither of us will come to a good end, that's for sure." Sumiko threw down the cards and lit a cigarette. Seiko's cheeks were white.

Seiko glared at Sumiko, "You sure are acting funny lately . . . depressed and mean." Then she quickly changed her mood and continued on in her old flighty tone, "Oh, yes, John has been transferred to Fuji and I'm going with him." She stood up, smiled, and strode to the door. Sumiko could tell she was only bluffing. Her defiant gestures confirmed how helpless her position really was.

Seiko turned when she reached the door. "Good-by. We may leave suddenly, so I may never see you again."

"You will come to see me if you return, won't you?" Sumiko said, trying hard to be gentle.

Seiko went without answering. Vain Seiko, poor Seiko, she is through with John. She must be going to Fuji and the new camp there to seek another partner, Sumiko decided. She had heard that already hundreds of girls had gathered there.

Sumiko could see a bit of herself in Seiko and a cold chill ran down her spine. She lay on her bed, her arms crossed on her breasts and her eyes closed. If she had only waited for Kazuo. . . . She pictured herself in her mind's eye, baby tied on her back, shopping bag on one arm and worn-down getas on her feet, going from shop to shop looking for bargains, and she longed, with all her heart, to be as she pictured. "I wonder what he is doing?" and she felt a million little pangs in her heart.

The sound of Robert's scooter broke her reverie. Lately, she had noticed he was always in a bad mood. She knew it was not entirely because of her gloominess. The peace talks that had been going on all summer had gotten nowhere and the hopes that she was sure Robert entertained of going home to his wife and children had dwindled. Robert never told Sumiko that he was married, she just assumed it and felt a womanly sympathy towards him and his loved ones at home.

"Let's go down to the Ginza and have something good to eat," Sumiko coaxed.

"Okay, anything you want to do," Robert consented.

When they reached the station, Sumiko saw Harue, a butterfly, buying a ticket to Kure, Kyushu. When she saw Sumiko, she bowed, showing a respect a lower person always shows to his superior. Harue had come to this base from Hokkaido last spring; now she was already leaving for Kyushu! What would become of these girls? Sumiko sighed to herself.

Sumiko had heard that Harue had been a nurse once. Going home late one night, she was picked up and raped. Her parents never saw her after that. She was too ashamed to go home and had taken up the trade.

While waiting for the train, they met Robert's friend, William, with his Japanese girl and their son. The boy, a beautiful child of four, had his father's features and his mother's complexion. Robert picked up the boy and held him high in the air, much to the child's delight. Sumiko saw in this how much Robert must be longing for his family. She felt cold and lonely inside.

The peace conference continued to drag on in Korea and Robert continued to fly on his missions. He never talked much about it to Sumiko and she never cared to hear about it. To live on the money he had earned by killing other people, was that all her life amounted to? The less she talked about it the better it was.

Then Robert stopped coming. It was not like him. It was not likely that he had gone on to another girl. Maybe, he had been shot down. She felt little emotion about the latter possibility.

Early one morning a note came from William's girl. Robert's plane had not returned from one of his missions. There was no way of knowing if he was safe or dead. He was merely listed as missing.

Her heart went cold and she could feel the blood leave her face. She felt dizzy and laid herself down on her bed. But she could not cry.

I am free, she thought. Then she thought of how she would have to make her living. She felt dizzy again, but still there were no tears. She felt sorry for Robert, yes. He had wanted so much to go home and with that close at hand to have to die seemed cruel and unjust. But there was herself to think of now.

She spent the following few days in a despondency never experienced before. She had lost all ambition to go find another partner, as Seiko had done; she knew there was nothing else she could do to earn a living—not the kind she had gotten used to since she had met Robert. One night an American plane crashed nearby and burned several Japanese homes. That night she had a nightmare in which thousands of her own people stood before her screaming accusations at her for the accident. She woke up in a sweat. The dream shook her spirits, and she made up her mind to quit her present life forever.

She dressed as modestly as possible and went to visit her brother Noboru. He had recently found a job in a butcher shop. When she entered the store, Noboru threw down his butcher knife and hurried her out to a tea shop a few doors away.

"Good Lord, Sumiko. People can tell right away," Noboru began even before Sumiko sat down. "You just don't look like a decent Japanese girl anymore. Don't embarrass me."

"Don't be like that, please," Sumiko pleaded faintly. "I tried to dress sensibly, today."

Noboru dragged on his cigarette, his eyes cast downwards. "I went home the other day," he started, "they were worried about you. Cousin Taichi was talking about your Kazuo. It seems he's become a big shot in the Communist party . . . He's married again . . ."

Sumiko's breathing stopped. She could hear her pulse beating in her head.

". . . Taichi is in a movement to liberate *buraku* people. Wants me to go in with him, but I'm not smart at all, you know . . ."

Noboru went on, but Sumiko only half heard. After the first of
the shock was over, she was able to look into her own heart objec-
tively and realized that she had still held a faint hope of going
back to Kazuo or she wouldn't have been shocked so much.

"Why don't you wash your feet," Noboru suddenly remarked,
"and start anew?"

Sumiko sat up. That's right, that's why she had come—to get
Noboru's help. But suddenly she realized that it wasn't as easy as
she thought. The gap between herself and society was deeper and
wider than she had ever dreamed possible. She lost courage altogether.

"That's what I came to talk to you about, but I have to think it
over some more."

"What do you mean, think it over?"

"I just realized that life isn't as easy as it seems. I don't think I
can ever lead a straight life again."

"You fool, you would continue being an embarrassment to your
family?" Noboru screamed at her. These words stung deep and only
served to wound her more. She went white with rage.

"What a thing to say. What a help you are. If that's all you're
worried about, I'll never bring you embarrassment again. I'll
never come to you again." And she walked out, her brother staring
at her back, dumfounded as she disappeared from his life.

She went to the nearby house of Maki, a friend of hers. Maki had
married a third national last year, but lived with him only three
months. He was a Formosan, a dollar broker. He also ran dope in
the Tachikawa district and was hooked up with international gambling groups on the Ginza. Three months after their wedding, he
got wind that the police had something on him and disappeared.
Now Maki rented a room in Showa-machi, the tremendous new gay
quarter, and was in business again as a butterfly.

Maki was in her room. She greeted Sumiko sympathetically in her
usual open manner. "You might as well realize, Sumiko," she
started, while preparing tea, "yes, you'd better realize that once you
fall into this life, you can't get out. It don't do you no good to yearn
for a home life."

There was more truth in Maki's words than Sumiko would con-
cede, or Maki, too, for that matter.

"Why, we can't even cook rice proper. We don't know how to

sew or wash. Too much trouble to raise kids." She laughed hollowly. "All we know how to do is rub a man's back.

Yet Maki seemed to enjoy her life. Sumiko envied this, just as she had envied Seiko. Maki was the type born to the life. Even Sumiko, a woman, was aware of the sex that oozed from Maki's being. Sumiko watched the smoke of their cigarettes rise and disappear into nothingness and her own spirit went with it.

The realization that she could never go back to a decent life, that she could never walk the same road with the rest of her people, not even her own brother, let alone Kazuo, hit her harder than anything else had so far. The year was drawing to its end, and people everywhere hustled about preparing to greet the new year. The rush of their movement seemed to stir up cold breezes that flowed into Sumiko's already cold heart.

One day just before Christmas, she made up her mind to end her meaningless life. To her great disappointment, mingled, however, with a slight joy she could not deny, the overdose of sleeping tablets she took proved no poison to her system. Too long had she been addicted to the tablets to get a normal night's sleep. When she came to, the sun was setting in the west and its faint cold winter light filled her drab room.

If I can't die, I must live, she thought to herself. And to live I must do the only think I know. She closed up her house and rented a small room in Showa-machi near Maki.

"You can bring guests in," the old landlady said, "but I don't want you bringing business here." Sumiko didn't mind this. At least this way, she could keep some remnant of independence and decency. She was through being an only one. Better to be a butterfly and free even if a butterfly of a cheaper type than she had been before she had met Robert.

She decided to make the Tama-no-ya her regular hotel. She took her first guest there and a boy brought in some cheap whiskey and a light snack. She got up and locked the door and went back and sat on the edge of the bed. Her guest poured a big shot of whiskey and downed it in one gulp. He glared at Sumiko and appraised her body, her past, her present, her future, and all its immediate possibilities and potentialities in one long lewd glance. Sumiko winced at the passion and violence she saw in that glance. She expected him to pounce on her with a bestial growl and to give vent in one violent spasm to all that had been behind that long glance. All he required of her was a piece of flesh to get his money's worth. In her mind's eye she pictured the fight between some pre-human stone-age man and woman, and prepared herself.

He looked down at her, the soul of a primeval male subjugating the female to his will reflected in his eyes. Sumiko killed all her emotions and coldly set about to calculate the other's ardor and desire. She would measure mechanically how animal-like are the desires of those who satisfy their hungers through money and physical power.

She despised more and more her inability to wash her hands of this life. She learned techniques to please men more. The hotels where she went with her guests took a large percentage of her earnings, but still she thought it better than suffering the loss of her last escape into decency and independence by using her own room.

The year ended and the world rejoiced at the new year, the year in which the peace treaty was to take effect and Japanese would once again be free men. But to Sumiko it all made little difference. She stood at her street corners rain or snow.

One time she picked up a blue-eyed youngster who had no money to pay when the business was over. She had to stand the hotel fee. After that she checked whenever he came to the hotel looking for her. She would ask sarcastically, "Got money today?"

"Sure," and he would pat his breast pockets.

"Let's see," she would ask. But the bills he took from his pocket were all military scrip of small value.

"You think you can buy me with this?" she shouted in his face. "You must think you're some slick operator. Now, get out!"

She walked back to the kitchen, opened the cupboard where she kept her own bottle, lifted it to her mouth, and sucked several large gulps. She fell to the bed in a heap, her face down. She didn't want anyone to see her cry.

She stayed in her room for the next few days. In her veins a living venom, capable of rotting her very brain, was advancing into the final stage of its attack; a condition so inevitable she had never bothered to think about it.

Winter and spring came and went. On the first of May, not realizing what day it was, she went to a movie. On her way home, she saw a crowd gathering talking excitedly of what had happened in downtown Tokyo that day.

"It was awful. All those beautiful automobiles all upset and burnt."

Sumiko could only catch fragments of their conversation. First she couldn't figure what it was all about, but as it gradually came to form a coherent picture in her mind, she trembled with fear.

You will be next, she heard the whispers inside, and she knew she couldn't run away this time.

Pon-pon! the voice inside her whispered again.

When the news of the anti-American riots were confirmed on the radio that night, she groaned. She pictured herself being dragged about over flaming coals by a demon, the hot flames licking at her face and body. She saw the flames engulfing her and the hideous grin of the devil laughing at her, his lips parted from ear to ear.

The laughter of the devil echoed sharply in her head as she staggered across the room to her bureau drawer. The cackle grew louder as she took Robert's old jackknife from the drawer.

Could it be that the venom had finally reached her brain?

She held it high, ready to plunge it deep into her throat the instant she heard the devil laugh again.

ECHOES FROM A MOUNTAIN SCHOOL

REFLECTIONS UPON MOTHER'S DEATH AND OUR HARD LIFE

by Eguchi Koichi

TOMORROW will be the thirty-fifth day after mother's death, and I have been thinking about her and the miserable condition of our home all day. We are so poor that after the ceremony tomorrow my little brother will be taken away and adopted by our uncle. I hate to see him go. He is such a good boy and does everything I tell him. Tsueko, my little sister, is going to be adopted by another uncle, but she will not go until she gets over whooping cough, which she got after mother died. After that only grandmother, who is seventy-four and scarcely able to cook our meals, and I will be left. Mother did her best to keep us together, but now that she is dead, we have to be separated.

We have a two-third-acre field, our house and the land on which it stands. Ever since father died, mother struggled alone to make this land support us, and when I say support, I mean just that, for, outside of public relief, we had no other means of livelihood. Now I have to work the land and support myself and grandmother. Mother's one hope was that I would soon grow up and help her. She was never very strong, but she worked all the time to feed us and to pay the taxes. Even after she lost consciousness, I heard her muttering, "Have you brought in the wood?" "Did you put the dried radishes into the salt and rice bran to pickle?" "Are the green vegetables washed, ready to pickle?" I am sure that she died more from exhaustion than illness. I did my best to help her, often staying home from school when there was work that required the strength of more than one person, but still I didn't realize what a burden mother was carrying until I heard her talking like that on her deathbed. Then I couldn't stand it and ran out to work, even though I wanted to stay with mother.

On November 12, the day before she died, the neighbors came and helped me bring in the wood. I don't know what I should have done without that help. On the next day they sent word from the village hospital where we had taken mother that she was dying. When we were all gathered around her bed, I told her how the neighbors had helped me with the wood, and she smiled. As long as I live, I will never forget that smile. I don't remember ever seeing her really smile before. Her lips rarely formed themselves into a smile, and when they did, it seemed that she smiled to keep from weeping. The expression that lighted up her face on her deathbed was something quite different. It was a grateful and contented heart that spoke. Her face with that smile upon it will remain in my memory forever.

Certainly she had had very little reason to smile. Ever since her marriage, and especially since our father's death, she had been absorbed body and soul in the losing struggle of trying to keep her family alive. Day after day, month after month, year after year, she struggled to improve our way of living. She fought with all her strength against asking for public assistance but the debts piled up, and, at last, in 1948, she and grandmother went to the village office to ask for help. She was never the same after that. She and grandmother never failed to remind us that our family was a public charge and could not be regarded like other families in the village who were able to support themselves.

A year and nine months later, mother became too ill to leave her bed. She insisted that she would soon be well, but she got worse and worse. Grandmother kept saying that we should send for the doctor, but mother stubbornly refused, saying that we could not afford a doctor. "The time comes," said grandmother, "when the last field has to be sold to get medical attention." But the field was never sold and mother got no better. One day Taro San happened to drop in, heard grandmother talking about the doctor. "Do you mean to say," he exclaimed, "that you haven't had the doctor yet? Don't you know that everyone receiving public assistance is entitled to medical attention? I will send the doctor to you at once."

When the doctor examined her, he said that she must go to the village hospital immediately. She had a serious heart condition. The word *hospital* always causes difficulty in a family, for it means that someone in the family has to go to look after the patient. I have heard that in some foreign-style hospitals, everything is done by nurses and that meals are prepared in the hospital kitchen for all the patients. This is a wonderful arrangement. I wish it were done in Japanese hospitals.

Our first problem was to decide who could be spared to go with mother to look after her and cook her meals. If I went, there would be no one to do the work. Grandmother was too old. There was no one left but little Tsueko; we wondered how a nine-year-old girl, who had no experience in looking after a sick person, could possibly take care of mother, prepare her own and mother's meals, and do all the other things which had to be done by a hospital attendant. There was no one else, so it couldn't be helped. Tsueko had to go.

After taking lunch with us, the doctor left, and grandmother and I got ready to send mother to the hospital.

The next day, uncle borrowed a cart drawn by a man on a bicycle. We piled the bedding on it and put mother on top of the quilts, covering her with one and spreading oil paper over everything as a protection against the rain. We then fastened an open umbrella over mother and at her back placed vegetables, rice, dishes, pots and pans. It was bumpy ride for her, but she endured it patiently. I was glad to have her in the hospital, but now the entire responsibility for the farm work rested upon me. I wanted to be with mother, but there was no time. Going to school was out of the question. There was nothing for me to do but work. That was when the people of the village came to help me. Then, on the thirteenth of November, mother died.

Two of our teachers came to the funeral with some of my classmates who had collected money from the boys for the funeral offering. When all the funeral expenses were paid, grandmother said, "We have seven thousand yen (seventeen and a half dollars) left. That is more than we had when your father died." When, however, we tried to pay off our debts, the seven thousand yen disappeared, and we found that we still owed four thousand five hundred yen (eleven dollars). How could grandmother think we were better off than when father died?

When my father died, I was only six, but I knew all about it, for mother and grandmother told me so often that I could not possibly forget. After the funeral, we had only five yen left (at that time about one dollar and twenty-five cents), but even that had to go in taxes. We were in a dreadful state. Mother and grandmother didn't know each day where the rice for the next day was coming from. Grandmother and mother made straw sandals which they exchanged for rice. The sandals they made in one day could be exchanged for about six pounds of rice, a good price, mother said. We were small, so we could live on four pounds. This gave a little reserve in time.

They worked so hard that they were able to save a little money. Mother hoped they could go on like that until I grew up, that we might be able to get along. Then the war came and everything became unbearably difficult. How often I heard mother say, "When Koichi grows up, he can help us and we may be able to pay off some of our debts."

This was her only comfort, but she was never able to realize her dream. She was simply overwhelmed by poverty; all her labor got her nowhere. Why did it have to be like that? I wonder if mother really believed that things would be better after I finished school and began to work. After all, what could I do more than she had done? When I think of this, I can scarcely sleep. I thought so much about it that I decided to make out a plan and send it to our teacher.

Next year will be my third year in junior high school, the end of compulsory education, and I want to attend school every day without having to work anywhere except on my own farm.

The year after that, I will work as hard as I can and pay my debts. If I can ever save a little money, I want to buy a rice field, for with only a vegetable field such as ours, we can never have enough food. I want to see my family have a little comfort. I must continue to improve myself so that I can work like a man, not be fed like a sheep. This is what I wrote to my teacher. But as I thought the matter over, I found how mistaken I was. In the first place, how could I ever save enough money to buy a rice field? And in the second place, the rice field that I should buy would have to be taken away from another family who would then be as poor as we are now. At present our entire income comes from the tobacco we raise on one-tenth of our field, or one-tenth of two-thirds of an acre. The rest we need for vegetables for the family.

No matter how I work, there seems to be no way of increasing this income. In January of this year we sold our tobacco for twelve thousand yen. After paying seven thousand yen which we had borrowed the year before, we had just five thousand yen left. This, added to the one thousand six hundred yen a month we received in public assistance, was all we had to live on for the entire year, twenty-two thousand yen (about sixty dollars) in all.

Is it any wonder that I could not believe it when grandmother said we were better off when mother died than we were at the time of father's death? I could see no possible way for the family to remain together and make enough money to survive. That is the reason why it was decided to ask our uncles to adopt my brother and sister.

Even without the children, grandmother and I will need at least two thousand yen a month for a bare living. This does not count clothes and fuel, which would bring it up to two thousand five hundred yen (about six dollars) a month. These will just be covered by our tobacco and public assistance, but what about the debts we still owe? So my beautiful plan of buying a rice field is only a dream.

Our poverty is not due to inability or laziness. It is simply that we haven't enough land for our needs. How can a family of five subsist on two-thirds of an acre of land? There is nothing ahead but a losing struggle and final destitution. It was the fate of my father and my mother and will probably be mine.

When my teacher and the principal called on me a few days after the funeral, I intended to ask about my future, but before I had a chance to say anything, teacher Muchaku said, "Are you still carrying wood every day? How long will it take for you to get enough for the winter? What do you have to do next?"

I told him that in spite of the help I received from the neighbors, I had a good deal more wood to carry, and after that I had to sort and smooth out the tobacco leaves.

"How long will that take?" he asked.

"I don't know," I replied.

"Don't you keep a record? Why don't you look at last year's record?"

I told him that there was no record for last year.

"No record?" he exclaimed. "That is no way to work. You should keep a record of the time it takes to do your work each year.

How do you expect to make out a work schedule without a record? Begin from this very day to make a record. What do you do next?"

"I have to cover the house with mats before the snow comes. After that, I think I can go to school."

"Which means that you will have only a few days at school this term," said Mr. Muchaku. "That will never do. Tomorrow when you go to get your rice ration, come over to school. You haven't been there for more than a month, and you have to see the boys and girls to thank them for what they did for you when your mother died. When you come, bring a plan of your work, written in a table form, and I will have a look at it."

When I heard this, a weight seemed lifted from my heart. When I finished my schedule, I found that, as my teacher had said, I had only a day or two in December for school. The next day I took my work plan to school and showed it to Mr. Muchaku. He looked at it carefully for a few minutes and then said, "Will you, Tozaburo, Soju, Shunichi and Tsutomu, go to the room of the teacher on night duty and wait there for me?"

When he came, he handed my work schedule to Tozaburo, saying, "What do you think of this?"

Tozaburo read it and handed it to others. When they had all finished, the teacher said, "Well, how about it?"

"We can all finish up that work in no time," said Tozaburo, "can't we, boys? Then he can come to school like the rest of us." The boys smiled and nodded.

I couldn't say anything and had to blink hard to keep back the tears.

"Be sure you do the work systematically and efficiently," said the teacher. "Divide it up among you and get it done as quickly as possible." I could no longer keep back my tears, and they fell shamelessly on my lap.

By early in December, the boys and some of the villagers had finished up all my work, and I did not have to worry about going to school. How happy I am to have such a teacher and such friends.

Tomorrow is the thirty-fifth day after mother's death. I will report all these things to her spirit. I will also promise her that I will study hard and try to find out why she had to work so hard with so little result and why people cannot earn enough to live on, even if they work every minute of their lives as she did. I also want to find out if I can buy a rice field without causing the man who sells it to suffer. In our school there is another boy, Toshio, who is even more unfortunate than I. He almost never goes to school, for he has to work nearly every day, rolling down logs and burning charcoal. Perhaps if we all get together, we can help him just as the boys helped me.

RICE WEEVILS

by Wada Den

THE GREEN LEAVES were all out. Sparrows played in pairs on the thatched roof, kicking up old rotten straws. When they fell, tripping over themselves, instead of landing on the grass, they fell right into the rice hulls; surprised, they flew away. The pile of rice hulls had been made by Suke, who, of all things, had started rice hulling at this time of the year. It was an unwritten law among the farmers that rice was to be hulled and packed away before the end of the year. It was only the slow pokes who left it unhulled over the year's end. If because of some unforeseen disasters the rice could not be hulled within the old year, it was usually finished within the New Year month. No one in his right mind left the task until this time of the year.

But Suke smiled at the sparrows that kept falling into the hulls. It was a smile that showed complete contentment. It was nice to have everything working out as planned. It was not because Suke was an incurable slow poke that he was doing what he did now. It was all included in his plan of things.

Last year his schedule had dragged nicely, or rather he had caused it to drag, taking only his son into his confidence; when he finally got around to the business of hulling rice, it was well into the month of December and time to prepare for the new year. Unmindful of his wife's cries of protest, he stopped hulling when he had enough for the government quota and to last them until May. He told her that his hulling a little at a time from now on meant they would lose less each year to rats and rice weevils. It was true that the amount of rice farmers lost annually because of rats and worms was considerable, but they had been losing rice like this for centuries. Lately everyone was putting their sacks in tin drums as a protection for the hulled rice. Suke not only gave no thought to buying such, but thought it a ridiculous idea.

Rats and rice weevils are ills ages old. There is nothing one can do about them. But at Suke's house the rats and weevils were not the same as those that bothered his neighbors or his ancestors; the pests demolished five and ten *sho* in one night, almost a sack a week. Suke remembered his own youth; when his son came of age, he was not so mean as to make much ado about the increased "rat" loss, but lately he had found out that the rats and worms were not his son alone.

When his son took on a wife, it became apparent. It was his son who started the fuss. He had stopped acting the rat when he married. Leaving the government rice aside, Suke measured out the rice for the family in front of them, telling them there was just enough to last them till May. That stopped the rat raids.

Ume, Suke's wife, had gone to her brother's house that morning for three days. His daughter was getting married. Suke was to follow her on the day of the ceremony. "I'll take a present when I go," he said to Ume.

"Yes, that's all right," his wife answered. "But I can't go empty-handed today. I'd like to take some little thing, like cosmetics to the bride and some sweets to the kids."

He should have given her money without being asked, but his innate stinginess, together with his suspicions that she might have some money secretly put away, kept him from offering. When he finally did put out some money, with reluctance, Ume pouted at the small amount.

"It's different from an ordinary visit, you know," she whined. "I can't take any cheap stuff. There are no more tenant farmers, don't forget."

He gave her a little more, but the way she had complained had angered him. Maybe it was this that had moved him to take out the milling machine.

Ume was his second wife, younger by ten years. He had a son by his first wife. Ume had married him in spite of this son because her family had been tenant farmers; Suke's family, on the other hand, had been landed farmers for generations back. It had been considered quite a Cinderella marriage. But her family held her good fortune against her, forever reminding her that while she had risen above her station, they had not; then the change in the land law, practically forced upon the Japanese by the Occupation Forces, changed everything. It was ironical that it was Ume, for years the wife of a landed farmer, who had rejoiced over the new land law rather than her brother who, replacing his father as the head of the family, had benefited as much by the revolution as Suke and Ume had lost. Though it was now six years since the change, Ume rubbed it in every chance she had for the years of humiliation she had undergone. It infuriated Suke every single time.

"Enough to hold us till rice planting," Suke said to his son. "And about three sacks for selling should be plenty."

"I think so, if we sell hogs," his son said.

Their minds were perfectly matched. Suke never mentioned to his son that he had intended to sell his hogs while Ume was away, but that too had been silently settled between them. "If we sell the hogs, then perhaps we need only about three bags." His son turned off the motor of the milling machine.

His son went to the hog dealer and the dealer came by early the next day. The price of hogs was going down, he said. The dealer told Suke to hang on a little longer until the price went up, but Suke would not hear of it.

"You always buy high, sell cheap," the dealer said. "Then you blame it on me."

Suke saw the foolishness of selling his hogs now, but if he wished to sell them without Ume knowing anything about it, now was the only time.

The dealer was telling the truth. But Suke said that it was only the rich farmers who could afford to raise hogs when feed was expensive. He wrapped a part of the money from the sale to take as the customary wedding present.

Ume was awakened by the noise her brother and his wife were making in the pig sty behind the house. Thinking maybe one of the litter was being squashed to death, she got up and went out to see.

The talk during dinner had been all about hog raising. Fifteen newborn was quite a litter in this time of low prices. "A hybrid may be cheap," her brother had boasted, "but mine are registered hogs. They will bring not less than three thousand each."

"What happened, one squashed?" Ume shouted.

Her brother Kisuke looked excited, squatting in the middle of the pen. He held a tiny wriggling pig in his arms and his wife was counting the litter with both hands.

"What happened?" Ume asked again.

"What happened?" her brother repeated the question. "If some one had stolen one of my litter, I could understand it. But no, we have sixteen instead of fifteen. How do you figure that?"

Kisuke babbled on. The one he held was the added member, he said. He had spotted it as a stranger and after a careful check, sure enough, he found he had one extra. A newborn like this couldn't have come of its own. Somebody must have planted it there. But what for?

"Maybe somebody came to change it for one of your good breeds," Ume said, "then was interrupted and couldn't finish the job."

Her sister-in-law interrupted, saying, "That's just what I said myself, just before you came. It's better to have one stolen. This gives you a queer feeling."

Just then a man walked through the dirt-floored kitchen and came out back to where they were. "Say, Kisuke-san, you didn't have a baby pig stolen, did you?" He too held a baby pig in his arms.

"Nakatsugawa-san, it's the darndest thing, it's the other way around," Kisuke almost shouted. "They didn't steal one, they put one here instead."

"What?" Nakatsugawa exclaimed, round-eyed.

Nakatsugawa was a hog-raising specialist working in the Prefecture's Domestic Animal Laboratory. He and Kisuke were on good terms because Kisuke was a conscientious hog raiser. Nakatsugawa explained he had been awakened by the squeals of a baby pig in the back of the house; when he went out to investigate, he found the little pig in the woods. Thinking it stolen from the lab, he had awakened the caretaker and checked, but the lab's litter had not been touched. Then he thought somebody had stolen it from somewhere nearby, and that because it squeaked so much, the thief had left it where he found it. So he came first to Kisuke to inquire.

Kisuke came out of the pen, still holding the baby pig he had just discovered in his own pen, and when he put his next to Nakatsugawa's, he exclaimed, "Look, it's from the same litter!"

"So they have started throwing them away," Nakatsugawa remarked gloomily. "My gosh, Kisuke-san—"

"You think that's it?"

"But it's an interesting thought—instead of throwing them into a river or something, they do it this way."

"No concern to me," Kisuke grumbled. Only rich farmers could raise stray hogs at a time like this.

"What shall we do?"

"*Sah* . . . It's got me."

The sight of the bewildered twosome, each holding a baby pig, was so funny that Ume started to laugh.

Kisuke remarked. "Why don't you take it and raise it?"

Ume was thinking the same thing and was on the verge of speaking out her mind when Nakatsugawa joined Kisuke. "Don't buy a pig to raise," he said. "Raise a stray pig, that's the motto. In the fall, the price is sure to go up," he assured.

"When Suke-san comes, I'll speak to him for you," Kisuke said.

"At any rate, in this wedding uproar you must have your hands full, Kisuke-san," Nakatsugawa said, offering to take care of the stray pigs at the lab, and the two of them went across the field, each still holding the baby pig twins.

Ume's mind was made up to raise them. No matter what Suke said, she was going to keep them. Now that the rat holes were stopped up, she must think of some way to make her own money. She was tired of asking Suke to buy even her underwear. Unless she acted smart now, her stepson would be treating her the same way in her old age.

She waited for Suke to come. There were more reasons besides the question of the pigs that made her impatient to see Suke. Suke hadn't been here since the war ended. "When he comes, he will see with his own eyes how this place has prospered. Wonder what face he will make?" Ume chuckled.

"Huh, nothing but a tenant farm," he had often said derisively of the place before the new land law. But look at it now, a barn with an upstairs where they raised silk worms, the house newly roofed with zinc with the whole south side porch enclosed by glass sliding doors, a chicken-coop big enough to hold fifty, and a pig sty for four, all modern, up-to-date buildings. Suke boasted of being an independent farmer, but he can't even rethatch his roof. Its rotten straw fell on her neck and gave her shivers everytime sparrows took their exercise upon it and, worst, Suke did not seem to mind.

In this day and age when there was no longer any difference between the independent and the former tenant farmers, there was no reason still to have a feeling of inferiority, to feel Suke had rescued her from poverty and hopelessness; she was going to have it out with her husband once and for all. With that in mind, she went to look the place over just as Kisuke came back with a guest. "About the bride's escort, you don't mind going alone, do you?" Kisuke asked. "Suke-san doesn't have to go, does he?"

"Oh, it's all right, I suppose," she said readily.

"We have to match the number of our guests with the groom's, you know," Kisuke said apologetically.

The bride's escort party was composed of close relatives who took the bride over to the groom's house and stayed for the reception feast. Everyone took pains to match the numbers as closely as possible since the wedding expenses were being split by the two families, as was the custom when the social and financial standings of the two families were on the same level. Ume, who was the bride's aunt, and her husband should be included in the party as a matter of course. In Kisuke's tone she noted that he thought lightly of Suke's position and his opinion reinforced her own feelings of a moment before. There now, you see? Ume said to herself, highly satisfied. The new guest who was to replace Suke was her youngest sister's husband, who, Ume heard, was also making good lately because of the new land law.

With the feast after the wedding ceremony over, Suke, who was not included in the escorting party, went home. He had come late, the house was already full of guests, Ume did not have the chance to talk much to him about the pigs. She had brought up the subject but there had been no opportunity to discuss it. But she wasn't sorry. She couldn't expect much of an answer from him anyway.

During the three-mile walk to the groom's house her younger sister's husband came up beside her, saying, "Suke-san has sure aged lately, hasn't he?"

"Yes, all of a sudden," Ume answered.

"Like a father and daughter, with you," he remarked.

"Oh, you don't say." Ume laughed quietly.

"He isn't sixty yet, is he?" he asked.

"No, he is only fifty," she answered with emphasis.

"Well, he's sure aged."

"Yes, he's gotten so old, all the time he is worrying that rats and worms will eat his rice all up," Ume laughed openly. Remembering that this brother-in-law had been present when she talked to her husband about the baby pigs, she sensed that there was more on his mind than what he said.

"Is he the kind that leaves words written in the surface of the rice pile so no one can touch it without his knowing it?" her brother-in-law asked as her sister drew near too.

"That's not all," Ume answered, and then told them about Suke hulling just enough rice to carry over a certain period. Not only the escorting group but the groom's party laughed, and the procession began to pass the joke around. People were still laughing as the procession, passing through several vales and over hills terraced in irregularly partitioned fields now sown in wheat, came to the village of the groom's house. As they neared the outskirts, a group of men standing by the road—dressed in formal attire of crested *haori* and stiff silk *hakama*, the groom's relatives who were not included in the wedding party, but who were invited only for the reception—were waiting for them. The waiting group stood rigid, and only bowed as the wedding procession passed in front of them. Just then Ume saw a face. Startled, she looked away quickly. It couldn't—but then she saw him, she couldn't be mistaken. Why didn't she look at him closer, why did she look away so quickly? Yes, he must be Genji. What connection had he with the groom's house? He must have some or he wouldn't be standing there.

When the sake drinking started, Genji didn't even look at her. While the relatives were introduced, Genji stood back. The matchmaker was a poor talker and Ume couldn't understand half of what he said. Ume sat in the bride's group and Genji was sitting at the lower end at the groom's side. Ume tried to catch his attention several times, but he just sat drinking sake. He looked sturdy and with his healthy tan had the air of a well-to-do farmer. In his prime, too. The way he drank his sake, too, reminded her of his aggressiveness of twenty years ago. She envied men, they didn't change as quickly as women, nor age as fast.

When the formality of the ceremonies began to break, it went down with the force of a landslide. Dancing and singing started and the seats on both sides of Ume emptied quickly. The parties of the bride and groom mingled in merry making while twosomes sat here and there, talking loudly and exchanging drinks. Those who could not drink sat by the porch. Ume missed her younger sister, but soon found her talking among the women of the groom's side. Not able to stand their open, ribald jokes, she was just getting up to join the porch group when suddenly, a sake bottle in one hand, Genji came and sat down in front of her. "Here, O-ume-san, have a drink on me," and he shoved a sake cup under her nose.

Overwhelmed by his insistence, all she could do was take the cup and utter faintly, "Why, it's Genji-san, isn't it?"

"Well, it's about time—I recognized you a mile away, and paid my courtesy then, a courtesy of twenty years. Anyway, drink it up," he ordered.

"Don't force me . . . please," she protested.

"But it's been twenty years, hasn't it? Haven't I got a right to force?"

Yes, it had been twenty long years, but Genji hadn't changed a bit. Ume looked at him with renewed interest. Genji, too, became a little sober and changing his sitting position slightly, started in on his tale. Genji now owned the house in the next village which Ume had passed on the way. He was a *yoshi,* a marriage arrangement in which the family name of the wife, who is usually the oldest or only daughter of a son-less house, is taken by the groom, who would be a second or third son since the first son must continue his own family name. Besides having quite a large farm, he was one of five big hog farmers in the village and quite naturally the conversation turned to the subject of hog raising.

"No, no, don't pick a stray pig to raise," Genji advised. "It can't be much of a pig. I'll give you a good one, a thoroughbred. You take it and raise it." He was dead serious.

"But I can't afford a thoroughbred," Ume replied.

"I said I'd give it to you, didn't I? For nothing. I'll take it to your place when it comes. My sow Yamabuki is expecting any time now. Yamabuki took a second prize at the Fair," he boasted. "A breeder from another prefecture offered two hundred thousand for her. But I didn't sell her. She is a beauty."

"But I can't take such a high-class hog. A cheap one is good enough for me," Ume said weakly.

"Don't be a fool. Cheap ones eat just as much."

When it came to hogs, Genji had much to say. He said he'd spent twenty years raising them. He had made his fortune with them, starting with only one sow, the sole inheritance that his brother had left him. The word brother, not father, puzzled Ume, but Genji's rapid speech left no room for her to ask questions. "Anyway, it's right close by. Come and look at my place, will you?" And he was already up, pulling Ume with him with one hand. The boisterous singing and dancing was still going on, no telling when it would end. Ume was thankful for the chance to get away.

Genji's house stood on the edge of the village, surrounded by zelkova and oak trees; like Kisuke's house, it had been rebuilt after the war. She remembered that Genji's parents had been tenant farmers like hers. Walking close to the man she had once allowed to make love to her, she thought again of those times. At that time he had had Korea fever, like all the second and third sons of tenant farmers.

He had asked her to wait for him, he would come to get her when he had made his fortune. He had gone to Yokohama to make money to go to Korea, just about the time her marriage to Suke was settled without her knowledge. She didn't remember which happened first.

"And it was the damndest thing," Genji started again. "Only about a half year after I got to Yokohama, my brother upped and died and I was called back to take his place."

"Then how came you to be a *yoshi?*" Ume asked, still puzzled.

"How come?" Genji turned to her. "It was the second brother, who'd married into this family, that died, that's how come." He continued, "Left two kids. They lost grandpa the year before. Couldn't make a go of it for one day without a man and I was put there to take my brother's place."

"Oh! Now I understand."

"When I came, there were two kids, a woman fairly worn out by my brother, and a sow. But this sow was a beauty . . ." He disappointed her by talking some more about pigs. But then it didn't matter to her what he talked about.

"It's wonderful, your being so prosperous," Ume said, turning back to look at Genji's house again from the distance. But Genji started to laugh, and there was a faint hollowness in his laugh.

"But look at me now. I've spent the best years of my life being a stud horse." There was even a bitterness in his tone of voice. "Just think. A young man of twenty-five, given a woman over thirty. She is seven years older. And as she is the head of the house, I cannot raise my head from my perpetual subservience to her all my life. Now that I think of it, the way I put my heart and soul into hog raising was maybe to distract myself and fill up an empty spot in my heart."

He continued brooding over it, till Ume said, "If you've had no romance on the side, you regret your past. But you can't say that, can you?"

"Don't be a fool. I told you it was all hog raising, and nothing else. It was different then," he said.

The course of life was mapped out by one's parents. A boy replaced a dead brother, a girl took her dead sister's place. It was an unwritten law, he had had no choice.

"A big river dividing us, and I didn't know a thing." Ume blamed it on the river. Then she wondered if Genji had heard anything about her and she asked.

"If I had heard anything, I suppose I wouldn't have let it go at that. You can't forget a person you once held in your arms." And without even a smile, he took hold of Ume's hand and squeezed it tight. She returned the squeeze and as if that were a signal, he stopped, pondered a second, changed their course and walked on into a dark grove of trees. After they walked a few paces into the darkness, through which Genji walked with sure steps, leading Ume by the hand, they came to an open space.

"An old race track," he explained. He kept on walking, and Ume followed blindly, her heart quivering with expectation. "Aren't you going to ask where we are going?" he asked, in a throaty voice.

Her heart was too full to answer.

Presently, he stopped at a spot where the grass was soft and dry under their feet, and put his arm around her waist. Without any hesitation, she threw herself into his arms.

Ume did not think Suke would consent as easily as that about the pig, but he simply said, "Okay, let's raise him, then."

"It takes guts, like the folks across the river." Folks across the river was a pseudonym for her brother's.

"Yeah, some guts." And there was no sarcasm in his tone either.

He certainly must have had his eyeful seeing with his own eyes the way her brother, whom he had always tended to look down upon, was doing so well. Then she got dressed to go to Genji, not listening to Suke's remark that she could send the reply by mail. Ume simply had to see Genji again.

Genji was working in the field. It was the biggest field she had seen and when she remarked about it Genji said there weren't very many fields as big as that in his neighborhood either.

"And it's all yours, too?"

He simply nodded, as if to say, of course. The fact that he said it so matter-of-factly reminded Ume that it had been some time since the new law went into effect. In fact, it could hardly be called new now. Yet it was just recently that she had begun to feel its effects.

"My, but it's wonderful," she said, half enviously.

"You too can do it," he added, half smiling. "Don't be taken for a rat or a rice weevil all your life."

"Then you know?" and she laughed. "Besides I'm not a daughter of a tenant farmer anymore, you know"

She said it with an implication, but she wondered if Genji could get her meaning, or begin to understand the ordeals of the years of humiliation she had undergone. Then she was caught in the emotion of the loss of twenty years of happiness.

"You know, it was you I really came to see today," and she looked at him as wistfully as a maid of sixteen.

"You go ahead, and I'll follow you shortly," he said, moving the hoe all the time he talked.

She had walked about a quarter of a mile toward the town in the opposite direction from her village when Genji caught up with her on a bicycle. She got on behind him and the two rode toward the town where they would stop at an inn.

A DATE

by *Saisho Foumy*

IT BEGAN RAINING when Asa reached her flat. There was a strange intimacy about the somber, ivied flat in the rain, dimly lit from inside. She knew René was in.

"*Bon soir,* madame." René's resonant voice greeted her from the deep divan into which he was sunk, evidently reading. "I have just come in."

"How are you, René?" Asa said mechanically, empty in heart.

"You look fatigued, *chérie,*" René was quick to observe. "Let's have a glass of wine, it's six o'clock anyway." René got up, his well-shaped limbs emphasized by white shirt sleeves.

Tomorrow, ten o'clock, Asa repeated in her mind. Suddenly nothing seemed as important as that ten o'clock breakfast appointment with Yugo—she'd never had a date with Yugo before. It was impossible tonight to banter with René.

"You are dreaming. What happened?" he said, half seriously, half pretending to tease her.

"My dear man, I've never consulted you about the affairs of my heart before. Please don't expect me to now." Asa was surprised at her own tone.

"Oh, you have a heart?" René countered. "That's news to me." The patter did not quite come off. His eyes were not laughing, but gently apprehensive.

This was what Asa liked about René, about the French, they allow women freedom of emotion; they were not arrogant about love.

"Stop that. Maybe I need your wisdom, but just now I don't want to be particularly wise."

"That's better," René said, studying Asa with his fascinating black eyes directly on hers.

"René, would you object if I lived with a man?" Asa said suddenly.

"What sort of a man?"

"Oh, René, someone I like extremely well, and who likes me too."

"That sounds trite, doesn't it? You don't need any comment from me, do you? You are free, but I don't want you to be too foolish."

"You think I am? I don't want to be particularly clever with this man."

"Nor very proud?" René insinuated.

"Oh, I don't believe in marriage, you know that, René."

"And he doesn't?"

"I never asked. I met him only two weeks ago and spoke to him only today."

At this, René did not, as Asa had half hoped and expected, gesticulate to loosen the tension. He did not move. He looked straight at her. No chance expression on Asa's face could now escape his gaze now.

"Who is the man?"

"Sogano Yugo."

"Not that playwright?"

"Yes."

"Going in for reflected glory?"

"Why should I now? You reflect your glory on me already," Asa said tenderly.

"Enjoy yourself, then," René said. "Anything's a pastime in this floating life, this, what you call it, Ukiyo."

His deliberately chosen words—"enjoy yourself," "pastime"—outraged and hurt Asa and from this she knew that he was more hurt than she.

René reached for another glass of wine. The rain was getting heavy. Rain drops spattering against the window-panes emphasized the stillness and intimacy of the night. Rain spattering on the roof, Asa thought, is one of the few things I live for. There is a sense of gladness of the mere fact of living, however lived. Asa loved this moment—not yet committed to a new love which would no doubt bore her in the end, yet not yet terminating the old love still warm.

The one mortal fear Asa had was to be bored, to be bored of everything, including herself, bored of men she loved and everything else that was supposed to be good in life. Better dead than bored: That was the main reason she had stopped smoking—cigarettes only emphasize the emptiness of life. She did not mind dullness at all if it got anywhere, if it produced anything.

Asa could not bear the end of things and this was not quite an end or a beginning, the thin dividing line which allowed you to linger between your remembered happiness and hoped-for-moments. This too will end soon and we may become strangers, Asa thought and looked at René lounging gracefully on the sofa in his white shirt sleeves. The sardonic glint in his eyes was gone, and he was quite his usual self, oblivious to what has been said. Their eyes met and they unconsciously smiled.

SAZANKA

by Kawachi Sensuke

RIGHT AFTER LUNCH, Mrs. Nakagawa Sumiyo, who arranged the
negotiations for this marriage, and Mr. and Mrs. Ikeda, who consented to be formal go-betweens at the wedding ceremony, arrived.
The beauticians soon came and started readying Miyoko for the
wedding. As the household got caught up in the excitement of
the approaching wedding hour, Kosuke lost all his equanimity. He
went to look in at his dead wife's altar, stood there for a moment
looking at its ebony black surface and the gold letters which shone
in the flickering candle light. He went into his study to lie down,
but could not stay more than five minutes. He got up and went into
the dining room to get something, but forgot what he had gone
there for.

"Surely, I am not getting old," he muttered, and waved his hand
before his face as if to throw off the idea. Coming from the dining
room he passed in front of Miyoko's room. They must have forgotten to shut the door for he saw, reflected in the tall mirror, Sumiyo
in her bright undergarment. His heart missed; he swallowed hard,
and walked quickly away. To his great surprise an old forgotten
emotion was aroused and stirred inside him. He blushed. His heart
was still thumping when he entered the dining room for the third
time and sat down.

"You look like a stray pup," his sister Katsue laughed at him.

"You know, aunty," his oldest son said, "There is a saying in

Europe that when young grape vines bloom, old wine ferments also. Maybe father wants a new wife, too."

This, coming from his own son, embarrassed him and Kosuke turned crimson. "Don't say that," he said, weakly. "At a time like this, a father doesn't know what to do."

Katsue did not know that Kosuke was aroused and bewildered at seeing Sumiyo. She had only seen him standing forlornly before his dead wife's altar, and thought to herself, I suppose he thinks of her at times like this, and that as soon as Miyoko's wedding was over, she must settle the question of marrying Sumiyo off to Kosuke.

"You had better get dressed too," Katsue said. "Miyo-chan will be ready before you are."

Kosuke had known Sumiyo thirty years before when he was still in college. Kosuke's family villa had been next to Sumiyo's in the summer resort town near Osaka where they used to spend summers together. They had been in love, but neither of them had confessed it to the other. In those days life was easy, not so rushed as it was now, and people took these things more leisurely. Kosuke entered a university in Tokyo. One day in the autumn, as he was absently watching the fine, thread-like rain fall on the brilliantly yellowed gingko leaves in the back yard of the boarding house where he stayed, the mailman rang. It was a letter from his sister, Katsue, telling him that Sumiyo had married a rich man's son in order to save her father's declining fortune. He remembered reading it as if reading a cheap pulp magazine story.

It was not very long after this that he fell blindly, madly in love with Aiko, the daughter of the boarding house owner. His father took this as a disgrace to the family and disowned him. It was only due to his mother that he was able to finish university. His father had a large store which had been handed down through many generations. Being a merchant through and through, he did not like Kosuke's going to the university. The only reason he did not oppose it entirely was because Kosuke was a second son; the first son had given up schooling after he finished high school to help his father. Kosuke often thought that his father would have been happier had he taken a course in business instead of literature.

"Ah well, I entered the university against my father's wishes," he told Aiko. "I might as well go all the way and marry you."

In spite of Aiko's deep affection for him, he was bothered for a long time by Sumiyo's image coming over the face of Aiko every time he held her in his arms.

After he finished at the university, he taught school to make a living. It was not until he became the father of four children that he was able to depend solely on his writing for his income. The war with China developed into the Great Pacific War, and in its third year his first son, Ichiro, a student in college, was drafted.

He was missing for a long time, and it was not known whether he was dead or alive. One day, late in the spring of the year after the war ended, he came back. Both Kosuke and Aiko had turned gray with worry. And yet, Kosuke remembered, during the time Ichiro was missing, neither of them hardly ever talked about him. Perhaps it was because each knew what was uppermost in the mind of the other.

When he returned, the family suddenly came alive. It was as though oil had been freshly added to a dying lamp whose light, in its renewed strength, now reached every corner of the house. And yet, and yet, in spite of all this rejoicing Ichiro turned his back to them all. He remained silent and glum.

"Did you eat lizards, too?" Shinji, the second son would ask.

"I bet you ate snakes, also," Ryozo, the youngest would pipe in.

"Oh, shut up and go away," Ichiro would shout. The little ones were just at that inquisitive age when they wanted to know everything about strange lands. They would look at their brother hurt and disappointed, while Ichiro would look as though an old wound had been torn open. He was drunk most of the time and spent all the money his father gave him on drink and gambling. When he ran out of money, he would sell his overcoat and his clothing on the spot. Although, as time passed, he lost some of his emaciated look, due to his mother's and sister's loving care, his behavior did not improve.

"Like a hoodlum," his mother said sadly.

Newspapers at the time were full of news about gang holdups and robberies by repatriates who had lost their spiritual sustenance in the defeat. They had been led to believe deeply in their country's final victory.

"If he should be led to take part in one of those robberies—" Kosuke and Aiko could not sleep on nights he was out.

The atmosphere of the family returned to darkness, darker than the time when he was missing.

"Father and Mother don't say much to you, but you have no idea how much they are worried," Miyoko cornered him one night. "I think I can appreciate how you feel, but to me a life of nihilism is a living hell. It is only by fighting against this temptation that our lives take on any meaning. You know that, without my telling you, and I know that you are not such a weakling."

At first Ichiro refused to listen to her; he pretended that he didn't hear. But she kept it up, gently but firmly. Suddenly Ichiro's face took on an expression of extreme agony and he turned aside. "No, I am a weakling," he said. "I just don't know how to continue to live in this topsy-turvy world of ours," and Miyoko saw, though Ichiro did his best to hide it, tears in his eyes. Miyoko felt that she had won.

It was not only Ichiro, but Kosuke too, for that matter, who found himself unable to cope with a world that had changed so suddenly. His being able to remain calm was perhaps due to his age; he was able to submit instead of straining against circumstances. Even so, he remembered how he used to sit all day, doing absolutely nothing but listening to the waves of the sea as it washed the side of his house on the Kugenuma beach. He might have stayed like that until death claimed him had it not been for his wife Aiko's sudden death.

One day in autumn, when the sound of the waves was high, and the delicate pale pink blossoms of the *sazanka* tree quivered in the wind that had changed to the north, his wife Aiko came down with acute peritonitis. She suffered only one week. "I am so grateful that I saw Ichiro back and alive. And I am also grateful that I am able to die on *tatami*. Please find a loving bride for Ichiro and a fine husband for Miyoko. Ichiro, my only worry is about you. You take care of Shinji and Ryozo, will you? And take care of father. Don't make him sad." These were her last conscious words. After she fell into a coma, all she talked about was Ichiro. She died holding Kosuke's hand. She was fifty, and had been married to Kosuke for twenty-six years.

For a while Kosuke felt as though he had lost his spiritual support, like a boat that had lost its course in the foggy sea. He would remain inert for hours on end, then suddenly a gust of sadness and misery would come over him and he would work furiously to overcome it. But above all, what hurt him most was the realization that he had not remained emotionally faithful to Aiko through all those years. He thought that he must live until all four children became independent and found their happinesses, that it was the only way he could repay his debt to Aiko's departed soul.

Three years had since passed. Ichiro had gradually regained his composure, landed a job in a publishing company and was busy running about, getting articles and stories from writers like Kosuke.

"You have recovered from your repatriate sickness, haven't you?" Kosuke teased him one time.

"Repatriate sickness? Well, I wouldn't brush it off as easily as that—but—" He grinned sheepishly. "It was a form of psychoneurosis, I guess."

And they both laughed it off happily. Kosuke felt that it was Aiko's prayer on her death bed that had saved Ichiro. But Ichiro was now twenty-eight and Miyoko twenty-six. He must find them good partners and life companions, as he had promised Aiko. He wished that they would find someone by themselves. Come to think of it, Ichiro seemed to have found a girl friend, though he hadn't admitted it yet. But Miyoko had no opportunity since she kept house after her mother's death. She had by nature great perseverance. Aiko often used to say that she wished Miyoko and Ichiro were reversed in their nature. Miyoko would never complain about her own hard lot.

Then Kosuke took notice of Miyoko for the first time; that her hands were chapped, her complexion, which she never had time to look after, had coarsened, and that all in all, she looked not at all the way a marriageable girl should look. What chance had she to get a husband, looking like that? From the next day he put on his old clothes and helped her clean around the house, something he had never done all his life.

"Please father, don't," Miyoko teased. "Don't make it rain, I want my washing to dry."

One day Kosuke did his own washing and Miyoko was furious. She said he was doing it to spite her; was he dissatisfied with her ways of housekeeping? She burst into tears. Kosuke watched her cry herself into hysteria and decided that something really must be done.

He wrote to as many friends as possible, sending Miyoko's pictures with his letters. An answer soon came back from his sister Katsue. She said that Sumiyo, whom Kosuke must remember, was in Osaka recently, though she really lived in Tokyo. She had become widowed and, when told about Miyoko, said that she knew of a young man who would be just the type for Miyoko. "At any rate she will call as soon as she gets back to Tokyo."

The letter concluded, "Sumiyo still uses her married name, but recently she was legally divorced from her former husband's family register. She also said that her folks want to marry her off again. When I told her about your being a widower, her face brightened, and she hinted that she might refuse the marriage talk of her folks."

Kosuke had to smile at Katsue's usual busybody attitude; she was always meddling in someone else's affairs. And yet he could not really get angry with her. Why? Then he realized that he had not, after all these years, really forgotten Sumiyo; that it was she, or rather her image, that had always stood between him and Aiko.

Sumiyo came about ten days later. Kosuke received her full of anticipation, like a young boy meeting a girl for the first time. Sumiyo was reticent at first, but after their business about Miyoko's prospective husband had broken the ice, the talk turned to the old days. The years disappeared and there hovered around her an air of womanly charm that was most bewitching to Kosuke.

"Do you have children?" he asked.

"No, I was never blessed with any," she answered, and the way she blushed when she said this fascinated Kosuke.

"No wonder you are so young," he said.

That night his old heart itched for the first time since his wife died.

The negotiations for Miyoko's marriage were carried out smoothly. At first Miyoko refused to be married off, saying there will be no one to take care of the family. "You marry first," she said to Ichiro, "then there will be someone, a woman in the house, to take care of you all."

"No, I can't agree with you," Ichiro said flatly. "Of course I appreciate . . . we all appreciate . . . how you took care of us after mother died. But I don't want you to stay with us at the sacrifice of your own marriage. I would feel obligated to you too deeply; the feeling would be a burden to me, to all of us, and would nag at us. I can't express myself very well, but you know what I mean don't you, father?" he concluded.

"Yes, yes," Kosuke said. "I know exactly what you mean."

Ichiro smiled at his father. "This is as good a chance as any, so I am going to tell you now and have your understanding," Ichiro continued. "I am going to marry soon. You remember Matsunaga Shusaku, a college chum of mine? It's his sister. It's all right, isn't it, father?"

"Why, of course, if you like her," Kosuke said happily. "It's perfectly all right with me. But my finances aren't in good enough shape for both of you to get married at the same time."

"That you don't have to worry about," Ichiro said. "Miyoko has been working for the family for nothing, so you will naturally have to pay for her wedding. But I have been saving, and with my savings and my fiancée's savings together, we should be able to have our own apartment."

"Then what are you going to do about the *yuino* exchange of gifts and money between the families of the betrothed couple, and the wedding?"

"I don't believe in *yuino*. That custom should be done away with," Ichiro said strongly. "The wedding ceremony—well, I am going to have a simple one, just with close relatives. And the reception will be very small also."

Kosuke agreed with him in every way, but he felt as though there was an empty space somewhere in his heart.

Ichiro is terribly matter of fact, he thought to himself. *But then I suppose you can call it American rationalism.* Just then Miyoko looked up.

"I think I will marry, father," she said bashfully, but with a bright smile.

"By all means," Kosuke said emphatically. "Don't worry about us. We'll manage. I might marry too, who knows!" And they all laughed happily.

Yuino for Miyoko was exchanged and the wedding date set. The formal go-between was decided upon as Mr. and Mrs. Ikeda, old family friends, because Sumiyo, the actual go-between, was a widow and could not act in that capacity at the ceremony. While the wedding preparations were going on, Sumiyo practically lived in Kosuke's house and looked after motherless Miyoko. But nothing was mentioned about the marriage between Kosuke and Sumiyo, although it seemed tacitly assumed by both.

"Don't sit there like a borrowed cat," Katsue teased him again with her sharp tongue. "Have a cigarette."

Kosuke smiled and sat down by the hibachi.

"What are you going to do about Sumiyo?" Katsue asked. "If you settle that, I can go back to Osaka in peace of mind. Sumiyo says that nothing definite has been decided upon."

"Yes, I suppose it really is the best, but—"

Katsue looked at him uncertainly.

Just then the two younger boys came home. When he heard their happy young voices at the front door, Kosuke, undecided till now, suddenly made up his mind.

"I don't think I'll go through with it," he said decisively. "The two boys are at critical ages. I don't want to risk their unhappiness because of my marriage. Aiko would never forgive me if anything should happen to them."

He felt empty inside, but light. He felt a bit guilty toward Sumiyo, but then he had never actually proposed to her.

I shall continue to cherish her image deep inside my heart, he thought.

A slanting ray of sunlight filled their small dining room. The dressing of Miyoko for the wedding would soon be finished.

A CRANE THAT CANNOT COME BACK

by Seto Nanako

I must live through the realities of life
Too cruel and irretrievable,
Though I feel much pain in myself.
Supposing
That my days are numbered.

Aug. 25, 1958

Profuse bleeding!
How painful I've felt in both mind and body.
Words simply fail me in expressing myself to others.
Thinking I'd be lost, I stoutly stood it, even while I cried. Gritting my teeth, I stoutly stood it, telling myself that I must live. Then, at the very moment that I was feeling relieved, I burst into tears in the excess of my joy. Soon after a feeling of anxiety grew in me, a fear lest I should shortly be attacked once more by that *horror,* and again be lost.
I *must* think about it against my will. I do not belong to myself alone.
I must live as long as I can for the benefit of my daughter, my mother, husband, and brother, although I have become weak and disabled.
Oh, God, let me live, and in peace.

Nov. 12

I recall it was about this time . . .
Like terrible dreams . . . almost one year has passed already.
My throat has become swollen, it is clearly visible.
I have had a sore throat for several days.

Nov. 14

The bloody phlegm continues, though I am careful still to keep quiet.
Impossible for me to rid myself of a feeling of fear.
Unthinkingly, gave a scolding to Mami, my child, for her mischief.
Now I repent.

Nov. 15

Mother has made a large purchase for me.
I feel very sorry for her.
I hear she has stopped smoking . . . only because of me.
How hard it must have been for you, mother!
I must live at any cost, for the sake of my family, especially Mami
. . . poor thing.
A verse suddenly came to me:

> *I that am now sick in bed*
> *Do want to live as long as possible;*
> *I am fighting*
> *For my only daughter.*

A poor verse . . . just a passing thought. I'd be ashamed if anyone else saw it.

Nov. 16

Caught a slight cold. Mami also feels bad, being a little feverish.

Nov. 17

It makes me very uneasy to take so much medicine.
Another new disease would be fatal to me.
How long will it be until we can joyfully look at each other again?
I am weeping . . .

Nov. 18

Have a constant headache. My sore throat continues as usual.
Whenever I have a singing in my ears, I feel unable to endure it.
But I am trying to take as little medicine as possible.
Another person had died of pernicious anemia, it is said . . . Recently, I get tired easily. Feel stiff in my shoulders, despite being in bed.

Nov. 21

I'm very surprised to hear that there is something abnormal about my chest.
Now I know the reason for the bloody phlegm, and also why I have been given streptomycin continually.
Out of the frying pan into the . . .
I have symptoms of Basedow's disease. That gets on my nerves, too.

Nov. 22

I've got a slight fever all the time. I am always in fear that something else is wrong with me.
Last night I was terribly confused, because a disgusting arthralgia began; however, it has now passed.
Feel relieved. May nothing be abnormal!

Nov. 23

Tears after tears,
Looking at the town by night,
Seeing Mami off from the hospital,
Longing for the time I shall recover from illness,
Fear grows that I may never be well again.

> *How long will it be*
> *Before the time I can lead a happy life*
> *With Mami?*
> *Listening to the sound of the peace bell*
> *Traveling over the autumn night*
> *Growing deeper and deeper.*

Nov. 26

Bleeding for five minutes . . .
Being caused by menses?

Nov. 27

Mother gives me so much food . . . I can't eat it all.
Filled with much gratitude.

Nov. 30

Feel so happy when Mami comes here.
Feel so bad when Mami goes home . . . unspeakable sorrow.

Dec. 1

Time flies like an arrow. The last month of the year has stolen upon us!
It is likely that my beauty parlor will be reopened.
I am a constant source of anxiety to my mother.

Dec. 2

Kikusada-san visits me. I speak too much about my illness and have hardly time to thank him for his kindness.

Dec. 3

Feeling better these days. Because of my liver?
Hoping this good condition continues.

Dec. 8

Begin to put my pictures in order. They bring back pleasant memories of when I was in good health.

Dec. 10

We could manage to buy for my husband an overcoat which he has long wanted. Sorry for him having done without it until now. I think that he will have to get the clothes he needs from now on . . . little by little.

Mami's need for clothing is also pressing heavily on me; however, it seems to be hardly possible to do anything about it.

Have a vague bad feeling in my body and try not to tell others about it.

Shortly the light is turned out and I go to bed listening to the sound of the peace bell.

I feel lonely.

Dec. 11

The blood count of leucocytes is 4,500.
May everything go well, at least until the New Year,
when I may visit home.

Dec. 12

Receive a small package from Tokyo containing a pair of pretty gloves for Mami. I kiss them impulsively.

Get tired seeing TV again, after such a long time.

Stiffness in my shoulders and pain in my back makes me so gloomy.

My only wish is that I may become healthy again, at least by the New Year holidays.

Dec. 13

I can't move my arms and neck today.

The doctor says that I may be out of the hospital in a few months if nothing abnormal interferes.

God, preserve me!

On hearing Shimizu-san is said to have cancer, I fall into low spirits as if it were my own disease.

Dec. 14

Am sorry for giving a scolding to Mami, and think, Mami, please forgive my thoughtless heart.

When she grows ripe for marriage, I am afraid, she will have to face many obstacles. . . . Until that time, oh, I wish I could live on . . .

Mami, please don't think ill of me, since only your father's uncontaminated blood runs in your veins. Thus, you must never consider yourself unfortunate, Mami. And so, get married to a person like your papa, you know.

Dec. 17

Feel many pains in the various joints of my body. My face appears to be a bit swollen . . . a reaction of Amipylo?

Dec. 21

My roommate has left the hospital.
Bedding and equipment have all been taken out of my room.
I'll be alone from tonight.
In my loneliness, tears stream ceaselessly down my cheeks.
Although thinking that I shall get used to my vacant room soon, tears come at once.
Make up my mind to ask my nurse, Shigehiro-san, to explain to me my medical record.
She advises me to take it easy for a few months so that I will make no failure of my life. I grit my teeth . . .
The count of leucocytes is 6,400. The doctor says that all the parts of my body which have been abnormal seem to be gradually returning to a normal condition.
Even with little or no blood transfusions, my condition should take no turn for the worse!

Dec. 22

I felt so lonely that it took much time to get to sleep last night.
I never hear the voice of Mami through the phone, or news about Mami from my husband, without tears.
When my husband had to go home, it was very hard for me to keep back my tears.

Dec. 24

The New Year is just around the corner. Many patients are leaving the hospital. I was at last moved into another room yesterday, in which I've been left alone again. I cannot stand such utter loneliness. Whenever night nears, my feeling of solitude grows more and more.
It is Christmas Eve tonight. Listening to gay Christmas carols sung

under the windows, I become sad to tears, wondering how soon I can return to good health and a happy life.

I hear that the patient who was operated on for his pancreas is dangerously ill. When the doctor inclines his head as if in doubt at seeing me, I always fear that I might be in the same position as that patient.

How long has it been since I saw Mami last? All day I think about driving home without permission from the doctors, to meet lovely Mami.

Dec. 25

I did not expect anybody to come to celebrate the holy night, but my brother, Hiromi, and his friends dropped in to say Merry *Christmas,* bringing a piece of Christmas cake they bought together down town. Weep for joy.

Dec. 26

Became feverish from last night. I cannot quite feel comfortable about it when relapses seem to occur.

Am making efforts not to think about my illness going from bad to worse, but a feeling of uneasiness inevitably attacks me.

Hoping that blood transfusions may not bring on fever, and that my temperature may not rise any more.

Dec. 27

According to thermometer at 6:00 a.m., I have 99° though slept like a log last night by the help of an injection.

Slight drop to 98.4° at noon.

May I never develop a higher fever than tonight's!

But, alas! I have an attack of fever of 100.4° although the pains have been gradually abating.

Must I give up all hope of visiting my home?

What an irony of fate!

Patent medicine for a cold is liable to reduce a higher feverish attack.

Take medicine, Ilotycin (erythromycin). I know it has a drastic action.

I am simply dying to go home, only so that I can see Mami play from my bed.

May I return home!

Dec. 28

I have had quite a weak appetite for a couple of days.

Urine suddenly decreased to a small amount today.

Received a slight feverish attack, because I broke into a cold sweat when the doctors took the blood from my chest.

I am not feeling much better.

Soon comes the hour of putting out the lights.

A sudden attack of unbearable solitude again.

Seem to be slightly feverish.

I catch at, and open every nerve to, any slight changes that happen.

I cannot possibly live long since I am a broken person.

I cannot know very well how things stand with Hiromi, however . . .

Poor fellow!

How can we help him find his life worth living?

Mother and I are being tormented by it.

Jan. 2, 1959

Began a new year of life in the hospital.

As nobody else is yet here—after going home for New Year's Day —there is much quiet and loneliness . . .

Gather up my courage, looking forward to the day of leaving the hospital.

About half the blood transfusions I've already taken before—100 cc.

Jan. 5

The highest fever is 98.6° for today.

Five days have already passed, too soon.

A patient in the next room has returned to the hospital.

Since the 27th of last month, my fever refuses to go down to a normal one.

It seems not to be serious enough to worry about, but it is always weighing heavily on me.

Spend lonely the long awaited New Year, in the hospital.
How hateful to be tried by God!
Feel like sinking through the earth.
My husband is very kind to me in every way possible.
One more has died this morning. The second victim this year.

Jan. 6

Scarcely had the fever been reduced when it rose to 104° last night.
Lose the power of resistance and feel myself easily running down day by day.
My husband leaves nothing to desire in nursing me.
I am much indebted to him.
I haven't seen Mami for quite a while. I hope she is fine. I cannot help feeling depressed.
102.2° in the evening.

Jan. 7

One more has died. Third victim this year.
Am sorry for having wasted a lot of money on the medicine; about four thousand yen (about $11) just simply to go home.
Besides, I made Mami happy by promising to return home.
Want very badly to be in bed together holding her tight in my arms if only for one night.
The count of leucocytes was 5,300 on the 27th of last December.
But erythrocyte and color index rather decreased.

Jan. 10

Mami and I meet after a long separation.
Shed tears.
Knowing that I must not move, Mami never comes close to me.
Feeling of loneliness . . .
There are still white signs in my throat like diphtheria.
We have been having troubles that are a bit different from before since the day before yesterday.
We are all black sheep, including me!
Hiromi has finally left home to go to Tokyo. I can't help feeling uneasy about Hiromi. Speaking little, showing his feelings hardly at all,

but I suppose he must be filled with much suffering. I'm sorry I couldn't meet him, for all his coming, before he left for Tokyo.

I that am already disabled cannot possibly do everything as I want. I can't stand by myself.

Wish my earliest possible recovery not only for my sake but also for my lovely daughter, Mami.

Mami is now my only hope to get well.

Jan. 12

Much menses after two months.

The count of leucocytes was 1,100 on the 30th of last December, but fortunately returned to a normal 5,000 on the 10th of this month. Yesterday Mami and I had a merry time together all day long after a long absence. She says, "Mommy, shall we go with Papa to Fukuya Department Store, with its many facilities for play, in the day after sleeping for one night together?" That makes me cry! May our happiest day come soon. I answered, "Mami, I wonder if the day will be after a lot of nights." Mami looked confused as she knew nothing about how long I must stay. Feel sorry for her. Shed tears.

Jan. 13

Spent the whole day all right without any sense of boredom.

Having a wonderful time with Mami makes me tired.

Bad headache. Feel very ill in my chest tonight.

I have never felt as sick as I do these days.

I am also out of sorts around my stomach.

Perhaps it might be my imagination.

Feel relieved to know that mother intends to come home and settle down.

I am anxious when I think about Hiromi; tears run down out of my eyes.

Hoping that I may have enough sleep tonight and get up happily tomorrow morning.

Shadow of restlessness.

Writing this diary while in bed five minutes before the lights are put out.

It is now raining. That makes me very sad.

Jan. 14

The head consulting physician comes round to see me, and says, "Perhaps you may be able to leave the hospital around the end of March."

I was very glad to hear it. I wish I could pay a day visit, at least before March. But I fear that I may cause much trouble by catching a cold, since I am too sensitive to that. Unwillingly, I control myself.

May I feel quite well by the day when Mami enters kindergarten.

Opinions about my blood test sound pretty good.

I know it is not good to be so gloomy about everything.

The doctor says that there is no reason to worry about my chest trouble.

My face seems to be a bit swollen now; I have been growing stouter. The blood transfusions are reduced to twice a week from today. I am very happy to know that I am getting better than ever.

I have not seen my husband for three days. Oh, yes, the temperature of my body has been returning to normal; besides, there is no need to test the urine quantity any more; the examinations of urine and feces become reduced to once a month from now on. I wonder if I am expected to go home around March. May everything pass off quietly. And may I soon recover. . . .

Jan. 15

My husband kindly called on me after a long absence. He seems to be tired out. I never miss two days without seeing Mami.

I find her fascinatingly pretty hearing her voice through the phone "Mommy, see you again. . . ."

Jan. 16

Permission for bathing.

Dr. Ishida said only in play that I am leaving the hospital by the end of this month. I know it is not true, but my heart beats with joy. The doctor says leucocytes are normal. There seems to be nothing wrong.

Tears for joy. Pleased with myself.

The blood transfusions will be only on Monday and Thursday every week.

Please God, I will not be long in getting well for the sake of Mami.
In the evening Sanae brings Mami to the hospital.
Mami's little face looked very cold, but she didn't seem to be catching
a cold. I was reassured by that. But I feel an unaccountable com-
passion for her . . .
I do not know, does Mami miss me and feel lonely?
I hope I may live long enough to protect my only daughter, as
long as possible.

Jan. 18

It has been awfully cold for a couple of days. Through the windows
I see many people in good health, and envy them very much.
Mami came in the afternoon.
Her hands were a bit swollen with the cold. I suppose she must have
felt cold, but she did not mind at all. She was very fine.
I notice there have been some changes about Mami that she never
had before, in her way of reading a book or doing something by
herself.
Since she is now growing, she is eagerly asking me many questions.
"Mommy, what is this? Well, how come—"
I am afraid, may my family be so kind as to answer her questions,
though it takes much trouble to do so. It is now one of the most
important times in her passage through life.

Jan. 19

Only three drops of kenacort (triamcinolone).
I pray to be back safely in March. I'm feeling better.
Mami has become simply mad in asking about everything lately.
People say that the future depends on the ages between three and
four.
I hope everybody will kindly use easy language in teaching Mami.
May I be able to be back home around March as the doctor says.
And may what he says contain absolute truth for this one time.
Shige-kun, Hiromi's good friend, brought me a piece of pie yesterday.
He dropped in today again because he can't come tomorrow.
Thanks to him I spent the whole day without any boredom. Re-
member Hiromi suddenly and think about him. I hope he may
not be discouraged by Miss Kuwada, who was one of his best girl
friends and killed herself, and make some mistakes.

Jan. 21

The head physician—unexpected on Wednesday—comes around to see me. It is a pleasure for me since he shows me my medical record. Leucocytes are 4,400. May this result be an error.

The test of my medulla taken yesterday appears to be not so bad. Have a little too much fever in the afternoon. That is haunting me. Besides, I feel a headache every day. I am worried because there still remain some white symptoms in my throat, which I hope will soon die away.

There is no use in thinking or in writing for the purpose of expressing myself. But mother and my husband who know me best are so busy that they have little time to talk with me.

Nevertheless, I do want to talk and to make myself heard—too much.

That is why I use my pen like this. By doing so, I drown my anxiety to a degree. No, I try to force it away . . .

It is a holiday today for my family. They are all bright and happy. Their faces are full of the delights of working. I envy them very much.

Jan. 26

The day before yesterday I was so happy as to be moved to tears when I met Hiromi after a long absence. But I was very surprised to hear Hiromi left home again yesterday; mother called on me unannounced and told me about him, her face turning pale. What a foolish thing you have done, Hiromi!

I thought we had been leading our lives quietly and peacefully for these last few days . . .

What worries my mother has!

I don't now know how I can keep mother in good spirits, but I hope she takes enough care of herself at least.

Mami is always reading our adult faces. Please be careful of the influence of your moods on the child.

Mami is my only child. I greatly appreciate having her.

Jan. 27

I hope Hiromi may return home safely.

I have been restless since yesterday as there are some problems left in my mind. I never feel refreshed unless I work out my troubles. It might be enough to grow up spiritually for my age though it will take a long time to be matured psychologically.

I will be relieved on one count if only Hiromi gets married and becomes a good merchant. Our family cannot afford even the time to say hello to each other every day since we are now living apart, individually.

But I firmly believe that we are, anytime and anywhere, always bound by the same spirit.

While I have been on the earth, I know mother, Hiromi, my husband, and Mami will have had some things to complain of about me. And I about them.

But we have been too careful in our speech and behavior to each other. Mother is a woman born to be filled with troubles.

Besides, she makes herself more miserable by making plenty of worries of her own. Mother was born and bred in loveless circumstances. She has been striving extraordinarily to live, though being exposed herself to cold treatment. That is because she is a person of strong affection, as is not seen in everybody. Her precious affection is never closed to anyone, neither to her children, nor to those who have no connection with her.

To be frank, such a precious love can be considered at once her strong point and her weak point, because it is a blind love.

I know it will be almost impossible for my mother to grant my request to her to be more selfish or less kind to other persons. I wish she would not give her love so freely to everybody.

Perhaps I may express myself so poorly that nobody can follow me. But I shall be quite satisfied if she alone understands me.

Don't remain a miserable mother any more.

Mami has come three days running. I enjoy myself while she is with me, but after she leaves the hospital, I become too lonely to bear it. "It is amazing that you should recover from your illness so fast," said the head physician.

My heart beats with joy.

I wonder *when* I shall be home?

Jan. 28

Leucocytes were 4,400 on the 20th of this month.

Whenever I have taken a blood examination, leucocytes have been increasing, 200 each time, and became 4,800 in all by the 27th of this month.

I hope my leucocytes may increase like this. Then I will be able to leave the hospital temporarily around March.

Well, I should rather say "take a long stay out," instead of "leaving the hospital."

Anyway nothing can keep me in the hospital longer.

Mami, I'll be very happy to take you along to Tenmaya Playland on the condition that I leave the hospital.

Even if people think their marriage for the best, it does not always succeed.

But ours is an exception.

Being young, we thought only of ourselves and at the same time, were passionate. Nevertheless, we made a nice start.

As the time passed, our affection deepened, becoming more real. I sometimes believe there are few couples who feel as happy as we. Our marriage is very wonderful.

But, too bad—this happiness is completely spoiled by my illness.

Jan. 29

The weather being rainy since last night, I feel a bit gloomy when I get up this morning.

Hearing Mami speaking, I become a little bright and happy.

According to my mother, Mami was crying while my mother went out for thirty minutes—poor thing.

If I am only in good health . . . I always think about it one way or another. It is said that children's character is influenced by such circumstances to a great degree.

I think of the future of Mami; I do want Mami to be a well-educated woman despite being a girl. She is my only child. And I do want Mami to be brought up with warm domestic affection. It reminds me that when my brother and I were little children, our mother was in bed for a long time. I do not want Mami to have such experiences as mine. I fear that family troubles are liable to complicate home life.

Being threatened with my illness, I am so sorry for not being able to give full play to my fondness for Mami. Dotage? Blind love? Well, call it either, but in any event, I wish I could embrace Mami in my arms with all my might. However, I am afraid that Mami forgets me when I do not see her often.

Thinking so, I feel lonely and miserable sometimes.

Jan. 30

No blood transfusion since Tuesday. This way, I may perhaps leave the hospital around the end of next month.

I am so sensitive as to easily catch a cold, but I will be all right as far as that goes.

May nothing abnormal happen, and have mercy on me to live one day longer on the earth. I exist not only for the sake of myself, but—

Feb. 3

I see visitor after visitor all day long: Shige-kun and Mrs. Morikazu, who have both come to see me four times, and Mrs. Wada, and Sanae.

How happy I have been today without any boredom, thanks to them.

But when they must be going: left all alone, I feel all the more sad. I have been not up to the mark from the day before yesterday.

Mami comes for the first time since we met nine days ago.

She has been so quick learning how to speak. I feel very sorry for Mami since I could not celebrate her birthday at all. Hiromi has not come back yet. It is surprising that he should have changed like this; he was so kind and meek when a little boy. I wonder if he has some trouble with being an A-bomb sufferer. Yes, he must have, I am sure. It seems to be a great problem for us to gain a better understanding about him physically and mentally. My home is full of black sheep! I feel like praying with folded hands to my mother and husband. My stepfather and my aunt are taking good care of Mami. Much obliged.

I am a bit tired today. Blood transfusions were stopped yesterday.

Feb. 4

There is still some fatigue left. Have a little high temperature this morning. Try to keep quiet today.

I will feel better again by tomorrow morning. My body seems to be growing weaker day by day.

Feb. 7

Isolation becomes doubly acute. Tears stream down ceaselessly.
Receive an express package containing a style book from Hiromi.
You silly fool, Hiromi!
Weep.
At last, yesterday, I got permission to leave the hospital on February 27, I am simply mad with joy.
I think the twenty days left till I leave much longer than they are.
Hoping time flies fast.
May nothing abnormal happen!
I feel uneasy to receive a letter from Hiromi in Hirano.

Feb. 9

I feel a bit feverish, but it is not much fever.
My top temperature has been 99° for today. So the more nervous I am the higher it gets. My pulse is pretty high, too.
At any rate, I am dying to go home; I'll stop thinking anything about my illness.
Time, fly, quickly, quickly!
Time, fly, quickly, quickly!
May nothing abnormal happen!
Shigeru kun comes to see me.
A bit cold.
Send some money to Hiromi.

Feb. 12

Mami does not come.

Feb. 22

My sweet home! I have not seen it for almost nine months.
I entirely drown memory of my illness for a while.

Come back again to the hospital, after staying for one night at my home.
Chilliness of the passage in the hospital.

I act selfishly to my husband in loneliness. Sorry for him.
Time to put off lights soon—lonely.
Tears. Tears stream down—ceaselessly . . .
Unfortunately, one more has died tonight.
I don't want to die.
Mami, my only daughter!
Nanako, Mami's only mother!
"Oh, this feeling . . .
"This lonely feeling . . .

(These are her last written words during her second experience in the hospital. She died at 10:45 A.M., April 10, 1959.)

BRINGING UP MOTHERS-IN-LAW

by John Fujii

ONE OF THE PLEASANT THINGS about life in Japan are the unexpected complications. Just about the time I thought I had everything licked, comes this cable from the folks in the good old U.S.A.

Father and mother were born in Japan but spent the last forty years in California, with time out for an occasional excursion to visit their grandchildren in Washington, D.C., and Chicago. Now they had decided to see Japan before they faded away. So like a couple of "Urashima Taro," they returned to the land of their birth.

Urashima Taro was the legendary Japanese character who befriended a lonely turtle; the turtle took him to a fairy Neptunian princess who lived at the bottom of the sea. He went to live in the mythical wonderland at the bottom of the sea until one day he got homesick for his old homeland and came riding home on the back of the turtle only to find that everything in his homeland had changed —he had been away too long.

So father and mother came riding back to Japan—by Japan Airlines instead of on the back of a turtle—to find everything had changed except the smell.

Nothing was left of the Japan that mother knew as a girl except Fujiyama, the Imperial Palace and Shimbashi Station. They oh-ed and ah-ed all the way into Tokyo from Haneda Airport and were happily pleased to find everything at the house in Stateside shape, including the plumbing. Mother kept on saying that she would have made the trip much earlier except for the memory of the old *benjo* and the ordeal of a public bathhouse while father kept on asking whether the tap water was safe to drink.

During the first few weeks and our daily brushes with the traffic, father was glad he had given up driving ten years ago. "Too many people on the streets and they drive on the wrong side anyway," he complained.

Everytime we ate *sushi,* it was always the same routine, "Do you think the tuna is safe to eat raw?" I assured them that the only thing radioactive was their imagination.

In our trips around the countryside, it was all I could do to curb my filial temper. They compared the Kamakura Buddha with the Statue of Liberty, Kegon Falls with Niagara, the Tsubame Express with the Super-Chief. I finally squeezed a begrudging concession out of them. They admitted that Fujiyama was unsurpassed. I noticed that they stood stiffly at attention one morning at Shinagawa when the Emperor's special train roared through the station.

They burst out with such unexpected observations that it was hard to keep from laughing. They expressed surprise that their grandchildren, going on four and six, spoke such good Japanese. They wanted to know whether the fresh milk was imported and who baked the bread. Now that they've slept on *futon* and *tatami* and eaten off the floor, they remember the vivid colors and bright spring days of their childhood. They recalled some of the ethereal beauties of ancient Japan and faced the realities of modern Japan. In the brief three months they spent in Japan, I got them to admit that life in Japan was pleasant and comfortably leisurely for a couple of exiles, seventy-odd years old, even without color television.

If you think you have mother-in-law troubles, a Japanese mother-in-law adds additional complications. All through the "beautiful friendship," one often wonders whether he is marrying the girl or her mother. Every time you go courting, the mother serves the tea and cooks the dinner. When winter comes, you get a hand-knitted sweater which old mama-san has produced.

After the first few weeks, if your intentions are not strictly honorable, mama-san is a pretty hard obstacle to face. If your intentions are on the up-and-up, you have problems, too. Mother treats you like one of the family already. Eventually, you break the news of the impending nuptials and mama-san rushes down to the nearest shrine to determine the best day for the wedding. It doesn't make any difference whether it's in mid-summer heat or winter cold, it's mother who arranges the wedding details.

Mother tells you where you should spend the honeymoon and looks a mite unhappy when you decide to leave her at home during the nuptial excursion. As soon as the newly-weds are back from the honeymoon, mother is back sniffing around to find out when the baby is coming. If you haven't quite decided on a family, mother goes back to her priests and then announces the most auspicious day for a son. The parents don't count at all. They are expected to cooperate fully.

If the prospective heir is delayed for any of a thousand and one domestic reasons, the mother-in-law flutters about with a determination to thwart the apparent catastrophe. She worships at a temple dedicated to the phallic gods, she consults her herb doctor for a bitter tea that is supposedly good for future fathers, and otherwise creates such confusion around the household that the parents finally decide that it's probably better to have the baby now than wait a year.

Once the fateful pronouncement is made by the doctor that the wife is pregnant, then the mother-in-law really gets down to business. She moves in bag and baggage to supervise the household. She directs the prospective father's diet and the future mother is forbidden to eat anything but tradition-prescribed food. It doesn't matter whether you get food parcels from the States or your friends help you with commissary supplies. Food that was good enough for her and for her grandmother is good enough for her daughter and the cans of nutritious food go on the pantry shelves. The next few months are pretty hectic and rather than face the inquisition of an irate mother-in-law, it's recommended that the father stay out of the way.

You don't worry about a name—she's got one picked out for the future offspring, which she has already decided is a son. If the baby should turn out to be a daughter, then mama-san won't speak to you—until the next confinement. If you are blessed with a son on the second try, mother is all smiles.

Japanese mothers-in-law may be a nuisance when it comes to having babies, but they are sort of nice to have around when you have problems. If you want to buy a piece of property to build a house, they usually scrape up the collateral. If you even casually mention that it's difficult to get some item of food, the old mother shuffles in from the country on the next Tokyo-bound train laden like a black-market peddler.

Once the youngsters are well on their way to adolescence, mother-in-law limits her visits to the New Year's holidays or a children's festival, when she insists they have a new kimono. When you try to explain that your current income does not warrant such foolish fineries, she usually trundles in with a kimono which she has stitched herself or provides a bolt of kimono silk.

She insists that the Japanese customs be maintained and you reluctantly comply.

But a good mother-in-law is one's best friend in Japan.

THE COMMUNIST

by Abe Tomoji

Suzuta was a defendant in the 1952 May Day riot trial. He came out of the public courthouse and was walking toward Hibiya when he ran into Ino. "Why, Suzuta," Ino exclaimed, walking towards him smiling.

But how he has changed, Suzuta thought. He had not seen Ino since a year ago, when he had had coffee with him; when he had last seen him Ino was dirty and miserably dressed. Now he is the picture of prosperity, he thought. Why, he even wears a red necktie. And he's smiling.

"I'm really glad to see you," Ino said. "But what are you doing in this neighborhood?"

"The public trial," Suzuta answered, as if irked at Ino's absent-mindedness.

"Oh, that's right," Ino smiled, a bit embarrassed. "I'm sorry. Well, I wish you all the luck. I suppose I shouldn't be walking through this neighborhood. They say they are still pinching those who 'went' that day."

"You'll be all right, I'm sure," Suzuta said.

"Anyway, have supper with me, won't you?" Ino asked. "I know a place near here—an inexpensive Chinese restaurant, but the food is excellent."

Suzuta looked at him, puzzled.

"Don't worry, I didn't rob anybody," Ino laughed. "I happened to fall into some money."

Suzuta did not possess the power to resist. His stomach, too long used to eating poor food, stirred inside him; it would not allow him the luxury of refusing. He followed Ino hungrily. They came to the broad intersection of Toranomon, the Tiger Gate, when Ino suddenly stopped. "Hey, Suzuta, wasn't it around here where we started our zig-zag snake dance that day?"

"Yes, I believe so," and Suzuta remembered that day two years ago as if yesterday. It had been a bright day like this. He and Ino, their arms locked tight, marched at the head of the students' group of the long parade that followed. They were covered with dust and sweat and their voices were hoarse from yelling "*Washoi, washoi.*" They passed by the Tiger Gate and marched into Hibiya Park, then rested a bit. Suddenly, as if possessed, they streamed out of the Park, passed the Hibiya intersection and the American G.H.Q. building, headed toward Babasaki-mon intersection, and stormed into the Imperial Palace Plaza. The last he remembered was being trampled by the counter-attacking police and struck on the back of the head by a night stick.

He lost his glasses, got up and tried to run away. Everywhere there were whirls of dust, and he heard a pistol shot. He picked up a bamboo stick and, waving it high in the air, rushed toward a group where several police had caught a rioting student. Knocked down again, he was grabbed by the police and arrested, taken to jail, indicted for trial.

Suzuta had first met Ino at a rally in the Outer Garden. Seeing that Ino, too, was a student, Suzuta joined him and they locked arms together in the march. They had become friends and often had coffee together.

Suzuta was questioned many times and asked to reveal the names of those who were with him at the May Day riot, but Suzuta did not once mention Ino's name. Suzuta considered himself a strong Liberalist. He did not know anything of Ino's political ideology, nor did he particularly care. It was simply that he did not think it right to reveal the names of those who were with him; his imprisonment gave him a chance to nurture a long dormant fighting spirit.

He was bailed out in the winter of the following year, and that was when his fight for existence began. His family, never well-to-do, stopped his allowance completely. His body became run-down after working at cheap manual labor. He was on his way back from one

prospective clerical job that he hadn't gotten and was in extremely
low spirits when he first ran into Ino after his release, who had
stopped his milk delivery bicycle in front of Suzuta, stuck out his
hand and gripped Suzuta's bony hand. Suzuta perceived that Ino
thanked him in silence for having protected him. "Come to my
place for a minute," Ino said that day over a year ago. "I ran under
cover immediately after that mess and came here. There is always a job delivering milk, thank god." Ino led him into a back
street that was dark and dirty, with the atmosphere of the bottom
of a gulley. Suzuta guessed that Ino had come to a place like this
to escape the police. That meant Ino knew where to go to get away.
Then, unlike himself, who had gone to the May Day parade more
out of curiosity than conviction, he thought, this Ino, dirty and
disheveled, must be a regular member of the Communist Party. I
had better look out for him, Suzuta thought over his cup of coffee.

Ino had gone on talking about the hardships of the life of a milk
delivery boy and had ended by saying that he was just about at the
end of his physical endurance. He had not attended school for
months, he said. "I appreciate your protecting me by not divulging
my name," Ino thanked him that first time, offering him a cake in
that small, dirty shop near the station. "I understand you are asking
for an individual trial, instead of a collective trial like the rest. May
I ask why?"

Suzuta wondered, How could Ino, living under cover in a place
like this, know such a thing so fast? He really must be a big figure
in the party, he thought. Suzuta decided he would put Ino to test.
"I wish to promote May Day as the day of peaceful festival for free
workers. I wish to advocate this as a Liberalist, and not as a Communist."

"I wonder if that lot would understand such a fine difference?"
Ino answered.

Just then a tall young man walked in. His dark gold hair was wet,
his eyes were bluish, and his skin fair. He looked like a half-breed,
but he was as miserably dressed as Ino. The young man nodded to
Ino and sat at their table. When Okijima left them after a cup of
coffee, Suzuta could not help asking who this strange-looking young
man was.

Ino explained that Taro Okijima was half Japanese, half Russian. His father, a white Russian, had escaped the revolution by
fleeing to Japan and there he had married a Japanese woman. Taro

had lost his parents during the war and his aunt in Osaka had taken
him in, but she had not been very kind to him. Eventually he left
her and made a living as best he could—which included a number
of fringe enterprises. He was a good fighter, so everybody feared and
respected him. He was always getting into trouble with women, too.
He sold dope, but one of his partners cheated, ran away with all the
profits. "He must have done something terrible, and come to Tokyo
to take cover in this neighborhood," Ino added.

"Taro got a job teaching Russian to a group of university students. I'm in that group, but all the girls seem to fall in love with
Okijima. I can't keep pace with the feverish way the girls study.
One of the girls seems to have won out and at present Okijima is
head over heels in love with her. But the girl's father is a very strict
government official and has practically imprisoned her in the house.
Okijima goes near her house every evening, hoping to get a glimpse
of her." Okijima had come in, Ino explained, to get a cup of coffee
to fortify himself against the long hours of freezing vigil near her
house.

While listening to Ino, Suzuta had been seized with an uncanny
feeling that Ino was making up his story, that Okijima was actually
more than just a teacher of Russian. He had thought that Ino
might be trying to make use of the class as a means of getting to the
women students for political reasons, and that Suzuta had decided
that day that he had really better stay clear of Ino.

The conversation in the coffee shop had taken place a year before.
A short time after his first encounter with Ino, he changed his
mind, decided to ask for a collective trial instead, and has been attending it twice or three times every week.

The two entered a small Chinese restaurant near Toranomon.
"Please order anything you like," Ino said. "You will have some
beer, of course."

Suzuta was still puzzled. Is this the same Ino that he saw over
a year ago, on that snowy day, looking so gaunt? "Ha, Ha. Why do
you stare at me like that?" Ino asked. "Is there some secret written
on my face?"

"That's what I am trying to find out," Suzuta answered. "The
change is so great."

"It's nothing. I just happened to fall into a little money," Ino
answered cheerfully. "That is, I am going to. I think my *arbeit* is
going to make a hit."

Suzuta had an uncanny feeling that Ino must be doing something extraordinarily unusual. He was overwhelmed with curiosity. "What are you doing, anyway?" he asked.

"Well, I don't know quite how to explain—it's a sort of racket, with Americans as 'clients.' It's called 'consulter.'"

"Is there such an English word?"

"I think there is."

"Does that mean one who consults, or one who receives consultation?" Suzuta asked, curious.

"You are still the same. What difference does that make? A name doesn't mean anything; it's the business I'm interested in."

"I see. And what is the business?"

"We find, through classified ads, that there are people who want to sell their cars or something. We telephone them," he explained. "We call and say, 'you want to buy a dog,' or 'your dog has run away,' 'you need a maid,' or 'you have old books to sell,' or 'electric ice box to sell,' something like that. By the way—do you know of anyone who wants to buy an electric ice box?"

"No, I don't know anyone who wants to buy one. But you've certainly thought up some business, haven't you?"

"No, I didn't think of it. I was working for a fellow until recently who thought it up. He made a mess of the business by getting himself tangled up with women. I took it over. I got the job through school. I saw a want ad for a student fluent in English. There were four who answered it. Two didn't pass the test. The other fellow and I passed the test, carried on the business, and for a while made quite a lot of money. You want to come in on it?"

"No, I'm no good at a thing like that."

"It's nothing difficult. Just a little bluff. I use 'living' English. Not the stuffy, dead English they teach in school. I call up colonels, majors, even generals. They call me back. I go to their homes, offices, wherever they want me to. Everywhere I go, I use 'living' English and I get what I want. I get my business done."

Suzuta was again caught with that strange feeling that Ino was making up his story, to cover up something else. Suzuta thought it was possible Ino might be thinking of something big for his Communist group, hiding behind the cloak of this new consulter, consultant, or whatever he called his business, to gain access to American military officers.

ONE WORLD

by Serizawa Kojiro

THE 15TH OF AUGUST was here again.
Madame Sonoko dreaded this day.

On this date in 1945, she had listened awe-struck to the voice of the Emperor over the radio, listened and cried over the sad fate of Japan. Her life, too, had gone topsy-turvy as of this date. Little did she realize it then, however, for she was thinking only of her country, as befitting the wife of a high officer of the Imperial Navy of Japan.

But it is not because of the memory of this that she dreads the return of this day. It is the never-failing annual visit of Tokuda Kakuko that weighs most heavily on her heart, for Kakuko's visit always leaves a big ripple in the peace of this House of Abe.

On this day in 1945, while she was still wiping the tears that kept flowing, Kakuko ran in. "Madame, it's over! It's all over at last," she had cried. "His Excellency will return unhurt, and my husband too. It's peace! Peace has returned at long last." Stuttering excitedly, she bowed low before Sonoko, and cried tears of happiness. It was so unlike Kakuko to lose her composure so, but then, who was she to blame her? Sonoko took Kakuko's hands into hers.

"There will be no more Imperial Navy, Madame," Kakuko said. "His Excellency, and my husband, will leave the sea forever, and you and I can lead normal lives, free from worrying about whether they

230

will be killed. We've had enough of it, haven't we?" And Kakuko's face looked infinitely bright.

She talked over and over about the return of peace and their husbands. Sonoko stared at her face, wondering if she had lost her mind. While I lamented over the fate of Japan, this woman cried in happiness because her husband was coming home unhurt—this thought never once entered Sonoko's mind.

Kakuko's husband, Lieutenant-Commander Tokuda, had become her husband's adjutant some two years before, and the two left for a base in the Southern Islands. The women met often in Sonoko's house to console and to encourage each other. There never was any discord between them during those two years, but now . . . Sonoko was bewildered. She could hardly sympathize with the feelings of her good friend.

It was not until Kakuko went home and she was left alone on the upstairs veranda that the realization began to take form and make sense. She saw the ocean before her eyes, shining blue under the August sun, and saw its quiet waters for the first time in a long while. She had not seen it thus since the American air raids began. She realized for the first time that peace had really returned, for she saw it written over its surface, spelled out by the white ripples.

Yes, this was a part of the Pacific Ocean; Pacific, peace. . . .

And with this thought she was able to realize fully the meaning of the words which she said first to herself, then out loud. "He is coming home. . . ." And as she heard herself repeat the words, her eyes blurred, and she understood Kakuko's tears. Her own tears, this time different tears, flowed down her cheeks . . . warm, they warmed her heart. Then suddenly she became hot, the hot blood ran through her body.

Just as suddenly, she was chilled through, for her mother-in-law was standing behind her.

"Sono-san, even if Jusuke does come home safe," the old lady said calmly, "he must commit harakiri in apology to His Imperial Highness, mustn't he?"

Her mother-in-law's late husband had been a civil official, and at one time a member of the Privy Council. Even when the air raids became severe, he turned a deaf ear to all their pleas to evacuate with the other aged folks. He insisted that as long as the Imperial Family remained in the capital, he could not quit Tokyo. On April 1945, in one of the worst bombings of the capital, his house caught fire and he was trapped. This old lady, a stout woman despite her small size, cremated the body of her husband in the blazing fire of her own home before she escaped to Sonoko's house here in the small town by the Sagami Bay.

"You must be prepared for it," the old lady continued.

"Yes, mother," Sonoko answered. But how was she to quiet her hot blood and her heartbeat. She blamed Kakuko for the loss of her own poise.

Just minutes earlier Sonoko had sat before the radio with this mother-in-law, who had changed into her formal kimono because she was going to listen to the voice of the Emperor.

A few days later, before her son and daughter came home from their labor corps demobilizations, Kakuko had come running in again, quite out of breath. She reported that she had been to General Headquarters. She was told that Sonoko's husband had left Keelung, Formosa, on a submarine headed for Japan, but that there were no reports of his arrival anywhere in Japan.

"They said that he must have known of the end of the war. And so did the enemy, so it is not likely that he was bombed on the way." She became indignant. "I realized then for the first time that we've lost the war. Everyone of them was at a loss as to what to do. Yes, those once high-and-mighty officers, such a poor lot. I was quite disgusted with them."

"You say Abe's boat was lost?" Sonoko mumbled, her face had turned pale.

"They couldn't even make that clear," Kakuko sneered. " 'If His Excellency did arrive in some Navy yard, he should contact the headquarters.' That's all they said."

"If Abe left Formosa knowing of the defeat, he left but with one thought . . ." Sonoko's voice did not shake. "He would not have reached Japan."

"You mean . . . to commit . . . suicide?" Kakuko's voice was clearly shaking.

Sonoko nodded in silence and stood up. She must not lose her composure before this woman, the wife of her husband's subordinate. A bag of this year's powdered tea had been sent from the father of another subordinate of her husband. This may be the last grind of tea, the letter that came with it had said. She got her equipment out for a tea ceremony. The cup was the favorite of her husband; it had been held lovingly in his hands over many years. He had wavered many times over the decision to take it with him.

Kakuko remembered it, too. She had helped Sonoko in the packing. Kakuko took hold of the cup in her hands, and closed her eyes. Its smooth surface was soothing to her uprooted nerves.

"The tea was sent to me by First Lieutenant Oishi's father," Sonoko said, and prayed inwardly that the young lieutenant be safely returned to his father.

Kakuko drank the tea, and placed the empty cup before her on the *tatami*. Then she covered her face with both hands and began to sob. Sonoko's calmness touched her heart, and this time she cried in sheer sympathy for this senior wife. But, while crying, somewhere in her heart was a faint hope that His Excellency would not have taken her young husband on the journey of death.

On the 15th of August of the following year, Kakuko came in deep mourning.

Sonoko was taken by surprise. Defunct Navy Headquarters had not yet formally announced the death of her husband; she herself had not performed any of the Buddhist rites for the deceased. Her husband's smiling portrait still adorned her dining room. She had not yet removed it to the family altar room.

Kakuko clasped her palms before the altar for a while, then walked into the dining room.

"Is Taro-san home?" she asked in a most casual voice.

"No, he went to Hiroshima."

"To the Peace Festival?" Kakuko smiled. "So unlike Taro-san, isn't it?"

"I haven't the slightest idea what for," Sonoko answered with a slight bitterness.

Her first son had graduated that year from junior college in Okayama, and entered the medical college of Tokyo University. But he seemed to have lost interest in his studies. He left home everyday, then instead of going to school wandered the streets of Tokyo all day.

A few days ago he announced suddenly that he was going to Hiroshima, and left. Not even a post card had come from him. She did not have train fare for him, but he took his father's watch, a souvenir of his days as a navy attaché in London. Taro must have hocked it for his fare. When asked why he was going to Hiroshima and where he was going to stay, he simply stared at her with his huge eyes and muttered, "It was awful in Hiroshima, you know."

The year before, when the war had ended, he had not returned until late in September, thin and pale, his big eyes burning dark like two big holes in a skeleton's head. "I was in Hiroshima," he had said. "It was awful there," and gazing deep into her face, huge tears formed beneath his hollow eyes.

"What do you mean, 'awful'?" she had asked. "How come you are unhurt?"

But his lips only quivered, and no words came out of them. In the year that followed there was never any conversation between the two pertaining to Hiroshima, even after she had learned through newspapers about the "awful incident of the atom bomb." She had been too busy with the cares of living.

"Fumiko-san is out too?" Kakuko asked.

"She is at work," Sonoko answered simply.

"I wanted to ask the young folks' opinion. I thought it would be quicker that way." Kakuko took some American cigarettes from her hand bag. "But if they are out, I am going to be direct, and ask you."

It was the first time Sonoko had ever seen Kakuko smoke, but there was nothing awkward about the way Kakuko smoked. She had rouge on her lips and her finger nails were manicured red. Kakuko looked infinitely young, and Sonoko stared at her, amazed. Unmindful of Sonoko's curiosity, Kakuko came directly to the point of her visit. The deep respect due to the wife of her husband's senior officer had disappeared from Kakuko in the course of one year. Sonoko's house was big and Kakuko wanted to know if she would let her two Western-style rooms to an American officer.

Sonoko had spent her days during the war without knowing the hardships and scarcity of food. From somewhere, someone always sent food that was hard to obtain. With the termination of the war all that had stopped, and almost every day someone's kimono went in exchange for more needed everyday clothes, or a family treasure laden with past ancestral memories went for rice. Kakuko, on the other hand, made use of her youth, her good looks, and some workable English. She had become a manager of a social club in Yokohama catering to American officers. It was no use hiding anything from this woman, Sonoko thought. She had come to the rescue of the Abe family's finances.

"He is a gentleman, and casual about money," she coaxed. "Take all the money you can. I haven't forgotten they were my husband's enemy. Our government won't take care of us. It is our only lot to take all the money we can from them."

Sonoko was amazed at the way Kakuko talked. When she stopped, she told her that she must first consult with her mother-in-law and her children.

Ten days later Kakuko called and said she was bringing the American officer. Unmindful of Sonoko's protest that she had not yet talked with her family, Kakuko came about an hour later with a tall officer.

A year before, just before the Americans began the Occupation, Sonoko had, like everyone else, sent her only daughter Fumiko away to a relative in Shizuoka. The government had sent out warnings, telling the young girls not to smile at the American soldiers, that they must retain the pride of Japanese womanhood. When the streets and towns had become filled with GIs and sailors, Sonoko failed to hear of any dreaded incident. Not only that, the Japanese people welcomed them with open arms, saying the Americans had saved them from the long oppression of the Japanese warmongers and from hunger. Within a year, they watched, with no disgust, as their daughters walked hand in hand with GIs in broad daylight.

But Sonoko could not receive an American into her home. He might not be a foreign devil, but he was—or had been—her husband's enemy. She went to the door with every intention of refusing him, but after the introduction Kakuko would not let Sonoko open her mouth.

"Shattuck-san loves the sea," she said. "He is happy also that he will be able to enter into a Japanese family." So saying she let the Major take off his shoes.

"We have not decided yet," Sonoko sputtered. "And I have not cleaned the rooms yet," she added.

Kakuko ignored Sonoko's protest, and showed the Major the two rooms that faced the sea. Then she took him to where the young folks were. After a short introduction, she started in with the financial advantages of renting the rooms to the Americans.

Fumiko ignored Kakuko's financial arguments, and tried her faltering English. "When you say you will use your rooms only at night," she asked with dignity, "does that mean you will bring your girl friend here?" She looked direct into the Major's blue eyes. "This is our home, it is sacred to us."

The Major listened to her with a grave expression.

"No, I sleep alone every night," he said in slow, distinct English Fumiko could understand. "I want to know the sanctity of Japanese home life. That is why I want to live in your home."

Sonoko stood outside the room, wondering anxiously over the conversation. She called Kakuko outside and told her she would give her answer in a few days. The Major bent over Sonoko's hand and kissed it. It might be an American custom, but her hand smarted a long time afterward. She felt she must refuse the Major no matter what. Her mother-in-law came in.

"Sono-san," she called, and declared with dignity, "If you let an American into this house, I shall leave."

A year later in 1947, when the 15th of August came around again, Sonoko was sitting in the upstairs veranda with a pair of binoculars. She scanned the ocean for a boat which might possibly carry Major Shattuck and Fumiko. She dreaded this day, as she had in the past, thinking of Kakuko's inevitable visit.

When noon came, Fumiko would not leave for work. "I am thinking of quitting my work," she said when asked. Then she blushed and added timidly, "Shattuck-san wants to marry me."

Sonoko's heart stopped.

"But don't worry, mama," Fumiko continued. "I won't do anything rash. And I won't ask for your opinion until my mind is made up either. Only I didn't want to have any secrets from you."

"What did the Major say? You know it's against the American rule."

But Fumiko only repeated, "I know, I know," and went out.

She wondered if Fumiko had made a rendezvous with the Major. Sonoko held her glasses close to her eyes.

In each boat was a pair or two of GI's with Japanese girls. They all looked so happy. Sonoko thought of her own youth, devoid of such freedom. The feeling of remorse for the freedom she never had, and apprehension for the youth of today passed through her own heart. She wondered if it had not been a mistake to let Major Shattuck stay in her house.

At that time a year ago, Sonoko and the old lady were dead against the idea, but the young people insisted. To be ostentatious was not in their vocabulary. They said they should be grateful to Kakuko.

The old lady fretted and said she would go to the home of her second son, who operated a hospital in Shizuoka. Fumiko took her there in the end.

"I don't think she will stay there more than a month."

To be sure, she returned exactly a month later.

"I met Mr. Ando who was a member of the Privy Council at the time of grandfather," she said. "Mr. Ando had been to the Imperial Palace, to pay his respects," and she told in detail what she heard from Mr. Ando, and about how the Imperial family live.

"The carpets are worn out and have holes in them. Mind you, holes. The Emperor tripped over one of them, looked at Mr. Ando, and smiled. Mr. Ando could not return the smile. Instead, he looked down, and wept." The old lady wept anew. "After I heard that, I made up my mind that I should be able to live with an American under one roof," and she bowed her head to Sonoko.

But she avoided Major Shattuck, and did not return his morning greetings, pretending to be hard of hearing. She ignored him completely. If Sonoko should tell her that Fumiko had been proposed to by him, she would surely have heart failure.

To Sonoko, Major Shattuck was a gentleman. He was polite and quiet, and not once was there any distasteful occurrence of any kind. He was humorous, too, full of fun. Takeo, her second son, regarded him as his idol. Not only that, but it was all due to his staying with them that her family of five had been able to lead a normal life. She wished that he would stay until Taro finished his college. Would he leave if she refused to consent to Fumiko's marriage?

But how had it happened? She thought she had watched over them very closely. She heard a rustle of silk, and turned. Her mother-in-law was standing there.

"Mrs. Okada is here," she said.

Kakuko came not in mourning this year, but dressed in a white linen suit. She wore a strand of pearls and a pair of matching earrings—every inch the woman manager of a social club. She did not ask to be shown to the altar room, she was so excited.

"You did know all the time, didn't you? You must have," she said a little breathlessly. "Then please tell me, if it is true, that His Excellency and my husband are still living, that their submarine did arrive in Japan."

Sonoko's body swayed forward involuntarily.

"Who said such nonsense?"

"You know this is the third year, and I was about to hold the third-year Buddhist rite." She dropped her voice to show that it was a grave secret. "Mrs. Akutsu came in and told me the news. She said she even saw Lieutenant-Commander Ohba selling old shoes in Shitaya. She said someone is sure to contact His Excellency's home."

"I have not received any information," Sonoko said.

Two or three months before, Taro had told her the same thing; that he had seen Commander Haruki selling old shoes in Shimbashi.

"Kakuko-san, do you think such a thing possible?"

"The way things happen nowadays, anything is possible." Kakuko laughed. "Look at me, before the war, who would have thought that I could hold my present job, manager of a social club?"

"You actually believe they are alive?"

"I have to . . . There are many others who are waiting for the safe return of their missing husbands."

"But they can't, they are not the type to live under such humiliating conditions."

"You think not, Madame?" Kakuko's voice sounded strangely sarcastic. "We are not living in the Meiji Era. Remember how they used to love to get drunk and chase geisha girls? I no longer have the respect for them that I once had."

She got up and took up the binoculars Sonoko left on the table.

"Who knows but that they may be picking trash in someone's back yard right now, waiting for the peace treaty to be concluded, and for the return of their day once again . . . which even a ten-year-old knows will never return . . . is gone forever."

Sonoko got up to get a cold drink for Kakuko, who stood, looking into the binoculars.

"Why, Madame, is Fumiko-san with the Major today?"

She must have found the boat. Sonoko ran downstairs, pretending she did not hear Kakuko.

Kakuko returned quite often after that, and each time brought different news. One time she brought a batch of letters, saying they were from either her husband or his associates.

Once she came and asked Sonoko to consent to Fumiko's marriage to the Major.

The old lady always overheard everything. "If Jusuke should return safe and alive, I will assist him in committing harakiri," she said calmly. She always talked calmly, which sometimes aggravated Sonoko. But her dead seriousness was a joke to the young folks. Fumiko alone listened to her grandmother's lectures, and found such lectures caused her to waver in her decision to accept the Major's marriage proposal.

One day, in midwinter, the old lady suddenly said she wanted to visit her second son in Shizuoka, and asked the Major to take her to the Tokyo station. The Major was delighted at this sudden recognition. When they reached Tokyo, she asked through Fumiko that the Major drive around the Imperial Palace.

"Sha-do-ku-san, I love to watch these water birds in the moat," she suddenly spoke in English, to the great amazement of everyone. "I think this view of the moat around the Imperial Palace is the most beautiful scene in Tokyo."

Not only the Major, but Fumiko and Taro were taken by surprise at their grandmother's fluent English.

"I studied English from an Englishman back in the Meiji Era," she explained. "I am glad to find out that my English is understood by the American also."

Fumiko noticed that the old lady's accent was perfect.

A few days later she was found dead in their family cemetery in Shizuoka. No one could think of the reason why. There was only one tiny possible clue to the mystery.

When Taro went to get the body, he saw the priest of the family temple for whom his father had had great respect.

"She was in to see me four days before her body was found," the old priest said. "I was pruning my trees in the garden when she came. She stood watching me. Then she said, 'The old branches must be cut off to give room for the new.' Then she wanted to know if that was what I was doing. Come to think of it, these were the last words uttered by your grandmother."

For the forty-ninth-day rite of the deceased grandmother, held in Shizuoka, Major Shattuck was invited. After the ceremony Fumiko told her uncle, Dr. Abe, that she wanted to go to America to enter a college there.

"Does your mother know about it?" Dr. Abe wanted to know.

"No, I want you to tell her, please," she said.

In the car coming back, the two Mesdames Abe talked intimately.

"I am having such a time with Taro," Sonoko confided to her sister-in-law. "I never know what he is thinking."

"It seems that a big gap has opened between the young and the old since the war," the doctor's wife said. "We are having a hard time with our young doctors at the hospital, too."

"Well, the young ones are probably having a hard time with us, saying we have no understanding nor sympathy for them." The good doctor laughed it off. The gloomy atmosphere went out of the car with the breeze.

That night, after Sonoko got into her bed, she asked Fumiko, "Is what you told uncle true?"

"I don't know exactly what conversation took place in your car," Fumiko said. "Uncle may exaggerate, but he wouldn't tell a lie, I'm sure."

"Was your idea to go to America your own," the mother asked, "or was it the Major's?"

"No, I have not even told him," the daughter answered. "I will probably have to secure his help in obtaining the visa though."

"Did you give up the idea of marrying the Major because of your grandmother's suicide?"

"How preposterous," Fumiko cried. "What possible connection is there between the two?"

Sonoko could not explain her feeling very well. All she knew was that she wanted Fumiko to be happy. She felt that Fumiko's hesitation to accept the Major's proposal was due to the grandmother. But she had a premonition that because of the way grandmother had died, Fumiko had given up the idea entirely, and if that was so, Sonoko wanted Fumiko to know that she was sorry for everything.

She was satisfied in the end when Fumiko told her that before she made up her mind, she wanted to know the Major better by going to America. Fumiko told her also that the actions of the young people nowadays might seem perilous and uncertain, but the young had at least learned to be responsible for what they are doing. This was true even of those young girls who walk the streets with the GIs.

Kakuko came more often. She insisted each time that their husbands were alive, hiding somewhere, waiting for the Peace Treaty to be concluded. While Sonoko denied this, she still longed for her husband. She told him in her heart to come out of hiding, just for her.

One day, she was thus calling for her husband in her heart, watching the sun set over the horizon from the upstairs veranda, when she heard her husband's voice in the *genkan*, the entrance hall.

"Where's mother?" he said. "Is she upstairs?"

She heard him come up the stairs, just like he always did when he returned unexpectedly.

Her knees shook, and the voice would not come out of her throat. Tears came down involuntarily.

"Oh, here you are," and before her stood her son Taro. She could not open her mouth. Taro stared at her tear-stained face in wonder.

"What happened?" he asked, still puzzled.

Sonoko told him for the first time what Kakuko had been telling her, that his father might possibly be still alive.

"Your voice was so very much like your father's," she said, shamefacedly. "I was seized by an illusion that it was your father."

"So you believe it, do you? You want to believe it, don't you?" Taro's voice was harsh. "You never knew the hardships of war, mother. You think you do, but actually you never suffered the way most people suffered. That's why you allow yourself to entertain such a dream." He looked at her accusingly. "Of course you had hard times, in your own way, but you didn't lose your house, you never saw death with your own eyes. I did. I saw with my own eyes two hundred thousand people die in one flash. I can still smell their burning flesh. I can still hear young girls cry for water, water. Sometimes I feel I ought not be living like this. So if father should suddenly appear before me now, alive and unhurt, I couldn't stand it. I don't think I could live with him in the same house. I would leave this house immediately.

"I am glad he is dead. I wouldn't have it any other way. It's your own fault to let him live in your heart. He is our enemy, and we should not let our enemy live."

The 15th of August has returned again. The peace treaty will be signed in a short while in San Francisco, and the whole nation is in a festive mood. But Sonoko tries to remain outside it.

She received a letter from Fumiko, who is attending Columbia University, saying that she is going to marry Major . . . Mr. now . . . Shattuck in a short while. He is studying anthropology at the same university, getting his Ph.D., and he will find Fumiko a good assistant.

Taro has finished his internship and is now in a lab in Nagoya, preparing his thesis on his study to free the human race from color. It is his belief that only by making all human races one color could world peace be realized, for then and only then could they live in one world, and will there be no more wars.

Takeo, her second son, got a job as a live-in private tutor and is attending college.

Sonoko is now alone in the small house they have moved into, deep in the narrow alleys of a suburb of Tokyo. She waits for Kakuko's annual visit on this day. But she does not dread it as she had in the past, for no one ever comes to see her and she is glad to receive her.

But for some reason Kakuko is late. She usually comes early. Lunch time has passed. Three o'clock tea time has passed, but still no Kakuko.

Sonoko confirms her husband's death in Kakuko's failure to arrive on this day. She changes into her mourning clothes, moves her husband's portrait to the *tokonoma,* and places some fresh flowers before it. Then she prepares a tea ceremony, and drinks deep its fragrant liquid, as if receiving it from her husband.

"Where's mother?" she hears her husband's voice in the *genkan.* She starts and cannot get up. Her knees shake violently. She goes to the *genkan,* still shaking, but she only finds Taro taking his shoes off.

"I had to come to Tokyo on urgent business," he says, going into the dining room.

How his back has come to look just like his father's, she thinks.

Then Taro notices his mother's mourning.

"I was just informed of your father's death," she says quietly.

"Mrs. Tokuda was here?" he asks. "Then, Lieutenant-Commander Tokuda, too?"

"No, just your father," she lies. "Lieutenant Commander Tokuda is still alive, I believe. Your father committed harakiri as befitting the descendant of a samurai."

"I see," and Taro sits up straight, and prays in silence. Sonoko's conscience is clear.

"I didn't know that," Taro says. "I ordered a fish dinner from the corner restaurant, to save you the trouble. And some cold beer too. I am sorry," he apologizes in the realization that fish and meat are taboo during Buddhist rites for the dead.

"That's all right," Sonoko says cheerfully. "I'll drink with you, to pray for his happy ascent to Heaven."

THE JAPANESE AUTHORS

KON HIDEMI (*1903-*   ) majored in French literature at Tokyo Imperial University, started writing right after graduation and soon became editor of the magazine *Comedy and Tragedy*. In 1929-30 he joined other artists in opposition to the Proletarian literature of the Marxists—because Marx pointedly ignored art. In 1933 he opposed as well the rising tide of nationalism, along with Abe Tomoji and Serizawa Kojiro, who are represented in this book, and such writers as Kawabata Yasunari, Yuasa Katsuei, Dazai Osamu, Takami Jun. Twenty-nine in all who called for a "tough and realistic prose," and insisted that art be "autonomous and integral." No strict policy was set down. The Marxists denounced them as bourgeois, and the movement they had hoped to found fizzled into genre writing which did seem to fit the earlier Marxist denouncements.

Kon turned to what is classed as "midway literature," midway between writing for the masses and the "pure literature" of the hermits.

Kon's other works include: *The Tragic General, On a Fine Day,* and *Wandering in the Mountains.* He won the 23rd Naoki Prize in 1950 with *The Emperor's Hat.*

MIYAMOTO YURIKO (*1899-1951*), born Nakajo Yuriko in Tokyo, graduated from Ocha-no-Mizu Girl's High School in 1916 and studied English literature at Nippon Women's College for one term. She came to America with her father, attended Columbia University and married a student. She returned to Japan alone in 1919 and was divorced in 1924. Her interest in Russian literature took her to Moscow in 1927; after a stay there she traveled through Europe until 1930. On her return to Japan she joined KOPF, the Japan Proletarian Writers' group of bourgeois intellectuals led by Kurahara, Nakano, Kobayashi and Miyamoto Kenji. In 1931 Yuriko joined

the Communist Party, married Miyamoto in 1932, and was herself imprisoned for short periods in 1932, 1934, 1935, and again in 1941 for opposing
the war. Her writing was banned in 1938 and 1941. KOPF was dissolved in
1934 after Kobayashi died at the hands of the Tokyo police, and the other
leaders went to prison. Her husband's release in 1945 forms the core of the
novel *Banshu Plain,* from which our selection is extracted.

The range of her themes is narrow, generally limited to autobiography.
She is highly popular among present-day students. By Japanese critical
standards, her "poetic technique" and "power of suggestion" are weak, by
which is meant she is not ambiguous, and her directness is regarded as
critically "uninteresting." Her odd tempering of the slow, interminable
marching-forward-into-the-sun finale of the socialist realists, with the Japanese sigh, almost of *mono no aware,* is poetically successful. She was one
of the naïve humanist Communists, whose Western counterparts have long
since been disenchanted with the Party.

ABE TOMOJI (*1903-*   ), born in rural Okayama, entered the English
Literature Department of Tokyo Imperial University in 1923. In 1927 as a
graduate student he wrote *A Gypsy in Japan,* and in 1930 *Intellectualist
Theory of Literature.* He was especially active in the Proletarian literature
movement and led the rearguard *Action* magazine in 1933-35 against the
wave of nationalism. In 1933 he began teaching at Meiji University, where he
presently is professor of English Literature. A humanist, he does not engage
in dialectics as most of his so-called proletarian colleagues do, but fights
issues. He is a crusader in the Occidental sense and is active in the Peace
Movement, but he rejects the Communist-front line in favor of the Quaker
approach. The range of his work is phenomenal, from heavy political and
social criticism to literary scholarship, translations from the English, travel
accounts and humor.

The individualist and progressive-with-a-small-"p" is a *rara avis* in Japan
and certainly needs a sense of humor to survive, as Abe shows in *The Horse
Manure Record* and this collection's *The Communist.* The utter confusion
of the characters, their ignorance, naïveté and suspicion, form a perfect portrait of the Japanese student who would rather prance on the palace plaza
beneath pennants and police batons than tackle a real book or a smaller-
scale problem he might conceivably understand and attempt to solve. It is
by far the best analysis and description of a mentality as slippery and as
hard to grasp as soap, but, like it, the by-product rather than the source
material of political TNT.

Abe has traveled extensively, to Java in 1941, to Europe since the war,
and to mainland China in 1954 as part of a cultural delegation. Other works
include: *Winter Inn, Wind and Snow, Doyle of Africa, White Officer, Alte
Heidelberg, Peking;* the postwar *Flower Shade, Black Shade, Death
Flowers, The Wanderer, European Journey.*

SERIZAWA KOJIRO (*1897-*) was born in Shizuoka, south of Tokyo, where the winter-ripening tangerines on the steep-terraced, pine-topped hillsides instill an awareness of constant life and growth. He graduated from Tokyo Imperial University at 35, worked for the Ministry of Agriculture for three years and then quit and went to Paris to study in 1935. He returned in 1939, and his maiden work, *Bourgeois,* won the *Kaido* magazine novel prize. It was autobiographical, based on his illness-racked life in France. His father was a devout adherent of the Tenri religion (often regarded as the Japanese Christian Science), which inspired his *A Believer* and *A Record of Conventions.* Their lack of deep religious insight may accurately reflect this religion's own philosophical poverty other than untutored, unselfish action. Serizawa is a romantic idealist usually classed with the Esthetic school. His main postwar writings include: *Anonymous Confession* (1947), *The Closed Door, Marriage, Hope, The State of Europe, One World* (1954, part of which appears in this collection), *Repentance Record* (1961). He is one of Japan's principal Nobel prize hopefuls.

KAWACHI SENSUKE was born in 1898 and died in 1954 a few days after approving our condensation and translation of his novel *Sazanka.* He graduated from the Osaka Koshu School of Commerce in 1916, and worked as a magazine editor. His first novel, *Gunji Yubin* (Military Mail), was serialized in *Shincho.* Later works included *Ishi* (Will), *Waga Ane-no-Ki* (My Sister's Story), and *Kaze Sayuru* (The Cutting Wind).

NAKAMOTO TAKAKO'S (*1903-*) name almost didn't appear. *Gunzo* magazine in 1953 had a policy of running stories anonymously to encourage its public to read for the sake of the story, not the name of the author. *Kichi no Onna* (Camp Women, here translated as *The Only One*) appeared in July 1953. Nakamoto allowed translation only on condition that the author remain anonymous. Nakamoto was afraid that her story might be thought anti-American. In a way she was right, for the Americans in Tokyo were a super-sensitive lot. The title was changed to the corresponding local GI idiom. The Japanese *Kichi no Onna* carries other connotations— the first US Ambassador to Japan, Townsend Harris, allegedly kept a mistress named O-kichi who has become the titular deity of poor country girls sacrificed to the red-headed barbarians. The movie *The Barbarian and the Geisha* was a Hollywood perpetuation of this thoroughly discredited story, which was given further life in paperback by Robert Payne.

Her major prewar work includes *The Iron Kettle Tinkers of Nambu* and *White-Robed Workers,* which also deal with the affairs of people of the economic and social cellar.

WADA DEN (*1900-*   ) is the scion of an ancient feudal family, a graduate of Tokyo Imperial University's French Literature Department and a resident of his ancestral estate. Wada joined the *Nomin Bungeikai,* Agricultural Literature Society or "physiocrats." Agricultural literature was a pawn of both the Marxists and the Ministry of Agriculture. The Ministry had the writers do articles, in which their fiction training stood them well, of country boys who made good or who conquered the barren wilds of Manchuria —little that can be classed as literature.

Between 1945 and 1954 Japan underwent the most successful rural upheaval in mankind's history. The land reform of 1945 could not safely be considered a success until 1954, when the combination of technology, agricultural cooperatives and conscientious "traditional" farmers at long last conquered Japan's periodic famine. Yet this revolution has gone virtually unchronicled. Wada Den has managed to write of the farmer's life successfully, with sympathy and understanding and just that touch of humor so characteristic of village Japan.

His better-known works include: *The Last Grave* (1929) and *Fertile Soil* (1937).

ISHIKAWA TATSUZO (*1905-*   ), born in Akita, attended Waseda University, Tokyo, and made his mark early, winning the Asahi short story award in 1926. He came from a background of poverty and graduated into an emotionally nomadic life as dance instructor, writer-editor, pig farmer and foreign correspondent, which probably accounts for the rapport which the foreign reader establishes with him even when he cannot "agree with more than half his statements, especially those on social problems."

In 1935 he started the magazine *Seiza* and received the coveted Akutagawa prize for his novel *The People.* Sent to cover the China fighting, he wrote articles that caused trouble with the militarists. In 1938 *The Living Soldiers* earned him a conviction—with a reinforcement of his own convictions to attempt "reform rather by goodwill than by wanton criticism." Other fiction from the China front followed. After the war Ishikawa's *It Isn't As If There Were No Hope,* serialized in 1947, was adapted for the stage in 1948. Mostly it had to do with his own experiences in China, evidencing a desire to re-establish a moral consciousness amidst the postwar disorder.

He writes in the tradition of the "I" novel, but rejects the usual preaching and subjectivity. Japanese critics note his directness, his avoidance of innuendo. He writes of China with just enough detachment and depth to allow Japanese to develop sympathy and understanding and a desire to rebuild and rectify, while avoiding saddling them with a "mournful awareness" of an unexpiable inherited guilt.

In the small Oriental literary world of emotional attitudinarians, Ishikawa persists as a "Moral Democrat." He writes what is classified as "midway" and "adventure" literature and frequently, as with *The Affair of the Arabesque Inlay,* the story in this collection, adapts the detective story genre. Other works of note by Ishikawa Tatsuzo include: *Village in the Shadow, Green Grass of Wisdom;* the postwar *Wind-Swayed Reeds, The Last Republic, Pride of Three Generations, Tax Collector's Ballad, In One's Own Hole, Blue Revolution, The Joys of Evil,* and the especially noteworthy *Human Wall.*

In June 1962, despite Fascist threats against his life, he accepted the editorship of the bankrupt weekly magazine owned by the Sohyo labor union. His rejoinder to their accusations of communism: "A liberal can be a nationalist too, and I shall prove it."

KOYAMA ITOKO (*1901-*   ) was born in Kochi, in southern Shikoku, the land of the long-tailed roosters. Her education was limited to primary school plus five years at the old-style Kochi Girls' High School. She is primarily a novelist. In her early writing days she took a masculine pen name. Critics have called her style masculine, especially in her broad outlook—though on this standard the bulk of Japanese male writers could be classed as feminine. She stresses romantic love and adventure and prefers rather human, unconventional heroes, the sort of man who might be anyone's husband, as in the story in this collection, *Black-Out.* She edited a women's magazine, *Bird of Fire,* in 1918, and today frequently appears in such women's magazines as *Shufu no Tomo* (Housewives' Companion). Her better-known works include: *Hot Wind, Village, The Daughter's House, Koya Monastery, Putting Off the Action,* and the very successful serial which ran for two years in *Shufu no Tomo, My Empress.*

KOH HARUTO (*1906-*   ) was born in Kumamoto, in westernmost Japan, an area never thoroughly brought under the repressive thought control of the Shoguns in Tokyo. Kyushuites to this day stand out among other Japanese for their independent ways and their individuality, and their directness, which other Japanese consider coarse but which the Occidental long in Japan finds refreshing, if at first somewhat shocking. Yet they are conservative, clinging to old ways the central areas of Japan have given up.

Koh Haruto majored in English Literature at Meiji Gakuin—a school well suited to his personality, where English was taught by such iconoclasts as Dr. Paul Yoshiro Saeki (to whom this book is dedicated), Christian, Confucian sage, world traveler, a plague on narrow-minded militarists and missionaries alike, and himself a country boy from western Japan.

Koh is of the same age group as such "Lost Generation" stylists as Hemingway, who brought conciseness and directness of language into our literature, with whom English Literature buff Koh was certainly acquainted, and whose directness and simplicity and humanity would appeal to the same innate qualities of the traditional Kyushu cuss. The humor of futility in *Black Market Blues* appeals to the Western taste. Yet Western as the story and treatment and style may seem, it is typically rural Kyushu, a modern version of what the Kyushu farmers do to their ancient heroes and gods in the age-old autumn amateur performances of the Harvest Plays, the Kagura. Japanese college students whom I have assigned to read Koh were unanimous in praise of his simple, direct language and rapid development of theme. They especially noted the absence of any dialectic, of any attempt to explain or preach—further reasons why they had not earlier been introduced to him by their Japanese teachers. Yet they felt nothing "foreign" about him, felt at ease while reading him and, when finished, as several pointedly stated, "much refreshed." To the Westerner, this is especially evident.

His other works, not yet translated, include: *Marriage, Mulberry in Water, Delinquent Girl, Ticket, Dangerous Experiment, Fire, Clear Eyes,* and *A Certain Gorge.*

MISHIMA YUKIO (*1925-*) began his prodigious rise with the publication of *Confessions of a Mask* in 1949. A graduate of the Peers' School and Tokyo University (1947), he was first published in 1944. He is the principal literary spokesman for Japan's "Lost Generation," and has been compared with Truman Capote and France's Raymond Radiguet. His stories deal mostly with homosexuality, as well as demented love, religious and political dementia—the full armory of a youthful literature of shock, symptomatic of a more general cultural malaise. His earlier work especially was noteworthy for its irony, as in *Minister* (1949) and *Revenge,* herein. By 1955 he had already produced over 70 volumes of novels, short stories, poetry, plays in old, new and mixed genres, much of which he does not take seriously and confesses through his journalistic mask to be plain pulp. A good bit is deservedly successful; some, as his modern Noh Plays, noble experimental flops which indicate future promise, for the new forms perhaps more than for the writer. Thankfully, he has since slackened his pace. *Revenge* was the first of his stories to be translated, several novels have since followed and Off-Broadway has tried his modern Noh. He has been called the exemplification of the postwar "conservative resistance." He is a Nobel-prize hopeful.

MIZUKI YOKO (*1913-*), born and raised in Tokyo, reflects the temperament of the Edo-ko, child of Edo (Tokyo). She majored in Japanese literature at Nippon Women's University and later took up drama at Bunkagakuin and radio script writing. After the war she wrote movie scenarios, her first being *Onna no Issho* (The Life of a Woman). She has been far less loath than most Japanese writers to tackle the broader social problems. One of her first movies to gain international attention, if not notoriety, was *Himeyuri no To* (The Tower of Lilies), the idiotic sacrifice of a large group of young Okinawan school girls during the American invasion.

Kiku and Isamu was a movie about two illegitimate children, the product of a Japanese-Negro GI dalliance. The Negro origin was chosen because Caucasian and Japanese offspring are often able to pass for Japanese. Where most Japanese writers drown in maudlin sentimentality, Mizuki manages to express sympathy. Her works include: *Tide, Mother, Here Is a Fountain.* She was awarded the eleventh Kikuchi Kan Prize and the Geijutsusen Award.

SHIBAKI YOSHIKO (*1914-*), born in the heart of the Floating World, Tokyo's Asakusa district, graduated from the Tokyo Girls' High School and attended Surugadai Women's School of the YWCA. In 1942 she married, published *The Vegetable Market* and won the cherished Akutagawa Prize. In 1944 a stay in Manchuria provided the basis for several stories, including *Journey's Start* in 1944 and the delayed *Song of Wandering in a Strange Land,* 1949. She wrote her first long novel, *Flowing Days,* during the war. Other short stories include: *That Day* (1947), *Hope,* and *Truth* (1948). In 1956 she traveled through India, Pakistan, Thailand and Southeast Asia. Recent work includes the serials *Springtime of a Woman* and *City Without Sea.* Her stories *Suzaki Paradise, Woman of Suzaki, Suzaki Area* and *Black Flame* were published together as a novel under the title *Suzaki Paradise.*

THE MILITARY DIARISTS

YOKOI TOSHIYUKI, Rear Admiral, graduated from the Naval Academy in 1919, was trained as a pilot, and went to the Naval War College. He became skipper of the aircraft carrier *Hiyo* in 1943, extending his command to the entire 25th Air Fighter Wing for the crucial battle of Midway and the loss of his flagship recorded in this selection. At war's end he was Chief of Staff of the Fifth Air Force. Later he turned to recording the war. *The End of the Japanese Navy* became a best-seller in Japanese, and was translated by the United States Naval Institute in 1954. He personifies the flowering of British Naval tradition as grafted to a Japanese root.

TSUJI MASANOBU (*1902-1962?*), a staff colonel, exerted personal influence far outweighing his rank and earned a niche in history worth at least three stars. He is credited with blue-printing the conquest of impregnable Singapore. Tsuji was a fanatic, dedicated to the idea of a Greater East Asia as a commonwealth of colored equals, with Japan as first among equals. His sincerity and naïveté (traits necessary to a successful zealot) earned him many friends on both sides of the battle line and his efforts to bring about a rapprochement with the Nationalists were received with enough good will to earn him the protection of Chiang Kai-shek after the war. When the Imphal campaign fell apart in 1943 he was given a command on the Burma front. Wounded, he was transferred to Bangkok, to purge the geisha-house command, and stave off the threatening revolt of Japan's only "ally," Thailand, with her 150,000 troops. It was futile; Thailand changed sides, Tsuji disguised himself as a Buddhist monk and Thai friends helped him escape, as did former enemies among the Cambodians, Annamese and Nationalist Chinese. He eventually ended up as a secret advisor to Chiang. His first book, a runaway best-seller, recounts this trek of 7,500 miles, over two years in duration. Our selection is a composite of two parts from this *Senko Sanzenri* (Disguised Flight of 3,000 Leagues) (1950).

In 1952, consulting with Tsuji was like living a pulp magazine cloak-and-dagger thriller. Everyone suspected him, everyone wanted to hear what he had to say and no one wanted him to talk. The whole procedure was further flavored by his own obvious savoring of the excitement. He stood for election to the Japanese Diet and won, and each re-election was a record-breaking landslide. In 1961 on a "congressional junket" to Viet Nam he contacted former Imperial Japanese Army colleagues still in the area, variously serving any and all factions, then disappeared. Attempts to trace him have been futile and he is believed dead.

His second best-seller, *Singapore,* was translated into English and published in 1960. Both *Underground Escape,* herein, and *Singapore* are among the principal historical works to come out of Japan, recounting the loser's story.

Many of the older group of nisei—Americans of Japanese descent—born before World War I, opted for Japan, for the most part well before Pearl Harbor, out of varying degrees of reaction to their rejection by Caucasian-American society. The job shortage, aggravated by the depression of the thirties, was especially hard on the non-assimilated minorities, the "different." Japan's expansion needed skilled linguists, people with a knowledge of the Western world, and Japan offered the rejected binationals a haven. Many returned; some for jobs their superior education entitled them to, some seething for vengeance. Out of these came much of the staff of Japan's overseas propaganda bureaus, the several people known collectively as Tokyo Rose (one of whom took the whole rap), some of the most sadistic of the prison camp executives and some of the most sympathetic. Most important, these hardy graduates of the American and Japanese schools of hard knocks were among the first to rise like flowers out of the ashes of defeat, to serve as pontoons for the bridge between the derelict Floating World and the new reality. They were the editors and writers of the local English-language newspapers, the interpreter-translators who were virtually the sole link between the linguistically deaf-dumb-and-blind American press, occupationaire educators, reformers, cultural missionaries on the one hand and the equally parochial Japan on the other.

YAMAMOTO TOMOMI is a nisei who served as an intelligence officer in Harbin, Manchuria, where he received word of the Russian invasion in sufficient time to cover up his identity. Captured by the Russians and sent to Siberia, he served in various camps for four years. His repatriation was delayed, at one time seemingly cancelled, because of his political obstinacy. He wrote of his ordeal in both Japanese and English, the latter, published as *Four Years in Hell,* from which this excerpt, *Damoi—Homeward Bound,* was taken. His was the fate of hundreds of thousands of Japanese military and civilians, tens of thousands of whom have never been accounted for officially. It is the description of one half of the pincers in which the Japanese people were trapped; the other half is shown by Miyamoto Yuriko's *Banshu Plain.*

OKA MASAMICHI is a diarist, though no amateur, being a working journalist for the Asahi Newspapers.

FUJI SEII is an amateur diarist and a stringer photographer for *Preview* magazine. While our projects of collecting, editing and translating Japanese war accounts and postwar literature were in full swing, he showed symptoms of the endemic human ill, "Now I really have a story, if only I could write it." The story *Captured by Americans* was written for this translation, in which he cooperated.

THE CIVILIAN DIARISTS

This category, strictly speaking, would include many of the professional authors; but it is here arbitrarily limited to those who did not write primarily for commercial publication. The professionals, by the very fact of being trained writers, consciously affected the techniques of fiction writing to varying degrees; fictionalizing to make the facts more palatable and more believable, to contribute more directly to a specific end (*The New Yorker* calls this reportage); or embellishing an essential fiction with the decorative accessories of miscellaneous facts to lend greater credence to a representative tale.

EGUCHI KOICHI, at 14, was a student in an isolated mountain school, a poor boy even by the standards of his impoverished community. His teacher embodied most of the ideals that colleagues working in far more comfortable conditions claim to find unattainable. Teacher Muchaku Seikyo was impressed by his wards, aware of the inadequate material at hand, conscious of his duty to them. "Simply reading textbooks on social science did not seem sufficient," he writes in the introduction to his book *Echoes from a Mountain School* (Kenkyusha, Tokyo, 1953). "I received the idea of having the pupils write compositions about their own special-problems and their thoughts on life in general. I tried to encourage them to make these compositions a part of themselves, a real study in the social problems of our community." His selection became a best-seller and a full-length movie. Eight pieces were translated into English in 1952, the one included in this collection having been circulated by UNESCO in 1954.

SETO NANAKO (*1932-1959*) is an atomic age representative of one of the oldest forms of Japanese literature, the lady's diary. Seto Nanako, nee Hayashida, 13 years old when the atom bomb leveled Hiroshima, seemed unscathed. At 18 she opened a beauty parlor and at 21 married Seto Tsuyoshi, soon giving birth to a daughter, the Mami of the diary. In July 1957, she suddenly became ill. In October she entered the A-bomb Hospital. The following April, released to out-patient status, she suffered a relapse and was re-admitted. The diary takes up from August 25th of that year and continues on through February 22, 1959. She died on April 10, 1959. The diary was found by the translator among some books owned by a friend. After translation it was privately published by a special committee of the Hiroshima YMCA, July 15, 1961. I discovered it a few days later, as did the *Pravda* correspondent who arranged for its translation into Russian the very week Russia suddenly resumed atomic testing unannounced. The success of the English edition prompted a Japanese edition of the entire diary.

There is a literature on the atomic bomb, most notably by Ota Yoko and Agawa Hiroyuki. The latter's novel *Devil's Heritage* has an excellent English translation and I had intended to include an excerpt from it in this collection. I was on my way to the offices of the Hiroshima daily, *Chugoku Shimbun,* for which he writes (and to which I occasionally contribute cartions), when I discovered *A Crane.*

JAPANESE LITERATURE IN ENGLISH

An amazing facet of Japanese publishing for almost a century has been the English language press. This may not seem surprising at first glance, when one considers that Iran's finest modern author wrote simultaneously in French, that India and Pakistan have long supported numerous and healthy English periodicals, that Southeast Asian and Black African and Moslem African authors excel, if only locally circulated, in the languages of their occupiers. Then recall that Japan's local English press dates back almost to the day English was openly allowed (a few special interpreters had studied it before Commodore Perry came). Japan's excellent English dailies are supported by a readership over half of whom are Japanese. Japanese is the language of a vibrant and highly literate people, but the language is of no use in international communication. Japanese must use English (or some other Western tongue) to explain themselves to the world. The locally published magazines have usually (as with those I myself edited or published) been foreign-run—but not always. But whatever the proprietorship, a fair block of internal circulation and a major segment of the contributors have from the very earliest issues been Japanese. These writers may be foreign-educated or repatriated second-generation Japanese. Some may be writing in their second language. Some are native-born but educated overseas by diplomatic or commercial-emigre parents, speaking English as their mother language. A number of these, several working today on the English dailies, are illiterate in Japanese. There are also the Eurasians and Japan-born and naturalized Caucasians, several of whom are working journalists. And Japan has perhaps as legitimate a claim to Lafcadio Hearn as has America (never an American citizen, he was naturalized as Japanese).

While this is also a part of the literature of the English language, it is legitimately an aspect of the literature of the Japanese culture. It is written by men of that particular culture and about that culture. Nor is it exactly minor from a physical standpoint, for the circulation of some of the periodicals in which it appears is often as large as or larger than that of the vernacular literary magazines in which some of the major literature of the native language has gained recognition. Some of the non-fiction from Japan which has had the greatest impact on the West in recent years has appeared originally in English, since being translated "back" or re-rendered into Japanese—for example, the Zen philosophical works of D. T. Suzuki.

TAGUCHI SHU was a writer-director-producer of documentary movies, almost as much at home in English as in Japanese. He died in 1955. The autobiographical piece in this collection is biography enough on him, except to say that as an artist with the camera he was superb. He adapted this story, *Three Unforgettable Letters,* from an earlier scenario for a planned short movie.

SAISHO FOUMY is a movie reviewer for the *Japan Times* and a member of the Tokyo-based editorial staff of *Reader's Digest.*

JOHN FUJII was taken to the USA as an infant. He returned to Japan after completing college, and worked at various English editorial jobs until he went in 1942 to edit a captured Singapore English daily. Since the war he has held numerous editorial positions on local papers and for American wire services. His ignorance of written Japanese has earned him the nickname of "The World's Only Illiterate Journalist." His clipped and acid style owes more to his Edo-Tokyo environment than to his American journalistic experience and he reminds one, in both his subject matter and his style, of the popular paperback hacks of the Floating World of 17th, 18th and 19th century Edo (and of whom he would be the ideal translator, were he able to read them). He later purchased *Orient Digests* and edited several issues before discontinuing publication. At present, he is living in Tokyo, editing an entertainment weekly and free-lancing.

ABOUT THE EDITOR

JAY GLUCK was born in Detroit, Michigan, in 1927. After attending Columbia University, he graduated from the University of California in 1949 and later did graduate work in Asian studies. Mr. Gluck has lived in Japan for the past twelve years; during this time he has founded and edited several magazines (including *Orient Digests*) and is currently teaching English at Wakayama National University in central Japan. Mr. Gluck, who has traveled extensively throughout Asia, is also a roving editor of *France-Asie*, a contributor to numerous Japanese periodicals, and has frequently appeared on Radio Japan Overseas Service.